RONNIE & NANCY

Other books by Bob Colacello

Holy Terror: Andy Warhol Close Up

Studios by the Sea: Artists of Long Island's East End (with Jonathan Becker)

RONNIE & NANCY

THEIR PATH TO THE WHITE HOUSE
1911 TO 1980

BOB COLACELLO

DOUBLEDAY LARGE PRINT HOME LIBRARY EDITION

WARNER BOOKS

NEW YORK   BOSTON

This Large Print Edition, prepared especially for Doubleday Large Print Home Library, contains the complete, unabridged text of the original Publisher's Edition.

Grateful acknowledgment is expressed to quote from the following: *A Surgeon's Odyssey* by Loyal Davis, copyright © 1973 by Loyal Davis, used by permission of Doubleday, a division of Random House, Inc. *Behind the Scenes* by Michael K. Deaver, copyright © 1988 by Michael K. Deaver, reprinted by permission of HarperCollins Publishers Inc., William Morrow. *Dutch: A Memoir* by Edmund Morris, copyright © 1999 by Edmund Morris, used by permission of Random House, Inc. *Early Reagan* by Anne Edwards, copyright © 1987 by Anne Edwards, reprinted by permission of HarperCollins Publishers Inc., William Morrow. *First Father, First Daughter* by Maureen Reagan, copyright © 1989 by MER, Inc., by permission of Little, Brown and Company, Inc. *Governor Reagan* by Lou Cannon, copyright © 2003 by Lou Cannon, reprinted by permission of PublicAffairs, a member of Perseus books, L.L.C. *Jane Wyman: The Actress and the Woman,* copyright © 1986 by Lawrence J. Quirk, reprinted by permission of the author. *Nancy Reagan: The Unauthorized Biography* by Kitty Kelley, copyright © 1991 by Kitty Kelley, reprinted with permission of Simon & Schuster Adult Publishing Group. *Nofziger* by Lyn Nofziger, copyright © 1992, published by Regnery Publishing, Inc., all rights reserved; reprinted by special permission of Regnery Publishing, Inc., Washington, D.C. *Where's the Rest of Me?* and *An American Life* by Ronald Reagan, copyright © 1965 and copyright © 1990 by Ronald Reagan; with permission of Nancy Reagan. *Nancy, My Turn,* and *I Love You, Ronnie* by Nancy Reagan, copyright © 1980, copyright © 1989, and copyright © 2000 by Nancy Reagan; with permission of Nancy Reagan. Courtesy of Department of Special Collections, Oral History Program, Charles E. Young Research Library, UCLA: Oral histories of Neil Reagan and Stanley Plog. Courtesy of Center for Oral and Public History, California State University, Fullerton: Henry Salvatori, OH 1674, Holmes Tuttle, OH 1675, Justin Dart, OH 1676, Ed Mills, OH 1677.

Warner Books
Time Warner Book Group
1271 Avenue of the Americas, New York, NY 10020

Printed in the United States of America
ISBN 0-7394-4812-9

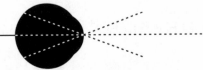

This Large Print Book carries the
Seal of Approval of N.A.V.H.

*To my father, John, who passed away
five days before Ronald Reagan;
and my mother, Libby,
his beloved wife of nearly fifty-eight years.*

*And to the late Jerry Zipkin,
who opened so many doors for me.*

Contents

LE CIRQUE
1981

You say there can be no argument about
   matters of taste?
All life is an argument about matters of taste.

> Friedrich Nietzsche,
> *Thus Spake Zarathustra*

Oh, those Greeks! They knew how to live. What
is required for that is to stop courageously at
the surface, the fold, the skin, to adore appearance, to believe in forms, tones, words, in the
whole Olympus of appearance. Those Greeks
were superficial—*out of profundity.*

> Friedrich Nietzsche,
> *Nietzsche Contra Wagner*

On Saturday night, March 14, 1981, President
Ronald Reagan, who had been inaugurated less
than two months earlier, and his wife, Nancy, went
to dinner at Le Cirque, then New York's most fashionable restaurant. The new President and First
Lady had been to see a Broadway show—*Sugar*

Babies, starring those Hollywood old-timers Ann Miller and Mickey Rooney—so it was about 10:30 when their motorcade turned into East 65th Street, where a small crowd cheered as they stepped out of their limousine. Caught up in the excitement, those of us in the restaurant spontaneously stood and applauded when the Reagans walked through the door, accompanied by their very close friends from California, Alfred Bloomingdale, the department store heir, and his fashion-plate wife, Betsy. Both women were wearing fur coats. Mrs. Reagan's was mink, Mrs. Bloomingdale's sable.

They were followed by the retired media tycoon Gardner Cowles and his wife, Jan, pillars of the Republican establishment, who had homes in New York, Southampton, and Miami and had been friends with the Reagans since the 1950s. Then came Jerry Zipkin, the acid-tongued Park Avenue bachelor who was Nancy Reagan's best friend in New York—*Women's Wear Daily*, which for years had dismissed him as "the Social Moth," now called him "the First Walker," walker being its term for a single man who escorts society ladies to parties when their husbands are unavailable. On one arm Zipkin had Claudette Colbert, the ageless movie star, who knew the Reagans from their Hollywood days. On the other he had Etti Plesch, an Austrian-born dowager from Monte Carlo known for her prize-winning racehorses and her six rich husbands.

All eyes were on the presidential party as Le Cirque's owner, Sirio Maccioni, showed them to the best table in the house—the corner banquette just to the right of the entrance, which Jerry Zipkin and his nemesis, *WWD* publisher John Fairchild, always fought over. Betsy Bloomingdale, who was giving the dinner, directed the seating, putting the President between her and Claudette Colbert, and the First Lady between Zipkin and Alfred Bloomingdale. One couldn't help but marvel at how young—fit, tan, handsome—the President looked for a man who had just turned seventy. He beamed when the model Janice Dickinson, sitting a table away with Peppo Vanini, the owner of Xenon, a midtown disco that rivaled Studio 54 in exclusivity and decadence, raised her champagne glass and, in a voice loud enough for the whole restaurant to hear, announced how proud she was to be an American now that Ronald Reagan was in the White House. The entire room erupted into applause again.

Sirio had obviously packed the place with friendly faces, having consulted the day before with Zipkin about who should, or should not, get reservations. Among those at tables near the President's were the octogenarian *New York Post* fashion columnist Eugenia Sheppard and her regular walker, Earl Blackwell, the octogenarian publisher of *Celebrity Service*; Princess Ira von Fürstenberg, of Salzburg and Paris, and the billionaire Spanish banker Alfonso Fierro, whose wife was an old friend of Zipkin's.

I had been invited to Le Cirque that night by one of Zipkin's favorite couples, Carolina Herrera, the

Venezuelan socialite who was just beginning to establish herself as a New York fashion designer, and her aristocratic husband, Reinaldo, whose family had lived in the same house in Caracas since the sixteenth century. The Herreras' other guests were Bianca Jagger, who had almost turned down their invitation, she told me that afternoon, because of Reagan's campaign attacks on her native Nicaragua's leftist Sandinista government; the Italian movie producers Franco Rossellini and Countess Marina Cicogna, the latter with her longtime companion, Brazilian actress Florinda Bolkan; and Andy Warhol, who published *Interview* magazine, of which I was the editor. "Gee, Bob, this is *so* glamorous. Oh, it's just so glamorous," he said, with his flair for repetition. He had voted for Jimmy Carter.

I had voted for the winner. Like the majority of voters in forty-four states, I was fed up with the anemic wishy-washiness of the Carter administration, particularly in foreign policy, and turned on by Ronald Reagan's full-blooded, unabashed patriotism, his clear delineation of right and wrong, his sense of certainty. Also, like William Safire, I was— and still am—"a libertarian conservative Republican contrarian iconoclast."

I was brought up in an Italian-American family where becoming a Republican was equated with becoming an American, and where any mention of Eleanor Roosevelt was invariably followed by the comment "she should mind her own business," usually uttered by one or the other of my grandmothers. Bess Truman, they never tired of saying, wore her corsage upside-down at the 1949 inauguration. My father, a World War II veteran who had fought in Europe and the Pacific and was one of the first Italian-Americans to hold an executive position in the Wall Street coffee trade, never got over Thomas Dewey's loss or Harry Truman's firing of General Douglas MacArthur, my father's hero. My mother was a Republican committeewoman in Plainview, the middle-class Long Island suburb where we lived from 1955 to 1968; in 1956 she had my sisters and me walk up and down the street waving signs saying, "I Like Ike," "I Like Dick," and "Vote Row A All the Way." Jackie Kennedy, my fashion-conscious mother and grandmothers used to say, dressed beautifully, but why shouldn't she, they would add, repeating a popular Republican rumor, she'd been given a million dollars by her father-in-law to stay married to his son. For some reason they didn't mind Lady Bird Johnson, but LBJ had to go—before I got drafted. By then I was at Georgetown University's School of Foreign Service and a raging radical—I'd even joined Students for a Democratic Society, although I never told my parents that.

And then, in 1970, I went to work at Andy Warhol's Factory, where in reaction to the lockstep liberalism of the New York art world, I found myself returning to my Republican roots. I voted for Ronald Reagan for the first time in the 1976 Republican primary, when he unsuccessfully challenged President Gerald Ford. It seemed to me that the Reagans were being unfairly portrayed by a largely Democratic press, which cast him as a B actor bozo invented and controlled as a politician by a sinister claque of ultraconservative Southern California tycoons, and her as the driven daughter of a John Bircher Chicago neurosurgeon who had played a major role in turning his dim-bulb son-in-law into a fanatical anti-Communist. Somehow this didn't square in my mind with a couple whose best friends were the fun-loving Bloomingdales and Jerry Zipkin, one of the most sophisticated men I had ever met. Zipkin had been friends with Warhol since the 1950s, and had taken me under his wing not long after I became editor of *Interview*; he was constantly calling with story ideas and sending gift subscriptions to his grand friends around the world.

And now here, at Le Cirque, was Nancy Reagan, the supposedly square and uptight First Lady, taking her social cues from Zipkin, who in his not too distant past had been known to give two cocktail parties on the same night—"Why waste the flowers?" he would explain—the first from five to seven for his international society friends, the second from seven to nine for "gents only." And here was Ronald Reagan, the most conservative president since Calvin Coolidge—one of his first acts was to have a portrait of "Silent Cal" hung in the Oval Office—seeming perfectly comfortable, sitting in a peach-and-gray room lined with murals of cavorting monkeys in eighteenth-century court dress, surrounded by assorted European titles and jet-setters, exotic mystery women from Central Europe and Central America, and male and female homosexuals of varying degrees of closetedness. Then again, he was also the first divorced president and the first movie star president. This president had dated Rhonda Fleming and Piper Laurie. In retrospect, the scene that evening—a circus crossed with a court—was a fairly accurate metaphor for the decade to come.

When we got up to leave, the Reagans and their friends were still dining. I headed straight for the coat-check room, trying hard not to stare at their table. Andy, who pretended he never knew what to do, followed me. Everyone else with us filed past the President's table, where they were introduced to the Reagans. As we stood waiting for our coats, I heard Alfred Bloomingdale's booming voice: "Where the hell is Bob Colacello? He's the only Republican in this group." "I think they want you at that table," Andy said. Coat in hand, I approached the table, with Andy still following. "Mr. President," Bloomingdale said, "I'd like you to meet the great American artist Andy Warhol, and Bob Colacello, the editor of *Interview* magazine. He's a real Republican." We shook hands. Then Alfred introduced first Andy, then me, to Mrs. Reagan. Taking my hand in hers, she looked me right in the eyes and said, "I'm so glad to finally meet you. I've heard so much about you from Ron and Doria." She was referring to their son Ron and his wife, Doria, who had recently started working as my secretary. "I've heard so much about *you* from Ron and Doria" was all I could think to say, but it made her laugh—a big coquettish laugh, sparkling, knowing, and warm, that was unexpected from someone who looked so proper. The moment we were on the street, Andy moaned, "She held your hand for so *long*. I think she really loves you."

Jerry Zipkin called early the next morning. "You played it just right," he pronounced, "not rushing over to the table with all the Italians and Brazilians and God-knows-whats. She said to me, 'Bob Colacello is so *not* pushy.'"

That evening I saw President and Mrs. Reagan again, from afar, at the Metropolitan Opera House, where Ron Reagan was making his debut with the Joffrey II Ballet Company. Zipkin had a few friends up to his apartment on Park Avenue at 93rd Street—"I live on the hem of Harlem," he liked to say—for chicken salad and champagne before the ballet. The friends included Jan Cowles, modern art collector Lily Auchincloss, society columnist Aileen Mehle (who wrote under the name Suzy), Andy, and me. We had orchestra seats at the Met, and rose to our feet with the rest of the audience when the Reagans entered the center box with Doria and the Bloomingdales. As young Ron leapt and spun through an abstract piece called *Unfolding,* we all agreed that he was pretty good for someone who had started dancing only four years before, at age eighteen. The second half of the program was a concert by Diana Ross. As she sang "Reach out and touch somebody else and make the world a better place to live," the President took his wife's hand, and she took Doria's. "That's your *secretary* up there, Bob," said Andy.

The next day every paper in New York ran a photograph of Ron, in full makeup and a terry cloth robe, being embraced backstage by his mother, in an off-the-shoulder Galanos evening gown, while his father, in a tuxedo, stood beside them smiling proudly. It wasn't exactly Camelot, but it was a long way from home on the right-wing range.

Two weeks later a madman named John Hinckley shot and almost killed Ronald Reagan in a misguided attempt to impress the movie star Jodie Foster. For the next seven and half years, there would be no more presidential dinners at Le Cirque, and Nancy Reagan would be obsessed with her husband's security (to the point of secretly consulting with a San Francisco astrologer about his schedule and travels). Within months Alfred Bloomingdale would be stricken with cancer and then engulfed in a tabloid scandal when his long-secret mistress, a Hollywood playgirl named Vicki Morgan, sued him for palimony as he lay on his deathbed. Betsy Bloomingdale went to Mass every morning, gathered her children and grandchildren close to her, and held her head high. "Nancy called every single day when Alfred was ill," she later told me. "She knows what a friend is." On the night Alfred Bloomingdale died, Betsy, who had visited him in the hospital earlier that day, was giving a dinner party at an obscure German restaurant in Santa Monica for friends from Europe and New York, including Jerry Zipkin, Reinaldo and Carolina Herrera, and me.

In the meantime, Nancy Reagan had started calling me at the office, causing no end of envy in Andy. She always had an ostensible excuse, such as asking what I thought Ron or Doria might like for their birthday, but invariably she would end up urging me to persuade her son and daughter-in-law not to give up their Secret Service protection. Both the Libyans and the Puerto Rican Liberation Front were threatening to kidnap Ron, she said. Then I got the idea of putting her on the cover of *Interview.* I called Zipkin, who called Michael Deaver, the White House aide closest to Mrs. Reagan, who liked the idea because he thought associating her with Andy Warhol would help lighten her imperious image. Unfortunately, Andy and Nancy did not hit it off when we went to the White House to interview her. "The funny thing about movie people," he told her, "is that they talk behind your back before you even leave the room." Looking at him as if he were unbalanced, she replied, "*I* am a movie person, Andy." Doria later told me that her mother-in-law had said she didn't understand how I could work for Andy. Whenever the interview got on track, she said, he seemed to undermine me. When the December 1981 issue hit the stands, the entire New York art world seemed to rise up in horror and outrage. How could I put that googoo-eyed harridan, that overdressed housewife, on the cover of Andy Warhol's magazine? The *Village Voice* even ran a parody by Alexander Cockburn in which Andy and I went to Hitler's bunker in Berlin and asked him the same softball questions we had asked the First Lady.

In January 1982, Mrs. Reagan invited me to attend the State of the Union speech with Ron and Doria. In June she came up to New York to attend the premiere of the movie *Annie,* which had been produced by Ray Stark, an old and close friend of the Reagans'. I remember her calling me over to her table at the party afterward and introducing me to her dinner partners, Cary Grant and John Huston, who had directed the film—and whose father, the great actor Walter Huston, she told me, had played on Broadway with her mother back in the 1920s. Jerry Zipkin was also at her table, along with retired CBS chairman Bill Paley; Elizinha Moreira-Salles, the ex-wife of the richest man in Brazil; Greek shipping tycoon George Livanos and his wife, Lita; and Rosemarie Marcie-Rivière, an aging Swiss socialite who had been married almost as many times as Etti Plesch. It was the same kind of mix—Old Hollywood's A-list and charter members of the jet set—that one would find at the small private dinners Mrs. Reagan liked to give upstairs at the White House.

I remember her having me tracked down at a friend's house in Southampton one weekend that summer and keeping me on the phone for nearly two hours, asking again and again, "Why does the press hate me so much?" She had been under constant attack since the day her husband was elected, it seemed—for trying to get the Carters to leave the White House early, for borrowing designer clothes and jewelry, for ordering up expensive White House china, for attending the royal wedding of Prince Charles and Lady Diana Spencer with an elaborate security entourage. But nothing raised the ire of the East Wing press corps—mostly younger feminists—more than the way she gazed at her husband with rapt adoration during his speeches. By the end of their first year in the White House she had the highest disapproval rating of any first lady in modern times. No wonder she sounded so hurt and bewildered. I agreed that the press had been unduly hard on her. Yet it crossed my mind that Nancy Reagan, like my grandmothers and mother, seemed to have a talent for playing the martyr.

In September, I was invited to a state dinner for President and Mrs. Marcos of the Philippines. Much to Andy's dismay, he wasn't. So I called Zipkin, who called Muffie Brandon, the White House social secretary, who prevailed upon the First Lady to have him. A month later Mrs. Reagan was in New York for a party at the Lincoln Center library to promote her book about the Foster Grandparents Program, *To Love a Child.* I had just returned from Thailand and brought her some souvenir seashells from Phuket Island. She hugged and kissed me as if I had given her pearls, and everyone on the receiving line wondered what I had done to deserve such a display of affection.

But I was beginning to realize that once Nancy Reagan liked you she really liked you. (Just as once she didn't, she really didn't.)

When I quit *Interview* the following February, a rumor arose that I was under consideration for a job in Nancy Reagan's office. That was followed by a second rumor: a photograph of me dancing with Truman Capote at Studio 54 had come to the FBI's attention, ruling me out. The truth was that I soon signed a contract with *Vanity Fair* and didn't have as much contact with Mrs. Reagan, partially because Tina Brown, the editor, preferred to deal with the White House herself, partially because Doria Reagan no longer worked for me. She and Ron moved to Los Angeles with the Joffrey Ballet not long after I left *Interview*.

But I remained close to Jerry Zipkin, and when he died of lung cancer in 1995, I was assigned to write his obituary by Graydon Carter, Tina Brown's successor at *Vanity Fair*. I called Mrs. Reagan at her house in Bel Air. She and her husband had been out of the White House for six years by then; he had announced that he had Alzheimer's disease in a letter to the nation the year before. Our conversation took off as if we had spoken days, instead of years, before, and as usual with her, it was a long conversation. "I don't know what I'm going to do without him," she said several times. "I feel as if I've lost the two most important men in my life now. Well, Ronnie's still here, but . . ." She told me she had visited Zipkin at his apartment just before he died, and had sat at his bedside for two hours. "I feel very strongly that he stayed alive until he saw her," their mutual good friend the designer Bill Blass told me. "It was all very planned, his departure."

In 1997, Graydon Carter called me into his office and said that he thought it was time to take a look back at the Reagan years, and that he wanted me to write the article. "I know you like them, which is why their friends will talk to you," he said. "But you will have to become neutral when you sit down at the typewriter." There is no such thing as true neutrality in journalism, and access is a two-edged sword, but I believe I was fair and balanced in the two-part article that was published in July and August 1998. In any case, I like telling stories more than making judgments, especially when writing relatively soon after the fact. I also like writing about the social side of life, not only because it is amusing but also because I have learned from experience that what seems silly often has serious repercussions, and that what seems superficial often reveals deeper truths. And if any subject was about the confluence of the serious and the frivolous, the social and the political, it was the Reagans and the era they came to represent.

I spent a large part of the next four years in California, researching first that article and then this book, and in the process growing much closer to Nancy Reagan than I ever would have thought possible that night at Le Cirque. We had many long lunches at the Hotel Bel-Air, which she liked because it was five minutes from home and her ailing husband. We spent many afternoons meticulously going through her White House scrapbooks at the former president's office high above Avenue of the Stars in Century City. She invited me to numerous events at the Reagan Library in Simi Valley, including lunches for George W. Bush and John McCain during the 2000 primary campaign. But although she had me to their house on St. Cloud Road, she never let me see Ronald Reagan. She may have mellowed in other ways, but Nancy Reagan was not about to stop protecting her husband's image when it needed protecting most. This was an exceptionally shrewd and determined woman, I came to realize, who did not give up, who never let go.

I have also been fortunate in having access to the Reagan Group, as Ronald and Nancy Reagan's oldest and closest friends in Los Angeles are called, and to what's left of its political subset, the Kitchen Cabinet, the wealthy businessmen who came together to elect Ronald Reagan governor in 1966, and who continued to support him through his bids for the presidency in 1968, 1976, and 1980, when he was finally triumphant. Most of these friends met the Reagans during the early years of their marriage. Some had known them separately before they married. Almost none of them had ever talked about the Reagans to a journalist or biographer (and they almost invariably checked with Nancy Reagan before talking to me). In the case of those who had died, I was usually able to interview their children, several of whom worked on Ronald Reagan's campaigns and, in two cases, in his White House.

Mostly in their seventies, eighties, and nineties, the surviving members of the Reagan Group were proud of their long association with Ronnie and Nancy, as they always called the Reagans, and were still jealous of one another's closeness to them. They actually referred to themselves as the Group. "She wasn't in the Group as early as some of us were," said Betty Adams, who took credit for introducing Nancy Reagan to many of the women in the Group in 1958, referring to Erlenne Sprague, who said she had sponsored Nancy's membership in the Colleagues, the exclusive Los Angeles charity, in 1962. "There were a lot of Johnny-come-latelys," Jean French Smith, the widow of the Kitchen Cabinet lawyer who became attorney general in the first Reagan administration, told me, "who say they were in the Kitchen Cabinet from the beginning but weren't. If you turn off your tape recorder, I'll tell you which ones."

The Kitchen Cabinet—the term goes back to the gang of cronies who unofficially advised President Andrew Jackson—was led by three self-made multimillionaires, auto dealer Holmes Tuttle, oilman Henry Salvatori, and drugstore tycoon Justin Dart, all long gone. Alfred Bloomingdale, steel magnate Earle Jorgensen, and oil equipment manufacturer William Wilson, the husbands of Nancy Reagan's three best friends, Betsy Bloomingdale, Marion Jorgensen, and Betty Wilson, were also in the inner circle. Somewhat removed but extremely influential were the Group's only billionaire, Walter Annenberg, the owner of *TV Guide* and President Nixon's ambassador to Great Britain, and his wife, Lee, who were based in Philadelphia but who spent several months each year in California.

Over the years, the Reagans and their friends came to resemble a court, and their social life, with its fixed calendar and closed guest list, took on the aura of ritual. Every Fourth of July these same couples trekked to the Santa Inez Mountains for Nancy Reagan's birthday picnic at the Reagans' Rancho del Cielo. Every New Year's Eve they celebrated at Sunnylands, the Annenbergs' palatial Palm Springs estate. Every New Year's Day they went to Holmes and Virginia Tuttle's bungalow on the grounds of the Eldorado Country Club. Every election night they watched the returns at the Jorgensens' house in Bel Air. When President Reagan turned seventy in 1981 and seventy-five in 1986, his black-tie birthday parties at the White House were paid for by the Annenbergs, the Jorgensens, the Wilsons, and the Armand Deutsches, who were also longtime members of the Group. "We all stood up when Ronnie cut the cake," recalled Harriet Deutsch, sitting in the screening room of their Beverly Hills house, surrounded by dozens of framed photographs of the Reagans and their friends. "Oh, he was so darling. The most loving, sweet man. I don't think he has a mean bone in his body. And Nancy is a darling friend. When she is your friend."

*   *   *

One of the advantages of taking a social approach in writing about the Reagans is that it highlights Nancy Reagan's role—the importance of which cannot be overemphasized—in Ronald Reagan's political career. As the pundit George Will once said, "Ronald Reagan has one best friend, and he married her." I would go further: one cannot figure out Ronald Reagan without figuring out Nancy Reagan, too.

Taking this angle has led me to three conclusions. First, the marriage of Ronald and Nancy Reagan is undoubtedly one of the great love stories of our time, with few rivals in fidelity, intensity, and longevity. Second, the social life that grew out of their marriage made Ronald Reagan's political career possible, mainly because, more than those of any other presidential couple, the Reagans' social and political lives were completely intertwined. Third, Nancy Reagan was one of the most powerful first ladies in history—although she was largely successful in her efforts to cover her tracks during the White House years and remained reluctant to reveal the extent of her influence for fear of appearing to be the power behind the throne and thereby diminishing her husband's legacy. Like Woodrow Wilson's wife, Edith, she shielded an aging and sometimes ill husband, though as president Ronald Reagan was never as incapacitated as Woodrow Wilson. Like Eleanor Roosevelt, she lobbied her husband on appointments and policy, though always privately, never publicly. Like Hillary Clinton, she stood by her man, particularly in times of crisis, though Reagan's crises were never as sordid as Clinton's. And like Jacqueline Kennedy, she understood the connection between style and substance, though she never quite matched Mrs. Kennedy in elegance and cultivation.

Ronald Reagan's five-day state funeral, at once grand and intimate, historic and moving, was his wife's finest moment. His death came on June 5, 2004, the day before the sixtieth anniversary of the Normandy invasion, which it eclipsed on the world's television screens. Nancy Reagan had begun planning the obsequies a decade earlier, concerning herself with every detail, determined to make this her final contribution to her husband's legend. From the first moment we saw her, standing outside the funeral home in Santa Monica, leaning on the arm of a brigadier general as she watched her husband's casket being lifted into a hearse, this frail eighty-two-year-old woman in a perfect black suit and pearls was a picture of dignity and grace.

More than 110,000 people filed past the casket at the Ronald Reagan Presidential Library in Simi Valley, and nearly as many paid homage in the Rotunda of the Capitol in Washington, where Reagan's body lay in state for thirty-six hours. The funeral service in Washington National Cathedral brought together four former United States presidents, and eulogies were delivered by former British prime minister Margaret Thatcher, former Canadian prime minister Brian Mulroney, Reagan's vice president, George H. W. Bush, and President

George W. Bush. Among the four thousand mourners were Mikhail Gorbachev, Reagan's partner in
ending the Cold War, and Lech Walesa, the Polish
union leader who led the struggle to overthrow
Communism in Eastern Europe; the current leaders of Germany, Great Britain, and South Africa;
and an array of Reagan friends from the East
Coast ranging from David Rockefeller to Joan
Rivers.

Prince Charles accompanied the Reagan family
on Air Force One back to California for the sunset
burial service that same day. Awaiting the party at
the burial site on a hilltop behind the Reagan
Library were the surviving members of the Group,
including Betsy Bloomingdale, Marion Jorgensen,
William Wilson, Erlenne Sprague, and Betty
Adams. Eulogies there were given by the three
surviving Reagan children, Michael, Patti, and Ron,
and at the end of the service Nancy Reagan broke
down for the first time. According to her old friend
Merv Griffin, an honorary pallbearer, she was
astounded and touched by the outpouring of sympathy across the land. "I thought people had forgotten Ronnie," she said. "They hadn't seen him
for almost ten years."

This work is not a full-scale biography of either
Reagan, but rather an attempt to paint a portrait of a
marriage that changed the course of history. I have
sought to expand and correct the rather limited
existing record of Nancy Reagan's life before she
became First Lady, which is riddled with errors and

distortions, partly because her most extensive biography to date was written by the sensationalistic Kitty Kelley, a dogged digger for documents but a relentlessly negative judge of character. Nancy Reagan herself contributed to the confusion by redacting and deleting, whitewashing and sugarcoating the more unpleasant and complicated facts of her life. Ronald Reagan was also prone, like most politicians, to sentimentalizing and mythologizing his past, but his many biographers, including Lou Cannon, Garry Wills, Stephen Vaughn, and the self-destructive Edmund Morris (who for some inexplicable reason virtually ignored Nancy Reagan), have done an admirable job of setting the record of his life straight. I have mostly summarized and interpreted that record in order to give the reader a clearer picture of the man with whom Nancy Reagan fell in love. This volume, the first of two, follows the couple up to 1980 and the start of Ronald Reagan's presidency.

"He never would have made it without her," I was told again and again in the course of interviewing nearly two hundred Reagan relatives, friends, colleagues, campaign aides, administration officials, and observers. "He never would have been elected Governor without her." "He never would have become President without her." They talked about her devotion, her protectiveness, her "antennae" for sussing out people who put their agendas ahead of her husband's. This was not to discredit Ronald Reagan's intelligence, talents, or achievements, they insisted. He was the simple man with the simple plan, the visionary, the dreamer, the great communicator, who had the big ideas he believed could change the country and the world for the better. She was the complicated woman of parts, the strategist, the fighter, the "personnel director of the Reagan operation," who created the atmosphere and forged the relationships that made it possible for him to carry out what both of them saw as his destiny.

One of the most telling conversations I ever had with Nancy Reagan was after I had appeared on the *Today* show to talk about my *Vanity Fair* story and had stressed the point that the Reagans were a great political team. "How was I?" I asked when she called that same day.

"You were good," she said, with a certain hesitation in her voice. "But you left out the most important word."

What was that? I asked.

"Love," she said. "Please don't make me sound like some kind of master backstage manipulator. Everything I did, I did for Ronnie."

CHAPTER ONE

EARLY RONNIE
1911–1932

We were poor and I suppose at the bottom edge of the town, but we thought of ourselves as typically middle-class Americans. . . . My father told Neil, two years older, and me, that he would try to help us get to college, but that we would have to do most toward it ourselves.

Ronald Reagan, in a *Saturday Evening Post* interview, April 1974

I was the one who . . . would go down to the one pool hall in town that was downstairs under a store, where your folks couldn't see you if they happened to walk by on the walk. [Dutch] would never do anything like that. He would rather be up there, just gazing at his birds' eggs.

Neil Reagan, UCLA Oral History Program, 1981[1]

Ronald Wilson Reagan was born at home on February 6, 1911, in Tampico, Illinois, the son of

John Edward Reagan, a shoe salesman everyone called Jack, and Nelle Wilson Reagan, a housewife who sometimes took in sewing. The Reagans lived in a five-room apartment over a row of stores on the town's one-block-long Main Street. Heated by three coal-burning stoves, the apartment, like most homes in Tampico at that time, did not have running water or an indoor toilet. Nelle's labor was extremely difficult and went on for twenty-four hours. Jack became so worried that he went out in a blizzard to get a doctor, who delivered the ten-pound boy at 4:16 in the morning and told Nelle she could not have any more children.[2]

In his 1965 autobiography, *Where's the Rest of Me?*, written as he was preparing to run for governor of California, Ronald Reagan painted the scene of his birth in patriotic colors: "My face was blue from screaming, my bottom was red from whacking, and my father claimed afterward that he was white when he said shakily, 'For such a little bit of a fat Dutchman, he makes a hell of a lot of noise, doesn't he?' 'I think he's perfectly wonderful,' said my mother weakly. . . . Those were their first opinions of me. As far as I know, they never changed during their lifetimes. As for myself, ever since my birth my nickname has been 'Dutch' and I have been particularly fond of the colors that were exhibited—red, white, and blue."[3]

His brother, Neil, born in September 1908, recalled the event in less glowing terms. "[T]hey came to me—I'd been sent to the neighbors for a couple of days—[and said,] 'Now you can go home and see your baby brother,' and I wanted to go in the opposite direction. I went home, and for two days after I was home, I would not go in the room where my brother and my mother were. I didn't want any part of a brother. I had been promised a sister by my mother and father. That's all I wanted. I guess that shows you how early in life I determined not to be queer. I was strictly a girl man."[4]

Neil Reagan also said, "Ronald is my mother's boy and I'm my father's boy." One way to illustrate what he meant is to compare how the two brothers remembered their youth. "We were poor, and I mean poor," Neil said.[5] "We were poor," Ronald said, "but we didn't know we were poor."[6] Another way to put it: the first son drank, the second didn't.

Reagan's biographers, following his lead, have presented Nelle and Jack Reagan as a case of opposites attracting. He was Irish Catholic; she was Scots-English Protestant. He could be moody, cynical, and stubborn; she was determined to be sunny, idealistic, and understanding. He was a charmer, a storyteller, a chain-smoker, a binge drinker. She was a do-gooder, a Bible-thumper, a teetotaler. He was a bit of a clown; she was a bit of a saint.

But they also had a lot in common, starting with their immigrant rural roots and their mutual desire to transcend those roots and make something of themselves. Both Jack and Nelle were amateur actors, autodidacts, and stylish dressers who stood out in the series of small Midwestern towns where Jack went from job to job and Nelle fixed up rented home after rented home. Both felt a need to be different, which expressed itself in Nelle's poetry writing and elocution recitals and in Jack's political views—he was an outspoken Democrat in solidly Republican rural Illinois. There was a whiff of bohemianism in their insisting that their sons call them Nelle and Jack, not Mother and Father. Both loved an audience; Jack's preferred venue was the saloon, Nelle's the church. Jack liked to joke: "Jesus walked barefoot . . . but then, He didn't have to deal with our Illinois winters, now did He?"[7] One of Nelle's mottos was "To higher, nobler things my mind is bent."[8]

The Reagans were strivers, joiners, dreamers— they wanted more out of life for themselves and their sons. Her bourgeois yearnings were matched by his "burning ambition to succeed," to use his son's phrasing.[9] In this they were hardly alone in early twentieth-century Main Street America, where Horatio Alger heroes were lining up for membership in newly constructed country clubs. Upward mobility has always been the great American motif; the self-made man and his social-climbing wife are all-American archetypes; the house on the hill is still the American dream.

But Jack and Nelle never made it. They never even owned a house until their son bought them one in Hollywood. As the Great Depression descended upon the Farm Belt in the late 1920s, and Jack's drinking became more and more of a problem, the Reagans were reduced to taking in boarders, and Nelle retreated further into religion. There would be good years in business and happy days at home, but Jack would never achieve his dream of financial independence and respectable status. As a family friend candidly put it, "Jack always wanted to be 'cut-glass Irish'; at best he was 'lace-curtain,' but that never had a way of registering with him."[10]

The O'Regans came from Ballyporeen, County Tipperary, Ireland. Jack's grandfather, a poor potato farmer, left home during the famine of the 1840s and lived in London for a few years, where he worked as a soapmaker and Anglicized the family name before crossing the Atlantic. Nelle's grandfather, a Wilson from Renfrewshire, Scotland, fought against the British in Canada during the Mackenzie Rebellion in the 1830s. Both families settled in the flat, fertile farm country of northwestern Illinois sometime before the Civil War. Illinois was on the frontier then—the last Indians had been driven out of the state only in 1832, after the Black Hawk War—and it was still possible to stake a claim to undeveloped land and homestead it. That is what both the Reagans and Wilsons did near the small Mississippi River port of Fulton in Whiteside County, about one hundred miles west of Chicago.[11] During this time Illinois came to be known as the Prairie State, and by 1860 it led the nation in wheat and corn production. But neither the Wilsons nor the Reagans prospered.

Jack Reagan was born in Fulton on July 13,

1883, and lived in a two-room farmhouse until he was orphaned at the age of six, after both his parents died of tuberculosis. He was raised by an aunt and uncle who had opened a general store in the new railroad town of Bennett, Iowa. He left school after the sixth grade to help out in his uncle's store during the depression of the 1890s. Around 1899 he returned to Fulton to work as a general clerk at J. W. Broadhead's Dry Goods Store.[12] According to Anne Edwards in *Early Reagan*, "Shoes became [his] specialty. He liked children, and particularly admired the graceful turn of a lady's ankle. He talked about someday traveling west to pioneer. . . . But he remained at Broadhead's for eight years, gaining a reputation as a young man a bit too fond of alcohol, a fact that made the parents of most eligible Fulton women (who were entranced by his beguiling manner and dark good looks) wary."[13] And then he met Nelle, who was earning her living as a milliner in Fulton.

Nelle Wilson, who was born on July 18, 1882,[14] also spent her early years on a farm. Her mother, Mary Anne Elsey, had been born in England and immigrated to Illinois to work as a domestic servant. When Nelle was seven, her father left the family and moved to Chicago for reasons unknown. Like Jack, Nelle left school after the sixth grade. Her mother died when she was seventeen. Although Nelle had been brought up as a Presbyterian,[15] and her father disapproved of Jack, probably because he was a Catholic, they were married in Fulton's Catholic church on November 8, 1904.[16]

It was said that Nelle didn't mind Jack's week-end benders at first, but when his older brother, William, was jailed for six months for drunk and disorderly conduct, she apparently had had enough. In February 1906, eighteen months after they married, the Reagans moved to Tampico, a country town with a population of about eight hundred, where the local Law and Order League prevailed and liquor licensing was banned twelve years before national Prohibition.[17] They were in their early twenties, full of hope, good-looking, and smart, even sophisticated by Tampico standards. Nelle was blue-eyed with auburn hair, petite and full-bosomed. Jack was almost six feet tall, well built and handsome, with wavy black hair rakishly parted in the middle, and always impeccably turned out for work in a freshly starched white shirt, a tie, and highly polished shoes.[18]

Jack and Nelle spent the next eight years in Tampico, the first five in the apartment on Main Street where Neil and Ronald were born. Three months after Ronald's birth, they moved up to a two-story frame house with modern plumbing that faced a small park with a Civil War monument and, just beyond that, the railroad tracks and a pair of tall grain elevators. Jack did well at H. C. Pitney's General Store. He was in charge of the shoes and clothing department and made occasional buying trips to Chicago. Energetic and outgoing, he was a natural leader, serving during the years in Tampico as a councilman, an assistant fire chief, a baseball manager, and, though not much of a church-goer, finance chairman of Saint Mary's Catholic Church.[19]

Neil was baptized at Saint Mary's, although Nelle had to be prodded by the priest to keep her marital promise to raise their children as Catholics. Neil's godfather, A. C. Burden, owned Burden's Opera House, located above the bank on Main Street. Nelle and Jack were soon appearing in plays put on there by the town's amateur dramatic group, for audiences of a hundred or so, seated on folding chairs. Neil recalled rehearsals at his parents' house. "When the rehearsal wound up at the end of the evening, they'd all sit down and have a bowl of oyster stew and crackers," he said. "Ronald and I'd sneak down the stairs partway and look . . . at all the goings-on down there."[20]

The most significant event of the Reagan family's years in Tampico was Nelle's conversion to the Disciples of Christ, a breakaway sect of Presbyterianism. On Easter Sunday, March 27, 1910, she was baptized by total immersion in the Hennepin Canal outside town. When Ronald was born the following year, she refused to have him baptized as a Catholic, and from then on she raised both sons as Disciples of Christ, taking them with her to prayer meetings on Sunday and Wednesday nights and to Sunday school, which she taught. She became a "visiting disciple," helping the poor and the sick, sometimes wrote the weekly church notes in the *Tampico Tornado*, and was elected president of the Missionary Society.[21]

The Disciples of Christ had emerged out of the great religious upheaval that swept the American frontier in the early nineteenth century, as the new nation spawned new churches, including the Unitarians and the Mormons. It was formally organized as a distinct denomination in 1832, and by 1900 had more than 1.2 million members. It was especially strong in the rural parts of Kentucky, Ohio, Indiana, and Illinois. The Disciples called themselves "simple Christians" and their church "the Christian Church." Unlike most other Protestant denominations, the Disciples made communion open to anyone who accepted Christ as the son of God and the New Testament as the means to salvation. They rejected the Calvinism of the old Presbyterians, with its emphasis on predestination and the depravity of man. Instead, they stressed individual responsibility, the work ethic, education, good works, and Protestant unity.[22]

Like many nativist churches, the Disciples had an anti-Catholic streak, seeing Roman Catholics as foreign and morally lax, particularly with regard to alcohol, so Nelle's choice of this church was something of a slap in the face to her husband. The Disciples of Christ were fanatically opposed to drinking, "the driest of the dries." They were closely aligned with the Women's Christian Temperance Union. One of the most famous Disciples was Carry Nation, who, in the 1890s, led a crusade of hymn-singing, hatchet-wielding women through the saloons of Kansas, smashing bottles and furniture. The Disciples used grape juice, not wine, in their communion service.[23]

In the summer of 1913, the Reagan family's peaceful life was turned upside down, literally and figuratively. Five years after Henry Ford brought out America's first affordable car, Jack bought a Model T and within a month had managed to overturn it, with his wife and two sons inside, by crashing into a stump. When it was repaired, it not only widened the family's horizons, making it easier for Nelle to visit her sisters in Morrison and Quincy, but also stimulated Jack's restlessness. His buying—and drinking—trips to Chicago and other "wet" towns became more frequent.[24]

In comparison to his brother William's alcoholism, which was so severe that Jack tried to have him committed in 1914, Jack's drinking seemed under control. He tended to binge on holidays and when things were going well, but otherwise he would remain sober for long stretches of time. Still, by the age of thirty-one he had apparently had enough of the smallness—and dryness—of Tampico.

The Reagans would move five times in the next five years. Their first stop was Chicago, where they spent a miserable eight months living in a cold-water flat. Jack hated being one of three hundred employees at the Fair Store, which billed itself as the largest department store in the world, and was fired after being arrested for public drunkenness.[25]

Then came three years in Galesburg, home of the country's largest horse and mule market, where Jack lost another job because of his drinking. (In Galesburg he tried to enlist for service in World War I, but as a father of two was turned down.) A year in Monmouth, a pleasant county seat best known as the birthplace of Wyatt Earp, followed. Finally, in 1919, Jack's former boss, H. C. Pitney, who was going blind, lured him back to Tampico with an offer of higher pay and the chance to become a partner. The Reagans moved into an apartment above the Pitney store, right across the street from the apartment where the boys had been born. After five years of wandering in an attempt to move up in the world, they had come full circle.[26]

Yet young Ronald thrived. Buoyed by his mother's faith and love, he was reading newspapers before he entered school, he earned a 95 average in first grade in Galesburg, and he skipped a grade in Monmouth. His teachers noted his nearly photographic memory, which he may have developed to compensate for his extreme nearsightedness, which was not diagnosed until he was thirteen. Although he was the perpetual new boy in town, he made friends easily. At the same time, he was also already learning to keep part of himself in reserve; he liked to draw, daydream, and wander in the woods. A girl in his third-grade class remembered him thus: "He was startling to look at (not only good-looking but he had this air about him). . . . His jaw was always set—as though somebody was going to take a poke at him and he was ready for the punches. I looked at his thrust-out chin every day, and wondered 'Why?' "[27] At nine he made his theatrical debut in the Tampico Christian Church with a recitation entitled "About Mother."[28]

Reagan later called the move back to Tampico "the most fortunate shift of my life. My existence turned into one of those rare Huck Finn–Tom Sawyer idylls.There were woods and mysteries, life and death among the small creatures, hunting and fishing; those were the days when I learned the real riches of rags."[29] He liked playing tag in the town's stockyard pens and having food fights with the refuse in the alleys behind the stores on Main Street, swimming in the "deep and treacherous" Hennepin Canal—he was the best swimmer among his friends—and learning to play football in the Civil War park. In the summer the Reagan boys picked strawberries for pay. In the fall they helped the school janitor rake leaves and were rewarded with a marshmallow roast. They carried coal to the Opera House in exchange for free admission to the silent movies shown there. Both boys loved the Westerns; Ronald's favorite stars were Tom Mix and William S. Hart.[30]

Most nights Nelle sat Neil and Ronald down at one end of the kitchen table and read aloud to them from such books as *The Three Musketeers* and *King Arthur and the Round Table,* while Jack read his newspaper at the other end of the table.[31] Ronald's grades were so good in the fourth grade—he got As in reading, arithmetic, and deportment—that he was one of five students in a class of twenty-two to be cited for excellence.[32] He was the kind of boy that grown-ups liked—scrappy but polite. He became particularly close to Jim and Emma Greenman, who owned Greenman's Jewelry Store next to Pitney's and lived above it. One might even say they were the first rich people to take up Ronald Reagan.

"An elderly childless couple, they took a special fancy to me," the future president recalled. "I had no grandparents and this sort of spoiling was delightful. The jeweler's wife gave me ten cents a week as an allowance (a magnificent sum in those days) plus cookies and chocolate every afternoon. The best part was that I was allowed to dream. Many the day I spent deep in a huge rocker in the mystic atmosphere of Aunt Emma's living room with its horsehair-stuffed gargoyles of furniture, its shawls and antimacassars, globes of glass over birds and flowers, books and strange odors; many the day I remained hidden in a corner downstairs in Uncle Jim's jewelry shop with its curious relics, faint lights from gold and silver and bronze, lulled by the erratic ticking of a dozen clocks and the drone of the customers who came in."[33]

The one member of the Reagan family who wasn't thrilled to be back in Tampico was Jack, especially after its single tavern closed when Prohibition went into effect on January 16, 1920. Nelle's church celebrated the event with a midnight service.

* * *

When Ronald was almost ten, his parents moved to Dixon, another county seat in northwestern Illinois, and there they stayed for the next seventeen years. They did, however, move five times within Dixon, always to a smaller place. Reagan considered Dixon, where he completed grade school and high school and spent his college summers, his hometown. "All of us have to have a place we go back to," he wrote. "Dixon is that place for me."[34] Dixon was where his commitment to the Disciples of Christ took hold, where his political views started to form, where his love of sports and his attraction to the stage began, and where his winning personality emerged—the cheerful determination that made his ambition seem more like helpfulness than selfishness.

Compared with Tampico, Dixon, which had a population of 8,191 in 1920, seemed like a city to young Ronald. In most ways it was typical of the small towns in rural Illinois—farmers brought their wheat and corn to market for shipment to Chicago, Omaha, and cities in the South on the Illinois Central and Northwestern railroads; dairy farmers supplied the Borden Milk Company's condensing plant; there was one hotel, and Lincoln had stayed there. But nearly half its wage earners were employed by manufacturing firms—the Grand Detour Plow Company, the Clipper Lawnmower Company, the Medusa Cement Company, the Reynolds Wire Company, the Brown

Shoe Company—and there was a large Irish Catholic minority among these lower-middle-class, blue-collar workers, many of whom were Democrats.[35]

That was part of Dixon's attraction for Jack Reagan—the speakeasies of Bootlegger's Knob on the South Side were perhaps another.[36] He had persuaded H. C. Pitney to sell his general store in Tampico and back him in a shoe store in downtown Dixon. The deal was that Jack's commissions would be deducted from his debt to Pitney, and when that was paid off, he would own half the business.[37] Jack now called himself a "graduate practipedist," because somewhere along the way he had taken a correspondence course from the American School of Practipedics—the newfangled, quasi-scientific study of the bones of the foot. There were already four shoe stores in Dixon, but Reagan's Fashion Boot Shop, as Jack named the store, was the first to use an X-ray machine for fitting shoes.[38] Despite the modern gimmicks, the shop did not get off to a good start, mainly because wholesale farm prices fell by nearly 50 percent between 1920 and 1921, and would not recover until 1926.[39]

The Reagans rented an old two-story frame house with a barn on South Hennepin Avenue, a few blocks from Jack's store. The boys shared a bedroom and a bed, and Nelle used the third bedroom for the sewing she took in when ends didn't meet. Years later, Neil recalled:

The downstairs part of the barn had just been made into a garage for a car, but there were still a couple of stalls there. Upstairs was just an empty hayloft. To this day, I can't remember what brought it about, but in some way I got interested in pigeons. I said something to my dad about it, and my dad brought home a pair of fancy pigeons, pouters, and said, "Now, build a little nest in a couple of boxes and put them into the haymow, keep the haymow door closed for three or four days. Feed them and keep them watered, but don't let them out for three or four days. That way, when you do open the mow door, they'll go out in the morning and they might stay all day, but they'll come back at night, because now this is their nest."

Well, over a short period of time, why, he bought two or three other pairs of different kinds of fancy pigeons; and, of course, as pigeons do, before long, when they came back at night, a thousand others would come back with them. The first thing you know I had practically the whole mow up there covered with boxes nailed to the walls and had pigeons up to our neck.

Dutch got interested in birds' eggs, collecting birds' eggs, and my dad got him an old glass display case from a store. . . . Then they put cotton batting on the floor of it, and that's where Ronald kept his bird egg collection. He'd punch a hole in both ends and blow the eggs, and he was climbing trees to get them out. This kind of stuff didn't interest me.

Then I got to raising rabbits and built quite a hutch out back of the barn. . . . Come Friday night, after the pigeons came in, if there were squabs up there, I'd get the squabs and a bucket of boiling water, and I'd snap their heads off and clean them. I'd kill four or five young rabbits, skin them and clean them. Then I'd take a market basket and go out the next day beating on doors, and I never failed to sell all the squabs and rabbits I had in the basket. I built up a little business.[40]

In March 1923 the Reagans moved to a smaller house on the North Side, where the brothers had to sleep on an enclosed porch but could attend the academically superior North Dixon High School.[41] The Rock River divided Dixon socially as well as geographically. Downtown was on the South Side, as were the factories and the working-class Irish Catholic neighborhoods. The North Side was a little leafier, a little wealthier, more Protestant—"the sissies' part of town," as Neil put it. He refused to switch from South Dixon High School, at which he had started the previous fall, preferring to trek across the bridge every morning and afternoon.[42] From then on, the Rock River also came to symbolize the division in the Reagan family.

On one side were Jack and Neil, on the other Nelle and Ronald. In talking about his father with a *Saturday Evening Post* writer in 1974, Ronald

Reagan said, "There was never any buddy-buddy relationship, because of either fear or self-consciousness."[43] While Neil frequented Red Vail's pool hall on the South Side with his friends, the sons of firemen and factory workers, Ronald was home taking elocution lessons from Nelle. "We just sort of went our separate ways," explained Neil.[44] On March 25, 1924, the Dixon Telegraph reported, "Neil Reagan was taken into Justice A. H. Hanneken's court yesterday afternoon on a warrant charging him with disturbing the peace, he being taken as the second party in Saturday night's fistic encounter staged near the corner of North Galena avenue and Boyd street, when police responded to a riot call."[45]

As a Dixon schoolmate put it, "Neil was all boy, Ronald was a momma's boy."[46] Perhaps young Ronald was aware of this perception of him, for he began to insist on being called Dutch, saying he hated the prissy-sounding Ronald.[47] Neil's South Side gang gave him his nickname, Moon, because he parted his thick head of hair down the middle like the popular comic strip character Moon Mullins.[48]

In the winter of 1922, coming home from playing basketball at the YMCA after school, Ronald found his father passed out drunk in the snow outside the South Hennepin Avenue house. He didn't tell his mother, but that spring he asked to be baptized into her church. On June 21, 1922, Ronald became a member of the First Christian Church of Dixon. At eleven, he was somewhat young to enter the Disciples of Christ, who rejected pedobaptism and believed that choosing the faith should be a rational adult decision. But Ronald's fervor was such that he even persuaded Neil to be baptized with him. There is some evidence that this happened behind their Catholic father's back.[49] In any case, Neil would return to his father's side of the religious divide and reconvert to Catholicism when he turned eighteen, in 1926.

Nelle's whole life had come to revolve around her church. She believed in tithing but could seldom afford to part with 10 percent of their income, so she made up for it in good works. She taught the True Blue Class in Bible study to a women's group every Sunday. She was song director of the choir and president of the Women's Missionary Society, and she raised funds to build a parsonage for the new minister, Reverend Ben Hill Cleaver. According to Neil, she regularly visited prisoners in the county jail, where she would "get all the inmates singing and drive the sheriff nuts." It wasn't unusual for her to have inmates released into her custody; she would put them up in her sewing room until they found a place to live. "Blacks, whites, we never thought about color," Neil said. "She would hear of a case and just know that person wasn't guilty and go to work on the state authorities who, I suspect, finally just gave up and paroled the person because it was too much trouble otherwise."[50]

In a compilation made by local historian Ron

Marlow of references to the First Christian Church congregation published in the *Dixon Telegraph* between 1920 and 1928, Nelle's name appears 136 times, Ronald's name sixty-six, and Neil's sixty. On November 24, 1923, for example, the *Telegraph* described a piano recital at the church in nearby Prairieville, at which "Mrs. J. E. Reagan . . . gave a number of delightful readings. . . . [She] captivated her audience, reading 'The Italian's Story of the Rose,' an exceptionally beautiful selection, and 'On the Other Train,' another pleasing number. . . . Mrs. Reagan is most versatile, and is equally happy in tragic, comic or descriptive readings. Every number on the program was heartily applauded. After the program the ladies of the Prairieville Social Circle served refreshments, clearing $19.45. Those taking part in the program were served free of charge, a compliment from the Circle and much appreciated."[51]

Once a month, Nelle and Ronald entertained the patients at Dixon State Hospital with banjo playing and recitations. She also wrote poems, essays, and plays with moralistic messages and, to quote her younger son, became "the dean of dramatic recitals for the countryside."[52] A typical Nelle verse, titled "On the Sunnyside":

> As you journey on the road of life
>   Observe as you push your way
> Some faces moodish, sullen, sad.
>   Others with smile so gay.
> These last ones are on the sunnyside

They see the best in life
Think lovely thoughts, ennobling the soul
  Keeping them from strife. . . .
The sunnyside's the only side
  Full of graces divine
Sometimes too bright for us to scan
  I'd seek to make them mine.[53]

A temperance play Nelle wrote for the Dixon church contained the telling line "I love you, Daddy, except when you have that old bottle."[54] Nelle's attitude toward Jack's drinking was complicated. On one hand she was a fervent temperance advocate; on the other, she told her boys that alcoholism was a sickness their father could not control. "She asked us to help him and love him," Ronald Reagan later recalled.[55] As he explained in a 1989 letter to the photographer Pat York, "Nelle drilled into us that if something went wrong, something that made us unhappy, we should take it in stride and not let it get us down. She promised that down the line something good would happen and we'd find ourselves realizing it wouldn't have happened had that other unhappy thing not taken place."[56]

Although they belonged to different churches, Jack and Nelle shared a strong belief in religious and racial tolerance. While the Disciples of Christ had an anti-Catholic slant, the "brotherhood of man" was very much part of their creed. Jack once slept in his car rather than stay in a hotel that did not accept Jews. He would not let Neil and Ronald see D. W. Griffith's *Birth of a Nation* when it came to town in a revival, because, as he put it, "it deals with the Ku Klux Klan against the colored folks, and I'm damned if anyone in this family will go see it. The Klan's the Klan, and a sheet's a sheet, and any man who wears one over his head is a bum."[57]

Dixon had twelve black families. They were not allowed in the town's hotel, beauty salons, or barbershops, but they could eat at its luncheonettes and go to the movie theater, though they had to sit in the balcony. Neil would sit in the balcony with two of his black high school friends, and Nelle thought nothing of having them over for dinner. Yet this was a town where the Ku Klux Klan had staged parades and burned crosses,[58] and where Ronald remembered a race riot that began when, as he put it, "a Negro bum slashed a white bum." As Reagan biographer Lou Cannon tells it, "The whites who ostensibly had been living in peace with the Negro community in Dixon now advanced on Negro homes and terrorized the inhabitants. Reagan recalls whites hurling Negro children onto freight-train boxcars and the screaming youngsters being carried hundreds of miles away in fear and panic."[59]

Still, no historic figure was more venerated in this Illinois town than the man who freed the slaves. On June 28, 1924, the *Telegraph* announced: "The life of Abraham Lincoln will be acted on the Dixon Athletic ground by 600 people for four nights starting July 9th. Besides the actors there will be 100 horses and two bands in the spectacle. The pageant is being given by Dixon Post No. 12, American Legion. . . . The vast epic of Lincoln's life will be unfolded in 24 memorable scenes [with] large groups of dancers for the six beautiful ballets that are part of the spectacle. But it is not a 'high brow' affair. There is nothing that a child cannot grasp and fully enjoy. The story is as simple as the life of the backwoods boy who got to be *president.*" Neil and Ronald played Union soldiers.[60]

At dawn on Easter Sunday, 1926, fifteen-year-old Ronald led his church's annual Sunrise Prayer Meeting on the Hennepin Avenue Bridge. By then he was already teaching Sunday school in the morning and occasionally leading the Christian Endeavor prayer meetings on Sunday nights. He was a sophomore at North Dixon High and had fallen in love with his classmate Margaret Cleaver, one of Reverend Cleaver's three very proper daughters. Margaret insisted on keeping things on a just-friends basis until their senior year. The popular minister became something of a surrogate father for the teenage Ronald and even taught him how to drive.

Reagan later noted that Margaret was like his mother, "short, pretty, auburn-haired and intelligent." She was the brightest girl in their class, down-to-earth, sure of herself, and rather serious. She terrified Neil, who said she "spat tacks."[61] Ronald tried to hide his father's drinking problem from her, but, as he later wrote in his post-presidential memoir, *An American Life*, "one day when I was out with Margaret, she brought up Jack's drinking; it was during one of the times when he had gone off the wagon, and somebody had given her a vivid account of his behavior. Coming from a very religious, strict family, she was quite upset. . . . I tried to tell her what Nelle had told us about Jack's problem, that it was a *sickness*, but she'd never heard anything like that before and didn't buy it. My heart was just about broken. I thought I was going to lose her. When I went home, I told my mother about it and said that if I did lose Margaret because of Jack, I didn't know what I'd do, but I'd probably disown him and never speak to him again. Nelle felt terrible for me but asked me again to be patient with Jack. In the end, Margaret decided that she was willing to accept Jack's drinking rather than break up our romance."[62]

From their freshman year, both Ronald and Margaret were in the Dramatic Club, which was run by the school's English teacher, B. J. Frazer, who was quick to recognize Reagan's talent. Under Frazer's direction they co-starred in productions of contemporary Broadway plays. In his senior year, Ronald was elected president of the club. He was also president of the student body (Margaret was president of the senior class), art director of the yearbook, and—what he considered the greatest accomplishment of his high school career—tackle on the varsity football team. In addition he found time to serve as vice president in charge of entertainment for the YMCA's Hi-Y Club, which was dedicated to "Clean Speech, Clean Sports, Clean

Living, and Clean Scholarship." His job was to invite local businessmen to give inspirational talks to the group. Only his grades suffered: he graduated in June 1928 with a B average.[63]

That month the Republicans nominated Herbert Hoover to succeed Calvin Coolidge, who had presided over the greatest economic boom the country had ever known, and the Democrats nominated New York governor Alfred E. Smith, the first Catholic to run for the presidency. Smith, who had been born on the Lower East Side, spoke with a heavy New York accent, played up his Irish background, and opposed Prohibition. The Republicans portrayed him as a lush and spread rumors that the Pope was going to move to Washington if Smith won. Jack hung Smith banners on his car, and was deeply disappointed when his candidate lost by a landslide in November.[64]

One wonders what Nelle, who apparently was also a Democrat, thought about the wet Al Smith. According to Garry Wills in *Reagan's America,* one of the men in her church used to kid her by saying, "I could really take a liking to you if you weren't such a Democrat."[65] Jack's sons shared his enthusiasm for the party of the people. Neil became part of the blue-collar working class when he took a job at the Medusa Cement Company after graduating from high school in 1926. Ronald's summer jobs, on the other hand—first as a caddie at Plum Hollow Country Club, then as a lifeguard at Lowell

Park—brought him into direct contact with the opposition: wealthy Republicans.

He started caddieing in junior high school and continued on and off all through high school. One of the men he caddied for regularly was Charles Walgreen, America's first drugstore tycoon. Walgreen, who had started with one store on Chicago's South Side in 1901 and built a national chain of 110 stores by 1927, had grown up in Dixon and often returned to his hometown. In the late 1920s he bought a six-hundred-acre estate overlooking the Rock River. In her memoir, his wife, Myrtle Walgreen, remembered that the young Reagan "came to one of the picnics which we gave for the caddies each year and I brought him his plate of food while he lay in the hammock. That was his idea of being king."[66]

In 1926, when he was fifteen, Ronald spent the summer as a construction worker, which he liked because it helped him build up his skinny body. "I was hired at 35 cents an hour—10 hours a day, six days a week," he wrote in a 1984 article for UPI. "First tools handed me were pick and shovel. . . . Before the summer was over I'd graduated to laying hardwood floor, shingling roof and painting the exterior."[67] The following summer, between his junior and senior years, he was hired as a lifeguard, a job he loved—perhaps because it allowed him to be narcissistic and altruistic at the same time. From Memorial Day to Labor Day, he worked seven days a week, from ten in the morning till ten at night. Three miles north of town, Lowell Park was a 320-acre heavily forested preserve with a beach on the Rock River and a posh hotel called the Lodge, where well-to-do Midwestern families, mostly from Chicago, spent their summers. Here he found another mentor in Sid Altschuler, a Kansas City businessman married to a Dixon girl, whose daughters he taught how to swim. Ronald even became a local celebrity, making the front page of a newspaper for the first time on August 3, 1928, when the *Dixon Telegraph* reported that he had rescued a drowning man[68]—one of seventy-seven lives he would save during his six summers at the park.[69]

In September 1928, Ronald and Margaret both enrolled in Eureka College, a small Disciples of Christ institution located a hundred miles south of Dixon. Only 8 percent of their graduating class went on to college, and Ronald was not actually sure he could afford it—tuition, room, and board at Eureka came to more than $300 a year. "While Margaret registered," he later wrote, "I presented myself to Eureka's new president, Bert Wilson, and Ralph McKinzie, the football coach, and tried to impress them with my credentials as a football player and as someone who could win some trophies for Eureka's swim team." Ronald was given a scholarship to cover half his tuition and a job washing dishes to cover his board at the Tau Kappa Epsilon fraternity house.[70]

A teachers college that had evolved into a liberal arts institution, Eureka had a faculty of twenty and fewer than two hundred students in 1928, but its handful of ivy-covered red-brick buildings set on a spacious campus of rolling lawns crisscrossed by gravel paths and shaded by elms looked like Princeton to the small-town shoe salesman's son. "I fell head over heels in love with Eureka," he later wrote,[71] and he was immediately caught up in campus life.

In his freshman year he took an active part in a student strike that led to the resignation of Bert Wilson, who had infuriated students and faculty with his plan for severe cutbacks in the academic curriculum. During the strike Ronald first became aware of his effectiveness as a public speaker, when a fiery speech he gave in the campus chapel, denouncing the "morally evil" president, brought the student body to its feet.[72] "I discovered that night that an audience has a feel to it and, in the parlance of the theater, that audience and I were together," he said.[73] One of the strike's organizers, Howard Short, would later explain, "We put Reagan on because he was the biggest mouth of the freshman class; he was a cocky s.o.b., a loud talker. Dutch was the guy you wanted to put up there."[74]

In October 1929 the stock market crashed, but on the surface the Depression did not seem to have much effect on Ronald's college life. That September, Neil had entered Eureka on a scholarship arranged by his brother. Ronald's days and nights were a whirl of extracurricular activities, occasionally interrupted by a bout of cramming.

He made the varsity football and track teams, captained the swimming team, and was the lead cheerleader for the basketball team. He was a sports reporter on the school newspaper for a year, features editor of the yearbook for two years, and president of the Eureka Booster Club, which was responsible for the college's public relations, for three years. As a senior, after two years in the student senate, he was elected student body president. Along the way he co-starred with Margaret Cleaver in several plays, including Edna St. Vincent Millay's avant-garde verse drama *Aria da Capo*, which won a prize for the Eureka Dramatic Society in the Eva Le Gallienne tournament at Northwestern University's School of Speech. Ronald played Thyrsis, a shepherd boy, in the one-acter, which was set in ancient Greece and had a strong pacifist theme; he was cited as one of the six best actors in the competition. Almost as an afterthought, it appears, he majored in social science and economics, and maintained an average that hovered between B and C. "He would take a book the night before the test," Neil recalled, "and in about a quick hour he would thumb through it and photograph those pages and write a good test."[75]

Things were not so carefree at home in Dixon. The *Dixon Telegraph* noted on April 3, 1928, that Jack Reagan had "severed his connection with the partnership operating The Fashion Boot Shop."[76] Jack took a temporary job at Dixon State Hospital, a mental institution, which he found "humiliating," before going to work at another shoe store in town in August 1929.[77] The Reagans had already given up their house on the North Side, and had moved from one small apartment to another. They were soon reduced to subletting all but one room and cooking on a hotplate. Jack spent most of 1930 and 1931 based two hundred miles away in Springfield, working as a traveling shoe salesman for the Red Wing Company, while Nelle remained in Dixon, working as a salesclerk and seamstress at the Marilyn Dress Shop. There was talk of a girl-friend in Springfield—and of divorce—but by late 1931 Jack and Nelle were reunited in an apartment on Monroe Avenue on Dixon's South Side. On Christmas Eve 1931, Ronald and Neil were home for the holidays when Jack received a special delivery letter firing him. Like millions of other Americans, Jack was unemployed throughout 1932.[78] Ronald, then in his last semester at Eureka and working part-time as the school's swimming instructor, would later recall sending his mother $50 to buy food. He was able to complete his final year at Eureka with a $115 loan from the Disciples of Christ–affiliated Henry Strong Educational Foundation,[79] but could not afford to buy his $30 class ring.[80]

On June 30, 1932, Franklin Delano Roosevelt was nominated for president at the Democratic convention in Chicago, and Jack went to work as a volunteer at the Dixon Democratic Party head-quarters for the patrician who promised a New Deal. Ronald was back on the lifeguard stand at

Lowell Park, where he would get into arguments over politics with his Republican boss. He was a twenty-one-year-old college graduate with no clear idea of what he was going to do with the rest of his life, except to spend it with Margaret Cleaver. "Soon after our graduation, I'd given her an engagement ring," he later wrote, "and we'd agreed to marry as soon as we could afford it."[81]

CHAPTER TWO

EARLY NANCY
1921–1932

After Mother and my father were separated, Mother had to go back to work. She didn't take any alimony and she didn't think that hauling me around from town to town and theater to theater was the best thing in the world. So I lived with my aunt and uncle and cousin in Bethesda, and it was very nice. I had a wonderful time. I've read that I was abandoned. I wasn't abandoned. I adored my mother. She could have, I suppose, sent me to I don't know where, but letting me live with my aunt and uncle and cousin—this is family. I was with my family.

> Nancy Reagan to author,
> June 4, 2000

When I had lunch with Peggy [Noonan, a speechwriter for Ronald Reagan], she said, "Well, you obviously had a couple of unhappy years." I said, "Well, no, I didn't." I didn't have a miserable, unhappy childhood. I was living with my aunt and uncle and cousin. And

Mother would come to Bethesda. Oh, that was a big thing when Mother came to Bethesda.

Nancy Reagan to author,
April 30, 2001

Among those attending the opening of the week-long Democratic convention that nominated Franklin Delano Roosevelt in Chicago at the beginning of that summer of 1932 was a chubby, well-dressed eleven-year-old girl named Nancy Robbins. She and her mother, Mrs. Loyal Davis, the wife of Chicago's first full-time neurosurgeon, were guests of Edward Joseph Kelly, the powerful Democratic machine politician who would become mayor the following year and rule the nation's then second-largest city with an iron hand through the Depression and World War II. While the twenty-one-year-old Ronald Reagan was back in Dixon deciding what to do with his life after graduating from Eureka College (and his unemployed father was rooting for Roosevelt from afar), his future First Lady was already well situated at the center of things. A photograph of Nancy and her mother at the convention ran in one of the Chicago papers.[1]

Nancy's mother, the former Edith Luckett, had been a theater actress of modest success until she married Loyal Davis, at the socially prestigious Fourth Presbyterian Church on Chicago's fashionable North Michigan Avenue, in May 1929—about the same time that Jack Reagan grudgingly took a job at the state mental institution in Dixon. Edith had separated from her first husband, a well-bred but unenterprising New Englander named Kenneth Robbins, barely a year after their daughter's birth in 1921 in New York, and Nancy had spent her early years in Bethesda, Maryland, living at the home of her mother's sister. Dr. Davis would not officially adopt his stepdaughter and give her his name until she was almost seventeen, in 1938, nine years after he married her mother.

For the rest of her life Nancy would refer to Loyal Davis as "my father," and for a long time she even went so far as to deny the existence of Kenneth Robbins and to falsify her birthplace. When she was First Lady of California, her official biography began, "Nancy Davis Reagan was born in Chicago, the only daughter of Dr. and Mrs. Loyal Davis." When confronted with her *Who's Who* entry, stating that she had been adopted by Loyal Davis, she said, "I don't care what the book says. He is my father. In my mind, he is my father. I have no father except Loyal Davis."[2] As she explained in *Nancy,* her 1980 autobiography, "Since Kenneth Robbins was such a small part of my life, it is impossible for me to think of him as my father."[3]

Nancy Davis Reagan was born Anne Frances Robbins on July 6, 1921, at Sloane Hospital in Flushing, a middle-class section of the New York City borough of Queens, where Edith and Kenneth Robbins were living at the time. "I was due on the fourth of July," she later wrote, giving her birth a patriotic twist, just as her husband had given his, "but my mother, as she tells it, was a baseball fan who was determined to see a doubleheader on that day. Knowing her, I believe it. When she arrived at the hospital two days later, she was told there was no room and she would have to go elsewhere. My mother is a strong-willed woman. She lay down in the middle of the reception room floor and said, 'Well, I guess I'll have my baby right here.' Everyone bustled around and miraculously discovered they had a room all the time. It was a hot day, and the last thing she remembered in the delivery room was the doctor talking about how hot it was and how he wanted to get it over with so he could get out on the golf course. It turned out to be a difficult forceps delivery, and when I was brought to her, my right eye was closed. The doctor told her I might be blind in that eye. She told him that she had heard what he had said in the delivery room, and that if my eye didn't open, she would kill him. Fortunately for him, after two weeks my eye opened."[4]

Although her mother called her Nancy from an early age, she was named after a great-great-aunt of her father's, Sister Anne Ayres, the first American Episcopalian nun. One of the ironies of Nancy Reagan's story is that the father she preferred not to acknowledge would provide the genealogical link she needed to be accepted into the Daughters of the American Revolution when she applied in 1983. Of Nancy and Ronald

Reagan's four biological parents and one adoptive parent, only Kenneth Robbins came from a certifiably old American family. One of his ancestors on his mother's side, John Root, arrived from England in 1640 and was among the earliest Puritan settlers of Connecticut.[5] Kenneth's great-great-great-grandfather, Ezekiel Root (1736–1808), moved the family to Pittsfield, Massachusetts, and was a captain in the American army during the Revolutionary War.[6]

Kenneth Seymour Robbins was born in Pittsfield in 1894, the only son of John and Anne Ayres Robbins. His father was vice president of the W. E. Tillotson Manufacturing Company, which made wool, and the family seemed fairly prosperous. Ken, as he was called, is said to have attended Princeton, but the university has no record of his application, registration, or attendance. He was reportedly employed as a salesman by the Berkshire Life Insurance Company in 1914, when he met Edith Luckett, who was then performing at the Colonial Theater in Pittsfield.[7]

Although Edith claimed to be two years younger than Kenneth, she was almost certainly six years older. Her birth date is as hazy as so much else about her background. She claimed to have been born on July 16, 1896, but 1888 is the more credible year. Edith took great relish in portraying herself as a Southern belle from one of the First Families of Virginia. Her parents, Charles Edward Luckett and Sarah Frances Whitlock, were married in Petersburg, Virginia, in 1868. Four years later

Charles, a railroad clerk with the Adams Express Company (the predecessor of Railway Express), was transferred from Richmond to Washington, D.C.,[8] where the couple's nine children were most likely born. Edith, however, maintained into her old age that her mother had returned to Petersburg for the birth of each child so that "they wouldn't be born damn Yankees."[9] The Lucketts lived in a series of row houses near the railroad tracks in Washington; some say Sarah ran a boarding-house.[10]

According to Nancy Reagan, "Times were tough for the Lucketts with their large family. Few of the children attended school for very long. They had to go to work."[11] Edith's older brother, Joseph, man-aged the Columbia Theater in Washington, where she first appeared on the stage. In 1900, when she was twelve, a local newspaper wrote, "Little Edith Luckett has beauty, wit and talent. She is the unusual child. Her prattle is as merry as the chirp of a cricket on the hearth, her eyes blue, and her hair brown and wavy. She has been brought to public notice by her remarkable cleverness as a dancer, her grace of movement and form, and her sweet, pretty face."[12]

By sixteen, Edith had left high school and was working steadily with various stock companies, including those of the famous Irish tenor Chauncey Olcott and the legendary Broadway producer, composer, and actor George M. Cohan.[13] Nick-named Lucky Luckett, she was a whirlwind of charm and energy, a pretty blonde with the riveting widespread eyes she would pass on to her daughter. She smoked, she swore, she told dirty jokes, and she was wildly popular. Yet she clung to her genteel Southern drawl. As Nancy Reagan would say again and again, in print and in private, "They broke the mold after they made my mother. If I could be half the woman she was, I'd be happy."[14]

In December 1910, *The New York Times* ran a picture of Edith in the stage production of *Shifting* at Nazimova's 39th Street Theater, one of Lee Shubert's houses, named in honor of his biggest money-making star, Alla Nazimova.[15] The great Nazimova was a charismatic Russian-Jewish lesbian who became a major attraction—and the incarnation of Ibsen's New Woman—when she toured America from 1907 to 1910 in *A Doll's House, The Master Builder*, and *Hedda Gabler.* Born in Yalta in 1879, she had been trained by the great Russian director Konstantin Stanislavsky in Moscow, where she was said to have worked as a prostitute to finance her studies. She came to New York in 1905 with her then lover, Paul Orleneff, and his St. Petersburg Players,[16] but, according to Diana McLellan in *The Girls: Sappho Goes to Hollywood,* she was soon seduced by none other than Emma Goldman, the fiery feminist crusader known as the Queen of the Anarchists.[17]

Edith had met Nazimova at a party given at the Irving Place townhouse of the literary agent Bessie Marbury, whose clients included H. G. Wells, George Bernard Shaw, and Somerset Maugham, and her lover, the society decorator Elsie de Wolfe, who were the reigning hostesses of Manhattan's thriving haute bohemia.[18] During this period, Edith had principal roles in the touring companies of Cohan's musical *Broadway Jones* and *The Fortune Hunter,* starring John Barrymore.[19]

At twenty-five, Edith reportedly became engaged to Edward A. R. Brown, the scion of a rich New York family.[20] A year later she met Kenneth Robbins, who was swept away by her looks, her humor, and her get-up-and-go. According to relatives, young Ken was sweet but weak, "kind of a momma's boy," one of them said, who was "kept [in] long golden curls until he went to school."[21] His mother, a formidable figure known in the family as Nannee Robbins, was also charmed by Edith. "Even though I think she might have been a little disturbed that her only son married an actress," Ken Robbins's niece Kathleen Young said, "Nannee thought the world of her."[22]

Edith and Ken were wed in Burlington, Vermont, on June 27, 1916, by a Congregational minister. Edith had promised to give up the stage, but after only a few months of living in a farmhouse in the Berkshires owned by her husband's family, she persuaded Ken to move to New York, where he floundered unhappily, working as an insurance agent according to one source, a booking agent according to another.[23] Edith contacted Alla Nazimova, who offered a role in her new production, *'Ception Shoals,* a melodrama "about incest, suicide, and bigotry, set in a lighthouse."[24] Edith's first Broadway play, it opened on January 10, 1917, ran to packed houses until March, and then went on tour until summer. By then Ken had enlisted in the Army—Congress having declared war on Germany on April 6—and Edith had formed a close friendship with Nazimova.

The following year, Nazimova went to Hollywood and quickly became one of the highest-paid actresses in silent pictures, starring opposite Rudolph Valentino in *Camille* in 1921. Two years later she produced and starred in the "ostentatiously homoerotic" *Salome,* with sets by Natacha Rambova, Valentino's second wife and one of Nazimova's many lovers.[25] Nazimova jokingly called the Spanish-style mansion she bought at 8080 Sunset Boulevard the Garden of Allah. Set on three and a half acres of lushly landscaped grounds, it was also known as the 8080 Club because of her constant entertaining, which included all-girl pool parties on Sunday afternoons. She attempted to cover up her lesbianism by, among other things, maintaining a fictional marriage with the actor Charles Bryant from 1912 to 1925.[26]

According to Nazimova's biographer Gavin Lambert, "Edith was probably Nazimova's main confidante for more than ten years," and their friendship led to rumors that they were lovers. Lambert plays down those rumors, citing the platonic tone of Nazimova's letters to Edith, in which the star is constantly thanking her admirer for favors large and small. "Enormously proud of her friendship with a great star, Edith seems to have felt to be privileged to do favors for her," Lambert explains, "and Nazimova . . . felt relaxed in the company of someone so exuberantly unshockable. The friendship lasted until Nazimova's death, and their correspondence over the years makes it clear that Edith was one of the very few people with whom she was frank about her sexuality." Lambert points out, however, that Edith's letters to Nazimova are not included in Nazimova's archives, even though the star was known to keep every letter she ever received.[27]

In January 1919, Ken Robbins was honorably discharged and rejoined Edith in New York. In late 1920, Edith became pregnant, and Ken, who had inherited a small amount of money from his father, wanted to move back to Pittsfield and bring up their child there. When Edith refused, he left her,[28] and he wasn't present when Nancy was born in July 1921—a fact Nancy would make much of in her memoirs. Sometime after his daughter's birth he returned, and Edith gave up acting for about a year. Nonetheless, the union between the lackluster Ken and the starstruck Edith was nearing its end. The last straw may have been Edith's decision to make Nazimova Nancy's godmother, which stunned her proper New England mother-in-law.[29] In 1922 the couple split for good. Edith took her baby on the road. Ken went home to Nannee Robbins, and for reasons unknown they soon moved to Glen Ridge, New Jersey.

At first Edith found it comforting to take little Nancy with her wherever she went. Colleen Moore, the silent screen star who would become one of Edith's closest friends, never forgot meeting her at a party at the Long Island home of First National Studios head Richard Rowland: "One of the women caught my eye. She was a beautiful blonde, and she had the biggest blue eyes you ever saw. And she was carrying a tiny baby in her arms." Fascinated, Moore asked her host who she was and if she always brought a baby to parties. Rowland explained that the baby was Edith's, and that she had just been divorced and didn't have a penny.[30] Moore, only twenty-one and soon to be hailed as the spirit of the Flapper Generation for her starring role in *Flaming Youth,* was impressed by the spunky Edith (who was already thirty-three, but telling people she was twenty-five). The two actresses struck up a friendship that would prove to be durable and mutually advantageous.

The following year, when Nancy was two, Edith decided to leave her with her sister and brother-in-law, Virginia and C. Audley Galbraith, in Bethesda, Maryland, just outside Washington. Edith rented a one-room apartment on West 49th Street in Manhattan's theater district, the first in a series of temporary quarters in converted brownstones and residential hotels that she would use as a base between extended stays as a leading lady in regional theater companies in Atlanta, Dallas, and New Brunswick, New Jersey. The scrapbook she kept is filled with favorable reviews and flowery

interviews, in which she goes on about her devotion to the Presbyterian Church and love of gar-
dening, but never mentions she has been married
or has a daughter. In 1924, Montague Salmon, a
columnist for one of the Atlanta papers, subjected
her to a "Theatrical Confession." Asked to name
her favorite cigarette, she answered, "Lucky
Strike." Her lucky day? "Pay day." Her greatest
ambition? "To be loved by the public." What would
she do if she were President for a day? "Have a
party at the White House."[31]

Among the many friends she made on the road,
one of her favorites was a struggling young
unknown named Spencer Tracy. "Spencer was a
darling," she later recalled. "And I liked his wife,
Louise. We played anywhere that anyone wanted
anything. Spencer and I would always be there.
We'd always play because we got paid for it, you
see. So we didn't care where we went. I had Nancy
to take care of, and he had Louise, and then their
son, John."[32]

"My favorite times were when Mother had a job
in New York," Nancy later wrote, "and Aunt Virgie
would take me by train to stay with her. Although I
saw her productions over and over, I was never
bored."[33] Other early memories she recorded
include having a stagehand build a dollhouse for
her one Christmas, seeing her mother being killed
on the stage and thinking she was really dead, and
having double pneumonia when she was four or
five and her mother not being able to visit her in
Bethesda. "My aunt and uncle took care of me as

well as anyone could, but I wanted my mother with me and she was somewhere out on the road away from me. No matter how kind someone is to you, it is just not the same as when it is your mother. I can remember crying at this time and saying, 'If I had a child and she got sick, I'd be with her.' Now that I have children myself, I realize how much it must have hurt my mother, especially since she had no choice. She had to work."[34]

Although Bethesda, then as now, was one of Washington's more affluent suburbs, with many large estates and several country clubs, the Galbraiths lived in "a tiny, tiny house"—Nancy Reagan's words—in the modest Battery Park section, which was popular with military families. "It was right up the street from the Army-Navy clubhouse," their daughter, Charlotte Galbraith Ramage, who was three years older than Nancy, said of the two-bedroom Dutch-colonial-style house at 123 Glenbrook Road. "I had my own bedroom before Nancy came, and then Mother and Dad fixed up the little sun porch, and that was her bedroom. We had a good time in Battery Park." Was Nancy a happy child? "As far as I knew." Didn't she miss her mother? "I'm sure she did. But Aunt DeeDee would come down anytime she could. And we'd go up to New York to see the plays she was in, when she was with Walter Huston and Kay Francis and Louis Calhern and Spencer Tracy and the rest of them."[35]

Talking about her mother's visits, Nancy Reagan told me, "Mother taught Charlotte and me the

Charleston, and I was dying to have long hair, so Mother went out and bought me a Mary Pickford wig." She and her cousin, she recalled, played hopscotch in front of their house, using coal to draw the lines, and went to a neighbor's for taffy pulls. "We both fell down in the cinder driveway, I remember, and I had to wear knee patches. I had a boyfriend who would come by while we were eating breakfast, and he would pull me around the block in his red wagon."[36]

C. Audley Galbraith was an assistant auditor of freight accounts for the Southern Railroad; Virginia Galbraith was a housewife. But somehow they managed to send Charlotte to Sidwell Friends School, the private Quaker institution where the children of high government officials and well-to-do Washingtonians had long been, and still are, educated. In the fall of 1925, four-year-old Nancy started kindergarten at Sidwell Friends, taking the bus with Charlotte four miles down Wisconsin Avenue through Northwest Washington. The Galbraiths covered the tuition for Nancy's first year, which must have been a burden on a railroad clerk's salary, and Edith paid after that.[37] School records show that Nancy was enrolled in kindergarten for only part of the 1925–26 school year, and then again for only part of 1926–27. Was her pneumonia the reason she missed so much school, or was her mother having trouble making the six-times-a-year tuition bills? Nancy Reagan vaguely recalled leaving school to spend stretches of time with her mother in New York. In any case, she started first grade in the fall of 1927, at age six, and completed it the following spring.

It might be said of Nancy's early years in Bethesda and at Sidwell Friends that she grew up with the wealthy, but was not of the wealthy. Charlotte Ramage recalled, for example, a Christmas party given by "the Hope Diamond gal," referring to Evalyn Walsh McLean, the silver-mining heiress whose husband, Edward B. McLean, owned The Washington Post in those days. The McLeans' estate, Friendship, with its own nine-hole golf course, was located directly across Wisconsin Avenue from the Sidwell Friends School. "Their son was in my class, or the class ahead of me, or behind me, I've forgotten which," Charlotte Ramage told me. "That's why I was included in that. And Nancy went. We saw the big tree, and they gave all the girls baby carriages, and the boys got little cars."[38]

The world of politics and power also seemed far away from the Dutch colonial in Battery Park, even though it was so near. Once, Nancy Reagan told me, Aunt Virginia and Uncle Audley took Charlotte and her to the White House Easter Egg Roll. She didn't remember how old she had been, but given the years she lived in Bethesda, Calvin Coolidge must have been President. I asked Charlotte Ramage if her parents were involved in politics. "No." Were they Republicans or Democrats? "Southern Democrats," she answered. "Just like Edith—to start off with."[39]

In fact, Edith was an active participant in the

1924 Democratic convention in New York City. Eleanor Roosevelt, the wife of New York's governor, had asked her friend Bessie Marbury to chair the Women's Committee of Nine "to prepare for the reception and entertainment of women delegates, alternates and visitors." According to *The New York Times* of May 18, 1924, Edith served on the Sub-Committee on Theatres and Restaurant Facilities, along with Mrs. Chauncey Olcott and Mrs. Condé Nast, wife of the owner of *Vogue* and *Vanity Fair.*

Ken Robbins is noticeably missing from accounts of this period. In both *Nancy* and *My Turn,* his daughter says that he pretty much ignored her until she was "older"—"He couldn't relate to me as a very young child"[40] is the way she puts it in her second book. But Charlotte Ramage said that Nancy's father and grandmother had visited Bethesda on more than one occasion, though she offered no specific dates or anecdotes.[41] And apparently Nannee Robbins was diligent in sending her only granddaughter presents or cards on her birthday and holidays. "Dear grandmother," reads an undated note written in a child's exceptionally neat block letters. "Thank you for the nice Halloween things. We had a fine time. Love, Nancy."[42]

In the summer of 1927, Edith Luckett met Loyal Davis sailing to England on the SS *New York.* Edith—thirty-nine and not yet a star—was said to be joining a company of English actors.[43] The thirty-one-year-old Loyal Davis, an associate professor of surgery at Northwestern University, was just starting his practice as Chicago's first specialist in neurosurgery, at a time when operating on the brain, spinal cord, and nerves was still an emerging field. He was going to London with a colleague, Dr. Lewis Pollock, to give a paper on decerebrate rigidity to a conference of American and British neurologists. He was still married to his first wife, Pearl, and they had a two-year-old son named Richard. According to Loyal Davis's 1973 memoir, *A Surgeon's Odyssey*, "I proposed that Pearl make the trip, thinking that her mother could come to Chicago and with Willa [their housekeeper] look after Richard. Perhaps I did not insist strongly enough, but at any rate I, alone, went to England with the Pollocks on the SS *New York*."[44]

Richard Davis, a retired neurosurgeon living on Philadelphia's Main Line, confirmed this story to me, with one crucial difference. "I've got a picture of Edith and Loyal on the ship. They were a very handsome couple. He was going to give a paper at the National Hospital in Queens Square. Dr. and Mrs. Pollock were traveling with him, and Edith was sitting at their table. Now, why she was going to London, I don't know. She was sitting across from Mrs. Pollock and had been talking to my father. And then she said—not in a whisper, but just moving her lips—'Is he married?' Of course, my father saw this, and he said to her, 'No.' There's a song called 'Hallelujah' and apparently they danced to that on the ship. And every time that was played on the radio, no matter what they were doing, they'd get up and dance."[45]

Had the young doctor removed his wedding band upon boarding the *New York*? Or fudged the date of his divorce when telling the story to his son years later? In any case, the invitation to Pearl was evidently a last attempt to save a collapsing marriage. Loyal Davis and Pearl McElroy were as mismatched as Kenneth Robbins and Edith Luckett. Loyal was an intern at Cook County Hospital in Chicago when they met on a blind date in late 1919. Pearl was a nurse at the hospital, who, in Loyal's words, "had left a small town for the attractions in Chicago." They married soon afterward, at the same fashionable Near North Side church where he would later marry Edith; neither Loyal's nor Pearl's parents were present. There was friction from the start. "I was unable to accept her dislike and ineptitude for housekeeping," Loyal later wrote.[46] Pearl, on the other hand, viewed Loyal's career as her rival.

"I think my father truly loved my mother," Richard Davis told me. "She was a beautiful young woman. He probably loved her a lot more than she loved him. But she had no vision at all. She was pretty footloose and fancy-free. He was anxious to climb the academic ladder of medicine, and wanted to be a pioneer in neurological surgery. She actually denigrated his ambitions. She was quite sarcastic about it. She made fun of that. I think that's what broke the marriage up. She was a very difficult woman. The only thing my father said about my mother was 'I never want you to grow up like her.' "[47]

A precocious and serious child who turned out to be an impatient and serious adult, Loyal Davis was born on January 17, 1896, in Galesburg, Illinois— one of the county seats where the Reagan family lived during their wandering years. He was the only son of Albert Clark Davis, a locomotive engineer on the Burlington Railroad, and Laura Hensler Davis, a housewife. The Davis family lived on a street called Scab Alley, because its row houses had been built by the railroad for workers who broke the strike of 1888. According to Loyal, his parents' "entire social life centered around the Masonic and Eastern Star lodges. Mother advanced through the various offices of the Violet Chapter, memorized her speeches, became Worthy Matron, and later held an appointive office in the Grand Lodge. Lodges were important in Galesburg. They afforded the social life for the working class."[48]

"My grandfather was highly intelligent," Richard Davis told me. "He was about six-two, quiet and self-disciplined. His son was the apple of his eye. On the other hand, my grandmother was short and very explosive. I think a lot of Dr. Loyal's unattractive characteristics were hers. Grandfather Al married her when she was about nineteen, and that was a love affair to end all love affairs. There's a cute story about them. He was tough—he made $16 a week, and would take the fast mail trains, or the best passenger trains, from Chicago out to Iowa and back to Galesburg. That's called deadheading. He came home from one of his runs, and Grandmother Laura was in the middle of the kitchen floor, crying her heart out. She'd bought a pattern for a dress and material, but instead of cutting the front and the back out of the material, she had cut two fronts out. Now this man has been up more than twenty-four hours doing really tough work, and here she was weeping. So he calmed her down and went to the store and bought more material and cut the dress out himself."[49]

In his memoir Loyal Davis recalls a single but telling anecdote from his childhood:

I went to Sunday School at the Grace Episcopal Church. I sang in the choir, wearing the black cassock and white surplice. I carried the cross, heading the choir's procession, and was often pressed into service in pumping the organ. I was proud, scared, and quavery of voice when I sang a Te Deum.

A prayer book was to be awarded to the boy and girl who had been perfect in attendance at Sunday school for the entire year. I was the only boy to have such a record and I knew that. The prayer book was given to the son of the owner of the largest department store in town. I was angered and crushed in spirit. When I got home, I announced I would never go back to church again. Mother cried and was angry about the unfairness of the action. Dad listened calmly.

"Did you miss one Sunday?"

"No, my teacher knows that but she didn't award the prayer book."

"I've always thought you could be good and follow the golden rule without having to go to church. You do what you think is right but don't keep talking about it to every Tom, Dick, and Harry."[50]

Although Loyal was only in grade school, he stuck to his guns and stopped going to church. He graduated from high school as valedictorian of his class at fifteen, winning a medal in shorthand and typing. "I expected to go to work for the railroad, so I took a three-year commercial course in high school," he told a reporter years later. "But a neighbor, a professor, urged me to go back for my fourth year, take college preparatory work, and, perhaps, he said, I might get a scholarship to Knox College."[51] He did, and breezed through Knox College in Galesburg in two years, then started Northwestern University Medical School in Chicago at eighteen. He earned his M.D. four years later, in 1918.

"We were sixty strong," Loyal wrote of his freshman class at medical school. "There were two Jews and two Negroes. One of each was liked and accepted totally by the class; the other two were wholly disliked. It was not a question of racism; it was character and personality."[52] Of the two

Jewish students, he noted, "Morrie Mazel . . . had been a chronic irritant to the whole class throughout our four years. Pushing, aggressive, confident, and smart, he pre-empted a front-row seat in every clinic. Being picked up and bodily passed back over the heads of his fellow students to a rear row didn't stop Morrie. The next time he'd take a front-row seat, grinning and inviting battle. The other Jewish boy in the class was jolly, fat Meyer Chapman; well-liked, quiet, friendly, and one of us."[53]

Loyal was just as sanguine in describing himself as a medical student. For part of his time at Northwestern he boarded at the house of a classmate named Howie Goodsmith, who was the son of a doctor but an indifferent student. Loyal records Dr. Goodsmith telling him "that Howie had a sense of humor, a personality that attracted people, the ability to relax, all of which, he said, I didn't possess but should try to develop."[54]

After marrying Pearl and completing his internship, Loyal took his bride home to Galesburg and set up a general practice with a Northwestern roommate, Robert Gunning. The return to small-town life lasted one year and one month. Loyal was eager to specialize, so in August 1920 he and Pearl moved back to Chicago, where they rented a one-room apartment on the South Side. Pearl went to work as a filing clerk,[55] while Loyal spent the next three years earning his master's and doctor's degrees in surgery at Northwestern. At the same time he served as surgical assistant to the distinguished Dr. Allen B. Kanavel, the chairman of the department of surgery at Northwestern, who became his lifelong mentor.

In the fall of 1923, on Kanavel's recommendation, Loyal was taken on as a voluntary assistant to Boston's legendary Dr. Harvey Cushing, generally considered to be the great pioneer of modern neurosurgery. The move to Boston worried Loyal: "I was concerned about how Pearl would occupy her days; I hoped she wouldn't work and we could live on my fellowship income. Maybe she would become more interested in my professional education and training."[56] Loyal now had a fellowship from the National Research Council, which provided a stipend of $166 per month.

Cushing was a forbidding figure, both professionally and socially. Born in Cleveland in 1869, he was fourth in a direct line of a family of physicians, at a time when doctors were close to the top of the American social scale. He graduated from Yale in 1891, from Harvard Medical School in 1895, and did his residency at Johns Hopkins University Hospital in Baltimore. When Loyal Davis met him, he had been surgeon-in-chief at Peter Bent Brigham Hospital for more than a decade. Three years later, his *Life of Sir William Osler*, the great nineteenth-century medical educator, would win the Pulitzer Prize in biography. His three daughters would become famous for marrying well: Minnie, the eldest, was the first Mrs. Vincent Astor; Betsy wed James Roosevelt, one of FDR's sons, and later the polo-playing Long Island multimillionaire Jock Whitney; Barbara, the youngest, known as Babe, struck it rich with her first husband, Standard Oil heir Stanley Mortimer, then reigned over the international jet set as the wife of William Paley, the head of CBS. "Babe's father was brilliant but austere—disconnected," Kay Meehan, a close friend of the Paleys', told me. "The mother ran the show."

"Dr. Davis was tremendously influenced by Dr. Cushing," said Dr. Nicholas Wetzel, a partner of Loyal Davis's in his Chicago practice. "He modeled himself very much after him. One of the funny things was that when he was with Dr. Cushing, he came in one day wearing a blue shirt—Oxford cloth probably—and Dr. Cushing made a snide remark: 'Well, that's what you'd expect from the son of a railroad engineer.' Dr. Davis never wore a colored shirt, as far as I know, from then on. He wore white-on-white, which I think is absolutely atrocious."[57]

In his memoir, Loyal Davis defends Cushing's strictness: "He rigidly disciplined himself and was unsparing in demands upon his energy and talents. It is difficult to find fault with him when he drove his residents and nurses relentlessly, because he asked even more of himself. . . . He could not help trying to direct the lives of everyone around him, trying to make them discipline themselves so they would be working at their greatest possible efficiency. . . . His philosophy was that those who did not like the work well enough to stay in spite of his treatment were not suitable to stand the rigors of a surgical practice in later years."[58]

According to Cushing's records, Loyal Davis was his junior assistant associate in surgery from March to October 1924. Upon his return to Chicago, he was given an assistant professorship under Kanavel at Northwestern. Kanavel, who was best known as a hand surgeon, generously turned over his neurological practice to Davis. "Dr. Davis was the first full-time neurological surgeon in Chicago," Wetzel explained. In 1926 he became involved with the reorganization of the Passavant Memorial Hospital, where he would become an attending surgeon in 1929, when its new building on the Near North Side was completed. The new Passavant, with its private suites facing Lake Michigan, was the city's most luxurious hospital, and Loyal Davis would remain associated with it until the end of his career.[59]

Things should have been looking up for Loyal and Pearl. Richard was born on June 15, 1925. "Our apartment was small," Loyal wrote, "and we moved to another, farther north, so the baby could have a separate room. Pearl's girl friends, her sister, and Willa, a black housemaid, helped her take care of our son."[60] But, according to Wetzel, "Pearl was very unhappy with Dr. Davis. I think she wanted him to be a general practitioner. In his first years, he would operate in the morning, work in the laboratory in the afternoon, and then take care of his patients in the evening. So I think they had very little of a life. She just didn't like that at all. She kept calling him the 'little professor' and all that sort of thing. He was extremely ambitious, Dr. Davis was."[61]

By the summer of 1927, when Loyal went to England without Pearl, the marriage was clearly in trouble. He was apparently in no hurry to return home after his London conference, for he joined the Pollocks for a week on the French Riviera and three days in Paris. The problems he left behind were still there when he returned to Chicago.

In retrospect, I am sure that my desire to excel in my profession contributed as much as, if not more than, Pearl's disinterest in my professional life, ambitions, and friends to the slowly progressive and ultimate disintegration of our marital relations. I accept the onus of not having insisted strongly upon her accompanying me on our trip to England. In an effort to try to save the situation, I agreed to move to Evanston, Illinois, to a larger, nicer apartment. Still, Pearl's use and reliance upon her girl friends and Willa in the care of our son became more pronounced. Suddenly, she made the decision to take Richard and visit friends in Los Angeles. It was but a week or so later that she informed me that she was going to Reno, Nevada, to seek a divorce.

I had never discussed my domestic affairs with Dr. Kanavel, but one day he took me into a patient's empty room at [the hospital] and without preamble said that he had been aware of the difficulty I was experiencing in my marriage and said, "Never hug a bad bargain to your breast." The opposite advice came from Lewis Pollock, also without solicitation. It was that a divorce would react unfavorably upon my professional career, and every effort should be made to avoid it. I did not contest the divorce.[62]

Loyal gave no dates for this sequence of events, though most likely the move to suburban Evanston happened in late 1927 and the divorce sometime in 1928. Nor did he mention the possibility that Pearl had been having an affair—according to Richard Davis, probably "with Dr. Robert Gunning, Dr. Loyal's best friend." Was his mother aware of his father's dalliance with Edith Luckett aboard the *New York* in the summer of 1927? "I don't think Edith had anything to do with their divorce."[63]

Yet Edith had evidently set her sights on marrying Loyal while crossing the Atlantic. "Years later I came across the journal of Mother's trip when she met the 'doctor she wanted to marry,'" Nancy Reagan says in her autobiography. "It had been a shipboard romance. . . . Each day she would describe her meeting with him and what they had done. But at the bottom of each page, she would write, 'How I miss my baby.' I cried when I first read it, and still get a lump in my throat at the thought."[64]

*   *   *

On November 21, 1927—just a few months after she had met Loyal—Edith Luckett and Kenneth Robbins filed a petition for an uncontested divorce, on the grounds of desertion, in Trenton, New Jersey. The decree was granted in February 1928, and soon Robbins married Patricia "Patsie" Cross, a Junior Leaguer from Montclair, New Jersey.[65] By April 1928, Edith was in Chicago, co-starring opposite Spencer Tracy in *Baby Cyclone*, a George M. Cohan farce about two couples quarreling over a Pekingese dog, which opened at the Blackstone Theater on April 16 and ran until the middle of June.[66] During its run, Edith picked up her friendship with Tracy, who in his late 20s was finally having some success on Broadway, and his wife, Louise. She also resumed her romance with Loyal Davis.

According to Lester Weinrott, a Chicago radio producer-director and Davis family friend, Loyal "had been cuckolded by his first wife and was living in a drafty hotel after his humiliating divorce. Edith took it from there. She saw Loyal as her lifeline and grabbed on without letting go. She wanted to legitimize herself and give her daughter a break. Over the years, she transformed herself and this dour little man from the wrong side of the tracks in Galesburg, Illinois, into something that Chicago society had to pay attention to. It was the greatest performance she ever gave, and I salute her for it."[67]

The week after *Baby Cyclone* closed, Edith was

back onstage at the Blackstone Theater in another George M. Cohan production, this time in a supporting role. *Elmer the Great*, a baseball comedy written by Ring Lardner, starred Walter Huston, then forty-four years old and a major star of the stage since his award-winning performance in Eugene O'Neill's *Desire Under the Elms* four years earlier. Edith had been recommended for the part of "a local scribe" by Huston's co-star and mistress, Nan Sunderland, who had taken a liking to her when they worked together and who would become the third Mrs. Walter Huston three years later.[68]

Elmer the Great opened in Chicago on June 18, 1928, and ran into August, which meant Edith was in Chicago for much of that spring and summer. At some point she took an apartment at 210 East Pearson Street on the Near North Side, a few blocks from Northwestern University Medical School and Passavant Hospital. And at some point her doctor proposed.

Typically, Loyal Davis does not provide a date for that event in his memoir, noting only that after he had invited Kanavel, Pollock, and their wives to a performance of *Elmer the Great* and dinner with Edith, "Dr. Kanavel invited himself to her apartment for her to cook dinner to make certain, he told her, whether it was right for us to be married."[69] As Richard Davis told me, "There was some jeopardy because Edith was an actress, and actresses weren't accepted."[70] There may have also been an element of pressing necessity on Edith's part.

Uncle Audley Galbraith had learned that he would be transferred to Atlanta by the Southern Railroad that fall. Where was Nancy, turning seven and about to enter second grade, going to go?

In both *Nancy* and *My Turn*, Nancy Reagan said that her mother made a special trip to Bethesda to tell her about Dr. Davis. Decades later she repeated the story almost word for word to me, emphasizing as always that Edith sought *her permission* to marry: "She came and she told me that she had met this man who had asked her to marry him, and she wanted to. But she wouldn't do it unless it was all right with me. And I said of course. I often wonder what would have happened if I'd said no. I'm sure Mother would have talked me into it. But anyway, I said yes. And then we moved to Chicago."[71]

She placed this event in the spring of 1929, but it must have happened the previous year. Nancy finished first grade at the Sidwell School in June 1928, and Charlotte Galbraith Ramage told me that her family moved to Atlanta in the fall of 1928. "When we moved, she moved to Chicago."[72] Meanwhile, after closing in Chicago that August, *Elmer the Great* opened on Broadway on September 24, with Edith still in the cast, along with Walter Huston and Nan Sunderland. It played for five weeks, which meant Edith was in New York until the end of October.[73] The most likely sequence of events, therefore, is that Nancy joined her mother in Chicago in November 1928, after Edith returned from New York and about the time the Galbraiths left Bethesda for Atlanta.

In an interview Nancy Reagan gave to Lawrence Grobel for his 1989 history of the Huston family, *The Hustons*, she revealed the previously undisclosed secret wedding of Edith and Loyal in New York during the run of *Elmer the Great*. "Uncle Walter and Nan stood up with my mother and father when they were secretly married in New York in October," she said. "Then when the play ended, they were remarried in May, in Chicago."[74] That was the first and only time a clandestine wedding has ever been mentioned, and she was the sole source. When I asked her why Loyal and Edith would have married secretly, she answered, "They just wanted to get married. They were married in front of a judge, I think." She said she "couldn't be there," which lends further credence to the probability that she was reunited with her mother a month later, in November 1928, and lived with her in the East Pearson Street apartment for a full seven months before Edith and Loyal's official marriage.[75]

I asked Richard Davis about the possibility that Edith and Loyal lived together before they were married and that the secret marriage was a yarn told to Nancy to cover up that fact. "No, no, no," he said. "Because if Dr. Kanavel ever knew that, Loyal Davis would have been finished." Richard couldn't recall for certain if his father had lived in a hotel between his marriages, but said, "I know he ate his dinners at a Greek restaurant, and that he was alone."[76]

On May 21, 1929, Edith Robbins and Loyal Davis were married in a chapel at the Fourth Presbyterian Church, with only two attendants. "The best man was Dr. Allen Kanavel, my new father's mentor," Nancy Reagan later wrote. "I was the bridesmaid, and I wore a blue pleated dress and carried flowers. I was happy for Mother, but I can remember, even then, feeling twinges of jealousy—a feeling I was to experience years later, from the other side, after I married a man with children. Dr. Davis was taking part of her away from me, and after being separated from Mother for so long, I wanted her all to myself. On their honeymoon, they went to a medical convention and then toured the battlefields of the Civil War—Dr. Davis was a Civil War buff."[77]

The day after their wedding, the *Chicago Tribune*'s society section noted, "Both Dr. Davis and his bride gave their ages as 33 years."[78] The bride was fibbing, but that was of little concern to the groom. "My professional and personal life became calm and happy," he later wrote. "My father and mother were devoted to Edith, as she was to them. . . . She taught me to change my asocial tendencies and habits, to develop a sense of humor, to retain my desire and energy to succeed but to relax and enjoy the association of friends."[79]

"They were a great couple" is how Nancy Reagan put it. "A really great couple. An ideal couple, if you think about it. Because they each gave the other something they didn't have."[80] Richard Davis saw it somewhat differently: "Edith was the giver. He was more of a taker. My God, for Edith the sun rose and set on Loyal Davis."[81]

In many ways their marriage, which endured for fifty-three years, until Loyal Davis's death in 1982, was the model for the marriage of Ronald and Nancy Reagan. Loyal's and Edith's shared big-time ambitions, their clear-cut roles of star husband and helpmate wife, his avid pursuit of leadership in professional organizations, her equally avid cultivation of rich and powerful friends, their attraction to glamour and style, their undying devotion to each other—all this and more would be repeated and magnified when Nancy married Ronnie. These were both marriages in which one plus one added up to much more than two, and in which a romantic partnership based on sexual attraction and emotional needs evolved into a joint venture based on power and prestige without losing love along the way. But there is an obvious twist in this comparison: in temperament and inclination, perfectionist Nancy was more like Loyal, and carefree Ronnie was more like Edith.

Like Jack and Nelle Reagan, Edith and Loyal Davis were a case of opposites attracting. She was an extrovert, a partygoer, fun-loving, funny, even a bit vulgar. He was an introvert, a taskmaster, a workaholic perfectionist, proper to a fault. A journalist once described them as "a short, gay Democrat" and "a tall, serious Republican."[82] Edith was the type who acquired nicknames—Lucky, DeeDee, Edie. Loyal was always Loyal.

Unlike Jack and Nelle, however, Loyal and Edith made it. The American dream came true for them: they *were* the self-made man and his oh-so-social wife, the picture of upward mobility triumphant. On their way up, they moved more times than the Reagans in Dixon, but, with the exception of a post-retirement pied-à-terre, always to a bigger apartment in a better building and always within Chicago's best neighborhood, the Near North Side off Lake Michigan, also known as the Gold Coast. The year before Loyal married Edith, he had been elected to membership in the small Society of Neurological Surgeons, which was led by such illustrious figures as Dr. William Mayo, the founder of the Mayo Clinic, and Dr. Harvey Cushing, Loyal's old idol. Five months after they exchanged vows, the stock market crashed and the Great Depression began to take its toll. Chicago would be one of the hardest-hit cities in the country, but that did not stop the Davises. As Loyal continued to put in long hours seeing patients in his office, operating at the hospital, and teaching and researching at Northwestern, Edith set about transforming herself from a stock company actress into a full-fledged socialite, giving up the stage— but not her stage friends—hosting small dinners for her husband's colleagues, and cultivating useful new acquaintances among Chicago's social and political elite.

"Within a year, she knew more people in Chicago than he did," Nancy Reagan recalled. "I had never seen my mother as a wife before, but she was terrific at it. She cared for her husband, she expanded his social circle—she helped him in every possible way. 'Now, Nancy,' she used to say, 'when you get married, be sure to get up and have breakfast with your husband in the morning. Because if you don't, you can be sure that some other woman who lives around the corner will be perfectly happy to do so.' "[83]

"At first Mother wasn't accepted by the other doctors' wives in Chicago," Nancy noted. "I once found her crying in her bedroom because she'd overheard another woman make a disparaging remark about this *actress* who had married that nice, handsome, highly eligible doctor. In the circles my father moved in, actresses were not looked on very kindly." One of the problems may have been Edith's irrepressible sense of humor. As her daughter recalled, "When my parents had company, she would tell the latest off-color jokes. If I was in the room, she would turn to me and say, 'Nancy, would you go to the kitchen and bring me an apple?' It took me quite a while to realize that this was a ruse to get me out of there until she had finished the joke. She ate a lot of apples in those years."[84]

Nancy's bohemian godmother, Alla Nazimova, was one of the first of Edith's old friends to give her approval of Loyal. In late 1930, the fifty-one-year-old actress went to Chicago on tour with Turgenev's *A Month in the Country*. She was accompanied by her twenty-one-year-old girlfriend, Glesca Marshall. Though Nazimova was very much in the closet, she confided her secrets to Edith, and presumably Edith told them to Loyal. Edith arranged for Nazimova to be the guest of honor at a Chicago Dramatic League luncheon, and that afternoon she took her and Glesca home to meet Loyal. Somewhat surprisingly, there was a meeting of the minds between the exotic Jewish Democrat and the starchy Protestant Republican. "I do hope he likes me half as much as I do him," Nazimova wrote Edith from the next stop on her tour. "He is grand."[85]

Nancy herself seems to have viewed her new stepfather with a mixture of awe and trepidation. "Soon after I arrived in Chicago," she wrote, "he sat me down and explained that he and my mother were in love, and that he would be good to her. . . . He hoped that he and I would come to love each other, and that we all would become one happy family. But both of us knew it would take time."[86]

In a eulogy delivered to the Chicago Neurological Society after Loyal Davis's death, Dr. Louis Boshes, who had assisted Davis and his research partner, Dr. Louis Pollock, at Northwestern, gave a telling picture of the newly formed Davis family: "Part of my neurology training consisted of buying cigars for Dr. Pollock and specific purchases for Dr. Davis. On Sundays, regularly, the two conducted experiments on a premise advanced by the late Dr. Lewis Weed of Johns Hopkins on intraspinal dynamics. The two scientists were attempting to prove or disprove Dr. Weed's theory, and they eventually advanced their own theory. On some afternoons would come Mrs. Pollock, 'Pinky,' and Mrs. Davis, 'Lucky,' who had been an actress on the legitimate stage. She would bring along a feisty little girl named Anne Frances, whose nickname became, and still is, Nancy. One of my jobs was to 'contain' Anne Frances. But it was pleasurable for me to gaze with only lateral vision upon Mrs. Davis's friend, whom she brought along now and then— Helen Hayes. And Mrs. Pollock and Mrs. Davis brought picnic luncheons for their husbands. I never rated one finger sandwich by invitation, or even as a leftover. But part of my neurological training included painting Easter eggs for Mrs. Davis and dressing and undressing Kachina dolls for Mrs. Pollock."[87]

It is clear from a short note from Loyal, typed on his office stationery, to his stepdaughter that the doctor quickly became the child's disciplinarian:

Nancy dear:
   I am sorry too that you had a little lapse of memory. We won't do that again, will we? You must always be the ladylike Nancy that you really are, regardless of what other little girls with whom you play do or say.
   Night, big boy. Sleep tight. I'll wake you in the morning when I leave.

Doctor Loyal[88]

Not long after Loyal and Edith married, Ken Robbins paid a visit to Chicago. Photographs from the summer of 1929 show Nancy and her father looking fairly comfortable with each other at a Lake Michigan beach or marina. Nancy, a chubby eight-year-old with a half-smile, is wearing a T-shirt with an airplane stenciled across the front, shorts, and a bathing cap. Ken, then a thirty-five-year-old real estate salesman with a receding hairline, looks rather prosperous, wearing a three-piece suit with a white shirt, silk tie, and pocket handkerchief in one picture, and a long terry cloth robe over a two-piece bathing suit in a second. In another photograph, most likely also taken that summer, because Nancy looks the same in it, she is standing between her grandmother and stepmother in a garden—probably at the house in suburban New Jersey that Ken and Patsie shared with Nannee Robbins.[89]

Although the terms of Edith's divorce from Ken are unclear, Kitty Kelley claims, "Edith made sure that Nancy spent part of every summer in New Jersey with him."[90] Nancy Reagan, on the other hand, has written, "I visited with my father only a few times when I was young. He had remarried, and his wife was a very nice woman who tried to make me welcome on my visits. They once took me on a trip to Niagara Falls. My father tried to please me, but too many years had gone by and we were really strangers to each other. As I look back, I am sure he was unhappy about it."[91]

There are photographs of Nancy with her father's family two summers later, including one of her, age ten and looking slimmer, standing under a Canadian flag at Niagara Falls. Another records the Robbinses' visit to Patsie's sister in upstate New York, probably on that same trip. "Nancy had beautiful manners," Patsie's niece, Orme Staudinger, told a reporter from *People* magazine years later. A shot of Nancy and her father swinging golf clubs appears to be from the same period.[92] Again, they seem to be getting along fine.

Nancy probably met her stepbrother, Richard, for the first time in 1930, when he came to spend the summer with his father under the terms of his parents' divorce agreement. His mother, he told me, "never remarried. She became really ill with tuberculosis in 1929 or 1930, which really frightened my father, because there was no treatment then—the only treatment for TB in those days was warm weather; streptomycin came out in about 1950. So she suffered terribly, and I watched her die. She died at the age of forty-three, on April 23, 1939." Until Pearl's death, Richard spent nine months of each year with her, first in Phoenix and from 1931 in Beverly Hills, and three months with Loyal and Edith in Chicago. According to Richard, he was five years old when he and Nancy met, and she was nine, and they took an immediate liking to each other. "We played a game called Help! Murder! Police!," he said, "with both of us jumping all over the furniture. We had a very, very good time."[93]

In all previous accounts of her childhood, including her own, Nancy was enrolled in Chicago's most elite private school immediately after moving to the city. According to records at the Girls Latin School of Chicago, however, she didn't start there until three years later. Her application indicated that she had come from the University School for Girls, a private school on Lake Shore Drive, which lacked the social cachet of Girls Latin. It is now defunct, so records that would show exactly when she started there are unavailable, though presumably she entered the second grade in the fall of 1928.

When I asked her about attending the University School, she said, "I just remember Latin School had a waiting list, and Mother could not get me in when she wanted to, so I went to this other school for a couple of years."[94] It may have been that the conservative Girls Latin School looked askance at the daughter of a divorced single actress, as Edith was her first year in Chicago, but was more amenable three years later, by which time she had consolidated her social position as the wife of an increasingly respected doctor.

Nancy started at Girls Latin in the fifth grade in September 1931. "She was very friendly and she fit in well," said Jean Wescott Marshall, who became her best friend at the school. According to Marshall, Nancy was already self-conscious about her weight—"She watched what she ate. She was very careful about it."—and she worshipped her stepfather. "She thought he was absolutely the tops. She really admired him. He was quite a person. Very strict. Very imposing. Her mother had a wonderful sense of humor. She and Nancy were very close."[95]

School records indicate that the Davises had

moved from Edith's old apartment on East Pearson Street by then. Their new apartment was two blocks north in a doorman building at 237 East Delaware Place, and, as Richard recalled, it had three bedrooms and a dining room. In 1932, Loyal was made chairman of Northwestern's department of surgery, the position formerly occupied by Dr. Kanavel. There was some concern about his age, thirty-six, but, as the dean of the school observed, "time would take care of that objection."[96] He also became chief of surgery at Passavant that year, again following Dr. Kanavel. And his reputation was growing: Dr. Franklin H. Martin, the founder of the American College of Surgeons, asked him to give the John B. Murphy Oration at the organization's annual conference, held in Chicago that fall. Loyal was already working on his biography of Murphy, the controversial Chicago surgeon who saved Theodore Roosevelt's life after a 1912 assassination attempt, which would be published in America and England the following year.[97]

In October 1932, Edith relaunched her show-business career, taking a part in one of NBC radio's first soap operas. After three years away from the stage, she couldn't resist the lure of the glamorous—and lucrative—new medium. On *Betty and Bob,* Edith played both a high-society matron with a pretentious British accent and her black maid, Gardenia, who had lines such as "Sho is good to have you back, Mistah Bob." The fifteen-minute melodrama was on the air five afternoons a week and ran for nine years. Sponsored by

Wheaties cereal, Gold Medal flour, and Bisquick, it "set the standard for all the washboard weepers that would follow,"[98] according to radio historian John Dunning.

According to Kitty Kelley, Edith earned between $500 and $1,000 a month from *Betty and Bob,* while Loyal was being paid "$150 for performing prefrontal lobotomies."[99] But Loyal wrote that his fee for a "brain operation" was $500 in the mid-1930s.[100] In either case, the additional income from Edith's radio work must have come in handy, because earlier that year the Davises had moved again—to the first of the three apartments they would occupy on East Lake Shore Drive, Chicago's equivalent of Fifth Avenue facing Central Park. The three-bedroom apartment at 219 East Lake Shore Drive was not much larger than the one on East Delaware Place, but it faced Oak Street Beach and was just around the corner from the Drake, Chicago's best hotel. Edith decorated it herself "in a very traditional style, not lavish at all," Richard Davis said, remembering that his stepmother was very proud of her "one antique—a piecrust table from England."[101]

At forty-five, Edith was finally where she wanted to be—on the best block in the city, up the street from Mr. and Mrs. W. Rockefeller Prentice, who would soon become good friends, and next door to Edward Joseph Kelly, the new political pal who invited her and Nancy to the 1932 Democratic convention. At the time, the rough-and-ready Kelly held two plum municipal posts, chief engineer of the Sanitary District and president of the South Park Board, and had a reputation for getting things done while enriching himself in the process. In February 1933, Mayor Anton Cermak was shot in Miami by an anarchist whose intended target was President-elect Franklin Roosevelt. After weeks of backroom machinations, the city council installed Kelly as mayor.

Lester Weinrott, who worked with Edith on *Betty and Bob*, described her in those days:

> Her face was beautiful, a classic face; her smile warmed the eye and the heart of the beholder. Her hair, under her Bes-Ben hat, had begun to gray. She wore a smartly tailored suit, white kid gloves, mid-heel pumps—and—a corsage made of two tightly wrapped white carnations. (No ribbon or fern—just the flowers.)
>
> She started each day at the Merchandise Mart (NBC). Her first stop was at Daskiel & Shapiro, the florists. Here she would select a single gardenia, two baby orchids, carnations or whatever. Here, too, she would tell a new joke. She seemed to have a new one every day.
>
> Where did she get her stories? From the policeman who directed traffic at Lake Shore and Michigan, from the Drake hotel doorman, from a cab driver—she knew them all and they all knew her. It was not uncommon to be walking down Michigan Avenue with Edie and have a cabbie shout, "Hi, Miz Davis!"[102]

CHAPTER THREE

IOWA

1933–1937

"Everything comes to him that waits"—But here is one that's slicker: The man who goes after what he wants, Gets it a darn sight quicker.

An optimist is the one who sees a light where there is none. A pessimist is one who blows it out.

A "specialist" is one who knows more and more about less and less.

Keep your head cool—feet warm—mind busy. Plan work ahead and stick to it—rain or shine. If you are a gem, someone will find you.

From *As a Man Thinketh* by B. J. Palmer, founder of WOC Radio, Davenport, Iowa[1]

The memories of friendships dear
Give strength that we endure
And the Great Purpose of it all
Hold steadfast, and more sure.

From "My New Year Poem 1935–36" by Nelle Reagan[2]

Edith Davis wasn't the only one pursuing a career in radio in the fall of 1932. After his lifeguard job in Dixon ended on that Labor Day, Ronald Reagan hitchhiked to Chicago in hopes of getting an interview at the National Broadcasting Company or the Columbia Broadcasting System, the booming new radio networks that had been established in the late 1920s by David Sarnoff and William S. Paley, respectively. Although the twenty-one-year-old Ronald didn't even get to see the program directors at NBC and CBS, by 1934 he was becoming well known across the Midwest as Dutch Reagan, sports announcer for WHO in Des Moines, Iowa.

It is hard to imagine how omnipresent, powerful, and glamorous radio was in the 1930s and 1940s. The biggest stars at NBC and CBS—George Burns and Gracie Allen, Jack Benny, Red Skelton, the ventriloquist Edgar Bergen and his dummy Charlie McCarthy—were as famous as, and made as much money as, the top movie stars at MGM and Paramount Pictures. *Amos 'n' Andy*, which starred Freeman Gosden and Charles Correll and went on the air in 1928 (it stayed on until 1960), was so popular that some movie theaters installed radios and interrupted their evening screenings so that audiences wouldn't have to miss a single fifteen-minute episode.

In *Where's the Rest of Me?*, Reagan makes much of the first time he heard a crystal set, as early radios were called, at Nelle's sister's farm near Morrison, Illinois: "I remember sitting with a dozen others in a little room with breathless attention, a pair of earphones attached tightly to my head, scratching a crystal with a wire. I was listening to raspy recorded music and faint voices saying, 'This is KDKA, Pittsburgh, KDKA, Pittsburgh.'"[3] According to Anne Edwards, "when the sound faded," the nine-year-old Ronald stood up "and imitated the announcer. Everyone laughed and he repeated the performance."[4] Edwards places this scene at Christmastime 1920, not long after KDKA, the first commercial radio station in the nation, had begun regular broadcasts that November 2 with the returns of the Harding-Cox presidential election.[5]

However, Edmund Morris quotes a 1984 speech in which Reagan said this momentous event took place "one Sunday afternoon" in Dixon. In this version, the Reagan boys had borrowed a crystal set from a neighbor: "My brother and I and a couple of other kids walked all over town trying to find if we could hear something. And finally we went down by the river and something was coming! We passed the headphones around and heard this orchestra playing, coming out of the air! Let me tell you, that was a miracle. 'This is KDKA Pittsburgh—KDKA Pittsburgh.' We were actually hearing this. . . . Can you imagine our sense of wonder? You know, none of the developments that came after, talkies and television and so forth, were ever such a revelation as that day I first scratched that crystal with a wire whisker under the bridge at Dixon."[6]

* * *

Ronald Reagan's decision to go into radio came after a talk with Sid Altschuler, the Kansas City businessman who had become a mentor to him at Lowell Park during the summer of 1932. After graduating from Eureka College, Dutch, as everyone called him by then, was back on his lifeguard stand with no clear idea about his future—the only certainty seemed to be that he would marry Margaret Cleaver. "This depression isn't going to last forever," the farsighted Altschuler told him, "and smart businessmen are willing to take on young men who can learn their business in order to have trained manpower on hand when things start to roll." Dutch, whose father was unemployed and spending most of his time campaigning for FDR, later wrote that it was "literally the first note of optimism I'd heard about the state of the nation." Altschuler then asked him the question he had been avoiding since graduating from Eureka that June: "What do you think you'd like to do?" Dutch said he didn't know. "When you determine what line of work you want to get in, let me know," Altschuler told him, "and if it's one of those areas where I can help, I'll get you a job."[7]

Dutch spent several sleepless nights mulling over his future before going back to Altschuler with an answer. "Out of the things that Sid had talked about came a new approach. No longer did I speculate about a paycheck and security. I really wrestled with the problem of what I would be happy doing for the next few decades." Thinking back on the thrill of winning a prize for his acting in *Aria da*

Capo the year before, he admitted to himself that he had a "secret dream to be an actor" but was afraid to declare it "in the middle of Illinois in 1932" for fear he would be institutionalized, as he half-jokingly put it. He also reasoned, "Broadway and Hollywood were as inaccessible as outer space," but there was a form of show business "closer to home" that attracted him—radio, which was then largely centered in Chicago. He went back to Altschuler and told him, "Way down deep inside, what I'd really like to be is a radio sports announcer."[8]

"Radio had created a new profession," he later wrote. "Broadcasting play-by-play reports of football games, people like Graham McNamee and Ted Husing had become as famous as some Hollywood stars and often they were more famous than the athletes they reported on." Parenthetically, he made an even more telling remark: "I'd seen several movies in which sports announcers played themselves and thought there was a remote possibility the job might lead me into the movies."[9] Reagan's recounting of the thought process involved in his decision reveals a clever willingness to move stealthily and incrementally toward a seemingly unattainable goal, as well as an ability to make compromises along the way. The goal, it is clear, was stardom.

Altschuler had no connections in radio, but he approved of Dutch's choice, because radio was one of the few growing industries during the Depression, and he urged him to "take any kind of job, even sweeping floors, just to get in."[10] In early September, Dutch went to Chicago. He didn't make it past the receptionists at the big networks, though he did have a stroke of luck. On his second attempt to see the program director at NBC, a secretary came out and sat with him. "This is the big time," he recalled her telling him. "No one in the city wants to take a chance on inexperience. Go out in what we call the sticks—we shouldn't but we do—and try some of the smaller stations. They can't afford to compete with us for experienced talent, so they are often willing to give a newcomer a chance. I think you will make it—come back and see me after you have some experience."[11]

He was only too happy to flee the big city: "I couldn't afford cabs and I was afraid of the damn buses—as a matter of fact, the city itself scared the bejesus out of me. Everybody seemed to know where they were going and what they were doing, and I could get lost just looking for a men's room."[12] He hitchhiked back to Dixon in the rain, borrowed his father's "third-hand Oldsmobile,"[13] and headed for Iowa.

His first stop was sixty-five miles west: WOC in Davenport, a small city sitting on a hill just across the Mississippi from Rock Island, Illinois. The station's call letters stood for World of Chiropractic; it was owned and operated by the Palmer School of Chiropractic and located on the school's campus. He auditioned for the program director, a tough old Scotsman named Peter MacArthur, who was impressed enough by his delivery—Dutch re-created the fourth quarter of a football game in which he had played for Eureka the previous fall—to offer him $5 and bus fare to announce a University of Iowa game the following week. Three more trial games followed that fall, but as the holidays approached Dutch still did not have a full-time job.[14] In November he voted for the first time—for Franklin Delano Roosevelt, who carried forty-two of forty-eight states, including Illinois. (Herbert Hoover was so despised by 1932 that in Detroit his campaign train was greeted by chants of "Hang Hoover! Hang Hoover!," and in many other cities his limousine was pelted with eggs and tomatoes.)[15]

Finally, just after the New Year, MacArthur called from Davenport to say that a position as staff announcer had opened up at WOC. The starting salary was $100 a month, which Dutch would apportion as follows: $32 for a room in a boardinghouse, $16.60 for meals at the Palmer School cafeteria, $20 for Nelle and Jack back in Dixon. After receiving approval from a Disciples of Christ minister, he also decided to send $10 a month to Neil, who was in his last year at Eureka, in lieu of his tithes to the church.[16] The remainder—$21.40—was his to spend or save as he liked. ("You could get a made-to-measure suit with two pairs of pants for $18.50," he wrote in his autobiography.)[17]

Ronald Reagan officially became a radio announcer on February 10, 1933. A month later, on March 12,

President Roosevelt gave the first of his Fireside Chats, reassuring Americans that it was "safer to keep your money in a reopened bank than under the mattress"—thus launching the first radio presidency. Like Adolf Hitler (who also took office in 1933), FDR was quick to recognize the power of radio to sway a mass audience, to connect a country's leader with its citizens in their living rooms, a possibility that had never existed before. One of the new President's most avid listeners was young Dutch. "I soon idolized FDR," he would later write. "During his Fireside Chats, his strong, gentle, confident voice resonated across the nation with an eloquence that brought comfort and resilience to a nation caught up in a storm and reassured us that we could lick any problem."[18]

Reagan would later criticize Roosevelt's "alphabet soup of federal agencies" as the first step toward "a form of veiled socialism [in] America."[19] In June 1933, however, he was grateful that his father's efforts on behalf of the Democrats were rewarded with a job in the Dixon office of the newly created Federal Emergency Relief Administration (FERA). That November, five months after graduating from Eureka, Neil Reagan was appointed district representative of the Federal Reemployment Bureau (FRB).[20] Neither Neil nor Ronald mentioned this government job in their later accounts of this period, and Ronald would often cite his father's supposedly frustrating experience with the federal bureaucracy as his first insight into why big government doesn't work. Neil often said that he had registered as a Republican "six months after Roosevelt's first inauguration"—perhaps *he* was frustrated by his New Deal experience. According to some sources, Jack considered Neil's defection to the party of the rich a personal betrayal.[21] In any case, his younger son was loyally defending FDR and the New Deal in heated arguments with Republican friends and colleagues in Iowa.[22]

Dutch did not get off to a good start at WOC, where his staff job involved "many hours of playing phonograph records, interspersed with the reading of commercials," as well as announcing the news, weather, and sports scores, from early morning until the midnight sign-off: "This is station WOC, owned and operated by the Palmer School of Chiropractic, the Chiropractic Fountainhead, Davenport, Iowa, where the West begins and in the state where the tall corn grows." Advertisers complained about the novice announcer's wooden readings, and after he neglected to plug the sponsor of a romantic organ music program, Runge Mortuary, he was fired. "It was the end of the world," Reagan recalled feeling. Fortunately, his replacement, a local schoolteacher, demanded a contract, and, as Reagan put it, "WOC was not in the habit of giving contracts." The teacher quit, and Reagan was rehired temporarily until a new replacement could be found. "I was mad, didn't give a damn," he recalled, and so he read his next commercial "freely, easily and with a pretty good punch. There was no more talk of a replacement."[23]

Advertising was gospel at WOC, which was

run by "Colonel" B. J. Palmer, the son of D. D. Palmer, the mesmerist turned chiropractor who had founded the Palmer School at the turn of the century and the radio station in 1922.[24] One of the Colonel's favorite mottoes was "Early to bed, early to rise; Work like hell—and advertise." Another was "Only mints can make money without advertising."[25] He was also fond of proclaiming, in lectures on salesmanship he gave throughout the Midwest, "Get the big idea and all else follows," "Sell yourself in all your business approaches," and "Smile your voice!" The Palmers lived in a mansion next to the school; their "world famous collection of spines" was housed on the third floor. The small garden between the buildings was called "A Little Bit O' Heaven."[26] Reagan leaves B. J. Palmer out of his books, probably because he considered him too weird: he had a full beard and long flowing hair, which he washed once a year; he slept with his head pointed toward the North Pole; and his late Saint Bernard, Big Ben, which had been stuffed, was kept under the piano.[27] Nonetheless, one can't help but think that the Colonel's assortment of peppy slogans, which were hung in the hallways of the school and radio station, had their effect on the future actor and politician.

Two years before Reagan went to WOC, Palmer had bought WHO, a larger station affiliated with NBC, in Des Moines, the state capital. He spent close to $250,000 upgrading its technical capabilities, making it one of only fifteen stations in the country with a 50,000-watt transmitter. WHO's

532-foot antenna tower was the tallest structure in Iowa, and its broadcasts could be heard throughout the Midwest.[28] In April 1933, MacArthur sent Dutch to Des Moines to broadcast the Drake Relays, a major national amateur track event held annually at Drake College. (Like Eureka, Drake was a Disciples of Christ institution, but eight times larger.)[29] The following month MacArthur was transferred to WHO, and he took Dutch with him as chief sports announcer. MacArthur would become the younger man's Iowa mentor, following in the line of Reverend Cleaver and Sid Altschuler. According to Reagan, MacArthur had come to America from Scotland with the celebrated Harry Lauder's vaudeville troupe; he eventually found his way to the Palmer School of Chiropractic, where he sought relief from his crippling arthritis, and was taken on as one of WOC's first announcers. (His strong Highland burr became his on-air trademark.) By the time Reagan met him, he was walking with two canes, and would soon be on crutches.[30]

At WHO, Dutch's salary was doubled to $200 a month; a year later it was raised to $300. He was now making enough money to marry Margaret Cleaver, but it was not to be. After graduating from Eureka, Margaret had taught high school for a year in a nearby town, then, to Dutch's dismay, decided to spend a year in Paris, where her sister was living.[31] In the summer of 1934 she wrote to say that she had fallen in love with an American diplomat named James Waddell Gordon Jr., and she enclosed Dutch's fraternity pin and engagement ring in her letter.[32] Reagan later reflected stoically, "As our lives traveled into diverging paths, we would find that it was true that before and after age twenty-one, people are often different. At any rate, our lovely and wholesome relationship did not survive growing up."[33] However hurt he may have been at the time, his feelings didn't stop from him buying his first car, a brand-new metallic-beige Nash Lafayette two-seater convertible, from Margaret's brother-in-law, who had a dealership in Illinois.[34]

Dutch asked Neil to drive the car to Des Moines. His brother was out of work again, so he introduced him to MacArthur, who guaranteed Neil $30 a week for announcing football scores and reading laxative commercials.[35] Neil moved into Dutch's apartment in a subdivided mansion in an old neighborhood near the radio station for a few months, before being sent to WOC in Davenport as a full-time sports announcer. In 1936, he was promoted to program director at WOC.

That same year he married Bess Hoffman, a Drake College graduate from Des Moines, two weeks after meeting her. Dutch urged him to wait, but Neil ignored his advice.[36] Meanwhile Jack, still chain-smoking, had suffered the first of his heart attacks and could no longer work. Dutch started sending his parents $100 a month. "I had the satisfaction," Reagan later wrote, "of being able to send a monthly check that removed all his economic problems for the first time in his life . . . it never entered his mind that he could apply for public assistance."[37] Nelle gave up her job at the dress shop in Dixon and frequently visited her son in Des Moines.

Dutch's official title at WHO was sports director. He announced football games, swimming meets, track meets, and car races. By 1934 he had his own show, *The Teaberry Sports Review,* which aired twice a day. He also interviewed visiting sports stars, most notably the world heavyweight champion Max Baer (in Reagan's words, "as beautiful a piece of physical machinery as ever stepped into the fight ring").[38] Occasionally he was asked to interview celebrities from other fields, including the movie star Leslie Howard ("I was so stage-struck that I forgot his name as I stepped up to the microphone") and the evangelist Aimee Semple McPherson, whose flamboyant style and dramatic voice so mesmerized him that he let her run away with the interview.[39]

He became best known for "covering" baseball games from Chicago's Wrigley Field without ever stepping out of WHO's studio in Des Moines. "To millions of sports fans in at least seven or eight middlewestern states," the *Des Moines Dispatch* reported on August 3, 1934, "the voice of Dutch Reagan is a daily source of baseball dope. Every afternoon at 2:00 o'clock, 'Dutch' goes on the air with his rapid-fire, play-by-play visualization of the home games of Chicago's major league baseball teams, the Cubs and the Sox."[40] Reagan called this technique "the magic of radio." A telegraph operator sitting in the stadium press box tapped out the game's plays in Morse code to an operator sitting in the radio studio opposite Dutch at his microphone. From these brief flashes he constructed the entire scene in the baseball park—the pitcher's form, the batter's gestures, the fans' reactions, even changes in the weather—out of his imagination. (He had visited Wrigley Field only once, when it was empty, to get a sense of what it looked like.) "You just couldn't believe that you were not actually there," remembered a WHO colleague of Reagan's decades later. In his four years at the station, Dutch made some six hundred baseball games come alive this way.[41]

Reagan lived in Des Moines between the ages of twenty-two and twenty-six—an attractive, enthusiastic, unattached young man, a local celebrity making good money in the middle of the Depression, a big fish in the small pond that was the capital of the Hawkeye State. Bland, drab Des Moines, with a population of 145,000 and the home offices of innumerable insurance companies, was the largest city Reagan had lived in, and he found it exciting. Civic organizations asked him to give speeches at their banquets, the Dispatch made him its sports columnist, he dated prairie beauties with names like Jeanne Tesdell and Gretchen Schnelle. Cy's Moonlight Inn, a former speakeasy on the edge of town, and Club Belvedere, the capital's only real nightclub, with chorus girls and a casino, were his regular hangouts. But he never gambled and was always careful not to drink excessively. He was most comfortable, it seemed, with the friends he made at Drake University, some of whom belonged to his fraternity (Tau Kappa Epsilon), many of whom were fellow Disciples of Christ. On fall weekends he was field announcer at Drake's football games, and for a year he shared an apartment with an assistant coach at Drake. When Nelle came to town, he and his Drake friends took her out with them. It was all very wholesome: Dutch and his buddies had formed a barbershop quartet and often sang at Cy's on Saturday nights.[42]

Reagan took up riding in Des Moines and, according to his memoir, it was there that he first heard the saying that would become a lifetime motto: "Nothing is so good for the inside of a man as the outside of a horse."[43] In order to ride the horses at Fort Des Moines, he joined the cavalry reserve, but he had to cheat on his eye test to earn his commission as a second lieutenant in the 14th Cavalry Regiment.[44] For a while he dated a blue-ribbon equestrienne he had met while emceeing a horse show; as the romance became more serious, however, their religious differences—she was a devout Catholic—became a problem.[45]

He kept in excellent physical condition by swimming regularly in the pool at Camp Dodge, another major military installation just outside the city. In Des Moines, too, he apparently developed his predilection for the brown suits that would raise eyebrows when he was president. He liked tooling around the Iowa capital in his beige convertible in tawny tweed jackets, puffing on a briar pipe, evidently aware of his snappy, color-coordinated image.[46]

On September 4, 1936, his hero came to town. FDR had been nominated for a second term that summer; in his acceptance speech he declared, "This generation has a rendezvous with destiny," a phrase Reagan would use twenty-eight years later in his famous speech for Republican presidential candidate Barry Goldwater. During the campaign Colonel Robert McCormick's *Chicago Tribune* claimed Roosevelt was the candidate of Moscow, and as election day approached the paper constantly reminded its readers of how many days remained "to save your country." (McCormick ordered his switchboard operators to repeat this message to all callers.) McCormick wasn't alone: across the country, from Beacon Hill to Nob Hill, America's rich were angrily telling one another that Roosevelt was "a traitor to his class." FDR counterattacked on the radio. "Never before in all our history have these forces been so united against one candidate as they stand today," he told his listeners. "They are united in their hate for me—and I welcome their hatred."[47]

Between broadcasts at WHO, Dutch entertained his colleagues, of both parties, with his affectionately mischievous imitations of the Fireside Chats. He also plugged his candidate whenever he could on his radio shows.[48] And it was with a mixture of awe and excitement that he watched FDR drive by the WHO building in his open limousine, waving to the crowds, on his way to the Great Plains Drought Committee conference with Midwestern governors.[49] Two months later, Roosevelt carried every state except Maine and Vermont as he trounced one of those governors, Alf Landon of Kansas.

As the fish grew bigger, the pond seemed smaller, and the Iowa winters seemed colder and longer. So in February 1936, Dutch Reagan, star broadcaster, came up with a way to get WHO to give him "an all-expense paid holiday under the California sun." Every winter the Chicago Cubs trained on Catalina Island; if the radio station let him accompany them there, he would agree to count the trip as vacation time. It was more than the weather that impelled him toward Los Angeles. He may have put off his dream of movie stardom, but he hadn't abandoned it. An interview he did shortly before that trip made him realize that Des Moines was not, after all, that far away from Hollywood.

Joy Hodges had started out as a child singing star on WHO and gone on to become a semisuccessful big-band singer in Hollywood, with hopes of a contract at RKO; the Des Moines press gave her star treatment when she came back to town to visit her parents. Dutch was only too happy to interview her at WHO. His first question: "Well, Miss Hodges, how does it feel to be a movie star?" Her answer: "Well, Mr. Reagan, you may know one day." As she explained many years later, "He sat across the microphone from me in riding breeches, which I found amusing. But he was very good-looking even with his glasses."[50]

After the interview he seemed reluctant to let her go. He grilled her about Hollywood, as well as her personal life: "Next thing I know he's got me to agree to a riding date in the morning. I change my mind overnight, and pretend to be out when he rings our bell. He just keeps on ringing, ringing, ringing. I thought he'd *never* go away! Ring, ring. I had to go stand in a closet and *cover my ears*. Well *finally* he stopped, but honey, you can't *believe* that *purposefulness*! And do you know, later on, when he and I became such *dear* friends, he *never once* mentioned how I'd stood him up! Like it never happened. That's why I've always known Dutch can't be hurt. It's water off a duck's back."[51]

Reagan didn't get to Hollywood on his first trip to California, and Joy Hodges was cool when, on the one night he was in Los Angeles, he looked her up at the Biltmore Hotel's nightclub, where she was the singer with the house band. (The Biltmore, with its 1,500 rooms, was the largest and most important hotel in town.) He spent three weeks on Catalina Island covering the Cubs. He arrived on a record-breaking 82-degree day at the beginning of March and couldn't wait to get into his swimming trunks and jump into the Pacific, which was freezing—"Everyone knew that except hick me." Three weeks later he packed his linen suits, white sports jacket, and white buckskin shoes and took the Southern Pacific Railroad back to Des Moines, thinking, he said, California was "a nice place to visit, but . . ."[52]

In 1937, WHO again sent him to cover the Cubs in Catalina. He arrived in Los Angeles on March 12, in the middle of a hailstorm, which made crossing to the island impossible that day. He checked into the Biltmore and caught a trolley out to Republic Pictures, where the Oklahoma Outlaws, a hillbilly group that had played on WHO's Saturday night barn dance program earlier that year, were filming with Gene Autry in one of his cowboy pictures. It was the first time he had been on a movie set, and he found it entrancing. That evening he looked up Joy Hodges again at the Biltmore Hotel's nightclub, and this time she joined him for dinner between floor shows. "I confessed to Joy," he later wrote, "that sports announcing had actually been chosen years before as a steppingstone to acting."[53]

"Take off your glasses," Joy Hodges told him. He did, and she promised to introduce him to her agent. The next day he flew to Catalina on a tiny seaplane. The flight was turbulent, the plane made him feel claustrophobic, and he vowed never to fly again.[54] The day after his return from Catalina two weeks later, minus his glasses and barely able to see, he met with George Ward at the Meiklejohn Agency, which represented Robert Taylor, Betty Grable, and the still unknown Jane Wyman, among others. Ward called Max Arnow, the casting director at Warner Bros. "Max," he said, "I've got another Robert Taylor sitting in my office." According to Reagan, he could hear Arnow bark back, "God only made one Robert Taylor." But he told Ward to deliver Reagan to the studio in Burbank for an interview that same day, which happened to be Good Friday. Arnow greeted the hopeful with a battery of orders and questions: "Stand up against that door. Are those your own shoulders? Let me hear your voice. Is that *your* voice?" "It's the only one I've got," Dutch told him. The casting director and the agent, he later wrote, "circled me like a pair of hummingbirds," talking about his face and body, "as if I wasn't even in the room."[55]

Finally Arnow handed Dutch a few pages of the Philip Barry play *Holiday* and told him to memorize them over the Easter weekend for a screen test early the next week. The actual test—opposite Helen Valkis, an actress from Iowa whom Warners had signed earlier that year—lasted but a few minutes. When Arnow informed Dutch that it would be several days before Jack Warner, the studio boss, could watch it, he said he couldn't wait around, he had to get back to his job in Des Moines. Both Arnow and Ward were taken aback, and Reagan himself later worried that he had "blown the whole thing."[56]

But on April 9, his first day back at WHO, he received a telegram from the Meiklejohn Agency: WARNER'S OFFER CONTRACT SEVEN YEARS STOP ONE YEAR'S OPTIONS STOP STARTING AT $200 A WEEK STOP WHAT SHALL I DO? Dutch wired back: SIGN BEFORE THEY CHANGE THEIR MINDS.[57]

On April 16, at the request of the sponsor of

his baseball broadcasts, Wheaties cereal, he addressed a meeting of sports announcers in Chicago. Four days later, back in Des Moines, he signed the contract that had come from Warner Bros. It was a standard-issue studio contract of that time, not quite indentured servitude but not exactly a fair deal either. He couldn't quit for seven years, but the studio had the option to fire him every six months. If they kept him on, he would receive a raise every six months, so by end of the fourth year he would be making $600 a week, and would then have his first opportunity to renegotiate. He was guaranteed his salary for only nineteen weeks out of every twenty-six, and any earnings he made from radio, advertising, or personal appearances would go to the studio. He had no right to choose which movies he appeared in, and he could be loaned out to other studios for a fee greater than his salary, with the difference going to Warners, not to him.[58]

In other words, he was giving up a sure thing—General Mills, the maker of Wheaties, had a made a counteroffer to keep him at WHO—for a high-risk dream. On his last night in Des Moines, May 21, 1937, the radio station presented him with a large suitcase at an on-air farewell party attended by some of the city's celebrities, including the mayor.[59] Reagan's contract required him to report for work on June 1. He set out for Los Angeles early the next morning in his open-topped Nash and drove six hundred miles a day through Nebraska,

Wyoming, Utah, and Nevada, reaching California on the third day.

"Sundown saw me driving that long stretch between the banked orange trees from San Bernardino to Los Angeles," he later wrote. "Today the orange trees are gone, replaced by tract homes even closer together than the trees had been planted, and smog has replaced the fragrance of blossoms."[60]

Four days after her son had left for Los Angeles, Nelle wrote a letter from Dixon to Reverend Cleaver and his wife, who had been transferred to Cerro Gordo, Illinois. It reads in part:

> I am enclosing some clippings regarding Ronald. I hardly know how to explain "our feelings," but when people ask me if I am not afraid to have him go to such a wicked place as Hollywood, all I can answer is that I feel I can trust him anywhere. He has never lost his high ideals of life, and when he called us to tell us the news, Pete MacArthur talked to me too and this is what he told me. (quote)
>
> "I am going to tell you something that your boy won't tell you. When the wire came from Hollywood and we were all overjoyed at Dutch's good luck, we missed him from the office and sent one of the fellows to look for him. He came back saying he had discovered Dutch in one of the smaller studio rooms on his knees, praying. He didn't let Dutch know

that he saw him, and when he told all of us there in the office, we cried like babies." (end of quote) Friends, he does love God and never forgets to thank Him for all his many blessings. When we visited him, he told me of all the nice things he would be able to do now for Eureka College if he won the seven-year contract with Warner Brothers.

You know he has been a wonderful son to us. His father hasn't had any work since the 15th of June last year, and during all that time I have received a $60.00 check the first of each month, and another one of the same amount the 15th of each month. If he signs the seven-year contract there, he is going to send for us. That is the thing that makes me so happy, to think I can live my last days making a home for him. It's almost more happiness than I ever expected in this life.[61]

CHAPTER FOUR

EAST LAKE SHORE DRIVE
1933–1939

Nancy was a year ahead of me at the Girls Latin School in Chicago. She was just as nice as she could be. And through the years I've read all this business in the newspapers, and I thought, My goodness, I don't think she turned into this evil person. In high school she was very, very friendly. She was not a personal friend of mine—I knew her just because it was a small private school and we played field hockey together. I think everybody just plain liked her. But I've had people come up to me and say, "Tell us about her. Was she such a witch?" I say, "No, she was just this delightful person. All we knew is she wanted to be an actress."

China Ibsen Oughton to author,
February 21, 2001

Nancy is well reared, not dragged up. It comes naturally to her to behave beautifully.

Jerry Zipkin, quoted in the
Los Angeles Herald Examiner,
October 30, 1980

The summer Ronald Reagan arrived in Hollywood from Iowa in his Nash, Nancy Robbins, as she was still called, was given a convertible of her own for her sixteenth birthday. It was a black 1937 Mercury with a red-leather interior, and it seems that Edith Davis paid for the gift with her *Betty and Bob* earnings.[1] Nancy loved the car so much that she drove it to school, which was just six blocks north of East Lake Shore Drive, where her family had moved up to a duplex apartment the year before.

Reagan was lucky enough to coast through the worst years of the Great Depression on a radio sportscaster's salary. Nancy was sheltered from the hard times by the ongoing success—professional, financial, social—of her stepfather and mother. And while the new Warner Bros. contract player was beginning to make the acquaintance of such stars as Dick Powell and Bette Davis, the private school teenager was already accustomed to coming home in the afternoon and finding "Mary Martin in the living room, or Spencer Tracy reading the newspaper, or the breathtaking Lillian Gish curled up on the sofa, talking with Mother."[2]

Edith had brought her daughter to Chicago at the height of the Roaring Twenties, which was called the Whoopee Era in the Windy City, where the decade's moral lapses and criminal excesses were particularly acute. In 1927 alone, the IRS estimated, Al Capone's organized-crime syndicate took in $105 million from its bootlegging, prostitution, and gambling enterprises.[3] Four years later Capone was jailed on tax-evasion charges, and the great metropolis of the Midwest was on the verge of economic collapse. As Roger Biles writes in *Big City Boss in Depression and War,* his biography of Mayor Edward J. Kelly, "The economic cataclysm of 1929–31 devastated Chicago, and the city veritably ceased to function. The signs of suffering and want were everywhere. As the nation's transportation hub, Chicago attracted thousands of transients to its already sizable stable of indigents and unemployed; throngs of uprooted men and women descended upon the city hoping for work and lodging, but they found only breadlines and cardboard shacks. By 1930 a shantytown had appeared at the very edge of the Loop on Randolph Street. Its residents named it 'Hooverville' and its streets 'Prosperity Road,' 'Hard Times Avenue,' and 'Easy Street.' The relief agencies strained to meet the demand for shelter—they used asylums, poorhouses, and veterans homes to house the needy—but like all departments of city government, they were ill prepared to deal with such large-scale misery."[4]

By 1932 the unemployment rate had hit 40 percent, and 130,000 families were on relief. In April 1933, the month Edith's friend Ed Kelly became mayor, fourteen thousand schoolteachers, who hadn't been paid for months, stormed the banks in the downtown financial district; the police repelled them with tear gas, and hundreds were arrested. A few days later, twenty thousand public high school students staged a one-day strike in support of their desperate teachers.[5]

None of this affected Nancy, however, who was completely shielded from any sign of this upheaval and suffering. Her entire day-to-day life took place within a twelve-block cocoon surrounding the grand apartment buildings of East Lake Shore Drive, where the Davises lived from 1932 on. Passavant Hospital, where Loyal Davis worked, was six blocks south, and it catered to the rich— patients' meals were served on linen tablecloths with china and silver.[6] And while Edith did a lot of charity work, it was more about raising money than ladling out soup to bums.

Every year for Easter vacation, beginning in 1930, Edith and Loyal took Nancy to the posh Arizona Biltmore Hotel in Scottsdale. Nancy spent eight weeks of every summer until she was fourteen at Camp Kechuwa—"darling" in Sioux—in Michigamme, Michigan. In an early letter to Loyal, she wrote: "Please excuse my writing. It is hard to write sitting up in bed. I think I told mother that I passed my red cap. So I am working on my green cap now. Will you please tell mother that I wove a rug for the guest bathroom. How do you like my book plates that I made? I hope you like them. I passed a safety test for canoeing so I can go out in a canoe alone. I have learned how to paddle. Are you and mother coming down to see me? I hope so. Doctor Loyal, there were a lot of girls from school that come here that I know so I know more than I thought. I miss you and mother a lot. Love, your daughter Nancy."[7]

* * *

From the time Nancy was ten in 1931 until she graduated in 1939, she attended the Girls Latin School, set in the heart of the Gold Coast at 59 East Scott Street. The Latin School of Chicago had been established in 1888 by newly rich Gilded Age parents who wanted their children to have a classical education. (Girls were admitted in 1896; Boys and Girls Latin became separate but associated schools in 1913.) In the years Nancy attended, Girls Latin was run by a strict New England spinster whom everyone addressed as Miss Singleton. The small student body, with no more than twenty girls in each class, was extremely homogeneous. "I'd say Protestant mostly," said Nancy's friend Jean Wescott Marshall, whose father was a corporate lawyer. "What percentage of the parents were Republican?" I asked. "Pretty much all." Most of these families lived on the Near North Side or in nearby Lakeview, another upper-class enclave. Were their daughters aware that there was a Depression going on? "We were told to turn out the lights," Marshall said. "That was about it. Isn't that awful?"[8]

"Girls Latin was a very conservative school," said China Ibsen Oughton, who was in the class behind Nancy's. "Academically it was very good. I don't know if I'd want to use the word 'best,' but it was the most social, the most prestigious. Our regular uniform was a dark blue skirt and a white or blue blouse. On Fridays we had to wear a special tunic top with a white collar and long sleeves. I don't think we liked those terribly well. They were sort of droopy. And we had these awful-looking outfits we wore as we went forth onto the hockey field—bloomers with a bright blue linen tunic that came over them, and a white shirt underneath, and knee guards, and black shoes. Oh, we were quite devastating. Nancy always looked very nice. I would not say glamorous, just very *nice*-looking, very fresh and wholesome—very ladylike."[9]

Along with most of her privileged friends from Girls Latin, Nancy took dancing lessons at Vourniques' Dancing School, on North Dearborn Street, near Boys Latin School. "It was where all the young men and young ladies from about seventh grade on were meant to go and learn ballroom dancing," recalled China Ibsen Oughton. "We wore little white gloves, and the boys sat on one side and the girls on the other."[10] Bruce McFarland, who attended Boys Latin at that time, told me, "Mr. Vournique and his wife were very impressive because of their size. She was a large woman, and he was a very slight little man. They were very proper and insisted on everyone being dressy. You didn't come in sloppy clothes and learn how to dance." McFarland remembered Nancy as "a very happy gal, the kind that you liked to be around because she was just a lot of fun. She was not a siren or anything like that. She was just a nice gal." Was she a good dancer? "Very."[11]

After classes and on Saturdays, Nancy and her friends would sometimes go to Woods restaurant, which was connected to the Drake Hotel by a pedestrian tunnel underneath Michigan Avenue, and just down the block from the Davises' apartment. "The waitresses were little ladies in white organdy aprons, that sort of thing," said China Ibsen Oughton. "They had the most scrumptious sandwiches. . . . Nancy was very popular with the young men, as well as with everybody else. One of her early beaus was Sangston Hettler, whom everyone called Sock. They were good high school friends, Nancy and Sock. His sister, Elizabeth Hettler—who's deceased; old Sock is, too—was also at Girls Latin, so we knew them and all that. Their family was in the wholesale lumber business."[12]

High school students from Girls and Boys Latin, the private coed school Frances Parker, and select public schools in the better suburbs—Evanston, Winnetka, and Lake Forest—were invited to dances at the Fortnightly Club. Another Chicago society institution founded in the Gilded Age, it was housed in a stately Georgian mansion on East Bellevue Place, a block north of East Lake Shore Drive. "Nancy loved to dance," said Girls Latin alumna Angie Johnson Galbraith. "And she used to stand up and sing—'Pennies from Heaven' was her favorite. I think she sang it once a month at the Fortnightly."[13] (Bing Crosby, the country's number one crooner, recorded "Pennies from Heaven" with the Jimmy Dorsey Orchestra in 1936; it was at the top of the charts for ten weeks late that year and in early 1937.)

"She had a lot of personality," said Jean Wescott

Marshall. "I don't want to say bubbly, but she was fun-loving. She was very at ease with the boys. And she had been with adults a lot, so she was very at ease with them, too. Nancy was the leader of everything."[14] In a television interview in 1997, Marshall elaborated on this description slightly: "Everybody looked up to her. She sort of ran the rest of us."[15] Nancy was freshman class vice president, sophomore class president, junior class vice president, and senior class judge.

Nancy's best friend chose a curious story to illustrate her leadership qualities: "At the end of our freshman year, Nancy got the great idea that we should go to boarding school. So I went home and told my family that I wanted to go to boarding school. Five of us went away for our sophomore and junior years. And Nancy stayed home."[16] (A look at the school's yearbooks shows that five students out of eighteen in Nancy's class, including Jean Wescott, left Girls Latin after their freshman year, in 1936; Wescott returned for her senior year.)

Practically the only time the Latin School kids left the Near North Side was to go to the movie palaces in the Loop. They usually took the bus downtown, which cost a dime, though they were occasionally driven by the chauffeurs of the richer families. McFarland recalled that such excursions made a deep impression on him: "You couldn't go downtown in the thirties—early thirties especially—and *not* see the guys selling apples on the corners and the soup kitchens and the people lined up where a job was available."[17]

Nancy saw nearly every movie, collected movie magazines, and made scrapbooks of her favorite stars.[18] "We were all wrapped up in movie stars," Jean Wescott Marshall told me. "I liked Ronald Reagan, and she liked Bing Crosby. She used to say, 'I don't see what you see in Ronald Reagan.' And I'd say, 'Well, I don't see what you see in Bing Crosby.' But we both liked Jimmy Stewart and kept pictures of him."[19] When Nancy was a junior, the Senior Class Will bequeathed her "a scrap book to hold all her pictures of Tyrone Power."[20]

It was far from unusual for teenage girls in the 1930s to be starstruck. But among her classmates, only Nancy had an Uncle Walter Huston and an Aunt Colleen Moore, not to mention a godmother named Alla Nazimova, whom she called Zim. As Garry Wills notes, "She was in touch with a very wide world, through her mother."[21] Although Edith had retired from the stage when she married Loyal, she kept up the relationships she had developed in the theatrical world, and her husband enjoyed meeting Edith's glittery friends. One of the advantages Edith had in maintaining her Broadway and Hollywood connections was that the fastest way to cross the country at the time was by train; passengers had to change trains in Chicago, which encouraged stopovers. Another was that Chicago was a big theater town.

It is also worth noting that Edith's friends were stars of the highest rank, not has-beens or wannabes. Spencer Tracy, her co-star in *Baby*

Cyclone back in 1928, had been discovered by the great Hollywood director John Ford two years later; by the mid-1930s he was one of MGM's most important leading men, winning back-to-back best-acting Oscars for *Captains Courageous* in 1937 and *Boys Town* in 1938. Walter Huston, Edith's friend since the 1928 Chicago and New York runs of *Elmer the Great*, had also become hugely successful in the movies while continuing to triumph on Broadway with the biggest hit of his theatrical career, the Sinclair Lewis play *Dodsworth*, which ran for 1,238 performances at the Shubert Theater in 1934 and 1935.[22]

In January 1936, Nazimova was in Chicago with her legendary production of Ibsen's *Ghosts*, which she not only starred in but also directed. ("Great is a word for sparing use," Brooks Atkinson wrote in *The New York Times* after its Broadway opening, "but there is no other way to characterize a transcendent performance of a tragic role.")[23] Edith and Loyal attended the Chicago opening, and a few nights later had Nazimova and her companion, Glesca Marshall, to dinner, a fact that Edith made sure was noted in the *Chicago Herald*'s gossip column. Nazimova recorded the evening in her diary: "To the Davises. Family. Peace. Contentment. Happiness? Must be."[24]

Edith put time and effort into these friendships. Nancy Reagan told me that it seemed every time the family was ready to go out, she and Loyal had to pull Edith away from her desk. "We used to tease her because she would always be writing a postcard to somebody. And we'd say, 'C'mon, Mother. C'mon.' She'd say, 'I just have to get this off.' "[25] After Nazimova had a partial mastectomy in June 1937, the Davises traveled to New York and visited her at her Westchester County estate.[26] Spencer Tracy, who seemed to get deeper and deeper into trouble as he achieved greater and greater success, could always count on Edith and Loyal when he needed a place to dry out, far from the prying eyes of Hollywood. Spence, as his friends called him, had been born on the right side of the tracks in Milwaukee in 1900 to a Protestant mother from a colonial New England family and an Irish Catholic father who managed a trucking company, and he was bright but bad from the start. He went to four high schools—parochial, public, Jesuit, and military—before moving on to Ripon College and the American Academy of Dramatic Art in New York. His binge drinking began after he and his wife, Louise, discovered their infant son, John, was deaf. At MGM he developed a reputation for disappearing on a week-long binge before the start of production on a film, but studio head Louis B. Mayer tolerated his behavior because he was so uniquely talented.

If Tracy was the glamorous but troubled kid brother in the Davises' life, Walter Huston was the grand seigneur. When *Dodsworth* played in Chicago in 1935, he and his third wife, Nan, who co-starred in the play, stayed with the Davises.[27] As Nancy recalled, Loyal "frequently stood in the wings watching the last act while waiting to drive them home. He had almost memorized Uncle Walter's climactic speech."[28] Walter had taken a liking to Loyal, and had even made him a member of his Crovenay Society, a tongue-in-cheek club dedicated to deflating "stuffed shirts of every kidney." Its members ranged from George M. Cohan and William Wyler, who directed Huston in the film version of *Dodsworth*, to the baseball player Ty Cobb and the boxing champion Max Baer.[29] Loyal became Huston's doctor and remained so until his death in 1950. "They were best friends," Richard Davis told me.[30] Walter's son, the director John Huston, wrote in his memoir, *An Open Book*, "[My father] was not unduly impressed by great names. The few people he thoroughly admired included Franklin D. Roosevelt, Eugene O'Neill, Bernard Baruch, [Broadway director] Jed Harris, Loyal Davis. He responded to quality."[31]

Four years older than Edith and twelve years older than Loyal, Walter Huston was a carpenter's son from Toronto who first appeared on the stage at eighteen, in 1902. After marrying his first wife, Rhea Gore, in 1905, he decided to settle down in her home state of Missouri and took a series of engineering jobs at utilities plants. In 1906 their son, John, was born. Three years later the marriage fell apart, and the restless Walter hit the vaudeville circuit as half of a song-and-dance team with the woman who would become his second wife, Bayonne Whipple. He made his Broadway debut in 1924, and that year won the New York Drama Critics' Circle Award for his performance in *Desire Under the Elms*. His movie career was launched in 1929, when he played a bad guy in *The Virginian,* a Western starring Gary Cooper in his first talking role. A year later he starred in the title role of D. W. Griffith's *Abraham Lincoln.*

President Franklin D. Roosevelt was one of Huston's biggest fans, and he had attended the February 1935 opening of *Dodsworth* in Washington, D.C. In fact, shortly before Walter and Nan arrived to stay with the Davises, they had been received at the White House, where FDR charmed them by serving the drinks himself.[32] Presumably they repeated the story to Loyal, who hated Roosevelt; if so, Loyal's reaction is unrecorded.

In the summer of 1937, the Davises took Nancy and Richard to visit the Hustons at their rustic but lavish hideaway in the San Bernardino Mountains near Lake Arrowhead, California.[33] When they had bought the four acres of land with its spectacular views and giant pines a few years earlier, Walter intended to build a log cabin with his own hands, but Nan talked him into a more substantial structure, as well as a tennis court, a gymnasium, and a swimming pool. He made eleven films in two years to pay for it, but he refused to have a telephone. Their only neighbors were the Hollywood agent Myron Selznick and the British actor Reginald Denny, both of whom were members of the Crovenay Society.[34] "The living room had a huge fireplace and a U-shaped sofa with its back even to the floor above—it was a sunken living room," Nancy Reagan told me. "Every night after dinner we'd sit in a circle and Uncle Walter would stand in front of the fireplace and read to us."[35]

And then there was Colleen Moore, the Auntie Mame of the Davises' circle. Edith had kept up a correspondence with the star since they met in 1922, but they didn't become intimates until fifteen years later, when Moore married Chicago stock-broker Homer Hargrave Sr. and moved to the Gold Coast. Although she was only thirty-five at the time, Moore was genuine Old Hollywood royalty—rich, glamorous, fascinating. She had retired from the movies three years earlier; her last great film, *The Power and the Glory*, was Spencer Tracy's breakthrough picture, and she always said it was her favorite of the hundred films she made between 1917 and 1934.[36]

Moore was born Kathleen Morrison in 1902 in Port Huron, Michigan, but she considered herself a Southerner because she grew up in Atlanta and Tampa. At fifteen she arrived in Hollywood with her grandmother as chaperone and signed a con-tract with D. W. Griffith that had been arranged by her uncle, Walter Howey, the *Chicago Examiner* editor who was the model for the tyrannical news-paperman in *The Front Page*.[37] Her first starring role was in *Little Orphan Annie,* and *Flaming Youth* in 1923 made her one of the two great symbols of the Roaring Twenties, the other being the less-refined Clara Bow. Moore had been ordered to cut her dark hair into a boyish bob for that picture; F. Scott Fitzgerald declared it "the most fateful haircut since Samson's." She was America's biggest box office draw in 1927 and 1928, earning $12,500 per week at First National Studio and living in a $1 million Spanish-style mansion in Bel Air with her first husband, John Emmett McCormick, an alcoholic producer.[38]

Those who knew her best said she was a "kick," a "dynamo," even a bit mad on the surface, given the obsessive extravagance of the project she called the Doll House or the Fairy Castle. Moore began building it in 1928, and by the time it was unveiled seven years later she had spent a reported $470,000 on it. Built at a scale of one inch to the foot, it was nine feet square and twelve feet high and weighed one ton. It was designed by her father, an engineer, and Horace Jackson, her set designer at First National. The drawing room floor was inlaid with rose quartz and jade, the dining room was hung with tapestries done in petit point, Peter Pan murals lined the Bedroom of the Fairy Princess, and the white bear rug in Prince Charming's Bedroom "was made by a taxidermist from the skin of a single ermine," to quote Moore's description. The Doll House held two thousand small objects, including miniature antiquities from Egypt, Greece, and Rome, and a $50,000 chandelier made of diamonds, emeralds, and pearls from Moore's own earrings and necklaces. It had running water, electric lighting, a radio, and a working organ in the chapel. Moore commissioned well-known writers such as Thornton Wilder, Willa Cather, Sinclair Lewis, and Anita Loos to create tiny books in their own handwriting for the library.[39]

Such fetishistic excess may have seemed objectionable at the height of the Depression, but Moore later defended her creation as "a beautiful toy, an extravagance, a folly, even, but one which had brought me more happiness than I'd ever known before."[40] It was also a distraction from her breakup with McCormick, which was followed by an unsuccessful second marriage to a New York stockbroker. On the suggestion of a public relations man for the May Company department store in Los Angeles, she took the Doll House on a nationwide tour of department stores to raise money for handicapped children.

In 1936, when Moore showed the Doll House at the Fair Store in Chicago (where Jack Reagan had been employed twenty years earlier), Edith took Nancy to meet her. On that trip, Colleen met Homer Hargrave, a well-to-do widower with two children. They were married on May 19, 1937. After their wedding ceremony, Homer took Colleen to the Riverview Amusement Park. "We rode on the roller coaster, had a wedding supper of hot dogs," she recalled. "Then we went to Europe."[41] Hargrave, who had been born in Danville, Indiana, had never been abroad. Not long after he married Colleen, he became a founding partner in Merrill Lynch Pierce, Fenner & Beane (later Smith), following a series of complicated mergers. "As he liked to tell it," his son, Homer Hargrave Jr., said, "he left

Indiana after the war, went to Chicago, joined a brokerage firm, and never changed jobs—it was just the name on the window that kept changing."[42]

Colleen Moore Hargrave and Edith Luckett Davis quickly became the closest of confidantes—two actresses with social ambitions checking in with each other on the telephone every morning. The retired flapper also became an important influence on Nancy, who was entranced by her Doll House, her Hollywood stories, and her somewhat kooky personality, all of which obscured a shrewd and unshakable inner core. Nancy was apparently deeply impressed by this combination of fabulousness and practicality.

"Colleen was the best. She was bubbly. She was fun," recalled Abra Rockefeller Wilkin, whose mother, Abra Rockefeller Prentice, became a close friend of both Edith's and Colleen's in Chicago. "She built the wonderful Fairy Castle, and she sort of thought she was one of the fairies. I mean, everything was magical. Yet she always had great advice. She'd say, 'If you're feeling blue, just get yourself dressed up and go out, because that's what I did, and I met Homer.' Her first husband was gay. Whatever has been done, Colleen did it. But she made it sort of respectable, and she told it in a ladylike way. Colleen was more ladylike than Edie. Colleen could be fun and bawdy, too, but she just pulled it off a little better."[43]

"She had it all," said Homer Hargrave Jr., who was thirteen when his father married Colleen. "She had all the street smarts. All of them."[44] His younger sister, Judy Hargrave Coleman, added, "She was wise in the ways of the world. People-smart. Astute. She knew people. She understood them. I don't remember her ever saying she had a great dislike for anyone. I know she didn't like a phony. She could pick them out. She was a very wise lady. She knew what she was doing and what she wanted."[45]

The Hargraves had a duplex apartment at 1320 North State Parkway, eight blocks north of the Davises' and next door to the Ambassador West Hotel, where Colleen would take visiting movie star friends such as Lillian Gish to the Pump Room and hold court with Edith in the first booth inside the entrance. The Hargrave apartment was decorated in a grand style with English antiques and Oriental rugs. "She entertained a lot," said Judy Hargrave Coleman. "She loved a party. She was a wonderful mother and a wonderful wife. My father was all business. But he had a dry wit."[46]

According to Homer Hargrave Jr., his father was greatly helped by Colleen, who was greatly helped by Edith. "She was very kind to my mother. Colleen moved to Chicago knowing no one, and Edie Davis helped her a great deal." Wasn't his father already well established in Chicago? "In business. But not socially. Colleen made him. First place, everybody falls in love with a movie star. Colleen did a great deal for my father." Like Edith did for Loyal? "Yes. Because Loyal was absolutely concentrated on medicine. And he was tough."[47] Judy Hargrave

Coleman found Loyal Davis intimidating. "You almost wanted to curtsey to him."[48]

The two couples were alike in many ways—a hard-headed all-business husband promoted and supported by a lighthearted, loads-of-fun wife. Although it was the second time around for Homer, and the third for Colleen, the Hargrave marriage would prove to be as durable as the Davises'—and one might even say it reinforced Nancy's idea of what an ideal marriage ought to be. Homer and Loyal grew to be almost as close as their wives. And in Colleen, Edith finally had the social collaborator, the high-spirited accomplice, she hadn't found in Edna Kanavel, Pinky Pollock, or the other doctors' wives.

These were not women who could be bossed around by men. Colleen Moore had single-handedly made her joke writer Mervyn LeRoy into a major director and later insisted that he give the fourteen-year-old Loretta Young a screen test.[49] Edith, her daughter assured me, wasn't intimidated by anyone. "Edith was impossible," said Abra Rockefeller Wilkin. "The stories, the antics. She was demanding. She was exacting. Difficult. And Loyal had to have enjoyed her, or he wouldn't have put up with her. I think they probably had more fun backstage than the rest of us realized."[50] Both Colleen Hargrave and Edith Davis realized that in enhancing their husband's status, they were enhancing their own.

"She and Mother were such a pair in Chicago,"

Nancy later wrote. "When my father would leave for the hospital each morning, and her husband, Homer, would leave for the office, she and Mother would be on the phone with each other planning their day. What one didn't think of, the other did."[51] She told me, "They would figure out what kind of mischief they were going to get into that day. And Colleen would be miffed if for some reason she couldn't get Mother on the phone."[52]

Both women served on the Women's Board of Passavant Hospital, along with such prominent social figures as Abra Rockefeller Prentice and Narcissa Ward Thorne, whose father-in-law was a co-founder of Montgomery Ward & Company. Narcissa Thorne shared Colleen Moore's passion for grandiose dollhouses. The Thorne Miniature Rooms, like the Doll House scaled one inch to the foot, were first shown publicly at Chicago's "Century of Progress" World's Fair in 1933, and were eventually put on permanent display at the Art Institute of Chicago. The Doll House went to Chicago's Museum of Science and Industry.

Narcissa Thorne maintained a studio near her Gold Coast apartment, where skilled craftsmen and society ladies sat side by side, the former carving miniature reproductions of period settees, the latter stitching tiny pillows to put on them. Nancy Reagan told me that Mrs. Thorne had given her one of the more modest rooms she made for the children of friends. "I have it in the guest room," she said, adding that she was impressed by Narcissa Thorne because she was so refined and "always looked perfect. Her posture was so straight and erect. You know, she was from that old school. And she was crazy about my father."[53]

Chicago's society was relatively open, more like New York's than Boston's or Philadelphia's. Accomplishment counted as much as lineage, and giving back in the form of charitable donations and deeds was a recognized means of social advancement. The city's leading families had made their fortunes in trade and industry in the late nineteenth century: the Armours and Swifts in meatpacking, the Palmers and Fields in retailing; the McCormicks in farm machinery; the Wrigleys in chewing gum. When Edith moved to town, second- and third-generation members of those families dominated the boards of the city's great institutions. Unlike Colleen, however, Edith never made it onto the most elite boards—those of the Art Institute of Chicago and the Lyric Opera—perhaps because the Davises weren't rich enough, perhaps because her bawdy jokes crossed the line of decorum. Nonetheless she dedicated herself to such charities as the Red Cross and the Seeing Eye and moved comfortably in upper-class circles. "She was a doer," said Judy Hargrave Coleman about Edith's fund-raising abilities. "You couldn't say no to Mrs. Davis."[54]

"Edith was a total extrovert—uncontrolled," said Richard Davis.[55] "You couldn't help but love her," said Lester Weinrott, Edith's friend and radio producer. "She was this adorable darling little woman with a phony theatrical Southern accent who always made you feel good just being around her. Yes, she swore like a drafted Turkish sailor and told smutty toilet jokes, but Loyal pretended not to hear, because she was paying all the bills and introducing him to the right people. I was so crazy about her I ended up being her educated slave for forty years. She could get people to do anything for her, and I have to say that Nancy, who never had her mother's spontaneous charm and warmth, certainly learned how to manipulate from a genius. She was schooled by a social mechanic of the first order."[56]

Edith liked giving small dinner parties, especially after she and Loyal moved to their duplex at 199 East Lake Shore Drive, which had a living room, dining room, and library downstairs and three bedrooms upstairs. Like her charity work, Edith's dinners revealed a social agenda. According to Richard Davis, who moved in with Edith and Loyal after his mother's death in 1939, his father was initially a reluctant participant in Edith's efforts. "She had to force him, really, to have people in. She was very gregarious and interested in social contacts—not only for him, but for Nancy." He added, "Dr. Loyal was an opinionated man. When friends were invited over, he had to dominate the conversation."[57]

Davis described these dinner parties as jovial but serious affairs. "There was never a lot of drinking. It was one drink and then into the dining room. Except for a very occasional cocktail party, they never had more than eight or ten people, because that was all the dining room would hold."[58] Although Edith wasn't much of cook—the Davises had a housekeeper who came in every day and fixed the evening meal—she sent the local society editors homemade mustard at Christmas, in jars labeled "From the kitchen of Mrs. Loyal Davis."[59]

Among those who sometimes came to dinner were Mayor Kelly and his second wife, Margaret, who became one of Edith's best friends. The rough-and-ready Kelly always seemed to be denying involvement in one corruption scandal or another—among other things, he was accused of not reporting $450,000 in income and settled with the IRS for $106,390 to avoid prosecution[60]—but he had managed to put the city's financial affairs in order soon after assuming office in 1933. Two years later, riding high on the repeal of Prohibition and the success of the 1933 World's Fair, Kelly was elected to the first of three full terms by the greatest margin in Chicago history—799,060 to 167,106 for his Republican opponent. There were credible charges that as many as 300,000 of the votes were stolen, but that didn't stop Kelly from putting his vote total on the license plates of his Cadillac.[61]

"I learned many things about the workings of city, county, and state government from Ed Kelly," Republican Loyal later wrote of the Democratic mayor. "A tall, redheaded Irishman with a quick wit, uneducated beyond grade school, he attracted people mainly, I think, because they identified with him in his mispronunciation of words and his laboring-class background."[62] Edith, still a self-professed Southern Democrat, was as usual less condescending and more practical: she gave Mayor Kelly elocution lessons and helped him write his radio addresses.

Meanwhile, Loyal's star continued to rise in the world of medicine. In 1936 he was elected to membership in both the American Surgical Association, which in his words was "the most prestigious surgical society in the United States," and the snobbish Southern Surgical Association, which held annual meetings at expensive resorts such as the Homestead in Hot Springs, Virginia, which were attended by the doctors' wives. (Loyal claimed that Edith's Southern background was the real reason he was invited to join.) In 1938, six years after he succeeded Dr. Kanavel as chief surgeon at Passavant and chairman of the surgery department at Northwestern, Loyal's great mentor was killed in a car crash while vacationing in California, and Loyal was named to replace him as editor in chief of *Surgery, Gynecology & Obstetrics*, the professional journal of the American College of Surgeons. For all his honors and titles, Loyal was hardly making a fortune. His university position was unpaid, which was not unusual for medical schools at the time. "The majority of the medical profession," Loyal wrote, "held that doctors were not subject to the temptations of average human beings and would resist the lure of money."[63] While Lester Weinrott's assertion that Edith paid for everything was exaggerated, her substantial radio earnings were what made their affluent way of life possible.

On January 17, 1938, Edith started working in a new radio soap opera called *The Stepmother*, produced and directed by Weinrott at CBS, while continuing to do *Betty and Bob* at NBC. Sponsored by Colgate toothpaste, the serial was about the daughter of a Chicago newspaperman who becomes the second wife of a small-town widowed banker with two children. According to John Dunning's *On the Air:* "*Stepmother* posed the question 'Can a stepmother successfully raise another woman's children?'" Edith, with her knack for Southern accents, played the family's "faithful colored servant," Mattie.[64] If the plot echoed the Hargraves' domestic situation, the theme was not unfamiliar to the Davis household. Three months after *The Stepmother* premiered, and nine years after her mother had remarried, Nancy, at age sixteen, was adopted by her stepfather on April 20. Nancy Robbins was finally Nancy Davis. A sign of how eager she was for that to happen can be seen in the Girls Latin yearbook of the previous June, in which she had already dropped her birth father's name for her stepfather's.[65]

In later accounts of what was one of the most important events of her life, Nancy Reagan was consistently vague about the time that elapsed between her mother's remarriage and her adoption. That is partly because of the two years she subtracted from her age when she went to Hollywood, but also it must have been hard for her to face the fact of Loyal's reluctance. It wasn't that he didn't love her; he worried about hurting Ken Robbins. Richard Davis explained that Nancy was his father's favorite: "She'd sit in his lap, or at the foot of his chair. I wouldn't say she was in awe of him, but there was an enormous respect. They were very, very close."[66]

In the end Nancy initiated the adoption process, not Loyal. For nine years she had sought to live up to his standards and values. In doing so, she had shaped herself into what he wanted her to be: neat, disciplined, agreeable, perfect. Along the way she must have learned valuable lessons about how to persuade the powerful man to see things her way. But that's not something she would ever admit. In her telling, she did what Dr. Loyal wanted her to do, and Dr. Loyal was always right. As she wrote in *My Turn,* "Loyal Davis was a man of great integrity who exemplified old-fashioned values: That girls and boys should grow up to be ladies and gentlemen. That children should respect and obey their parents. That no matter what you did, you should never cheapen yourself. And that whatever you worked at—whether it was a complicated medical procedure, or a relatively simple act like sweeping the floor—you should do it as well as you could. . . . When I started going out at night, I always had a curfew. But although he was a strict father, he was always fair. He was, I felt, what a real father ought to be."[67]

Or, as she put it in *Nancy*: "Some people you meet in your life make you stretch to reach your fullest capabilities. I found my new father to be one of these people, which is why he was such a good teacher when he was Professor of Surgery at Northwestern University. He always demanded the best of you and made you want to give the best you had. He was strict but fair with me, as he was with his students. They came to respect him as I came to respect him. When he took privileges away from me as punishment for some misdeed, I understood I deserved the discipline. He was, I feel, the way a father should be."[68]

She did everything possible to please him: She chewed her food thirty-two times.[69] She was always on time. ("He was a stickler about punctuality. When he said six o'clock, he didn't mean two minutes after six.")[70] She tagged along on emergency calls outside Chicago. After she entered her teens, he permitted her to watch him operate, usually from a glassed-in balcony but on at least one occasion standing beside him in the operating room. (Years later she told a reporter that she had always worried about getting sick to her stomach and embarrassing him.) She promised not to drink or smoke until she was twenty-one, and kept her promise. (Loyal kept his, too, and rewarded her with $1,000.)[71]

She became as interested in clothes and grooming as he was. In fact, in my interviews with Davis family friends, they almost always brought up Loyal's style and appearance, but rarely mentioned Edith's. "He was immaculately dressed," Abra Rockefeller Wilkin told me.[72] "My goodness, that man was very, very meticulous about his appearance and clothes," said racetrack owner Marjorie Everett, a close family friend from both Chicago and Arizona. "Loyal Davis epitomized what you'd like to see in a doctor. Very distinguished-looking. Great style. Beautifully groomed. I'm certain that some of the qualities that we see in Nancy—the discipline especially—came from him."[73]

One of the most important ways that Nancy got closer to her stepfather was by accompanying him on his trips home to Galesburg. "Since my mother's parents passed on early, I never knew them, so my father's parents were especially important to me," she later said. "They treated me as if I were their real grandchild, and I felt as if I were. They were good, hard-working people, proud of their son, happy with the second marriage he had made, happy with Mother and me. I adored my grandfather and vividly recall the last time I saw him. He was dying of cancer and I went to visit him in Galesburg. We both knew it would be our last time together, although those words were never spoken. We said our good-byes, and as I was leaving, I turned to look back before getting in the car. He was standing at the window and managed a weak wave. I waved back, threw him a kiss, and hurried into the car so he would not see the tears streaming down my face."[74] (Albert Davis died in 1938.)

Meanwhile, her relationship with Ken Robbins was deteriorating. In recounting her "last visit" to her father in New Jersey, she wrote that "things went badly. He said something about Mother I didn't like and it made me angry. I said I was going to call my mother and go home. He got upset and locked me in the bathroom. I was terrified, and it seemed suddenly as if I were with strangers. Recalling the incident brings back a flood of memories I would rather forget. To this day I dislike locked doors and feel trapped behind them. His wife felt terrible and later wrote to my mother to apologize, but there were no more visits."[75]

But when did this traumatic incident occur? It seems unlikely that it happened in the apparently happy summer of 1931, when she was ten, because in *My Turn* she refers to visiting her father during her adolescence, which would mean that she spent time with him until she was at least thirteen or fourteen. Marian Robinson, whose father was Ken's first cousin, placed Nancy in New Jersey in the late 1930s, adding, "[Nannee Robbins] told me . . . that I should learn some of the social graces that Nancy had."[76] Another Robbins cousin, Kathleen Young, talked about visiting the Davises on East Lake Shore Drive in 1936, indicating that relations had not broken down between the two families. "I was awed by Nancy," said Kathleen, who was four years younger, "because she was very pretty and she had angora socks hanging in the bathroom. The Davises bought me all new clothes and took me to the best French restaurants in town, and I ordered for them because I spoke French."[77]

Nancy Reagan never gave a date for the time her

father locked her in the bathroom. "Oh, dear, I don't remember," she said when I asked her how old she was then. "That's going back a lot of years."[78] Could it be that she exaggerated her birth father's behavior in an effort to win her stepfather's sympathy and get him to adopt her?

In any case, she finally took matters into her own hands and one day in the elevator approached a neighbor who was a retired judge. "I asked him, 'How can I go about getting adopted?' [He] called my mother, and she must have approved because he volunteered to help me with the paperwork. I already knew that according to Illinois law, a child who reached the age of 14 could make her own decision on matters of adoption. By then there was no longer any question in my mind, and I finally made it official by going to see Kenneth Robbins in New York. He came with my grandmother to meet me under the clock at the Biltmore Hotel. I explained what I wanted to do, and they agreed, reluctantly. I'm sure it hurt my grandmother terribly. When Kenneth Robbins signed the papers, I sent a wire to Chicago to tell my family that the adoption had gone through. I didn't have much experience with telegrams, but I knew they had to be brief. This one read: HI DAD."[79]

She explained to me that she had passed through New York on her Easter break. "I was going to Bermuda to spend the vacation with some girls from my school, and I wrote my father that I'd like to see him. I felt badly. But then, you know, this was obviously the right thing to do."[80]

Loyal Davis matter-of-factly confirms the extraordinary role his stepdaughter played in her adoption: "Nancy had taken the initiative and consulted Orville Taylor, an attorney who lived in the same apartment building, about the steps necessary for me to adopt her. I wished it very much but was somewhat hesitant to institute the proceeding because her father and paternal grandmother were alive. After she was advised by her attorney, she made a trip east . . . obtained her father's signed agreement, and upon her return I soon had my daughter legally."[81]

According to Cook County records, her petition for adoption, filed on April 19, 1938, stated "that the natural parents of said child are divorced, and that the mother of said child has since married Loyal Davis . . . and that the father of said child, Kenneth S. Robbins, consents in writing to the adoption of said child by the petitioners, and . . . that said minor child being more than 14 years of age likewise consents in writing to her adoption." The petition also requested that her name be legally changed from Anne Frances Robbins to Nancy Davis.[82]

Even after Nancy was adopted, she continued to address her stepfather as Dr. Loyal. "I knew he would have loved it if I had called him Dad," she wrote in *My Turn*, "and in retrospect I wish I had. But at the time I just couldn't. Although we became very close, it wasn't until my own daughter was born that I finally dropped the formal title. When Patti was too young to say 'Grandpa,' she called him Bapa—and so did I."[83]

* * *

In the spring of 1938, Nancy was in her junior year at Girls Latin. Pretty, happy, and popular, she was dating the equally popular Sock Hettler, who was in the same year at Boys Latin. She was on the hockey team, in the Glee Club, and president of the Drama Club. That summer she turned seventeen and went to Lake Arrowhead with her parents to spend several weeks with Uncle Walter Huston. One day her idol Jimmy Stewart—tall, slim, a big star at thirty—turned up with the director Joshua Logan, who wanted to feature Huston in the Maxwell Anderson and Kurt Weill musical *Knickerbocker Holiday* on Broadway.

"Walter was the best American actor on the stage, no question about it," Logan later said. "I flew out to California and then I rented a car and drove to Lake Arrowhead. . . . He had visitors staying with him: a young girl named Nancy Davis and her mother and father. [Walter] arranged immediately for me to read them the play aloud. So I put on a big show. And Nancy Davis sat there and howled and laughed, she was the best audience I ever had."[84] Nancy later wrote that when Uncle Walter asked her opinion, she advised him against taking the part. He ignored her counsel, and would be remembered long after his death for his recording of "September Song" from *Knickerbocker Holiday.*[85]

Another day, when Nan Huston took Edith off to Los Angeles on a shopping excursion, Uncle Walter suggested making a "radio broadcast" of a scene from *Othello*. He played the title role, as he had on Broadway the year before, Loyal played Iago, and Nancy was Desdemona. When the women returned that evening, Huston played the record for them. "They were easy on me," Nancy said, "but teased Father unmercifully. Mother told him, 'You just got hammier and hammier.' He took it with good nature. He was used to it."[86]

Nancy later said that she had always wanted to be actress, "like my mother,"[87] but surely being exposed to the top of the profession at such an early age and in such a special way made it seem almost predestined. "I can't remember a time when I wasn't interested in the theater, and in school my main interest was drama," she wrote in *My Turn*. "I was only an average student . . . [but] I acted in all the school plays. In my senior year, I played the lead in *First Lady*, by George S. Kaufman. I don't recall much about the story, but I do remember that I wore a black dress with a white collar, and that when my classmates forgot their lines, I was able to jump in and start talking until we got back on track. Everyone was terribly impressed—including me."[88]

In *First Lady*, a comedy by Katharine Dayton and George S. Kaufman, Nancy played the wife of one of two candidates running for the presidency. With lots of behind-the-scenes help from her, her man wins. *Vita Scholae*, the school yearbook, described a rehearsal: "In one corner of the gym two or three girls are desperately trying to learn their lines, but in the other corner, Nancy, with by far the longest role, is perched gaily on top of the radiator, apparently telling a grand story to judge by the vigorous gestures and the hilarity of her appreciative classmates. The group has broken up, Miss Magowan having pleaded at length with the uproarious cast. For the moment Nancy is not 'on.' She sits on the gym floor, her books spread around her, doing her homework with the amazing concentration that is hers. Nothing seems to bother her, neither the chatter of her friends, the frantic coaching of Miss Magowan, nor even Jimmy Stewart's handsome face grinning up at her from her notebook cover."[89]

Homer Hargrave Jr., who was a freshman at Boys Latin that year, told me that he had a crush on Nancy. "I remember when I first fell in love with Nancy," he said. "We had a dance club that was just for freshmen in high school. It was called Miss Pratt's Dancing Class, and they had it in the gym at Girls Latin. Nancy just sort of crashed the dance. I still remember the young man she was with, who I think died during the war. But anyway, she sang 'My Heart Belongs to Daddy.' It was really great."[90]

Nancy may have molded herself to Loyal's demanding specifications, but there was obviously a lot of Edith in her. An anecdote told by Hargrave shows how bossy she could be. "One Saturday," he said, "I went to the movie house, and they had changed the prices and I didn't have enough money. The Davises lived only a block and a half from that theater, so I went to see Mrs. Davis to borrow a dollar. She wasn't home, but Nancy was. And Nancy wanted to know first who my date was. When I told her it was Joanie Johnson, she approved and gave me a dollar. But that night at dinner, my father asked, 'What did you do all day?' And I told this story. My father got furious. I had to get up from the dinner table. And it was a cold winter night, and we lived about six or eight blocks from the Davises. I had to walk over there and give that dollar back. With the admonition, 'Don't you ever, *ever* borrow any money from friends of mine again!' "[91]

Nancy Davis graduated from Girls Latin in June 1939, with a B average. The text under her photograph in the yearbook read: "Nancy's social perfection is a constant source of amazement. She is invariably becomingly and suitably dressed. She can talk, and even better listen intelligently, to anyone from her little kindergarten partner of the Halloween party, to the grandmother of one of her friends. Even in the seventh grade, when we first began to mingle with the male of the species, Nancy was completely poised. While the rest of us huddled self-consciously on one side of the room, casting surreptitious glances at the men, aged thirteen, opposite us, Nancy actually crossed the yawning emptiness separating the two groups and serenely began a conversation—with a boy."[92]

That September she entered Smith College, in Northampton, Massachusetts—just days after Hitler invaded Poland, beginning World War II in

Europe. On December 28, 1939, while home for Christmas vacation, she made her debut at the Casino Club, the exclusive dining club in which the Davises had recently been accepted as members. Despite the Depression, this was the era of famous debutantes—Barbara Hutton, Doris Duke, Brenda Frazier—when high-society families spent tens of thousands on lavish coming-out parties for their eighteen-year-old daughters. In Chicago there were balls every night during the holiday season, and all kinds of lunches, cocktail parties, and dinners in honor of that season's debs. Edith had arranged for one of the city's grande dames, Mrs. Patrick A. Valentine, an Armour heiress, to give a dinner for Nancy at her Gold Coast mansion. The biggest bash of the week, at the Blackstone Hotel with the Glenn Miller Orchestra, was for Priscilla Blackett, the daughter of an advertising tycoon. The night before Nancy's debut, Jean Wescott's parents gave their daughter a ball at the Casino.[93]

Nancy's late-afternoon tea dance was a simpler affair, though the attendance of thirty Princeton boys assured its social success. (One of those young men, Frank Birney Jr., the son of a Chicago banker, would soon become Nancy's first college beau.) To mark the occasion of their daughter's introduction to society, Edith and Loyal gave Nancy a single strand of pearls, which she wore with her silver-trimmed white gown.[94] The trunk baby had become a debutante, the near orphan a near princess.

CHAPTER FIVE

WARNER BROS.
1937–1941

In those days at the studios, which governed everything we did, we generally saw the people who were at the same studio. Joe Mankiewicz, the screenwriter, said it was like living in a duchy, in a moated castle. From 1938 to 1941, I was in the Warner Bros. duchy, because my first husband, Wayne Morris, was an actor at Warners. He and Ronald Reagan and Jane Wyman acted in the same movies, so we saw them all the time. They were not married when I first met them. Jane, as a matter of fact, was married to a man called Myron Futterman, and it used to send me into fits of laughter. He was a perfectly nice man. I don't know why, the name tickled me. What were Jane and Ronnie like then? They were adorable. But what did I know? I was eighteen years old. They were young and beautiful. But everybody was beautiful.

Leonora Hornblow to author,
February 10, 2000

Los Angeles in 1937—the year Ronald Reagan arrived—was a place apart, a paradise some would say, far away from the rest of the world and its problems. Its leading industry—moviemaking—employed nearly forty thousand people in the manufacture of fantasies, illusions, and myths for a nation still struggling with the grim reality of the ongoing Depression. The hard times had only increased the public's appetite for Busby Berkeley musicals, high-society comedies starring Carole Lombard and Myrna Loy, and Saturday-matinee Westerns with Gene Autry and William Boyd as Hopalong Cassidy. The Spanish Civil War, with Nazi Germany and Fascist Italy backing one side and the Soviet Union the other, had started the year before, Japan invaded China in July 1937, and a nervous Franklin Roosevelt was beginning to rearm America. But that meant stepped-up orders for Southern California's burgeoning oil, rubber, and aircraft industries. Bad news was good news, it seemed, in this upside-down Shangri-la.

The landscape itself was a mirage come true, semidesert transformed into semitropics by sheer human willpower and the massive importation of water from the Owens Valley in Central California, carried over the world's longest aqueduct, a 233-mile marvel of engineering built between 1906 and 1913 by an itinerant knife sharpener turned municipal water czar named William Mulholland.[1] Where there was once sagebrush and mesquite, there was now jasmine and oleander, hibiscus and bougainvillea, and acre upon acre of perfectly

manicured and constantly watered lawns surrounding mile upon mile of mock Spanish, Tudor,
Italian, and New England mansions, from
Pasadena to Palos Verdes, from Hancock Park to
Beverly Hills. Even the palms that lined the boule-
vards to the beaches were imported, and every
two-bedroom bungalow in the most modest
neighborhoods seemed to come with a flowering
orange or lemon tree in its tiny front yard. If New
York was the ultimate vertical metropolis, Los
Angeles was the ultimate horizontal one, sprawling, spacious, languid, preternaturally pretty. The
newest city in the world, they called it, the city
without a past.

This was the city of upward mobility and self-
invention, hedonism and fundamentalism; the
mecca of beauty queens and musclemen, swamis,
psychics, evangelists, and astrologers, asthmatics
and arthritics, rich retirees fleeing the boredom of
Peoria and Omaha, poor Okies fleeing the desperation of the Dust Bowl, Jewish intellectuals and
artists fleeing Hitler; the land of the white picket
fence and the kidney-shaped swimming pool, of
the open shop and the gated community, where
the myth of the American Dream was invented by
the Eastern European moguls who ran Hollywood.

Between 1900 and 1940 the population of Los
Angeles grew from barely 100,000 to almost 1.5
million,[2] making it the fifth-biggest city in the country, after New York, Chicago, Philadelphia, and
Baltimore.[3] A relentless campaign of annexation—
the only way for neighboring towns to tap into the

city's water supply was to be annexed—had made it the largest city in area in the country, encompassing 442 square miles from the San Fernando Valley in the north to Venice, San Pedro, and the man-made Port of Los Angeles in the south. This was also the city of the car (one for every 1.6 residents by 1926, a ratio the rest of the country would not match until 1950),[4] the single-family home (a remarkable 94 percent of all dwellings in 1930),[5] and the feverishly promoted residential subdivision (at the height of the 1920s boom, there were 43,000 real estate agents).[6]

Unlike the older, industrialized cities of the East and Midwest, whose growth was fueled by European immigration, Los Angeles was the result of a great internal migration from the heartland of America. As Mike Davis noted in *City of Quartz*, the railroad magnates, real estate developers, bankers, and boosters who took over the seedy cattle town in the 1880s "set out to sell Los Angeles—as no city had ever been sold—to the restless but affluent babbitry of the Middle West."[7] The newcomers, in John Gregory Dunne's words, were "already thoroughly Americanized, with roots going back several generations—hardworking, white, English-speaking Midwestern smalltowners seeking a Protestant Eldorado with a temperate climate and no foreigners fresh from the boat."[8] Until well after World War II, Los Angeles was the most homogeneous large city in America—90 percent white and two-thirds Protestant[9]—and had been kept that way by the Chinese exclusion acts of the 1890s, the periodic repatriation of Mexican nationals, and the widespread deed covenants and block restrictions excluding blacks and Asians that took hold in the 1920s.[10]

Yet set within this WASP utopia was the most ostentatiously powerful Jewish community in the nation, led by the self-made moguls who founded and ran the Hollywood studios. The two most important men in prewar Los Angeles were probably Harry Chandler, the publisher of the *Los Angeles Times*, the city's dominant newspaper, and Louis B. Mayer, vice president and head of production of Metro-Goldwyn-Mayer, the largest and grandest of the five major and three minor studios. Chandler, the de facto dictator of the downtown oligarchy that ran Los Angeles, used his newspaper as a promotional vehicle for his vast real estate ventures, and was by far the city's richest citizen, leaving an estimated $500 million fortune at his death in 1944. Mayer, the undisputed king of the movie industry, owned stock in 20th Century Fox and Columbia Pictures as well as MGM;[11] he was the highest-paid individual in the country in 1937, earning $1.3 million in salary and bonuses, and would remain so until 1946. Though they were hardly friends, both men were union-hating, moralistic, conservative Republicans— Mayer was actually chairman of the California Republican Party's central committee in the 1930s.[12]

On matters of politics and industry standards the other studio heads kowtowed to Mayer—except for his great rival, Jack Warner, vice president and head of production at Warner Bros., the second-largest studio. If Mayer and his family were Herbert Hoover's first dinner guests at the White House in 1929, Jack Warner would brag in his autobiography that he "virtually commuted" to the Roosevelt White House—"court jester, I was, and proud of it."[13] If Metro was the Tiffany's of the studios, Warners was the Ford, an efficient assembly line known for its low budgets and long hours. The Warners—Jack's older brother Harry was the studio's New York–based president—saw themselves as upstarts, outsiders, innovators, whose movies made up in realism and relevance what they lacked in gloss and sophistication. They had made the first talkie, *The Jazz Singer* with Al Jolson, in 1927, and pioneered the gangster movie, the headline movie based on news stories, and movies about such controversial subjects as labor disputes and race relations. The studio motto was "Combining good citizenship with good moviemaking." "The motion picture," Harry Warner told *Fortune* magazine in December 1937, "presents right and wrong, as the Bible says. By showing both right and wrong we teach the right."[14]

Although Harry and Jack Warner were not really liberals—they counted FBI director J. Edgar Hoover and the jingoistic newspaper tycoon William Randolph Hearst among their closest friends—many of the studio's producers, directors, and writers definitely leaned to the left, including Hal Wallis, the executive producer responsible for most of the studio's A movies, and Jerry Wald, its most important writer (and later producer). With the exception of Dick Powell, a dedicated Republican, most of the studio's major stars—Edward G. Robinson, Paul Muni, James Cagney, Humphrey Bogart, Bette Davis—were also prominent liberal Democrats.

One can see why an idealistic FDR fan from a working-class background like Ronald Reagan would fit in at Warner Bros. One can also see why an optimistic Disciple of Christ from Illinois by way of Iowa would feel at home in Los Angeles.

On May 24, 1937, as night fell over the glittering coastal metropolis, twenty-six-year-old Dutch Reagan drove into town in his open-topped Nash. The first thing he did, after checking into the Biltmore, was to thank Joy Hodges, who had made the introduction that led to his contract and who was still working in the hotel's nightclub. The next day, wearing a new white sports coat and blue trousers, he presented himself at Warner Bros. in Burbank—a week early. "Where in hell did you get that coat?" was the way Max Arnow greeted him. Summoning a young assistant, the casting director ordered, "Take him over to Wardrobe and see what the tailor can do with this outfit. He looks like a Filipino."[15]

Over the next few days he was put through the studio makeover mill. The makeup department told him his head was too small and gave him a new hairstyle. The wardrobe department said his shoulders were too wide and his neck too short and sent him to Jimmy Cagney's shirtmaker for custom-made shirts with trick collars (which he would continue having made for the rest of his life). The publicity department hated the name Dutch Reagan, even though he insisted it was known throughout the Midwest. When he told them his real name was Ronald, they said they loved it— Ronald Reagan!—and acted as if they had thought it up themselves. In an industry where most of the stars had their names changed, the name Ronald Reagan had the alliterative symmetry the studios considered classy and commercial. And so he came to be called by his proper name for the first time in his twenty-six years.[16]

In his first six months at Warners, he had the lead in two B movies and supporting roles in two A movies, a pattern that would prevail over the next four years. He played a radio announcer in *Love Is on the Air*, a sports reporter in *Swing Your Lady*, a cavalryman in *Sergeant Murphy*, and an assistant to Louella Parsons in *Hollywood Hotel*, which was based on the gossip queen's CBS radio show of the same name. Meeting Parsons, one of the two dominant columnists in Hollywood—the other being her bitter rival, Hedda Hopper—would prove to be a boon to Reagan's career. She took an immediate liking to him when she learned that he was from Dixon, Illinois, her beloved hometown, and from then on seized every opportunity to promote him in her daily column in the Hearst-owned

Los Angeles Examiner, which was syndicated in six hundred newspapers worldwide.

Among the Warners stars he worked with in these early movies were Humphrey Bogart and Dick Powell, who would become a close friend. During the three weeks it took to complete *Love Is on the Air,* he started dating his co-star, the beautiful June Travis. The daughter of a vice president of the Chicago White Sox, she had another suitor at the time, a rich playboy from Philadelphia named Walter Annenberg.

Annenberg was only three years older than Reagan but had already been romantically involved with Lillian Vernon, a Ziegfeld Follies girl (and later a mail-order entrepreneur), and Ethel Merman, then the hottest new star on Broadway, among others. He had been coming out to California since 1932, when his father, Moses Annenberg, the multimillionaire owner of the *Daily Racing Form*, started a Hollywood-based fan magazine called *Screen Guide*. (Walter always took the train, because Moses, who had seven daughters but only one son and heir, wouldn't let him fly.) He was introduced around town by Louis B. Mayer, and he knew everyone there was to know from William Randolph Hearst and his movie star mistress, Marion Davies, to Jack Warner and his glamorous second wife, Ann. The press scion cruised around town in a custom-made Lincoln convertible, stayed in a bungalow at the Beverly Hills Hotel, and spent weekends partying and gambling in Palm Springs, then the Hollywood elite's favorite hideaway.[17]

Nonetheless, June Travis preferred her co-star from Iowa, and Annenberg graciously withdrew. But he kept up a passing friendship with Reagan all through the late 1930s and 1940s, though the Republican Annenberg, whose father had bought the *Philadelphia Inquirer* in 1936 and made it a rabidly anti-FDR organ, often disagreed with Reagan's liberal views. Eventually, however, they would come to see eye-to-eye, and Walter Annenberg would be one of the most important backers of Ronald Reagan's political rise.

Love Is on the Air was released in September 1937, to generally good reviews. *Variety* called Reagan a "find." The *Hollywood Reporter,* the other major trade paper, called him a "natural." "Bill Meiklejohn assured me it was safe to send for Nelle and Jack," Reagan recalled, and that same month he sent his parents train fare.[18] He rented them an apartment at 1842 North Cherokee Avenue in Hollywood, a few blocks from his own in the Montecito Apartments at 6650 Franklin Avenue, a ten-story Art Deco building constructed in 1931. Not long after, Neil and Bess Reagan joined the rest of the family, and Neil was hired as an announcer at the Warner Bros. radio station, WFWB.[19]

Three of Reagan's Drake friends from Des Moines also followed him west that fall; three more moved to Los Angeles a few months later.[20] For a while Reagan was "the group's sole support," in

his words, but he was only too happy to be surrounded by familiar faces. After a long day at the
studio, he would drive out to Santa Monica to join
his buddies for bodysurfing or volleyball on the
beach, followed by onion soup, chili, and beer at
Barney's Beanery, a West Hollywood bar that
became their hangout.[21] Reagan frequently took
Joy Hodges—another Iowan—out to dinner,
though they were never romantically involved. "We
discussed politics more than any other subject,"
she recalled. "I was so fond of him, but he was a
passionate Democrat and I a Republican and we
used to go round and round about that. . . . He
loved anything and everything about government,
history and politics. So did I, and I loved hearing
him relate accounts of Indian battles."[22]

On December 1, 1937, Warner Bros. picked up
his option, raising his salary to $250 a week. He
bought his parents a small house in West
Hollywood, at 9031 Phyllis Avenue, just over the
Beverly Hills line, the only piece of real estate they
would ever own. Its small yard was filled with
rosebushes, which Jack discovered he liked to
tend. After his heart attack, Jack had finally given
up drinking, but not chain-smoking. He was fifty-
four and in failing health. "Every morning he would
take the slow, careful walk his doctor had prescribed," his son later wrote. According to Reagan,
Jack always joked about the new neighborhood,
"There's nothing, by God, but real estate offices
and hot dog stands."[23] For Christmas, Reagan
gave his father a club chair with an ottoman so that

he could put his feet up and listen to sports—and FDR—on the radio, which was also a gift from him. When Reagan's option came up again in June 1938, he persuaded the studio to give his father a $25-a-week job helping with his fan mail.[24]

On Sunday mornings, Reagan usually accompanied his mother to the Hollywood-Beverly Christian Church on Sunset Boulevard, and Nelle often fixed dinner for his Iowa friends on Sunday nights. "They were in and out more than I was," he later recalled, "and I think Nelle would have given someone an argument if he pointed out she hadn't really given birth to the whole gang."[25] The fact that they all came from a Disciples of Christ college no doubt pleased Nelle, whose life in Los Angeles, as in Dixon, revolved around her church and lay missionary work. She made regular trips to the Olive View Sanitarium in the San Fernando Valley, where she entertained the tuberculosis patients with dramatic readings, and Christmastime 1938 found her wrapping five hundred presents her church had collected for "needy folks."[26]

In a letter Nelle wrote to an Illinois friend that year, she gives a sense of the new life the Reagan family had in Hollywood. "Ronald said he was very glad to get your letter. Although he was so small when he left Tampico he still holds a soft spot for the home of his birth. I am acting as Ronald's secretary and open all the mail, and there is a lot to open. Of course, all the mail from former friends from the old hometown is turned over for him to read, so you can rest assured that he read yours.

Last month he received mail from forty-two states and three foreign countries, so you see if he had to answer his mail he would have not much time for work. . . . Ronald has finished three pictures now that he has taken the lead in, and is very well thought of at the studio. But really I don't yet know how to act with these people. I don't just fit in somehow—I get my fork in the wrong hand but I don't care, just so the boy gets along."[27]

By the end of the year, Reagan's salary was up to $350 a week, and he had rented a cottage at 1128 Cory Avenue, a block north of Sunset Boulevard and three or four blocks from Jack and Nelle's.[28] He was a seeing a recently divorced actress from the studio named Jane Wyman. When their engagement was announced by Louella Parsons eleven months later, Nelle wrote a friend in Dixon, "I hope my Ronald has made the right choice. I was in hopes he would fall in love with some sweet girl who is not in the movies."[29]

Jane Wyman, "a little, loud, brassy blonde," according to Hedda Hopper,[30] was not the sort of girl most mothers would choose for their son: a high school dropout, a former chorus girl, a divorcee twice over at twenty-one, beautiful to be sure and eager to please, but also touchy and tough, impulsive and needy. Nelle probably didn't know most of this; for one thing, it is highly unlikely that Wyman told Reagan about her first marriage, which she kept a secret, as she did so much about her past. This was not uncommon in Hollywood, where studio biographies were masterpieces of ellipsis and embellishment, but Wyman seemed to take things a step further. A decade later, when Nancy Davis signed with MGM, she would take two years off her age and erase the existence of her real father; Jane Wyman erased *both* her real parents, upgraded the professional status of the man she claimed was her father, and *added* three years to her age, just in case her teenage marriage to Ernest Eugene Wyman, the mysterious first husband, from whom she took her screen name, ever came out.[31]

Jane Wyman was born Sarah Jane Mayfield in St. Joseph, Missouri, on January 5, 1917, to Manning and Gladys Hope Mayfield, seven and a half months after they were married. Her parents separated in late 1921, and her father took a job with a shipping company in San Francisco. Her mother filed for divorce and moved to Cleveland, leaving Sarah Jane, not quite five, with friends named Richard and Emma Fulks. Manning Mayfield died of pneumonia the following year; a trip Emma Fulks made to California with Sarah Jane that winter may have been to see him on his deathbed and to arrange for the girl's guardianship. According to a neighbor of the Fulkses', although Gladys Mayfield occasionally visited her daughter in St. Joseph, the child went by the name of Sarah Jane Fulks, and she maintained that Richard and Emma Fulks were her real parents.[32] In the 1986 authorized biography, *Jane Wyman: The Actress and the Woman*, author Lawrence J. Quirk makes no mention of the Mayfields and states that she was "christened" Sarah Jane Fulks,[33] choosing that word perhaps because he knew the truth but was not allowed to print it. In contrast to Nancy Reagan's eagerness to substitute Loyal Davis for Kenneth Robbins as her one and true father, Jane Wyman's embrace of the Fulkses, and theirs of her, seemed to be based more on necessity than devotion. The prominent neurosurgeon took his time in making Anne Frances Robbins his legal daughter, but there is no record of Richard and Emma Fulks having adopted Sarah Jane Mayfield.

The Fulkses were both in their fifties when Gladys Mayfield left her little girl with them. Both had been previously married: Richard had a son from his first marriage; Emma, a daughter and a son; all three offspring were a generation older than Sarah Jane and living away from home when she was taken in. According to Quirk, "the Fulks house was a Victorian gingerbread horror, the furnishings lank and forlorn."[34] Richard Fulks was said to be a remote and tyrannical figure; the German-born Emma was more approachable, but equally demanding and strict.[35] Warners would later claim Wyman's "father" had been mayor of St. Joseph; in reality he was a frustrated politician who had been elected county collector for one term (as a Democrat) in 1916, and then joined the police department, where he rapidly rose from patrolman to chief of detectives.[36]

Emma Fulks dressed her charge in "drab, utilitarian clothes," Quirk writes. "Bows or furbelows of any kind were *verboten.*"[37] Strangely, she waited until September 1923 to register Sarah Jane in first grade, when she was nearly seven. Very occasionally, she would take the girl downtown for lunch and a Saturday matinee.[38] In interviews Wyman gave after she became famous, she mostly remembered feeling inferior, isolated, unwanted. When she was eight, a neighbor woman "hurt her deeply" by announcing loudly enough for her to hear, "With that turned-up nose and those bug eyes, no one will ever take that child seriously." She told Quirk, "Shyness is not a small problem; it can cripple the whole personality. It crippled mine for many years. As a child, my only solution to the problem of shyness was to hide, to make myself as small and insignificant as possible. All through grade school I was a well-mannered little shadow who never spoke above a whisper." But somehow she persuaded the Fulkses to let her take dance classes at 50 cents a throw with a local hoofer known as Dad Prinz.[39] Not surprisingly, this gloomy little girl had dreams of becoming a movie star.

On March 25, 1928, after a long, unspecified illness, Richard Fulks died at age sixty-three, leaving his widow little more than their house. Emma decided to rent it out and move to Los Angeles, where her children by her first marriage lived. She took Sarah Jane, then eleven, with her. They moved in with Emma's daughter, Elsie Weymann; her son, Morie Weymann, an eye-and-throat doctor, helped them out financially. No doubt motivated by the need for an income, Emma turned into a full-fledged stage mother, taking her "daughter" to singing and dancing lessons, scrimping to buy her pretty clothes, sending her photographs to talent agencies and movie studios, all without evident success.[40]

By 1932, Sarah Jane, then fifteen, had left Los Angeles High School without graduating, started working as a coffee shop waitress to pay for her lessons, and bleached her hair platinum blond à la Jean Harlow. That year she appeared in her first film, *The Kid from Spain*, a Samuel Goldwyn musical starring Eddie Cantor, kicking her legs in the air alongside two other young hopefuls named Betty Grable, then sixteen, and Paulette Goddard, then twenty-one. Between 1933 and 1935, she worked as a model, a switchboard operator, a manicurist, and a secretary, as well as a waitress, and had bit parts in six more movies, mostly at Paramount, mostly in the chorus line.[41]

"It was work when the family badly needed the money," she later said of her chorus line days, "but for a girl who had grown up in terror of being looked at, it was also agony. Then I made a discovery: a good shield for shyness is a bold exterior. Did my heart turn over when the man with the megaphone bellowed out my name? Were all the other dancers prettier? Never mind. I covered up by becoming the cockiest of all, by talking the loudest, laughing the longest, and wearing the curliest, most blatantly false eyelashes in Hollywood."[42]

On April 8, 1933, she married Ernest Eugene

Wyman, whom she may or may not have met in 1931, when they were both high school students, and who may or may not have been a salesman. She said she was nineteen on the marriage certificate, the beginning of the lie about her age. According to a 1957 *Movie Life* story, "Still in her teens, she impulsively entered marriage. Jane never talks about her first heartbreak, but in less than a month she knew it was a terrible mistake and the marriage was dissolved."[43] Other sources say she wasn't divorced until 1935. Much confusion surrounds this period of her life. In the summer of 1933, according to one report, she returned to St. Joseph, where she stayed with a woman named Gladys H. Johnson, who may or may not have been her real mother with a new surname. A neighbor remembered her having been married then and sitting in the yard trying to write.[44] Another version, in the 1949 *Current Biography*, which usually relies heavily on the subject's word, had her returning home in 1935, very briefly enrolling at the University of Missouri, then touring the Midwest and South as a radio vocalist, using the name Jane Durrell. Lawrence Quirk says she never went back to St. Joseph, a place which she disparaged as "oppressive, strait-laced, hypocritical."[45]

All sources agree that in May 1936, on the recommendation of William Demarest, an older actor who was also an agent, she was given a standard contract by Warner Bros. She was in the chorus line in her first film there, *Stage Struck*, a Busby

Berkeley musical featuring two of Warners' biggest stars, Dick Powell and Joan Blondell, and didn't get a leading role until a year later, in her tenth film for the studio, *Mr. Dodd Takes the Air*, opposite the crooner Kenny Baker. Still, she was thrilled to be at Warners, and when asked "What is your long-range ambition?" in a 1937 studio questionnaire, she answered, "To be not just *an* actress but *the* actress at the studio."[46] (No wonder Bette Davis, then queen of Warners, wasn't that friendly.)

In the meantime, Jane was willing to take on such starlet tasks as showing up at parties for potential investors and wealthy cronies of the studio brass. It was at one of these parties that she reportedly met Myron Futterman, a middle-aged businessman from New Orleans who owned a dress company in Los Angeles. Futterman was divorced and had a teenage daughter a few years younger than Wyman, but that seemed to make little difference to either of them, because on June 29, 1937, they were married—Quirk calls it an elopement—in New Orleans.[47] The strange thing is that only six days before a story had appeared in the daily *Variety* under the headline JANE WYMAN HOSPITALIZED FOR NERVOUS BREAKDOWN.[48]

June 1937 happened to be Ronald Reagan's first month at Warners, and in one version of events he and Wyman were introduced in the commissary soon after his arrival on the lot. In another, they met in the publicity department while having their pictures taken. Wyman later said that from the first moment she saw him, she thought to herself, "That's for me." "The knight on a white charger had finally showed up," William Demarest said. "Ronnie was the dream of true, perfect manhood personified that this little girl had always held in her heart through thick and thin. She was the aggressor, the intent pursuer, from the start. . . . I think Ronnie at first was somewhat bewildered by her fast come-on; then he started to like it, then her, and then he fell in love."[49]

Futterman and Wyman separated sometime between October 1937 and January 1938—he wanted her to tone down her look, give up acting, and play hostess for his business associates, none of which she had any intention of doing.[50] Reagan and Wyman started discreetly dating sometime during those months, though both would later insist that they hadn't started going out with each other until 1939, *after* she had divorced Futterman.

They definitely drew closer to each other during the filming of *Brother Rat,* from July 5 to August 11, 1938. It was the first of five films they would appear in together at Warners, and the first A movie in which either had a principal role. Reagan, Wayne Morris, and Eddie Albert played cadets at the Virginia Military Academy, known as the West Point of the South; Wyman, Priscilla Lane, and Jane Bryan were their respective love interests. The plot line reflected the state of the emerging Reagan-Wyman relationship: because she is the commandant's daughter, he has to proceed with caution, and when they finally kiss for the first time in the boys' dormitory, the heat seems to be coming more from her than from him. Their reported behavior on the set was more indicative of where the relationship would eventually go: while a loquacious Reagan held forth on New Deal policies and Hitler's demands on Czechoslovakia for fellow liberal Eddie Albert, a moody Wyman made lumpy clay models of other Warners actresses and stuck pins in their eyes.[51]

Leonora Hornblow, then married to Wayne Morris and a frequent visitor to the set, told me that she and Reagan often discussed politics. "That's why we became such friends. Ronnie was devoted to Franklin Delano Roosevelt and the Democratic Party. So was I. So we would talk. The studio bosses were all Republicans. And they'd say things like, 'that cripple in the White House,' which would make me crazy, and Ronnie too." Was Reagan critical of these rich Republicans? "Not at all. Ronnie was never against rich people. There was no such talk." Hornblow noted that her own husband and Jane Wyman were "apolitical."[52]

Reagan went out with three other co-stars during 1938—Anita Louise, Susan Hayward, and Ila Rhodes—some say for real, others for publicity purposes. He was even reported to have been "briefly engaged" to the obscure but apparently voluptuous Rhodes. None of these relationships seems to have been intimate, and some have suggested that Reagan may have been a virgin when he met Wyman.[53] His description of a studio-arranged date indicates his innocence at that time:

"A publicity man asked me to escort a young girl under contract to the studio, who had recently done a great deal for sweaters in a Mervyn LeRoy picture. She was very young and very beautiful and we were both very scared—she in a gown borrowed from wardrobe, and I in a dinner jacket from the same place. Lana Turner and I went to the premiere in a taxi because I was afraid to drive my old convertible. I hadn't learned how easy it was to rent a limousine and play big shot."[54]

Jack Warner's right-hand man, Richard Gully, described Reagan when he got to know him in the late 1930s. "There was always an aloofness about him. He was warm, but he had the extraordinary ability to stop any familiarity. He would be horrified if you went up and slapped him on the back. He was not that kind of man, but he was never disagreeable." Gully added, "He was not a womanizer or oversexed, believe me. He was not interested in women in the way Errol Flynn or Clark Gable was interested. He and Jane were just a great fun couple when I knew them as kids."[55]

Wyman filed her divorce petition on November 10, 1938, alleging that Futterman was obsessively jealous and refused to have a child with her. The divorce was granted on December 5, 1938. She got $1,000 in cash, her legal expenses, the car that Futterman had bought her, and the furnishings of their apartment, which she continued to occupy.[56] It was a big two-bedroom with a private entrance and a fabulous view at 1326 Londonderry Terrace, directly above the Sunset Strip and less than a mile from Reagan's place on Cory Avenue. By the spring of 1939 he had moved into her building (though it's not clear whether to her apartment or an adjacent studio). "We all knew he was living with her," was how Leonora Hornblow put it.[57] But Reagan and Wyman would later primly claim they had their first date at about that time. She said he took her to dinner and the premiere of *Second Fiddle*, starring Sonja Henie, the Norwegian ice-skating star.[58]

In all versions, the courtship reads a bit like a campaign, waged by Wyman, rather than Reagan, with persistence, guile, and some emotional black-mail. She wooed everyone around him that mattered: the Drake College friends, Nelle Reagan, Louella Parsons. The girl who had loved making entrances in nightclubs wearing fancy clothes and big hats suddenly became "a bug for outdoors" and "a swell scout,"[59] playing volleyball on the beach with Reagan and the guys, going to Disciples services with Nelle, signing up for committee assignments at the Screen Actors Guild (SAG), and taking Reagan with her to meetings. It was an amazing performance, though perhaps not entirely convincing.

"Jane and Ronnie really made a strange combination," observed her friend Jerry Asher, a fan magazine writer. "She was so experienced, hard-boiled, intense, and passionate, and he was so pragmatic, down-to-earth, not overly imaginative. Sure everyone respected . . . his clean-living ways and solid character, but he was—well, rather a square. Serious, respectful of women, steady of mind and manners. In short, predictable and a little dull. He was a very sexy-looking man, of course—looked wonderful in swimming trunks, great body and all that, but he was a little earthbound for someone like Jane."[60]

Wyman herself explained, "It was Ronnie's easy friendship which attracted me to him first. Everyone liked him and it seemed to me that he liked nearly everyone. I began to analyze what it was in *me* that *he* liked . . . and to try and have more of it!"[61] She also said, "For the first time in my life I truly trusted someone."[62]

Brother Rat, released that fall, was "a top picture and a big money maker," according to Reagan, but it didn't do for his career what he had hoped. "My part was enough to provide a steppingstone to stardom," he wrote. "Unhappily I learned another lesson. There is room for only one discovery in a picture. Eddie Albert stole all the honors, and deservedly so."[63] Nor did it do much for Wyman's career. Warners gave her the lead in four B movies after *Brother Rat*, playing boxers' girlfriends in two and Torchy Blane, girl reporter, in the other two. Reagan, meanwhile, in 1939 blew his one big chance, *Dark Victory*, starring Bette Davis and Humphrey Bogart; "wooden" is the adjective most frequently used to describe his performance as a rich young lush. In the fall of 1939, Warners reassembled the *Brother Rat* cast for a sequel, *Brother Rat and a Baby*, which in retrospect is most memorable for a line Wyman delivers to

Reagan: "You might as well back down, because I'm gonna get you."[64]

On October 4, 1939, as they were about to begin shooting the picture, Wyman was taken to the Hollywood Receiving Hospital with what was officially recorded as a stomach disorder. Years later Nancy Reagan told Edmund Morris that it was an overdose of pills, that Jane had sent Ronnie a suicide note, and that he rushed to the hospital and gave in to her demand that he marry her.[65] According to a previous version told by Anne Edwards, "Jane suffered a recurrence of an old stomach disorder," and when Ronnie went to the hospital, her sister—Emma Fulks's daughter, whose married name was Elsie Wyatt—told him that Jane didn't want to see him. The next day, "he refused to be barred from her room. When he left, they were engaged to be married."[66]

Louella Parsons announced the engagement of "two of Hollywood's very nicest young people" in early November, adding that Reagan had given Wyman a ring with a 52-carat amethyst—his semiprecious birthstone.[67] To make sure the deal stuck, Parsons took them on a nine-week, cross-country "Stars of Tomorrow" tour, along with six other young actors, including Susan Hayward and Joy Hodges. After a tryout in Santa Barbara, Louella's troupe opened at the Golden Gate Theater in San Francisco, where their forty-minute variety show, with Reagan as master of ceremonies, played to full houses as many as five times a day. They then flew east on a chartered TWA DC-2, refueling in

Albuquerque, New Mexico, where Louella was made an honorary member of the Pueblo Indian tribe and given the name Ba-Ku-Lu, which means starmaker. The plane was forced to land in a snowstorm in Chicago, and Reagan once more swore he would never fly again—and didn't for twenty-five years. From there they traveled by train to Philadelphia, Pittsburgh, Baltimore, New York, and Washington—all cities that Reagan and Wyman were seeing for the first time. It was also the first time that Reagan found himself pursued by clamoring young female fans, screaming his name and pulling at his clothes. On New Year's Eve morning, their one day off in Washington, he persuaded Wyman and Hodges to drive out to Mount Vernon, George Washington's house in Virginia. Hodges later recalled how fascinated Reagan was, "especially with Washington's personal writing desk." Wyman took note, and bought him a replica for his study.[68]

On January 26, 1940, three weeks after they returned to Los Angeles, Jane and Ronnie were married, following in the footsteps of such two-star couples as Mary Pickford and Douglas Fairbanks, Paulette Goddard and Charlie Chaplin, Betty Grable and Jackie Coogan, and Warner Bros.' own Joan Blondell and Dick Powell. The ceremony took place at Wee Kirk o' the Heather, a small chapel with a Scottish theme in Forest Lawn Memorial Park, the burial ground of Old Hollywood. "It was doomed," noted Leonora Hornblow, who was a bridesmaid. "But they were very attractive together and crazy about each other."[69]

The bride wore a pale blue gown of heavy satin, high-collared and long-sleeved, set off by a mink hat and a mink muff on which she had pinned a purple orchid corsage. The groom wore a dark suit. In their wedding photograph, Reagan looked waxen, perhaps because he had been in bed with the flu and was still running a fever.[70] The ceremony was performed by Reverend Cleveland Kleihauer of the Hollywood-Beverly Christian Church. The wedding party was mostly family: Jack and Nelle, Neil and Bess Reagan, Emma Fulks and Elsie Wyatt, who was matron of honor. Reagan asked one of his Iowa friends, Will Scott, to be his best man, passing over Neil. Louella Parsons's third husband, Harry "Docky" Martin, an alcoholic urologist who specialized in venereal diseases, walked the bride down the aisle.[71]

Parsons, who had been ceaselessly promoting Jane and Ronnie as the ideal all-American couple next door and took credit for engineering the marriage, gave the reception at her house on North Maple Drive in Beverly Hills. Hornblow thought Nelle seemed out of sorts at the party: "She looked like a pioneer woman. I don't mean she wasn't well dressed, she was. She wasn't forthcoming. She was cold and uncommunicative. But everyone was extremely nice to her. Who would be rude to Ronnie's mother?"[72] Louella drank almost as much as her husband, which may have been the cause of her chronic incontinence—she was famous for leaving a puddle wherever she sat—and perhaps that bothered Nelle.[73]

The newlyweds drove to Palm Springs that night. As if getting married in a cemetery wasn't omen enough, it rained in the desert for most of their one-week honeymoon. Fifty years later I asked Jane Wyman if she remembered the first time she went to Palm Springs—which was on that honeymoon. "No, not particularly," she said, flashing me such a cold and angry look that I thought she might murder me right there in her pink-and-lavender retirement condominium.[74]

"Theirs is the perfect marriage," Louella Parsons proclaimed in a column shortly after the wedding. "Jane always seemed so nervous and tense before she found Ronnie. She was a girl on the make—for life, for love. I think she wanted—well, *everything*. But steady, solid, decent young Ronnie has slowed down her pace, and it is all for the best. Yes, it was an 'opposites-attract' thing, but I'm predicting here and now that these opposites will celebrate their twenty-fifth *and* fiftieth wedding anniversaries—together."[75]

The first two years of the marriage were full of promise and good news. Their daughter, Maureen Elizabeth Reagan, was born on January 4, 1941. The Meiklejohn Agency was bought by the increasingly powerful Music Corporation of America, and Lew Wasserman, the slick young protégé of MCA founder Jules Stein, became their agent. By the fall of 1941 Wasserman had renegotiated both of their contracts at Warners, tripling their salaries overnight. Ronnie was now making $1,650 a week, Jane $1,500, and both of them had been elected to the SAG board.[76] They bought a plot of land on Cordell Drive, high up in the Hollywood Hills with a view that extended from the Pacific Ocean to downtown Los Angeles, and built an eight-room "English farmhouse," with big picture windows and a huge stone fireplace, inspired by Rosalind Russell's house in *This Thing Called Love*. (They actually borrowed the plans from Columbia Pictures.)[77] They continued to see the Iowa crowd, but they were also becoming friendly with such established stars as Claudette Colbert, then the highest-paid actress in Hollywood.[78] Reagan was proud of being included by James Cagney, Humphrey Bogart, Pat O'Brien, and Dick Powell at their regular table in the studio commissary.[79] Powell took a particular liking to Reagan, who had made three movies with him, and offered to sponsor him as a candidate for Congress, if he would become a Republican.[80]

Bogart, Powell, and many other Warners stars were members of the Lakeside Country Club, in nearby Toluca Lake, as were Bing Crosby, Bob Hope, and Walt Disney. Reagan was accepted for membership, but he resigned when he realized the club did not allow Jewish members or guests. "What happened was Ronnie took a Jewish friend to play golf," Nancy Reagan told me. "And he was informed afterward that you couldn't do that. Ronnie said, 'You mean Jewish people are not allowed?' They said that was right. Ronnie was furious and resigned. They were mad at Ronnie and he was mad at them. It was a Mexican stand-off. They put his membership card on the bulletin board and threw darts at it. And then Hillcrest made him an honorary member."[81]

The Hillcrest Country Club, near Beverly Hills, was known as the Jewish club because it had been founded in 1920 by Jewish businessmen who could not get into the city's oldest country club, the Los Angeles Country Club, which excluded not only nonwhites and Jews but also movie people. By 1940, Hillcrest was the bastion of the Jewish elite of Hollywood: studio chiefs Louis B. Mayer, Jack and Harry Warner, Adolph Zukor, and Harry Cohn were all members. At Hillcrest, Ronnie and Jane became part of the social set centered on the great husband-and-wife comedy teams Jack Benny and Mary Livingstone and George Burns and Gracie Allen. "Popular legend had it that one could be a part of the Jack Benny–George Burns group just by being able to tell a good, funny joke," notes Jill Robinson, the daughter of producer Dore Schary, in her memoir, *With a Cast of Thousands.*[82]

Jack Benny's annual salary for his Jell-O-sponsored radio show had just been raised to $350,000, and he was earning another $200,000 a year in movies for Paramount.[83] Burns and Allen, who were also under contract to Paramount, were making $9,000 a week for their radio show on CBS. Although both Benny and Burns were a good decade older than Reagan, these friendships would last all their lives, and no doubt helped him hone his sense of humor. "I've taken up golf," Jane Wyman told a reporter in 1941. "You just can't keep me away from the club. I have a date with Mary (Livingstone) Benny this afternoon. Ronnie and I play together when we're both not working."[84]

"Jane was completely self-satisfied," said Leonora Hornblow of the new bride. "And Jane was Mrs. Full Charge. I don't think she ever asked Ronnie if he wanted a blue sofa—she just ordered what she wanted. The house was perfectly nice but very banal. And there were literally no books, just the news magazines for Ronnie and the ladies' magazines for Jane. Jane wasn't a great reader either."[85] Reagan may not have been a bookworm, but he reportedly immersed himself in current events by reading both the *Christian Science Monitor* and the *Wall Street Journal* in addition to the local papers.[86]

Louella Parsons was a constant presence on Cordell Drive. Little Maureen called her "Aunt Lolly" and later wrote, "She was pretty much a fixture in our household during the early years of my childhood." In fact, Parsons thought the child should have been named for her, and was not above trying to get usable information out of the toddler. As Maureen put it, "One of my most enduring memories about Louella Parsons is that she was someone I wasn't supposed to talk to too much."[87]

The Reagans also grew close to Lew Wasserman, who was not yet all-powerful but was working on it, and his equally ambitious wife, Edie. Their daughter, Lynne, played with Maureen (and gave her the nickname that would stick for the rest of her life, Mermie). Jane Wyman told producer William Frye, a longtime friend of Reagan's and Wasserman's, "Ronnie and I started going to Chasen's when it was just a stand. We'd go there with Lew and Edie almost every Saturday or Sunday night for a hamburger and chili." Frye told me, "Lew and Edie were very, very close to Jane and Ronnie. Lew was behind both of them in a very big way in those days."[88]

Evidently Jane wasn't much of cook. "Ron and I practically lived at the Derby," she later wrote in the introduction to a book about the Brown Derby at Hollywood Boulevard and Vine Street, one of four restaurants in the chain. Their favorite dish was Catalina Sand Dabs Meunière, and they sometimes played gin at their table after dinner.[89] Soon Ronnie became an enthusiastic wine connoisseur. "He got me started on a wine collection," recalled actor Robert Stack, who became friends with Reagan around 1940. "He got me a cellar, and, being a class act, he got me Romanee Contis and Pomerols and Montrachets."[90] Reagan may have been trying to impress Stack—who was from a socially prominent Los Angeles family and eight years younger than he—with his newfound sophistication.

On the other hand, Nelle's son couldn't help disapproving of Stack's wild ways and friends, who included another future president of the United States. "Jack Kennedy was also a friend of mine," Stack told me. "He was a just a young guy who happened to be the son of Joe Kennedy, who was then the ambassador to the Court of St. James's. Jack had a key to my apartment, which I could never get into because he was always there with a pretty girl. We had a little room called the Flag Room. It had flags going up the walls and over the ceiling and one very large triple bed. The object of that room was that the girl had to match the flag to the country or otherwise pay a penalty. There were more penalties paid and more happy customers came out of that Flag Room." According to Stack, "Ron kept trying to get me to settle down. 'It's high time you became a responsible citizen,' he would say. 'Okay, sure, Ron. Very good. Thank you. I think I'm busy now.' "[91]

Ronnie, who clearly loved being married, called his wife Button Nose, leading the movie magazines to dub Maureen "Button Nose the Second." Completing this picture of young marital bliss in Hollywood was a pair of Scottish terriers—the same breed as FDR's famous Fala—named Scotch and Soda.

Warners put Ronnie and Jane in two more movies together after they married, *An Angel from Texas* and *Tugboat Annie Sails Again*, both in 1940. But her career stalled as his took off with the two A films that would make his name: *Knute Rockne,*

All-American, in 1940, and *Kings Row*, filmed in 1941 and released in early 1942. In the first he played George Gipp, a famous halfback for Notre Dame known as the Gipper, who died of a strep infection at age twenty-five in 1920. Reagan took the idea to Warners, then had to fight to get the part, and probably succeeded only because his friend Pat O'Brien, who was cast in the title role of the famous Notre Dame coach, pushed hard for him. Reagan's parting words in his deathbed scene, "Win one for the Gipper," would become a battle cry for his supporters in his political campaigns. His most memorable line in *Kings Row* was also delivered from bed, and would become the title of his autobiography: *Where's the Rest of Me?*

Everyone involved in *Kings Row* was first-rate: the producer Hal Wallis, the director Sam Wood, the screenwriter Casey Robinson, the cinematographer James Wong Howe, the composer Erich Wolfgang Korngold, and a cast that included Robert Cummings, Claude Rains, Charles Coburn, and Judith Anderson. Its budget exceeded $1 million, an exceptional amount for frugal Warner Bros., and larger than that for any previous Reagan film.[92] It was based on a controversial best-seller by Henry Bellamann, which involved incest, insanity, euthanasia, and homosexuality in a small Midwestern town, and which had to be severely diluted to get the script approved by the Hays Office censors. Reagan gave what he and most critics considered the best performance of his career as the thoughtless young rake who loses his inheritance to a crooked banker and his legs to a sadistic doctor, but finds a uniquely American kind of redemption in the love of a girl from the wrong side of the tracks, played by the stunning Ann Sheridan, who marries him and helps him become a successful real estate developer. (Interestingly, Sheridan's character is wiser than Reagan's, she consults with a psychiatrist about how to handle her husband's depression without telling him, and his first real estate project is her idea, though she pretends it was his.)

Reagan took his father to the premiere of *Knute Rockne* at Notre Dame in October 1940. Warners invited two train cars full of stars and press from Los Angeles, and an estimated 250,000 fans crowded into South Bend, Indiana, for the three-day publicity event, which included a football game between Notre Dame and the College of the Pacific. Franklin Roosevelt Jr. read a letter from his father at the banquet following the opening. As Reagan later told the story, he had been eagerly anticipating the trip for weeks:

> Nelle cornered me one day and told me that someone else was excited. Jack would never let me see it, but the dream of his life was to make this trip. Here was an Irishman who had really worshipped from afar: he'd never seen a Notre Dame team play; he'd never even been to South Bend. He thought Pat O'Brien was the greatest man since Al Smith. And he sensed somehow his youngest son would

pass a kind of milestone before the trip was over.

What a simple thing this would be for me to fix—still, I felt a chilling fear that made me hesitate. We had all lived too long in fear of the black curse. Nelle's optimism was in full tide—she'd tell Jack how important it was that he vote dry on the trip and she knew he could be trusted. Whatever happened, I'm glad that she was so persuasive. It only took a phone call and the studio said yes before I got the question out of my mouth. . . . Saturday was the big day with lunch in the dining hall of St. Mary's followed by the game and at night the premiere.

First thing in the morning I called Jack's room, but there was no answer. All unsuspecting, I called the desk to ask if he had gone out. I was informed he and Pat had just come in. His weakness was prosperity, and this was prosperity in capital letters. The evening before at the university banquet he had sat with an old Dixon friend, and heard students, faculty, and distinguished alumni greet us with a thunderous ovation. Then while I peacefully slept, he had been taken into the inner circle, so to speak, by Pat who had adopted him in his warmhearted way. Some time later I was told of their early morning return to the hotel— it must have been quite a scene. Jack was sure the empty streets were a trap and that the quarter-million fans were lurking in an alley,

just waiting to swoop down on Pat for autographs. At each intersection he would halt Pat
while he tiptoed up to the corner, and peered
cautiously around; then he would signal Pat to
join him and they would scamper across the
street to the shelter of the buildings. Pat loved
every minute of it.[93]

If any movie star was the perfect friend for Jack
Reagan it was Pat O'Brien—the grandson of four
Irish immigrants, a devout Catholic, a faithful
family man, a hard drinker, and a fervent FDR supporter. Famous for playing Irish cops and priests,
he was also a Milwaukee schoolmate and Navy
buddy of Spencer Tracy's (and, like Tracy, a friend
of Edith Davis's from their theater days). Ronald
Reagan and O'Brien, who was eleven years his
senior, had hit if off on the first film they made
together at Warners, *Submarine D-1*, three years
earlier; Reagan's part ended up on the cutting room
floor, but it was the beginning of a friendship that,
as he later wrote, "would play an important part in
all that has happened to me."[94]

O'Brien kept up with Jack Reagan after their
South Bend bender, taking him to the Hollywood
Democratic Party headquarters to help out with
the Roosevelt campaign. Barely six months after
they celebrated FDR's November 1940 victory
over Wendell Willkie together, Jack dropped dead
of a heart attack on May 18, 1941, at age fifty-
seven. According to family lore, he died while waiting for an ambulance that never came; Nelle had

called the nearest ambulance service, not knowing that, because of a jurisdictional dispute, Beverly Hills ambulances were not permitted to cross the boundary into West Hollywood.[95] Ronnie was in Atlantic City, on a Warners promotional tour. When Nelle reached him by telephone, she urged him not to fly, saying she would delay the funeral until he and Jane could return home by train.[96]

Pat O'Brien was among the small group of mourners at St. Victor's Catholic Church in West Hollywood. Ronnie, as he told Maureen years later, was "beyond crying. My soul was just desolate, that's the only word I can use. Desolate. And empty. And then all of a sudden I heard somebody talking to me, and I knew that it was Jack, and he was saying, 'I'm OK, and where I am it's very nice. Please don't be unhappy.' And I turned to [Nelle], who was sitting with me, and I said, 'Jack is OK, and where he is he's very happy.' And it was just like it went away. The desolation wasn't there anymore, the emptiness was all gone."[97]

Four months later, in September 1941, it was Nelle's turn to share in her son's stardom. This time the junket was to Dixon, Illinois, for Louella Parsons Day and the premiere of *International Squadron*, starring Ronald Reagan—the man who hated to fly—as a daredevil American pilot fighting with the British Royal Air Force against the Nazis. This double homecoming started with the biggest parade in Dixon's history, with five bands and fifteen floats, followed by the dedication of the Louella Parsons Wing at the Dixon Hospital, a banquet at the Masonic temple, the premiere at the Dixon Theater, and a Hollywood Ball at the town armory.[98] Ronnie invited Nelle's old friends from her True Blue Bible class to the premiere, which was a benefit for the hospital, and mother and son were put up at Hazelwood, the Walgreen estate on the Rock River, along with the rest of Louella's entourage, including Bob Hope, Ann Rutherford, George Montgomery, and Joe E. Brown.[99] Charles Walgreen's widow, Myrtle, gave a lunch for two hundred on the lawn where a decade earlier young Reagan, then a caddie for Mr. Walgreen, had lolled in a hammock.[100]

"I want all of you to know that I did not sleep last night, thinking of my trip back to Dixon, where I could meet my old friends," Reagan said in his speech at the kickoff of the parade. "I counted the 77 persons whom I have been credited with pulling out of the Rock River at Lowell Park many times during the night."[101] As Louella rose to cut him off, Bob Hope's sidekick, Jerry Colonna, whispered, "This fellow must be running for Congress!"[102]

"During the couple of days it took to reach Dixon, I got to know Ronnie quite well," recalled Ann Rutherford, then an MGM starlet, who was also traveling with her mother. "You know, who else are you going to talk to? Picture people stuck with picture people when you went into the dining car, and over a couple of dinners my mother and I were so impressed with him. He had an idea about everything, especially political things. My mother shook her head and said to me, 'He is *not* going to stay in the picture business. He has far more important fish to fry, and he'll do it.' He really had suggestions on *everything*. For instance, he said to me, 'You do have a three-check bankbook, don't you?' And I said, 'Yes, why?' He said, 'Well, what do you do with your canceled checks?' I said, 'I put a rubber band around them and throw them in a shoe box.' And he said, 'Well, what you should do is, when you get them back, take a little Scotch tape and tape them to the stubs. That way you know where everything is.'"[103]

Clouding the festivities in Dixon was the inevitability of America's involvement in World War II. The war had started two years earlier with Germany's invasion of Poland on September 1, 1939, and as country after country fell to the Nazis, including France in the summer of 1940, an increasingly bitter and urgent debate divided America. On one side were the isolationists, who were opposed to America's entanglement in any foreign wars; on the other the interventionists, who believed it was America's duty to fight beside Britain, the only Western European democracy still resisting Hitler.

Although Roosevelt had been reelected in November 1940 promising to keep the country out of war, he was secretly plotting with Winston Churchill to do just the opposite while publicly promoting preparedness, rearmament, and aid to Britain. For most of 1940 and 1941, the isolationists, led by the influential America First Committee, were ascendant. By May 1941, eight months after it had been founded, the AFC had almost 850,000 dues-paying members,[104] and among its most prominent supporters were Charles Lindbergh, Frank Lloyd Wright, Alice Longworth Roosevelt, and former ambassador Joseph Kennedy, who had been recalled from London by FDR for being too eager to appease the Germans.

The AFC was headquartered in Chicago, where its principal backers were General Robert E. Wood, the chairman of Sears Roebuck, and *Chicago Tribune* publisher Colonel Robert McCormick. The only movie star on its national board was Lillian Gish, who during 1940 and 1941 was starring in the Chicago production of *Life with Father*[105] and, through her good friend Colleen Moore, seeing a lot of Loyal and Edith Davis. Although the AFC would later come to be seen as a reactionary and even anti-Semitic group, its membership included such leading liberals as future ambassador Chester Bowles, and it began as a student antiwar group at Yale that included Gerald Ford, Sargent Shriver, and future Yale president Kingman Brewster.[106] It should also be remembered that between August 1939, when Hitler and Stalin signed a nonaggression pact, and June 1941, when Germany invaded the Soviet Union, the American Communist Party and its left-wing sympathizers were also vociferously isolationist.

Indeed, the American political scene during the prewar period was so complicated that the House Un-American Activities Committee (HUAC), which had been started in 1938 by Congressman Samuel

Dickstein, a far-left Democrat from Manhattan's Lower East Side, to investigate pro-Fascist and pro-Nazi organizations such as the German-American Bund, was soon taken over by Congressman Martin Dies, a far-right Democrat from Texas, who promptly launched an investigation of the Hollywood Anti-Nazi League, claiming it was "under the control of Communists."[107] As the Brown Scare turned into the Red Scare, and Hitler and Stalin carved up Eastern Europe, the Anti-Nazi League—which had been formed in 1936 and had in its vanguard everyone from Lillian Hellman, Dashiell Hammett, and Dorothy Parker to Lucille Ball, Henry Fonda, and Groucho Marx[108]—changed its name to the Hollywood League for Democratic Action and lost many of its movie star members.[109]

Nonetheless, Congressman Dies spent the month of August 1940 in Hollywood personally interviewing many of the stars associated with the Anti-Nazi League and like-minded groups. "One by one, the accused came to his hotel to seek absolution," Neal Gabler writes in *An Empire of Their Own*, "Humphrey Bogart, Fredric March, Luise Rainer, Franchot Tone, even Jimmy Cagney, who left telling reporters that the charges claiming Hollywood was permeated by Communism were 'so exaggerated that they are ridiculous.'"[110]

Cagney was papering over the fact that the Communist Party in Hollywood had been steadily growing since the start of the Spanish Civil War in 1936, and had a strong appeal for the socially conscious intellectuals in the community. As Paul

Buhle and Dave Wagner write in *Radical Hollywood*, "In this world where networking meant everything, the Communist Party's Popular Front was, from the middle thirties until the late forties, *the* network for the cerebral progressive, the inveterate activist, and the determined labor unionist."[111] Ring Lardner Jr., for example, was drawn into the Party by his co-writer on *A Star Is Born*, Budd Schulberg, in 1937. In his memoir, *I'd Hate Myself in the Morning*, he says, "I thus became one of about two dozen party members in Hollywood. (Five years later, the count was well over two hundred.)"[112]

In *Dutch*, Edmund Morris repeats a startling claim by the screenwriter Howard Fast, that Ronald Reagan tried to join the Party in 1938. "Reagan got carried away by stories of the Communist Party helping the dispossessed, the unemployed, and the homeless," Fast told Morris. "Some of his friends, people he respected, were Party members. So he turned to them. Said he wanted to become a Communist." According to Fast, who was in the Party at the time, Reagan's *Brother Rat* costar Eddie Albert and his far-left Mexican wife, Margo, talked him out of it, at the behest of the local Party hierarchy, who thought Reagan was a "flake."[113] Leonora Hornblow told me she was "shocked" by Morris's story, and said Ronnie "never gave any indication" of Communist leanings in their political discussions on the *Brother Rat* set.[114]

The first HUAC investigation of Hollywood fizzled out, but a year later the movie industry was under attack again. "[The movies have] ceased to be an instrument of entertainment," declared the isolationist Senator Gerald B. Nye of North Dakota in an inflammatory speech he gave at an America First rally in St. Louis on August 1, 1941. "They have become the most gigantic engines of propaganda in existence to rouse . . . war fever in America and plunge this nation to destruction." The studios had the power to "address 80 million people a week," he pointed out, and were run by executives who came from "Russia, Hungary, Germany, and the Balkan countries." As he shouted out their names—Mayer, Warner, Goldwyn, Cohn—the crowd booed.[115] "Are you ready to send your boys to bleed and die in Europe, to make the world safe for Barney Balaban and Adolph Zukor and Joseph Schenck?" he railed, naming the president and chairman of Paramount and the president of Fox.[116]

One month later, on September 11—just four days before Louella Parsons Day in Dixon—Lindbergh, the AFC's most popular spokesman, weighed in with a speech in Des Moines that created a national uproar and would tarnish his reputation forever. "The three most important groups," he said, "who have been pressing this country toward war are the British, the Jewish, and the Roosevelt administration." He went on to say that the Jews' "greatest danger to this country lies in their large ownership and influence in our motion pictures, our press, our radio, and our government."[117]

On September 25, 1941—ten days after the Dixon festivities—Harry Warner was called before the U.S. Senate Subcommittee on Moving Picture Propaganda. The subcommittee, chaired by Senator D. Worth Clark of Idaho, a leading isolationist, had compiled a list of fifty films it said contained pro-war propaganda, including eight made by Warner Bros. Harry Warner didn't flinch. "You may correctly charge me with being anti-Nazi. But no one can charge me with being anti-American," he told the committee.[118] "Shortly after Hitler came to power in Germany I became convinced that Hitlerism was an evil force designed to destroy free people, whether they were Catholics, Protestants, or Jews." He added that he had "always been in accord with President Roosevelt's foreign policy."[119]

Warner Bros. wasn't making propaganda movies so much as historical movies, Harry Warner calmly claimed. But as both proud Jews and the most conspicuous Roosevelt supporters among the Hollywood hierarchy, the Warners had taken the lead in opposing the Nazis and preparing the American public for eventual intervention in Europe. In April 1938, to give one example of their high-profile efforts, Jack and Ann Warner had hosted a $100-a-plate dinner at their Beverly Hills estate to raise money for refugees from Germany, with the exiled Nobel Prize writer Thomas Mann as guest of honor.[120] In a 1939 article Harry Warner wrote for the *Christian Science Monitor*, he stated that the film industry had "implied duties to ethics, patriotism, and the fundamental rights of individuals."[121] Despite his demurrals to the Clark subcommittee, Warners was definitely making propaganda movies, including at least two starring Ronald Reagan.

Murder in the Air, which Reagan began shooting a few days after the war started in Europe in September 1939, was originally titled *The Enemy Within* and briefly retitled *Uncle Sam Awakens* before its release in early 1940. It was the fourth and last in a series in which he played Brass Bancroft, a nonchalantly heroic Secret Service agent who defends America from smugglers of illegal aliens, international counterfeiters, foreign saboteurs, and home-grown subversives.[122] These were the films in which he earned his self-described reputation as the "Errol Flynn of the Bs,"[123] with "one fight per every 1000 feet of film."[124] To promote the third in the series, *Smashing the Money Ring*, Warners filled theater lobbies with fingerprint booths, wanted posters, and "crime clue boxes," in which patrons were encouraged to drop the names of suspicious neighbors.[125] *Murder in the Air* introduced a futuristic weapon that could shoot enemy aircraft out of the sky, and the trailer beckoned: "Join Ronald Reagan battling 20,000 unseen enemies to protect . . . the most deadly weapon ever known to man . . . a death ray projector . . . the greatest force for peace ever discovered."[126]

International Squadron, the other Reagan movie cited by the Clark committee, actually opened with an on-screen dedication to the men of the RAF and, like all Warners war movies, was made with the full cooperation of the Department of Defense. "I was a rascal who ferried Lockheed bombers to London, joined the R.A.F., and squared all my sins by taking a suicide mission," Reagan would describe his role as a bomber pilot in this "timely production about the Battle of Britain. . . . Twin engine Lockheed planes were rolling off the line a few blocks from the studio and being flown directly to England. If we needed one of those in our picture, we'd jolly well use it in a Lockheed hangar from 8 p.m. until 4 a.m. and then it was on its way to a real war."[127]

According to Stephen Vaughn in *Ronald Reagan in Hollywood*, "Warner Brothers estimated in 1940 that it based a fifth of its movies on newspaper headlines."[128] Historians have suggested that this was where Reagan's tendency to blur fact and fiction, to dramatize the political with the anecdotal, began, and point to the death ray projector as the model for his Strategic Defense Initiative, commonly known as Star Wars, forty years later. Yet as his description of the use of U.S. military planes in *International Squadron* indicates, Reagan was quite aware of the difference between the fake and the real, and of the ironies that grew out of basing the former on the latter.

Lest anyone miss *International Squadron*'s pro-British message, Warners flew Bebe Daniels and Ben Lyon from London for the splashy premiere in Dixon. This American comedy couple had become immensely popular in England for continuing to broadcast their weekly radio show during the darkest days of the Blitz. In Dixon they gave interviews to the local press in which they spoke of the fear and bravery of the English people, who had lived through nine months of nightly air raids by the Luftwaffe during the previous fall, winter, and spring.[129]

It's clear which side Reagan was on—that of his bosses at Warners and his idol in the White House. As someone who avidly followed the news, he was keenly aware of the desperate situation in Europe—Hitler's troops had laid siege to Leningrad, and German submarines were blockading Britain, trying to stop American supplies released under the Lend Lease Act from getting through. Yet, as late as that November, a Gallup Poll disclosed that only 17 percent of the American public supported going to war against Germany.

On December 7, 1941, the debate between isolationists and interventionists was rendered moot by Japan's surprise attack on Pearl Harbor. A day later, the United States Senate, with only one dissenting vote, declared war on Japan. On December 11, Germany and Italy declared war on the United States. America was at war whether it wanted to be or not. And suddenly the world apart didn't seem so far away from the rest of the world and its problems after all.

CHAPTER SIX

NANCY AT SMITH
1939–1944

I was in Chicago in September 1941, until I went into the Navy in late 1943. I was doing the evening news on WBBM at the time and narrating one of the soap operas as well. Edith Davis was one of the people around WBBM, and we would drink occasionally in the Wrigley Building bar—WBBM was in the Wrigley Building. She was a very attractive, interesting woman. If she was bawdy, she was bawdy in a funny way. She was just a funny woman who was enjoying her life and was very happy to have met Loyal. I got to know her and her child. Her child was very ladylike, a Smith girl, with the Peter Pan collar and the black patent leather shoes and the white gloves and the pearls. Nancy was—her father's darling. Utterly, utterly unlike her mother.

Mike Wallace to author,
May 30, 2002

After high school, I went to Smith College, where I majored in English and drama—and boys.

Nancy Reagan,
My Turn[1]

In the summer of 1939, Richard Davis, Nancy's stepbrother, came to live with Edith and Loyal in Chicago, after his mother died of tuberculosis in California. "Nancy was terribly nice to me," Richard recalled. "She never said, 'Well, I'm sorry your mother died,' but she was very kind. Of course, she was going out with boys, and they would always take me along to the movies. We had a lot of fun together as a teenager and a college student."[2] Though Nancy and Richard had hit if off from the time they met as children, a closeness was established between them during these years that would last for the rest of their lives, perhaps because they were both only children, of opposite sexes, and far enough apart in age so that they didn't threaten each other's position in the family. "My most positive memories of Nancy are from those days," he said. "She was a very happy person. She had a great smile, she was always laughing, she was the life of the party."[3]

That fall Nancy started her freshman year at Smith College. She had promised Dr. Loyal that she would complete at least a year of higher education before pursuing an acting career, but she soon discovered that life at the exclusive girls' school suited her. Situated on two hundred acres in Northampton, Massachusetts, Smith, with 2,500 students, was the largest of the prestigious group of women's colleges known as the Seven Sisters. It had been founded in 1875 with a bequest from Sophia Smith, a deaf local spinster, with "the design to furnish for my own sex means and facilities for education equal to those which are afforded now in our Colleges to young men."[4] Nancy arrived at the end of the tenure of Smith's greatest president, William Allan Neilson, who had vastly expanded the campus and the curriculum, transforming the high-minded provincial retreat into an internationally recognized liberal arts institution, well known for its Junior Year Abroad Program, which he started in 1924.

Tuition, room, and board were $1,000 a year, and Nancy received an allowance of $100 a month.[5] Students lived and took their meals in residences called cottages, which were staffed by uniformed maids. For her first two years Nancy roomed with her friend from Girls Latin Jean Wescott, and struggled with the required courses, particularly science and math.[6] Her first college boyfriend, Frank Birney Jr., was also from Chicago. The son of a banker, Birney had attended the private Lake Forest Academy before enrolling at Princeton University, where he was invited to join Tiger Inn, one the school's eating clubs. Wealthy, well liked, and "utterly handsome,"[7] Frank seemed to have everything Nancy wanted. He even shared her theatrical ambitions and was an officer of the Triangle

Club, Princeton's musical theater organization, whose alumni included Jimmy Stewart.[8]

During Nancy's freshman and sophomore years at Smith, Hitler would conquer most of Europe, and in her junior year the United States entered the war, but for her "those were very happy and care-free days." As she wrote forty years later, "The students were much less serious than they are today, much less politically involved. I knew nothing about politics. I don't say this with any pride, but it didn't seem important then."[9] As her stepbrother said on a television show decades later, "I used to like to kid her that she spent more time at Princeton with her boyfriends than studying. But she was extremely well liked and very personable, had a great sense of humor, and didn't seem to be burdened by anything."[10]

She was, however, in need of occasional reassurance, as evidenced by a letter Loyal sent her on December 6, 1939, a week before she would return home for her debutante party. "Nance dearest," he wrote. "I'm sure you know I love you, but I'm afraid I haven't told you so enough. I'm repaid more than enough by your love and respect . . . and by knowing that you are honest, frank, direct and dependable. These are things which many of us have to acquire in later years, but you have them already. There has never been, and will not be ever, any question in my mind that you are trying to do a good job."[11]

*   *   *

The Davises enrolled Richard in the ninth grade at Boys Latin School, where he became friends with Homer Hargrave Jr. and Joseph Kelly, one of the mayor's sons. Like his father, Richard was an avid Civil War buff, and in previous summers Loyal and Edith had taken him on trips to some of the historic battlefields. Much to the delight of Edith, who had given him a biography of Robert E. Lee, *The Gray Knight,* young Richard saw himself as "an unreconstructed rebel."[12] Loyal's son was fascinated by military matters, so for the next three summers the Davises sent him to camp at the prestigious Culver Military Academy in Indiana.[13]

While Edith was happy to have her stepson living with them, there was a certain amount of tension involved in suddenly having a teenage boy around the house. "Edith was very, very sensitive," Richard Davis told me. "I remember one Saturday afternoon when I was about fifteen, the three of us were sitting in the library. And my father and I were going down to the Drake to get a magazine or a chocolate soda. Dr. Loyal said, 'You and your mother ought to kiss each other before we go out.' So I turned my cheek, because I thought Edith was going to kiss me. Jesus, she interpreted that as me turning away from her. Edith could be very, very tough, especially when it involved my father. If anybody said anything critical of Loyal, Edith didn't mince any words. It didn't matter where she was or who was there."[14]

This was "the same sort of protective attitude," Davis pointed out, that Nancy would later show toward Ronald Reagan. On the surface everything at the Davises' seemed to revolve around the husband's career, schedule, and wishes. "Nancy and me," Richard Davis recalled, "if we said, 'Oh, it's chicken again tonight, DeeDee.' Not exactly a complaint, but she took it very seriously. 'Your father *likes* chicken.' And therefore *you* like chicken. It was just about that simple."[15]

There was an underlying insecurity, Davis thought, in Edith's feelings toward Loyal. As a teacher, his father "was constantly promoting young people and stimulating their interest," whereas Edith sometimes seemed threatened by the younger generation, including her own daughter. Perhaps this was because she was hiding the fact that she was eight years older than her husband. "I was always told that they were both born in 1896," Richard said. "It was interesting, because I didn't know why she was absolutely gray in 1940. Her hair was *white*."[16]

As Edith began to show her age, Nancy was blossoming. She was home for Easter vacation in April 1940, when Alla Nazimova spent a night with the Davises on her way to Los Angeles, where she was making her first movie in fifteen years, *Escape,* directed by Mervyn LeRoy at MGM. On the train the next day the actress wrote a letter to her girl-friend, Glesca Marshall, in which she rhapsodized about her "extraordinarily beautiful" goddaughter. Nancy's face, she wrote, "which has every right to be bold and assertive has instead a soft dreamy quality. And add to this a figure of 'oomph!' You'd be crazy about the child."[17]

Nancy had grown accustomed to having her mother's show business pals stay for a night or two, but for Richard it was a new experience: "All my football friends and I called our home Ma Davis's Boardinghouse for Actors. It really was terribly stimulating."[18] Some of these visitors observed that Edith really ran the show on East Lake Shore Drive. As Katy Weld, the wife of Walter Huston's colleague John Weld, the writer, saw it, "Edie Davis was the power behind her husband, behind the *whole* thing. She ran their lives. Loyal Davis was a famous surgeon, very high up in his profession, but she pushed him up in society also. Edie was always behind everything." John Weld added, "Edie was *very* ambitious about Nancy, about getting her in the movies. And Nancy was ambitious, like her mother."[19]

In early 1940, another major star entered the Davises' life. Lillian Gish, "the First Lady of the Silent Screen," was in Chicago with the touring company of *Life with Father,* which opened on February 19 and ran for a record-breaking sixty-six weeks. Gish had been a friend of Colleen Moore's since they were both under contract to D. W. Griffith. After the advent of the talkies, Gish had moved to New York, where she became an acclaimed theatrical star and met the love of her life, George Jean Nathan, the brilliant drama critic and ultra-sophisticated dandy who co-edited both

The Smart Set and *The American Mercury* with H. L. Mencken.[20] Through Nathan, Gish took a seat among the fast livers and sharp wits of the Algonquin Round Table, but she always retained her pure, almost virginal, image. She never smoked or drank. She never married either, seeming to prefer the company of her mother and her actress sister, Dorothy, to that of a husband. Memories of her father, an alcoholic who had deserted the family when the girls were youngsters and died in an insane asylum in 1912, doubtless colored her views on both alcohol and men.[21]

"Marriage is a business," Gish declared in a 1919 interview, when she was twenty-six. "A woman cannot combine a career and marriage. . . . I should not wish to unite the two." Twenty years later she reaffirmed her opinion in an article titled "Why I Never Married": "I believe that marriage is a career in itself. I have preferred a stage career to a marriage career."[22] She was forty-seven when she arrived in Chicago, and had ended her relationship with Nathan four years earlier, allegedly because she discovered that he was Jewish by birth, although his mother was a convent-educated convert to Catholicism and he himself had markedly right-wing views, not unlike her own.[23]

A lifelong Republican and early anti-Communist, Gish went to her grave denying that D. W. Griffith's *Birth of a Nation*—in which she starred as a Northern senator's daughter who turns sympathetic to the Southern cause after she is almost raped by her father's mulatto protégé—was the slightest bit racist, despite ongoing protests that it was a glorification of the Ku Klux Klan. She was thrilled when Warren Harding invited her and Dorothy to lunch at the White House after the Washington premiere of Griffith's *Orphans of the Storm* in 1921,[24] and she gushed with admiration about meeting Benito Mussolini while filming *Romola* in Italy in 1923.[25] While Gish loved spending time in Europe, she was a flag-waving patriot and a practicing Episcopalian, proud that her mother's ancestors had emigrated from England in the 1630s and included President Zachary Taylor. Yet she endorsed FDR in 1936 and resigned from the Daughters of the American Revolution when the organization refused to allow Marian Anderson, the black opera singer, to perform at its 1939 convention in Washington.[26] In the 1940 election, she refused to vote for Roosevelt or Wendell Willkie, saying both "were more interested in other countries than in their own."[27]

Gish's year and a half in Chicago coincided with the rise of the America First Committee, and her closest friends there, General Robert E. Wood and Colonel Robert McCormick, were the leaders of the isolationist organization. According to Colleen Moore, McCormick declared Gish "the most fabulous woman he had ever known and asked her to marry him."[28] As Gish wrote in *Silver Glory*, her unpublished history of Hollywood, "My days were filled happily by knowing Robert E. Wood and his family [and] through them the idols of us all, Charles and Anne Lindbergh."[29] Gish became the

AFC's most prominent spokesperson after Lindbergh. On April 1, 1941, she gave a radio speech urging Americans to keep the country out of war. Among those who sent her congratulatory letters was Edith's co-star on *The Stepmother,* Francis X. Bushman, who wrote, "I can think of no one woman who I would rather place beside our National Hero Lindbergh, than yourself. I am sure a National Shrine will in days to come, be erected to you."[30]

In June, Gish joined Lindbergh at an America First rally at the Hollywood Bowl, where the crowd of eighty thousand chanted, "Lindy! Our next president!," and she called for a national referendum on the war.[31] But on September 1, 1941, one month after Senator Nye's startling attack on the Hollywood moguls in St. Louis, she suddenly resigned from the AFC's board—some say at the urging of her old friend Mary Pickford, others say to avoid testifying before Senator Clark's Subcommittee on Moving Picture Propaganda, which was then convening in Washington. Ten days after Gish's renunciation, Lindbergh gave his notorious speech in Des Moines accusing the British, the Jews, and the Roosevelt administration of pushing America into the war. By then the AFC was viewed by many as more pro-Nazi than antiwar, and according to Lindbergh biographer A. Scott Berg, "talk of Col. McCormick's and General Wood's anti-Semitism was rampant."[32]

There is no record of the Davises' being friendly with either Wood or McCormick, though the latter was close to their friend Mayor Kelly. It has been reported, however, that Loyal Davis was an "active member" of America First.[33] "If he had been a member, I probably would have known," asserted Richard Davis, who doubted that he was. "He was an Anglophile, so I think he was sympathetic to the British. I never heard him say we have to stay out of the war. Maybe he did in 1937 or 1938, but he never did anything about it politically. He was very *interested* in politics, but he was not a joiner."[34] The only organizations Loyal belonged to, his son said, were medical associations.

Loyal's friend Homer Hargrave Sr., while admiring of America First, was not a member, according to his son. "He was very sympathetic to Lindbergh and Senator [Burton] Wheeler," Hargrave Junior said,[35] referring to the Montana Democrat who was in the forefront of the isolationist movement and whose wife was on the AFC's board. Hargrave added that his father, having lived through World War I, was adamantly opposed to going to war again but was neither pro-German nor anti-Semitic. He told a story to illustrate his point, though it also conveyed a sense of how nonchalant the Davises' social set seemed about the rise of right-wing authoritarian regimes in Europe (an attitude shared by many Americans, including Louis B. Mayer and Jack Warner, both of whom had entertained Mussolini's son Vittorio in Hollywood in 1937).[36]

"In 1938, when Colleen and my father went to Europe on their honeymoon, she said she wanted to bring me a present. I said I'd like a black shirt from Italy and a swastika. She was trying to make friends with me, so she brought both back. I put the swastika up on my bedroom wall with the college pennants. One day I came home from school and the swastika was gone. I asked Colleen where it was. 'Your father couldn't stand it anymore. It went down the incinerator.' "[37] According to his son, this was Homer Hargrave Sr.'s reaction to Kristallnacht, the first organized attack on Jewish communities in Germany, which occurred on November 9, 1938.

Richard Davis recalled his parents' lunching with the Lindberghs at the Arizona Biltmore, probably in the spring of 1940. "I don't think Dr. Loyal was impressed by Charles Lindbergh at all. He was very impressed by Anne Morrow Lindbergh, who was a marvelous author." Davis also recalled, "Walter and Nan Huston were very much against Hitler. This went back to when we spent two summers with them, and I heard a lot of conversations at the dinner table. They were very pro-European. They were oriented to the British and the French."[38]

On the other hand, Edith and Loyal saw a lot of Lillian Gish in Chicago in 1940 and 1941. Richard Davis said he had never heard any talk of America First during the dinners they had with the actress, but of all Edith's actress friends, the conservative Gish was his father's favorite. "She and Loyal were very close. I always thought they had a thing for each other."[39]

*   *   *

Historians have made much of Loyal Davis's political views and his influence on those of the future First Lady and her husband. According to the stock portrayal, the doctor was a relentless right-wing bigot who turned his stepdaughter into a Republican zombie and through her converted Ronald Reagan from a New Deal liberal to a New Right conservative. As former California governor Pat Brown, whom Reagan defeated in 1966, put it, "There is no doubt that Reagan's move to the far right began after he met and married Nancy."[40]

Loyal Davis was a Republican, but he was neither a party activist nor a significant donor to any candidate other than his son-in-law. Whether he was particularly right-wing is difficult to say—his friends insist he wasn't, his enemies insist he was. Allegations of his racism and anti-Semitism appear to be exaggerated, though not far-fetched. In discussing such matters, there is a natural but simplistic tendency to apply the standards of the present to those of the past. What can be said unequivocally about Loyal Davis is that he was very much of his time, place, class, race, sex, and profession. Only his negative attitude toward religion in general was unusual. As a self-proclaimed Southern Democrat, Edith held views that were even more clichéd than her husband's.

Nancy Reagan always maintained that her stepfather had little interest in politics and no influence on her views or Ronald Reagan's, which is somewhat disingenuous and clearly overstated. "His life was medicine," she told me. "I never heard him say that he was a Republican. My mother was a Democrat—Southern Democrat, y'all. And I knew nothing about politics."[41]

Richard Davis told me his father was a standard-issue Republican: "He didn't like Roosevelt, but no one in upper-middle-class America did." Davis was uncertain as to whether Edith ever voted for Roosevelt: "If she did, she didn't tell Loyal, that's for sure."[42] Edith's political hero, he noted, was Senator Carter Glass, an eminent conservative Democrat from her home state of Virginia and the last surviving member of the Senate born in the antebellum South; he had authored the Federal Reserve Act of 1913 and been secretary of the treasury under Woodrow Wilson. Nicknamed the Unreconstructed Rebel by FDR, Glass led the fight against his attempt to abolish the poll tax, which effectively deprived blacks of the vote in many Southern states, and he opposed Roosevelt's renomination in 1936 and 1940.[43]

Edith was "as bigoted as her husband," according to Kitty Kelley, who relied heavily on the recollections of Lester Weinrott, Edith's producer and director, to reach this conclusion. "Loyal was the worst bigot in the world," Weinrott told Kelley. "He was a racist who called all blacks niggers, and an anti-Semite who called all Jews kikes. He hated every Catholic he ever met. His mother . . . was president of the Eastern Star [a Masonic order], and she spat on the floor every time a Catholic entered the room. Loyal was the same way. We had a federal judge in Chicago named Mike Igoe, who married a nice Catholic girl from Galesburg, and Loyal never referred to Mrs. Igoe as anything but 'that Catholic bitch.' Not to her face, of course, just behind her back."[44]

"I never heard any racial or anti-Semitic utterance from my grandparents, nor Dr. Loyal or Edith," Richard Davis insisted. "My father's best friend and colleague all of his life was Dr. Louis J. Pollock, who was Jewish. A Jewish surgeon, Jacob Bookbinder, operated on my grandfather, Albert, for cancer of the bowel. My father trusted him to take care of his own father. Edith would go out to black churches on the South Side of Chicago on Sunday afternoons and participate in their activities. Lester Weinrott knew all of this. He and his wife, Betty, were at the house all the time. Les Weinrott was a very, very dear friend of Edith and Loyal. And I was extraordinarily fond of him. I don't understand why he said what he said to Kitty Kelley."[45]

Mike Wallace, the CBS newsman, whose long friendship with the Davises began in the early 1940s when he worked at the same Chicago radio station as Edith, told me, "I'm Jewish, and I never had that feeling from anybody in that family. I never heard a whisper about anti-Semitism." Asked why Lester Weinrott, whom he also knew, would have made such statements, Wallace answered, "He was probably bitter, because he was left behind, so to speak. He disappeared after doing radio soap operas."[46]

"Dr. Davis was certainly not anti-Semitic," said

Dr. Nicholas Wetzel, who started as a clerk with Loyal Davis in 1945 and was a partner in his practice until 1977. "He brought any number of Jews on the staff at Passavant."[47] Both Wetzel and Richard Davis cited Loyal's intervention in 1946 or 1947 on behalf of Dr. Harold Laufman, a talented surgeon whose appointment was actively opposed by many doctors at the hospital because he was Jewish. "My father absolutely blew everybody away who objected to it," Davis recalled, "because Dr. Laufman was an outstanding surgeon."[48] Although this incident took place after the end of World War II, when the revelation of the concentration camps put a muzzle on American anti-Semitism, quotas on Jewish students persisted at some colleges and universities into the 1960s.

Wetzel also said that he saw no evidence of anti-Catholicism in Loyal, pointing out that he himself was a Catholic. He added that, while Edith was a regular attendant at the Fourth Presbyterian Church, her husband seldom accompanied her. "I don't think he was atheistic, but he was certainly irreligious," said Wetzel, "and that dated back to his grade school days, when he had perfect attendance at Sunday school and the prize was given to the son of the local department store owner. I think that totally soured him on the church."[49]

"I never joined a church," Loyal wrote. "I have tried to practice the golden rule. I have never been able to subscribe to the divinity of Jesus Christ nor to his virgin birth. I don't believe in his resurrection, or a heaven or a hell as places. If we are remembered and discussed with pleasure and happiness after death, this is our heavenly reward and mortality for having led a good life. I have never thought these beliefs necessary to the recognition of the great influence Christ's teachings have had and which I have tried to follow. . . . I have always been affected by flagrant acts of injustice."[50]

"My father loved to discuss serious topics," Nancy Reagan explained, "and I can remember more than one conversation about whether there really was such a thing as a human soul. I don't remember the answers, but I recall, unlike my mother, Loyal wasn't religious. I once asked him what happiness was. 'Nancy,' he said, 'the answer to that question is almost twenty-five centuries old, and it's basically what the Greeks said. Happiness is the pursuit of excellence in all aspects of one's life.' "[51]

One of the most oft-repeated—and damning— stories about Loyal Davis was originally reported by Lou Cannon in his first book about Reagan, in 1969: "A California physician who interned under Dr. Davis remembers that his fellow interns chafed under his strictness. In those days the interns were frequently called to deliver babies in the city's Negro districts and they would, on occasion, be asked by the mother to suggest a name for the child they had helped bring into the world. The interns invariably suggested the name Loyal Davis, a practice that was brought to the attention of the esteemed surgeon and finally prompted a bulletin board edict that interns were in no case to assist in naming an infant."[52] (Cannon repeated this story in his second Reagan book in 1982 , but not his third in 1991.)

In her version, Kitty Kelley omits Cannon's reference to Loyal's strictness as the basis of the resentments against him: "The prejudices of Loyal Davis were not hidden from the medical community, or from the interns and residents who worked for him. Some were so appalled by his virulent racism that when they went into the Chicago ghetto to deliver babies, they persuaded the black mothers to name their children 'Loyal' out of spite."[53]

Although Cannon based the story on a single source, who apparently didn't date it, there probably was some truth to it. "I've heard that story, but an equal number of babies were named after Irving Cutter," Wetzel said, referring to the dean of Northwestern University Medical School. "It was probably before the war, because Dean Cutter quit in 1942."[54] Loyal Davis's other longtime partner, Dr. Daniel Ruge, concurred. "I had a patient one time whose name was Loyal Davis Washington. I think it was done more as a joke, but you can't tell. It's true, a lot of people didn't like him. He was a strong personality."[55]

"It was always a joke," said Richard Davis, who told an anecdote suggesting that Loyal was less a racist than a snob. When Richard was in medical school at Northwestern in the 1950s, pairs of students would go to the South Side and other neighborhoods "where people couldn't afford hospitalization to have babies. Dr. Loyal always used to kid us— 'Dicky, you better take a good catcher's mitt, just to catch the babies as they fly out.' The students would name not only the black children but all the others after their professors.

"Before and after the war, Dr. Loyal had a very famous class for junior medical students, which they nicknamed the Hour of Charm," Davis continued. (*The Hour of Charm* was a popular radio show, featuring Phil Spitalny and His All-Girl Orchestra, that aired from 1934 to 1948 on CBS and NBC.) "Now, if you came to that without a necktie and a coat, you were thrown out. He taught doctors to be doctors. To act like doctors and to think like doctors. In neurosurgery you can't be sloppy."[56]

No discussion of the Davises' political attitudes would be complete without considering their relationship with Mayor Edward Kelly, which began in the early 1930s and lasted until his death, in 1950. Kelly's wife, Margaret, was almost as close to Edith as Colleen Moore Hargrave was. Loyal and Ed Kelly also grew quite close, the train engineer's son from Galesburg and the policeman's son from the Southwest Side having developed a deep respect for each other as neighbors on the Gold Coast. The Kellys lived just down the block from the Davises, at 209 East Lake Shore Drive, which was considered the finest address in the city.

In the 1940s, Kelly was at the height of his power. Along with Cook County Democratic Party chairman Pat Nash, he ran one of the most powerful political machines in the country, rivaling those of Boston's James Michael Curley, Kansas City's Tom Pendergast, and Jersey City's Frank Hague. A member of FDR's inner circle, he engineered the President's nomination to a third term at the 1940 convention, and also the replacement of his left-wing vice president, Henry Wallace, with the middle-of-the-road Harry Truman at the 1944 convention. Both conventions were held in Chicago. Kelly supported the New Deal, but at heart he was a law-and-order fiscal conservative who knew how to get along with the city's Republican business establishment, especially Colonel McCormick (who had roomed with Franklin Roosevelt at Groton and hated him ever after). He was also cozy with the heirs to Al Capone's organized crime syndicate, which along with other criminal interests was said to provide the Kelly-Nash machine with an estimated $12 to $20 million annually in return for lax enforcement of the anti-gambling laws.[57] Pat Nash's nephew was Capone's lawyer.[58] (The Mafia boss had been convicted of federal income tax evasion the year Kelly became mayor; released from prison in 1939, he died in 1947.)

Kelly is not even mentioned in either *Nancy* or *My Turn,* but Nancy Reagan confirmed that he and his wife were close to her mother and stepfather. "I remember there was a picture of Mother and Margaret Kelly in our apartment," she said. What was Mrs. Kelly like? "She was very nice. You know, they were what they were."[59]

"Margaret Kelly was a fireball—a beautiful

woman and a lovely person," Richard Davis recalled. "We would go over to the Kellys' every Sunday. They had a spectacular apartment. It was really something else."[60] In his memoir, Loyal Davis recounted a night in the early 1940s when the Democratic mayor and the Republican governor of Illinois, Dwight Green, came for dinner at the Davises' apartment. Loyal naively assumed that Edith must have mistakenly invited them on the same evening. But, he writes, "they greeted each other warmly, and my embarrassment quickly disappeared. After dinner, they were in earnest conversation, and the governor asked to use our telephone. When he returned, he said quietly to the mayor, 'I've taken care of it.' Until then, I thought that political rivals must be dyed-in-the-wool enemies but soon learned that this is more apparent in campaigns than it is in the day-to-day administration of government."[61]

What Edith understood and Loyal would learn was that power transcends political affiliation, and ideology need not get in the way of social success. In other words, whom you know is more important that what you believe. The Davis dining room was not so much a hotbed of political activism as a celebrity salon whose luster was heightened by the presence of not only powerful politicians but also movie stars, society figures, and prominent doctors. Loyal and Edith got along with everyone from the conservative Lillian Gish to the liberal Walter Huston to the bohemian Alla Nazimova precisely because those people's political views—or sexual morals, for that matter—didn't matter as much as their stardom. These were lessons that Nancy learned as a young woman, and that she would apply most effectively as she and her husband made their way through the hybrid society of Los Angeles.

At the beginning of her third year at Smith, in September 1941, Nancy was one of only eleven students out of a class of five hundred to choose drama as her major.[62] That December, Smith announced the appointment of Hallie Flanagan Davis as dean of the college and professor of drama. A remarkable and controversial figure, the fifty-one-year-old Davis had been the first woman to win a Guggenheim Fellowship, had started the Vassar Experimental Theater in 1925, and from 1934 to 1939 had run the Federal Theater, part of FDR's Works Progress Administration, which at its peak employed fifteen thousand theater workers and presented the works of such playwrights as Eugene O'Neill, George Bernard Shaw, T. S. Eliot, and W. H. Auden to millions across the country. It also created a politically oriented series called the Living Newspaper, which drew criticism from conservatives and which led to Davis's being called before HUAC in late 1938. The following year Congress cut off the Federal Theater's budget.[63]

At her first class with the drama students, the redheaded, tweed-caped Davis said, "I wish to say that this is a much warmer group than the last time I stood in front of a table like this. That was the

[House] Investigating Committee for Un-American Activities." Davis cast Nancy in her first production at Smith, *Susan and God,*[64] and later said of her, "She was a very good student, interested in the backstage as well as on stage, and she always had a feeling for her audience."[65]

By that time Nancy was certain that she wanted to act, having spent the two previous summers as an unpaid apprentice at "rickety old summer-stock theaters on the eastern seaboard."[66] Between her sophomore and junior years she was at the Bass Rocks Theater near Gloucester, Massachusetts, which was run by Martin Manulis, a young producer whose father-in-law, Ralph Austin Bard, a prominent Chicago entrepreneur, was an acquaintance of Loyal Davis's. "I did not know Nancy before she came to Bass Rocks," Manulis said, "but she was very knowable and likable and vivacious. She was quite serious about being an actress, even then. She wanted to do something in the theater. I don't think she was talking movies in those days."[67]

Bass Rocks, Manulis explained, "was real old-fashioned summer stock. Plays ran only one week, and they rehearsed a week. We didn't have much money, so we tried to have unusual leading players who didn't demand high salaries. We did former Broadway hits, and some kids were quite lucky and got bit parts in a play."[68] In her memoir Nancy Reagan writes, "As an apprentice, I did everything—painted scenery, upholstered furniture, ran errands, tacked up announcements in the town, cleaned dressing rooms, and so forth. I learned a lot about the actors from the way in which they left their dressing rooms. Some couldn't have cared less about the condition of their rooms and the fact that others would occupy them after they left. Others were clean, calm, and neat people, whose performances were as orderly as their dressing rooms."[69] If Nancy acted that summer, Manulis didn't remember it. But she did develop a "big crush," as she put it, on a thirty-three-year-old actor and dancer named Buddy Ebsen, who had just starred in a movie called *Parachute Battalion* and would eventually become a household name playing the cornpone grandfather on *The Beverly Hillbillies*.[70]

Apparently that was also the summer when Nancy saw Ken Robbins for the last time. A pair of snapshots in a Robbins family scrapbook, dated 1941 and labeled Massachusetts, show father and daughter standing together in front of what appears to be a beach house, Ken looking portly in a business suit, Nancy stylish in a light-colored shirtwaist dress. He was forty-seven and a partner in a New Jersey Chrysler-Plymouth dealership, although within three years he would lose his share of the business and never hold a steady job again.[71] When I asked Nancy Reagan about this visit, she insisted that she never saw her father during her college years, and that the photos must have been taken at least two years earlier. One of these pictures was found in Robbins's wallet when he died in 1972.

When Nancy returned to Smith that fall, she had a new roommate, a Jewish girl from New York who was also a drama major. "She was better suited to Nancy than I was," Jean Wescott told me, adding that Nancy "got in with some people that I didn't care for, and we just sort of grew apart for a while."[72]

According to Kitty Kelley, "Homosexuality was an unspoken fact of life in the all-female environment of Smith College," and Nancy had a "secret but romantic" relationship with a "classmate who later became an avowed lesbian. The lesbian classmate was involved in the theater and very popular on campus."[73] When I asked Richard Davis about this, he told me, "I remember Nancy joking one Christmas when she came home from Smith that some girl had fallen in love with her, and given her flowers."[74] Davis pointed out that Nancy was always comfortable around homosexuals of both sexes. "As a matter of fact," he said, "the men she gets along with are a little effeminate."[75] Davis put Nancy's high school beau, Sock Hettler, whom he said she continued to see when she was home from college, in this category, as well as James Platt White Jr., the Amherst man she would start dating in her senior year at Smith, but not Frank Birney, whom she later called "my first serious boyfriend."[76]

Nancy and Frank had started seeing each other after her coming-out party in December 1939. "I would go to Princeton for football games and dances, he would come to Smith for dances, or we would meet in New York for a weekend, 'under the clock' at the Biltmore Hotel," she later wrote, hastening to add that she stayed on the hotel's girls-only floor. "Frank and I went together for about eighteen months," she continued. "We talked a little bit about getting married, but it ended in tragedy before that ever happened."[77]

On December 15, 1941, Birney's life came to a mysterious end. In Nancy's telling, he was accidentally killed while running across the tracks to catch a train from Princeton to New York, where she was waiting for him. But a strong case can be made that Birney, despondent about having to spend part of Christmas vacation at Princeton making up bad grades and perhaps in emotional turmoil one week after Pearl Harbor, deliberately threw himself in front of the train. Bruce McFarland, one of Nancy's Boys Latin friends, told me, "I knew Frank fairly well at Princeton. His roommate, Geoffrey Montgomery Talbot Jones, was my best friend. Frank was a neat guy, but I'm almost certain he was a manic-depressive. And he committed suicide—no matter what Nancy says."[78]

In his memoir, Christian Gauss, the dean of Princeton at the time, states that several Tiger Inn members told him that Birney had been "much depressed" and that a telegram from his sister was found in his room, "indicating she was clearly worried about his depression." The account that Gauss gives of Birney's death clearly suggests that suicide was the probable cause, and his use of the initials "J.S." to disguise the student's identity supports the assumption that it was not an accident:

> I learned at the station that J.S. had tried to catch a train to the Junction to meet one for New York at 6:40, but the train pulled out while he was rushing across the platform. A taxi man drove him to the Junction but too late for the connection. J.S. gave him a dollar. He walked down the tracks one-third of a mile toward Philadelphia. What thoughts led him to this pass? And yet it is possible to believe, as his parents would so like to do, that he was robbed and thrown upon the tracks. It is odd that his ring was missing and there was nothing, not even a penny, in his pocket when he had at the outset clearly intended to go to New York.[79]

The *Daily Princetonian* reported the following day that the train's engineer "saw the victim leap from behind the pole to the track, [and] he gave a long blast of his whistle and applied his brake but was unable to bring the train to a stop before it struck the man."[80] According to Kitty Kelley, "a close Princeton friend" found a suicide note in Birney's wastebasket and gave it to Birney's brother-in-law, who had come down from New York to identify the body. Kelley claims that Birney was on his way to New York to see his sister, not Nancy, and that "Nancy's Talbot housemates, none of whom ever met Frank Birney, remember her being at Smith the weekend she got the news of his death."[81]

Nancy may have been protecting Frank's family by leaving them out of her pared-down recollection. Though she doesn't reveal her source, Anne Edwards writes in *Early Reagan* that when the call came Nancy was at the apartment of Birney's "brother and sister-in-law." They were so concerned about his mental state that they had persuaded him to come up to New York for a night, and had also contacted Nancy at Smith, who "offered to come down to see if she couldn't help to cheer up the despondent Birney."[82] Another of Birney's Princeton friends, Richard E. Pate, recalled, "We had to bring the body home for the funeral right before Christmas, which was really rough on Frank's parents. Nancy was almost constant in her attendance on Mrs. Birney during that time, and I would say that she as much as anyone made life halfway livable for the Birneys then."[83]

"It was the first time that anybody I was close to had died," Nancy later wrote, "and it was a tremendous shock. My roommate forced me to go out and take long, brisk walks. Frank and I skirted around the subject of marriage, and even though I doubt it would have worked out, he was a dear friend and I felt a great loss. His mother gave me his cigarette case as a memento—a silver case I had given him the previous Christmas with his name engraved on it. He had been carrying that case when he was killed, and I still have it."[84]

Bruce McFarland, who continued to see Nancy

in Chicago when she was home from Smith and he from Princeton, told me she had never mentioned that she was dating a classmate of his. "Apparently it was a terrible blow to her," McFarland said. "But I was unaware of that at the time. Totally unaware. I didn't even know they knew each other. She's very close-mouthed about things like that. And we weren't romantic at all. We just happened to see each other at parties and went out occasionally together."[85]

"I remember how depressed Nancy was," Richard Davis said. "But she never mentioned suicide. No one could be sure. You know, all those kids drank a lot. And he just ran across the railroad tracks one night."[86]

America's entry into World War II at the end of 1941 brought major changes to the Smith campus. Maid service was suspended, and there were regular air raid drills. Some nine hundred Smith students joined the Waves, the women's volunteer branch of the Naval Reserve. Gas shortages also meant less driving back and forth to Amherst, seven miles away.[87] Nonetheless, a group of Smith and Amherst students, including Nancy, formed an ad hoc theater group they called the Bandar-log, after the wild and lawless "monkey people" in Rudyard Kipling's *The Jungle Book*. In the spring of 1942 they put on a musical comedy titled *Ladies on the Loose*, which sent up college life. Nancy did a sexy song-and-dance routine wearing a banana headdress à la Carmen Miranda.[88]

That year she invited a new beau to spend Easter vacation with her family at the Arizona Biltmore. Brent Starck was from Chicago; his family owned P. A. Starck & Company, a manufacturer of pianos and player pianos. "Brent was a red-blooded American boy," Richard Davis recalled. "He was in college someplace in Illinois. I don't think he went to school in the East. But the Starck family was very prominent, very wealthy. We went out to Phoenix on the *Super Chief* together."[89]

That summer Nancy did summer stock with the Coach House Players in Oconomowoc, Wisconsin.[90] A Chicago society columnist reported that the "company was domiciled in the fine old coach house of Danforth Lodge, Mrs. Patrick Valentine's beautiful home on Lac La Belle."[91] Mrs. Valentine was the friend of Edith's who had given a dinner party for Nancy when she came out. This was Nancy's third summer in summer stock, and as she would later write, "Only once in those summers did I actually appear on stage, in a play with Diana Barrymore. I played the maid who announced, 'Madam, dinner is served.' "[92]

Nonetheless, according to Richard Davis, she was so determined to have a theatrical career that "she threatened not to go back to Smith to graduate. My father was five thousand miles away in Europe, but he raised the roof: she *had* to graduate."[93]

* * *

In July 1942, Loyal had been summoned to Washington by Dr. Fred Rankin, a Lexington, Kentucky, surgeon who had been appointed chief of surgery of the U.S. Army. Rankin asked Loyal to go overseas as a senior consultant in neurological surgery in the European theater of operations. He accepted with alacrity, but panicked on the flight back to Chicago: "I was obsessed with the idea of getting home quickly; my disturbing affliction of nostalgia had recurred in a serious attack. I wondered what I would do in England suffering from homesickness." After consulting with Edith, Dr. Pollock, and Dean Cutter, he decided to stick with his decision to accept the appointment.[94] "It all happened so fast," Richard Davis recalled. "He was called to Washington the first week of July '42, and my God, he was gone six weeks later. But it was a great honor."[95]

"The night before Loyal left, Edith had a little party at home," Davis continued. "It was more like a wake. All of our friends came in and out—Colleen and Homer, Margaret and Ed Kelly, Dean Cutter— like they were passing the coffin. This thing went on and on. Betty and Les Weinrott and the Pollocks were the last ones to leave. It was a grim night. Jesus, we were upset. I mean, he was going overseas for God knows how long."[96]

Before flying to England in September, Loyal spent ten days in Washington being documented, immunized, and fitted for his uniform, helmet, and gas mask. In his memoir, he records being taken to "an unforgettable cocktail party" by Chicago socialite Mrs. Henry "Patsy" Field, who introduced him to the wife of General Dwight D. Eisenhower: "Mamie Eisenhower quickly realized that the doctor before her was uncomfortable in his strange clothes, ill at ease in the crowd, and awed by the wife of the general whom he was sure he would see at mess daily, and with whom, undoubtedly, he would have the opportunity of talking at table, even though he might well sit at the foot. She graciously steered the conversation so that a rather detailed recital of my life came pouring out. I was convinced that soon I would be living and working close to the commanding general of the European theater of operations when in excusing myself at Patsy's insistence, Mrs. Eisenhower instructed me to tell Ike she sent her love."[97]

Loyal never laid eyes on Eisenhower during the ten months he was stationed in England, mainly in Oxford, where he consulted with American, British, and Canadian surgeons on the treatment of airmen and soldiers with cerebral, spinal, and peripheral nerve injuries. He was eventually credited with designing an improved protective helmet for airplane crewmen, as well as diagnosing high-altitude frostbite in airmen and recommending ways to prevent and treat it, though he had to fight military bureaucrats every step of the way to have his innovations accepted.[98] In late 1942 he was nearly court-martialed for sending memorandums of his that had been ignored or rejected to colleagues outside the military, but he found a protector in

General Paul R. Hawley, the chief surgeon of the European theater.[99]

"The trials and tribulations that he had in World War II were extraordinary," his son told me. "He actually designed plastic headgear for the Eighth Air Force, and he went through all sorts of ballistic tests at Oxford—and they turned that down. Even more devastating to him was that he recognized high-altitude frostbite in the airmen, but the Air Force physicians insisted that the airmen were burned—and of course they were absolutely wrong. For someone at the age of forty-seven who was a very accomplished neurosurgeon—and used to having his own way, too—it was a real blow to him. He simply couldn't tolerate the bureaucracy. But nevertheless, he was given the Legion of Merit, and he came out a colonel."[100]

While her husband was overseas, Edith apparently had difficulty making ends meet. *Betty and Bob* had been canceled in 1940, and *The Stepmother* in July 1942, though she still sometimes played on the long-running soap opera *Ma Perkins.*[101] According to Richard Davis, "The rent at 199 [East Lake Shore Drive] was $500 a month—I remember hearing that. My father's salary as a lieutenant colonel was about $850 a month, and he probably sent all of that home. I would think that Edith got a lot of help from the mayor. No question. Somebody had to pay the rent while Loyal was away. I don't know who paid Nancy's tuition at

Smith. I don't know who paid my tuition at the Latin School."[102]

If Kelly helped Edith, she also helped him. When he was nominated for a third term in January 1943, she signed on as head of the women's division of the Citizens' Committee for Mayor Ed Kelly. That summer she was given a $75-a-week job as an announcer for the city-sponsored concerts in Grant Park. All through the war years, Edith, along with Colleen Moore Hargrave, put in countless hours as a volunteer at the servicemen's canteens run by Margaret Kelly.[103]

The mayor had inaugurated the main Servicemen's Center in the Loop in August 1941, when America's armed forces were being built up in anticipation of war. Open twenty-four hours a day, the twelve-story renovated former Elks Club offered military personnel everything from hot meals and beds to bowling alleys and big band entertainment free of charge. In 1942, Kelly opened an outdoor facility on twelve lakefront acres in Lincoln Park and an auxiliary canteen for black servicemen on the South Side. As chairman of this enormous undertaking, his wife often put in twelve-hour days, according to Roger Biles. "Her volunteer helpers ranged from society matrons to maids given time off. Approximately thirty-five hundred women, many of them members of the U.S.O. [United Service Organizations], acted as hostesses. . . . An average of ten thousand soldiers passed through the center on a week night, with as many as forty thousand counted on a weekend. . . . The centers constituted such an unqualified success and engendered such good-will for the city—soldiers from across the nation spoke glowingly of their time spent in Chicago, even years later—that reporters called their operation one of Mayor Kelly's finest achievements in office."[104]

In her final semester at Smith, Nancy starred in *Make with the Maximum: A Factory Follies,* "the first musical show ever staged by college girls to entertain war workers."[105] During the spring of 1943, the thirty-three-member cast performed the half-hour revue for more than five thousand workers at defense-related companies, including Westinghouse Electric and U.S. Rubber, in the Connecticut Valley. Wearing a black sheath and long gloves, Nancy played "the Glamour Gal—a Sophisticated Singer." At the start of the show, she complains that the war has deprived her family of their butler and yacht, singing, "Cocktails at five/Dinner at the Stork/Long drives in the country/To get away from New York."[106] At the end, however, she joins the rest of the cast in the show's title song: "Make with the maximum/Give with the brawn!/Make with the maximum/Smother that yawn!"[107]

They performed the show one last time at the Class of 1943's graduation ceremony, on May 23, 1943. Neither Loyal nor Edith was present; he was still in England, and she could not travel owing to wartime restrictions. Despite Nancy's desire to pursue an acting career, she returned to Chicago to stay with her mother until her stepfather completed his tour of service. She found Edith embroiled in a rather ridiculous mess.

From 1942 to 1946, according to several Reagan biographers, Edith was secretly employed as an "undercover policewoman" by the city, at a salary of $2,141 a year. On May 8, 1943, she had invited several underage sailors to meet young women at her apartment, where a police captain and a lieutenant commander of the shore patrol gave the boys money to take their dates to particular bars; when they were served drinks, police swooped in and arrested the bartenders and owners. The charges were thrown out of court later that month on the grounds of entrapment, "after one of the sailors testified that the raids had indeed been planned at the apartment of a 'Mrs. Davis on the North Lake Shore.'"[108] Edith denied everything, but reporters pursued her persistently. When one got Nancy on the telephone, she answered repeatedly, "Not that I know of."[109] For several days in early June, all four Chicago newspapers ran front-page stories with headlines such as IS MRS. DAVIS A LIQUOR COP? SHE WON'T TALK and MRS. DAVIS, SOCIALITE, IS A POLICEWOMAN.[110]

Nancy would later tie her mother's police job to her volunteer work at the Servicemen's Center. "There was a navy yard nearby," she writes in *My Turn*, "and when she learned that some of these young kids were being picked up by prostitutes and infected with venereal diseases, she had herself sworn in as a policewoman so she could go out on the streets of Chicago and protect those boys."[111]

Richard Davis was more forthcoming. "She must have been on the city payroll," he told me, "because one night she went on a raid with the police. Some reporter took a picture, which was on the front page of the *Chicago Tribune*. And she didn't have her teeth in. It was a god-awful sort of mini-scandal. I remember this appeared in the Saturday morning paper. Sunday morning she took me to lunch at the Casino Club. All the old biddies greeted her, and she aimed her fingers at them and said, 'Bang, bang! Stick 'em up! I'm Dick Tracy!' You know, deflecting all the gossip—and she got away with it. It was amazing what she could get away with."[112]

Edith had become something of a legend in the Windy City. Lillian Gish, whom she always picked up at the station, later remarked, "When I'd get in the car and come down Michigan Avenue with her, all the people would stop and ask her to do something for them. The police, too; she practically ran Chicago."[113]

That summer Edith sublet their apartment, and she and Nancy moved into a suite at the Drake Hotel. Nancy was invited to join the Junior League of Chicago and was a bridesmaid at Jean Wescott's wedding.[114] She volunteered as a nurse's aide at Cook County Hospital, where she was assigned to the men's ward. "The hospitals were all terribly shorthanded and needed all the help they could get," she recalled. "I did a lot of dirty work, but it was a job that had to be done." She also took a job as a salesgirl at Marshall Field. "I wanted to work to make some money and keep myself occupied. My most unforgettable experience there was catching a shoplifter."[115] Her account of that incident is one of the most dramatically told stories in *Nancy*:

> A woman was circling around a display case in the center of the floor, and I looked up just in time to see her put a piece of jewelry in her purse. I looked around for the store detective, for anyone, but no one was available. I went up to the woman and asked if I could be of help to her. She said, No, she was just looking. . . . No one had really prepared me for what to do in such an emergency. She started to leave and I was frantic. As calmly as possible, I said, "Don't you think you better give me back the jewelry before you go?" Whereupon she broke away and started to run for the elevator, with me hot on her heels. When I think about it now, we must have made quite a sight. The store detective appeared miraculously from nowhere, and the woman was stopped at the elevator. She turned, took hold of the top of my button-down dress, and tore it right down the front. The detective took both of us and hustled us to the store offices. Here he found that her shopping bags were full of loot she had lifted from this and other stores. I had to tell the whole story, all the while certain

this woman was putting some kind of curse on me as she glared at me. . . . Later, I was reprimanded for stopping the shoplifter in the store. I learned that you have to wait until the shoplifter has left the store to substantiate the charge that the customer had no intention of paying for whatever was taken. I was given a twenty-five-dollar check as a reward, and even though I had gone about it all wrong, I was very proud![116]

In June 1943, General Hawley appointed Loyal to the first Anglo-American medical mission to the Soviet Union. Accompanied by two agents of the Soviet secret police, the seven members of the mission flew to Moscow via Gibraltar, Tripoli, Cairo, and Tehran. Their suite at the National Hotel was bugged, Loyal noted in his memoir. He also noted the large portraits of Charlie Chaplin and Paul Robeson on display beside those of Churchill, Stalin, and Roosevelt at the headquarters of the Soviet's cultural exchange organization. After spending the Fourth of July at Spasso House, the residence of the American ambassador, watching Mickey Mouse cartoons and lunching on hot dogs and Coca-Cola, and attending a performance of *Swan Lake* with an audience of factory workers whose body odor Loyal found "overpowering," their tour of Moscow hospitals and research institutes began. One of his American colleagues, Harvard professor Elliot Cutler, Loyal writes, "had insisted upon taking a million units of penicillin as an introductory gift, like taking wampum to the Indians. The drug had just been released for use and was scarce. It was received coldly with the statement that it was nothing new to them and was available for the care of their wounded. This was the first bald demonstration of their facility for lying to support their claims to priority and superiority."[117]

At the Institute for Neurological Surgery, Loyal was so dismissive of a demonstration of the Russians' nerve graft technique, which he undiplomatically pointed out had been proven "completely useless" during World War I, that the other members of the mission "were not hesitant later in indicating that my doubting attitude might well impair the entire success of the mission and, if carried into other fields, might even destroy the alliance between the Western nations and the Soviet Union and allow Germany to win the war."[118] But at dinner that evening the institute's head, General Burdenko, rearranged the place cards so that Loyal was next to him, and he heaped praise upon the American for his bluntness and honesty; Loyal saw this as a lesson in how to handle Communist apparatchiks. On July 11 the mission traveled to the front, 125 miles southwest of Moscow, where they toured the wards of a casualty-clearing station hidden in a thick forest and were served caviar, smoked fish, strawberries, and large quantities of vodka. A second feast awaited them that evening at an evacuation hospital, and although Loyal refused to participate in all the obligatory vodka toasts, he still became violently ill during the night. The next morning at breakfast, the Russian medical officer who had mocked him for switching to water the night before complimented him for standing up to his hosts' demands.[119] One wonders how many times Loyal told these tales of how to handle the Soviets to his son-in-law before including them in his 1973 memoir.

His wartime Russian experience became part of the Loyal Davis legend. A 1962 magazine profile summarized it thus: "He was greatly impressed by the prompt field treatment given the wounded by the Red Army doctors—both men and women. He found, however, that Russian surgeons at times used inferior techniques because the Kremlin did not permit a free exchange of knowledge between them and their American counterparts."[120]

By the beginning of August, Loyal had returned to Oxford and resumed his battle with his nemesis, General Malcolm Grow, the surgeon to the Eighth Air Force, who was now taking credit for first recognizing high-altitude frostbite. A week later Loyal was ordered to Washington to present his studies at the Pentagon. At a meeting with Colonel Walter Jensen, a top Air Force medical officer, Loyal was again confronted by General Grow, whom he angrily attacked for placing "every kind of an obstruction in the way." The meeting ended with Jensen's demanding that Grow apologize to Loyal. "Grow mumbled that there were no hard feelings on his part," Loyal later recounted, "but I said that there were hard feelings on my part and they concerned the dishonest statements that had been made and were continuing to be made."[121]

Suffering from amebic dysentery picked up in Russia, Loyal was sent from Washington to an Army hospital in Chicago. After a stay in a second hospital in Michigan, he was finally cured at the Walter Reed Hospital in Washington and discharged from the Army. In an anecdote told by Richard Davis, pitting Loyal against Morton Downey, the popular entertainer, his father was still capable of combativeness. "Morton Downey was a great friend of Ed and Margaret Kelly's, and we would see him at the Sunday dinners at 209. It so happened that the day Dr. Loyal returned from Europe he stayed at the Waldorf-Astoria in New York, and Morton Downey was the first person he saw. They were in the elevator, along with several generals, and Dr. Loyal started to embrace Morton Downey, who just turned away and talked to the generals. The next summer Downey was visiting the Kellys, and at dinner Dr. Loyal absolutely ripped him to pieces in front of everybody. He said, 'I'd been overseas doing all these things, and you were so impressed by the stars on their shoulders that you didn't even say hello to me, Morton. You weren't gentleman enough, and I don't even want to be in the same room with you.' It was absolutely devastating. And Morton Downey left. It didn't faze Ed Kelly a bit. He knew Dr. Loyal was principled, and he didn't want to see his good friend treated this way by Morton Downey, who was a real lightweight."[122]

* * *

Life slowly returned to normal in the Davis household after Loyal came home and resumed his work. In March 1944, Edith and Loyal made a trip to Los Angeles to visit Walter and Nan Huston, Spencer Tracy, and Nazimova. By June they had moved back into their apartment. Richard Davis, who had spent one term at Princeton in 1943 before joining the Army, recalled being home on leave in July 1944 when Franklin Roosevelt was nominated for a fourth term in Chicago. He attended the convention with his parents, the Kellys, and Spencer Tracy.

"The big issue was black voting rights," he said, "and Spencer Tracy just went bananas about this. He could not understand why there were all these ridiculous rules about blacks voting in the South, and he didn't waste any time telling Mayor Kelly. I can't say that my father disagreed with Spencer Tracy. I don't think he said anything. He respected Spencer Tracy's viewpoint. They were very, very close. Spencer Tracy and Katharine Hepburn both spent time in our apartment."[123] Dr. Daniel Ruge, who became Loyal's clerk that fall and partner in 1952, pointed out that Loyal tended to keep his views to himself around Edith's more liberal friends, adding, "But that doesn't mean he agreed with them."[124]

Tracy had been thought of as a "hidebound arch-conservative" in the 1930s,[125] but his political views became more moderate after 1941, when he began his celebrated affair with Katharine

Hepburn, a Connecticut blueblood with decidedly progressive views. They would remain semisecret lovers until his death in 1967, but Tracy, a devout Catholic who had once seriously considered becoming a priest, could never bring himself to divorce his wife. According to Nancy Reagan, Edith managed to remain friends with Louise Tracy even while playing hostess to "Spence and Kate."[126]

For all Edith's show business worldliness, however, she was not about to accept adultery in her own marriage. "When Dr. Loyal was in England, he had a love affair with his English driver," Richard Davis revealed. "And this woman came over to the United States, presumably to get married. I remember there was a big blowup in the summer of 1944, when she appeared in Chicago. That was the only time I've ever heard or seen Edith hysterical. Edith was just off her rocker because this woman had shown up. Apparently Loyal was so homesick, and this woman was, I'm sure, of great solace and comfort to him. But it certainly upset Edith. I didn't know what was going on, but I remember how steady Nancy was. She said, 'Dick, don't worry. Everything will be all right. Just go somewhere now, and I'll take care of it.'" After calming her mother down, Nancy had a talk with her stepfather, although she never told Richard what was said. "There were a lot of things between Loyal and Nancy that I never knew about."[127]

That summer was a time of romantic turmoil for Nancy as well. In her senior year at Smith she had "started going quite seriously" with James Platt White Jr., an Amherst student from a well-to-do Massachusetts family. They decided to get engaged on a visit she made to California in May 1944, when he was stationed on a Navy aircraft carrier off San Diego.[128] This was Nancy's first trip on her own to California, and she spent much of her time in the company of her mother's friends. She stayed with Lillian Gish, who had returned to Hollywood in late 1941 and, perhaps hoping to put her America First stigma behind her, accepted the part of a Norwegian resistance fighter's wife in *Commandos Strike at Dawn*, her first movie in ten years. Nancy told me that Gish took her to a party at the home of Lady Mendl, the decorator also known as Elsie de Wolfe.[129] Nearly thirty years earlier Edith Luckett had been introduced to Alla Nazimova at the New York townhouse of de Wolfe and her then companion, Bessie Marbury, whom she had left in 1926 to marry British diplomat Sir Charles Mendl.

Nancy saw her godmother for the last time on this trip. At sixty-five, Nazimova was in failing health, living in one of the bungalows on her old Sunset Boulevard estate, which she had been forced to turn into a hotel in 1927, when her silent film career came to an abrupt end. (The Garden of Alla had become the Garden of Allah.)[130] "It was so small, nicely furnished but. . . . How terrible it must be for her after all that fame and glamour," Nancy told Nazimova's biographer years later. One night Nancy went to the theater with Glesca Marshall and Emily Woodruff, a Coca-Cola heiress who would become Glesca's lover after Nazimova's death from a blood clot the following year. Another night, Nancy took her fiancé to meet Nazimova, who was quite impressed. "I think I met one of our great future statesmen," she recorded in her diary, "perhaps even a president."[131]

On June 24, Loyal and Edith gave a party at home to announce Nancy's engagement to James Platt White Jr. His parents presented Nancy with a diamond engagement ring from Tiffany's on their son's behalf, and the Chicago and Boston papers ran the announcement on their society pages.[132] Later that summer, however, Nancy broke off the engagement. As she writes in her memoir, "It was a heady, exhilarating time, and I was swept up in the glamour of the war, wartime engagements, and waiting for the boys who were away. I realized I had made a mistake. It would have been unfair to him and to me. It wasn't easy to break off the engagement, but it was the best thing for us both. We were not meant to be married, but we remain friends to this day."[133]

"Jim White was the nicest guy," Richard Davis said, "handsome, upright, straightforward, courteous. But Edith told me—'gay' wasn't used then—'He's just a homo, Dick.' I could never figure out how a girl like Nancy could have missed that."[134]

White never talked about Nancy or their engagement. When she was First Lady, he discreetly contacted her through her friend Jerry Zipkin to let her know that he was seriously ill. Zipkin told a friend,

"I heard from the man Nancy was engaged to after college. He was gay."[135]

As fall approached, Nancy was getting bored and frustrated working at a department store and living at home in Chicago. She later wrote, "Soon a call came from ZaSu Pitts. I suspect that Mother had a hand in it. ZaSu told me there was a part available for me in a play she had on tour, *Ramshackle Inn*. That first part is the hardest to get. Until then, when producers or casting directors or agents ask you what you have done, you can only speak of college plays or summer stock. When you get your first part in a professional production, then you have a credit. I grabbed the offer and joined the company in Detroit, where the girl who had been playing the part was leaving. I played the role of a girl who has been held captive in an upstairs room. At one point, I came downstairs, spoke my three lines, and was returned to my room. It wasn't much but it was a start, and I was out on my own with the best wishes of my parents."[136]

Ramshackle Inn had opened on Broadway in January of that year to mediocre reviews—the newspaper *PM* called it "a dreary piece of hocus-pocus with a soporific first act and a helter skelter second and third."[137] But ZaSu Pitts was a big draw, with a long career behind her as one of America's most prolific and popular comediennes. Everything about her was funny, from her name, which was real, to her "blinking eyes, fluttering hands, and quavering voice."[138] Yet she gave two of the most highly praised dramatic performances of the silent film era in Erich von Stroheim's *Greed* and *The Wedding March*. Born in Kansas and raised in Santa Cruz, California, she was made a comedy star by the director King Vidor in the 1920s. She was forty-six when Nancy went to work with her. Off screen, she was married to a Pasadena business-man and best friends with Hedda Hopper, with whom she shared a devotion to Catholicism and high fashion and an antipathy to Communism.

Pitts took Nancy under her wing, sharing her hotel rooms and dressing rooms with the young actress. "It was a brand-new world to me and, not being used to the road, having a friend was very comforting. ZaSu had been a great beauty in her youth and at this point in her career looked age-less," Nancy wrote. "We traveled with the play across country and wound up in New York, playing the 'subway circuit.' We played theaters in Brooklyn, Long Island, The Bronx, and so forth."[139]

When *Ramshackle Inn* ended its tour in New York, Nancy decided to stay and pursue a theater career. She told me many years later, "When I graduated from college, I hadn't found the man I wanted to marry, and I certainly didn't want to sit in Chicago and be a post-deb. So I decided I wanted to be an actress. I'd done summer stock when I was in col-lege, and I had been exposed to actors all those years. Of course, I'd seen the best. You know, I'd seen people who were very successful."[140]

CHAPTER SEVEN

RONNIE AND JANE
1941–1946

From Stettin in the Baltic to Trieste in the Adriatic an iron curtain has descended across the Continent. . . . In a great number of countries, far from the Russian frontiers and throughout the world, Communist fifth columns are established and work in complete unity and absolute obedience to the directions they receive from the Communist center.

> Winston Churchill, "Iron Curtain Speech," March 5, 1946

Show people are emotional. You'll find very few in this business who participate in politics on an intellectual level. Slam-bang convictions, violent loyalties, passionate enmities, purple principles, and utter naïveté—these are the ingredients of political action in show business.

> Robert Ardrey, quoted by Stephen Vaughn in *Ronald Reagan in Hollywood*[1]

On December 2, 1941, five days before Pearl Harbor, Warners' publicity department announced that Ronald Reagan had received more fan mail that year than any other male star at the studio except Errol Flynn; James Cagney was in third place.[2] A few months earlier, a Gallup survey had ranked Reagan 82nd among the top 100 stars. By the beginning of 1942, he was tied for 74th place with Laurence Olivier, and Gallup estimated that he was earning $52,000 per film, while Flynn was earning $157,000 and Clark Gable, America's box office king, $210,000.[3]

Reagan was getting leading roles in A movies consistently now, and in early 1941 Warners had even lent him to MGM for *The Bad Man,* with Wallace Beery and Lionel Barrymore. He was "duly impressed" by the poshest of the studios but was also happy to return to "the meat and potatoes atmosphere of Warners,"[4] where executive producer Hal Wallis promptly cast him as a concert pianist in *Million Dollar Baby*. He was in such demand that he had to do reshoots for *International Squadron* and the opening scenes of *Nine Lives Are Not Enough* on alternating days during June 1941; the latter would win him critical praise for his comic turn as a hapless newspaper reporter.[5]

Reagan was filming *Kings Row* when he received his first call to active duty in August 1941, but the studio was able to secure a deferment for him until the end of production. "The first time I ever met Ronald Reagan was on the set of *Kings*

Row," the set designer and producer Jacques Mapes told me. "Ann Sheridan was a friend of mine, and she was shooting *Kings Row* in the morning and *The Man Who Came to Dinner* in the afternoon. That's the way they used to work at Warners. I thought what he was doing was really remarkable—that role was such a stretch for him. It's too bad that he didn't have more properties like that earlier. And then the war came in."[6]

Reagan received two more deferments and starred in two more A movies produced by Hal Wallis—*Juke Girl,* a message movie about migrant farm workers in Florida, co-starring Ann Sheridan again, and *Desperate Journey,* a pro-British war picture directed by Raoul Walsh and co-starring Errol Flynn—before he went into the Army on April 20, 1942. Jack Warner tried to pull strings in Washington until the last minute, hoping to pair Reagan and Sheridan for a third time in the upcoming *Casablanca,* after the tremendous box office success of *Kings Row,* which had been released that February. There was also talk of the studio's casting Reagan in Frank Capra's *Arsenic and Old Lace* and giving him the title role in *The Will Rogers Story,* a biography of the plainspoken cowboy-philosopher.[7]

One of Ronnie's major concerns before going away was arranging for his fifty-nine-year-old mother's well-being. He had no trouble supporting Nelle on the $1,650-a-week salary that Lew Wasserman had secured when he renegotiated his contract with Warners the previous fall. But Jane, who was making $1,450 a week, would now have to pay the mortgage and support herself and Maureen on her own. There was no question of Nelle's moving in with her daughter-in-law. According to Leonora Hornblow, Jane was not very fond of Nelle—or her brother-in-law, Neil, for that matter—and "had them around as little as she could."[8] Reagan tried to get the studio to pay his mother $75 a week to answer his fan mail, but Jack Warner refused on the grounds that other stars going off to war would make similar demands. He finally agreed to give Reagan an interest-free loan of $3,900, from which Nelle would draw a weekly salary for one year.[9] (The arrangement was not renewed at the year's end, though Warner, in a typically paternalistic gesture, later forgave the loan.)[10]

Although Ronnie and Jane had bought the land on Cordell Drive and started building their dream house in 1941, they did not move in until March 1942. Jane was still furnishing it with decorator Connie Rennick on the eve of her husband's departure for Fort Mason, in San Francisco. On Saturday, April 18, she gave Ronnie a surprise farewell party at home with many of their Hollywood friends, including Pat O'Brien, Ann Sheridan, Jack and Mary Benny, and Barbara Stanwyck and Robert Taylor. Ronnie knew something was up when he returned home from a baseball game with Bob Cobb, the owner of the Brown Derby restaurants, and saw sixteen Cadillacs lining the driveway.[11] On Sunday night the Reagans were photographed having dinner at the Hollywood Brown Derby—he in uniform, she in a dark dress, matching hat, and fur wrap—before driving to Glendale, where he boarded the overnight train to San Francisco.[12]

The following morning Reagan reported for duty as a second lieutenant in the Army Cavalry and was given a physical examination. His eyesight was so poor that one of the examining doctors told him, "If we sent you overseas, you'd shoot a general." A second added, "Yes, and you'd miss him." Thus disqualified for combat, he spent his first seven weeks in the armed forces as a "liaison officer loading convoys with troops bound for Australia."[13] His greatest triumph was persuading Jeanette MacDonald, the favorite movie star of Fort Mason's commanding general, to give a concert on I Am an American Day—a new national holiday created by Congress earlier that year—for seventeen thousand soldiers waiting to be shipped overseas.[14]

Three days before Reagan reported for duty, Jack Warner had been sworn in as a commissioned officer in the Army Air Corps, the predecessor of the U.S. Air Force. The patriotic mogul had been lobbying Washington for months to establish "a very effective propaganda department" at his studio, with him in charge.[15] At a meeting in March with General Henry "Hap" Arnold, chief of staff of the Army Air Corps, Warner, not entirely in jest, proposed that he be made a one-star general. He didn't get the rank he wanted, but by late June the newly established First Motion Picture Unit of the Army Air Corps (FMPU) was temporarily installed at Lieutenant Colonel Warner's Burbank studio, and Second Lieutenant Reagan had been transferred there from San Francisco.[16]

"Jane Wyman and wee daughter are probably the happiest people in town since husband and daddy Ronald Reagan has been temporarily sent back to Burbank to make Government shorts," reported *Photoplay.*[17] The new assignment meant that Reagan frequently spent evenings and week-ends at home, a comfort to Jane in the jittery atmosphere of wartime Los Angeles. Fear of an imminent Japanese attack was acute during the first half of 1942, when the Japanese fleet still dominated the Pacific. Paranoia about a fifth col-umn among the city's large Japanese population was so widespread that on February 19, 1942, President Roosevelt signed Executive Order 9066, authorizing the internment of 112,000 Japanese and Japanese-Americans at inland military camps for the duration. On February 23, a Japanese sub-marine shelled an oil field near Santa Barbara, damaging a derrick and a pier. The following night, Los Angeles residents were awakened at 2:30 in the morning by air-raid sirens responding to reports of as many as one hundred unidentified aircraft flying over the coast, and antiaircraft fire lit up the sky for five hours. The so-called Battle of Los Angeles was a false alarm,[18] but the city remained on complete war status, with gun batteries installed at Pacific Palisades, Playa del Rey, Manhattan Beach, and Redondo Beach, klieg lights spaced along the shore at five-mile intervals scanning the ocean nightly, and frequent air-raid drills and blackouts keeping people on edge.[19]

Although Reagan would later quip that he "flew a desk" during the war, his military service, in Hollywood terms, fell somewhere between that of Captain Jimmy Stewart, who volunteered as a bomber pilot and won a Distinguished Flying Cross for his 25 combat missions over Germany, and that of John Wayne, who was so determined not to put his career on hold that he managed to secure deferment after deferment while making movies with—and love to—Marlene Dietrich at Republic Pictures.[20] Errol Flynn, Cary Grant, and Frank Sinatra also avoided wartime service, while Robert Montgomery and Robert Taylor joined the Navy, and Tyrone Power became a Marine. Jack Warner wasn't the only mogul who signed up: Darryl F. Zanuck, the head of Fox, "donated his entire string of 20 Argentine polo ponies to West Point"[21] before flying off to the European front as a colonel in the Army Signal Corps. Director John Ford, who served as a captain in the Navy, earned a Purple Heart for wounds suffered during the tide-turning Battle of Midway in June 1942.[22] According to Otto Friedrich in *City of Nets: A Portrait of Hollywood in the 1940's,* "By October 1942 some 2,700 Hollywood people—12 percent of the total number employed in the movie business—had joined the armed forces."[23]

Those who did not don uniforms entertained the troops and promoted the sale of war bonds—337 stars sold almost $850 million in bonds in September 1942 alone.[24] Bette Davis was the president and MCA chairman Jules Stein the chief underwriter of the Hollywood Stage Door Canteen, where every night thousands of GIs danced and socialized with gorgeous movie stars. Bob Hope kicked off his Hollywood Victory Caravan at a White House garden party in April 1942; after touring sixty-five military bases across the country, he took the show overseas.[25] Hedy Lamarr and Lana Turner sold kisses, for $25,000 and $50,000, respectively, to aid the war bond drive, which had been initiated by Treasury Secretary Henry Morgenthau and was spearheaded by MGM publicity director Howard Dietz. As head of the actors' division of the Hollywood Victory Committee, Clark Gable sent his wife, Carole Lombard, on one of the first tours, in January 1942, to her home state of Indiana, where she sold $2 million worth of bonds. Lombard, her mother, and her publicist were killed when the plane taking them back to Los Angeles crashed near Las Vegas. After six months of heavy drinking, Gable enlisted as a private in the Army Air Corps, where he served as a combat cameraman in Britain, rose to the rank of major, and eventually was furloughed to Fort Roach, as the First Motion Picture Unit headquarters came to be known. Gable's discharge papers were signed by Ronald

Reagan, who by then had risen to the rank of captain.[26]

Reagan would later claim that he had turned down a promotion to major—"who was I to be a major for serving in California, without ever hearing a shot fired in anger?"[27]—and he was undoubtedly self-conscious about his lack of combat service. But the FMPU was doing important work at Fort Roach, and Reagan was well suited for his assignment. As Stephen Vaughn explains in *Ronald Reagan in Hollywood*, "General Arnold's headquarters used its films to several ends: to increase enlistments, train servicemen, build morale, define the enemy, create unity, and promote air power. . . . Reagan seemed an appropriate choice to narrate and appear in the FMPU's films, even if in reality he did not like to fly. Warner Bros. had already created an image for him as a pilot-hero skilled at using aviation technology in *Secret Service of the Air, Murder in the Air, International Squadron,* and *Desperate Journey.*"[28]

Reagan's first film for the military was *Rear Gunner*, which was designed to make turreteers seem as heroic as bomber pilots. He would go on to act in or narrate such indoctrination movies as *Target Tokyo, Beyond the Line of Duty, Fight for the Sky, Land and Live in the Desert, Fighter Bomber Against Mechanized Targets,* and *For God and Country* (in which he played a Catholic chaplain whose two best friends are a Protestant and a Jew and who dies in battle trying to save an American Indian buddy).[29]

Reagan also emerged as an effective administrator in the military. Shortly after arriving at Burbank, he was made personnel director of the FMPU, charged with interviewing and processing producers, directors, writers, technicians, and fellow actors. "A great many people to this day harbor a feeling that the personnel of the motion picture unit were somehow draft dodgers avoiding danger," he later wrote. "The Army doesn't play that way. There was a special job the Army wanted done and it was after men who could do that job. The overwhelming majority of men and officers serving at our post were limited service like myself, or men who by reason of family, age, or health were exempt from normal military duty."[30]

In the fall of 1942, Jack Warner gave up his commission—though he still insisted on being called Colonel—to turn out his own war movies at his own studio, and the FMPU leased the nine-acre Hal Roach complex in Culver City, which had five soundstages and state-of-the-art special effects facilities. Warner was replaced as commanding officer by Major Paul Mantz, a stunt pilot who won his appointment because he was the only man at Fort Roach—also dubbed Fort Wacky—who could actually fly a plane. For all the jokes, however, by early 1943 the "Culver City Commandos" numbered more than one thousand enlisted men and officers who were turning out eight films a month, featuring such stars as Alan Ladd, Arthur Kennedy, and Lee J. Cobb.[31] That July, Reagan received his promotion to captain, and in December he was made post adjutant, the second-highest position at Fort Roach.[32] He was known as a stickler for following rules and respecting rank. When Lieutenant William Holden was transferred to Fort Roach in early 1945, Captain Reagan kept him standing at attention for twenty-five minutes while he recited the regulations. Holden called him a son of a bitch behind his back, but the two actors soon became best friends.[33]

Warner Bros. did its best to keep Reagan in the limelight while he was in uniform. Ronnie and Jane were on *Modern Screen*'s January 1943 cover, and they were frequently photographed on his weekend leaves at events such as the premiere of *Yankee Doodle Dandy* and the California State Military Guard Ball at the Hollywood Palladium. In February 1943, Jack Warner arranged for Reagan to take the lead in *This Is the Army*, a musical based on Irving Berlin's Broadway show of the previous year. The premiere at the Hollywood Theater in July was a major publicity event—Ronnie wore his dress uniform, Wyman a hot-pink cocktail dress with a silver-fox cape and gobs of amethyst jewelry. The movie was a huge hit, taking in $10 million at the box office, with Warners donating its profits to Army War Relief.[34] As a result of its success and that of *Kings Row*, Reagan was rated Hollywood's top box-office draw for 1942–43.[35] He was on the cover of *Modern Screen* solo in October 1944, looking as handsome and comfortable in uniform as he had in ten of the thirty movies he had made at Warners before he entered the military.[36]

Jane's career, however, remained in the doldrums, with Warners continuing to cast her in run-of-the-mill comedies, musicals, and war movies. In early 1944 she went on a twelve-week tour to promote war bond sales and *The Doughgirls*, "a honey of a funny—about love and money!," as the ad campaign put it, in which she co-starred with Ann Sheridan and Alexis Smith.[37] Like a good soldier's wife, Jane also put in many hours at the Hollywood Canteen, and was rewarded with a part in Warners' 1944 musical of the same title, along with the studio's reigning triumvirate of strong-willed leading ladies: Bette Davis, Joan Crawford, and Barbara Stanwyck. At the end of that year she was finally given a dramatic role in a major picture when Warners loaned her out to Paramount for *The Lost Weekend,* directed by Billy Wilder and starring Ray Milland as an alcoholic writer. Jane was cast as Milland's almost masochistically devoted girlfriend. It would prove to be her breakthrough role to stardom.

In August 1944, as Allied forces pushed the Japanese back across the Pacific, the FMPU embarked on a top secret project designed to assist in the bombing and invasion of Japan itself. The film unit's set designers and special effects wizards built a miniature replica of Tokyo and other targets on the floor of one of the soundstages and mounted cameras on cranes above it so that simulated bombing runs could be filmed and sent to the front to brief bombing crews before they took off for Japan. In turn, footage from the actual raids was sent back to Fort Roach, where the model was adjusted to reflect bombing damage. Security surrounding the project was so tight that, Reagan later wrote, "it was enough to make all of us fearful of talking in our sleep, or taking an extra drink. We knew the bomb targets well in advance, including the proposed time of the bombing raid, because our geniuses—informed in advance of possible weather conditions—were even floating the right kind of clouds between the camera and the target."[38]

He played the briefing officer in these films, directing the pilots toward their targets as if he were sitting in the cockpit with them, thirty thousand feet above the Pacific, rather than in a projection room in Culver City—a task not so different from giving play-by-play descriptions of baseball games he wasn't actually watching. "I would usually open with lines such as, 'Gentlemen, you are approaching the coast of Honshu on a course of three hundred degrees. You are now twenty miles offshore. To your left, if you are on course, you should be able to see a narrow inlet. To your right . . .'" His closing line was always the same: "Bombs away."[39]

Reagan later said that his disillusionment with big government—"the first crack in my staunch liberalism"—began during his last year and a half in the Army. He attributed his nascent doubts to his experience with the civil service bureaucrats who arrived at Fort Roach halfway through the war. Until then, the FMPU, because of the sensitive nature of its work, had made do without civilian workers. According to Reagan, the new arrivals were transferred to Culver City after the Army, acting under pressure from Congress, ordered a 35 percent cut in civilians at all installations that employed them. "Neither Congress nor the military had figured on the ability of the Civil Service to achieve eternal life here on earth," Reagan later wrote. "As fast as reductions took place, new positions were found for the displaced."[40] Whereas the FMPU's personnel section had eighteen employees to handle the records of 1,200 men, he noted, the civil service sent more than twice that number to keep track of the 250 civilians assigned to Fort Roach. Furthermore, Reagan asserted, incompetent workers could be removed only by promoting them to better jobs, supervisors opposed reductions in the workforce because their own pay was based on how many workers they had under them, and requests to destroy unnecessary documents were met with orders from Washington to copy each document before destroying it. Although Reagan would one day deride such inefficiency and empire building as "the peculiar ways of the federal bureaucracy," and use his Fort Roach anecdotes in political speeches, during the war years his New Deal beliefs were still strong.[41]

While filming *This Is the Army*, he spent his lunch hours debating politics with his Republican co-star, George Murphy, who like Reagan had been brought up a Democrat and was hooked on politics at an early age. Murphy, however, had switched parties in 1939, and was heavily influenced by his good friend FBI director J. Edgar Hoover, who told him that the New Deal was a Communist plot.[42] For all their heated arguments, the two actors grew close. Two decades later Senator Murphy and Governor Reagan would be the first and second movie stars, respectively, to hold high government office, and the latter would write of the former, "I owe a great deal to this cool, dapper guy who had to deal with me and my early white-eyed liberal daze. There were some of our associates, I'm sure, who believed I was as red as Moscow, but Murph never wavered in his defense of me even though I ranted and railed at him as an arch-reactionary (which he isn't)."[43]

As his words make clear, Reagan moved left—not right—during the war, along with the Roosevelt administration and most of the movie industry's liberal Democrats. The Soviet Union was now America's ally, and once again Hollywood Communists, leftists, and liberals were united in the great anti-Fascist battle, as they had been from 1936 to 1939, when the Hitler-Stalin pact tore the first Popular Front apart. Even Louis B. Mayer and Jack Warner, prodded by the White House, joined the pro-Soviet campaign, releasing *Song of Russia* and *Mission to Moscow,* respectively, in 1943: the first was scripted by secret Communist Party members Paul Jarrico and Richard Collins; the second, written by leftist Howard Koch, was so soft on Stalin that conservative critics called it *Submission to Moscow.*[44]

In 1943, Reagan became friendly with Bernard Vorhaus, an FMPU writer-director who had been active in the Hollywood Anti-Nazi League in the late 1930s and would be blacklisted as an alleged Communist. The New York–born, Harvard-educated Vorhaus was Fort Roach's resident left-wing intellectual, and Reagan was no doubt flattered to be taken seriously by him. Vorhaus directed Reagan in the instructional short *Recognition of the Japanese Zero Fighter* in January 1943, and according to Edmund Morris, Reagan and Vorhaus developed the same kind of "political intimacy" that Reagan would later share with his longtime California aide and national security adviser, William Clark. Although Vorhaus was never able to win Reagan over entirely to his pro-Moscow views, he told friends at the time, "Dutch R. knows more about politics than any other actor in Hollywood."[45]

That year Reagan joined the Hollywood Democratic Committee—curiously, for someone so highly opinionated, he had managed to avoid joining any political organization until then. The HDC had been formed as a "support group" for the Roosevelt administration after the Republicans made significant gains in the 1942 midterm elections, but it was more radical than its name suggested. Several Communists, including the Party's not-so-secret Hollywood leader, screenwriter John Howard Lawson, sat on its board, alongside such liberal stalwarts as Walter Huston, Gene Kelly, Olivia de Havilland, and Ira Gershwin. So did Herbert Sorrell, the fiery Hollywood union leader, who may have been a Communist. Officially chaired by liberal screenwriter Marc Connelly, the HDC was actually run by George Pepper, "an energetic young violinist whose career was cut short by a hand injury" and who was later identified as a Communist Party member.[46]

With nearly one thousand members by January 1944, the HDC had "emerged as the most sophisticated partisan political organization Hollywood had ever seen: well-funded, fluent in the latest campaign technology, and committed to hardball campaigning," according to Ronald Brownstein in *The Power and the Glitter: The Hollywood–Washington Connection*.[47] In the July primaries, it was credited with unseating anti-FDR Representative John M. Costello—a Rita Hayworth broadcast castigating him as a "renegade Democrat" was thought to be the final blow—and with securing the party's nomination in a second Los Angeles congressional district for one of its members, actress Helen Gahagan Douglas.

As the influence and prestige of the HDC grew, the movie colony's frustrated right wing reacted by forming an activist organization of its own. In February 1944, one hundred industry conservatives, including Clark Gable, Gary Cooper, John Wayne, Ginger Rogers, Irene Dunne, Barbara Stanwyck and Robert Taylor, Adolphe Menjou, and

Walt Disney, met at the Beverly Wilshire Hotel to announce the formation of the Motion Picture Alliance for the Preservation of American Ideals. Director Sam Wood, with whom Reagan had argued politics on the set of *Kings Row*, was named president, and MGM screenwriter and producer James Kevin McGuinness, a favorite of Louis B. Mayer's, became executive committee chairman. Both were fanatic anti-Communists, eager to purge Hollywood of what they saw as a dangerously subversive minority and convinced that the Roosevelt administration was a Trojan horse packed with Reds and pinkos poised to take over the government.[48]

"The American motion picture is, and will continue to be, held by Americans for the American people, in the interests of America, and dedicated to the preservation and continuance of the American scene and the American way of life," Wood declared at the Beverly Wilshire meeting.[49] The group's Statement of Principles—which attempted to cross Harry Warner with Abraham Lincoln, but now sounds proto-Nixonian—was reprinted in full-page ads in the trade papers the following morning:

In our special field of motion pictures, we resent the growing impression that this industry is made of, and dominated by, Communists, radicals, and crackpots. We believe that we represent the vast majority of the people who serve this great medium of expression. But unfortunately it has been an unorganized majority. This has been almost inevitable. The very love of freedom, of the rights of the individual, make this great majority reluctant to organize. But now we must, or we shall meanly lose "the last, best hope on earth."

As members of the motion-picture industry, we must face and accept an especial responsibility. Motion pictures are inescapably one of the world's greatest forces for influencing public thought and opinion, both at home and abroad. In this fact lies solemn obligation. We refuse to permit the effort of Communist, Fascist, and other totalitarian-minded groups to pervert this powerful medium into an instrument for the dissemination of un-American ideas and beliefs. We pledge ourselves to fight, with every means at our organized command, any effort of any group or individual to divert the loyalty of the screen from the free America that gave it birth.[50]

The launching of the Alliance, as it came to be known, was timed to coincide with a dinner in honor of Vice President Henry Wallace hosted by the liberal Free World Association, and it was the opening shot in the ideological war that would dominate Hollywood politics well into the 1950s. Less than three months after its first meeting, *The New York Times* reported, "A wide cleavage in Hollywood's political and economic thought . . .

has resulted in the breaking up of some long-established writing teams and has even extended into the colony's social life. The factional spirit is most pronounced in studio commissaries at lunchtime. Talent groups—particularly writers and directors—have broken previous bonds of friendship, the so-called liberal thinkers grouping at certain tables, the conservatives at others. But in their references to one another they are 'Fascists' or 'Communists.'"[51]

As the 1944 presidential election approached, the fledgling Alliance was no match for the thriving HDC, which went all-out to win a fourth term for FDR, despite his replacement of Henry Wallace, the darling of the left, with the provincial but less controversial Harry Truman. Working closely with the California State Democratic Committee and the Democratic National Committee, George Pepper deployed hundreds of movie stars across the nation, culminating in an election eve broadcast on all four major radio networks. Humphrey Bogart narrated, Judy Garland sang, Groucho Marx told jokes, and lyricist E. Y. Harburg, who had written "Over the Rainbow," provided jingles. As a finale, one star after another stepped up to the microphone and endorsed the Democratic ticket: Tallulah Bankhead, Joan Bennett, Irving Berlin, Joseph Cotten, John Garfield, Rita Hayworth, George Jessel, Danny Kaye, Gene Kelly, George Raft, Edward G. Robinson, Lana Turner, Claudette

Colbert, and even the supposedly apolitical Jane Wyman.[52]

Although Reagan did not take part in the broadcast, he gave $100 to the HDC during the 1944 campaign.[53] Along with Wyman, he was among the horde of stars who turned out to hear Roosevelt's secretary of the interior, Harold Ickes, give a speech attacking the Republican candidate, New York governor Thomas Dewey. Neil Reagan recalled the endless political arguments he and Ron had then: "On Sunday afternoon up at his house above Sunset Boulevard . . . there used to be a big gathering of the [Jack] Bennys and the [George] Burnses. . . . If they were all out around the pool, in about thirty minutes the Reagan brothers would have driven everybody into the house with our battles on politics. His statement to me always was: 'That's the trouble with you guys. Anybody who voted for Roosevelt is a Communist.' And I used to agree with him heartily, at which point he'd get the screaming meemies."[54]

Ronald Reagan was crushed to hear the news of FDR's death on April 12, 1945. Nearly fifty years later, Elvin Crawford, who served with Reagan at Fort Roach, remembered how upset he looked: "That weekend I had to stay over at the base, and Ronnie was Duty Officer. Saturday afternoon the whole place was empty. I saw him coming down Main Street, past Stage 2, with his head down and slowly shaking. He seemed really stricken, like he had a migraine. When he looked at me I saw he was in despair. 'Oh, sergeant, I don't know what's going to happen to this country.' "[55]

Eighteen days after the President's death, Hitler committed suicide as Allied troops closed in on Berlin; Victory in Europe was declared on May 8. Shortly after, raw footage filmed by FMPU combat-camera crews at German concentration camps arrived at Fort Roach to be edited for viewing at the Pentagon. Reagan was among the handful of officers on the base to see the "ghastly images," an experience that only intensified his anti-Fascism, as well as the sympathy for Jews and other minorities drilled into him by his father. Reagan would later say that he kept a print of one of these films to show his children.[56]

Japan surrendered on August 14, 1945, and Reagan was released from active duty later that month, although he was not officially discharged until December 9.[57] "By the time I got out of the Army Air Corps," he would later write, "all I wanted to do—in common with several million other veterans—was to rest up awhile, make love to my wife, and come up refreshed to a better job in an ideal world. (As it came out, I was disappointed in all these postwar ambitions.)"[58]

Reagan had every reason to be optimistic. The victorious Allied Powers were in the process of setting up the United Nations, Lew Wasserman had a seven-year, million-dollar contract from Warners ready for him to sign, and Jane and Maureen were waiting at home with an adopted baby boy named

Michael Edward Reagan. What's more, he was now looking at the world through contact lenses and, as cumbersome as they were, he found them preferable to the options he'd had since age thirteen—thick glasses or extreme myopia.[59]

With his uncommon ability to be sentimental and elegant at the same time, Reagan writes in his memoir: "Michael came to us in March of 1945—closer than a son; he wasn't born unasked, we chose him."[60] The legal arrangements had been handled by Betty Kaplan, one of Jane's bridesmaids, and her lawyer husband, Arthur; on March 18 they delivered the infant to the Reagan house, where Lew and Edie Wasserman were keeping the new parents company. Michael had been born three days earlier to a twenty-eight-year-old would-be actress from Kentucky who had had a wartime fling with a married Army Air Corps man. Jane had gone to meet her first in the hospital.[61]

Modern Screen reported, "In a world where there are many children who never have proper care or love and who never know real home life, Jane thinks it is important for people like herself and Ronnie to add, from the outside, to their family—and then to regard the newcomer as flesh of their flesh, bone of their bone."[62] The family would later say that four-year-old Maureen had wanted a baby brother so badly that she tried to buy one on a shopping trip to the toy department of Saks Fifth Avenue in Beverly Hills with her father, and that when Michael was brought home, she ran to her room to get her piggy bank and gave her entire savings, 97 cents, to a woman from the adoption agency who had presumably accompanied the Kaplans.[63]

In her 1989 memoir, *First Father, First Daughter*, the late Maureen Reagan wrote, "It's always been my understanding that my parents didn't think they could have any more children naturally. I've also sensed that my mother didn't want to go through the pain and suffering of childbirth again, not after what I'd put her through. She can tell you the most adorned story of the day I was born—right down to what she was wearing when she went into labor and how much pain she endured throughout. You can hear every minute of eight and a half hours of agonizing labor, and a minute and a half about me. That's my mother."[64]

Reagan's new contract, guaranteeing him $3,500 a week whether he worked or not, went into effect on September 12, and Jack Warner told him, "Just relax until we find a good property for you."[65] He spent his first weeks out of uniform in a rented house at nearby Lake Arrowhead, where Jane, on loan to MGM, was filming *The Yearling*. Her career was about to ignite: *Lost Weekend* opened that fall to rave reviews, and *The Yearling*, a big-budget Technicolor drama co-starring Gregory Peck, would win her an Oscar nomination the following year. While "Nanny" Banner, their Scottish governess, took care of the children, Ronnie spent his days speed-boating around the lake and building models of ships.[66]

Decades later, Neil Reagan would complain that he, and not his former lifeguard brother, had to teach little Maureen how to swim.[67] Maureen, however, recalled her father as an attentive parent: telling her stories about growing up in Illinois and reading her fairy tales at bedtime; acting out her favorite poem, Robert Service's "The Shooting of Dan McGrew"; doing vaudeville routines with her when they had company. Both parents, noted Maureen, "encouraged me to be independent. One of [my mother's] favorite expressions was, 'If I get hit by a Mack truck tomorrow, you'll have to take care of yourself.' At four I had the dubious distinction of being the only kid on the block who knew what a Mack truck was." She also noticed that her mother tended to become more involved in her roles than her father did in his: "When she was doing Ma Baxter in *The Yearling*, we hardly saw her smile for six months. No exaggeration. She was this earth-mother-dirt-farmer-starving-to-death-type person every hour of the day."[68]

Jane "would come through the door thinking about her part," Reagan later said of his wife at this time, "and not even notice I was in the room."[69] Jane Wyman explained to a reporter in 1948, "It was my biggest chance yet, and I was determined to make the most of it. I determined to act from the inside out, to disregard all surface effects, and delve into the character of a sturdy woman who endured hardship stoically and who concealed a deeply emotional nature under a frosty, pragmatic exterior. I meditated on the role at great length; I wanted to get to the bottom of this woman's psyche. And in doing so, I dredged up all the early hardship and disappointments in my own life, looking constantly for some points of reference that would link our respective inner schemes."[70]

By the time Jane finished shooting *The Yearling*, in January 1946, Warner Bros. still hadn't put her husband to work, and Ronnie could not have been happy to read in *Photoplay*: "Will there be room for both the male wartime and male peacetime stars in movies, Hollywood is asking? During the war an amazing number of men stars burst into being: Van Johnson, Peter Lawford, Robert Walker, Tom Drake, Cornel Wilde, Gregory Peck, John Hodiak, and many more. But already out of uniform or soon to don mufti again are such peacetime favorites as: Jimmy Stewart, Tyrone Power, Robert Montgomery, Henry Fonda, Clark Gable, Ronald Reagan, Lon McCallister, Donald O'Connor, Gene Kelly, Victor Mature, Wayne Morris, and many other golden boys."[71]

Reagan's first postwar picture, *Stallion Road*, did not begin shooting until April. A black-and-white melodrama co-starring Alexis Smith, this tale of a selfless veterinarian who gets the girl but contracts anthrax would prove noteworthy only for the fact that it led to the purchase of the first of four Reagan ranches. "I'd been a long time away from horses," Reagan recalled, "and I desperately wanted to do my own riding and jumping."[72] An army friend, Oleg Cassini, the designer who would dress Jacqueline Kennedy in the White House, introduced Reagan to Count Nino Pepitone, who impressed him because he had been an officer in the famously stylish Italian cavalry. Reagan hired Pepitone as his riding coach, and when shooting was finished on *Stallion Road* that summer, they decided to go into racehorse breeding together. Reagan bought an eight-acre ranch at Northridge in the San Fernando Valley, then still largely agricultural, which Pepitone and his wife managed for him.

"Nino was amazed to discover that my idea of fun was to do what needed to be done, myself," Reagan wrote. "This included building paddock fences—even a quarter-mile track with the inner rail posts slanted at the proper angle and every post hole dug by hand, by me."[73] Ronnie named the Northridge ranch Yearling Row, for *The Yearling*, which won Jane raves when it opened at the end of the year, and *Kings Row*, his biggest screen success.

"Meanwhile I was blindly and busily joining every organization I could find that would guarantee to save the world," he would write of this crucial transition period in both his personal and professional life, when his movie work "at times seemed to be a sideline, what with everything else that was happening."[74] Whether he realized it or not at the time, during these years Reagan was launching his third successful career—after radio announcer and movie star—as a political activist and industry spokesman. "I found him totally changed after the war," recalled producer Frank McCarthy. "He had gotten so serious, to the point that he was talking about the world and politics all the time. People started listening to him at parties."[75]

In June 1946 he was approached to run for Congress again—this time as a Democrat. "Heck, I couldn't do that," he told the *Los Angeles Times*. "If I did, I'd be the subject of criticism as a politician. I couldn't go around making speeches without feeling I was doing it for self-glorification. No, I don't want to have any ax to grind."[76] Wyman was quoted in another paper: "They wanted him to run for Congress. He's very politically minded. I'm not."[77]

Reagan's postwar political activities began the day after he left Fort Roach in late August 1945, when he won a seat on the board of the Hollywood chapter of the American Veterans Committee. The newly formed AVC's high-minded internationalism stood in contrast to the raw anti-Communism of such traditional organizations as the American Legion and the Veterans of Foreign Wars, and it enlisted such notables as Franklin D. Roosevelt Jr., theologian Reinhold Niebuhr, cartoonist Bill Mauldin, and Audie Murphy, the most decorated American soldier of World War II. Even General Eisenhower was an early supporter.[78]

"I myself observed more than forty veterans' organizations arise," Reagan later wrote. "[M]ost of them seemed to be highly intolerant of color, creed and common sense. I joined the American

Veterans Committee because of their feeling that the members should be citizens first and veterans afterward—and, as it worked out, I became a large wheel in their operations."[79] The Hollywood chapter was the second largest of some seven hundred chapters; as chairman of its membership committee, Reagan personally enrolled at least one tenth of its two thousand members.[80]

Reagan also stepped up his involvement in the Hollywood Democratic Committee, which continued to wield considerable clout in California politics after the impressive role it had played in Roosevelt's 1944 reelection. In early 1946, the HDC merged with its New York counterpart, the Independent Citizens Committee of the Arts, Sciences, and Professions (ICCASP), and became its Hollywood affiliate, known as HICCASP. Harold Ickes was named executive chairman of the combined organization, and FDR's Hollywood-based son, James Roosevelt, became executive director of HICCASP. George Pepper, who had run the HDC, became the executive secretary of HICCASP. By mid-year, "3,300 professional exhibitionists," as *Time* dubbed the Hollywood contingent, stood beside Albert Einstein and sociologist Max Weber in support of both legitimate progressive issues, such as repeal of the poll tax, and hidden Communist party-line positions, such as transferring control of America's atomic weapons to the United Nations.[81]

"In the old days," *Time* noted, "a motion picture star had needed nothing but a white Duesenberg and 175 suits to round himself out socially. In the words of Dorothy Parker, there was no 'ism' in Hollywood but plagiarism. But modern studio life has become much more complicated. Today few stars, male or female, would be caught dead at a commissary lunch table without a Cause. Most of them, horrified at the thought of being considered bloated capitalists, favor leftish causes of one kind or another." Edward G. Robinson told the magazine he belonged to HICCASP "because the atom bomb, when it exploded over Hiroshima, blew up every ivory tower in the world." Humphrey Bogart signed up "because I believe in the principles promulgated by Franklin Delano Roosevelt."[82]

Reagan became one of the most active stars working the "rubber-chicken and glass-tinkling circuits" on behalf of the AVC and HICCASP. "It fed my ego," he said, "since I had been so long away from the screen. I loved it."[83] He started wearing his glasses again for these public speeches—an indication of how seriously he took his new role. His first speech, at Santa Ana on December 8, 1945, was to promote racial harmony by honoring Japanese-American veterans. In four brief lines, he displayed his innate idealism with eloquence: "The blood that has soaked into the sands of the beaches is all one color. America stands unique in the world—a country not founded on race, but on a way and an ideal. Not in spite of, but because of our polyglot background, we have had all the strength in the world. That is the American way."[84]

Two nights later, at an opening dinner for

HICCASP's conference on "Atomic Power and Foreign Policy," Reagan's reading of "Set Your Clocks at U-235," a Norman Corwin poem warning of the danger of nuclear annihilation and calling for world unity, was followed by speeches by Congresswoman Helen Gahagan Douglas, Harvard astronomer Harlow Shapley, and novelist Thomas Mann.[85] During the winter and spring of 1946, Reagan delivered speeches and wrote articles on the necessity of international cooperation, the promotion of racial and religious tolerance, and the threat of a neo-Fascist conspiracy to keep the world divided and unstable.

In an article for the *A.V.C. Bulletin* of February 15, 1946, he lambasted the American Order of Patriots, a whites-only veterans organization, and the anti-Semitic demagogue Gerald L. K. Smith as "home-grown fascists" intent on installing "a strongman government in America" and starting World War III. He ended: "I think the A.V.C. can be a key organization in the preservation of democracy for which 300,000 Americans died, and because I have attacked the extreme right does not mean I am ignorant of the menace of the complete left. They, too, want to force something unwanted on the American people, and the fact that many of them go along with those of us who are liberal means nothing because they are only hitching a ride as far as we go, hoping they can use us as a vehicle for their own program."[86]

Yet later that month, along with Gregory Peck, bandleader Artie Shaw, and director Edward

Dmytryk, he lent his name to an anti-colonialist ad taken by the Los Angeles Committee for a Democratic Far Eastern Policy in the *People's Daily World*, a local Communist Party newspaper.[87] After giving a speech to the men's club of the Hollywood-Beverly Christian Church, he was approached by the pastor, Reverend Cleveland Kleihauer. Kleihauer had married Jane and Ronnie, and Reagan admired him for his sermons against discrimination. "Don't you think," the minister asked, "while you're denouncing Fascism, it would be fair to speak out equally strongly against the tyranny of Communism?"[88] At his next speaking engagement, filling in for James Roosevelt, Reagan tacked an explicitly anti-Communist paragraph onto the end of his stock text, only to have it met with total silence—even though he had received "riotous applause" more than twenty times during the previous forty minutes. Startled, Reagan began to reassess the implications of his political commitments.[89]

After watching a small but dedicated Communist faction outmaneuver the liberal majority at the American Veterans Committee's state convention in April, he wrote a letter expressing concern to Charles Bolté, the chairman of the organization's national planning commission.[90] A few weeks later, he was angered to learn that the location for a meeting of the Hollywood chapter had been inexplicably moved from KFWB's 750-seat auditorium—which Reagan had secured free of charge from Warners—to a seventy-five-seat hall owned by the leftist-dominated Screen Cartoonists Guild. When Reagan arrived at the meeting, he recalled, "hundreds of A.V.C. boys were milling about outside, unable to get in. The KFWB hall was still available and gratis—but someone preferred a hall which could hold only a 'small, working majority.' It was an old Communist trick but new to me."[91]

Using such tactics, the Communists took over the AVC's Los Angeles–area council, but their attempt to gain control of the entire organization was thwarted by the liberals at its national convention in Des Moines in June, which Reagan was unable to attend because he was filming *Stallion Road*.[92] But soon after the convention he wrote to *Hollywood Reporter* publisher Billy Wilkerson, who had called the AVC a Communist front, informing him that the organization had dealt with "a tentative pink infiltration . . . in true democratic fashion."[93]

That same month, Olivia de Havilland set off a similar power struggle within HICCASP when she refused to deliver two speeches in Seattle as written by her fellow executive council member Dalton Trumbo, one of Hollywood's highest-paid screenwriters and a secret Communist since 1943. She felt that Trumbo's text was too left-wing and worried that the organization was becoming "automatically pro-Russian." In her rewritten speech, she sought to stake the liberal claim for the soul of the organization while answering right-wing accusations that groups like HICCASP were controlled by party-liners loyal to Moscow by unequivocally stating, "The overwhelming majority of people who make up the liberal and progressive groups of this country believe in democracy, and *not* in communism. We believe that the two cannot be reconciled here in the United States, and we believe that every effort should be exerted to make democracy work, and to extend its benefits to every person in every community throughout our land."[94]

Trumbo was outraged, but at the next meeting of the executive council, on July 2, James Roosevelt weighed in with his concern about the growing perception that the organization was dominated by leftists, and he proposed a resolution supporting the democratic, free enterprise system and rejecting Communism. Reagan, who had been asked to fill a vacancy on the council, was attending his first meeting and was amazed by the hysterical reaction to Roosevelt's suggestion:

A well-known musician [elsewhere identified as Artie Shaw] sprang to his feet. He offered to recite the USSR constitution from memory, yelling that it was a lot more democratic than that of the United States. A prominent movie writer leaped upward. He said if there was ever a war between the United States and Russia, he would volunteer for Russia. . . . After this hubbub of dismay had continued for a while, I decided that an Irishman couldn't stay out. . . . I took the floor and endorsed what [James Roosevelt] said. Well, sir, I found myself waist-high in epithets such as "Fascist" and "capitalist scum" and "enemy of the proletariat" and "witch-hunter" and "Red-baiter" before I could say boo. . . . Dalton Trumbo, the writer, was very vociferous. Most vehement of all, however, was John Howard Lawson. . . . You can imagine what this did to my naivete. Here was a H.I.C.C.A.S.P. that I had admired and honored. Suddenly it was broken up into a Kilkenny brawl by a simple statement which I thought any American would be proud to subscribe to.[95]

This tumultuous meeting ended with the formation of a seven-member policy committee—including Roosevelt, Trumbo, Lawson, and Reagan—which was to draft a resolution in time for the next executive council meeting. As Reagan was leaving, producer Dore Schary, who was then working for David O. Selznick, invited him to Olivia de Havilland's home. There he found Roosevelt and a small group of HICCASP's leading liberals, including the screenwriter Don Hartman and the composer Johnny Green. According to Reagan, Roosevelt and de Havilland revealed that they had deliberately provoked the dissension that night to flush out the "others." In turn, he helped them write what they called a "disinfecting resolution" to force the hand of the Communist faction at the next meeting. Reagan had co-starred with de Havilland in *Santa Fe Trail* before the war, but he didn't know her well. They had a good laugh, he said, over the fact that each had suspected the other of being a Communist until that night.[96]

The ideological wrangling went on for the rest of the month, but Lawson and Trumbo blocked all attempts to clearly dissociate HICCASP from the Communist Party. Fed up, Roosevelt and de Havilland submitted their resignations, as did a number of other liberals. On July 30, what was left of the executive council adopted a resolution declaring HICCASP independent of "any political party or organization, Republican, Democratic, Communist, Socialist, or other."[97]

That week, Arthur Schlesinger Jr., a young associate professor of history at Harvard and a Pulitzer Prize winner for *The Age of Jackson*, published an article titled "The U.S. Communist Party" in *Life* magazine. Its publication in the country's most widely read weekly indicated how central the subject had become to the national conversation. Schlesinger began:

> For better or for worse, the Communist Party of the U.S. is here to stay. It grew when the U.S.S.R. was still a gamble; it will grow faster as the gamble pays off, and it will persist if repressive legislation forces it underground. . . . The Center, as party members call the smoky brick headquarters on 12th Street in New York City, controls an active and disciplined following through the country. . . . Communists are working overtime to expand party influence, open and covert, in the labor movement,

among Negroes, among veterans, among unorganized liberals.

Schlesinger used the AVC and ICCASP as examples of "groups of liberals" that were "organized for some benevolent purpose, and because of the innocence, laziness and stupidity of most of the membership, perfectly designed for control by an alert minority." He went on to make his most urgent point: "The Communist Party is no menace to the right in the U.S. It is a great help to the right because of its success in dividing and neutralizing the left. It is to the American left that Communism presents the most serious danger. On the record, Communists have fought other leftists as viciously as they have fought fascists. Their methods are irreconcilable with honest cooperation, as anyone who has tried to work with them has found out the hard way."[98]

When HICCASP regrouped, Dore Schary succeeded Jimmy Roosevelt, and the young Frank Sinatra took de Havilland's place as vice chairman and the group's most tireless public speaker.[99] Its membership roster still boasted stars ranging from Humphrey Bogart to Gypsy Rose Lee, as well as Ronald Reagan. When *Time* questioned national executive director Hannah Dorner about alleged "Communist influence," she dismissively replied, "Says who and so what? If the ICCASP program is like the Communist line, that is purely coincidental."[100]

After Henry Wallace criticized Truman's hardening policy toward the Soviet Union at an ICCASP rally in New York on September 12, and was fired as secretary of commerce, the Hollywood group passed a resolution supporting Wallace and calling for "permanent cooperation with the Soviet Union."[101] By October even Eleanor Roosevelt was saying privately that the organization was "Communist-dominated," and Jules Stein was warning his client Bette Davis, "You had better get out."[102]

Reagan had been getting similar warnings from his brother for months. HICCASP "was as bad as you could get," Neil Reagan recalled in a 1981 interview. "I used to beat him over the head, 'Get out of that thing. There are people in there who can cause you real trouble.'" Neil also boasted that he had been spying on HICCASP for the FBI: "I was doing little things. . . . You know, 'Neil, we'd like to have you go out and lay in the bushes and take down the [license plate] numbers off of the cars that are going to be at this little meeting in Bel Air. Put it in a brown envelope, no return address. And always remember, if you get caught in the bushes, you can just forget about saying, well, you're doing this for the FBI, because we'll just . . . say, We never saw this guy in our lives.'"[103]

According to Neil, late one night his brother had an epiphany of sorts and summoned him to "a Nutburger stand at the corner of Sunset and Doheny." Reagan shared his suspicions that the HICCASP board was being packed with Communists and their allies and showed him minutes he had "filched" to prove his case. "I just looked at him," Neil recalled, "and said, 'Junior, what do you suppose I've been talking about all these weeks and weeks and weeks?'"[104]

Neil doesn't date this incident. Nor is it clear when Reagan severed ties with HICCASP. He would later say that he had resigned via telegram in July, a claim contradicted by HICCASP records (which show him being appointed to its labor committee in late August) and by de Havilland's recollection that he remained involved for three months after she quit. "He always seemed to be observing," she told an interviewer in 1989. "And then I learned much later he was with the F.B.I." (Some people said she was, too.)[105]

Reagan's FBI file was made public in 1985, after the *San Jose Mercury News* had obtained it under the Freedom of Information Act. The FBI first contacted Reagan in September 1941, at Warner Bros. In November 1943 he was interviewed by an agent at Fort Roach and reported that he had almost come to blows at a party with a fellow actor who had made pro-German and anti-Semitic remarks.[106] By March 1946, Reagan himself was being watched by the bureau's Los Angeles office as a suspected Communist sympathizer because of his involvement with HICCASP, the AVC, and other left-leaning groups.[107] In June an agent reported that Reagan had introduced a pro-Communist speaker at an AVC luncheon.[108] But sometime later that year—most likely between mid-July and late September—he agreed to help the bureau monitor Communist activity in Hollywood.

According to his 1965 memoir, Reagan was visited at home by "three men from a well-known government agency" several months *after* he quit HICCASP. "Now look, I don't go in for Red-baiting," Reagan told them, but after being convinced that national security was at stake, "we exchanged information for a few hours."[109] At a 1955 trial involving the Screen Extras Guild, however, he had testified under oath that he received confidential information from government agents while still in HICCASP,[110] and in his 1990 presidential memoir he would confuse matters further by saying that two FBI men had knocked on his door shortly *before* he went on HICCASP's executive council.[111] His FBI file doesn't resolve this contradiction, but it does show that by 1947 he was one of at least eighteen informers for the bureau within the motion picture industry. Reagan's code name was T-10, and his fellow moles most likely included Walt Disney and Billy Wilkerson, the publisher of the *Hollywood Reporter* and owner of the Sunset Strip hotspots Ciro's, La Rue, and Trocadero.[112]

Reagan's willingness to work with the government law enforcement agency most anathema to the Hollywood left was one more sign of the political metamorphosis he was undergoing during the summer and fall of 1946. Reagan's disillusionment with the AVC and HICCASP, his cooperation with the FBI, his rise to leadership at the Screen Actors Guild during Hollywood's worst period of labor strife—all these were taking place almost simultaneously. One experience reinforced the other and perhaps made the transformation from "near-hopeless hemophiliac liberal"[113] to anti-Communist crusader seem something like an act of fate.

Reagan returned to the SAG board in February 1946 on the recommendation of his conservative debating partner from *This Is the Army*, George Murphy, who had succeeded another conservative, Robert Montgomery, as Guild president. Although several liberals, including James Cagney, Gene Kelly, and Henry Fonda, sat on the board, it tended to be dominated by its more middle-of-the-road and conservative members, among them Reagan's friends Pat O'Brien, Dick Powell, Robert Taylor, and William Holden. Jane Wyman had stayed on all through the war, and was one of only four women on the forty-four-member board.[114] One of those women, Anne Revere, was an outspoken leftist who would later recall that Reagan let down his liberal colleagues within a matter of months.[115]

In the spring of 1946, SAG was considering forming a tri-guild council with the somewhat more liberal Screen Directors Guild and the decidedly left-wing Screen Writers Guild. But the attempt to draft a statement of purpose for the proposed council led to a sharp disagreement on SAG's board: Murphy and Montgomery insisted on language condemning Communist, as well as Fascist, "influence in the motion picture industry or the ranks of labor."[116] When the wording came up for a vote in mid-June—just two weeks before Jimmy Roosevelt and de Havilland raised the very same issue at HICCASP—Reagan voted with the board's anti-Communist majority. He also joined Murphy and Montgomery in rejecting the tri-guild council after the directors and writers agreed to the entire statement of principles *except* the condemnation of Communism.[117] He was proving himself a valuable liberal ally to SAG's conservative powers that be and, perhaps, was starting to see things their way. Murphy and Montgomery, he would later write, were "equally aware of the strange creatures crawling from under the make-believe rocks in our make-believe town."[118]

On July 1—the day before the showdown at HIC-CASP—Herbert Sorrell, the head of the Conference of Studio Unions, called a strike. It was the latest skirmish in the sometimes violent struggle for control of Hollywood's thirty thousand studio workers between the upstart CSU and the entrenched International Alliance of Theatrical Stage Employees (IATSE) that had been raging on and off since early 1945. The July strike was settled in two days by an agreement known as the Treaty of Beverly Hills because it was negotiated in a bungalow at the hotel of the same name by union and studio representatives brought together by an emergency committee of SAG's board.[119] Reagan was one of the committee's six members,[120] and from that moment on he would play a central role as SAG's point man in the increasingly byzantine—and ideologically charged—conflict.

Hollywood's labor war had begun almost absurdly—with a decision by the seventy-seven member Society for Motion Picture Interior Decorators to switch its affiliation from IATSE to the CSU—and quickly engulfed the entire movie industry. Despite rulings by the National Labor Relations Board and the War Labor Board, IATSE refused to recognize the switch. The battle was engaged in earnest on March 12, 1945, when the CSU's ten thousand members went on strike in support of the decorators and began picketing the studios. The studio bosses backed IATSE, the older and less militant of the labor coalitions, partly because it included the projectionists union, which could close down their theaters, and partly because of right-wing accusations that the CSU was Communist-controlled—accusations that had some basis in fact. The Hollywood left, including HICCASP and the AVC, backed the CSU, claiming that IATSE was run by racketeers, which until 1941 it had been. While Dalton Trumbo wrote speeches for CSU leader Herbert Sorrell, a hotheaded former boxer from Oakland, the rabid anti-Communists of the Motion Picture Alliance rallied around IATSE head Roy Brewer, a onetime projectionist from Nebraska whose deceptively mild manner cloaked an obsessive hatred of Communists.[121]

Both sides vied for SAG's support, because if the stars honored the CSU's picket lines, the studios—which were being kept running by IATSE's seventeen thousand members—would be forced to shut down. From the start Murphy and Montgomery took the position that the strike was jurisdictional—a dispute between unions, rather than labor and management—which meant that under American Federation of Labor (AFL) rules SAG members were not obligated to honor the picket lines. The CSU called for a national boycott of stars who crossed the lines, but it didn't stop most marquee names—including liberals such as Bogart, Judy Garland, and Lucille Ball—from continuing to report for work.[122] (Edith Davis's Republican friend Lillian Gish waved demurely at the strikers on her way into the Selznick studio, where she was filming *Duel in the Sun*.)[123]

The 1945 strike dragged on inconclusively for seven months before reaching a violent climax outside Warner Bros. On the morning of October 5, some one thousand CSU strikers massed at the studio's front gate and began overturning cars to block the entrance to IATSE workers. Warners' security force, backed by local police, responded with fire hoses and tear gas. In the ensuing riot, each side accused the other of using chains, pipes, clubs, and knives. Black Friday was followed by Bloody Monday, and the fighting went on for two more weeks, spreading to MGM, Paramount, and Republic. Earl Warren, California's moderate Republican governor, refused demands to send in the National Guard. The so-called Battle of Burbank was finally brought to an end on

October 25, when the AFL's national executive council issued the Cincinnati Directive, ordering the strikers back to work and both sides to the negotiating table. Three AFL vice presidents— W. C. Doherty, head of the mail carriers, Felix Knight, head of the railway car-men, and W. C. Birthright, head of the barbers—were chosen to arbitrate outstanding disputes. The day after Christmas, the Three Wise Men, as they were called, handed down a ruling that gave the CSU jurisdiction over the set decorators. But it also allowed the studios to transfer 350 set-construction jobs from CSU carpenters to IATSE stage-hands. The carpenters protested to the AFL, and Sorrell threatened to shut the studios down with another strike. Jack Warner declared that the studios were victims of "a gigantic Communist conspiracy" and swore he would never make another "liberal" movie, because "liberalism was just a disguise for Communist propaganda." He also swore that he would never vote for a Democrat again.[124]

That is where matters stood when Reagan entered the picture with SAG's emergency committee in July 1946 and helped settle the two-day strike. Six weeks later, however, the Three Wise Men delivered their August Clarification, which appeared to favor the carpenters. In response, IATSE leaders threatened to shut down not only production but also distribution if the studios complied. In secret meetings held in August and September, the Producers Labor Committee plotted with IATSE representatives to break the CSU once and for all. Their plan was for the studios to demand that CSU carpenters and painters work on sets started by IATSE stagehands. If they refused, as expected, they would be fired for violating a moratorium on work stoppages agreed to in the Treaty of Beverly Hills, and be replaced by IATSE workers.[125]

SAG's emergency committee, including Reagan, who had been nominated third vice president of the Guild, met with IATSE chief Roy Brewer and suggested that he abide by the August Clarification until the matter could be taken up at the AFL's national convention in October, but Brewer argued that Sorrell wouldn't be satisfied until the CSU controlled every union worker in Hollywood. Reagan attended at least one of the Producers Labor Committee's secret meetings with IATSE leaders, on September 11, so there is some basis for believing he knew of their plans.[126] That same day he called Sorrell on behalf of SAG and urged him not to call another strike.[127] According to Reagan, Sorrell rebuffed him, probably because he had already ordered CSU painters and carpenters not to work on IATSE-built sets, thus making a confrontation inevitable. Both sides were clearly spoiling for a fight, and had already lined up muscle: the longshoremen's union for the CSU; the Teamsters for IATSE.

SAG's leaders tried to cast themselves as innocent bystanders. "The Guild is not interested in the merits of the case," Montgomery proclaimed at the board's September 17 meeting, "but feels that all possible steps should be taken to prevent a strike which would throw 30,000 people out of work because of 300 jobs."[128] Reagan spoke out strongly for a motion stating that "members of the Guild be instructed to go through picket lines and live up to their contracts . . . and that the Guild make every effort to see that the studios provide adequate physical protection for its members when crossing picket lines." The motion passed with only two dissenting votes, from Boris Karloff and Anne Revere.[129] The board also called an emergency meeting of the entire membership for October 2 and asked Reagan to prepare a speech explaining SAG's strike policy.

A few nights later, Reagan and Bill Holden, his closest friend on the SAG board, "crashed" a meeting of SAG's leftist contingent at Ida Lupino's house. According to Reagan, the seventy-five actors gathered on Lupino's patio were "astonished and miffed" by their arrival. The meeting was chaired by Sterling Hayden, who would later testify to HUAC that he had been assigned by his Communist Party cell to line up SAG support for Sorrell. "The whole thing was a brainwash job," Reagan recalled. "The C.S.U. was lauded to the skies, the I.A.T.S.E. was damned, and the SAG drew faint praise indeed for trying to be blessed with the peacemakers." When he defended SAG's policy, he was booed and heckled. John Garfield, who also sat on SAG's board, tried to quiet the group, but was pulled aside by Howard Da Silva—

both Garfield and Da Silva were secret Party members at the time.[130]

The next day Reagan was filming a beach scene at Point Mugu for *Night Unto Night*—he had started shooting his second postwar movie on September 20—when he was called to the phone. "There's a group being formed to deal with you," an anonymous caller said. "They're going to fix you so you won't ever act again." He was escorted back to the studio, where the security office issued him a .32 Smith & Wesson pistol and a shoulder holster. The fear was that CSU hotheads were planning to throw acid in Reagan's face; he claimed not to take the threat seriously until he saw a police car guarding his house that night. "Thereafter, I mounted the holstered gun religiously every morning and took it off the last thing at night. I learned how much a person gets to lean on hardware like that. After months of wearing it took a real effort of will to discard it. I kept thinking: 'The very night you take it off may be the night when you need it most.' "[131]

Meanwhile, between September 12 and September 24, 1,200 carpenters and painters had been fired, and they started picketing the studios. On September 26, the CSU called a strike to halt work on the fifty films then in production at the eight largest studios. In a repeat of the previous fall's Battle of Burbank, CSU and IATSE workers clashed outside Warners' gate, and Burbank policemen fired shots into the air.[132] The following morning the *Los Angeles Times* quoted Sorrell as saying, "There may be men hurt, there may be men killed before this is over. But we are in no mood to be pushed around any more."[133] For his part, Brewer declared, "I.A.T.S.E. and the [CSU] cannot exist together in Hollywood. It is war to the finish."[134]

Over the next several days ugly battles erupted outside MGM, Universal, Columbia, and Paramount. The AVC's Hollywood chapter voted to support the CSU and ordered its members to join the picket lines in full military uniform, a move an outraged Reagan saw as proof that it had become "a hotbed of Communists." By October 1 more than two dozen veterans had been hospitalized for injuries suffered in clashes with police.[135]

On October 2, Reagan gave his speech urging SAG's membership to support the board's policy of neutrality and to honor their contracts by crossing the picket lines. Three thousand actors had gathered for the mass meeting at the Hollywood Legion Stadium, an old boxing arena, where a podium was set up in the ring. Outside, some two thousand pro-CSU demonstrators were handing out leaflets and shouting taunts demanding that SAG support the strike. Reagan's friend Robert Stack recalled the tense scene: "There was a group outside and inside that was trying, supposedly, to take the Guild away from us. I don't know if they were Communists, but when we arrived at the stadium they were about ten deep, and we had to walk in single file. There was a guy standing on the marquee taking pictures as we walked in, saying, 'You better know how to vote, because we'll know how you vote.' Inside people were yelling. Bob Mitchum got up and said, 'Look, as an American you can ask me what to do, but damn it, don't *tell* me what to do.' There was a racket going on; they were marching in cadence on the roof. Ronald Reagan stood up in the middle of the boxing ring and said, 'Ladies and gentlemen, I implore you, stay to the bitter end tonight. Because if you don't, you're going to lose your union. I don't care how early your call is, but please stay tonight.' And he went on and on. He'd had death threats. In fact, Chuck Heston told me that they were flattening Ron's tires and stuff."[136]

After the meeting, a half-dozen Teamsters led Reagan and Wyman through a gauntlet of hecklers to their car. "A group of us went to Trader Vic's," Stack remembered. "And I said, 'You know something, Ron, I was very impressed by you. I can't think of anyone else who could have gotten up there and done what you did. And I feel strongly that if you're as gifted as you are and if you believe in democracy, as an American, you have an obligation to do something for your country. You really should do something with that leadership quality.' He looked at me kind of funny, gave me a quizzical smile, and said, 'You mean if I run for president, you'll vote for me?' I said, 'Yeah, you bet your ass.' And everybody laughed."[137]

SAG members voted 2,748 to 509 in favor of the board's—and Reagan's—position.[138] Thus empowered, Reagan stepped up his efforts to keep the studios open and end the strike. He persuaded SAG's board to let him lead a delegation to the AFL's Chicago convention, and Warners suspended production on *Night Unto Night* so that he could go. The star-studded group—Wyman, Murphy, Edward Arnold, Robert Taylor, Gene Kelly, Walter Pidgeon, Alexis Smith, Dick Powell and June Allyson—threatened to tour the country condemning the AFL's leaders if they didn't do more to mediate the dispute. Back in Los Angeles, Reagan met with the technicians at Technicolor who had voted to switch sides from IATSE to the CSU, but they walked out anyway, a major setback for the studios because they had no other way to process color film. In late October, Reagan organized a SAG-sponsored roundtable of forty-three local unions at the Hollywood Knickerbocker Hotel, which ended badly, with Sorrell screaming at his friend Gene Kelly and Reagan telling Sorrell, "Herb, as far as I'm concerned . . . you do not want peace in the motion picture industry."[139]

According to Reagan, "Now various homes of the I.A.T.S.E. members were bombed at night; other workers were ambushed and slugged."[140] Warners employees were being brought to the studio each morning on buses driven by Teamsters; CSU picketers threw rocks and bottles as the buses whizzed through the gate.[141] On November 13, Reagan watched as the Warners bus on which he usually commuted went up in flames on Beverly Boulevard, not far from his house.[142] Two days later, in violation of a court injunction prohibiting more than eight pickets at any studio gate, 1,500 strikers led by Sorrell marched on Columbia. The CSU boss was among the nearly seven hundred arrested on charges ranging from unlawful assembly to assault and conspiracy and held on bail of $500 each, a steep sum for carpenters and painters in 1946.[143]

That same week, SAG left-wingers, including Sterling Hayden, Howard Da Silva, and Hume Cronyn, tried to persuade the Guild's board to reverse its "anti-union, anti-labor, anti-democratic policy" and support the strike. When the board refused to change course, three hundred SAG members signed a petition demanding another mass meeting on strike policy.[144] On December 19, Reagan again addressed his fellow actors at the Hollywood Legion Stadium. Edward G. Robinson and Katharine Hepburn spoke for the other side. Reagan later dismissed Hepburn's speech as "a word-for-word copy of a CSU strike bulletin several weeks old."[145]

By a ten-to-one margin this time, SAG members voted to support their board.[146] Without the actors, the CSU's days were numbered. SAG executive director Jack Dales congratulated Reagan on a brilliant performance, and Jack Warner announced, "Ronnie Reagan . . . has turned out to be a tower of strength, not only for the actors but for the whole industry, and he is to be highly complimented for his efforts on behalf of everyone working in our business."[147] Others thought he was an opportunist, a bastard, a scab. One actor called him a Fascist to his face. Both the compliments and the insults testified to the crucial role Reagan had played in isolating Sorrell and the CSU.

And all the while he was acting as a labor leader by night, he was playing an epileptic biochemist by day. Shooting on the abysmal *Night Unto Night* dragged on through the Christmas holidays. Reagan didn't get along with either his director or his co-star, the young Swedish sex-pot Viveca Lindfors, who found him bland and untalented. "I don't remember a single conversation with him of any substance," she later wrote. "I do remember some chitchat about sex, which was up my alley. . . . 'It's best in the afternoon, after coming out of the shower,' he said, and then he laughed."[148]

Supporting actress Rosemary DeCamp was more sympathetic. "He worked 18 to 20 hours a day," she remembered, "at night trying to resolve an ugly industry strike . . . then all day on that baffling film about a man with epilepsy. But he remained cheerful and loquacious with three or four hours of sleep a night. This went on for months and may have been the cause of his divorce from Jane Wyman, who must have had a difficult and lonely time as Mike and Maureen were very young."[149]

At the end of the year, the North Hollywood Women's Professional Club named Jane Wyman its "Ideal Working Mother."[150] But according to the wife of a Hollywood personality who saw a lot of

Ronnie and Jane in those days, it was clear that all was not well in the marriage. "Ronnie used to sit around with Adolphe Menjou and George Murphy and talk about Communism—at parties, when it was boring to talk about this evil force that was penetrating our society. People would say, 'There go Adolphe and George and Ronnie talking the Red Menace.' Don't you think Jane was bored by all that talk? She wasn't interested in politics. Jane was a very pert, fresh-faced little thing who wanted to dance with George Burns at parties—she didn't want to hear about Communist infiltration. She could dance like a son of a son, let me tell you."

"Jane was restless and bored," said Leonora Hornblow. "Ronnie talked all the time. All his life he talked all the time. In the beginning she had been so stuck on him it didn't matter, although she never hung on his every word. She said to me, 'I'm so bored with him. I don't know what's going to happen—whether I'll die from boredom or I'll kill him.' "[151]

CHAPTER EIGHT

NANCY IN NEW YORK
1944–1949

I lived at 34 Beekman Place, on the corner of 51st Street, and Nancy was just around the corner in a brownstone. I can see her now in my mind's eye, walking down the steps all ready to go make the rounds. She was a charming, wholesome, lovely girl, very pleasant to be with. A little overweight. And an extremely pretty face.

> Anne Washburn to author,
> May 7, 2003

Nancy picked a particularly exciting moment to settle in Manhattan. The war was still on, but victory was a few months away, and the city was full of footloose young soldiers and sailors returning from Europe, as well as rich and glamorous European exiles, including almost the entire Surrealist pantheon, who had sat out the war in New York and gave the town a high-style, Continental air. The expensive nightclubs and restaurants—El Morocco, the Stork Club, Toots

Shor's, Sardi's, "21"—were packed every night with café society, Hollywood stars between pictures, debutantes, gigolos, and gossip columnists.

Broadway was booming. The 1944–45 season was the best—financially and creatively—in nearly twenty years, with eighty-three new plays and twenty-four hits, including John Van Druten's *I Remember Mama*, Rodgers and Hammerstein's *Carousel*, Tennessee Williams's *The Glass Menagerie* (starring the incomparable Laurette Taylor), and Jerome Robbins's *On the Town*, which had a book by Betty Comden and Adolph Green and music by Leonard Bernstein. Held over from the previous season, *Oklahoma!* approached its 1,000th performance, Tallulah Bankhead drew crowds to Philip Barry's *Foolish Notion*, and Mae West reigned in the risqué *Catherine Was Great*. (Prudery was not entirely extinguished, however: the city's license commissioner refused to renew the Belasco Theater's license until it ceased performances of *Trio*, a drama about "the unhealthy subject of Lesbianism.")[1]

On December 7, 1944—just about the time Nancy arrived in New York—the impresario Billy Rose unveiled his handsomely refurbished Ziegfeld Theater, with a $350,000 extravaganza titled *Seven Lively Arts*, featuring the combined talents of Beatrice Lillie, Cole Porter, Igor Stravinsky, Alicia Markova, Bert Lahr, George S. Kaufman and Moss Hart, and the Benny Goodman Band. Opening night seats went for an unheard-of $24 and, as one observer noted, "there was a veritable flood of newly pressed tuxedos and feminine dinner ensembles for the first time since Pearl Harbor."[2]

Nancy's first address in New York was the Plaza Hotel, but she soon found it too costly and moved to the Barbizon Hotel for Women on East 63rd Street, where she shared a room with another aspiring actress from Smith.[3] The Barbizon was where good girls from proper Midwestern and Southern families stayed; the rates were reasonable, and male visitors were not allowed beyond the lobby. A few months later Nancy rented her own apartment, a one-bedroom, fourth-floor walk-up at 409 East 51st Street, just off smart Beekman Place. "It was a wonderful apartment," she recalled. "It had a fireplace. And I think I paid $150 a month."[4] One friend remembered it as "impeccably done," another as nicely furnished but "very small—a small living room and bedroom and kitchenette thing."[5]

Living on one's own was still a fairly daring thing for a respectable girl to do in the 1940s, but Nancy and her parents were comforted by the fact that several family friends had apartments nearby: Uncle Walter and Nan Huston were right around the corner on East 50th Street; Lillian Gish lived with her sister, Dorothy, and their aged, invalid mother on East 57th Street, off Sutton Place; Katharine Hepburn had a house on East 49th Street. Therefore, the young actress never lacked for a proper meal, or advice on agents, acting coaches, and suitable young men to go out with. "It was wonderful," Nancy Reagan recalled, "I went

PHOTO CAPTIONS

1 Ronald Reagan and his brother, Neil, at a Warner Bros. radio broadcast, 1943. *(The Everett Collection)*

2 Nelle Reagan visiting her son Ronald on the set of Stallion Road, 1947. *(©Underwood & Underwood/ Corbis)*

3 A publicity photo of Ronald Reagan shortly after his arrival in Hollywood in 1937. *(Imageworks/Time Life Picture Collection/Getty Images)*

4 Dr. Loyal Davis and Edith Luckett on the SS *New York* in 1927, two years before their marriage. *(Collection of Richard Davis)*

5 Nancy with her stepbrother, Richard Davis, circa 1930. *(Reagan Family Photo Collection)*

6 Nancy with her father, Kenneth Robbins, who visited her in Chicago in 1929. *(Camera Press/Retna)*

7 Nancy Davis onstage with ZaSu Pitts, a friend of her mother's and her theatrical mentor, circa 1946. *(Reagan Family Photo Collection)*

8 Colleen Moore Hargrave, the silent screen star turned Chicago socialite, with her famous Doll House. *(A.P. Wide World Photos)*

9 Reagan with gossip columnist Louella Parsons, who also hailed from Dixon, Illinois. *(Photofest)*

10 Jane Wyman and Ronald Reagan on their wedding day, January 26, 1940. *(Culver Pictures)*

11 Wyman with her Academy Award for *Johnny Belinda,* March 1948. *(A.P. Wide World Photos)*

12 Lieutenant Reagan with Jane and little Maureen the day he reported for military service, April 19, 1942. *(A.P. Wide World Photos)*

13 Screen Actors Guild leaders Robert Montgomery, George Murphy, and Ronald Reagan after testifying before HUAC, October 23, 1947. *(A.P. Wide World Photos)*

14 Reagan and Lauren Bacall with President Harry Truman during his 1948 campaign. *(Al Humphreys/Los Angeles Times)*

15 Nancy Davis and Ronald Reagan on a date at a Beverly Hills Hotel gala. *(Globe Photos)*

16 Nancy in a 1950 promotional photo for Metro-Goldwyn-Mayer. *(Photofest)*

17 Loyal and Edith with Nancy in Hollywood, July 1949. *(Collection of Richard Davis)*

18 Nancy with her co-star James Whitmore, filming *The Next Voice You Hear,* 1950. *(Lester Glassner Collection/Neal Peters)*

19 Ronnie and Nancy on their wedding day, March 4, 1952, photographed at the home of their witnesses, William and Ardis Holden. *(Reagan Family Photo Collection)*

20 The newlyweds on their honeymoon at the Arizona Biltmore Hotel in Phoenix. *(A.P. Wide World Photos)*

PHOTOS 1–20

1

2

3

4

5

6

9

10

11

12

13

14

15

16

over to the Hustons' a lot to have dinner with them. And I also had dinner a lot with Lillian and Dorothy, and then we'd go to a movie. It was funny, because Lillian always seemed so meek and Dorothy was just the opposite. But somehow we always ended up seeing the movie Lillian wanted and never the movie Dorothy wanted."[6]

On Sunday afternoons the Gishes regularly received friends "4:30 at 430"—the number of their apartment building—and Nancy was almost always included in these sophisticated but cozy gatherings.[7] The Gish sisters were in their fifties then, but both were still working in films and the theater, as was Uncle Walter, who was well into his sixties. All three starred in Broadway plays during the time Nancy lived in New York: Dorothy Gish starred in *The Magnificent Yankee*, opposite Louis Calhern, another close friend of the Davises'; Walter Huston was in *The Apple of His Eye*; and Lillian Gish played in *Crime and Punishment*.

For most of the fall of 1945, Spencer Tracy was ensconced in a suite at the Waldorf-Astoria. Tracy, in his mid-forties and still a major Hollywood star, had nervously agreed to appear in his first Broadway play in fifteen years, *The Rugged Path*, a heavy-duty drama written by three-time Pulitzer Prize winner Robert Sherwood and directed by Garson Kanin. Nancy loved watching Spence, as she called him, rehearse at the Plymouth Theater; once again, she was being exposed to the best.[8] She was also continuing to learn about the hard realities hidden behind doors with stars on them.

With Katharine Hepburn's constant support, Tracy managed not to drink during the play's rehearsal and run. But he fought with Sherwood and Kanin, treated Hepburn like a servant, disparaged the play in interviews, and generally made things as difficult as possible for everyone around him. *The Rugged Path* received lukewarm reviews and closed after ten weeks.[9]

"There are times when mutual failure draws the participants closer," Garson Kanin lamented in his biographical memoir, *Tracy and Hepburn*, "but, in this instance, the result was wreckage."[10] Tracy remained in New York during the winter of 1946, and he was said to be binge drinking so badly that MGM had him secretly committed to Doctors Hospital, a private institution on the Upper East Side, where he was put in a straitjacket and guarded by studio security men.[11] According to Richard Davis, Tracy was hospitalized in Chicago later that year as a patient of his father's. "There was a very private floor at Passavant—the top floor—and I remember he was there maybe six weeks getting dried out. Loyal and Edith kept that very quiet."[12]

Despite these family connections, Nancy did not land a single acting job during her first year in New York. To supplement monthly checks from Edith and Loyal, she signed up with the Conover Modeling Agency and posed for a few advertisements, mostly for hats and one for Colgate toothpaste. (Some contemporaries said her "thick legs" kept her from getting more assignments.)[13] She took acting classes and faithfully made the rounds of auditions, though she often found herself dreading the thought of being judged and rejected.

"Tryouts are frightening and embarrassing," she would later write of her struggling-actress days. "But if you are beginning in the theater and your ability is not established, you have no choice but to try out. And even if you pass, you remain on trial. There is a period after a show goes into rehearsal when many performers are replaced. In the days when I was in the theater, the first five days of rehearsal were critical. You could be fired at any time during that period and not be paid." She continues:

I got a part in one play on the basis of a tryout, but I was fired after a few days. I don't even remember the name of the play or the director. Maybe I don't want to remember. I do recall that when we broke for lunch during the rehearsal, the director caught up with me, took my arm, and led me out the stage door into the alley. "I hate to have to tell you this," he said, "but it's just not working. You're just not right for the part. I have to let you go."

Maybe I wasn't right for the part. Or maybe I just wasn't any good. We cannot all be right for every part on the stage or in life. We cannot all be good at everything. But I found out how painful it is to be rejected. It was the first and last time I was ever fired from anything and it hurt horribly. I was so embarrassed. I begged the director to go back to the dressing room to get my coat and purse as I did not want to face the other people in the show. Even if they did not yet know I had been fired, they would know soon enough. I did not want them to see me leaving. He brought me my coat and purse, and I left, humiliated and depressed.[14]

In December 1945 another family friend came through. Mary Martin, who had made her name seven years earlier singing a torrid "My Heart Belongs to Daddy" in Cole Porter's *Leave It to Me*, was a pal of Edith's and a patient of Loyal's. That fall, Martin had stayed at the Davises' apartment for several days, and to return the favor she saw to it that Nancy was given a part in her new play, *Lute Song*, an opulently produced musical fantasy based on the two-thousand-year-old Chinese classic *Pi-Pa-Ki*. Nancy played Si-Tchun, a lady in waiting to Martin's princess; Yul Brynner, in his first starring role on Broadway, played the prince. Apparently some effort was made to make Nancy think she had gotten the part on her own, since she was hired after auditioning for producer Michael Myerberg, who told her, "You look like you could be Chinese." Years later, director John Houseman confirmed in his memoir that "the usual nepotistic casting" was behind the hiring of "a pink-cheeked, attractive but awkward and amateurish virgin by the name of Nancy Davis."[15] After a week or two of rehearsals, Houseman tried to fire her, but Martin wouldn't hear of it. "John, I have a very bad back," she told the director, "and Nancy's father, Loyal Davis, is the greatest [neurosurgeon] in the U.S.A. *We are not letting Nancy go!*"[16]

Nancy dyed her brown hair black for the part, and took the crosstown bus to and from the theater. "I'd have to get out on 50th, then walk a block to my place," she recalled. "New York was so great then. You never thought about it being dangerous or anything like that."[17] Loyal and Edith came from Chicago for the play's opening at the Plymouth Theater on February 6, 1946, which was followed by a big party at Sardi's. "Nancy was the ingénue," recalled Robert Fryer, an aspiring young producer who met her when she was in *Lute Song*. "And we became good friends. I didn't drink, and Nancy didn't drink, so after the theater at night, we'd go have our cereal. Cornflakes—that was the big treat."[18] According to Nancy, they usually went to a Horn and Hardart automat, "and if we were really feeling flush, we'd have bananas." As for drinking: "I tried . . . but I just didn't like the taste of it."[19]

"That's absolutely true," said Richard Davis, who told me that his stepsister had shunned alcohol during her college years as well and would continue to do so all her life. He remembered how furious she was with him when he visited her in New York with three buddies from Princeton and got so drunk that he vomited in her bathtub. "She gave me hell," Davis said, and it was two years before she invited him back.[20]

* * *

When *Lute Song* closed in the summer of 1946 after a six-month run, Nancy continued to spend a lot of time with Fryer and his boyfriend, James Carr, a young actor. "Bobby and Jimmy lived right around the corner from me," she recalled. "My building had a little backyard, so in the warm weather we would barbecue hot dogs and hamburgers and eat outside."[21] Anne Washburn, a Yale drama school graduate who lived in Fryer and Carr's building, told me that she and Jimmy and Nancy spent their days going to auditions "trying to get parts. No parts ever seemed to be forthcoming, but Nancy could handle any situation. She was a very down-to-earth person."[22] Fryer, who later became a successful Broadway and Hollywood producer, would remain a lifelong friend of Nancy's. On a television biography of her in 1997, he noted, "The theater and films both are strange, in that you don't keep your relationships usually beyond the shooting schedule or the run of the show. But she was one of the people that kept her friends closely held."[23]

Ron Fletcher, a principal dancer in *Lute Song,* also became close to Nancy. "I found her to be a delightful creature," he told me. "She had a wonderful sense of humor and was bright and curious. However, she didn't seem worldly at all, which is what I liked about her. I would tell her tacky, slightly obscene stories, and that wonderful laugh would come out." Fletcher said that, before the

Broadway opening, they were in New Haven, Philadelphia, and Boston for twelve weeks of try-outs. "When you're on the road, people pair off. I don't remember how Nancy and I first started to talk—we just decided to go out and eat one night, and people were dancing. She was a marvelous dancer and loved to dance, and I'm a very good ballroom dancer."

Another Nancy Reagan biographer has implied that Fletcher was homosexual.[24] "I was living with a girl when I went into the show," he explained. "I later realized that I had always been gay, but I was also very attracted to unusual females, and I found Nancy very sexy. We had a little romance on the road, but I don't think she was in love with me, and I can't say I was in love with her. We were just liv-ing in the moment and enjoying each other. After we came back to New York, we drifted apart. I went to her apartment a couple of times and real-ized what kind of a lifestyle she had. Maybe that intimidated me, because I'm from the backwoods of Missouri and didn't finish ninth grade." Nonetheless, he told me, they kept in touch. "Nancy was the type of person you may not see for ten years, but the minute you see each other, you just start laughing."[25]

Nancy's affinity for homosexual men has been frequently remarked upon, but it would hardly have been so noteworthy if she had stayed in show business instead of marrying an actor who went into politics. She was close to a number of lesbian and bisexual women over the years, starting with her godmother and her circle of friends, but this, too, is not unusual in the entertainment world. If gay men were attracted to the young Nancy Davis, it was probably for the same reasons that straight men were: she was pretty, lively, well dressed, a good dancer, a great listener, and, like her mother, a natural-born coquette. She knew how to flirt with a man in a way that was flattering and unthreatening, which may explain why gay men felt especially comfortable with her. And when she was out with a man, she gave him her full attention.

There was also something nurselike about Nancy Davis. She had been a volunteer nurse's aide in Chicago, and one can easily imagine her in a white uniform and pinned-back cap, hovering over a patient's bed with care-filled eyes and a troubled brow, telling him that everything will be all right if he follows doctor's orders and takes his medicine as prescribed. From high school on, by all accounts, she enjoyed spending time with the opposite sex, hearing their problems and their hopes, comforting them and encouraging them. Moreover, she had the examples of her mother, her Aunt Colleen, and even Katharine Hepburn to impress upon her that a woman's job was to bring out the best in a man, to make him feel better about himself, to fix and improve him.

One of the most heartfelt—and nurselike—stories in her autobiography concerns a visit she had from Spencer Tracy's handicapped son while she was living in New York. John Tracy had been born deaf, was nearly blind, and had been stricken with

polio as a youth—"so much affliction for one boy,"
Nancy wrote. Despite his disabilities, he had graduated from college and wanted to visit New York.
Louise Tracy, who stuck with her marriage despite
her husband's relationship with Katharine Hepburn, called Nancy and asked if John could stay
with her. Nancy put him up on the sofa-bed in her
living room and took time to guide him around
town, accompanying him to the theater and
museums. ("He enjoyed musicals," she noted.
"Somehow, he sensed the music through the
vibrations he felt.")

The highlight of his trip was to be a date with a
girl he had met in California. Without telling him,
Nancy called the restaurant in advance to advise
the maître d' of John's "difficulty in communicat-
ing." But the girl canceled the morning of the date,
and an infuriated Nancy told her off: "I took the
telephone call, turned away from Johnny so he
couldn't read my lips, and told her what I thought
of her leading him on. . . . I could tell she wasn't ill,
she just did not want to go out with Johnny. It had
been one thing to meet Spencer Tracy's son and
therefore meet Spence in Hollywood; it was
another thing to date his handicapped son in New
York. Well, she was a lot more handicapped than
he was as far as I was concerned. . . . I tried to
soften the blow, but he was hurt. I went out to dinner and dancing with him as his date, and we had
a good time. He was a marvelous young man, and
I admired his courage enormously. . . . I remember
the night he left me in New York. A representative

from MGM came to take him to the airport. The man took one of his two bags, and I started to take the other to help him down to the car. He said, 'Oh, no, you're my princess, and I'm your slave,' and took his own bag. I kissed him good-bye and dissolved into tears."[26]

Nancy did not want for dates in New York—her suitors included assistant directors and producers, as well as a young Navy doctor based at the Brooklyn Naval Yard[27]—but, as she recalled in *Nancy*, "I had no serious romances."[28] She loved being taken to the Stork Club, where the Duke and Duchess of Windsor held court and Walter Winchell recorded the goings and comings of showgirls and playboys. She would always slip a dinner roll or two into her evening bag for breakfast the next morning, and one night the owner, Sherman Billingsley, who didn't miss a trick, decided to have a little fun. "On the way out," Nancy recalled, "the captain handed me a little package. I opened it right in front of my date. There was a card from Mr. Billingsley which said: 'For the rolls,' and inside was a pound of butter."[29]

"Nancy was very charming, very outgoing, very friendly," recalled retired publisher Kenneth Giniger, who started dating her while she was in *Lute Song*. "She was a very nice-looking girl. I didn't think of her as a great beauty." At the time, Giniger, a graduate of the University of Virginia and New York University Law School fresh out of the Army, was publicity director of Prentice Hall. "I knew her mother, who in those days had a radio show in Chicago on which I placed authors," he explained. "And her mother mentioned to me that she had a daughter in a show in New York, and I ought to look her up, which I did. She was very close to all her mother's friends. She sort of flowed with the tide, I think. Of course, she had a very social mother and stepfather, and they helped her a great deal." Nancy, he said, "was quieter than Edith, more reserved, I would say. Edith was somewhat effusive." He took her to "the Stork Club a great deal, or El Morocco," and placed the occasional item about her in the columns. Although he was actively involved in New York's Republican Party, they rarely discussed politics. "She wasn't particularly interested," Giniger said.[30]

In August 1946, shortly after *Lute Song* closed, ZaSu Pitts offered Nancy a supporting role in her new play, *Cordelia*. Though it was scheduled to open on Broadway that fall, the old-fashioned comedy didn't make it beyond tryouts in New England, and Nancy did not get another theater part for almost a year. She started a scrapbook of her press clippings at that time, meticulously dating each clipping and underlining all mentions of her. The first were a pair of reviews of *Cordelia* from New Haven and Boston, the latter dismissing the play as "hoked-up" and "amateurish" but praising her as "unusually talented and attractive."[31] These were followed by a flurry of items from Chicago society columns noting her attendance at various parties and charity events during an extended visit home for Thanksgiving 1946. "Enjoying the music of two bands against a back-drop of red velvet," a typical item read, "Nancy Davis here from New York, wearing Kelly green brocaded satin with a large red cabbage rose on her matching purse. Her dancing partner was Warner [sic] G. Baird Jr."[32] She also pasted in clip-pings—sent to her by her mother, no doubt—charting her parents' social and professional progress: Edith, "with orchids pinned to her mink coat," arriving at a Chicago theater opening in December 1946; Loyal, now president of the Society of Neurological Surgeons, lined up with his colleagues at a Vanderbilt University medical con-ference that April.[33]

In the spring of 1947, Nancy's agent, Max Richard, persuaded RKO Pathé, which was based in New York, to use her in several short documen-taries for its "This Is America" news series, includ-ing one about the National Foundation for Infantile Paralysis—not exactly the most glamorous of movie debuts. Her SAG application, dated May 20, 1947, notes her memberships in the Actors Equity Association and the American Federation of Radio Artists. Where it asks for a reference, Nancy put Walter Huston.[34]

She was still seeing Walter and Nan Huston quite frequently, but not under the happiest of cir-cumstances. The Hustons' marriage, like the Tracys', was a case of misery wrapped in tinsel: tense, complicated, fundamentally unhappy. While

Walter's career continued to thrive, his third wife's had withered away, and she fell into frequent and severe depressions, often requiring hospitalization. "Their marriage got to be very rough," said John Huston, Walter's son by his first wife. "I think Nan was very jealous of my father and his popularity. She wanted to be a star."[35] Since suffering a nervous breakdown in 1942, Nan had been treated by a psychiatrist recommended by Loyal Davis. In February 1947, however, she was so unstable that, on Loyal's advice, Walter agreed to have her undergo a series of electroshock treatments at Passavant Hospital. He spent the next two months by her side in their New York apartment,[36] and then left for Mexico to film *The Treasure of the Sierra Madre*, which was directed by John and would win Oscars for both father and son. Nancy visited them during this New York stay, and her sympathy went mostly to Uncle Walter. "Nan was a very difficult woman," she said. "Very difficult. She wanted parts in plays that she couldn't possibly get. But he was so darling. Just darling."[37]

That summer ZaSu Pitts found another job for Nancy, a supporting role in George Abbott's revival of *The Late Christopher Bean,* which was touring the stock circuit. For three months the comedy warhorse and her protégée spent each week in a different town, working with actors from the local theater company—a learning experience for Nancy, but a step down for Pitts. As James Karen, who played opposite Nancy at the Olney Theater, in suburban Maryland, pointed out, the largely older audiences were mainly there to see how stars who were popular in the 1920s and 1930s had aged. "Some were happy, beautiful, and well-off financially," he recalled, "others were old, beaten up, and broke, defeated by a hard profession. I was never sure about ZaSu's status, because she complained a lot publicly about Roosevelt's New Deal robbing her, but she seemed to be well-off. Nancy was very much under ZaSu's control. They lived together and dressed together and ate together. They never socialized with us or with any of the locals. They came to the theater, did their job, and then went back to their hotel in Washington."[38]

The tour began in Ogunquit, Maine, on July 7, the day after Nancy's twenty-sixth birthday, and she was showered with telegrams—all saved in her scrapbook—wishing her happy birthday and good luck, from "Mother and Pops" and Richard at Princeton, from Colleen Moore Hargrave and Louise and Spencer Tracy, from her Chicago dancing partner, Warren Baird Jr., and even her former fiancé, James Platt White. (The most intriguing was sent from La Guardia Airfield and signed Tommy: "A birthday message between we two to let you know I'm thinking of you.")[39] The following week, at the Olney Theater, Nancy received a card backstage from General and Mrs. Omar Nelson Bradley saying, "We are in seats F7 and 8. If you have time, we'd love to say hello. We met your mother in Chicago last month."[40] General Bradley had led the American army at Normandy and would soon be named chairman of the joint chiefs of staff by President Truman; this was one more example of Edith's ability to charm powerful figures and enlist them in her daughter's cause.

That same week, the American Newspaper Women's Club gave a tea honoring ZaSu and Nancy at its Washington headquarters, which drew a mix of reporters, socialites, and government wives, including those of Florida senator Claude Pepper and Montana congressman Mike Mansfield (the future Senate majority leader and ambassador to Japan under Presidents Carter and Reagan). "Conversation hummed about politics, the theater and press," *The Washington Post* reported. "Miss Pitts told a small group, 'I'm definitely 'agin communism. I'd like to get on a soap box and warn everybody against supporting it or any other isms.' "[41]

Nancy had a fairly substantial role in *The Late Christopher Bean*, playing the younger and nicer of a greedy country doctor's two daughters, and she got several good reviews. "Nancy Davis, the likeable sister, is spirited and good-looking," wrote one critic. "She manages to make what might have been a sappy, cloying girl into a real person." "Nancy Davis does a splendid job," declared another. "She has lots of charm and grace as well as ability."[42]

When the summer season ended, Pitts decided to take the show on a fall tour of regional theaters in larger cities, including Philadelphia, Boston, Cleveland, and Milwaukee. *The Late Christopher*

Bean opened at Chicago's Civic Theater on October 20, 1947, and once again Nancy's dressing room was papered in congratulatory telegrams from family friends and assorted beaus, including the Tracys, the Hustons, Lillian Gish, Louis Calhern, Mary Martin, and Illinois governor Dwight Green. There were flowers from Mr. and Mrs. Philip Knight Wrigley, of the super-rich chewing gum clan, with a card reading "Chicago is proud of you, Nancy," and from Orville Taylor, the lawyer who had arranged Nancy's adoption a decade earlier, who wrote, "For my adorable Nancy from your general counsel and greatest admirer."[43] Loyal and Edith gave an opening night party, with a guest list that included the governor's wife, the Hargraves, Narcissa Thorne, Mrs. Alden Swift, and millionaire retailer Leon Mandel and his wife, Carola, who was considered Chicago's best-dressed woman. The party was noted in the next day's papers, as was the performance of "a sleek brunette named Nancy Davis, who plays the love interest with an appealing dash of wistful charm."[44]

Nancy had been on the road with ZaSu Pitts for nearly six months when *The Late Christopher Bean* tour came to an end, in December 1947 in Detroit, and from there she returned to Chicago for the holidays. The Davises had moved from 199 to 209 East Lake Shore Drive earlier that year. The eighteen-story limestone fortress built in 1925 by Benjamin Marshall, the architect of the Drake Hotel, was considered the city's premier apartment building and counted the Davises' good friend Mayor Kelly among its residents. Their new place was also a duplex, but it had only two bedrooms, and the main rooms were on the ground floor; according to Richard Davis, "it was the cheapest apartment in the building."[45] Bruce McFarland, Nancy's old Latin School friend, who was now working at a Chicago radio station, recalled going to the apartment to take Nancy out and finding her in her usual good spirits. "I could hear Dr. Davis upstairs reading the riot act to his son, Dick—he was really ticked off and letting him have it. Nancy and I just looked at each other and smiled and got the hell out of there." On a second occasion, Loyal and Edith were "playing charades using medical terms" with a couple of other doctors and their wives when McFarland arrived.[46]

Nancy returned to New York in January 1948. She next appeared on the stage that July, for a two-week run in Detroit, where her pal Robert Fryer was producing a revival of Lillian Hellman's *The Little Foxes*. Nancy played the demure daughter of the venomously evil Southern Gothic matriarch Regina Hubbard, a character made famous by Tallulah Bankhead on Broadway and by Bette Davis in the 1941 movie. Ruth Chatterton, one of the great leading ladies of the stage in the 1920s and 1930s, took the part in Detroit. Nancy Reagan told me that she didn't remember having been in this play,[47] and it is not listed among her stage credits in her memoirs or in books and articles about her. But her scrapbook contains seven clippings about it, as well as a sheaf of telegrams—from her parents, the Mandels, Bruce McFarland—she received at the Shubert Lafayette Theater opening night, July 5, 1948, the day before her twenty-seventh birthday. Perhaps she had a falling out with Fryer. A telegram sent from him in Detroit to Nancy in New York on August 5 sounds both conciliatory and foreboding: "Hoping a new future opens for you and you know what's happening to you. Best luck to my best girl. Love Bobby."[48]

The Detroit engagement marked the end of Nancy's stage career. Meanwhile, her romantic life seemed stymied as well. She still went out once a week or so with Kenneth Giniger, but he told me, "I wouldn't call it a romance. We were just good friends and that was it."[49] According to Kitty Kelley, she had a "short affair" with Alfred Drake, the married star of Oklahoma!, in early 1948, and subsequently pursued Max Allentuck, the general manager for Kermit Bloomgarden, an important Broadway producer. Giniger, who knew Drake fairly well, doubted that he and Nancy ever met. A clipping from March 1948 in Nancy's scrapbook may confirm her link to Allentuck, noting that he and "Norma Davies [sic], actress, have joined the steady set at Sardi's." An unnamed secretary of Allentuck's told Kelley that he would sometimes slip out a back door when Nancy—"lovely looking and beautifully dressed in her suits and fur coats"—dropped by his office. "Let's put it this way," the secretary said. "She liked Max much more than he liked her."[50]

One night in September 1948, Nancy got a call from Edith telling her that Spencer Tracy had given her number to Clark Gable. "The King," as Gable was universally known—he had actually been "crowned" in a ceremony at the MGM commissary in 1938—was planning a trip to New York and would be calling Nancy to ask her out for dinner. "Be sure not to say," Edith warned Nancy, " 'Sure, and I'm Greta Garbo.' "[51]

Gable's visit was the highlight of Nancy's New York years, an experience she would still be talking about at dinner parties in her seventies and eighties. Gable spent a week in New York, and after their first dinner date, he took Nancy out every day and every night. Gable was a big baseball fan, so in the afternoons he and Nancy would be driven uptown to Yankee Stadium, where the crowd got so excited by his presence that the police had to escort them to and from their seats. On the days when the Yankees weren't playing, they lunched at "21." Then it was dinner at the Colony (the Le Cirque of its day), followed by a stop at the Stork Club. "When we got up to dance," Nancy recalled, "I never knew I had so many friends. 'Nancy! How nice to see you!' And then, of course, I had to introduce them to my date."[52]

Gable, a bachelor since the death of his beloved third wife, Carole Lombard, five years earlier, was forty-six when Nancy met him and not quite the swashbuckling he-man who had carried Vivien Leigh up the stairs in *Gone With the Wind*. He had put on weight, drank heavily—according to Gore

Vidal, "after a few drinks [he] would loosen his false teeth, which were on some sort of peg and then shake his head until they rattled like dice"[53]— smoked three packs of cigarettes a day, and admitted to being a so-so lover. His postwar pictures had flopped at the box office, but when he took Nancy to see Phil Silvers and Nanette Fabray in the hit musical *High Button Shoes*, the audience stood and applauded him and would not sit "until he waved his hand."[54]

Nancy was enchanted by him and thrilled with the attention she received simply by being at his side. "I knew all sorts of stars as family friends," she later wrote, but this "was my first experience going anywhere with a star of that magnitude." One night he took her to a fancy showbiz party at the Waldorf Towers: "I was sure I would be forgotten and left in a corner somewhere when some of the gorgeous and famous glamour girls got to him. They were certainly aware of his presence! But nothing like that happened. When he was with you, he was with you and only you, and never looked over your shoulder to see who else was in the room. I think the secret of his charm was that he made whoever he was with feel important. He made me feel important, and I must say it gave my ego a boost."[55]

In *My Turn*, she describes Gable's attentiveness as "a quality that good courtesans also have," but she makes it clear that things went only so far between them. "Clark was sexy, handsome, and affectionate, but I found him less the seducer he was reputed to be than a kind, romantic, and fun-loving man. He sent me flowers and we held hands, but I think that in his case the lover image had been so built up that it was a relief for him to be with someone like me, who made no demands on him."[56]

Their week of dates won her more press coverage than any of her stage appearances had. All the leading New York columnists—Walter Winchell, Ed Sullivan, Earl Wilson, Dorothy Kilgallen—ran items, as did Louella Parsons in Hollywood. "Has something at last happened to Clark Gable," asked *Modern Screen* magazine, "something, to be exact, in the form of a slim, brown-eyed brown-haired beauty named Nancy Davis—that is changing the fitful pattern of his romantic life? Has he, in other words, finally found the Gable woman, for whom he is more than willing to give up the Gable women? The answer seems to be yes—even though, if it is love at all, it is so far a love in hiding."[57]

A year later, Gable married Sylvia, Lady Ashley, in Santa Barbara. It was a fourth marriage for both of them, and it lasted a little more than a year. In *My Turn*, written a year after she left the White House, Nancy relived her dates with the King:

Perhaps I missed some of the signals he was sending out. He lived in Encino, and he referred to his house as a ranch. One night, at dinner, he asked me, "How would you feel about living on a ranch?"

I mumbled something foolish like, "Gee, I don't know, I never have." But I have often looked back at that moment and wondered: Was Clark Gable sounding me out about a possible future together? And if so, how should I have responded? I wasn't in love with him, but if we had seen more of each other, I might have been. I was certainly taken by his attentiveness and his kindness, and by his modesty. It just wasn't what you would have expected from such a star.[58]

Aside from her dates with Gable, the only bright spot during her last year in New York was a modicum of success in the emerging new medium of television. Nancy had appeared on television for the first time while she was in Chicago the previous fall, most likely in a celebrity show for the Community Fund organized by Edith, who was chairman of the charity's women's division. Television was just beginning to take hold of the American living room—there were only 136,000 sets in the whole country in 1947—and the technology was not yet perfected. "I had to wear green makeup and black lipstick," Nancy recalled, "to look good on those early, primitive black-and-white sets."[59]

In 1948, according to *Mademoiselle*, she "had feature roles on the Kraft Television Theater and the Lucky Strike dramatic series."[60] The fashion magazine noted her progress in its November issue with a small photograph and a paragraph of text, concluding with: "Enthusiastic about television, Nancy looks forward to the day when video will have its own stars, [and] would like a dramatic show of her own." At the end of the year, ZaSu Pitts arranged for Nancy to reprise her three-line part in *Ramshackle Inn* on NBC's *Philco Television Playhouse,* another one of the live dramatic anthology series that dominated the small screen's early years.

"I wasn't setting show business on fire," she later wrote, trying to put a realistic but cheerful face on this period of her life. "However, I honestly don't think I even thought of that. I was doing something I wanted to do and having a good time."[61]

Nancy Davis at twenty-seven, it would seem, was not that much closer to a successful acting career than she had been when she left Chicago four years earlier. Nor had she found Mr. Right.

CHAPTER NINE

DIVORCE

1947–1948

I have turned down quite a few scripts because I thought they were tinged with Communistic ideas. . . . I could never take any of this pinko mouthing very seriously, because I didn't feel it was on the level.

Gary Cooper, testifying before HUAC, October 1947

The year 1947 began on a high note for Ronnie and Jane, with her Oscar nomination for *The Yearling* and his being cast in *The Voice of the Turtle*, a romantic comedy based on John Van Druten's long-running Broadway play, which Warners saw as one of its top films of the year.[1] On January 26, shortly after their seventh anniversary, Jane learned that she was pregnant. If they had a girl, the movie magazines confided, Ronnie wanted to name her Veronica. Jane reportedly had her heart set on a boy, who would be named Ronald Reagan Jr.[2]

On March 10, Robert Montgomery stepped down

as SAG president, citing a conflict of interest, as he had recently begun to co-produce his own movies. In a secret vote by board members, Reagan was chosen to serve out Montgomery's term, winning over the more liberal Gene Kelly and the more conservative George Murphy, who were then elected first and third vice presidents, respectively. William Holden—nominated by Jane Wyman—was made second vice president.[3]

Four nights later, Jane and Ronnie attended the Academy Awards with Mary Benny—Jack Benny was emcee—and watched Olivia de Havilland win over Jane to take the Best Actress award for *To Each His Own*. As they left the Shrine Auditorium, Reagan tried to make light of his wife's loss, telling reporters that maybe they'd name their expected child Oscar—"Jane deserves one around the house."[4]

On April 10, sitting in their living room with an FBI agent, the couple named at least six SAG members as suspected Communists.[5] According to Anne Edwards, who interviewed a close friend of theirs, "Wyman . . . was in an emotional state, torn, not knowing what to do but not agreeing with his decision."[6] According to the agent's report, "Reagan and his wife advised that for the past several months they had observed during the Guild meetings there were two 'cliques' of members, one headed by Anne Revere and the other by Karen Morley, which on all questions of policy confronting the Guild followed the Communist Party line."[7] Both Revere and Morley were Party members; the latter had recruited Sterling Hayden, whom Reagan apparently also named because of his leadership of the pro-CSU faction in SAG.[8]

By then the strike that had violently disrupted the industry for a large part of the previous year was sputtering to an end, and Herbert Sorrell was a desperate figure, the victim of his own dema- gogic excesses and the relentless right-wing cam- paign to hang the Communist noose around his neck. After SAG led twenty-four other Hollywood unions in declaring the CSU "a rump organization, conflicting with our duly constituted A.F.L. central labor council of Los Angeles," workers deserted the picket lines in droves. "The CSU dissolved like sugar in hot water" is the way Reagan put it.[9] "Crushed to powder" was more like it, said liberal screenwriter Philip Dunne, adding that Reagan was "always careful to hide his own aggression."[10]

Larger forces were at work, too, creating a climate in which left-wing union activism was increasingly untenable. In the November 1946 elections, Republican majorities took control of both houses of Congress for the first time since 1928; among the newcomers were Senator Joseph McCarthy of Wisconsin and Representative Richard M. Nixon of Southern California. On March 12, 1947, the White House announced the Truman Doctrine to defend Greece and Turkey from Soviet aggression. That same month Harry Truman signed an executive order requiring loyalty oaths of all federal employ- ees.[11] In June the new Congress passed the Taft-

Hartley Act over Truman's veto; it outlawed the closed shop, prohibited jurisdictional strikes, forbade unions to contribute to political campaigns, and required elected union officials to take an oath that they were not Communists.

Across the nation, the right was resurgent, and the left was divided and on the defensive. In the last week of 1946, ICCASP merged with the National Citizens Political Action Committee, another left-wing group, to form Progressive Citizens of America (PCA), laying the groundwork for a third-party challenge to Truman in the 1948 election by Henry Wallace. In Hollywood, the remains of HICCASP—including Gene Kelly, Lillian Hellman, John Howard Lawson, and Dalton Trumbo—voted to go along with the merger.[12]

One week later, in January 1947, a group of nationally prominent liberals met in Washington to launch Americans for Democratic Action. The organization had "two objectives," wrote Arthur Schlesinger Jr., "to infuse the Truman administration with the spirit of the New Deal, and to liberate the democratic left from Communist manipulation."[13] Schlesinger was an ADA founder, along with Eleanor Roosevelt; Harold Ickes, the former executive director of ICCASP; Hubert Humphrey, then Mayor of Minneapolis; economist John Kenneth Galbraith; columnists Stewart and Joseph Alsop; labor leaders Walter Reuther of the United Auto Workers and David Dubinsky of the Ladies' Garment Workers; and AVC national head Charles Bolté.[14]

"The liberal split was crystallizing," Schlesinger explained. The two new organizations "were in substantial agreement on domestic issues, but they disagreed on qualifications for membership. A.D.A. rejected 'any association with Communism or sympathizers with Communism as completely as we rejected any association with fascists or their sympathizers. Both are hostile to the principles of freedom and democracy on which this Republic has grown great.' P.C.A., on the other hand, welcomed 'all progressive men and women in our nation, regardless of . . . political affiliation.' . . . And the admission of Communists moved P.C.A. toward the Soviet side in the Cold War."[15] Mrs. Roosevelt agreed: "The American Communists seemed to have succeeded very well in jeopardizing whatever the liberals work for. Therefore, to keep them out of policy-making and staff positions seems to be very essential even at the price of being called red-baiters."[16]

Actor Melyvn Douglas became ADA's California chairman in early 1947, and Reagan joined fellow liberal anti-Communists Walter Wanger and Philip Dunne on its organizing committee.[17] Olivia de Havilland, Bette Davis, and Will Rogers Jr. also signed on.[18] At the same time, Reagan was working closely with Jimmy Roosevelt and Douglas trying to save the AVC's Hollywood chapter from a total Communist takeover. By that spring they gave up, and started the separate, anti-Communist Hollywood Chapter No. 2.[19]

"Our highest aim should be the cultivation of

freedom of the individual for therein lies the highest dignity of man," Reagan told Hedda Hopper in an interview published in May. "Tyranny is tyranny, and whether it comes from right, left, or center, it's evil. Right now the liberal movement in this country is taking the brunt of the Communist attack. The Reds know that if we can make America a decent living place for all of our people their cause is lost here. So they seek to infiltrate liberal organizations just to smear and discredit them."[20] Hopper, the avenging angel of the Hollywood right, was obviously taken by Reagan, despite his defense of liberalism, and told her readers that he "commanded the respect of his most bitter opponents."[21]

That same month, HUAC came to town. The committee was now chaired by New Jersey Republican J. Parnell Thomas, a former insurance salesman whose office featured a picture of the American flag with the slogan "These colors do not run."[22] But the committee's driving force was a reactionary Mississippi Democrat named John Rankin, who terrified the larger part of Hollywood because of his tendency to conflate Communism and Judaism. On May 8 and 9, Thomas and two other committee members held closed hearings at the Biltmore Hotel on Communist influence in the movie industry, and then Thomas announced to the press that "hundreds of very prominent film capital people have been named as Communists to us."[23]

Nearly all of the fourteen "frank and cooperative" witnesses—including screenwriters James Kevin McGuinness, Howard Emmett Rogers, and Rupert Hughes, an uncle of Howard Hughes's—were from the Motion Picture Alliance for the Preservation of American Ideals, which itself had an anti-Semitic taint. Alliance stalwart Robert Taylor told the congressmen that the Roosevelt administration had delayed his entry into the Navy in 1943 so that he could finish shooting *Song of Russia*, a film he considered pro-Soviet propaganda. Ginger Rogers's mother, Lela, testified that her daughter had insisted on cutting the Marxist line "Share and share alike—that's democracy" from Dalton Trumbo's screenplay for *Tender Comrade*.[24] Veteran character actor Adolphe Menjou swore that if the Communists took over Hollywood, which he thought was close to happening, "I would move to the state of Texas . . . because I think that Texans would kill them on sight."[25]

Jack Warner was the only studio chief to testify, and he did so secretly, one week later. Some said that he was still fuming over the CSU siege of Warner Bros. during the 1945 strike, others that he was eager to clear his name as the head of the studio that had invented the liberal-message movie. The other moguls, led by Mayer, hoped that if they ignored the committee it would go away. But Warner told the inquisitors what they wanted to hear, and in doing so assured that they would be back. There was, he testified, a conspiracy to slip anti-capitalist, un-American propaganda into

Hollywood films, and it was led by the screenwriters. "They endeavor to inject it," he said. "Whatever I could do about it—I took out." Stretching the truth, he added, "Anyone I thought was a Communist or read in the papers that he was, I dismissed at the expiration of his contract." He then listed sixteen suspect writers, including Lawson, Trumbo, Ring Lardner Jr., Irwin Shaw, and Clifford Odets, many of whom were still typing away in studio bungalows in Burbank.[26]

Like the moguls, the anti-Communist liberals of ADA, including Reagan, didn't pay too much mind to HUAC's Hollywood foray. But four nights after Jack Warner testified, PCA held a rally for Henry Wallace at which J. Parnell Thomas and "all their ilk" were denounced by the star speaker, Katharine Hepburn. Her fiery speech had been written partly by one of Warner's listees, Dalton Trumbo; another, Ring Lardner Jr., had scripted the movie that launched her on-screen partnership—and off-screen romance—with Spencer Tracy. A Bryn Mawr graduate, Hepburn inherited her progressivism from old-money East Coast parents who prided themselves on their unconventionality: her father, a prominent Hartford surgeon, was a long-time Henry Wallace admirer; her mother, born a Houghton in Boston, was a suffragette and early birth control militant. By 1947 the thirty-eight-year-old actress had already won her first Oscar and been nominated for three more, but she was more respected than beloved in Hollywood, where she was perceived as a lock-jawed snob and an eccentric radical. Yet she managed to get along with Loyal and Edith Davis when she and Tracy were their houseguests in Chicago.

The playwright Arthur Laurents, then a young screenwriter at MGM, accompanied Hepburn, Tracy, and Irene Selznick (the more unconventional of Louis B. Mayer's two daughters) to the PCA rally that night. In his memoir, *Original Story By*, Laurents captures the drama and glamour, the sheer spectacle, of Hollywood politics at the time—and also reveals its preciousness:

> The Progressive Citizens of America held a big rally at Gilmore Stadium for Henry Wallace as part of a drive to stem right-wing attacks on unions and the arts. . . . At the most dramatic moment, at the peak of excitement, a very high platform was hit with blazing spotlights and there was Katharine Hepburn in a red Valentina gown. The stadium roared. Hepburn's grin carried to the top of the bleachers and she delivered magnificently a speech fighting the destruction of culture. The crowd wouldn't stop cheering. Henry Wallace could have been elected president if Katharine Hepburn, in that red dress, on that blazing tower, could have been transported from city to city all over the land.
>
> Afterward, she, Tracy, Irene, and I went back to her house on Tower Drive, high in the Beverly hills. She was euphoric, proud of her

speech. I had been one of the writers of that speech. . . .

Tracy was bothered by the speech, more that she had made any speech at all. Actors had no place in politics, period, according to Spencer Tracy. I'd heard that before, I was sure I'd hear it again, but I never once heard it from a liberal. Only from the most conservative—and Spencer Tracy, congenial and pleasant as he was, was a right-winger. So was Louis B. Mayer. So were Cecil B. DeMille and Sam Wood. So were Barbara Stanwyck and Ronald Reagan and George Murphy, John Wayne, Ginger Rogers—stars born on the wrong side of the tracks who thought playing footsie with conservatives would allow them to cross over.[27]

Ronald Reagan was not yet a full-fledged right-winger in mid-1947—and George Murphy was born on the Yale campus, where his father was a famous track coach—but the point Laurents makes is a valid one. Consciously or not, social motives often color political views. So does the company one keeps. Reagan's postwar friends— the guys he went out for a drink with after SAG meetings, the couples he and Jane saw at Saturday night dinner parties and Sunday afternoon barbecues—were mostly self-made and mostly Republican. Even those who generally avoided party politics—the Bennys, George Burns and Gracie Allen, Claudette Colbert—were intrinsically conservative, patriotic, entrepreneurial, and obsessively concerned with the high taxes they were paying on their six-figure incomes.

Reagan considered Bill Holden, who was seven years younger, his best friend. A moderate Republican, the handsome actor was known as Golden Holden, partly because his first hit film, released in 1939, was *Golden Boy*; partly because he had grown up in monied South Pasadena and his mother was descended from George Washington.[28] Ronnie and Jane were also close to Dick Powell and June Allyson, the vivacious young blonde Powell had wed in August 1945, a month after divorcing Joan Blondell. Powell had been in films with both Ronnie and Jane: *The Cowboy from Brooklyn*, among others, with him, and two musicals, *Gold Diggers of 1937* and *The Singing Marine*, with her. June Allyson recalled in her 1982 memoir, "Ronnie and Richard were close buddies— a love of arguing politics drew them together just as a distaste for the same subject brought me and Jane Wyman together in a fortuitous blending of couples."[29]

Powell and Allyson were both major stars in the late 1940s: after a decade of crooning and swooning with Ruby Keeler in Warner Bros. musicals, he had miraculously transformed himself into a leading man in noir classics such as RKO's 1944 *Murder, My Sweet*; she had been signed by MGM in 1942, and had gone from hit to hit, starting with *Girl Crazy* with Mickey Rooney and Judy Garland. Both were from the wrong side of the tracks—he from the Ozarks, she from the Bronx—and both loved life among the swells. Louis B. Mayer gave her away at their wedding in the Holmby Hills house of Johnny Green, MGM's musical director. Powell played polo and golf, owned a yacht, which he sailed with Humphrey Bogart, and piloted his own plane.

In 1947, Powell and Allyson bought a Tudor-style mansion on Copa del Oro Drive in Bel Air, and Dick, according to June, "began ordering beautiful old oaken pieces directly from England. And when everything was in place I couldn't imagine it any other way—it was indeed like living in an old English castle complete with swords, shields, armor, mugs, and even a wishing well outside."[30]

"Ronnie and Jane and George and Julie Murphy were among our first dinner guests," Allyson remembered.

> Jane asked me to show her around the house so we could both get away from the men talking politics. I took Jane upstairs and showed her our separate bedroom suites. I am glad to say that Richard did not use his much, but he liked having a bedroom in masculine colors—brown and beige. . . . My bedroom suite was in a misty rose. And it had a niche for my collection of stuffed animals, witches, and, especially, Raggedy Ann dolls.
>
> Back downstairs Jane Wyman and I joined the men, and Julie Murphy, around the fireplace. It was a riot to listen to Ronnie, a

staunch Democrat, try to convert Richard while Richard argued just as hard to turn Ronnie into a Republican. I figured the only way to get into this conversation was to pop some basic questions at Ronnie.

He answered me carefully, methodically. When Ronnie got through explaining something to me, Jane Wyman leaned over and said, "Don't ask Ronnie what time it is because he will tell you how a watch is made.". . .

Jane Wyman seemed more upset with her husband's obsession with politics than I. I tried to make her laugh. "He'll outgrow it," I told her. To her it wasn't funny. But even more annoying to her was the fact that it took Ronnie so long to make up his mind about anything she asked him.[31]

The Reagans and the Murphys, Allyson recalled, were among a half-dozen "important and affable" couples who entertained one another regularly. This close-knit group included the ventriloquist Edgar Bergen and his wife, Frances, a former Powers model; tire heir Leonard Firestone and his wife, Polly; and drugstore tycoon Justin Dart and his wife, Jane Bryan, a co-star of Ronnie and Jane's in Brother Rat and its sequel, who had retired from acting after marrying Dart on New Year's Eve 1939. Bridge and square-dancing were among the group's favorite pastimes.

Except for Reagan, the men were all Republicans. Firestone and Dart would later be members of Reagan's Kitchen Cabinet, but back then Dart tried to avoid talking politics with the future Governor and President. "When we'd go out with Jane Wyman and Ronald Reagan, my wife would say, 'For God's sake, no politics, please!,'" Dart said years later. "The night we first met we fought like cats and dogs."[32]

Dart, who was forty in 1947 and a millionaire several times over, did not suffer fools—or those who disagreed with him—lightly. A nationally recognized business leader who had been profiled in *Time*, *Life*, and *Business Week* the year before, he ran the giant United-Rexall Drug Company and sat on the boards of ABC and United Airlines. While he would later say of Reagan, "I don't think he's the most brilliant man I ever met," he sized him up from the first as a "real leader" and exceptional communicator who could "get on his feet and influence people." Reagan, he observed, "can sell people on what's good for them, not just what they want."[33]

Like Reagan, Justin Whitlock Dart was Illinois-born, but he had grown up in Chicago's expensive North Shore suburbs. His father was a successful shirt salesman. "He worked a circuit, going from store to store," Dart recalled. "And he worked like hell. When I was eight years old—in 1915, or whenever it was—he was making $15,000 a year! In those days, that was upper, upper, *upper* middle class."[34]

In the late 1920s, while Reagan was caddieing for Charles Walgreen, Dart was courting the chain drugstore king's daughter at Northwestern University, where he played tackle on the football team and was twice selected All-Big-Ten. He was senior-class president, president of his fraternity, and already something of a "kingmaker," as he later put it. "Every year, four or five of us would sit down and decide who the class presidents were going to be," he told a *Los Angeles Times* reporter in 1982. "And then we'd start campaigning. Our guys always won."[35]

He married Ruth Walgreen in October 1929, the month the stock market crashed, and went to work in the stockroom of one of her father's stores. Three years later he was head of operations for the entire 345-store chain, and he kept the company profitable during the Depression by streamlining its purchasing and distribution systems and ruthlessly closing laggard stores. He also took credit for such marketing innovations as moving the prescription counter to the back of the store so that customers had to pass display shelves holding Walgreen's 25,000 products, ranging from pots and pans to golf balls. "Make money," he exhorted employees, "but have fun doing it!"[36]

His grateful father-in-law gave him shares in the company, put him on its board, and in 1939 appointed him general manager. Dart was already flying out to Los Angeles to woo Jane Bryan by then, and that April he divorced Ruth Walgreen, with whom he had had two sons. On Christmas

Day, Charles Walgreen died suddenly at age sixty-six, and control of the company passed to Ruth and her brother, Charles Walgreen Jr. It took them almost two years to force Dart out, but in 1941 they fired him. According to Dart, Walgreen senior had been closer to him than to his own children, and left him with "quite a little nest egg."[37] Dart also claimed to have cornered the bourbon market before the repeal of Prohibition and made $1 million in a few months by selling it as prescription whiskey for medicinal purposes. "It was borderline, but it was legal," he explained.[38] Dart himself was a teetotaler, and discouraged drinking among his subordinates.[39]

In November 1941, Jane and Justin Dart left Chicago for Boston, where he took charge of the Liggett Drug Company, a subsidiary of United Drug, Inc., a sprawling, inefficient conglomerate, which also licensed the Rexall name to more than twelve thousand independent druggists in the U.S., Canada, England, and Ireland. In April 1943, he was made president of the parent company, which he renamed United-Rexall. In 1945 he persuaded the board to move the headquarters to Los Angeles—"I thought it was the promised land"—and started construction on a $2 million headquarters at the intersection of Beverly and La Cienega Boulevards with "the world's largest drugstore" on its ground floor.[40]

The Darts built a house, which they named Winds Aloft, at 944 Airole Way in Bel Air, not far from Dick Powell and June Allyson's new mansion.

Like Powell, Dart was a passionate aviator; he frequently flew company planes, with Jane as his co-pilot, to inspect United-Rexall stores around the country. He was said to breeze through his daily office appointments in four hours, and his 1946 *Current Biography* entry noted, "President Dart concerned himself only with the establishment of broad policies, leaving their execution entirely to his associates." This left time for a full plate of civic activities; Dart was active in the Chamber of Commerce, the Community Chest, the Boy Scouts, and the Republican Party. He was invited to join the Los Angeles and Bel Air Country Clubs, as well as the California Club, the bastion of L.A.'s downtown Protestant elite, and the Rancheros Vistadores, a Santa Barbara–based group of wealthy businessmen who spent weekends riding, roping cattle, and sleeping under the stars on members' ranches.

Jane Dart was the "exact personality opposite from her husband"—shy, reserved, self-effacing.[41] A dark-haired Irish beauty, she had been born Jane O'Brien in Los Angeles, and was renamed Jane Bryan when she went to Warners in 1936. Bette Davis took her under her wing, and Jane was cast in four of Davis's films—*Marked Woman, Kid Galahad, The Sisters,* and *The Old Maid.* She happily gave up her promising career to devote herself entirely to her husband and the three children they had in short order, and she liked being called by the nickname Dart gave her, Punky. In some ways, she was also the opposite of Jane Wyman, but they became good friends at Warners and stayed close after they both married.

Two other future Kitchen Cabinet figures—Holmes Tuttle and Jack Wrather—also came into Reagan's life at this time. Tuttle, a wealthy automobile dealer, sold Reagan a Ford coupé in 1946, and he and his wife, Virginia, occasionally dined with Ronnie and Jane. Wrather, a Texas oilman, moved to California in 1946 to go into the entertainment business and married the actress Bonita "Bunny" Granville the following year; Bunny and Ronnie had been friends since working together in the 1939 Dead End Kids vehicle *Angels Wash Their Faces*. Like Punky Dart, Bunny Wrather put acting aside after her marriage.

Holmes Tuttle, who was already active in local Republican politics, and Jack Wrather, who was then a conservative Southern Democrat, later recalled arguing politics with Ronnie. "He was quite outspoken in his beliefs," said Tuttle, "and several times when we were together we had—I'll put it this way—some spirited discussions."[42] It seems that Reagan talked politics wherever he went and with whomever he met. But where a Robert Stack or a Justin Dart saw charisma and confidence, others detected insecurity and detachment. "He was a boring liberal," said actress Marsha Hunt, a leftist actress—later black-listed for suspected but unproven Communist ties—who went on the SAG board in 1947. "He would buttonhole you at a party and talk liberalism at you. You'd look for an escape."[43]

Robin Duke, the widow of diplomat Angier Biddle Duke and later President Clinton's ambassador to Norway, came to know Reagan and Wyman fairly well while she was married to actor Jeffrey Lynn in the 1940s. "Jane was outgoing and fun," Duke told me. "Ronnie was always perfectly nice, but you could never get close to him. He put up this barrier, which I thought was based on fear." Talking politics, she felt, was his way of avoiding more personal subjects, and she found it hard to take his views seriously, even when she agreed with him. "He was an airhead," she said. "No one would have ever dreamed that he could become president."[44]

One of the things that aggravated Jane Wyman most was her husband's insistence on screening *Kings Row* when they had dinner guests. "Jane had a violent aversion to . . . *Kings Row*," fan magazine writer Jerry Asher told a biographer. "It wasn't that she envied Ronnie his one serious success in films. It was just that the morbid, repressed, baleful ambience of the picture brought back her Missouri past much too vividly. [She] knew the picture itself to be a fine one, but Ronnie's compulsive efforts to foist continued screenings on his guests to underline his pride in one of the few pictures he thought showcased him decently, drove her wild, and depressed her. Ronnie was a hell of a bright guy, but he lacked, I'm afraid, the sensitivity to discern that he was opening old wounds in Jane by rubbing that picture into her."[45]

Others felt it was Jane who was insensitive and self-centered. Leonora Hornblow, who *liked* talking politics with Ronnie, recalled visiting her one afternoon around this time. "I remember saying, 'Jane, could I have a cup of coffee? I'm dying for a cup of coffee.' She said, 'No, there's no coffee in the house. I'm allergic to coffee.' Imagine! I'm sure Ronnie drank coffee—I know he did. But she didn't want coffee, so why should there be coffee in the house? I always thought that was so typical of Jane."[46]

In early June 1947, Reagan started shooting *That Hagen Girl* with Shirley Temple, a film he considered beneath him creatively and morally. It was the famous child actress's first adult role, playing a sultry small-town teenager who is rumored to be the illegitimate daughter of Reagan's character, a lawyer returning from the war. Reagan hated the fact that the script called for them to fall in love, and tried to have their romance written out of it. He succeeded only in winning an "oddball finish in which we climb on a train—Shirley carrying a bouquet—and leave town. You are left to guess as to whether we are married, just traveling together, or did I adopt her."[47]

In one scene, Maureen Reagan later wrote, Temple "tries to commit suicide by jumping into a lake, and Dad, playing her older suitor, had to jump into the lake to rescue her. Over and over again.

They shot take after take, until the director was grudgingly satisfied . . . the water was freezing. The numerous retakes took their toll on Dad; he woke up feverish the next morning, and within a few days, as he was leaving a premiere, he doubled over with a pain he described as 'being stabbed in the chest.' It turned out he had a serious case of viral pneumonia; in fact, it almost claimed him. I vividly remember the night later that week when an ambulance came to take him to Cedars of Lebanon Hospital."[48]

Ronnie was admitted to the hospital on June 19, and Jane, six months pregnant, kept a bedside vigil for five days and nights as his fever rose to 104. By the time the fever broke, on June 25, Jane had gone into labor. She was taken to the Queen of Angels Hospital, where at 11:26 the next morning she gave birth to a girl they named Christine, who died nine hours later. Reagan was released from Cedars of Lebanon that day, seventeen pounds lighter, overwhelmingly exhausted, but grateful for life: "The ambulance ride home made quite an impression on me. I couldn't get enough of looking at the world as it went by, and even the most ordinary, everyday things seemed strangely beautiful."[49]

Christine Reagan was cremated on July 2. One might say that her parents' marriage perished with her, as the broken couple pursued their separate obsessions: his with politics, hers with acting. Ronnie went back to work on *That Hagen Girl*, while continuing to devote five nights a week to

SAG, immersed in the contract negotiations with the Motion Picture Producers Association that had begun in April and would extend into September. He also found time for yet another cause, the International Rescue and Relief Committee, which was helping refugees from the recently installed Communist regimes in Eastern Europe. Robert Montgomery chaired the IRRC's Hollywood branch, and Dick Powell was on its founding committee. For Reagan, this was another small step rightward.[50]

A depressed Jane Wyman started preparing for her role as a deaf-mute teenager in *Johnny Belinda*, which was scheduled to start shooting in Northern California after Labor Day. She spent the summer practicing sign language and lip-reading with a deaf Mexican girl who came to the house several times a week. For days on end, she would stuff her ears with wax to block all sound, and refuse to speak a word to her husband and children. Six-year-old Maureen was sent off to summer boarding school for several weeks, and upon her return learned a bit of sign language to communicate with her mother. Two-year-old Michael was left in the hands of Nanny Banner. On Saturday nights Ronnie dropped the children off at his mother's, and he picked them up on Sunday after Nelle had taken them to church. Whether the children were home or not, Ronnie now slept in his study.[51]

For the Warners publicity department, the perfect couple still had the perfect marriage. The day after Ronnie came home from the hospital, Louella Parsons quoted him extolling his wife for being by his side until she herself was hospitalized. In the August issue of *Movies*, Jane printed an open love letter to her husband celebrating their seven years of marital bliss:

> You and I have been married seven years, Mr. Reagan. During this period, at least once a week you've reminded me (kiddingly) how lucky I am to have you for a husband. I think I *am* lucky. . . .
>
> I don't think I have ever seen you *really* angry—but I'd hate to cause you to lose your temper. There was that one time: I was wrong and we both knew it. You believe there's a reason for everything, so as usual, you were tolerant and took an objective viewpoint. I think your understanding is your greatest of many sweet qualities.
>
> . . . there isn't a single thing about you I'd want to change. You've been wonderful for me in many ways. You know how easily I blow up and have to get things off my chest. You're just the opposite, and it has a soothing effect. Actually, you are a serious person, but you use a humorous approach. It's a great gift, Ronnie. Calmly and quietly, with that keen analytical mind, you get the most amazing results. . . .
>
> Your love of sports has given you a clean mind, to say nothing of a clean body. How well I know! Two baths and two bath towels a day.

Remind me to tell you a bedtime story about the laundry situation. Your room is always neat, everything you own in immaculate order. You never even put away a pair of shoes without first buffing them. You're a sentimentalist: you remember holidays; you've never forgotten an anniversary. On these occasions you buy me presents, and a card always comes with them. I love these cards and I save them. They're witty and tender. You write as well as you act—and jump horses.

If you promise to do something you never go back on your word. . . . I guess the only thing we heartily disagree on is dancing—together. We get along so beautifully with other partners but I suspect that I unconsciously do the leading. You never say anything.[52]

The week after Labor Day, Ronnie drove Jane to Mendocino, a hundred miles up the coast from San Francisco, where she would spend the next six weeks filming *Johnny Belinda.* Jane had wanted this part since she saw the original play by Elmer Harris on Broadway in 1939, while she and Reagan were touring with Louella Parsons. Producer Jerry Wald, who had first worked with Jane as the screenwriter on *Brother Rat,* pushed hard for the studio to buy the rights and give her the lead.[53] Lew Ayres was cast as the compassionate doctor who teaches Wyman's character to speak. Charles Bickford played her father, Agnes Moorehead her spinster aunt, and Stephen

McNally the rapist she kills when he tries to kidnap their baby. This was high Hollywood melodrama, but filmed with such spare artistry and directed with such subtle intelligence that the finished product transcended the genre.

Away from home, the thirty-year-old actress seemed to blossom. The cast and crew lived in an old lumber camp outside town and spent their evenings singing songs around a campfire. After getting over their mutual wariness—he assumed she was an insipid chorus girl, she had hoped Joseph Cotten would get the part—Jane and her leading man became nearly inseparable.[54] They spent hours together every day, talking, listening to classical music, discussing philosophy and poetry. Jane told friends that Lew really *listened* to what she had to say and took her ideas seriously—in contrast to a husband who usually dismissed her thoughts with a "That's fine, Jane," and then went back to expounding his own views and opinions. Ayres was only two years older than Reagan, but to Jane he seemed years wiser, much more refined and thoughtful. If Ronald Reagan was the eternal lifeguard, Lew Ayres—tall, dark, and tweedy—was the perpetual professor.

A Quaker from Minnesota, Ayres was the son of divorced musicians. He had been signed by MGM in 1929, when Greta Garbo chose him out of a line of young actors to play opposite her in *The Kiss,* and he won fame the following year as the lead in *All Quiet on the Western Front*. Between 1938 and 1942, he solidified his stardom in the title role of

nine Dr. Kildare movies. But when he declared himself a conscientious objector in March 1942, the
studio was flooded with letters branding him a
coward and a traitor. He turned public opinion
around by serving as a battlefield medic in the
Pacific, and by the time he was discharged in
1945, even Hedda Hopper was calling him a man
of principle.[55]

It was rumored that Wyman and her co-star had
an affair while making *Johnny Belinda*. She always
denied it, and the consensus seemed to be that
the relationship was more spiritual than carnal. "It
was platonic," said studio publicist Jim Reid,
adding "but it was intense."[56] Ayres had been married and divorced twice in the 1930s, to actresses
Lola Lane and Ginger Rogers. (Of the latter, he
said, "Ginger Rogers was married to her career
and that mother of hers. I interfered with both relationships.")[57] There can be little doubt that working
with and being around Ayres did wonders for
Wyman's confidence personally and professionally. "No matter what they do," she told director
Jean Negulesco, "the Oscar is mine this year."[58]

While his wife was in Mendocino, Reagan was
between pictures and almost totally focused on his
duties as SAG president. The Guild finally concluded negotiations with the producers in mid-
September, though the new contract, unlike the
ten-year pact it succeeded, was for only two years.
In Reagan's account, "Actors had gotten raises
ranging from 52 to 166 percent. Working condi-

tions had been vastly improved and we had wearily agreed to a stopgap clause that settled nothing with regard to movies someday being reissued on television—but then everyone said they'd be crazy to sell their movies to a competing medium."[59]

SAG members approved the agreement 3,676 to 78, but there was little cause for celebration. On September 15 the board was shaken by the resignation of its treasurer, Anne Revere. A well-liked character actress who had won an Oscar as Elizabeth Taylor's mother in *National Velvet* in 1945, Revere had been identified to the FBI by Reagan in April as someone who always voted the Party line, though the rest of the board did not know that he had done so. Now she was the only Guild officer who refused to sign an affidavit stating that she was not a Communist, as required of union officials by the Taft-Hartley Act.[60]

Reagan and the board had been struggling with this issue since the controversial labor law was passed in June. The following day Reagan offered an explanation in a *New York Post* guest column. Speaking for himself and former SAG presidents Montgomery, Murphy, and Edward Arnold, he wrote, "We are violently opposed to indiscriminate Red-baiting, but believe that every union in our country must awaken to the menace of Communist party members who are seeking to destroy our trade unions by boring from within."[61] Most of the board resented the government's intrusion into union affairs, a position shared by the AFL's national leadership, which considered the legislation unconstitutional and supported its repeal. Reagan said he agreed, but he also argued that the Guild faced sanctions from the National Labor Relations Board if its officers did not comply, and he convinced his three vice presidents, Kelly, Holden, and Murphy, to sign the affidavits "voluntarily."[62]

On September 19, U.S. marshals began serving bright pink subpoenas on more than forty Hollywood figures, including Reagan, commanding them to appear before HUAC in Washington the following month for hearings on "Communist Infiltration of the Motion-Picture Industry." Since the committee's visit to Hollywood in May, its chief investigator, Robert E. Stripling, abetted by the right-wingers of the Motion Picture Alliance, as well as the Los Angeles office of the FBI, had been compiling lists of suspected subversives. As Stripling later wrote in *The Red Plot Against America*, "We obtained enough preliminary testimony to make a public hearing imperative."[63] In Stripling's opinion, Hollywood was the headquarters of a plot to "communize the country" and its films were saturated with subliminal propaganda: "The rich were grasping, greedy exploiters of the poor, who were always honest and down-trodden. Bankers were generally despotic; landlords cruel, and tenants noble. Judges and political figures were either crooked or fatuous fools."[64]

A large number of those subpoenaed were Alliance members, including Sam Wood, Walt

Disney, Gary Cooper, Robert Taylor, and Adolphe Menjou. These so-called friendly witnesses couldn't wait to get to Washington and publicly point fingers at those they had already named in secret. A second group, dubbed "the unfriendly nineteen" by the *Hollywood Reporter*, included eleven screenwriters, six directors, the actor Larry Parks, and the German playwright Bertolt Brecht, who had been living in exile in Los Angeles since 1940. Occupying the middle ground, sort of, were a handful of industry leaders, including Louis B. Mayer and Jack Warner, as well as the former SAG presidents George Murphy and Robert Montgomery.

Reagan apparently owed his place among them to Warner, who had told J. Parnell Thomas that he would make an effective public witness.[65] HUAC's newest member, Richard Nixon, apparently also had a hand in Reagan's selection. According to Irwin Gellman in *The Contender: Richard Nixon: The Congress Years, 1946–1952,* the freshman congressman had been impressed by the SAG president when they crossed paths for the first time in California that spring, and he thought that Reagan should be called to testify in Washington, since he was, in Nixon's words, "classified as a liberal and as such would not be accused of simply being a red-baiting reactionary."[66]

Most of Hollywood reacted to HUAC's summonses with outrage. The Unfriendly 19 gathered at the house of director Lewis Milestone—the director of *All Quiet on the Western Front*, and the only one in the group who had definitely never been a Party member[67]—with a team of five lawyers to plot a legal strategy. A few days later, John Huston, fellow director William Wyler, and the screenwriter Philip Dunne founded the Committee for the First Amendment "to protest the procedures of the House Committee and to head off [a] blacklist and censorship."[68] The first meeting was held at Ira Gershwin's house. "You could not get into the place," one attendee recalled. "The excitement was intense. The town was full of enthusiasm because they all felt they were going to win. Every star was there."[69]

"In my estimation, Communism was as nothing compared to the evil done by the witch-hunters. They were the real enemies of this country," declared John Huston.[70] The younger Huston was realistic about the political sympathies of the unfriendly witnesses. "They were mostly all Communists," he later said, "well-intentioned boobs, men mostly from poor backgrounds, and out in Hollywood they sort of felt guilt at living the good life."[71] But for Huston the issue was bedrock civil liberties: Parnell Thomas and company were infringing on the rights of free speech and free assembly, and therefore must be stopped. The Committee for the First Amendment took full-page ads in the trade papers, deploring the investigation and the mass hysteria it was encouraging. "Our position was greeted with unanimous enthusiasm in Hollywood," Huston noted, "but HUAC was not deterred."[72]

Huston, Wyler, and Dunne quickly rallied more than five hundred Hollywood personalities to their cause—not only such committed liberals as Humphrey Bogart, Rita Hayworth, Frank Sinatra, Gregory Peck, Burt Lancaster, and Judy Garland but also such moderate Republicans as Irene Dunne, Jimmy Stewart, and William Holden, and even the anti-political Spencer Tracy.[73] Reagan apparently decided not to get involved. "Willy Wyler has told me he was present at an early meeting," Dunne wrote in his memoir, *Take Two*.[74] But one of the Unfriendly 19, screenwriter Lester Cole, remembered "the conspicuous absence of such self-proclaimed liberals as Ronald Reagan." According to Cole's memoir, *Hollywood Red,* early one evening he went "to Ronnie Reagan's . . . house to ask him to a meeting of the First Amendment group. . . . Wyman told me Reagan was lying down, not feeling well, but she'd talk to him. She was back in moments, seemingly embarrassed, and asked me to tell Humphrey Bogart and Willie Wyler that he was not well, but was thinking seriously about joining them. He would let them know the next day. He didn't."[75]

Perhaps Reagan was just too busy to join one more committee. He was in Illinois doing a celebrity turn at Eureka's annual Pumpkin Festival when the first subpoenas were served in Los Angeles, which, given his aversion to flying, meant a three-day train ride each way. He was still an active member of ADA's Hollywood organizing committee, which ran ads of its own in the trades urging HUAC to respect due process and "creative freedom." He continued to assist the ADA's recruitment drive, and was one of fifty guests at a cocktail party Melvyn Douglas, its California state chairman, gave in early October to enlist new members, with Hubert Humphrey as guest of honor.[76] The day after the party, Reagan set out for Mendocino, an eighteen-hour trip by car, and he spent ten days there waiting for Jane to finish location shooting on *Johnny Belinda*. They returned home on October 17, and that night he left for Washington by train, a four-day trip. If Lester Cole came calling that afternoon—and it appears to be the only day before the HUAC hearings when Ronnie and Jane were both home—is it any wonder he was sent away?

HUAC's "Big Show," as *The New York Times* called "the most thoroughly publicized investigation [the committee] has ever undertaken," opened on Monday, October 20. The hearings were held in the Caucus Room of the Old House Office Building, the largest auditorium on Capitol Hill after the House and Senate chambers, with batteries of klieg lights aimed at the witness table and floodlights hanging from the chandeliers. Six newsreel crews, announcers from the three major radio networks, and 120 newspaper and magazine reporters covered the proceedings, and D.C. police had a hard time holding back the throng of movie fans who rushed the doors as each session opened, hoping to get one of the four hundred seats reserved for spectators.[77]

Jack Warner was the first to testify. "Ideological termites have burrowed into many American industries," he declared in a prepared opening statement. "Wherever they may be, I say let us dig them out and get rid of them. My brothers and I will be happy to subscribe generously to a pest-removal fund. We are willing to establish such a fund to ship to Russia the people who don't like our American system of government and prefer the Communistic system to ours."[78] Mayer, who came next, also read an opening statement designed to please his inquisitors, asserting that he had personally "maintained a relentless vigilance against un-American influences" at MGM and calling for "legislation establishing a national policy regulating employment of Communists in private industry. . . . It is my belief they should be denied the sanctuary of the freedom they seek to destroy."[79]

The tough-talking studio chiefs were thrown off balance, however, when pressed to name names. When Warner hesitated, Stripling read out the list of sixteen screenwriters the mogul had so willingly fingered in May. Mayer coughed up Dalton Trumbo, Lester Cole, and Donald Ogden Stewart as MGM writers he had heard *might* be Communists. Asked why they hadn't fired such employees, Warner waffled, and Mayer blamed his lawyers. Congressman Nixon asked Warner why his studio had made so many anti-Nazi movies but no anti-Communist ones, and both bosses were stunned to find themselves defending the pro-Russian films they had produced during the war.

Warner, who would later brag in his memoir that he had made *Mission to Moscow* at the personal behest of FDR, claimed he wasn't quite sure where the idea had come from. Mayer was reduced to insisting that *Song of Russia* was just another boy-meets-girl picture, which, "except for the music of Tchaikovsky, might just as well have taken place in Switzerland."[80] As Representative Emanuel Celler of New York later commented, "If Chairman Thomas sought to strike terror into the minds of the movie magnates, he succeeded. They were white-livered."[81]

To make matters worse, Mayer's shilly-shallying was directly contradicted by the next witness: Ayn Rand, the Russian émigré author of the 1943 best-seller *The Fountainhead*, which would soon be made into a movie starring Gary Cooper. Rand was the intellectual star of the Alliance, and her scene-by-scene analysis of *Song of Russia* left little doubt that MGM had put a positive gloss on conditions in the Soviet Union. "Anything that sells people the idea that life in Russia is good and that people are free and happy would be Communist propaganda. Am I not correct?" she argued, adding that she believed such was the case even if it had been done for the sake of Allied unity.[82]

The parade of Alliance witnesses who followed Rand lacked her rhetorical finesse. Sam Wood asserted that if you pulled down the pants of Communists "you would find the hammer and sickle on their rear ends,"[83] and he accused four fellow directors of trying "to steer us into the red river."[84] Walt Disney mistakenly included the League of Women Voters on his list of Communist front organizations and had to issue a public apology.[85] "This may sound biased," said matinee idol and Reagan's pal Robert Taylor. "However, if I were even suspicious of a person being a Communist with whom I was scheduled to work, I am afraid it would have to be him or me, because life is a little too short to be around people who annoy me as much as these fellow travelers and Communists do."[86]

The message that came through—from both the committee's loaded questions and the friendly witnesses' loaded answers—was persistent and threatening: Hollywood was riddled with Reds, and the studios were doing nothing about it. Adolphe Menjou reprised the Hollywood strikes of 1945 and 1946, labeling CSU boss Herbert Sorrell a card-carrying Communist and praising Reagan for "the magnificent job" he had done in trying "to settle this strike in every way possible."[87] He carried guilt by association to new extremes in a prize exchange with Congressman Nixon:

> MR. NIXON: Have you any other test which you would apply which would indicate to you that people acted like Communists?
>
> MR. MENJOU: Well, I think attending any meetings at which Mr. Paul Robeson appeared, and applauding or listening to his Communist songs in America. I would be ashamed to be

seen in an audience doing a thing of that kind.[88]

It was against this backdrop of hype and hysteria that Reagan testified, on the fourth day. If the press covered the hearings like a spectacle, Reagan seemed to approach his appearance like a performance. He had observed the proceedings of the previous afternoon from the spectators' section and had rehearsed his testimony in his hotel room with Stripling.[89] "There was a long drawn-out 'ooooh' from the jam-packed, predominantly feminine audience," *The New York Times* reported, as Reagan strode to the witness table the following morning, dressed for the part of youthful white knight in a tan gabardine suit, white shirt, and navy knit tie.[90] Lest he come across as too glamorous or lightweight, he carefully put on his glasses as he began his testimony. One could say that this was the moment when Ronald Reagan perfected the public persona he had been developing since he took to the speaking circuit at the end of the war— a finely calibrated mixture of small-town friendliness, movie star shine, and political gravitas. His testimony was balanced, sober, clear, and forceful.

"As president of the Screen Actors Guild," Stripling asked, "have you at any time observed or noted within the organization a clique of either Communists or Fascists who were attempting to exert influence or pressure on the guild?"

"Well, sir, my testimony must be very similar to that of Mr. Murphy and Mr. Montgomery," Reagan replied, referring to the former SAG presidents whose testimony had just been heard. "There has been a small group within the Screen Actors Guild which has consistently opposed the policy of the guild board and officers of the guild, as evidenced by the vote on various issues. That small clique referred to has been suspected of more or less following the tactics that we associate with the Communist Party."

MR. STRIPLING: You have no knowledge yourself as to whether or not any of them are members of the Communist Party?

MR. REAGAN: No, sir, I have no investigative force, or anything, and I do not know.

MR. STRIPLING: Mr. Reagan, what is your feeling about what steps should be taken to rid the motion-picture industry of any Communist influences?

MR. REAGAN: Well, sir, ninety-nine percent of us are pretty well aware of what is going on, and I think, within the bounds of our democratic rights and never once stepping over the rights given us by democracy, we have done a pretty good job in our business of keeping those people's activities curtailed. After all, we must recognize them at present as a political party. On that basis we have exposed their lies when we came across them, we have opposed their propaganda, and I can certainly testify that in the case of the Screen Actors Guild we have been eminently successful in preventing them from, with their usual tactics, trying to run a majority of an organization with a well-organized minority. In opposing those people, the best thing to do is make democracy work. In the Screen Actors Guild we make it work by insuring everyone a vote and by keeping everyone informed. I believe that, as Thomas Jefferson put it, if all the American people know all of the facts they will never make a mistake. Whether the Party should be outlawed, that is a matter for the Government to decide. As a citizen, I would hesitate to see any political party outlawed on the basis of its political ideology. We have spent a hundred and seventy years in this country on the basis that democracy is strong enough to stand up and fight against the inroads of any ideology. However, if it is proven that an organization is an agent of a foreign power, or in any way not a legitimate political party—and I think the Government is capable of proving that—then that is another matter. I happen to be very proud of the industry in which I work; I happen to be very proud of the way in which we conducted the fight. I do not believe the Communists have ever at any time been able to use the motion-picture screen as a sounding board for their philosophy or ideology.

When Reagan finished, Thomas spoke up, hoping to seize the high ground that the actor had claimed so gracefully with his short soliloquy on the nature of democracy. "There is one thing that you said that interests me very much," Thomas said. "That was the quotation from Jefferson. That is just why this Committee was created by the House of Representatives: to acquaint the American people with the facts. Once the American people are acquainted with the facts there is no question but that the American people will do the kind of job that they want done: that is, to make America just as pure as we can possibly make it. We want to thank you very much for coming here today."

But Reagan was not about to let the New Jersey congressman hijack Jefferson for his own purposes. "Sir," he rejoined, "if I might, in regard to that, say that what I was trying to express, and didn't do very well, was also this other fear. I detest, I abhor their philosophy, but I detest more than that their tactics, which are those of the fifth column, and are dishonest. But at the same time I never as a citizen want to see our country become urged, by either fear or resentment of this group, that we ever compromise with any of our democratic principles through that fear or resentment. I still think that democracy can do it."[91]

Reagan's performance impressed a wide range of observers, from Nixon on the right to ADA executive secretary James Loeb on the left. Loeb, whom Reagan met with before leaving Washington, thought his testimony was "by all odds, the most honest and forthright from a decent liberal point of view" and called him "the hero" of the hearings.[92] The press was also adulatory: *The New York Times*, *The Washington Post*, *Life*, and *Motion Picture Daily* singled him out for his credibility and refusal to name names. "Intelligent Ronald Reagan stole the show from his better known colleagues," wrote Quentin Reynolds in *Collier's* magazine. "Reagan, it was obvious, had done a good deal of thinking on the subject in question."[93] Even the recently installed Communist government of Rumania paid him the compliment of being the only star among the friendly witnesses whose movies were not banned by its Ministry of Information Censorship Division.[94]

Eleven of the Unfriendly 19 were called to testify the following week. When asked the fateful question—"Are you now or have you ever been a member of the Communist Party?"—ten refused to give a direct answer, choosing instead to lecture the committee on the Bill of Rights, compare its members to Hitler, Goebbels, and Himmler, and otherwise make themselves look, in John Huston's phrase, like "belligerent buffoons."[95] In doing so, the Hollywood 10, as they would be known from then on, played right into the hands of Parnell Thomas, who pounded his gavel and charged them with contempt of Congress.

"I am not on trial here, Mr. Chairman. This Committee is on trial here before the American people. Let's get that straight," shouted John Howard Lawson in a typical outburst.[96] After ordering police officers to remove the screenwriter from the stand, Thomas had Stripling read a nine-page memorandum detailing Lawson's long and extensive involvement with Communist activities in Hollywood.[97] A second investigator produced a copy of Lawson's 1944 Communist Party registration card. Dalton Trumbo wouldn't even say whether or not he was a member of the Screen Writers Guild. Albert Maltz, Alvah Bessie, Samuel Ornitz, Herbert Biberman, Edward Dmytryk, Adrian Scott, Ring Lardner Jr., and Lester Cole gave equally truculent performances before the hearings were abruptly suspended by Thomas on October 30, some say because of the negative publicity, others because by then he had realized his goal of instilling the fear of God into the studio moguls. Only Bertolt Brecht, who as a resident alien felt his position was especially precarious, had outrightly—and probably falsely—denied Party membership and escaped a contempt citation.

"It was a sorry performance," wrote John Huston in his 1980 memoir, *An Open Book*. "You felt your skin crawl and your stomach turn. I disapproved of what was being done to the Ten, but I also disapproved of their response. They had lost a chance to defend a most important principle. . . . Before this spectacle, the attitude of the press had been extremely sympathetic. Now it changed."[98] Huston and two dozen other luminaries from the Committee for the First Amendment, including Humphrey Bogart, Lauren Bacall, Gene Kelly, and

Danny Kaye, had flown to Washington the day before the unfriendly witnesses began testifying.[99]

The First Amendment group also produced an anti-HUAC radio show, titled *Hollywood Fights Back*, which was broadcast nationwide on ABC the day they flew to Washington. The half-hour program featured brief remarks by four U.S. senators as well as a slew of film personalities, beginning with Myrna Loy announcing, "We question the right of Congress to ask any man what he thinks on political issues," and ending with Judy Garland urging listeners to write their congressmen to protest the inquiry.[100] But as Huston and his colleagues sat in the back-row seats that Thomas had assigned them, watching the men they were there to support sink to the chairman's level, they felt increasingly let down and hopeless. President Truman decided not to have them to lunch after all, *Life* magazine mocked them as "lost liberals," and the right-wing Hearst papers began a campaign to portray Huston as "the brains of the Communist Party in the West."[101] On his way back to Los Angeles, Bogart told a Chicago columnist that the Washington trip had been "ill-advised, even foolish," and not long after that he called himself a "dope" in a *Photoplay* article titled "I'm No Communist."[102] Reagan, it seemed, had been wise to avoid the Committee for the First Amendment from the beginning. He would later write that "it was for suckers only."[103]

New York Governor Herbert Lehman, Broadway's George S. Kaufman and Moss Hart, publishing executives Bennett Cerf and Clifton Fadiman, and composer Leonard Bernstein lent their voices to a second *Hollywood Fights Back* broadcast in early November, all to no avail. The American Legion threatened to organize a boycott of movies on which the Hollywood 10 worked, and a Gallup Poll showed that Americans favored punishing the uncooperative witnesses by a margin of 46 to 29 percent (though only 30 percent approved of the way the investigation had been handled).[104] On November 24, the House of Representatives voted overwhelmingly to uphold the contempt citations against the Hollywood 10.[105]

The next day a conclave of film industry chieftains, including Mayer, Jack and Harry Warner, Joseph Schenck of 20th Century Fox, Barney Balaban of Paramount, and Harry Cohn of Columbia, met at the Waldorf-Astoria hotel in New York and unanimously agreed to dismiss the ten without compensation. "We do not desire to prejudge their legal rights," the studio heads maintained in a press release that came to be known as the Waldorf Declaration, "but their actions have been a disservice to their employers and have impaired their usefulness to the industry."[106]

The moguls didn't stop with the Hollywood 10. Prodded by Eric Johnston, the president of the Motion Picture Producers Association, who had sworn at the hearings that the industry would never institute a blacklist, they now put the beginnings of one in place. "On the broader issue of alleged subversive and disloyal elements in

Hollywood," the producers' statement continued, "our members are likewise prepared to take positive action. We will not knowingly employ a Communist or a member of any party or group which advocates the overthrow of the government of the United States by force or by any illegal or unconstitutional methods."[107]

The New York Times called the producers' decision "an action unprecedented in American industrial fields."[108] RKO fired Scott and Dmytryk the next day, Fox let Lardner go the day after that, and Trumbo and Cole were banished from MGM the following week; the other five were not under contract to a studio. All ten were subsequently indicted by a federal grand jury, tried, convicted of contempt, and, after the Supreme Court refused to take up their case in April 1950, imprisoned for up to one year.

"Hollywood is going to clear up its back yard," Mayer announced upon his return from New York.[109] At two meetings, in late November and early December, Mayer and other top executives urged the leaders of the directors, writers, and actors guilds, including Reagan, to endorse the Waldorf Declaration, arguing that their harsh new policy was necessary to mollify public opinion and protect the industry from more government interference. "It was generally agreed that Louis B. Mayer, at the second of these sessions, hit on the most graphic way of expressing the official point of view," screenwriter Gordon Kahn recalled sarcastically in his 1948 memoir, *Hollywood on Trial*. "The British people, he said, had their Royal Family, in veneration of which a certain deep human impulse was satisfied. American democracy had to have a similar object of worship, and it had found it in the personalities of the motion picture business. That was why any word or act from Hollywood which shook the loyalty of even a fraction of the royal subjects was a matter for grave alarm and a potential contribution to national disintegration."[110]

Reagan had been reelected SAG president in mid-November; in that same vote his fellow actors backed his policy of requiring Guild officers to sign loyalty oaths. Still, he had serious misgivings about denying anyone employment because of his or her political affiliation, as the producers were setting out to do. He made this clear in the pointed questions he asked Mayer and his cohorts at the December 3 meeting—Why had they suddenly reversed their policy? How could they prove someone was a Communist? What about members of Communist fronts who were not Communists themselves?[111]—and in a statement he prepared for the December 8 meeting of SAG's board, in which he wrote, "We have no desire to protect communists. However, liberty cannot be held in water tight compartments. Once suppression, backed by the pressure of fear, breaks down one bulkhead, the other compartments are soon flooded."[112] Mayer responded by saying that he knew a Commie when he saw one, and the SAG board rejected Reagan's proposed statement as not tough enough.[113]

By December 19, when Reagan met with the FBI for the second time that month, he had apparently come around to the producers' point of view:

> T-10 advised Special Agent [blacked out] that he has been made a member of a committee headed by L.B. MAYER, the purpose of which allegedly is to "purge" the motion picture industry of Communist Party members, which committee was an outgrowth of the THOMAS committee hearings in Washington and the subsequent meeting of motion picture producers in New York City.[114]

Reagan was not the only would-be liberal floundering ideologically; nor was he alone in giving in to the rising tide of reaction. Shortly after the HUAC hearings, the Directors Guild followed SAG in adopting a loyalty oath, with only a furious John Huston and a hesitant Billy Wilder, among the 150 or 200 directors present, voting against it. Even William Wyler, who had founded the Committee for the First Amendment with Huston, raised his hand in support.[115] Dore Schary, then vice president of RKO, and the prominent independent producer Walter Wanger, both longtime liberal activists, had reluctantly gone along with the Waldorf Declaration, had then helped Mayer sell it to the guilds, and now took an active role in setting up Mayer's purge–cum–public relations committee, officially called the Motion Picture Industry Council (MPIC). Reagan represented SAG at the council's first meeting in early 1948; six months later, he was made co-chairman of this increasingly powerful group, which brought together the leaders of the studios, the guilds, and the unions under a single anti-Communist banner.[116]

"You bore me! Get out!" Those were the words with which Jane Wyman greeted Ronald Reagan upon his return home from the Washington hearings in late October 1947. Reagan was accustomed to his wife's moodiness, but this was the first time she told him—in no uncertain terms—that she wanted a divorce.[117] "Jane wasn't interested in what Ronnie was interested in," Nancy Reagan told me, "and she wasn't about to try to become interested."[118]

"It just horrified him and shocked him," said their old friend Leonora Hornblow. "He just didn't think he'd ever be divorced. His mother had put up with an awful lot from the father, and they remained married."[119]

"I suppose there had been warning signs, if only I hadn't been so busy," Reagan later wrote, "but small-town boys grow up thinking only other people get divorced. The plain truth was that such a thing was so far from even being imagined by me that I had no resources to call upon."[120]

Ronnie's first reaction was to talk Jane out of it. "We'll lead an ideal life if you'll avoid doing just one thing," he told her. "Don't think."[121] But it was just that dismissive attitude, all the more demeaning because it was so unconscious, that exasperated her. She had had it with his endless debates over politics with their friends, his late nights at SAG meetings, his foreign policy lectures at the breakfast table when all she wanted to do was get ready for work. "I got along without you before," she shouted at him outside the Beverly Club as they waited for their car, "and I certainly can get along without you now!"[122] When California's then lieutenant governor, Goodwin Knight, stopped by their table at Ciro's one night and started talking politics, Wyman practically yawned in his face.[123]

As soon as shooting on *Johnny Belinda* was finished in mid-November, she took off for "a long rest" in New York. On December 5, while Christmas shopping in Beverly Hills, Ronnie was stopped cold by a headline in the *Los Angeles Examiner*: JANE WYMAN, MATE IN RIFT.[124] "There is no use in lying," Jane was quoted as saying. "I am not the happiest girl in the world. It's nothing that's happened recently, it's an accumulation of things that have been coming on for a long time. . . . We will talk things over and I hope and believe that we will solve our problems and avoid a separation."[125] A *Photoplay* article titled "Those Fightin' Reagans" soon followed, reporting that Wyman had confided to a friend in New York, "We're through. We're finished. And it's all my fault."[126]

Louella Parsons was the first to reach Ronnie after the news broke. "Right now, Louella, Jane needs very much to have a fling and I intend to let her have it," he told the columnist who had given them their wedding reception. "She is sick and nervous and not herself. . . . Jane says she loves me, but is no longer 'in love' with me, and points out that this is a fine distinction. That, I don't believe. I think she is nervous, despondent, and because of this she feels our life together has become humdrum."[127] "I love Jane, and I know she loves me," he insisted to Hedda Hopper. "I don't know what this is all about, and I don't know why Jane has done it. For my part, I hope to live with her for the rest of my life."[128] He reminded movie reporter Gladys Hall that Jane had lost a baby only six months earlier and almost immediately after had taken on "a taxing, difficult role" in *Johnny Belinda*. "Perhaps, too," he added, "my seriousness about public affairs has bored Jane."[129]

On December 14, back in Los Angeles, Jane Wyman announced that she was separating from her husband. Reagan moved into the Garden of Allah. "If this comes to divorce, I think I'll name Johnny Belinda as co-respondent," he joked to Hedda Hopper, fueling the rumors that Lew Ayres was the real reason Wyman had left him, which Reagan then vehemently denied, insisting that no other man was involved.[130]

Warner Bros. announced that Wyman would not co-star with Reagan in *John Loves Mary,* a Jerry Wald production scheduled to begin shooting in January. Wyman's replacement, Patricia Neal, then a twenty-one-year-old ingénue, was introduced to Reagan at a party on New Year's Eve. "He said,

'Well, we're going to do a film together.' And I thought, Good, good, good," the actress told me. "Then midnight came and we all went outside, and he wept and wept on an older woman's arm. He was heartbroken. He really was."[131]

"Hollywood sympathy in this case is one hundred percent with Ronnie, who is a prince," *Silver Screen* magazine's Fredda Dudley informed her readers in early 1948. "Jane is a moody person, temperamental, ambitious, restless and seeking; furthermore, she is not now and hasn't been well for some time. It is to be hoped, that as her health improves, Jane's other problems will vanish, and two of the town's favorite people will resume their marriage."[132]

Friends, including Bill Holden and his wife, Ardis (who acted under the name Brenda Marshall), tried to coax the couple back together at small, tense dinner parties, but Jane refused to waver. On Ronnie's thirty-seventh birthday, February 6, 1948, she gave him a turquoise Cadillac convertible that she had ordered months earlier as a surprise, but she signed the gift card with Maureen's and Michael's names. Later that month, she checked into the Flamingo Hotel in Las Vegas to establish residency for the divorce. After a few days, however, she returned to Los Angeles and asked Ronnie to move back in with her and the children. In May she asked him to move out again, and filed for divorce in California on the grounds of extreme mental cruelty.[133] At the divorce trial the following month, which Reagan did not attend, the *Los Angeles Times* reported, "Miss Wyman told the court that she and Reagan engaged in continual arguments on his political views. Despite her lack of interest in his political activities, Miss Wyman continued, Reagan insisted that she attend meetings with him and be present during discussions among his friends. But her own ideas, she complained, 'were never considered important.' 'Finally, there was nothing between us,' Miss Wyman said."[134]

A divorce decree was granted on June 28, 1948. Wyman received custody of the children, $500 a month in child support, a $25,000 life insurance policy paid for by Reagan, and horseback-riding privileges at their Northridge ranch; the house on Cordell Drive was to be sold and the proceeds evenly split.[135] Jane left it to Ronnie to break the news to seven-year-old Maureen; Michael, then three, was too young to understand. "I can still hear Dad saying," Maureen later wrote, "'Just remember, Mermie, I still love you. I will always love you.' His voice was cracking a little as he spoke."[136]

"No marital separation since I broke the story that Mary Pickford, America's sweetheart, was leaving Douglas Fairbanks, has had the effect of the parting of the Reagans," wrote a crushed Louella Parsons. "Just as Mary and Doug stood for all that is best in this town, so have Ronnie and Jane. . . . For eight years they have shared a beautiful life that has earned them the respect and admiration even of people who did not know them personally. To those of us who are close friends, they were an ideal Mr. and Mrs. That's why this hurts so much."[137]

"They would not have gotten a divorce had their careers not been going in opposite directions," said their good friend Dick Powell. "Hers up, his down."[138]

"Perhaps I should have let someone else save the world and have saved my own home," said Reagan.[139]

CHAPTER TEN

RONNIE AND NANCY
IN HOLLYWOOD
1949–1952

It looks as though Nancy Davis, Dr. and Mrs. Loyal Davis' talented actress daughter, may have the break for which she has hoped and persevered. She is in Hollywood now, waiting for the cameras to start rolling on "Death in the Doll's House," in which she has a role.

Cholly Dearborn, *Chicago Herald-American*, March 24, 1949

Hollywood is bounded on the North by legend, on the East by rumor, on the West by scandal and on the South by superstition. Somewhere within those boundaries lies the actual Hollywood community so many talk about and so few really know.

Dore Schary, *Case History of a Movie*, 1950

A few days after the television adaptation of *Ramshackle Inn* aired on January 2, 1949, Nancy

Davis received a call from her agent telling her that "someone from Metro" had seen her performance and suggested that she come out to the coast for a screen test. Nancy was so excited that, as she put it in her autobiography, "I started packing before I hung up the phone." She added proudly, "This was one opportunity that none of my family friends had anything to do with."[1]

Nonetheless, she immediately called her mother in Chicago, and Edith began working the phone on her daughter's behalf, starting with a call to Spencer Tracy, urging him to make sure that Nancy was handled with kid gloves.[2] By mid-January, Edith and Loyal were in Phoenix, a month earlier than they usually arrived for their annual six-week stay at the Arizona Biltmore Hotel, and Nancy joined them. So did Spencer and Louise Tracy, who were traveling with their good friend Benjamin Thau, MGM's vice president in charge of talent and the executive who supervised screen tests at the studio.[3]

Benny Thau was forty-nine and still a bachelor. ("Thau pronounced his name like winter thaw," noted Leonora Hornblow. "The joke was Benny never thawed.")[4] A short, heavyset man who wore his thinning hair slicked back, he spoke in a deliberate near-whisper that forced people to listen closely to what he said. He had started out in show business as a vaudeville booker in New York and was made casting director of MGM by Louis B. Mayer in 1928. "From then on," according to Mayer biographer Charles Higham, "Thau's casting couch was the busiest in Hollywood."[5] Thau was notorious for demanding sexual favors from starlets whose careers he advanced, for carrying on affairs with married actresses (most notably Greer Garson, whom he made an overnight star), and, according to Higham, even for organizing Christmas Eve orgies on the MGM lot during the 1930s.[6] He was immediately taken by Nancy's ladylike looks and manners.

"It was my impression that Benny was there to see Bob Rubin, who was with Metro in New York," Nancy Reagan told me, referring to MGM's long-time East Coast vice president and general counsel, J. Robert Rubin. "Bob and his wife stayed at the Biltmore every year and became good friends of my parents'."[7] Richard Davis said that his father had taken an instant dislike to Benny Thau and strongly disapproved of Edith's backstage machinations on Nancy's behalf. "Dr. Loyal was all for someone getting ahead on his or her own," Davis told me. "To have the inside track was against his principles. And he didn't want his daughter to be mixed up with this man at all. I think my father thought this whole Hollywood thing was a little unsavory for his daughter. But Edith encouraged it. Edith would say, 'Well, you have to make a few compromises if you want to get anywhere.' My father was not that way. He wouldn't compromise for anything or anybody."[8]

A newspaper photograph of the Davises, Thau, and Louise Spencer at the opening of the new Sombrero Playhouse confirms their presence in

Phoenix that month, as well as Richard Davis's take on his parents' conflicting attitudes: as Edith studies the Hollywood big-shot with interest, Loyal casts his wife a stern glance. Nancy is not in the picture, but she saved it in her scrapbook, a rare piece of printed evidence linking her to a man she never mentioned in any of her books or talked about in interviews.[9] Her silence only fueled suspicion that she had something to hide, and several previous biographers, unaware of their meeting in Phoenix, have written that Nancy met Thau on a blind date in New York shortly before her screen test and that she became his girlfriend in Hollywood.[10]

This version of events was largely based on an interview Thau gave, at age eighty, to Laurence Leamer, the first Reagan biographer to research Nancy's background in some depth. Recalling a trip to New York in early 1949, Thau said that a friend had suggested, "If you want to take somebody out to a show, call Nancy Davis. She's a nice girl who likes company." Over dinner after the theater, Thau said, he uttered the magic words: "Nancy, why don't you come out and make a screen test?" Thau's memory was not airtight, however; he told Leamer that he had taken Nancy to see a play starring Spencer Tracy, but Tracy's last play, *The Rugged Path*, had closed more than two years earlier.[11]

Nancy Reagan told me there was no blind date—or love affair. "I never had dinner with Benny in New York," she said. "When I came out to Los

Angeles to do the test and stayed—yes, then I saw him, had dinner with him, and so on. . . . I was *not* his girlfriend. He took a liking to me, that's true . . . and I liked him as a friend. But that was it, as far as I was concerned."[12]

In any event, Spencer Tracy had lined up another powerful MGM executive on Nancy's behalf, Dore Schary, vice president in charge of production. Schary had been brought over from RKO the previous year by Nicholas Schenk, the head of Loew's Inc., MGM's New York–based parent corporation, and it was generally thought that it was only a matter of time before he replaced the aging Mayer. Schary, a former screenwriter, had been close to Tracy since 1938, when he wrote the script for *Boys Town*, which won Oscars for both of them. At some point before Nancy's screen test, Tracy called Schary and, playing to the executive's preference for intellectual message films, recommended Nancy as a serious actress. "The girl," he said, "knows how to look like she's really thinking when she's onstage."[13]

Schary was drawn into Nancy's camp by other means as well. Like Mary Martin, he suffered from chronic back problems, and shortly before Nancy was signed, he had called Loyal Davis for advice about an operation.[14] It is not clear who recommended Nancy's stepfather to Schary, but he became a regular patient. According to Nancy's New York publishing pal Kenneth Giniger, it was Schary "who brought her out to the coast. That's what I understood from her at the time."[15] However, there can be little doubt that meeting Thau in Phoenix advanced matters immeasurably.

"You can say I helped her" was how Thau later summed up his role. "Stars like Norma Shearer, Elizabeth Taylor—she couldn't compete with that. She was attractive, but not what you'd call beautiful. She [was] a very nice behaved girl."[16]

Nancy Davis's screen test was like few others in the history of Hollywood. Ordinarily, tests were directed and filmed by whatever studio technicians were available. Nancy's was directed by George Cukor, one of MGM's most important directors, and filmed by George Folsey, the prestigious cinematographer. Both were known for flattering female stars, Cukor so much that he was dubbed "the women's director." Over the years, he had elicited exceptional performances from Jean Harlow in *Dinner at Eight*, Greta Garbo in *Camille*, Katharine Hepburn in *The Philadelphia Story*, and Norma Shearer, Rosalind Russell, and Joan Crawford in *The Women*. Fortunately for Nancy, he was extremely close to both Hepburn and Tracy, whose long-term love affair was conducted in a guesthouse Tracy occupied on the director's Hollywood Hills estate. When Tracy asked him to direct Nancy's test, Cukor found it hard to say no.[17]

On Thau's instructions, the studio's drama coach, Lillian Burns, spent three weeks working with Nancy on her acting, voice, dancing, deportment, and appearance. As Lucille Ryman, the head of MGM's talent department, explained, "I had told Lillian to give her extra special care because Benny had asked me to do the best I could with her."[18] Despite all her advantages, Nancy was so nervous on the day of the test that she had a friend of her mother's, Nathalie Moorhead Dunham, a retired actress, accompany her to the studio. "I remember Nathalie standing there," Nancy told MGM's "hairdresser to the stars," Sydney Guilaroff, years later, "while you were doing my hair, the two of you talking and her making suggestions and you saying what you thought and me just sitting there. I was terrified."[19]

Nancy read a scene from *East Side, West Side*, a high-society melodrama that was scheduled to begin shooting that summer. Howard Keel, a handsome newcomer who would soon become a star in *Annie Get Your Gun*, played opposite her. As Nancy remembered it, Cukor was "kind and understanding."[20] According to his biographer Emanuel Levy, Cukor "told the studio Nancy had no talent," and he would make nasty remarks about her for the rest of his life.[21]

Mayer reportedly agreed with Cukor's assessment, but the combination of Thau and Schary prevailed. On March 2, 1949, MGM signed Nancy Davis to a seven-year contract starting at $250 a week, with forty weeks a year guaranteed; if the studio renewed her option every six months, by the last year she would be making $1,250 a week. "I grabbed it," she later wrote. "I was finally earning a regular paycheck, which meant I would no longer have to accept money from my parents."[22]

Shortly after being signed, Nancy was asked to fill out a four-page biographical questionnaire for MGM's publicity department. Dated March 15, 1949, it offers a glimpse into her personality at a moment that, in her words, "marked the end of one period of life and the beginning of another."[23] She stated her height as five-feet-four, her weight as 117 pounds, and shaved two years off her age, making herself twenty-five instead of twenty-seven, a fib she would stick to even as First Lady. She listed knitting as her hobby, tennis and swimming as her sports, "dancing and anything that gets me into the sun" as her favorite forms of recreation, and said she liked to sleep in "tailored nightgowns" with the "windows wide open." Her most treasured possessions: "Two baby pictures of my mother and father—never am without them—and a locket of my great-grandmother's with a baby picture of my mother inside. Why? Because I'm a sentimentalist, I guess."

She named as her favorite actors Walter Huston and Spencer Tracy. Her favorite actresses: Nazimova and, in keeping with her serious-actress image, Laurette Taylor. She admitted to believing in hunches and superstitions ("All of them and then some"), and produced a list of her phobias: "Superficiality, vulgarity, esp. in women, untidiness of mind and person—and cigars!" One can hear echoes of her stepfather in her answer to the question "Do you govern your life by any rule or rules?" "Do unto others," she typed, "as you would have them do unto you. I believe strongly in the law of retribution—you get back what you give."

She left several questions unanswered, including "Your favorite childhood memory?" Her childhood ambition was "to be an actress."

Any ambitions outside present career? "Sure."

Greatest ambition? "To have a successful happy marriage."[24]

"I arrived in the Last Days of the Glamorous Empire," wrote the screenwriter and playwright Arthur Laurents, who was signed by MGM not long before Nancy was and whose description of Hollywood in the late 1940s captures both its insularity and seductiveness: "Everybody in town was in pictures or wanted to be in pictures. The aircraft industry was booming and paid well but nobody knew anybody in airplanes except Howard Hughes—who owned a movie studio. The oil wells on Signal Hill pumped day and night, there was even one pumping away smack in the middle of LaBrea Boulevard in West Hollywood but nobody knew anybody in oil, either. There was no smog, everybody played tennis, and everybody drove everywhere in convertibles to get a tan and flirt at stoplights."[25]

Until she found Mr. Right, Nancy was thrilled to be at MGM, which was not only the biggest and most important studio but also the most glamorous and the most social—and the most protective of its stars. Ann Rutherford, who was under contract there at the time, compared it to the White House, a place where everything was taken care of for you. "I had no ambition when I was there," she told me. "All I wanted was to make it last as long as I possibly could. I would carry a tray for someone—I didn't give a rip—so long as I could stay forever. It was just the most wonderful life on earth. If I wanted to go to New York between pictures, all I had to do was go see [publicity chief] Howard Strickling and say, 'Would you arrange some interviews for me in New York?' And he'd say, 'What shows do you want to see?' And they'd come up with house tickets to anything. . . . I *loved* Metro-Goldwyn-Mayer. . . . And they really had more stars than there are in heaven."[26]

In 1949 the MGM roster included Clark Gable, Jimmy Stewart, Frank Sinatra, Judy Garland, Lana Turner, Ava Gardner, Fred Astaire, Ginger Rogers, Gene Kelly, June Allyson, Deborah Kerr, Gary Cooper, Mickey Rooney, Esther Williams, Elizabeth Taylor, and Lassie. Louis B. Mayer, who had opened the studio twenty-five years earlier with a ceremony that included Army and Navy planes dropping roses from the sky, saw these stars as his children, who needed to be shaped and coddled, reprimanded and controlled by "their stern but loving father."[27] (Dore Schary may have been more liberal politically, but he was just as paternalistic.) Some found this atmosphere oppressive, but it suited Nancy. She was accustomed to being disciplined and sheltered, and with Uncle Walter

Huston and Spence and Aunt Kate all making movies at Metro in 1949, it felt very much like the "home" that Mayer insisted it was.

"In those days, if you were under contract to a studio, the studio was your life, six days a week," Nancy later wrote. "If you weren't making a movie . . . you were doing publicity for one you *had* made. . . . When I was making a movie, I'd have to be on the lot at 7:30 A.M.—women always had early calls for hair and makeup—which meant that I had to be up extra early to drive myself to work. . . . I'd stay on the lot until five or six every evening. And then, even on the days when I wasn't working, I'd come in and visit other sets."[28]

Of course, she was off to a late start—Lana Turner and Ava Gardner, who were more or less her age, had started out as teenagers; Elizabeth Taylor was *still* in her teens. "Mysterious indeed are the ramifications of Hollywood," wrote Inez Wallace, the first reporter to interview Nancy after she arrived at MGM. "Certain actors are pointed out to writers as 'comers.' This means that the studio is putting everything it has behind an actor to make him or her a star. When Nancy Davis was pointed out to me on the MGM lot I couldn't believe they intended to build her up. She looks more like a character actress than a leading lady."[29]

Nancy's publicity was personally overseen by Ann Straus, Howard Strickling's elegant and low-key deputy. "Ann was one of the old-timers in the PR department," said Bill Fine, who ran the West Coast office of *McCall's* magazine. "She was very much a lady, and she would be very careful to make sure that the ten or twelve people she was sort of nanny for got good mannerly press. She wasn't married, so she could always go out and have dinner with you. She had a very deep voice, very soothing, and you could tell her anything. I think the reason Nancy felt strongly about having her as a friend is she never blabbed about anything. She always kept her counsel."[30]

Straus introduced Nancy to Amelia Gray, a former department store buyer from Baltimore, who had recently opened an exclusive dress shop in Beverly Hills. Gray, a soigné woman in her late thirties who always wore her jet-black hair swept back in a chignon, attracted both fashion-conscious movie stars such as Rosalind Russell and up-and-coming Los Angeles socialites such as Betsy Bloomingdale. "I was new out here and I didn't know where to go," Nancy Reagan told me, "so Ann took me to Amelia, and we became friends. She was a wonderful woman. I never went any-place else. I'd go there and sit in Amelia's little office or the fitting room and we'd have a sand-wich. That's how I met Jimmy—through Amelia."[31]

James Galanos, who would become California's leading designer, was a Greek-American in his twenties, just starting his own business after having apprenticed at a couture house in Paris. "Amelia discovered me," Galanos told me. "She had heard about me, and she propositioned me: if I would sell to her exclusively, she would make it worth my while. So I decided to go with her. It was unbelievable—every day she'd reorder. And I'd deliver the things—I was still delivering on my own. We'd sit in the back in her office. I'd sit up on the table, and Nancy was always there. Amelia just loved her, and took her on like a daughter. At the end of every season, Amelia would want all my samples. And that was when Nancy started buying Galanos, because they were a terrific price that she could afford. She *loved* clothes." How expensive were his dresses then? "When I first started with my little cotton dresses, they retailed for $89 to $125. Cocktail dresses were $275 to $395, which was a lot of money in the fifties."[32]

"I remember the first dress of Jimmy's that I got," said Nancy Reagan. "I was so excited about it. It was black with a high neck. I remember Amelia turning to one of the salesgirls and saying, 'See, that's the way it should be. Those other dames come in here, and they're so blasé and bored.'"[33]

Nancy was almost immediately cast in *Shadow on the Wall* (originally titled *Death in the Doll's House*), a murder mystery starring Ann Sothern and Zachary Scott. It was a B movie, and they were B stars, but Nancy was given a featured role, playing a child psychiatrist. Before shooting began in late March, the studio allowed her to fly to Phoenix to get some "authentic pointers" on how to play a doctor from her stepfather, who was still vacationing at the Biltmore. For one of her scenes, the costume designer chose an antique gold locket that still had a tag on it from the last time it had been used: by Nazimova in *Escape*, in 1940. Nancy saw that as a positive sign; she was already carrying a gold watch from her late godmother in her purse for good luck.[34]

The film's plot revolved around a six-year-old girl who has witnessed her mother's murder but blocked out all memory of it. The role of Dr. Caroline Canford was a good fit for Nancy, requiring her to be caring, patient, and inquisitive as she coaxed the truth out of the child through play therapy and free association. "There is a fine line in acting, and I've never heard of a textbook that can define that line," Nancy later remarked. "You play the character the writer has created, but you also play the role partly the way you yourself would react in a given situation."[35]

She barely had a day off before starting *The Doctor and the Girl*, in which she was typecast as the daughter of a prominent Park Avenue neurosurgeon. Once again Nancy's role called for her to be patient, understanding, and smart as she tries to make peace between her domineering father, played by Charles Coburn, and her rebellious younger siblings, played by Glenn Ford and Gloria DeHaven. Apparently her diplomatic skills came in handy off the set when Coburn, who was in his seventies and wore a monocle, asked her to dinner. "It seems he was a lecherous old fellow," said her Chicago friend Bruce McFarland, who called Nancy once a week during her first year in Hollywood. "She indicated that she spent the entire evening keeping him away from her. She thought it was hysterical."[36]

Life seemed to fall into place fairly easily for Nancy in her newly adopted city. She found a nicely furnished two-bedroom bungalow with a flower-filled garden in Santa Monica. Nancy told Inez Wallace she had "a girl who comes in three days a week, cleans up the place and cooks my dinner. At night I study my script for the next day, or read or listen to the radio. I'm never lonely."[37]

Van Johnson, who had become one of MGM's top leading men during the war, and his wife, Evie, lived next door, and kept an eye on her. Clark Gable took her to lunch at the studio, and John Huston, at his father's behest, gave a dinner party at Chasen's to welcome her to town. "That was the first time I met Nancy," recalled Leonora Hornblow. "She was very nice. Un-actressy. Very simple, very good manners, cheerful, bright, charming."[38]

"It was a very clubby feeling at Metro," recalled Armand "Ardie" Deutsch, who met Nancy soon after she signed with the studio. "I don't believe I ever took Nancy out on a quote-unquote date. But hosts would call and see if I could pick her up to come to dinner. And we got to be good friends. I developed an ability to make her laugh by just looking at her. One day we were going into a big soundstage—L. B. Mayer was going to lecture us on the evils of Communism or something of that sort—and Nancy and I happened to meet at the entrance. I said, 'Nancy, don't laugh. We could get fired.' She said, 'Why would I laugh?' Well, she sat a few seats from me, and I called, 'Nancy, Nancy.' And she looked at me and I said, 'Don't laugh.' Well, she was gone. She had to take out her handkerchief and hide her laughter."[39]

Ardie Deutsch had come to Hollywood the same way Nancy had: via the social route. A grandson of Julius Rosenwald, an early partner in Sears, Roebuck, he had gone from private schools in Chicago and New York to Dartmouth and the University of Chicago, and from radio to the Navy to Wall Street, never quite sure what he really wanted to do. He met Dore Schary at a dinner party in New York in 1946 and formed a fast friendship that led to a job as Schary's assistant at RKO and a brief marriage to nightclub singer Benay Venuta. When Schary jumped to MGM two years later, Deutsch jumped with him and became a producer; he was producing his first film, *Ambush*, a Western starring Robert Taylor, when he and Nancy met. Within three years' time, Ardie would marry a stylish young widow named Harriet Simon, Nancy would marry Ronald Reagan, and the Deutsches would become charter members of what eventually would be known as the Reagan Group.[40]

One of the hostesses who sometimes asked Deutsch to pick up Nancy was Dore Schary's wife, Miriam. Although the Scharys saw themselves as bohemians—Miriam was a dedicated artist who showed her paintings in a New York gallery—they were quite snobbish about their guest lists, and not every newly signed actress was asked to dinner at their home in Brentwood. As Esther Williams wrote in her memoir, *The Million Dollar Mermaid*, "You didn't just hang out with people like that. You bore their scrutiny. 'Were you from a good family?' 'Did you come from money?' 'Was your talent intellectual or even avant-garde?' "[41] Miriam Schary, a difficult woman whose face was partially disfigured from a childhood accident and whom some of the town's more fashionable hostesses considered "a bit batty," was won over by Nancy's deferential manner.[42]

Nancy was also taken up by Kitty LeRoy, the very social wife of the director Mervyn LeRoy—and the complete opposite of Miriam Schary. Petite and beautiful, Kitty was from Chicago, and one of her three previous husbands was the owner of the Pump Room, where she came to know Edith Davis and Colleen Moore. Coincidentally, Mervyn owed his first directing job, back in 1927, to Moore, and they had remained close friends after she retired and he went on to make countless hits at Warners and then at MGM, including *Little Caesar* and *The Wizard of Oz*. He had been married to Harry Warner's daughter and was thought to be one the richest men in the business. The LeRoys entertained in the grand manner at their house in Bel Air, and the guests almost always included MCA chairman Jules Stein and his wife, Doris, who was Kitty's best friend. "Kitty saw herself as Nancy's *duenna*," said her stepdaughter, Linda LeRoy

Janklow. "She tried to protect her and make sure she had a good life in California."[43]

When Mary Astor dropped out of LeRoy's next movie, *East Side, West Side*, he decided to offer her part to Nancy, and Dore Schary gave his okay. Two weeks later, at the beginning of September, the studio picked up her first six-month option, and she finally felt secure enough to move into an unfurnished apartment closer to work and have her belongings shipped out from New York.

Richard Davis came to visit Nancy at the end of that summer, just before she moved out of the Santa Monica bungalow. He had graduated from Princeton in June and taken summer courses at Northwestern University Medical School, so Loyal and Edith rewarded him with a ticket on the *Super Chief*. He told me he remembered two things about his stay: Katharine Hepburn lent him her beat-up old Ford so that he could drive to Santa Barbara to see a girlfriend, and one night he and Nancy had dinner at Benny Thau's house in the Hollywood Hills.

"It was all very much on the up and up," Davis said. A butler served dinner, and Thau "didn't paw Nancy or fawn over her. . . . But you could see he was a controller—sort of reminiscent of a Mafioso type."[44] During dinner Thau told a story about growing up in New York. "He said he was very, very poor," Davis recalled, "and it was Thanksgiving and he had just enough money to buy dinner. The floor of the restaurant was covered in sawdust, and apparently his dinner spilled. There was a good-looking girl sitting next to him, alone, and he was just too embarrassed to pick the dinner up out of the sawdust and eat it. I didn't have a soft spot in my heart for Benny Thau, but it was a very touching story. Whether it was a ploy to get Nancy's sympathy, I don't know."[45]

Nancy was seeing a lot of Benny Thau, and rumors about their relationship were so widespread that the studio put out stories suggesting that Clark Gable had been the hidden hand behind her "gilt-edged" screen test.[46] Nothing was written about her evenings out with Thau—the studio made sure of that—but according to MGM talent chief Lucille Ryman, "Benny took her to premieres and benefits and parties."[47] "People said he was her beau," said Leonora Hornblow, noting the general perception at the time. "I don't think this was a great passion on her part. It couldn't have been. But as far as her career went, it didn't hurt."[48] Thau's receptionist later claimed that Nancy would visit his office every Saturday morning, presumably for a quick tryst.[49] Nancy Reagan vehemently denied this—"I did not!"—and her brother backed her up: "I think Nancy would only go to bed with someone she was in love with," he told me.[50] As far as her family could tell, it was a classic case of a powerful older man falling for a younger woman who finds him interesting and supportive but is not attracted to him romantically. Such relationships can go on for only so long before something gives, and theirs would not be an exception. In the meantime, Nancy continued to enjoy the benefits of Thau's patronage while trying not to hurt his feelings.

Along with her princess upbringing (which the publicity department played up to the hilt), her famous family friends, and her instant A-list social life, Nancy's closeness to Thau stirred up a certain amount of envy. What's more, her reputation as Thau's paramour scared off younger, less powerful suitors. Amid all the studio-inspired fluff in her scrapbook there is not a single item about her dating *anyone* until November 1949, eight months after she arrived in Hollywood. And then her date was Ronald Reagan, a power in his own right as president of SAG and chairman of MPIC, the alliance of studio, guild, and union chiefs that had been formed in the wake of the 1947 HUAC hearings to restore Hollywood's image and cleanse the industry of Communist influence.

Production on *East Side, West Side* began in September. Once again, Nancy was cast close to type as the socialite wife of a New York press baron. She appeared in only two scenes, but they were with the film's star, Barbara Stanwyck, and Mervyn LeRoy made sure Nancy had her fair share of close-ups. The big-budget, high-gloss film also starred James Mason as Stanwyck's unfaithful husband, Ava Gardner as his mistress, who is murdered, and Van Heflin as the reporter who solves the crime.

On October 28, 1949, the *Hollywood Reporter*,

which was owned by the ultra-right-wing nightclub impresario Billy Wilkerson, published a list of "Communist sympathizers" who had signed an amicus curiae brief urging the Supreme Court to overturn the convictions of John Howard Lawson and Dalton Trumbo. To Nancy's horror, her name was on the list.[51] Since she had also been receiving unsolicited mail from left-wing organizations, she called LeRoy in a panic. "She drove over that evening to show me some of the propaganda that was being slipped under her door," the director wrote in his memoir, *Take One*. "We were both anti-Communist, and strongly so, so the whole business was annoying."[52]

Nancy's concern was not unreasonable. Behind the facade of klieg-lit premieres and glittery dinner parties, Hollywood was an increasingly divided and frightened community in late 1949: the right saw a Red under every bed, the left an FBI agent; according to Arthur Laurents, people even suspected their analysts of being government informers.[53] The *Los Angeles Times* was running as many as twenty anti-Communist articles a day, and California state senator John Tenney, who chaired a mini-HUAC in Sacramento, had launched investigations into the political activities of Charlie Chaplin, Orson Welles, Gene Kelly, Gregory Peck, Frank Sinatra, and Nancy's friend Katharine Hepburn.[54]

The American Legion threatened to boycott studios that employed Communists, and freshly sprouted newsletters such as *Red Channels* and

Counter-Attack printed lists of suspected Party members, friends of suspected Party members, and friends of friends of suspected Party members. ("We don't care whether an individual cannot be proved to be an outright Communist," asserted Myron Fagan, whose Cinema Educational Guild distributed hundreds of thousands of pamphlets with titles such as *Red Stars in Hollywood*. "As far as we are concerned any man or woman who is a fellow traveler, or belongs to a Red front organization, or has supported Communism with financial or moral support, a la Charlie Chaplin, or has come out in open support of the ten branded men who defied the Parnell Thomas investigation, or associates with known Communists, openly or in secret, is just as guilty of treason, and is just as much an enemy of America as any outright Communist.")[55] Although the studios continued to deny that they were blacklisting anyone, some of those whose names appeared on such lists suddenly found auditions were canceled, or parts were cut from movies in which they had already been cast, or their agents stopped returning their calls.

At MGM, Louis B. Mayer, clinging to power in his all-white office lined with framed photographs of Herbert Hoover, J. Edgar Hoover, and New York's Cardinal Francis Spellman, sometimes whispered that he wondered if Dore Schary was a Communist, and Schary threatened to sue Hedda Hopper for referring to the studio as "Metro-Goldwyn-Moscow" because it employed him. Schary was one of the few studio executives who tried to resist the rising tide of guilt-by-association blacklisting.[56] Gale Sondergaard, a well-regarded character actress who had a supporting role in *East Side, West Side*, was married to one of the Hollywood 10, director Herbert Biberman, and under investigation by both the FBI and HUAC while the film was being shot. Not surprisingly, Sondergaard had signed the amicus curiae brief. Seeing a fellow cast member's name on the *Hollywood Reporter*'s list made Nancy all the more nervous.[57]

LeRoy tried to reassure Nancy by telling her that the studio would take care of her problem, and on November 7, Louella Parsons ran an item declaring her "100 percent American" and pointing out that there was *another* Nancy Davis, who supported "leftist theater" and "Henry Wallace's politics."[58] The *Hollywood Reporter* also ran an item clarifying the matter, but Nancy was still not satisfied. LeRoy told her he would talk to his old friend from Warners, SAG president Ronald Reagan, and ask him to call her. As she later wrote, she sat up all night waiting for the phone to ring. "I had seen him in films and, frankly, I had liked what I had seen." She continued, "On the set the next day, a beaming Mervyn reported that Ronnie had checked me out . . . and the Guild would defend my name if it ever became necessary. I told Mervyn that was fine, but I was so worried I'd feel better if the Guild president would call me and explain it all to me."[59]

"She had her heart set on meeting Ronnie," LeRoy told a reporter years later. "I knew they'd make a great pair, so I went along with it and fixed them up."[60]

The phone rang soon after Nancy got home that afternoon. Reagan said he had an early call the next morning, but if she was free they could have a quick dinner to discuss her concerns. She told him it was awfully short notice and added that she, too, had an early call. "I didn't, of course, but a girl has to have some pride," she would write. "Two hours later, my first thought when I opened the door was, This is *wonderful*. He looks as good in person as he does on the screen!"[61]

"The door opened," Reagan wrote in describing the same scene, "not on the expected fan magazine version of a starlet, but on a small, slender young lady with dark hair and a wide-spaced pair of hazel eyes that looked right at you and made you look back. Don't get ahead of me: bells didn't ring or skyrockets explode, although I think perhaps they did. It was just that I had buried the part of me where such things happened so deep, I couldn't hear them."[62]

A year and a half had passed since Ronald Reagan and Jane Wyman were divorced, in June 1948, and although he put on his usual cheerful face, bachelorhood did not agree with him. To cope with his loneliness, he was going out too much, drinking too much, and spending too much—his nightclub bills alone were running $750 a month.[63] And while he dated a succession of actresses, singers, and models, including Ann Sothern and Ruth

Roman, the word around town was that he was still obsessed with Wyman. Reagan would later brag to a buddy that he was sleeping with so many different women that he woke up one morning at the Garden of Allah and "couldn't remember the name of the gal I was in bed with. I said, 'Hey, I gotta get a grip here.' "[64] But, according to Kitty Kelley, some of the women he was linked with in 1948 and 1949 described him as sexually "passive" and sometimes so drunk and heartbroken over Jane that he couldn't perform.[65]

"Reagan was a lonely guy because of his divorce," said Eddie Bracken, a co-star in *The Girl from Jones Beach*, which was filmed during the summer of 1948, "but a very level-headed guy. He was never for the sexpots. He was never a guy looking for the bed. He was a guy looking for companionship more than anything else. But I wouldn't say he was strait-laced."[66]

"I just can't get it right," Reagan told Doris Lilly, a tall, fetching blonde who later became well known as the author of *How to Meet a Millionaire*. "I'm no good alone." According to Lilly, Reagan proposed to her a few months after they met, but she turned him down because she knew he wasn't in love—just desperate for someone who "was willing to make the big moves, push, be there, encourage him, never leave him alone for a moment. . . . I couldn't do it."[67]

Reagan continued to drive the Cadillac convertible Jane had given him before they split, and he moved back into the Londonderry Terrace apartment they had shared as newlyweds, claiming he couldn't find anything else because of the postwar housing shortage.[68] He and Jane dined together regularly to discuss the children, and she seemed to play with his hopes of reconciliation, telling reporters at the October 1948 opening of *Johnny Belinda* that she was wearing a dress he had given her, then announcing at a big Hollywood dinner party the following month that "Lew Ayres is the love of my life," setting off speculation about an eventual marriage.[69] Such behavior did little for Reagan's self-confidence, and one can only wonder how he felt when his ex-wife, with Ayers at her side, won the best actress Oscar in March 1949. By then she had signed a new, ten-year contract with Warners.[70]

Reagan's own situation at Warners was going from bad to worse. He had no films in release in 1948, and two of his three 1949 releases—*John Loves Mary* and *Night Unto Night* (which had been held back for three years)—were flops, with only *The Girl from Jones Beach*, a cotton-candy comedy designed to show off shapely Virginia Mayo in a variety of bathing suits, scoring at the box office.[71] "Ronnie wasn't considered a big leading man then," recalled Connie Wald, the widow of Jerry Wald. "We used to see him after he broke up with Jane. He'd come over to the house, we'd go out to dinner, and the girls were after him like mad. I don't think he was ever with anybody—seriously—until he went with Nancy. He was such a sweet man. We always liked him so much. But as far as his career went, it was really going downhill. . . . Who knows what he felt inside. As warm as he was, he was always a very distant person. Charming, but very private—that was Ronnie."[72]

Reagan was convinced that if only he could star in the kind of Western that had made John Wayne a top box office draw his popularity would rebound. To please Jack Warner, he agreed to take the second male lead in *The Hasty Heart*, a wartime drama set in a military hospital, on the condition that his next movie would be *Ghost Mountain*, a Western based on a short story he had persuaded the studio to buy. He spent four cold months filming in London—it was his first trip abroad, and he complained incessantly about the weather, the food, and the austerity policies of Britain's Labour Party government—only to read in *Variety* on the day he returned that *Ghost Mountain* was being assigned to Errol Flynn.[73]

Hurt and angry, Reagan refused to take his next assignment, a loan-out to Columbia—a big step for someone who had always been one of the studio's most accommodating stars.[74] Lew Wasserman let his client sulk for a month, then persuaded him to accept a compromise: Reagan would make one picture a year for Warner Bros. for the remaining three years of his contract, his $150,000 annual salary would be cut in half, and he would be free to work for other studios. Indeed, even before the Warners deal was finalized in May 1949, Wasserman announced that Universal had signed

Reagan to a five-year, five-picture deal at $75,000 per picture.[75]

As bad luck would have it, Reagan broke his right thigh in six places in a charity baseball game three days before he was to start shooting his first film for Universal, and was hospitalized for seven weeks. He had a hard time getting around on crutches when he was released in early August, so Jane let him stay in her fully staffed new house in Holmby Hills with the children while she was in London filming *Stage Fright* for Alfred Hitchcock. When she returned, he moved into his mother's house, on Phyllis Avenue, for a few weeks. If anyone could make him feel better about himself, it was Nelle, who in her late sixties was still driving her old Studebaker to the Olive View Sanitarium, where she now showed patients movies her son got for her from the studio. After he moved back into his apartment, he continued to stop by her place every Sunday for brunch and spiritual support.[76]

By November things were looking up. Jerry Wald came through with a part in what promised to be a good film, *Storm Warning*, the story of a courageous district attorney who busts the Ku Klux Klan in a Southern town. On November 13, two days before his first date with Nancy, Reagan won his third full term as SAG president by an overwhelming majority.

There is a conflicting version of how Ronnie and Nancy met. According to Miriam Schary, several weeks before the *Hollywood Reporter* printed its list, Nancy told her that she would like to meet Ronald Reagan, and Miriam invited them both to a small dinner party at the Scharys' house. The dinner, as described by the Scharys' daughter, writer Jill Robinson, bordered on the disastrous: Miriam, an outspoken liberal, and Ronnie argued about the seriousness of the Communist threat to the film industry; Dore tried to mediate, and Nancy, who was seated opposite Ronnie, "kept smiling at him in agreement." "I don't recall his saying much to Nancy," Miriam said, adding that she had asked Ronnie to pick Nancy up, but he said he would be coming directly from a SAG meeting. She had then hoped he would offer her a ride home, but he was the first to leave, explaining that he had to depart for New York early the next morning.[77]

Reagan did indeed travel to New York in early October on SAG business.[78] However, Nancy consistently maintained that the Schary dinner never took place, and Mervyn LeRoy always told the story more or less her way. So did her husband in his two books. No matter: if she wasn't introduced to Reagan at the Scharys', she seemed determined to meet him that fall. In mid-October, according to SAG records, she called the Guild and "indicated her willingness and desire to run for the Board, but due to some confusion in membership records (two Nancy Davises) her name was not included on the ballot."[79] In addition, one of Nancy's MGM acquaintances remembered her "jokingly" making a list of Hollywood's most eligible bachelors, including producers, directors, agents, lawyers, and actors, and putting Ronald Reagan's name on top.[80]

In any event, there is little doubt that they hit if off on their first date. Ronnie arrived at Nancy's apartment on the dot at 7:30, still using a pair of canes. She greeted him in a trim black dress with a crisp white collar, the kind of always-right, good-taste classic she had favored ever since she graduated from her Girls Latin uniform. He took her to LaRue's, on the Sunset Strip. On the way, he came up with what he thought was an ideal solution for her name problem.

"Have the studio change your name," he said. "You would hardly be the first."

"He had no way of knowing," she later wrote, "how long I had waited to be called Nancy Davis, and how much that name meant to me. 'I can't do that,' I told him. 'Nancy Davis is my name.'"[81]

"Without her amplifying the statement by a single word," he later wrote, "I knew that whether there were three or thirty Nancy Davises, they could do any name-changing that was going to be done."[82]

Reading their separate accounts of that first dinner, it is clear that he was impressed and she was mesmerized. "One of the things I liked about Ronnie right away was that he didn't talk only about himself. . . . He told me about the Guild, and why the actors' union meant so much to him. He talked about his small ranch in the San Fernando Valley, about horses and their bloodlines; he was also a Civil War buff, and he knew a lot about wine. When he did talk about himself, he was personal without being *too* personal. The whole world knew that he had recently been divorced from Jane Wyman, but he didn't go into details, and I wouldn't have liked him if he had."[83]

He was fascinated to learn that her mother had been on Broadway, that Nazimova was her god-mother, and that Walter Huston had been staying with her parents in Chicago when his son, John, called to offer him a part in *The Treasure of the Sierra Madre*. He told her that he had been offered a part in that picture, but Warners had made him turn it down for *The Voice of the Turtle*. He then segued into his miserable time in London, turning his misadventure into an extended comedy routine about too little sunshine and too many Brussels sprouts.

She laughed at his stories, and he was so enchanted by her laugh that he asked if she'd like to catch Sophie Tucker's act at Ciro's, which was just down the Strip, so that he could hear her laugh some more. They ended up staying for the second show—they even managed to dance despite his injured leg. It was almost three in the morning when he took her home, both of them a little giddy perhaps, because, as he told Edmund Morris, the usually abstemious Nancy had helped him con-sume two bottles of champagne during the course of evening.[84]

"Why do people fall in love? It's almost impossi-ble to say," she reflected in the introduction to a book of his love letters that was published on their fiftieth wedding anniversary. "If you're not a teenager or in your early twenties, you've gone on a lot of dates and met a lot of people. When the real thing comes along, you just know it. At least I did. . . . I loved to listen to him talk. I loved his sense of humor. I saw it clearly that very first night: He was everything that I wanted."[85]

Yet after a spate of dates over the next few weeks—"Ronald Reagan and Nancy Davis together again at Kings," "Ronnie Reagan doing Mocambo with Nancy Davis," "Newest telephone number in Ronald Reagan's book is Nancy Davis, attractive M-G-M actress," "Ronnie Reagan's romancing Nancy like mad"—Reagan pulled back.[86] During most of 1950, the couple saw each other now and then, and both dated other people. "Ronnie was in no hurry to make a commitment," Nancy later explained. "He had been burned in his first marriage, and the pain went deep. . . . My mother reminded me that Loyal Davis had been badly burned in his first marriage. He had been terrified of making another mistake, and she had had to wait until he was ready."[87]

Eager to make up for lost time and income after being incapacitated for months, Reagan completed four films that year: *Storm Warning* at Warners, *Louisa* and the infamous *Bedtime for Bonzo* at Universal, and finally a Western, *The Last Outpost*, at Paramount. With the exception of Bonzo the chimpanzee, the Hollywood press linked him with every one of his co-stars—including the flame-haired Rhonda Fleming in *The Last Outpost* and even the nineteen-year-old Piper Laurie in *Louisa*—but these "romances" lasted only as long as the shooting schedules. "He danced well and he had a pleasant personality," Doris Day, who played opposite him in *Storm Warning*, said of their dates. "When he wasn't dancing, he was talking. It really wasn't conversation, it was rather talking at you, sort of long discourses on subjects that interested him. I remember telling him that he should be touring the country making speeches."[88]

If any woman had a hold on him in 1950, it was still Jane Wyman. Although one of the columns had Wyman and Lew Ayres "ga-ga" over each other as late as November 1949,[89] by early 1950 he had decided not to marry her, and Jane once again focused her attentions on her ex-husband. For his thirty-ninth birthday in February, Reagan was honored by the Friars Club at a black-tie dinner in the ballroom of the Beverly Hills Hotel, and Wyman was among the six hundred attendees. It was a big night for Reagan—Cecil B. DeMille and Pat O'Brien made speeches extolling his virtues; Al Jolson sang "Sonny Boy" and said he hoped his son would grow up "to be the kind of man Ronnie is."[90] Jane sat at a table close to the dais, beaming. A few nights later, when she received *Photoplay*'s Gold Medal in the same ballroom, Reagan had a ringside seat, and "clapped louder than any other person in the audience," according to the magazine's reporter, who added, "So many in town are still hoping that these two will reconcile."[91]

Nancy saw in the New Year with her family in Chicago. She must have been happy to get away: not only had Ronnie stopped calling, but a few days before she left, the studio announced that the part she saw as her big chance and was sure she had—the female lead opposite Cary Grant in *Crisis*—was going to Paula Raymond. Another disappointment came as she arrived in Chicago: *East Side, West Side* opened in New York to generally favorable reviews but with nary a mention of her. Her mother was waiting at Dearborn Station, along with several photographers from the Chicago papers, which treated Nancy's arrivals and departures as major celebrity events. Edith organized the first annual Passavant Cotillion and Christmas Ball that season—another rung up the Windy City social ladder for her and a moneymaker for Loyal's hospital. Nancy attended with her old standby Bruce McFarland, who was about to get married to a Chicago girl.[92]

Upon her return to Hollywood, she, too, started playing the field, dating the actors Robert Walker and Robert Stack and the playwright-producer Norman Krasna. Perhaps coincidentally, but probably not, Stack and Krasna were friends of Reagan's. Nancy had met Stack—who would later play Eliot Ness in *The Untouchables* on TV—when she first arrived in town, with a letter of introduction from Colleen Moore to his mother, a grande dame of old Los Angeles society who had bought

Moore's Bel Air mansion.[93] They didn't really click, and even now he bored her a bit, but she was pleased when he called and asked her out. She was more amused by Norman Krasna, who had a production deal at Warners with Jerry Wald and was bright, Jewish, and twelve years her senior. For his part, Krasna was crazy about her, and started proposing marriage soon after they started dating.[94]

She became quite involved with Robert Walker, one of the most talented leading men on the MGM lot—and definitely the most troubled. Three years older than Nancy, Walker had been married twice, to the movie star Jennifer Jones, who left him for producer David O. Selznick in 1945, and then to director John Ford's daughter, Barbara, who asked for a divorce after five weeks in 1948, reportedly because he beat her up when he drank too much. When Nancy met him, he was putting his life back together after spending nearly a year, on Dore Schary's orders, at the Menninger Clinic in Topeka, Kansas, where he was treated for what *The New York Times* called "a severe psychological crackup."[95] He was still under psychiatric care and prohibited from drinking, and Nancy made it her mission to make sure he stayed sober. She also helped him furnish his house in Pacific Palisades and look after his two young sons by Jones when they visited on weekends.[96] By April 1950, one Hollywood columnist was reporting, "Someone close to Bob tells me he is happier with Nancy than he has been at any time since his parting from Jennifer Jones."[97]

Nancy's best shot at stardom came that winter, when she was cast in Schary's pet project, *The Next Voice You Hear*, which was based on a magazine story that imagined how people would react if the voice of God suddenly came over the radio. The script focused on an American Everyman named Joe Smith, who works in a Los Angeles aircraft factory, his wife, Mary, who is about to have a baby, and their eleven-year-old son, Johnny. Schary saw the picture as an experiment in a new way of moviemaking, a low-budget, high-concept antidote to the bloated, schmaltzy period pieces that Mayer favored.

Both Schary and the director, William Wellman, a veteran realist, felt strongly that the principal roles should be played by unfamiliar faces, not well-known stars who they thought would be less believable as such utterly average types. James Whitmore, whose second movie had been directed by Wellman the previous year and won him a nomination as best supporting actor, was quickly cast as Joe Smith. Miriam Schary suggested Nancy for Mary. "This idea took a bit of getting used to," Dore Schary wrote in *Case History of a Movie*. "This would be an exacting star role and Nancy had had only three small parts in pictures, and all of them had been on the 'society' side rather than a middle-class housewife and mother. But in her favor was the fact that her looks and manner and inner self were 'nice' rather than cover-girl glamorous."[98]

Schary asked her to read for the part with Whitmore: "I remember . . . her waiting next to Jim on one of the straight chairs in the anteroom, her fingers clasped tight in her lap to conceal the turbulent emotions which her enormous brown eyes betrayed." He feared he might have to tell her "she wouldn't do." But he and Wellman were so impressed by "the way these two superb young people began making the story live and breathe" that they gave her the part without further ado.[99] On the first day of shooting Nancy found a note in her trailer from Schary: "If 'Mary' turns out to be as real and as sincere and as sweet as you are, then everybody is going to be happy and we're going to have the kind of picture we're hoping for. All the best to you, darling."[100]

The Next Voice You Hear was shot in fourteen days in late February and early March, and came in under budget at $460,000, less than half the standard cost of MGM films at the time.[101] It was a demanding regime, but Nancy proved herself up to the challenge. "It was the first starring role for both of us, and we worked intensely because [we] were very serious about our careers," James Whitmore recalled. "Nancy was definitely not a frivolous person. When it came to her career, she was deadly earnest. She was delightful to work with, very affable, and had a good, hearty laugh. She'd throw her head back and just let loose from somewhere in the center of her being. But we didn't socialize off the set, and there was never any personal conversation about her boyfriends or anything like that. I do recall, though, that she held very strong political opinions which weren't exactly mine."[102]

Nancy's role required great subtlety: although Joe Smith comes across as capable and good-natured, it is Mary who quietly holds the family together and gently directs her husband when he stumbles. On Wellman's instructions, Nancy wore no makeup, combed her own hair, and was fitted with a wire-framed pregnancy pad under her $12.95 maternity smocks. "He wanted everything to be as natural as possible. I did what he wanted, and he helped me make the most of my part. . . . I'd heard he was strictly a man's director and hated directing women. But he was a tiger who turned out to be a pussycat, even though he was known as 'Wild Bill Wellman.' "[103]

"Nancy Davis is considered a new 'perfect wife' type on the strength of her portrayal of James Whitmore's spouse in *The Next Voice You Hear*," the *New York Herald Tribune*'s Hollywood correspondent reported on April 5. "MGM feels that she can be groomed to follow Myrna Loy, who first earned the title as Nora Charles in the Thin Man series. Studio head Dore Schary has instructed MGM producers to be on the lookout for likely material for the young actress."[104]

Schary himself immediately cast her as a small-town schoolteacher opposite Fredric March in *It's* a *Big Country*, which he had co-written and was personally overseeing. He also pushed her for the role of Justice Oliver Wendell Holmes's wife in *The Magnificent Yankee*, a part that would have required her to age from sixty to ninety during the course of the film. Ardie Deutsch was the producer, and he gladly tested Nancy in mid-April. She also had the support of Louis Calhern—Edith's old friend and a patient of Loyal's—who was set for the title role. But that was before John Sturges was assigned to direct, and he apparently decided Nancy wasn't up to the demands of the role.[105]

Later in April, Walter Huston suddenly fell ill on the night of his sixty-sixth birthday. "It was an aneurysm of the abdominal aorta," Richard Davis recalled. "He was in god-awful pain and kept calling Dad. Of course, there wasn't anything you could do about it."[106] Loyal, after sending a Los Angeles colleague to see Huston, flew in the next morning, but he arrived a few hours too late to bid his friend farewell. Nancy remembers going with him to the Beverly Hills Hotel, where Walter had been staying, and comforting Nan Huston. More than six hundred people, including the Davises, attended the memorial service at the Academy Award Theater. Spencer Tracy gave the eulogy. "Professionally, he's easy to rate," Tracy said. "He was the best."[107]

In May, Nancy's first movie, *Shadow on the Wall*, was released after nearly a year's delay, with some very good notices for her. A few days later, Mayer and his new wife, Lorena, hosted the first screening of *The Next Voice You Hear* at their Benedict Canyon home. Nancy was so anxious she broke her string of pearls and spilled coffee all over Bill Wellman's wife.[108] Happily, the early reviews in the trades were glowing. "The screen has never had a better example of husband-wife affection and understanding than that which Wellman builds between James Whitmore and Nancy Davis," said the *Hollywood Reporter*. "And they play it to boff results."[109] *Variety* added, "Nancy Davis gives her role high realism and full polish."[110]

The studio flew Nancy to New York for ten days of interviews and personal appearances before the June 29 opening at Radio City Music Hall. She was thrilled to see her name above the title on the marquee of Manhattan's most prestigious movie house. *The New York Times*'s Bosley Crowther found Nancy "delightful," and *Time* praised her for "a fine, attractive piece of well-balanced acting."[111] The critics were less enthusiastic about the film itself—"a naïve theological hodgepodge," sniffed *Time*—and it did not do as well as Schary had hoped. Still, because he pushed it so hard, *The Next Voice You Hear* received tremendous coverage, and Nancy was highlighted in national publications ranging from *Look* and *Seventeen* to *The American Magazine*, which titled its profile of her "Silver-spooned starlet."[112]

Nancy frequently mentioned how much she missed major league baseball in Los Angeles, sometimes adding that she rooted for the New York Yankees and the Boston Red Sox because she had crushes on Joe DiMaggio and Ted Williams. "Although she's a bachelor girl," one interviewer said, "Nancy states emphatically that she doesn't wish to remain so. . . . Her role of the wife and mother in *The Next Voice You Hear* . . . made family life so appealing that she's eager to try it in real life!"[113]

On July 6, 1950, wearing a black dress, a white hat, and a big corsage, Nancy was photographed celebrating her twenty-ninth birthday with Benny Thau and the Mayers at the Cocoanut Grove. Although she looked pleased to be seen with the head of the studio—one wonders if Mayer gave her the advice he always gave his daughters, "Be smart, but don't show it"—all was not well between her and Thau. Despite his coldhearted reputation, the jaded old roué had fallen in love with his proper young protégée and was pressing her to marry him. This became increasingly problematic, especially after she started going out with other men, who were much closer to her in age. When I asked if her dates with Reagan, Walker, and Stack made Thau jealous, she snapped, "I don't know. I was not *his*. . . . He would have liked to have married me. I did not want to marry him. . . . He was a strange little man, really. He gambled a lot. I think he gambled all his money away. I finally got through to him that the answer was no. And that was it."[114]

Before his death in 1983, Thau was asked if he had wanted to marry Nancy. "I was friendly with her folks, and me being Jewish, I don't know," he answered. "I thought about it, but that's all I did."[115]

According to Richard Davis, it was Loyal who insisted that Nancy bring the Thau situation to a head. "Dr. Loyal laid down the law," Davis told me. "Nancy talked to Dr. Loyal very, very frequently, and he was very negative in terms of this man. It was for Nancy's own good."[116]

Nancy saw a lot of her family that summer. In early July, she flew to San Francisco, where her parents were attending a medical convention. Later that month Richard Davis visited Nancy in her new two-bedroom duplex on Hilgard Avenue in Westwood. The highlight of that trip for him, he said, was accompanying her to a dinner party at Dinah Shore's house, where he met Groucho Marx and golf champion Ben Hogan.[117] In August, Nancy traveled to Chicago for Richard's wedding to Shirley Hull, a socialite from suburban Wheaton. According to clippings in her scrapbook, she had been "quite ill" before leaving Los Angeles, and "on reaching Chicago, collapsed of nervous exhaustion and had to be hospitalized." She missed a private screening of *The Next Voice You Hear* that Edith had organized, but after being treated for a "vitamin deficiency," she was released in time for the August 25 wedding. The studio said Nancy "wore herself to a frazzle plugging her film in New York recently," but surely breaking with Benny Thau while juggling the fragile Robert Walker, the irrepressible Norman Krasna, and the elusive Ronald Reagan added to the strain.[118]

Ronnie and Nancy had seen each other infrequently since that first rush of dates in late 1949, but the relationship took off again in the fall of 1950. In a photograph taken at the Ice Capades in September, Nancy looks wan and thin, and Reagan has his arm reassuringly around her shoulder: maybe he needed to feel she was weak as well as strong, in need of support as well as capable of giving it.[119] In an interview a few days later, Louella Parsons asked Nancy, "Any one man in your life?" The gossip queen expected her to name Walker, but Nancy was noncommittal. "Not yet," she answered. "I won't be trite and say I'm married to my career, but that's pretty much the truth."[120]

On October 2, Nancy started shooting *Night into Morning* with John Hodiak and Ray Milland—she played a "sturdy war widow" whose big scene involves talking Milland out of committing suicide—and later that month Reagan left for Tucson, where *The Last Outpost* was being filmed. He wrote her while he was on location—"Just a quick line. . . . I'm balancing this on my knee while I wait to ride gallantly over another hill"—the first of hundreds of letters, postcards, and telegrams he would lavish on her over the years.[121] After he returned, there were more nights out—a cocktail party, a Friars Club roast, supper at the Sportsmen's Lodge.[122]

Yet, she continued to entertain proposals of marriage from Krasna—"Norman Krasna, alter ego of producer Jerry Wald, is so currazy about Nancy Davis that he's already popped the all-important question," Hollywood columnist Edith Gwynn reported on October 13. "Nancy and her whole family are thinking it over at the moment."[123] Maybe the Davises were just being practical: Krasna and Wald had recently signed a $50 million deal with Howard Hughes to produce twelve movies a year for five years at RKO.[124] Or maybe Nancy was trying to make Ronnie jealous. By mid-December, she had turned Krasna down, and for Christmas Ronnie gave her a gold key from Ruser Jewelers in Beverly Hills to congratulate her on getting her own dressing room at MGM.[125]

Nancy worked to get closer to Ronnie in other ways as well. She took a few riding lessons from Peter Lawford, the handsome British-born Metro actor and future brother-in-law of John F. Kennedy. She put aside her distaste for alcohol and let herself have a weak cocktail or two when Ronnie took her out to dinner. "I'd drink a little," she told me. "Nothing very strong like a martini—that would taste like gasoline to me. But some orange juice and vodka I would drink."[126]

Perhaps the most important factor in drawing Ronnie and Nancy together was her appointment to fill a vacancy on the SAG board, a goal she had been pursuing for almost a year. The minutes for October 9, 1950, open with, "President Reagan welcomed Nancy Davis to her first Board meeting." The following November she was elected to a full three-year term.[127] Although the SAG board was deeply involved in such controversial issues as loyalty oaths, Nancy Reagan told me, "I don't remember any tension. Maybe it's my memory, or maybe it's that I was falling in love."[128]

Going on the board meant that Nancy now saw Ronnie every Monday night. "After the meetings," she said, "we'd all go—Ronnie and I and whoever else—to this little place nearby and sit and visit."[129] It also meant that Nancy witnessed firsthand and over an extended period of time how Reagan functioned as a leader: how he took advice, how he could be influenced, how he dealt with opposition, how he achieved a consensus, how he reached a decision. She may have ended up with a clearer understanding of Reagan's decision-making process and leadership style than he had.

For Reagan, the SAG presidency, which he held until 1952, was half of "my double life."[130] Yet he clearly relished every moment, from traveling to New York for meetings with the American Federation of Radio Artists about which union would represent the growing numbers of television performers to wrangling with the studio bosses to get actors a five-day week. ("Thanks to Ronnie, we had *Saturdays* off," exclaimed Ann Rutherford. "We could go away for a *weekend*.")[131] On nights when he didn't have a date, Reagan worked late at SAG headquarters, and was often seen dining alone at Chasen's, sipping a glass of wine while reviewing Guild papers.[132] At a time when his movie career was faltering, running the Guild kept his profile high and boosted the ego he hid so well.

Closely related to Reagan's SAG duties were his activities as "a leader in the industry drive against Communists and their sympathizers," in Nancy's words.[133] Although his term as chairman of MPIC had expired in July, he remained on its executive board and met with State Department officials that fall to discuss ways in which the industry could help the government fight Communism over-seas.[134] He had also become heavily involved in the Crusade for Freedom, a new national organization supported by the recently created CIA and headed by General Lucius Clay, the Army commander who had organized the 1948–49 Berlin Airlift.[135]

In September 1950, the Crusade held mass rallies at every major Hollywood studio, at which speakers ranging from liberal producer Walter Wanger to the ultra-right-wing John Wayne called for the liberation of the Soviet-dominated nations of Eastern Europe. Reagan participated in these rallies, and he fired off a telegram to General Clay, pledging the support of SAG's "more than 8,000 members . . . in the battle for men's minds now being waged around the world."[136]

By then, after Mao Zedong's takeover of China, the North Korean invasion of South Korea, and the arrest of Julius and Ethel Rosenberg for giving atomic secrets to the Russians, anti-Communism had become something akin to a national religion. The movement's wild-eyed ayatollah, Senator Joseph McCarthy, a Wisconsin Republican, had burst from obscurity that February with a fiery Lincoln's Birthday speech accusing the State Department of harboring 205 "card-carrying Communists." Its holy grail, the Internal Security Act of 1950, which provided for the registration of Communist and Communist front organizations and for the internment of Communists during a national emergency, was passed over Truman's veto in September.

Reagan wisely refrained from praising McCarthy—he would later say that McCarthy was "using a shotgun when he should have been using a rifle"—perhaps because McCarthy never targeted Hollywood, perhaps because Reagan still considered himself a Democrat.[137] In the November 1950 election for a Senate seat from California he campaigned for Congresswoman Helen Gahagan Douglas, the wife of actor Melyvn Douglas, against Richard Nixon, who had made a name for himself with HUAC by helping to expose Alger Hiss, a high-ranking State Department official, as a Soviet spy, and who now accused the liberal Douglas of being "pink right down to her underwear."[138]

There is reason to believe, however, that Reagan's loyalty to the party of his father, as well as to Douglas, was wavering—and that Nancy may have had something to do with that. Nancy Reagan told me, "I knew nothing about politics, and I wasn't even registered when I met Ronnie."[139] Reagan, however, later wrote that the girl he had met "was more than disinterested in Leftist causes: she was violently opposed to such shenanigans."[140] Once, when I asked her if she believed that there was a Soviet-backed plan to infiltrate Hollywood, she declared without a moment's thought, "Damn right there was. And they were trying to get their message into the movies."[141]

In her memoir, *A Full Life*, Helen Gahagan Douglas recalls that Nancy's old acting mentor and would-be political instructor, ZaSu Pitts, "who was livid on the subject of communism, made a particularly vicious speech about me."[142] Anne Edwards quotes Pitts referring to Douglas as "the Pink Lady who would allow the Communists to take over our land and our homes as well." Unbeknownst to Douglas, Reagan was in the audience that night with Nancy, and he apparently liked what he heard.[143] Robert Cummings, Reagan's co-star from *Kings Row*, recalled Ronnie calling in the middle of the night to ask him to support Nixon. "We're giving a party for him tomorrow night," he said. "Can you come?" "But isn't he a Republican?" Cummings asked. "I've switched," said Reagan. "I sat down and made a list of the people I know, and the most admired people I know are Republicans."[144] Reagan would not formally change his party registration for another twelve years, but he never endorsed another Democrat.

In 1951, Reagan stepped up his anti-Communist activities. He took to the dinner speaker circuit on behalf of the Crusade for Freedom, and even made a short film for the organization that was "circulated to schools, civic groups, and churches around the country."[145] That spring HUAC held another round of hearings on Communist influence in the film industry, which both the SAG and MPIC boards endorsed. The SAG board refused to support Gale Sondergaard—Nancy's colleague from *East Side, West Side*—after she took an ad in *Variety* announcing she had been subpoenaed by the committee and intended to take the Fifth Amendment. Sondergaard wouldn't make another movie until 1969.[146] Actor Sterling Hayden, on the other hand, testified that "joining the party was the stupidest thing I ever did," identified three industry associates as Communists, and praised Reagan for his handling of the 1945–46 strike, calling him "a one-man battalion" against Communism in Hollywood.[147] Hayden went right back to work at Fox, and was rewarded with an official statement from the SAG board congratulating him on "his honesty and frankness."[148]

Along with the other industry potentates in MPIC, Reagan had come to believe that confessing one's own sins was not enough; one also had to do penance by exposing the sins of others before one could be redeemed. He and IATSE head Roy Brewer proposed the creation of a Patriotic Services Committee at MPIC, and spent much time and effort clearing the falsely accused, rehabilitating cooperative penitents, and screening prospective employees for the studios.[149]

"Any American who has been a member of the Communist party at any time, but who has now changed his mind and is loyal to our country should be willing to stand up and be counted, admit 'I was wrong' and give all the information he has to the government agencies who are combating the Red plotters," Reagan wrote in the *Hollywood Citizen News* in July 1951. "We've gotten rid of the Communist conspirators in Hollywood. Let's do it now in other industries."[150]

"Ronnie Reagan . . . is a happy man these days," Hedda Hopper reported that summer. "He has a new 350-acre ranch that he loves and it's very obvious that he's in love with Nancy Davis."[151] For months, the Hollywood press had been describing Ronnie and Nancy as an "everynightem," predicting an imminent marriage, or even an elopement. Ronnie refused to take calls from reporters; Nancy would say only, "He hasn't asked me yet."[152] That spring, she had stopped seeing Robert Walker; in August—a few days after completing *My Son John*, in which he played a Communist who is turned in by his mother—Walker died from a sedative injection administered by a psychiatrist.[153]

Ronnie and Nancy were occasionally photographed at premieres and nightclubs, and frequently dined at their favorite restaurant, Chasen's, "especially on Tuesday nights, when the special was Beef Belmont," as she remembered it. But they spent many more evenings at her apartment watching TV, or having quiet dinners at Bill and Ardis Holden's "charming Tudor house" in Toluca Lake.[154] Almost every Saturday, Ronnie invited Nancy to accompany him and the children to his new ranch in Malibu Canyon.

"As far as we all knew at the time, she was the first woman in his life since Mother," Maureen Reagan wrote in her memoir, *First Father, First Daughter*. "You could tell the two of them were crazy about each other. They weren't lovey-dovey or anything like that, at least not in front of us kids, but they had a natural, easy way of being with each other that suggested that they belonged together."[155] The ten-year-old Maureen took to her future stepmother immediately: "I especially liked Nancy because when the four of us were at the ranch, she would happily perform one of my most hated chores—whitewashing the thousands of feet of redwood fence that Dad was building. . . . He'd spend hours in the hot sun building paddocks for the horses, a riding ring, or whatever, all with a manual posthole digger."[156]

Michael, who was six, liked the way Nancy would let him sit on her lap and massage his back on their rides out to the ranch. "She was always cheerful, unlike Mom who had constant mood shifts," he wrote in his memoir, *On the Outside Looking In.* An unhappy child who cried himself to sleep most nights, Michael craved attention and stability. The previous year, he had joined Maureen at the Chadwick School in Palos Verdes; Jane and Ronnie took turns having them on weekends. While Michael blamed his mother for the divorce— and took pleasure in annoying her with stories about his good times at the ranch—he idolized his father. "Dad taught Maureen and me to ride by leading us around the corral. He was a pussycat as a teacher, always calm and patient," Michael recalled. "I was in total awe of him. He was a man's man and everyone loved him. I wanted to be just like him."[157]

Reagan bought the Malibu Canyon property, a wild stretch of oak-covered hills a half-hour's drive inland from the Pacific Coast Highway, and the run-down old farmhouse on it, for about $85,000 in March 1951. It was almost completely surrounded by a 2,500-acre reserve where 20th Century Fox filmed its Westerns. Nino Pepitone, his partner in the much smaller Northridge horse farm, which had been sold for an undisclosed sum, continued to train Reagan's thoroughbreds at Malibu. Curiously, Reagan kept the name Yearling Row. But, at Maureen's suggestion, the first foal born at the new ranch, "a gorgeous dapple filly," was named Nancy D.[158]

Not surprisingly, Jane and Nancy saw each other as rivals. Michael Reagan wrote that even in those early days the two women said "derogatory" things about each other—and, as children of broken marriages often do, he would agree with both of them.[159] According to Nancy Reagan, Jane "convinced" Ronnie that he shouldn't remarry before she did, "because it wouldn't be good for the children."[160] Someone close to the Reagans told me that when Jane realized Ronnie was getting serious about Nancy she made one last play to get him back, telling him she'd like to start over again. But it was too late.

In the February 1951 issue of *Modern Screen*,

Louella Parsons wrote, "Not long ago, I went to a dinner party at [Jane's] home and Maureen came in to cut her birthday cake. Her mother and father stood by her side, polite to each other and respectful—so different from those gay kids who went barnstorming with me. I turned away so they couldn't see the tears in my eyes. Since then, when I see Janie, she seems self-sufficient, independent, and oh, so gay. But I know that not long ago she said to someone, 'What's the matter with me? I can't seem to pick up the pieces of my life again. Will I ever find happiness ahead?' "[161]

Ronnie naively believed that the two women could get along, and even took Nancy to the premiere of Jane's film *The Blue Veil*, in September 1951. Jane's date was the Hollywood lawyer Gregg Bautzer, a slick playboy who had previously romanced Lana Turner, Merle Oberon, Sonja Henie, and Ginger Rogers. Although Jane had hopes of marrying him, by the end of the year he had resumed his long-term, up-and-down relationship with Joan Crawford.[162]

Meanwhile, Ronnie took Nancy to meet his mother. The Disciples of Christ lay missionary and the Chicago Gold Coast princess would seem to have had little in common, but Nelle approved of Nancy's sedate style and earnest personality. According to Nancy, Nelle "very quickly sized up the situation" between Ronnie and her. "You're in love with him, aren't you?" Nelle asked Nancy, who admitted she was. "I thought so," said Nelle.[163]

Nancy introduced Ronnie to Edith and Loyal

"over the telephone; I called my parents every Sunday, and Ronnie would get on and say hello."[164] On one of his trips to the East Coast he met Edith when he changed trains in Chicago. She brought Colleen Moore Hargrave and Lillian Gish along to look him over. Both of them had shared her concern that Nancy, at thirty, was in danger of never marrying. Colleen declared that Reagan reminded her of Loyal, which Edith saw as a good sign, given Nancy's adoration of her stepfather. "It will take," Gish reportedly predicted.[165]

Still, two years after they had met and a year after they started going steady, Reagan needed more time. Or maybe he was waiting for an auspicious alignment of the stars.

At some point during their extended courtship, Nancy began accompanying Ronnie to the sign-of-the-month parties given by Carroll Righter, Hollywood's reigning astrologer. These parties, attended by everyone from such old-time divas as Marlene Dietrich to young sophisticates like Lauren Bacall, were famous for their decor: a baby lion greeted guests at the Leo party, the swimming pool was filled with fish for the Pisces party, sets of twins formed a receiving line at the Gemini party.[166] "Ronnie went to all of Carroll's parties," I was told by Arlene Dahl, who had met both men shortly after she was signed by Warners in 1947. "They were very good friends. Carroll was helpful in choosing dates for Ronnie when he was president of SAG, and he told him early on that he would amount to much more than just an actor."[167]

According to Ed Helin, a longtime associate of Righter's, Reagan started consulting the "guru to the stars" when he was still married to Wyman, who was also a client. "They even picked the date astrologically to get a good clean divorce without any problems," Helin disclosed. "Whenever an occupation is kind of iffy, like show business, real estate, politics, the stock market," he added, "you're going to get a lot of people going to either psychics or astrologers."[168]

Righter's movie star clients depended on him to set the dates for signing contracts, starting films, taking trips, even conceiving children. "I don't ask Carroll when I should go to the bathroom," Van Johnson's wife, Evie, told *Time* magazine, "[but] some of our friends do."[169] Among those for whom Righter did monthly, weekly, or daily charts were Bette Davis, Clark Gable, Dick Powell, Bob Cummings, Lana Turner, Adolphe Menjou, Ann Sothern, Susan Hayward, Rhonda Fleming, and Peter Lawford, as well as the writer Erich Maria Remarque and Goodwin Knight, who would become governor of California in 1953. Buff Chandler, the wife of the publisher of the *Los Angeles Times*, sat on the board of the Carrroll Righter Foundation, which ran an astrology insti-tute at his Hollywood mansion.[170]

With his patrician air and gold-buttoned blazers, Righter reeked respectability. A confirmed bache-lor from a Main Line family, he had obtained a law degree and chaired the Philadelphia Opera before moving to Los Angeles in 1939. As a practicing Episcopalian, he assured his clients that astrology did not conflict with traditional religion. "If God works through other mediums," he told *Life* in 1954, "why not also through the planets?"[171] He virtually invented the syndicated daily horoscope column, and by the 1960s, when astrology had became gospel for the hippie generation, his prognostications could be read in more than three hundred newspapers.

The actor Cesar Romero took Nancy to her first Righter party, in January 1950, a month or so after her first date with Ronnie.[172] About the same time, Nancy befriended Arlene Dahl, who had moved from Warners to Metro in 1948 and was something of a fanatic about astrology. The earliest reference to Nancy's interest in the zodiac can be found in a Walter Huston biography and dates back to 1933, when she was twelve. In describing a dinner party hosted by Nan and Walter and attended by Edith and Loyal, author John Weld notes, "The conversation turned to astrology. Edith Davis's daughter Nancy had recently had her horoscope charted by Nan's friend Deborah Lewis, a professional astrologer and writer for *American Astrology*. She prophesied that Nancy would be a great success, no matter what she chose to do."[173]

That's not the way it looked as 1951 drew to a close. Nancy's film career was all but over, and the man of her dreams still had not proposed. In

September she was told that MGM would termi-
nate her contract when her next option came up,
in March.[174] It was clear by then that while her talent was substantial, her star appeal was limited.
Earlier in the year she had made her last two films
for Metro, turning in her usual solid but un-charis-
matic performances as James Whitmore's wife
(again) in *Shadow in the Sky*, and George Murphy's
wife in *Talk About a Stranger*. "After reading the
script of that frightful picture," Murphy later said,
"Nancy and I both realized the studio wanted to
get rid of us."[175]

Nancy decided not to go home for the holidays
that year, preferring to stay close to Ronnie.
"Ronnie brought over a small tree for my apartment," she recalled, "and on Christmas Eve I finally
got up the courage to ask him what was, for me, a
very bold question: 'Do you want me to wait for
you?' And he said, 'Yes, I do.'"[176]

What was holding him back? According to Kitty
Kelley, he was secretly seeing an actress named
Christine Larson at the time.[177] He was also mired
in his own career crisis and worried about his
financial situation. On January 15, 1952, Universal
cut his five-picture deal back to three after he had
rejected two scripts that he considered beneath
him.[178] Two weeks later he completed his forty-sec-
ond and last movie for Warners. For a change it
was a picture he wanted to make—*The Winning
Team*, in which he played Grover Cleveland
Alexander, the troubled baseball great—but that
was the end of his guaranteed annual income.

Both Ronnie and Nancy were now on their own, at a time when the studio system was collapsing all around them. The major film companies, battered on one side by the 1948 Supreme Court ruling forcing them to sell their lucrative theater chains and on the other by the ever-rising popularity of television, were in a state of upheaval. Weekly movie attendance had plummeted from a postwar high of 100 million to half that by the early 1950s, and the studios were dropping contracts, slashing budgets, and cutting back production to stem their losses. The King of Hollywood, Louis B. Mayer, who more than anyone had created and upheld the old order, had finally been toppled by Dore Schary in June 1951.

According to Nancy, sometime in January 1952 she told Ronnie that she was thinking of calling her agent to "see about getting a play in New York." "I decided to give things a push" is how she later put it. "As I recall, he didn't say anything, but he looked surprised. Not long afterward, while we were having dinner in our usual booth at Chasen's, he said, 'I think we ought to get married.'"

She quietly answered, "I think so too."[179]

A few nights later, during an MPIC meeting, Ronnie asked Bill Holden to be his best man. "It's about time," Holden blurted out.[180]

On February 20, MGM issued a face-saving press release stating that Nancy had asked to be let out of her contract.[181] That same evening Ronnie called Loyal from Nancy's apartment and asked for her hand in marriage. "Davis-Reagan Nuptials Set," Louella Parsons announced the next day, saying the wedding was scheduled for early March. "Ronnie stands for all that's good in the industry," added Louella about her favorite from Dixon. She also reminded her readers, "It was at my home that Jane and Ronnie held their wedding reception, so I have always felt very close to him through the years." (In her scrapbook, Nancy blacked out references to Ronnie's first marriage in the deluge of press items that followed Louella's scoop.)[182]

On February 27, MGM announced that the wedding would take place the following Tuesday at "some small church in Southern California." The day after that, Nancy and Ronnie were photographed at Santa Monica City Hall getting their marriage license: Ronnie looked a little pale in a turtleneck and trench coat; Nancy radiant in a white-collared black dress, just like the one she wore on their first date.[183]

There was one sad note leading up to the wedding: Nancy's grandmother, Nannee Robbins, whom she hadn't seen in years, heard about the upcoming marriage and decided to make the trip from New Jersey to meet her only grandchild's betrothed. "The three of us were having dinner at Chasen's," Nancy later wrote, "when she suffered a stroke. We rushed her to the hospital, and although she recovered, she died not too long afterward."[184]

Otherwise, the planets seemed to be aligned in their favor. According to Ed Helin, the couple consulted with Carroll Righter, and he gave their union his blessing.[185] For those who believe in such things, the combination of an Aquarius II (Ronnie) and a Cancer II (Nancy) is said to be extremely potent. As Gary Goldschneider and Joost Elffers write in *The Secret Language of Relationships*:

This relationship seems easygoing but conceals a tremendous thirst for power. Hidden beneath an amiable exterior is a core that no one who mistakes these two for an easy touch will quickly forget. Although Cancer is a water sign and Aquarius air, their relationship is ruled by earth and fire, here connoting smoldering desire and ambition. These volcanic seethings may cause tremendous frustration if not vented, but Cancer II–Aquarius II couples often have the patience and foresight to wait until they are called. Part of this pair's power lies in their popularity. Lovers, friends and mates in this combination may be in high demand in their social circle. Their charisma, often of the charming and light variety, is a kind of hook with which they can snag the hearts of their admirers. The process need not be at all unpleasant, and in fact a good time is often had by all in the long run.[186]

The couple themselves seemed to realize how perfectly suited they were. By then they had even chosen "their song"—George Gershwin's "Our Love Is Here to Stay."

CHAPTER ELEVEN

PACIFIC PALISADES
1952–1958

Nancy's marriage paralleled her mother's exactly. You had two men—got them on the rebound. They were lucky men. Very, very lucky.

Richard Davis to author, May 30, 2003

The Little Brown Church in the Valley, a Disciples of Christ outpost on the southern fringe of the San Fernando Valley, is everything its name suggests: small, simple, picturesque. A rose-covered white picket fence frames the church's neatly trimmed lawn, and the dark brown clapboard structure is topped by a squared-off steeple bearing a plain white wooden cross. Another unadorned wooden cross stands in the center of the altar: a bare table with the words "In Remembrance of Me" carved along its front edge. The walls are knotty pine, except for the one behind the altar, which is draped in red velveteen. There are only nine rows of pews, and the center aisle is just three feet wide. This is where Ronald Reagan and Nancy Davis were married on Tuesday, March 4, 1952, at five o'clock in the afternoon. He was forty-one, she was thirty.

The only attendants were the couple's witnesses, Bill and Ardis Holden. When I asked Nancy Reagan why the wedding was so small, she answered, "That was the way we wanted it."[1] Tellingly, the woman who had waited nearly a decade to be a bride had convinced herself that her groom's wishes were her own. "Came our wedding day," Reagan wrote in his autobiography, "and not one protest from Nancy over the fact that I cheated her out of the ceremony every girl deserves." Clearly referring to his resentment of the press's intrusive coverage of his breakup with Jane Wyman, he continues, "I can only confess that at the time to even contemplate facing reporters and flashbulbs made me break out in a cold sweat."[2]

Instead of a wedding gown, Nancy wore a smart gray wool suit with white collar and cuffs from I. Magnin—"I was so disappointed that Amelia [Gray] didn't have anything for me"[3]—and the single strand of pearls her parents had given her for her debutante party. Her dark hair was brushed back high off her forehead and crowned with a chic white-flowered hat and veil. Ronnie presented her with a bouquet of white tulips and orange blossoms when he picked her up at her apartment, where her German housekeeper, Frieda, had helped her dress. The brief nuptial service was performed by the Reverend John H. Wells, and

Nancy was "so excited" that she "went through the ceremony in a daze" and had no memory of saying "I do."[4]

If Ardis hadn't arranged for a photographer to meet the newlyweds at the Holdens' house a few miles away, there would be no visual record of the historic event. Ardis had also ordered a three-tiered wedding cake, and in the photograph of Ronnie and Nancy cutting it, they both look truly content. From the Holdens', they drove to Ann Straus's house in Beverly Hills, where the MGM publicist helped them prepare the press release announcing their wedding. "It was seven o'clock when they stopped by," recalled Bill Fine, who was taking Straus out to dinner that night, "and they were very bubbly."[5]

At some point they called Edith and Loyal in Chicago, Nelle at home in West Hollywood, and the children at Chadwick to say, "OK, it's official," as Maureen later put it, adding, "I think Michael and I both felt a little weird . . . waiting for a phone call like that, but Dad felt strongly that we should be a part of things in at least this small way."[6]

The happy twosome then drove off in Ronnie's Cadillac convertible to the Mission Inn in Riverside, the Spanish colonial-style hotel that was famous locally for hosting presidents going back to William Howard Taft and Theodore Roosevelt. Richard and Pat Nixon had been married and spent their wedding night there in 1940. A plaque in the lobby commemorates the Reagans' first night as man and wife:

Upon arrival, a bouquet of red roses greeted the couple, compliments of the hotel with wishes for a long and successful union. Before continuing on to Phoenix the following morning, the Reagans gave the roses to another guest of the Inn—an elderly woman staying across the hall from the newlyweds.

After a long day on dusty Route 10, Ronnie and Nancy checked into the Arizona Biltmore. Loyal and Edith arrived in Phoenix four days later. Ronnie later wrote, "Meeting her father, the doctor, wasn't the easiest moment I ever had. After all, here was a man internationally renowned in the world of surgery, a fearless stickler for principle, and a man who could no more choose the easy path of expediency than he could rob the poor box. My fear lasted about a minute and a half after we met— which was as long as it took to find out he was a true humanitarian."[7]

Ronnie related to his new mother-in-law on a less elevated plane. They quickly discovered a shared fondness for off-color humor and, according to Richard Davis, whenever they got together from then on "the first thing Edith would do was take Ronnie into the guest bedroom and lock the door. They would tell dirty jokes and stories for hours. . . . You could hear the hilarious laughter. . . . She just *adored* him."[8]

The Davises weren't staying at the hotel, as they had recently built a house in the adjacent Biltmore

Estates, which was considered Phoenix's best address. The white-brick ranch-style house with its gray slate roof and dark green shutters was tastefully landscaped and set along the edge of the Biltmore's golf course. Still, it was among the more modest residences in this posh enclave, where the Davises' neighbors included Senator Barry Goldwater, Vincent and Brooke Astor, and Henry and Clare Booth Luce.

A couple who were also honeymooning at the Biltmore that spring remember the Davises showing up every afternoon to join Ronnie and Nancy at their poolside cabana.[9] It was clear that Ronnie was impressed with his new in-laws, and not without reason. Two years earlier Loyal, then in his mid-fifties, had been elected to the board of regents of the American College of Surgeons and by the end of the decade would become chairman—"the most powerful position in American surgery," as the *Chicago Daily News* proclaimed upon his appointment.[10]

Edith, at sixty-four (pretending to be fifty-six), continued to amaze in her own way. A few months before her daughter's wedding, while Loyal was giving a lecture at Oxford University, Edith and her Chicago socialite pal Narcissa Thorne were having tea with the Queen Mother in London. (Thorne presented the dowager queen with a rare first edition of James Doyle's *History of England*; Edith confided to a Chicago society columnist that Her Majesty was "very folksy.")[11] The Davises' two-month European tour had also included a visit with

General Eisenhower, then commander of NATO, and his wife, Mamie, at their home outside Paris. Probably as a result, Ronnie and Nancy received a congratulatory telegram from the Eisenhowers two weeks after their wedding.[12]

Ronnie and Nancy spent ten sun-drenched days in Phoenix, leaving just in time for him to start shooting *Tropic Zone* with Rhonda Fleming at Paramount. On the way back to Los Angeles, the convertible's canvas top was nearly torn in half in a sandstorm, and Nancy had to hold it together. "From the start, our marriage was like an adolescent's dream of what a marriage should be," Reagan would later write. "It was rich and full from the beginning, and it has gotten more so with each passing day. Nancy moved into my heart and replaced an emptiness that I'd been trying to ignore for a long time."[13]

On March 13, while the new Mr. and Mrs. Reagan were still on their honeymoon, Louella Parsons announced Jane Wyman's engagement to Travis Kleefeld, the twenty-six-year-old scion of a locally prominent contracting family. The photographers went wild when both couples attended the Academy Awards later that month. Jane was up for best actress for *The Blue Veil* but lost to Vivien Leigh. A few days later she broke off the engagement with Kleefeld. Since Jane was at the height of her career—and an older woman going out with a younger man, which raised eyebrows in those days—the Hollywood press played the story for all it was worth. An irked Nancy told friends she was sure Jane had set up the whole thing to upstage Ronnie's marriage.[14] As Richard Gully, a Carroll Righter follower, remarked many years later, "Destiny planned to pit Jane Wyman against Nancy Reagan. Jane is a Capricorn and Nancy is a Cancer and it's a very bad mix. They were bound to clash. It was fate."[15]

Ronnie moved into Nancy's Hilgaard Avenue duplex but kept his place on Londonderry Terrace, because there wasn't enough room in her apartment for all of their clothes. Soon they found a three-bedroom Cape Cod–style house at 1258 North Amalfi Drive in Pacific Palisades. "We bought it for $42,000," Nancy Reagan recalled. "I loved that house. Pacific Palisades wasn't as built up as it is today. We had a wonderful garden—it was almost like living in the country."[16]

Before the war, Pacific Palisades had been considered too far west for the Hollywood crowd, though its steep hillsides covered with oaks, cedars, palms, and eucalyptus attracted artists and writers, most notably the Nobel Prize–winning novelist Thomas Mann, who settled there in 1940 after fleeing Nazi Germany. By 1952, however, with prices escalating in Beverly Hills and Bel Air, the Palisades was rapidly becoming an upper-middle-class suburb. Gregory Peck, Joseph Cotten, and Lawrence Welk were among the first entertainers to move there. "Jerry Lewis lived on our street," Nancy Reagan told me.[17] The summer the Reagans moved in, Mann, hounded by HUAC for openly supporting the Hollywood 10, sold his estate and returned to Europe. "The sick, tense atmosphere of this country oppresses me," he said. "I have no desire to rest my bones in this soulless soil."[18]

For Reagan, such a thought would have been inconceivable. "This land of ours is the last best hope of man on earth," he declared in a commencement address at William Woods College in June 1952, echoing Lincoln. Ronnie and Nancy had traveled by train to the Disciples of Christ school in Fulton, Missouri, and Reagan wrote his speech on the way. America, he told the graduating students, was "a promised land . . . in the divine scheme of things . . . less of a place than an idea . . . an idea that has been deep in the souls of man ever since man started his long trail from the swamps. It is nothing but the inherent love of freedom in each one of us, and the great ideological struggle that we find ourselves engaged in today is not a new struggle. It's the same old battle."[19]

The Reagans also attended the premiere of his last Warners film, *The Winning Team,* in Springfield, Missouri, where their train was greeted by some seven hundred fans, even though it arrived at midnight. President Truman was in Springfield for a reunion of his World War I artillery unit, but at the last minute he decided not to attend the film's opening. According to Stephen Vaughn, Truman had "considered inviting the Reagans for dinner, but after some thought concluded that he did not want any 'Hollywood riffraff.'" Reagan, who had done so much to fight the Wallacites in Hollywood during Truman's 1948 run, was miffed, as was Nancy, and the snub may have contributed to his decision to support Eisenhower instead of the Democratic candidate, Adlai Stevenson, that fall.[20] It would be the first time he voted Republican in a presidential election.

Eight weeks after they were married, the Reagans announced that Nancy was expecting a baby at Christmastime. In June, reporters in Missouri noticed, her condition was already showing. On the evening of October 20, Ronnie and Nancy were at a horse show at the Pan Pacific Auditorium in Hollywood, watching one of their horses—a mare named Mrs. Simpson after the Duchess of Windsor—jump. During the show Nancy started having labor pains, but she insisted it was just the baby changing positions or cramps. Ronnie wanted to take her to the hospital, but she made him take her home, an hour's drive along Sunset Boulevard. By the time they got into bed, the contractions were coming fast.

"There was a heat wave," Nancy Reagan told me. "It was so hot I thought I was going to lose the baby."[21] After fourteen hours of labor at Cedars of Lebanon Hospital, her doctor asked Ronnie for permission to perform a cesarean. Patricia Ann Reagan was born at 2:30 in the afternoon on October 21, seven and a half months after the wedding. Although she weighed a healthy seven pounds three ounces, Patti was always told by her parents that she had spent two months in an incubator. "This was the Fifties," she wrote in her auto-biography, *The Way I See It.* "Good girls weren't supposed to have sex before marriage. If they did, they were supposed to be ashamed of it and hide it. So, if you had a baby seven months after you got married, pretending prematurity was one option."[22]

"Nancy was pregnant when they were married," a longtime family friend told me. "It was common knowledge." Still, the question remains whether Nancy knew she was pregnant or had told Ronnie that she was *before* he called Loyal Davis and asked for her hand on February 20—about a month after the child was presumably conceived. "Go ahead and count" is all Nancy Reagan would ever say.[23]

"If you drive up to the house on Amalfi," Nancy Reagan told me over lunch at the Hotel Bel-Air many years later, "you'll see there's an olive tree out front that Ronnie had planted for me when I had Patti. When I came home from the hospital it was there with a big red ribbon around it that said, 'Welcome Home, Mommy.' Most people don't know this about Ronnie, but he was a very, very sentimental, romantic man."[24]

From then on, Ronnie would call his wife Mommy, in letters and in person, in private and among friends. In his autobiography he practically admitted that he wasn't thrilled with the idea of having to share his new wife with a baby so soon into their marriage. "I confess that at the moment her arrival didn't impress me much," he wrote about Patti's birth. "The only word I wanted concerned her mother."[25]

On doctor's orders, Nancy stayed in bed for six weeks after Patti's birth, and an English nanny named Penny was hired to look after the baby. The chubby little girl with a full head of dark hair was a problem child from the beginning. "Patti always, always wanted attention twenty-four hours a day from the day she was born," Nancy Reagan told me. "And you couldn't give anyone attention twenty-four hours a day."[26]

Nancy wore her wedding hat—minus the veil—to Patti's christening at the Hollywood-Beverly Christian Church in December. Bill Holden was the godfather, and Louise Tracy stood in for the godmother, Colleen Moore Hargrave, who was unable to leave Chicago. Edith and Loyal were there, as was Nelle, looking frail but proud in a black dress and light-colored shawl.

One week after Patti's birth, Jane Wyman made headlines again, by eloping with Fred Karger, a suavely handsome musician who had been dating a newcomer named Marilyn Monroe. Maureen and Michael, who were already feeling threatened by the arrival of a stepsister, were introduced to their "new father" and his eleven-year-old daughter by a previous marriage the night before the wedding.[27] Ronnie tried to make Michael feel better about this sudden turn of events by inviting Fred out to the ranch one Saturday, "so that I could see both of my fathers getting along together," as Michael put it.[28] Neither of his mothers, however, seemed will-ing to make that kind of effort.

"Dad and Nancy became a family unto them-selves after Patti was born," Michael recalled. "Until then, Nancy had treated Maureen and me like her own kids. It soon became apparent that we were becoming less and less important in her life and Dad's."[29] Like any new wife and mother, Nancy was understandably more focused on building a family than on fixing the one she had inherited. "I was just running our little house," she said when I asked her about her first year of marriage. "And wheeling Patti up and down the street."[30]

On November 10, 1952, Ronald Reagan formally stepped down as president of SAG at a meeting of the entire membership, who gave him a standing ovation and a gold lifetime membership card. He remained on the board and the executive commit-tee. Nancy also kept her seat on the board, but was glad to see Ronnie give up the presidency, feeling that after one appointed and five elected terms he had done enough for his fellow actors. "There's no question in my mind that Ronnie's political involvements had begun to hurt his prospects for work," she later wrote. "By the time I came along, he had become so identified with the Screen Actors Guild that the studio heads had begun to think of him less as an actor than as an adversary."[31]

He was succeeded by Walter Pidgeon, who four months earlier had been instrumental in persuad-

ing the board to approve one of the most controversial decisions Reagan took in his long tenure as
the Guild's chief: to grant an unprecedented blanket waiver to his own agency, MCA, allowing it to
produce an unlimited number of television shows.
Until then, waivers of the bylaw forbidding agents
to act as producers had been given on a case-by-
case basis for film production; the Guild was in the
process of drawing up a similar rule for television.
But MCA's chairman, Jules Stein, and president,
Lew Wasserman, approached Reagan with a
tempting proposal at a time when unemployment
among actors in Hollywood was at a record high,
live television production was booming in New
York, and the old-line studio moguls still saw the
new medium as a threat rather than an opportunity. According to Garry Wills, they told Reagan
that MCA's recently launched Revue Productions
"would undertake [television] production on an
ambitious scale, furnishing employment to
Hollywood actors, but they could only do this if the
Guild would not undercut the project at some
future date by making production an impermissible
activity for agents."[32]

In addition, MCA quietly agreed to pay actors
residuals when Revue shows they appeared in
were rerun, a concept the Association of Television
Producers had rejected out of hand in negotiations
with SAG earlier that year. The hush-hush deal was
worked out by MCA's freshly hired lawyer,
Laurence Beilenson, who had been SAG's lawyer
for years, and who had represented Reagan in his

divorce proceedings. (Ten years later, when Reagan was subpoenaed in a Justice Department investigation of alleged antitrust activities by MCA, he would claim that he had no memory of this backroom pact. And although the feeling that he gave special treatment to his own agents would persist, he was never formally charged with wrong-doing of any kind.)[33]

The blanket waiver proved to be a bonanza for MCA. "The Octopus of Show Biz," as it came to be known, would dominate television throughout the 1950s—producing shows for its own talent, including Jack Benny, Edgar Bergen, George Burns and Gracie Allen—and with its huge TV prof-its go on to acquire Universal Studios in 1958. Actors also benefited tremendously from Reagan's decision, because once MCA agreed to pay "reuse fees," other producers had no choice but to follow. As one MCA agent later put it, "Every writer, actor and director in this town ought to get down and kiss Ronald Reagan's feet."[34]

If there was a payoff for Reagan personally, it would be some time in coming. His contract with Universal was closed out with *Law and Order* in the fall of 1952, and he would not make another movie for fourteen months. "Ronnie was upset with Lew for the way things worked out with Universal," Nancy Reagan told me.[35] The Wassermans had also pulled back from Reagan socially after his re-marriage, probably because, as Nancy Reagan pointed out, "Edie and Jane were very close."[36] (In 1955, Revue Productions launched *Jane Wyman*

Presents the Fireside Theater.) In fact, Wasserman no longer actually represented Reagan, having turned him over to Arthur Park, a vice president at the agency.

"The phone continued to ring for Ronnie," Nancy later wrote, "but now he was being offered bad roles in bad films—pictures he described as 'They don't want them good, they want them Thursday.'"[37] She supported her husband in his refusal to make any more "clunkers," but the financial strain was considerable. Reagan was in debt to the IRS for income tax he had deferred during the war, the horse ranch was mortgaged and losing money, there were two mortgages on the Amalfi Drive house—and no furniture in the living room because they couldn't afford any.[38]

So Nancy made a clunker instead: "Five months after Patti was born, and despite my decision not to be a working wife, I went back to work for one picture. Quite simply we needed the money. This was a blow to Ronnie, but we had to face facts, and face them together. I could get work, but his movie career was at a standstill."[39] She was paid $18,000 for *Donovan's Brain*, a low-budget sci-fi thriller about a mad scientist who preserves the brain of an evil tycoon. In a master stroke of irony, Lew Ayres played the scientist and Nancy his wife. (She claimed they did *not* talk about Jane.) Her best line: "Call me when the brain quiets down." According to one critic, she "walked through the movie in a state of utter bafflement, giving a new dimension to the word *dumbfounded*."[40]

Although he was almost as dismissive of television as the studio bosses, Reagan agreed to go on *The George Burns and Gracie Allen Show* in May 1953, and later that year he started going to New York to make guest appearances on such shows as *Revlon Mirror Theater, Lux Video Theater,* and *What's My Line?* "Dear Nancy Pants," he wrote from the Sherry-Netherland on one such trip. "Yesterday I went directly from the train to rehearsal—only stopping to check in here. . . . Back at the hotel I put in a call to you and then I tried for Lew Wasserman—not in town! [MCA agent] Sonny Werblin—away on vacation! Nancy Poo Pants Reagan—away out yonder! Eight million people in this pigeon crap encrusted metropolis and suddenly I realized I was alone with my thoughts and they smelled sulphurous."[41]

Ronnie may have been feeling sorry for himself, but he was only down and out by Hollywood standards, staying as he was at a luxurious Fifth Avenue hotel and, as he went on to tell Nancy, enjoying a half-bottle of Pichon Longueville with his dinner at "21." Still, he couldn't resist expressing resentment of those who had it easier in life, namely a fellow at an adjacent table, "a Brooks Brothers character who was evidently a Fond Fathers junior partner with plenty of loot he never could earn for himself." Mainly, however, he missed Nancy: "Man can't live without a heart and you are my heart, by far the nicest thing about me and so very necessary. There would be no life without you nor would I want any." He signed off, "I Love You, the Eastern Half of Us."[42]

That Christmas, Reagan recalled, was "the lowest point of all." Then a script from MGM "came down the chimney to the sound of sleigh bells and tiny hoofs on the roof." Reagan earned $30,000— less than half his fee just two years earlier—for *Prisoner of War*, in which he played an American intelligence officer captured and tortured by the North Koreans. The script was based on interviews with POWs released after the end of the Korean War in June of that year, and the role seemed custom-made for an anti-Communist crusader. But *Prisoner of War* was a critical and commercial disappointment. "Unfortunately, production and release were both rushed, with the idea the picture should come out while the headlines were hot," Reagan rationalized. He also felt that the film was hurt by "the reluctance of extreme liberals to enthuse about anything that upset their illusions."[43]

Reagan was not in a position to say no when Art Park came up with another way to bring in some cash: doing a Las Vegas act. He found the idea "outlandish," but when Park told him that he could make $15,000 a week, Reagan agreed to consider it. On the morning of his meeting with Park, he and Nancy checked the daily astrology column of "one of our good friends . . . Carroll Righter." Reagan later wrote that he "almost suspected an MCA plot: my word for the day read, 'This is the day to listen to the advice of experts.' Cutting out the item, I walked into the meeting, and without even saying hello, asked, 'Are you guys experts?' "[44]

After assuring Reagan that he would have to do little more than what he had done at countless benefits over the years—tell a few jokes and introduce other acts—Park made a call to Beldon Katleman, the owner of the El Rancho Vegas Hotel Casino. Katleman was eager to book Reagan, whom he knew from the Friars Club, but when it turned out that he wanted him to emcee a show featuring a stripper, Reagan balked.[45] Instead, he was booked into the Last Frontier for a two-week stint in mid-February 1954.

MCA hired comedy writer John Bradford to help prepare Reagan's act. "I was scared to death because I had never heard of a performer who couldn't sing or dance doing a Vegas act before," Bradford recalled. "So I met with Ron and Nancy— she was always with him, always—to see what he could do. I tried him out singing, and he was great; I gave him a sample monologue, and his timing was perfect. He loved telling jokes in an Irish brogue, and he was good at it, so I felt a little better. My wife and I then spent every day for the next three weeks with the Reagans working on the act, and Ron was terrific; he really knocked himself out because he was on his uppers and needed the dough. . . . [Nancy] attended every rehearsal and took notes like a secretary; she was that concerned." Bradford added, "I remember he wanted me to put a lot of tax jokes in the monologue because he'd just been hit with a whopping bill for back taxes and he hated the IRS. He said the Internal Revenue Service should be abolished. 'Everyone should pay ten percent of their income and that's it,' he said."[46]

Reagan's ninety-minute show featured the Continentals, a male quartet that had appeared in nightclubs and on the Ed Sullivan television show. It also included the Honey Brothers, slapstick comedians known for their blue humor (though most of that was cut for Reagan's show), a musical duo called the Blackburn Twins, and a line of showgirls in feathered headdresses. Reagan wrote most of his self-deprecating monologue, and good-naturedly went along with skits that required him to crack lowbrow jokes in a German accent while wearing an apron advertising Pabst Blue Ribbon beer and get smacked on the head with rolled-up newspapers by his fellow performers. According to one of the Continentals, Nancy sat through two shows every night, "sipping nothing more than a glass of ice water."[47] "I never got bored," she said, putting a good face on what must have been a somewhat painful experience.[48]

Ronnie and Nancy didn't gamble in Las Vegas until their last night, and then bet only $20 at the blackjack table. At bedtime, they would read books side by side—history and politics for him, biographies and novels for her. After two weeks in the capital of honky-tonk, the couple had had enough.[49] "We couldn't wait to get back to the Palisades and that tiny queen who had taken us over," said Ronnie, referring to one-and-a-half-year-old Patti.[50]

"We had been very, very definite as to the kind of person we wanted. Good moral character, intelligent. Not the kind with the reputation for the social ramble. A good upright kind of person." So said Earl B. Dunckel, a General Electric public relations executive, explaining why the giant industrial corporation agreed to have Reagan take over as host of the struggling weekly drama series it had been sponsoring since early 1953. *General Electric Theater* was originally conceived by MCA, in collaboration with G.E.'s advertising agency, Batten, Barton, Durstine and Osborne (known as BBD&O), as a way to lure big-name movie stars—most of whom were still refusing to do TV—onto the small screen. Dunckel recalled meeting Reagan at an early planning session in New York in August 1954: "There was nothing of the posturing, nothing of the 'I am a star'—he was a regular guy . . . whom I liked instantly. . . . Nancy was there with him."[51]

Reagan had vowed he would never do a TV series, but the terms of the contract he was offered by Taft Schreiber, the MCA vice president who ran Revue Productions, which produced the show, were extremely attractive. For an annual salary starting at $125,000, he would introduce each week's half-hour episode, star in some, and tour the country for sixteen weeks visiting G.E. plants and making speeches as part of the company's Employee and Community Relations Program.

This last function, Reagan would later say, was the clincher for him. In addition, he was given the title of program supervisor as well as profit participation in episodes he starred in after they had run five times. The contract was for five years.[52] As it worked out, the G.E. job not only rescued him professionally and financially but also laid the groundwork for his emergence as a national political figure.

The revised *General Electric Theater*, hosted by Ronald Reagan, was a hit from its first airing on CBS at nine o'clock on Sunday evening, September 26, 1954, and by its third year only *I Love Lucy* and *The Ed Sullivan Show* had higher ratings. Nancy co-starred with Ronnie in the first season's third episode, "The Long Way Round," which was billed as "the tense story of a wife's attempts to help her husband recover from a breakdown," and she would appear in a handful of others over the years. Some episodes were broadcast live from New York, and some were filmed on the old Republic Pictures lot, where Revue had set up shop. Reagan's introduction of each episode was less than two minutes long, and he signed off every show with the company motto: "Here at General Electric, progress is our most important product."[53]

"Ronnie held it together. He was a wonderful host. We couldn't have asked for anybody better," said William Frye, who produced the filmed segments for Revue from 1955 to 1960. "There was a scriptwriter to write the intros, but Ronnie always contributed in his own way and always made them better. We had a TelePrompTer, but he very seldom used it—Ronnie knew his lines. Our deal with Ronnie was that he would star in three out of every thirteen episodes. I usually had one being written, one being shot, and one being edited, to keep ahead. Once in a while Ronnie would come into the office and say, 'Gee, I just read such and such a script. Who's going to do it?' I'd say, 'Well, I'm trying to get Charlton Heston,' or, 'I'm trying to get Fred MacMurray.' Because those guys hadn't done television at that point. And he would say, 'Well, listen, I would like to do it.' So it was kind of a touchy situation, because I wanted to keep Ronnie happy, but at the same time I was trying to build the show with important people who had never been on television. And within the first couple years we got Jimmy Stewart, Joan Crawford, Fred Astaire, Joan Fontaine—they all made their TV debuts on *G.E. Theater*." Frye added, "Of course, with Stein and Wasserman and Schreiber controlling everything, it made my job very easy."[54]

Reagan's first tour for General Electric began at a turbine plant in Schenectady, New York, where the company had its headquarters. He spent four hours walking through the thirty-one-acre factory, stopping to chat with almost every worker, signing autographs, and "generally having a hell of a good time getting acquainted," Dunckel recalled. It happened that several thousand high school teachers were holding a convention in Schenectady that weekend, and when their scheduled speaker fell ill, they asked Dunckel if he could get Reagan to give a speech on education. Dunckel turned them down, fearing that he would have to write the speech, but Reagan volunteered to write it himself. "He got up there and gave a speech . . . that just dropped them in the aisles," according to Dunckel. "He got a good ten minute standing applause afterward. This is when I finally began to realize the breadth and depth of his knowledgeability . . . everything that went into that mind stayed there. He could quote it out like a computer any time you wanted."[55]

This first tour, in the fall of 1954, lasted eight weeks. "At the beginning, I took Patti and went to see my family in Chicago," Nancy recalled. "The time apart seemed to drag on and on. Ronnie and I were both so unhappy that . . . we never allowed ourselves to be separated for that long again."[56] In the following years, G.E. reduced Reagan's time on the road to twelve weeks a year, broken into three or four trips, and Nancy sometimes joined him in New York or Chicago. Of the eight years Reagan worked for the company, he estimated, he spent two on the road. He always traveled by train, and Nancy always drove him to the station. He preferred to do his own packing, but Nancy "would slip little notes and jellybeans" into his suitcase; it was part of their "ritual," she said.[57]

By 1958, according to *TV Guide*, he had visited more than 130 G.E. factories in twenty-five states and met nearly 200,000 G.E. workers. "He delivers as many as 15 talks per day in an 18-hour day of corporate good will," the magazine reported in its November 22 issue. "Reagan speaks not only to employee groups in company auditoriums and cafeterias, but also . . . is available wherever he goes, free, to local groups. Lions, Kiwanians, Rotarians, high school principals, Great Book-worms, chambers of commerce or clergymen have only to phone their requests to the local G.E. plant manager . . . and lo, a live TV star from Hollywood . . . appears as if at the press of an electric button. . . . The community and employee relations aspect of his job is the part of which Reagan is apparently most proud."[58]

For Reagan, traveling through Middle America was an enlightening experience: "When I went on those tours and shook hands with all of those people, I began to see that they were very different people than the people Hollywood was talking about. I was seeing the same people that I grew up with in Dixon, Illinois. I realized I was living in a tinsel factory. And this exposure brought me back."[59]

As much as he related to his audiences and loved the glad-handing and applause, Ronnie never stopped missing Nancy and never ran out of new ways to tell her so. "My darling," he wrote from the Atlanta Biltmore on Sunday, March 20, 1955:

Here it is—our day and if we were home we'd have a fire and "funnies" and we'd hate anyone who called or dropped in.

As it is I'm sitting here on the 6th floor beside a phoney fireplace looking out at a grey wet sky and listening to a radio play music not intended for one person alone.

Nevertheless I wouldn't trade the way I feel for the loneliness of those days when one place was like another and it didn't matter how long I stayed away. With all the "missing you" there is still such a wonderful warmth in the loneliness like looking forward to a bright warm room. No matter how dark & cold it is at the moment—you know the room is there and waiting.

Of course when I say "you" anymore I'm talking a package deal—you and the two & a half year old you. Time goes so slowly and I'm such a coward when you're out of sight—so afraid something will go wrong if I'm not there to take care of you, so be very careful. . . .

I love you so very much I don't even mind that life made me wait so long to find you. The waiting only made the finding sweeter . . . I love you, Ronnie.[60]

A year after Reagan signed on, G.E. helped him build "The House of the Future." Ronnie and Nancy had found the perfect plot of land, as high up as you can go in Pacific Palisades, at the top of a twisting, unpaved road called San Onofre Drive. They hired the local architect William Stephenson to design their five-thousand-square-foot modern ranch house, but it was very much Ronnie's project. As Nancy Reagan told me, "Ronnie made a model, and he had it on the dining room table at the Amalfi house. He'd study it, and he figured out some things that were wrong—and how to improve some things. . . . He wanted it to flow; he wanted the rooms to go into each other, because he said when you have parties people always stay in the library. He didn't want that. He wanted people to spread out."[61]

In exchange for letting the house be used in advertisements, G.E. outfitted it with the company's full repertoire of electrical devices and gadgets, including intercoms in every room, an electric-eye security system in the driveway, a retractable roof over the central atrium, a heated swimming pool with underwater lights, an electric barbecue and rotisserie, a refrigerated wine cellar, a projection booth, three TVs, and a $5,000, state-of-the-art kitchen with two electric ranges, two ovens, three refrigerators, two freezers, a washer-dryer, and—G.E.'s latest innovation—a dishwasher with a built-in garbage disposal.[62] There was also a three-thousand-pound switchbox attached to the rear exterior wall that Ronnie liked to joke had a direct connection to the Hoover Dam. "I wasn't wild about having my home turned into a corporate showcase," Nancy said, "but this was Ronnie's first steady job in years, so it was a trade-off I was more than happy to make."[63]

In 1999, I was given a tour of 1669 San Onofre Drive by the owner, Norman Switzer, a retired executive, who assured me that very little had been changed. The house was well hidden behind a hedge of bougainvillea and an iron gate, which opened onto the short, steep driveway. The Reagans' original gray shag wall-to-wall carpeting still covered the floors of the living room, dining room, and den. Built-in black-lacquered book-cases lined two walls of the den, and a matching bar stood in one corner. All three main rooms had floor-to-ceiling sliding glass doors that opened onto the deck, the pool, and sweeping views of the city and the ocean. "The ceilings are eleven feet high," Switzer noted. "When I walked in, I said to my wife, 'This is it.' I wanted high ceilings, big rooms, and a view. We didn't buy it because of the Reagans."

The living room was dominated by a gray field-stone fireplace, and the lights over the dining room table could be changed from white to yellow, pink, or blue. "We have a letter from G.E. to Reagan say-ing that he should have this lighting system because everybody would look better," Switzer said, indicating the large metal panel on the wall studded with switches, buttons, and knobs. "There are so many switches in this house we're still not sure what some of them are for."

Traces of Nancy's favorite colors could be found in almost every room: the kitchen cabinets were buttercup yellow, the play area between the chil-dren's bedrooms was bright red, the his-and-her sinks in the master bathroom were pale peach. And every room flowed into the next—just as Ronnie wanted them to. Only the master bedroom was set apart, opening onto its own courtyard. "They could come in here right from the garage," Switzer pointed out. Along with a massive stone fireplace, the Reagans' bedroom had the largest control panel of all: "Flick this switch," Switzer said, "and every light in the house goes on one by one."[64]

Ronnie and Nancy would live on San Onofre Drive for the next twenty-five years.

In both Pacific Palisades houses, Nancy Reagan told me, "Ronnie drew a heart in wet cement and then wrote our initials and put an arrow through the heart. At the house on Amalfi he did it on the patio, and at the house on San Onofre he did it in front of the barbecue."[65] The new house was finished in December 1955, and Nancy softened its contemporary architecture somewhat by furnishing it with traditional sofas and club chairs in the living room and den and a black-lacquer dining room set that seemed to cross Chippendale with Art Deco. Ronnie's reproduction George Washington desk went into the master bedroom, as did a Paul Clemens oil portrait of Nancy hugging Patti in a white-and-gold frame. The Reagans' first house-guests were Loyal and Edith, who from then on would come to stay every Christmas. There was also a new addition to the family that holiday season: a collie named Lucky, "because that's the way I felt," said Ronnie.[66]

The Reagans' social life was far from glittering in the early years of their marriage. In memoirs and coffee-table books of the period, they turn up at major events such as the 1954 wedding of Jack Benny's daughter, Joan, which had a guest list of 1,200, but they are nowhere to be found at the A-list dinner parties of the Goetzes, the Goldwyns, and the Selznicks, or the even more exclusive get-togethers at the Ronald Colmans', the Gary Coopers', and the Jimmy Stewarts'. "As a couple during the fifties they had no social prestige," said Richard Gully. "They were not Gable and Lombard, or Tyrone Power and Linda Christian. They were not glamorous. They weren't in the top circles socially. No one ever saw them. They were never at Jack and Ann Warner's. Ann Warner thought Reagan was dull and had nothing in common with either one of them."[67]

"We really weren't part of that Hollywood scene," Nancy Reagan admitted. "I mean, we'd stay home at night and pop popcorn. . . . When we did go out, we mainly saw the Holdens, Dick Powell and June Allyson, and Bob and Ursula Taylor, who lived across the street from us on San Onofre."[68] After a string of brilliant hits, including *Sunset Boulevard*, *Stalag 17*, *Sabrina*, *Love Is a Many-Splendored Thing*, and *Picnic*, Bill Holden was the highest-paid actor in the business and the number one box office draw, but he hated fancy parties, preferring to share his extensive collection of fine wines with close friends.[69] The other two couples were equally rich and famous, but, like the Holdens, the Taylors shunned the social scene, and the Powells were considered a bit B-list.

According to Arlene Dahl, who married Fernando Lamas and moved to Pacific Palisades in 1954, the Reagans were still regularly attending Carroll Righter's sign-of-the-month parties. "Nancy had become pretty good at designing her own charts," Dahl added.[70]

The Taylors had also moved to the Palisades in 1954, shortly after they were married. Robert Taylor, "the man with the perfect face," was one of the all-time great matinee idols, best remembered for holding a dying Garbo in his arms in *Camille*. He had been on the SAG board in the 1940s, and he and his first wife, Barbara Stanwyck, had become friendly with Ronnie and Jane. He was divorced from Stanwyck in 1951, and, like Reagan, he apparently found happiness and stability in his second marriage. His movie career was also waning, though not so rapidly as Reagan's; he hung on at MGM until 1959, when he signed up for his own TV series, called *The Detectives*. The two men, who were the same age, shared an enthusiasm for horsebreeding and a love of words. If anyone could outtalk Ronald Reagan on the subject of the Communist threat, it was Bob Taylor. Reagan's relationship with Taylor, Patti would write, "was the only time I observed my father being close friends with another man."[71]

Nancy's friendship with Ursula Taylor revolved around the children. Like Nancy, Ursula had put aside a modest movie career, in her native Germany, to focus on her family; she had two young children by her first marriage, and two more with Taylor, a boy named Terrance in 1955 and a girl named Theresa in 1959. Nancy frequently turned to her for help with Patti, who even at that young age seemed to have a hostile relationship with her mother. When she was three, she asked her father to marry her, which can be seen as merely cute or disturbingly competitive. After they moved to San Onofre and her English nanny was let go, "Patti would throw up all over her bed," Nancy Reagan told me. "Ursula and I would go in and change that bed all the time. I remember Ursula would always say, 'I never saw a child try so hard to get you mad.'"[72]

Nancy was not as close to Dick Powell and June Allyson, though she often took Patti to play with their children, Pam and Richard. The Powells had moved from their Tudor mansion in Bel Air to a sixty-two-acre spread in Mandeville Canyon, replete with a stone manor house, a private lake, pastures for their Black Angus cattle and sheep, a barnyard for their chickens, turkeys, and pheasants, and stables for their horses. Powell had made a successful transition from leading man to TV producer with his own company, Four Star Television, and Allyson continued making movies at MGM all through the 1950s. They still had the same tight circle of friends—half showbiz, half big business—including the George Murphys, the Justin Darts, the Leonard Firestones, and the Edgar Bergens. And they were still square-dancing on Saturday nights. But they had their hip moments: when Ford introduced the Thunderbird in 1955, June and her girlfriends all got convertibles. Hers was pink, Punky Dart's yellow, and Frances Bergen's lavender.[73]

Of this group, Nancy gravitated toward Frances Bergen, who was by far the most stylish and social. A former fashion model, she had married Edgar Bergen in 1945, when she was twenty and he was forty, and gradually transformed the rich but reclusive ventriloquist into one of Hollywood's most esteemed and well-connected figures. The Bergens lived in Bella Vista, "a sprawling white-washed Spanish house that hung high over Beverly Hills," as their daughter, the actress Candice Bergen, described it in her 1984 memoir, *Knock Wood*, and it was at the Bergens' parties that the Reagans occasionally mingled with the cream of 1950s Hollywood society, including Jules and Doris Stein, Jimmy and Gloria Stewart, Ray and Mal Milland, David Niven, Rosalind Russell, David Selznick and Jennifer Jones, Judy Garland and Vincente Minnelli, and the Randolph Scotts (he was the only actor to be made a member of the Los Angeles Country Club).[74]

"Ronnie and Nancy lived rather quietly," Frances Bergen recalled. "They were not that much party people. They would have small dinner parties at the G.E. house, as they called it, and we were there quite often. Usually Bob and Ursula Taylor would be there, and the Holdens, and Henry Koster, who had made his name, more or less, directing Deanna Durbin pictures, and his very pretty wife, Peggy. Bob Arthur, who was a producer at

Universal, and his wife, Goldie, who was very involved in Republican causes and politics, were also very close to the Reagans then."[75]

Politics was almost always on the menu at the Reagans' dinners, even when it was just Ronnie and Nancy and Bob and Ursula in sweaters and blue jeans. Like most of the Reagans' friends, the Taylors were staunch Republicans; he was on the board of the right-wing Motion Picture Alliance for the Preservation of American Ideals. In contrast to Jane Wyman, who would roll her eyes and let out audible sighs of boredom when the conversation turned political, Nancy actively participated in these dinner-table discussions and even cultivated friendships with politically minded people, such as Goldie and Bob Arthur (who was also on the Alliance board). As Reagan himself recalled, "Even though I'd done a picture for Bob, it was Nancy who really brought me into the warm circle of their friendship. Bless baseball, she'd met them at a World Series game in New York and it was a sort of instant liking."[76]

Edgar Bergen was a staunch Eisenhower supporter, and through the Bergens the Reagans became friendly with Freeman Gosden, the President's Palm Springs golfing partner, and his second wife, Jane. Coincidentally, Gosden knew Edith Davis from his days in Chicago, where the *Amos 'n' Andy* radio show had been produced, and, according to Nancy, her mother was the only woman to have been on the program—once. In

1948, Gosden, along with his partner, Charles Correll, had sold the show to CBS for more than $2 million. He was an important behind-the-scenes player in national Republican circles; the brainy, elegant Jane was as passionate about politics as her husband.

Dick Powell and George Murphy, according to June Allyson, were still trying "to shift Ronnie Reagan into the Republican Party" over dinners at Mandeville Canyon.[78] So was Holmes Tuttle, the Ford dealer, who tried to persuade Reagan to run for the U.S. Senate in 1954. "I turned down the offer with thanks," Reagan told the *Los Angeles Daily News* at the time. "I'm a ham—always was and always will be."[79]

During the years he worked for G.E., most of Reagan's political energies were channeled into the speeches he gave on his tours. "He never directly hawked G.E. products," noted Paul Gavaghan, who was the company's publicity director for New England. "He promoted anti-communism and the free enterprise system."[80] From the beginning, Reagan realized that he "couldn't be a mouthpiece for someone else's thoughts. . . . I had to have something I wanted to say, and something in which I believed."[81]

As Reagan's reputation as a speaker spread, he found himself addressing increasingly powerful groups, including the National Association of Manufacturers and the Executives Club of Chicago, and his message evolved from a rose-colored defense of the unfairly maligned citizens of

Hollywood into a full-frontal attack on the dangers of big government, with its wasteful welfare programs and power-grabbing bureaucracy. "My speeches were nonpartisan as far the two major political parties were concerned," he later noted, "and I went out of my way to point out that the problems of centralizing power in Washington, with subsequent loss of freedom at the local level, were problems that crossed party lines."[82] In the late 1950s, according to Lou Cannon, Reagan was told by a G.E. executive that "he was more in demand as a public speaker than anyone in the country except President Eisenhower."[83]

"I heard Ronnie speak at a gathering of maybe two hundred people in Tennessee or Kentucky," *G.E. Theater* producer Bill Frye told me. "He was unbelievable. He sounded as though he were running for something. Of course, this was before one ever thought that he'd be running for governor, let alone president. Those people just loved him, and I was totally surprised. I *knew* he was good on-screen, when the camera was going, but he was just as good without the cameras. They used to say about Jimmy Stewart, 'He saves it for the camera.' Well, Ronnie didn't save it for the camera. Ronnie did just as much before a group of two hundred people as he did in front of that camera for a million people."[84]

Bill Frye and his friend producer James Wharton were among Hollywood's most popular extra men, and they frequently gave dinner parties at their house on Coldwater Canyon. "Every so often the G.E. people would come to town and I'd have to give a dinner for them," Frye told me. "I'd call my social Hollywood friends and say, 'Listen, the G.E. people are coming and I thought I'd have a little dinner for Ronnie and Nancy.' None of the A-list people wanted to come. Now, flash-forward ten years to 1966. Ronald Reagan is Governor of California and Nancy is the First Lady. All of those same people are *surrounding* the Reagans. They can't get *enough* of the Reagans. And I can't get any of them to come to my parties, including Ronnie and Nancy, because they're much too busy—seeing all the people who wouldn't see *them* ten years before."[85]

Despite the attitude of some of his snobbish friends, Frye grew fond of the Reagans. He sometimes went to dinner at San Onofre, and when Nancy asked for help in finding a live-in housekeeper, he recommended a Czechoslovak woman named Anne Allman. "Her sister Sophie worked for me," Frye explained. "Anne was crazy about the Reagans. She was just a big, lovable, capable, country-type woman who could not cook fancy food. And she was on the shy side, never had married. She must have been awfully good with the Reagans, or they wouldn't have kept her for thirty years. That's a long time to keep help."[86]

Even in those days, Frye found Nancy's devotion to Ronnie endearing, and he admired the subtlety with which she advocated her husband's cause. "She just adored him. He could do no wrong. I used Nancy and Ronnie together in maybe three *G.E.* episodes, and there was such a sweetness between them. . . . She was always behind him, but she never was pushy about it. Just to give you a comparison, I used Alan Ladd a few times on *G.E.,* and I was crazy about Alan, but his wife could be the worst pain in the ass! She would come in before he would, and say, 'Who is going to play this part? How tall is she? Is she married?' She wanted to know everything! Nancy never once came to the studio or interfered, with me at least. I always appreciated that. I mean, she knew what was going on. She knew that I'd offer Ronnie a part after it had been turned down by Charles Laughton, or Gregory Peck, or Jimmy Stewart. And she'd call me on it. She'd say, 'I heard Gregory Peck turned it down.' Or, 'So and so told me you sent her husband the script.' But she was nice about it.[87]

"I remember the Wassermans invited me for the weekend in Palm Springs," Frye continued. "And who should show up on Saturday morning but Nancy and Ronnie. Now, the Wassermans had two guest rooms, a smaller one, which I was in, and the larger one, which the Reagans took, with a bathroom in between, which we had to share. I got up in the middle of the night, and the bathroom door was locked. So I opened the sliding glass door and peed on the oleanders. The next morning I said to Nancy, 'Please don't lock the door tonight. I might have to do more than pee.' And she laughed and promised she wouldn't. But the same thing: I got up, the door was locked, and I peed on the olean-ders."[88]

An invitation from the Wassermans was consid-ered a command performance. Nancy Reagan told me, "You had to be nice to Edie or she could make life difficult for you at the agency."[89] One of the trickier feats Nancy—or any Hollywood wife with social aspirations—had to manage was staying on the good side of the Wassermans while cozying up to the much more socially significant Jules and Doris Stein. "The Steins were *it*," explained Leonora Hornblow. "Jules thought very highly of Lew professionally, but he used to say, 'I don't have to have dinner with him.' And Doris could not bear Edie."[90]

"That was a very bad mix, unfortunately," Richard Gully confirmed. "Edie handled it very gra-ciously, but it was endless snubbing—really unkind. Doris was a very autocratic woman, a great hostess, wonderful . . . but she did like the spotlight, and she regarded Edie Wasserman basi-cally as hired help."[91] Others said Edie Wasserman was less discreet about her feelings. "Edie Wasserman hated Doris Stein," Bill Frye told me, "and she used to call Jules 'the little eye doctor.' "[92]

Jules Caesar Stein, the Chicago ophthalmologist who founded the Music Corporation of America in 1924, and his imperious wife, Doris, who liked to forget that her Jewish father had changed his name from Jonus to Jones, took the town by storm from the moment they arrived in 1936. "I'm going to be king of Hollywood," Jules, who had just turned forty, told Hedda Hopper,[93] as he began gobbling up independent talent agencies, including the one that represented Ronald Reagan and Jane Wyman. He also bought 10 percent of Paramount's stock and began construction of MCA's 25,000-square-foot headquarters, a Beverly Hills version of the White House, complete with an oval office for the chairman. Ann Rutherford vividly recalled Stein at the time: "You should have seen him trying to teach these meticulous bricklayers, who were used to laying bricks and scraping off all the mortar so that you had a flush, even surface. *Au contraire.* Jules wanted *weeping* mortar, the kind they have down South, so he took off his coat and took a trowel—it was *the* sight in town. He'd go by every day and make them redo what didn't have enough weeping."[94]

Doris Stein formed firm alliances with Mary Pickford, Marion Davies, and Buff Chandler. The Steins became regulars at San Simeon, and returned the hospitality with seated dinners for fifty to a hundred at their Spanish-style villa, Misty Mountain, set high on Angelo Drive. Both MCA's offices and the Steins' house were decorated with the finest English antiques, and Doris set her tables with the largest collection of Flora Danica china in Los Angeles, complemented by orchids grown in her own hothouses. After conquering the local royals, she cast her net eastward, becoming *the* Hollywood hostess for visiting New York grandees and Europeans titles such as fashion arbiter Diana Vreeland, philanthropist Mary Lasker, and the Duke and Duchess of Bedford.[95]

In the 1950s, the Reagans were occasionally invited to Misty Mountain. Doris had been favorably disposed to Nancy by Kitty LeRoy, and was slightly acquainted with the Davises from Chicago. Jules had known Ronnie since shortly after they both arrived in Hollywood, and he was one of the tycoons who wished the well-spoken and well-informed actor would go into politics on the Republican side. Like his good friends Justin Dart, Alfred Bloomingdale, Edgar Bergen, and Freeman Gosden, the MCA chairman was a big Eisenhower supporter, though he was careful to maintain good relations with politicians of both parties, believing that was best for business. "Thanks to Jules, MCA had its bases covered," said Bill Frye. "Lew Wasserman was a big Democrat, Taft Schreiber was a big Republican, and Jules was for whoever was in power."[96]

Of the three, Taft Schreiber would play the most important role in Ronald Reagan's future political career. Schreiber had started out as an office boy during MCA's early days in Chicago, and as Stein's oldest and closest friend at the agency was the natural rival of Wasserman. Although Taft and Rita Schreiber were not as socially elevated as the Steins, they still ranked several tiers above the Wassermans in the 1950s, having established themselves among the city's pioneer modern art collectors. "Taft was very fond of Ronnie," Frye recalled. "Matter of fact, I went to Ronnie's forty-fifth-birthday party at the Schreibers'. They had a beautiful house, very modern, way up toward Tower Drive. I was pleased to be included, because it wasn't a big party. I can't remember who-all was there, but it wasn't a celebrity crowd."[97]

Reagan was evolving into a different kind of celebrity, not so much a Hollywood movie star as a national public figure: the amiably distinguished host of a television show that was watched by millions of Americans every Sunday night and the most famous corporate spokesman in the land. Even the few movies released after he signed on with G.E. added to this image. He played classic Western heroes in *Cattle Queen of Montana* in 1954 and *Tennessee's Partner* in 1955 and a real-life World War II submarine commander in *Hellcats of the Navy* in 1957. His co-star in the last was his real-life wife, Nancy, who, true to form, played the nurse who is in love with him.

One of the things Ronnie liked most about his G.E. job was that it gave him plenty of time at the ranch when he wasn't on the road. "I had television worked down to an average of about one day a week," he later said, "and I could spend four or five days a week at the ranch. My routine was just get up—the ranch was only a thirty-five-minute drive from our home—go out there for the day, back in the evening. I loved every minute of that."[98]

In the summer of 1957, Nancy became pregnant for the third time since Patti's birth. She had suffered two miscarriages in four years but was determined to have a boy. As Reagan later wrote, "Nancy had decided Patti should have a brother. Personally I would have settled for the three of us: I grew frightened every time I remembered that long night when Patti was born, and didn't want to take chances with a happiness already so great I couldn't believe it. At the same time I knew Patti would have that brother, because I couldn't say no to Nancy."[99]

Nancy was ordered to stay in bed for the last three months of her pregnancy. Frances Bergen and June Allyson gave her a small baby shower. Arlene Dahl, who was one of the guests, recalled, "I had just had my son, Lorenzo, and friends of mine had given me a blue candle that Nancy wanted in the worst way. She was hoping and praying that her second child would be a boy, and I gave her what was left of my blue candle, which had produced Lorenzo."[100]

Ronnie arrived home from a G.E. tour the day before Nancy went into the hospital for a planned cesarean. "Moral support for Papa," he recalled, was provided by Ursula Taylor and Edith, who had flown in from Chicago. At 8:04 A.M. on May 20, 1958, the eight-and-a-half-pound Ronald Prescott Reagan arrived.[101] Reagan again admitted that his primary emotion was relief that his wife had survived. For Nancy, a dream had come true, and people soon sensed that the little boy was her favorite.

That's certainly what five-and-half-year-old Patti

felt. "As much as I wanted to participate in this new adventure of having a baby in the house," she recalled, "I was usually ushered out of my brother's room. I didn't know it then, but Ron's and my relationship was being defined at that point. There were nights when I snuck into his room and stared at him sleeping, smelled his baby smells, listened to his breathing. I had to be very quiet because there were intercoms in both his room and mine. I knew I was taking a risk, but it was worth it. I used to ask my mother if I could hold Ron, but the answer was always the same. 'No. You might drop him.' "[102]

The Reagans asked the Taylors to be Ron's godparents, and in 1959 they became the godparents of Bob and Ursula's daughter, Tessa. In March of that year, Ronnie and Nancy celebrated their seventh anniversary, and when his G.E. contract came up for renewal not long after that, he was given 25 percent ownership of the show, making him a partner of MCA/Revue. The new contract also reduced his time on the road to ten weeks a year.[103]

"He was always glad to come home," a close family friend told me. "He knew Nancy would be there waiting for him with open arms. To be treasured like that is a wonderful, wonderful thing. I've never seen a marriage like that. He was nuts about her. He'd come into a room and look at her like she was the flower of the Nile."

CHAPTER TWELVE

THE GROUP
1958–1962

My mother always said, "You're known by the company you keep." And it's true.

Nancy Reagan to author, February 7, 1999

Nancy cherry-picked her friends.

A close friend of the Reagans' to author

Motion-picture people engage in civic, cultural and charitable activities, and individually appear occasionally in the doings of "downtown" society. But it is axiomatic that any function where movie people turn out in force automatically is not "society."

Gladwin Hill, "California Society Stems from Gold Rush," *The New York Times*, February 18, 1957

During the first five or six years of the Reagans' marriage, their close friends were mostly people Ronnie had known before he met Nancy—the

Holdens, the Taylors, Dick Powell and June Allyson, Frances and Edgar Bergen, Bob and Goldie Arthur. But gradually Nancy began reaching out to a wider circle, first among their Hollywood acquaintances and then to a whole social set beyond the film industry. These new friends— Armand and Harriet Deutsch, Walter and Lee Annenberg, Earle and Marion Jorgensen, Bill and Betty Wilson, Alfred and Betsy Bloomingdale— would come to be called the Group, and they would help to forge Ronald Reagan's entire political future.

Nancy had known Armand Deutsch since her MGM days, but after she married Ronnie and Ardie married Harriet, the two couples crossed paths only occasionally. Then, according to Harriet Deutsch, "Nancy called me one day, and said, 'Couldn't the four of us just have dinner alone?' We went to Trader Vic's. And from then on we became very close friends."[1] The Polynesian-themed Trader Vic's had opened in the new Beverly Hilton in 1955, and it instantly became a favorite of the Beverly Hills in crowd, of which the Deutsches were very much a part. Deutsch left MGM in 1957, along with his mentor and boss, Dore Schary, and would cap his career in the entertainment business three years later by producing *The World of Carl Sandburg*, starring Bette Davis, on Broadway. But as the grandson of a Sears, Roebuck partner and reportedly its largest shareholder, he still commanded a prized seat at the tables of such leading hostesses as Buff Chandler and Edie Goetz, and he would later be appointed to the Warner Bros. board. He and Harriet had been introduced by producer Ray Stark and his wife, Fran, in 1951, shortly after Ardie divorced Benay Venuta and Harriet was widowed by director Sylvan Simon, the heir apparent to Harry Cohn at Columbia Pictures. Fran Stark, the daughter of the legendary comedienne Fanny Brice, was one of Harriet's two best friends. The other was Cohn's niece, Lee Annenberg, the wife of the powerful newspaper and magazine publisher Walter Annenberg.

A slim beauty who had been a salesgirl and model in New York before coming west, Harriet was a clotheshorse of the first rank, one of Amelia Gray's best customers and Jimmy Galanos's earliest devotees. Perhaps more than any other woman in the Group, she fit the press image of a flighty socialite largely concerned with gowns, parties, and social status. But she could be warm, generous, and loyal, particularly to Nancy Reagan. According to Harriet, the loyalty went both ways. "Nancy has the capacity of being a great friend," she told me. "Never ever has Nancy forgotten a birthday or an anniversary of ours in forty-five years."[2]

"We used to go to parties a lot on San Onofre Drive," Ardie Deutsch added. "They often had barbecues for eighteen people—show business people pretty much. Bill and Ardis Holden. George Burns and Gracie Allen. And Jack Benny, who always referred to Ronnie as Governor—I don't know why, but he did. We also used to go to the

Reagans' every Christmas morning for eggnog, and her mother and father were always there. I remember Loyal and I were sitting on the sofa one day, and I said, 'Loyal, I hear you're to the right of Attila the Hun. Is that true?' He said, 'No, I'm just a bit conservative.' I said, 'Do you hear that I'm to the left of Stalin?' He said, 'Never actually heard it.'"[3]

Ardie Deutsch was the lone Democrat among the husbands of Nancy's new friends. He had refused to sign a loyalty oath at MGM and gotten away with it because of Schary's protection. In 1952, Deutsch and Reagan had joined forces with labor leader Roy Brewer and screenwriter Philip Dunne in the Democratic primary to oppose California state senator Jack Tenney, who they believed had unfairly criticized the film industry's anti-Communist efforts. Now, when the Reagans went to dinner at the Deutsches', the political discussions between the increasingly conservative Reagan and the steadfastly liberal Deutsch sometimes got out of hand. "Ronnie, that's enough of the political talk," Harriet remembered Ardie saying. "That's enough of that."[4]

In 1960 the Deutsches moved into a new house on Coldwater Canyon Drive, a sprawling white-brick-and-glass ranch with a matching annex behind the pool for their screening room (which Harriet, like most Hollywood hostesses, kept well stocked with big bowls of M&M's, Milky Ways, and Snickers). The only guests at their first dinner party were the Reagans and the Annenbergs, who were visiting from Philadelphia, where Walter's company, Triangle Publications, was based. The Deutsches' guest book records that intimate housewarming dinner:

Being the first houseguests of Harriet and Ardie is a privilege and responsibility of which we are proud. We are grateful for the privilege and find the responsibility inspirational.
Always devotedly,
Lee and Walter Annenberg

We have no hesitation, indeed it is with pride we take second billing to Lee and Walter. And besides, we'd sign anything anywhere just to be at the Deutsches'.
Ronald Reagan
Me too. Nancy. XX

Next to the kiss-kiss symbol, Nancy drew a little "happy face."

Ronald Reagan and Walter Annenberg first crossed paths in 1937, when Ronnie was a fresh face at Warners and Walter was a young publishing scion overseeing one of his father's publications, *Screen Guide*, and they both sought the affections of June Travis. Their paths crossed again when Reagan was traveling for General Electric. "On several occasions," Lee Annenberg recalled, "Walter and I would be coming back from

New York to Philadelphia on the train, and there would be Ronald Reagan."[5] Annenberg would later disclose that, as the owner of *TV Guide*, he had put in a good word with one of G.E.'s top executives when Reagan was up for the job: "I told him Ron was a great speaker, that he had been a very effective and respected head of the Screen Actors Guild, that he was a good-looking guy, genial and very able on his feet."[6] Lee shared her husband's high opinion of the actor. "As far back as I remember, he was always interested in issues," she told me. "I always thought he was a very thoughtful and discerning man. He wasn't just a Hollywood star, he was a thinking man. A lot of people didn't realize that."[7]

Reagan was on the cover of *TV Guide* in 1958 and 1961, but it was mainly through Nancy's growing friendship with Harriet Deutsch that the Reagans came to see more and more of the Annenbergs. Harriet and Lee had been inseparable since they were in their early twenties and married to their first husbands. They thought alike, dressed alike, and changed their hairdos in tandem—somewhere along the way the brunette Harriet and the redhead Lee both went blond. Yet there was always a lady-in-waiting quality to Harriet's relationship with the richer, more forceful Lee.

Leonore Cohn was born in New York in 1918. Her mother died when she was seven, and she and her sister were taken in by their Uncle Harry, who was considered the most tyrannical of the studio moguls. Cohn was an admirer of Mussolini and made a point of working on Yom Kippur even though he was Jewish—Lee herself would later admit that "his character was third-rate."[8] His wife, Rose, a convert to Christian Science, managed to instill a strong sense of faith in Lee. Aunt Rose was also an indefatigable hostess, who gave impeccably organized dinner parties for everyone from Irving Berlin to Rita Hayworth. By the time Lee and her sister were teenagers, they had sailed on the *Normandie* and stayed at the Dorchester in London and the Ritz in Paris, but as Annenberg biographer Christopher Ogden notes, "nothing was theirs. They were always treated as wards, never as family members."[9]

Lee graduated from Stanford in 1940. Her first two marriages, both largely motivated by her desire to escape Uncle Harry, were disasters. The first, in 1941, to Beldon Katleman, the son of a parking lot tycoon, whom she had met at the Hillcrest Country Club, and who later owned the Las Vegas casino where Reagan had declined to perform in 1954, produced a daughter but lasted less than three years. The second, in 1946, to Lewis Rosenstiel, the Schenley liquor king, a manic-depressive widower nearly twice her age, produced a second daughter.[10] Lee was still married to Rosenstiel in February 1950, and was spending the winter in Palm Beach, when Harriet and Sylvan Simon took her to a party where she met Walter Annenberg. The forty-one-year-old publisher, a somewhat stiff and formal workaholic, had just been asked for a divorce by his first wife, with whom he had two children. "We started to dance and we just kept dancing," recalled Lee Annenberg. "It was magic and magnetic," said Harriet Deutsch.[11]

It was a year and half before Rosenstiel would let Lee go, and then only on the condition that she leave everything he had given her behind, including her 10-carat diamond engagement ring and their daughter. Walter bought Lee a 27-carat diamond ring and put his lawyers to work on securing partial custody of the child. They were married in September 1951 at his mother's Fifth Avenue apartment. A few weeks later the newlyweds bought Van Gogh's *Les Oliviers* for $68,000 and Monet's *Femme à l'Ombrelle* for $27,000, thus beginning what would become one of the greatest private art collections in the world. Annenberg's income was then said to be $1 million a year.[12]

In many ways his rise had been as torturous as his new wife's. His father, Moses, a German-Jewish immigrant, started out in the newspaper business as a henchman for the Hearst organization in the Chicago circulation wars of the early 1900s and went on to make a fortune after buying the *Daily Racing Form* in 1922. When Walter was twelve, the family moved into a thirty-two-room mansion in Great Neck, Long Island. After graduating from the Peddie School in New Jersey, he spent a year at the Wharton School of Finance and then started working for his father. In 1936, Moses Annenberg bought the *Philadelphia Inquirer*, the nation's oldest daily newspaper. Three years later he was indicted for income tax evasion, some historians say because of his paper's relentless attacks on FDR. He spent two years in jail and died a month after his release in 1942, leaving his family in disgrace and Walter in charge of the nearly bankrupt Triangle Publications.

Within four years Walter had paid off his father's $5 million debt to the IRS and launched *Seventeen* magazine. He then began buying up radio and television stations in Pennsylvania, New York, Connecticut, and California, and started up *TV Guide* in 1953. His marriage to Lee was also a success, a love match that gave them both the sense of security that they had previously lacked. Lee redecorated Inwood, his fourteen-acre estate on Philadelphia's Main Line, and began entertaining the city's leading political and business figures.[13] Like her husband, she took an active interest in politics, and she was appointed to Pennsylvania's electoral college in Eisenhower's second term.[14]

By the 1960 presidential election, Walter was considered one of the most influential Republican media magnates in the country, right up there with his friends Time-Life chairman Henry Luce, *Los Angeles Times* publisher Norman Chandler, and Gardner Cowles, the owner of the *Des Moines Register* and *Look* magazine. Despite his disappointment over the defeat of Richard Nixon, whom he counted as a friend, he was careful not to repeat his father's mistake of being overly partisan. When Jacqueline Kennedy called to ask him to donate a 1767 portrait of Benjamin Franklin valued at $200,000 for her White House redecorating project, he readily agreed, and soon after that he and Lee were invited to a small private dinner by the new President and First Lady.[15]

Nancy was greatly impressed by the Annenbergs, especially Walter. "Walter was the kind of man that Nancy liked," said Leonora Hornblow. "He was rich, he was powerful, he was very nice. And she liked rich, powerful, and nice. I'm not saying this against her. I agreed with her."[16] Her feelings toward Lee were more complicated. The two women had much in common—both were shipped off to relatives as children, grew up tantalizingly close to fame and power, went to fancy private schools and elite colleges, and married men in their forties who were coming out of failed marriages. But Lee already inhabited a social universe that for Nancy was still a long way off. They understood each other, however, and enjoyed each other's company. Like Nancy, Lee didn't smoke or drink, and she was finely attuned to her husband's moods and needs. "I'm a pleaser," she once said. "And my first goal was to please Walter."[17]

Like Ronnie, Walter was a loner at heart. Both men were fanatically neat, a sign of needing to control the world around them, and capable of spending long stretches of time alone, lost in their own plans and visions. And for both, their wives were everything: lovers, confidantes, and protectors. Walter called *his* wife Mother.

* * *

Every August, Lee and Walter Annenberg took a bungalow at the Beverly Hills Hotel. Socially speaking, August was to Los Angeles what October was to New York or June to London—a time for parties and more parties, many of them for visiting New Yorkers and Europeans. The Deutsches, the Starks, and Jules and Doris Stein all lined up to give dinners in honor of the Annenbergs. So did Anita May, the grande dame of the Beverly Hills social set and another of Nancy Reagan's fashionable new friends. Anita May and her husband, Tom, the chairman of May Company Department Stores, have generally been over-looked by Reagan chroniclers, perhaps because both were dead by the time the Reagans reached the White House. But in the late 1950s and 1960s they were at the very center of what became the Reagan Group, and Anita especially played a sig-nificant role in promoting Ronnie politically and Nancy socially. As Richard Gully attested, "Anita May was a great power. And she helped Nancy Reagan a lot."[18]

"My ex-mother-in-law was very close to Nancy. Nancy virtually sat on her knee," said Ann Rutherford, who was married to the Mays' son, David, in the 1950s.[19] "Anita was a wonderful woman. Generous, kind, giving," Nancy Reagan told me. "And if she liked you, she wanted all the people she liked to like you, too."[20] "If she didn't like you, watch out," said Dr. Herbert Roedling, who was married to another one of David May's

ex-wives. "She had teeth. Tom was the opposite—
he liked everybody."[21]

Anita Keiler May, a bourbon heiress from
Kentucky, had come to Los Angeles in 1922, after
marrying Tom May and persuading his father to
open the first California branch of the family's St.
Louis–based department store chain. Tom and
Anita built a ballroom they called the Casino on a
lot next to their white-pillared mansion on Cañon
Drive in Beverly Hills, and gave elaborate parties
there even during the war years. In the late 1940s
they sold the house, tore down the Casino, and
had the architect Sam Marx put up an ultramodern
ranch in its place. When the Beverly Hilton opened
in 1955, the Mays moved into the penthouse,
where Anita entertained on a grand scale. They
also had a weekend place in Palm Springs. All of
the May residences were done by Billy Haines, the
openly gay silent screen star who had reinvented
himself as Hollywood's foremost interior decorator,
and who, along with his lifelong companion,
Jimmie Shields, was a regular on the social scene.

"Anita was the style queen out here," said society florist David Jones, who started doing the flowers for her dinners at the Hilton. "Everything had to
be just perfect. She had a daytime chauffeur and
an evening chauffeur. She had a daytime maid and
an evening one. She had a series of cooks—the
same cook didn't do every meal. But most important was how pretty the table was."[22]

Ann Rutherford said that Anita would spend a
month in New York in the spring and another in the

fall, staying at the Hampshire House on Central Park South and being fitted for her clothes at Saks Fifth Avenue. The store's couture salon was run by Anita's best friend, Sophie Gimbel, its resident designer and the wife of the owner of Saks and Gimbels. Anita's shoes and handbags were also custom-made in New York. In Los Angeles, she shopped at Amelia Gray's for "Palm Springs things," as Rutherford put it, but after Gimbel retired, Galanos became her preferred couturier. And she made a fetish of her makeup brands. "One time I was going off to Tahiti," David Jones recalled. "And Anita said, 'Isn't that a French colony?' I said, 'Yes, it is.' She said, 'Here's $5,000. I want my mascara. It's a French product, and I can't buy it anymore in this country. Bring me back as much as you can. And keep the change.' "[23]

May was already in her sixties when she discovered Nancy. "She kind of adopted four gals," explained Harriet Deutsch. "Anne Douglas, Edie Wasserman, Nancy Reagan, and me. We were her special girls." May loved giving her protégées advice on everything from clothes to china to how to handle their husbands' idiosyncrasies. She was also known to shower her favorites with gifts. According to Leonora Hornblow, if Nancy thought a dress was too expensive, "Anita would buy it. And if you were at Anita's house, you had to be careful. She was like the Spanish. You couldn't say, 'Oh, isn't that pretty.' It would be bundled up at once and in your car."[24]

"Anita did things with such class," said Anne Douglas, who had landed in Beverly Hills from her native Paris after marrying Kirk in 1954. "And with such taste. She never overdressed. She had the best jewelry—one of the most superb blue-white diamonds in the 20-carat range, that Tom gave her. Tom was a lovely man, and he adored his wife. He knew that everything she did was perfect, and she did everything that he admired. She really put her personal taste and her personal feelings into a party. Nobody was badly seated. Nobody had a bad time. And the caviar was flowing."[25]

The Reagans were invited regularly to the Mays' parties at the Hilton, where the guest list—"a mix of Hollywood and the Hillcrest Country Club," as Ann Rutherford put it[26]—often included Jimmy and Gloria Stewart, Frances and Edgar Bergen, Irene Dunne, Claudette Colbert, Dinah Shore, and the agent Irving "Swifty" Lazar. Anita, an ardent Republican who liked talking politics, grew very fond of Ronnie and predicted great things for him. "She was the first one to tell me, 'Ronnie is going to be governor,'" remembered Denise Hale, who became another of Anita's girls after she married director Vincente Minnelli in 1960. "And when Anita May said something was going to happen, it usually came true."[27]

As Ann Rutherford pointed out, Anita respected Nancy's total belief in her husband. "Nancy simply idolized him. There was no competition. I think she saw in him what Anita saw in him. I'm sure Nancy had no idea whether he was going to go far in the theatrical business or what. But she knew that wherever Ronnie sat was the head of the table."[28]

As the Reagans moved up on the Beverly Hills A-list, Nancy was seeking out another group that had little to do with the entertainment industry and was more connected to the Republican Party and the downtown Los Angeles business establishment. To be sure, the Jorgensens, the Wilsons, and the Bloomingdales had Hollywood friends and lived on the Westside, not in old-money Hancock Park or ultraconservative Pasadena. But they were considered "society" as opposed to "Hollywood," and in Los Angeles in the 1950s there was a strong distinction. As Dore Schary's daughter, Jill Robinson, writes: "All the society-oriented people in Los Angeles made a point of excluding show business people from their ranks. Show business people, like gypsies, were usually excluded from schools . . . from country clubs, and even from the society pages of the *Los Angeles Times* (except for Jimmy Stewart, who made it after he became an Air Force General, and Irene Dunne, who was such an active and charming Republican that the publishers couldn't resist her)."[29]

The whole notion of society in a city as new and spread out as Los Angeles was seen as something of a joke by East Coast experts and snobs in general—"Los Angeles Society," Ethel Barrymore once said, "is anybody who went to high school." Cleveland Amory, the ultimate arbiter of society in America, called the city a "social melee."[30] A 1957

New York Times article on California society noted that San Francisco had its own edition of the Social Register, but Los Angeles did not.[31] All of which may be why some of the local grandees took so much comfort in looking down their noses at Hollywood, and others felt the need to import New York socialites and titled Europeans to validate their place in the great scheme of things.

"I was Nancy's first California friend outside pictures," Betty Adams told me. "Before Betsy, before Marion, before Betty Wilson. I met Nancy at Amelia Gray's shop in Beverly Hills. She had told Amelia, 'I'd like to meet some girls out of the picture industry.' Just because she wanted to broaden her base and get into a little different group. Amelia said, 'I have the perfect person for you.' So we all had a sandwich at Amelia's office. We just had the best time, laughing and enjoying it. Nancy said that she belonged to the Junior League, but none of her Hollywood friends did, and she didn't want to go alone. She said, 'Would you go with me?' I said, 'I haven't been in years, but we should go.' So we went and sat through the whole boring meeting, and decided we didn't have to go anymore."

Adams was reminiscing over lunch at the Hotel Bel-Air in 1999. A tall, slim woman then nearing eighty, she was still attractive and still very much a part of the Group. A widow, she had been married three times, and all three of her husbands were from prominent Los Angeles families. The first, Alphonzo Bell Jr., was the son of the developer of

Bel Air—"This hotel used to be my father-in-law's office," Adams pointed out. From 1956 to 1959 the younger Bell was chairman of the California Republican Party, and two years after they divorced, in 1958, he won a seat in Congress, which he held until 1977. Her second husband, Harry See, was an heir to the See's Candies family, which had shops all over the state. Her third and longest marriage was to Robert Adams, whose family had been established in Los Angeles since the 1890s, when they developed the city's first exclusive residential enclave, West Adams, near downtown.

Betty Adams's father, Paul Helms, was the multimillionaire owner of Helms Bakery, which sold its goods in neighborhoods throughout the city from a fleet of five hundred trucks. He was also a powerful behind-the-scenes player in the Republican Party. "My father and Paul Hoffman, the head of Studebaker, went over to France to convince Eisenhower to run for president in 1952," Adams recalled. "And the first time President Eisenhower came to Palm Springs, he stayed with Mom and Dad at their home in Smoke Tree. I just *loved* President Eisenhower." She was wearing the gold-and-diamond cross her father, a Methodist, had given her for her sixteenth birthday, on a white Chanel suit.

According to Adams, Nancy "was really anxious to know the Wilsons and the Bloomingdales and the Jorgensens. I had a dinner party in 1958 so she and Ronnie could get to know those people."[32]

Marion Jorgensen, Betty Wilson, and Betsy Bloomingdale were all well-established social figures by then, and along with Adams members of the Colleagues, an elite charity organization that raised money for unwed mothers and was limited to fifty women. Their husbands were equally prominent: Earle Jorgensen had run his own steel-and-aluminum company since the 1920s; Bill Wilson's family went even further back, in the oil equipment business; Alfred Bloomingdale was president of the Diners Club. While none of these couples knew the Reagans well at that point, the Bloomingdales sometimes saw them at the Mays' and the Steins', and Marion Jorgensen had known Ronnie slightly since his early days at Warners, when she was married to her first husband, Milton Bren, an agent and producer.

"I met Ronald Reagan at a party at Jack and Mary Benny's house," Marion Jorgensen told me. "He was married to Jane Wyman—but we don't mention that." Sitting in the spacious Billy Haines–designed living room of the Bel Air house she had lived in since marrying Earle Jorgensen in 1953, she recalled her initial impression of the Warner Bros. actor who would eventually become one of their dearest friends: "He was good-looking, but I thought the idea of him as a leading man was the dumbest thing I'd ever heard. He wasn't a Clark Gable, he wasn't even a Bill Holden. He wasn't the kind of man that I would even think of in that way. That's what made me laugh when I read about how sexual he was in that book *Dutch*—before I threw it away. I remember he used to wear that white jacket, you know, typical movie star—it had a kind of belt in the back that made it fuller on top and tight in the middle. Milton had a gray one—they went to the same tailor, Mariani—and I hated Milton's. I used to say to him, 'Please don't wear that.' It looked so Hollywood to me."[33]

Marion Jorgensen, a decade older than Nancy Reagan and most of their friends, was called "the General" by her husband, and the name stuck. She was born Marion Newbert, the daughter of a well-to-do couple from Chicago who, in her words, "came out here on their honeymoon and never left." The money came from her grandfather, Thomas Griffin, an Irish immigrant who founded the Griffin Wheel Company, which made wheels for freight trains, in Baltimore in 1877; by 1923 the company's thirteen plants were turning out 1.5 million wheels annually. "My father never worked, it's that simple," Marion Jorgensen told me. "We lived in Hancock Park, but we moved out to Beverly Hills when it was still half farmland. We lived on the corner of Sunset and Alpine, and across the street lived Wallace Beery." Marion, however, continued to attend the exclusive Marlborough School in Hancock Park, which didn't accept the daughters of Jewish families. "It sounds so silly," she explained, "but people who lived in Hancock Park didn't know picture people."

At eighteen, Marion Newbert "ran away and married" the twenty-seven-year-old Milton Bren—

who was not only Jewish but in the movie business—before completing her senior year at Marlborough. Ironically, she had met Bren at the debutante party her mother insisted on giving her even though "they really didn't have them out here then," she said. "It was at the Ambassador Hotel, and somehow Milton got invited as a stag. And he was the only one there that intrigued me. The others were sort of puny-looking things, but he was already a man and already successful."[34] As for Marion, as Connie Wald recalled, "My brother always said she was the best-looking blonde in town. And she had the best legs."[35]

Milton Bren was an agent when he married Marion in 1930, but within a few years he was producing movies at MGM, starting with the *Topper* series starring Cary Grant. He also made money in Southern California real estate. The marriage produced two sons but ended in divorce in 1948. Shortly after they split, Bren married actress Claire Trevor, and Marion married insurance heir Tom Call, whose father, Asa Call, was the chairman of Pacific Mutual Life. Call senior was known as Mr. Big because of the enormous power he wielded as head of the secretive Committee of 25, the clique of Republican businessmen who dominated Los Angeles politics in the 1940s and 1950s. Along with his best friend, *Los Angeles Times* publisher Norman Chandler, Call was the driving force behind the rise of Richard Nixon from congressman to president. Marion's marriage to his son ended in divorce in 1952.

Marion had just turned forty when she was introduced to Earle Jorgensen, who was fifty-four and also divorced. "My friend Lucy Toberman, who was head of volunteers for the Red Cross, said to me, 'Homer and I would like to take you out to dinner to meet Mr. Earle Jorgensen. He's chairman of the Los Angeles Red Cross now.' I made all kinds of excuses. I really wasn't going out with anybody. You know, you can't have two marriages and then start over that fast. I just didn't feel like it. Finally, I was invited to a Christmas party at the old Romanoff's, and so were the Tobermans. So Lucy started in again. I said, 'All right, Lucy, I'll tell you what, why don't you and Homer bring Mr. Jorgensen and pick me up at my house and we'll go together?' So that's what we did. Earle was driving his car, and they were in the back seat. And when we got down to Robertson and Wilshire— there was quite a lot of light there—I looked at him and I thought, 'Damn, he's not bad at all.' Three months later we were married."[36]

The marriage lasted forty-six years, until Earle died in 1999 at the age of 101. He was still running his company in his nineties when he gave an interview to photographer Pat York for her book *Going Strong*. "Have courage, confidence, and determination is my motto," he told her. "I picked it up as a kid along with 'Never say die; say damn.' . . . I have enjoyed working hard since I started as a very young man. My dad died when I was about 13, and when I was 15 we ran out of money. I had to go to work as an office boy to support my mother. . . .

The one thing my mother taught me when we were poor was the importance of neatness and cleanliness. I've followed that all through my life. In all my plants, you can eat off the floor."[37]

Jorgensen's parents were immigrants from Denmark who settled in San Francisco in the late nineteenth century. His father was a sea captain, and he sometimes took his wife and three children on his trips. "I remember going around Cape Horn when I was six, in his schooner," Jorgensen told York.[38] After serving in the Army Tank Corps during World War I, Jorgensen moved to Los Angeles in 1921, arriving shortly after the discovery of oil at Signal Hill near Long Beach. He started the Earle M. Jorgensen Company, which provided shipyard surplus and scrap metal to oil drillers, his wife told me, "by selling his extra suit and getting two dollars and a half. That was the beginning of Earle. So to say the least he was a self-made man."[39]

"By 1923, he had created in essence a supermarket for steel and aluminum," according to the *Los Angeles Times*, buying in bulk from large manufacturers such as Bethlehem Steel and U.S. Steel and selling to local businesses.[40] With the emergence of the aircraft industry on the West Coast during the 1940s, his customers came to include Boeing and Hughes Aircraft, and by 1960 annual revenue was approaching $100 million.[41] Almost universally well liked for his modest, plainspoken manner and fun-loving attitude—he was known to stand on his head at parties—he was nonetheless a player in the Los Angeles business and political

community: a generous Republican Party contributor who sat on the boards of the Chamber of
Commerce, the Citizens National Trust and
Savings Bank, the California Institute of Technology, and Occidental College, as well as the
executive committee of Northrop Aircraft. Typical
of the time—and of the Reagan Group in general—
Jorgensen saw no contradiction in supporting the
National Conference of Christians and Jews while
belonging to the highly restrictive Los Angeles
Country Club.

Although the Jorgensens had occasionally
crossed paths with the Reagans at "buffets and
things" in the early 1950s, it wasn't until Betty
Adams got them together that a closeness began
to develop. "Ronnie was working for General
Electric," Marion Jorgensen recalled. "And they
were such a great couple. We saw quite a bit of
them in the evening. We'd go to Chasen's to dinner. Nancy and I often had lunch." Even though
they quickly became good friends, she observed
that "I don't care how close a friendship you might
have with Nancy, if she doesn't want to go your
way, she doesn't go your way. Nobody could influence Nancy that much. Nancy's Nancy, you
know."[42]

Nancy and Marion were usually joined for lunch by
Betty Wilson, Marion's best friend. *Her* nickname
was the Infanta, although some called her the Little
General. "Betty was a little mighty mite, and she
ran a tight ship," said Frances Bergen. "Betty and

Marion were both generals. Neither one of them was an adjutant."[43] Marion Jorgensen and Betty Wilson called each other every morning at seven to coordinate their social schedules, and their husbands were good friends. Bill Wilson was on Earle Jorgensen's board and had known him since 1936, when he went to work in his father's business, Webb Oil Tools, which bought metals from the Jorgensen Company.

William A. Wilson, a native Angeleno, graduated from Stanford University that year and married his college sweetheart, Elizabeth "Betty" Johnson, upon her graduation two years later. Her father, Luther H. Johnson, who died shortly after they were married, had founded the Pennzoil Company of California in 1913 and built it into one of the largest oil companies in the country. Her mother, a devout Catholic from an Italian immigrant family, had grown up in a Victorian mansion in downtown Los Angeles, and Betty was educated at Marymount, the elite Catholic girls school in Westwood. Bill Wilson, who was born an Episcopalian, converted to Catholicism when they were married. According to a close family friend, Betty's mother gave the couple $1 million "to help set them up." David Jones told me, "Betty Wilson ran Bill—she'd tell him, 'You wear this, you wear that.'"[44] Not long after the Wilsons met the Reagans, Bill left his family's business and became president of L.N.W. Investments, which mainly invested his wife's money.

As Bill Wilson remembered it, he and Betty were

introduced to the Reagans in the late 1950s at the Brentwood home of Bill and Frances Hawks. (Bill Hawks, a producer, was the brother of director Howard Hawks.) Wilson also recalled attending Betty Adams's dinner party for the Reagans not long after that. "Ron and I hit it off pretty well," he said. "He had a little ranch up in the Malibu mountains then, and I like horses, so we had some things in common. And, of course, Betty and Nancy got along very well." Wilson made the point that the women saw each other more often than the men did, but Nancy's friends generally acknowledged that Bill was the husband who would become the closest to Ronnie. With his extended sideburns and well-cut suits, the lanky, good-looking Wilson came across as an old-fashioned gentleman cowboy. "I always thought that Ron was very open and easy to talk to," Wilson told me, adding, "Ron wasn't born here, and he didn't really grow up here, but it does seem like he fit into California perfectly. He liked the outdoors. He liked horses. I think he was at heart a true Californian."[45] Like Justin Dart, Bill Wilson was a member of the exclusive men's riding club Rancheros Vistadores. The Wilsons were also long-standing members of the Los Angeles Country Club, extremely conservative politically, and probably the squarest, most right-wing couple in the Group.

Marcia Hobbs, one of their two daughters, told me that the Reagans were frequent dinner guests in the late 1950s and early 1960s. "It would just be the two families. I was ten or eleven, and Mr. Reagan would talk about world politics at the dinner table. He was very instructive, and he opened my eyes to many things that were going on."[46]

Of all the Reagans' new friends, the Bloomingdales were the most fun, the most sophisticated, and the most adventurous. Alfred was a big, tall man, not handsome but attractive because of his tremendous energy and charm. Betsy, with her curly locks and wide-eyed enthusiasm, sometimes came across as a high-fashion Shirley Temple, but that was something of an act, belying a sharp mind, a keen eye, and a strong will. The Jorgensens and the Wilsons may have been big-time in Los Angeles society, but the Bloomingdales set their sights higher and cast their nets wider.

"Alfred and I had a premarital agreement never to go to Pasadena," Betsy Bloomingdale told me, implying that the snooty suburb was unbearably provincial. More than any other couple in the Group, the Bloomingdales mixed with both society and Hollywood. Anita May gave Betsy her first baby shower, and her son David and Alfred were card-playing buddies. But the Bloomingdales also had the Old Guard—the Dohenys, the Ducommuns, the Kecks—to their parties. Betsy saw herself as another Doris Stein, a cosmopolitan hostess who rose above the local divisions. She idolized Merle Oberon, the glamorous 1940s movie star who had married the Mexican industrialist Bruno Pagliai, and was proud of the fact that when the British royal family's favorite photographer and artist, Cecil Beaton, came to Los Angeles to design the sets for *My Fair Lady* in 1963, "he only did two portraits—Merle's and mine."[47]

As an heir to the Bloomingdale's department-store fortune and a co-founder of the Diners Club, Alfred Bloomingdale was both to the manor born *and* a self-made multimillionaire who maintained offices in Los Angeles and New York and frequently traveled to Europe, Asia, and Latin America. The Bloomingdale family was very much part of New York's German-Jewish elite known as Our Crowd, and was related through marriage to three-time Democratic governor Herbert Lehman. Alfred and Betsy kept an apartment at the Carlton House on Madison Avenue, and she was a favorite of the fashion press, cited for her high style in the same breath as Jackie Kennedy, Babe Paley, and C. Z. Guest. The Bloomingdales' house in Holmby Hills was a big 1930s Spanish colonial that had been transformed into a modern Palladian villa and filled with an eclectic but elegant mix of English furniture, French paintings, and Oriental antiques by Billy Haines, whose work Betsy had first admired as a young woman invited to dine at the Jack and Ann Warner estate.

"My mother was Australian, and my father was English and Australian," Betsy Bloomingdale told me, sitting in her library on a red-and-green printed-linen sofa designed by Haines forty years earlier. "Daddy went to Harvard, to the medical school, and he loved America and wanted to live here. So he went home to Adelaide and got my mother and brought her back. I grew up right here on Maple Drive in Beverly Hills, and I made my First Communion at the Good Shepherd Church. Life hasn't changed much, but there have been many wonderful things in between."[48]

She was born Betty Lee Newling in Los Angeles in or about 1922. (She managed to keep her birth date a secret from even the FBI when it investigated Alfred for a possible ambassadorship in 1981.) Her father was an orthodontist who also taught at the University of Southern California. "I grew up never knowing Hollywood people at all," she told me. "They were patients of my father's, but Daddy wasn't so crazy about Hollywood people."[49] A long-time family friend told me, "The father was as dull as they come. The mother was a big Australian woman, extremely outgoing and ambitious." David Jones, who credited Betsy Bloomingdale with launching his career as a florist in the 1950s, recalled dining with Mrs. Newling in her later years. "She was called Vinnie. She was very funny. Very elegant. And she always called Betsy 'Betty.'"[50]

The Newlings were members of the Los Angeles Country Club, and Vinnie saw to it that her only child, who was as tall, vivacious, and ambitious as she was, had a proper upbringing. Though the Newlings were Catholic, Betsy was sent to the Marlborough School, graduating in 1939, one year behind Betty Adams. She was then sent east to Bennett Junior College in horsey Millbrook, New York. One summer she took courses at the Hillcliffe

School of Cookery in Beverly Hills, because "my mother firmly believed that every young woman should attend cooking school before marriage."[51] In 1941 she was a bridesmaid at the teenage Gloria Vanderbilt's scandalous but stylish wedding to the playboy Hollywood agent Pat di Cicco in Santa Barbara.[52] By then she had already decided that Los Angeles society was limiting. "I always had my nose up about the West," she admitted. "I always thought it was kind of hokey."[53]

"I introduced Alfred to Betsy," said Hollywood producer Fred de Cordova. "I was doing a picture with Robert Hutton, who was a young star at Warners, and he was going with Nathalie Thompson, Betsy's closest friend from Marlborough. Nathalie said, 'I'm going out with Bobby Hutton tonight. Why don't you take Betsy?' I said, 'I'd love to. Her father is my dentist. Maybe he'll learn to not hurt me so much.' So I met Betsy, and after that I introduced her to Alfred."[54]

De Cordova had been Bloomingdale's best friend since the early 1930s, when he was an up-and-coming theatrical producer and Alfred was a Park Avenue boy who had just discovered showbiz and showgirls. His parents' marriage had already unraveled by the time his father, a frustrated playwright who hated the retail business, took Alfred to his first Broadway play, at age fifteen. Soon after that he started hanging out at the Stork Club whenever he could get away from the Westminster School in Connecticut. Although his teachers found him exceptionally bright, he squeaked through with a 66.3 average and went on to Brown University. He dropped out three months short of graduation in 1939, because of a serious football injury that would also keep him from serving in World War II.[55]

On November 13, 1940, *The New York Times* announced that Bloomingdale and two associates had formed a production company, and five months later their first play, *Your Loving Son*, opened on Broadway. It closed two days later, but Alfred, undeterred, took a suite of offices in the Empire Theater Building, formed an alliance with Lee Shubert, of the theater-owning family, and put $40,000 of his own money into *High Kickers*, a vaudeville revival starring George Jessel.[56] It was a hit and provided the twenty-five-year-old Alfred with his first wife, a chorus girl named Barbara Brewster. "Alfred called me and said, 'I'm going to New Jersey tonight. I'd like you to come along,'" recalled de Cordova. "I said, 'I've been to New Jersey.' He said, 'Well, I'm sort of visiting a justice of the peace. I'm being married and want you to be my best man.'"[57] The marriage lasted less than two years, ending in divorce in 1943.[58]

By then Alfred had two successful shows running on Broadway: an updated version of *The Ziegfeld Follies*, starring Milton Berle, and *Early to Bed*, a comedy. He was also a partner in a shipbuilding company in Rye, New York, and was elected treasurer of Tammany Hall, as the Manhattan Democratic Party organization was known, in 1944.[59] But he missed the party's convention in Chicago that summer and opted out of a second term. After losing more than $100,000 on *Allah Be Praised*, a musical, his interest in the theater also seemed to wane.[60]

In January 1946 he moved to Los Angeles, hoping to produce a movie called *Petty Girl* at RKO. "Alfred came out here looking for a wife," a close friend recalled. "I think he thought it was time to settle down." Nine months later, on September 15, 1946, he married Betsy. Fred de Cordova was the best man again, and because of the difference in religion the ceremony was performed by a superior court judge at the home of Alfred's friend Buddy Adler, a producer at Columbia. "I'll never forget that wedding," Marion Jorgensen said. "Because only one of her parents was there—I forget which one. They were mad at her for marrying Alfred, just like my family when I married Milton."[61]

That would soon change, as Betsy set out to transform her husband into something more to her parents' liking. Two years after they married, Alfred converted to Catholicism and they had a proper church wedding. By the 1952 election, he was involved in the Eisenhower campaign. "I started out as a Jew and a Democrat," he liked to joke. "And the next thing I knew I was a Catholic and a Republican." Like Earle Jorgensen and Bill Wilson—and, for that matter, Ronald Reagan—Alfred Bloomingdale would always try to give his wife what she wanted. According to their friends, he thoroughly enjoyed indulging her expensive tastes, and it was he who insisted she use the grander-sounding "Betsy." As she herself told me, "Alfred was divine. He was a fascinating man. And warm and cozy and wonderful. He brought his barber from New York out here with him, and got him a job in a barbershop in Beverly Hills. He came to the house every evening to shave Alfred. Isn't that funny?" At the time of their marriage, Alfred was still hoping to produce *Petty Girl*, but at Columbia, where he had been hired by Harry Cohn. "We went on Harry Cohn's yacht," Betsy Bloomingdale recalled. "He was a rough old coot. Alfred was supposed to be a producer, but he really didn't like working at a studio. He was more of an entrepreneur." His first venture involved installing soda machines in movie theaters. "No one had ever done that before," said his wife. "But Alfred had so many businesses going. And then he started the Diners Club."[62]

While Bloomingdale did not invent the credit card, as is often claimed, in 1950 he was the first to see the possibilities in an infant company called Dine and Sign, the brainchild of Frank X. McNamara, a Brooklyn savings-and-loan executive. Two years later he bought out McNamara and took over the renamed Diners Club.[63] Until American Express introduced its card in 1958, Diners Club had a virtual monopoly on the credit card business. "Alfred Bloomingdale was a very colorful man," said Richard Gully. "I've never known a man with such bad table manners. And yet he was enormously likable. He really was beloved. I never met anyone who didn't like Alfred Bloomingdale."[64]

"Alfred had a great rapport with Ronnie," Betsy Bloomingdale told me. "He adored Ronnie. And Nancy adored Alfred." Nancy Reagan concurred, saying, "Alfred was a wonderful man, and wonderful with Betsy. It was a good combination."[65]

If Anita May was like a second mother to Nancy, Betsy was the sister she had never had, and one from whom she would learn much. Even more than Anita, Betsy was infatuated with the rituals and minutiae of entertaining on a grand scale, and while Nancy could not match either of her mentors' collections of china, crystal, or silver at that time, she was eager to soak up their expertise.

When the Bloomingdales traveled to Europe, as they did every summer, Betsy kept notebooks of dinners they attended at private homes in London, Paris, Rome, and Vienna, listing the guests and recording what was served and how the table was set. "I've always been fascinated by table settings," she explained. "And I was very influenced by what I saw in Europe and New York." After moving into the Holmby Hills house in 1959, she started keeping records of her own dinner parties.

"The first date I have for Ronnie and Nancy coming for dinner here was April 7, 1962," she said, reading from one of her party books. "I had the Wilsons, the Reagans, the Peter Douglases, and the Gordon Walkers. Peter Douglas's father was our ambassador to London then. And the Walkers were very social people here—she was in the

Colleagues and was always a dedicated Republican. We had beef Wellington, zucchini, limestone lettuce with two cheeses, strawberry sherbet, fresh raspberries, fresh strawberries, apricot sauce, oatmeal cookies, and Château Cheval Blanc."[66]

Betsy was not only a social dynamo but also a dedicated mother of three, who believed in being very involved in her children's upbringing. She often found herself giving advice to Nancy, who seemed to have a harder time raising her children, especially Patti—perhaps, as Richard Davis believed, because she harbored a lingering resentment toward her mother for not having been there during her early years; perhaps, as many others suggested, because she expended most of her emotional energy in keeping her husband happy. "She and my father were this country unto themselves," Patti Davis told me. "And we were these little islands kind of floating out there. As an adult I can now look at their love and be very impressed and moved by it—not so many of us can ever find a love like that. But I still recognize that as a child you absolutely got that you were excluded from that."[67]

Nancy Reagan never saw it quite that way. "Both of us were always there for the children," she told me. "We were not the people that they try to paint us as—you know, this disinterested mother and father. That's just a lot of malarkey."[68] Her friends tended to take her side. One of them told me,

"Nancy put a lot of time into those kids. Not him much, but she did, more than a lot of those Hollywood dames. She really loved them. Patti always gave her lip and trouble, but not little Ron. Nancy worshipped at the altar of little Ron."

Both Reagan children attended the exclusive John Thomas Dye School in Bel Air, Patti starting pre-kindergarten in 1956, Ron in 1961. John Thomas Dye is where Betty Adams sent her children, as did Dick Powell and June Allyson, Bob and Ursula Taylor, Jimmy and Gloria Stewart, Ray and Fran Stark, and Kirk and Anne Douglas. Judy Garland's younger daughter, Lorna Luft, was in the same class as Patti, who remembered being thrilled when the star of *The Wizard of Oz* turned up at Parents' Day one year. "It was an elite atmosphere, but it didn't seem so to us," Patti later wrote. "We just accepted celebrity as a part of life."[69]

The school had been founded in 1929 as the Brentwood Town and Country School by John and Cathryn Dye, and renamed in 1959 in honor of their son, who had died in World War II. Although the Dyes were upright Midwestern Republicans who believed in a strict classical education—Latin and French were compulsory—they ran their school in a distinctly casual California way. The 280 students, from nursery school to the eighth grade, began their day by reciting the Pledge of Allegiance and an inspirational poem called "The Salutation of the Dawn." The girls in the lower grades wore blue-and-white gingham dresses with heart-shaped abalone buttons and blue-and-white saddle shoes; the boys wore blue shorts and white shirts without ties. Set at the top of a ridge with spectacular views of the Pacific, the campus looked like a storybook horse farm, with its white fences and two-story yellow schoolhouse topped with a weathervane. Everyone called the headmaster and headmistress, who were in their sixties, Uncle John and Auntie Cathryn.

"The day before Thanksgiving, there would be turkeys roasting on a spit in the great big fireplace in the assembly hall," said Lanetta Wahlgren, a Hershey Chocolate heiress who was one of Patti's friends at the school. "Uncle John and Auntie Cathryn sat in these red high-backed chairs on either side of the fireplace, and we would sit at their feet. Every once in a while Auntie Cathryn would let us sit in the chair with her and cuddle up."[70] At Christmastime, the children were robed in white and sang carols while their parents were served hot gingerbread and wassail. "Ronnie would saw wood for the school," Betty Adams recalled. "And he and Bob Taylor would bring over piles of it, and we had our Yuletide drink, and Ronnie's enormous logs burned away."

She continued, "I happened to be president of the Mothers' Club board. Right after I met Nancy at Amelia Gray's and realized her daughter was going to the same school as my children, I said, 'Oh, good, you can join the Mothers' Club board.' Then Mary Jane Wick came along with her kids. So I said, 'Oh, good, Mary Jane, you can be on the board, too.' The three of us practically ran the school."[71] When the main building burned down in the 1961 Bel Air fire, the Mothers' Club raised a large part of the money to rebuild it, and Betty Adams and Mary Jane Wick arranged for classes to be held at the Westwood Methodist Church during the reconstruction. "Betty's father had given the land for the church years back," explained Mary Jane Wick. "And I taught Sunday school there."[72]

Mary Jane and Charles Wick, a show business lawyer who started a nationwide chain of nursing homes in 1956, would eventually become an integral part of the Reagan Group. In those days, however, the Wicks were not very social, and their friendship with the Reagans revolved around the school and the children. Charlie Wick, an inveterate joke-teller and all-occasion piano player, would eventually double as the Group's court jester. When I asked him where he and Mary Jane were from, he immediately shot back, "She was from Minneapolis and I was from Cleveland, before it closed." They met in Los Angeles in 1944. "Tommy Dorsey had sent me out here to buy the Casino Gardens in Ocean Park, where all the big bands played, and I was staying at Rudy Vallee's house," Wick recalled. "One Saturday I was coming down to the pool and there was this gorgeous creature sitting by the tennis court watching them play."[73] It was a case of opposites attracting: the short, dark, nominally Jewish Wick and the tall, fair, staunchly Protestant

Mary Jane Woods were married in 1947 and had five children, one right after another. Their eldest son, Charles junior, whom everyone called C.Z., was in Patti's class at John Thomas Dye, and their daughter Cindy was in Ron's.

"A lot of mothers didn't pick up their own children from school," Mary Jane Wick told me. "They had nannies, and *they* picked them up. Nancy always picked up her children. I always picked up my children. And I think we became friends because we would always get there early. She would get in my car or I would get in her car— Nancy drove a red station wagon. Nancy and Ronnie were both very involved with the school. They both worked in the hot-dog booth at the annual school fair in June, and they both came out with ketchup and mustard all over them when it was over."[74]

Betty Adams recalled teasing Nancy about her station wagon. "I'd say, 'Aren't you ever going to sell that old Ford?' She said, 'You'll be surprised when you see what I'm doing.' So I said to Mary Jane, 'Oh, she's getting a new Ford station wagon.' The next day she brought it to school, and she'd just had it repainted. That's the way Nancy was. She saved everything." Adams added, "One year after I married Bob Adams, he had a heart attack, and they put him in bed from December to June. Nancy never forgot me. I couldn't do anything for her, because my whole attention was to my husband, but she'd come by in the afternoon just to say hi."[75]

Patti was such a good student that, like her father, she skipped third grade. "She was smart, and musically talented, and one of the prettiest girls in our class," recalled C. Z. Wick.[76] According to Lanetta Wahlgren, she was also something of a tomboy. "Patti and I used to go down to Bristol Circle on Sunset with a bunch of our gang. It was all dirt in those days, and we would make these little mounds and jump off them on our bikes. Brentwood and Pacific Palisades were almost like the country then, and we were all really farm kids in a way, living in a very sophisticated environment."[77]

When Patti was about nine, Betty Adams recalled, "Nancy wanted her to go to dancing school at Miss Ryan's, which was near Hancock Park on Wilshire across from Perrino's." (Perrino's restaurant was to L.A. society what Chasen's was to Hollywood.) "My daughter, Fonza, was in the same grade as Patti, and we made sure they went places together, whether they wanted to or not. Ronnie and Nancy and I would drive our girls to the dancing school about five o'clock. Then we'd go to Perrino's, eat our dinner, pick up the little darlings, and go home. . . . We did have fun together with the kids. We sent them to Douglas Camp up in Carmel Valley, and Betsy and Alfred Bloomingdale sent their child. Nancy and I took Fonza and Patti to the train ourselves. We put them on the train and cried all the way home. Nancy was a good mother. You never read about that."[78]

Betsy Bloomingdale recalled driving the children

to camp with the Reagans some summers. "That's really how Alfred and I became friends with Nancy and Ronnie," she said. "The four of us would stay at John Gardiner's Tennis Ranch for the weekend. It was right next to the Douglas Camp, and they had beautiful bungalows and wonderful food. I remember the kids would all be lined up at the camp with their hands out, and Ronnie would inspect their fingernails."[79]

Betsy said Patti was a "sullen" child, and Patti describes how unhappy she was in her 1992 book, *The Way I See It.* She craved her father's attention and dreaded her mother's. Her father, she told reporter Nancy Collins years later, "was not terribly engaged" in family matters. Her mother, on the other hand, was "too engaged, her presence too much felt. Overwhelming. There was no balance."[80] In her telling, Patti and her mother argued about her clothes, her weight, her hair, her bathroom habits, even the way she would stare silently out the window of the car when her mother was driving her home from school. "Don't you ignore me, young lady," Nancy would scream. "Why can't you just do what I say?"[81]

Patti wrote that her mother slapped her for the first time when she was eight, and that it became a regular occurrence, but in 2004 she told me that her memoir had been written in anger, with a certain amount of exaggeration.[82] She also wrote that her mother's rage was worst when her father was away on his G.E. trips, and that when he came home, he refused to credit her complaints. On the contrary, he would tell Patti that her behavior was the reason Nancy was so nervous and had to take the tranquilizers that Patti had found in her mother's medicine cabinet.[83] "My mother is a woman who needs to control everything around her," Patti concludes. "Yet, inside, she doubts her ability to do so."[84] From Nancy's point of view, back then Patti was the control freak. "I remember at Christmastime my mother and father would be there, and Patti would write these little Christmas plays," she told me. "She'd give a part to Ron, but Ron never had anything to do. He'd just be standing in the background. Finally, one day he walked off. He wouldn't stand there anymore. It was always all about Patti. She had to be the center of attention."[85]

Even Patti's rosier memories seem to have strange endings. When she was eight, she recounted in a 1999 *George* magazine article, her pet fish, Blackie, died, and her father gave it a "fish funeral." He dug a small grave in the backyard, tied two sticks into a cross, and gave a eulogy. "I was so into this ceremony, and I was having so much fun, that when it ended, and after my father had asked me if I felt better, I said, 'Yeah, can we go kill another one?'"[86]

In 1959, at the recommendation of a child psychiatrist, Michael Reagan came to live with his father and Nancy. Now fourteen and severely troubled, he had not had an easy time of it since his mother eloped with Freddy Karger shortly after his father remarried. Jane's second marriage had fallen apart within two years, and she had moved several times. In 1955, with Loretta Young as her god-mother, Jane converted to Catholicism and had Maureen and Michael baptized alongside her. Maureen was dispatched to a Catholic boarding school in Tarrytown, New York, and in 1958 to Marymount College in Arlington, Virginia. Mean-while, Michael was bounced from the Chadwick School to a public elementary school in Westwood—he would later claim he was sexually molested at age eight by a male counselor at an after-school gymnastics camp[87]—and then to the Good Shepherd Catholic school in Beverly Hills for fifth grade. He had to repeat that grade at St. John's Military Academy, a Catholic boarding school in downtown Los Angeles, where he stayed for two years. He spent seventh grade at a private school in Newport Beach, where Jane briefly lived, and where he was a straight-D student. By then Jane had her own TV show at Revue Productions and was hardly ever at home, and when she was they fought bitterly.

He was thrilled when his father agreed to take him in—"I thought that at last I would be living with a family unit just like a normal kid."[88] But he would soon be let down once again: he was going to be a boarder, not a day student, at the Jesuit-run Loyola High School, despite the fact that it was only a half hour away from San Onofre Drive. He spent only weekends with his father and step-mother, and he slept on the living room couch.

Several months after he arrived, an additional bedroom was added onto the house for Ron's nurse, and Michael was given the daybed in the playroom.

"The first thing Nancy did when I moved in was send me to the dentist," Michael writes in his memoir, *On the Outside Looking In*. "I had not been to the dentist in years. . . . [He] discovered I had almost a dozen cavities. Nancy was livid with Mom because my teeth had been let go for so long. She also took me shopping for new clothes, something Mom rarely had time for." But, he adds, "like everyone else in the house, including Dad, I was a little intimidated by Nancy."[89] On Sunday mornings, when the family went to services at the Bel Air Presbyterian Church, Michael was left home, because he was a Catholic.[90] According to Patti, her parents avoided any mention of Jane Wyman, and she was never made to feel that Michael was her true brother.[91]

Both Patti and Michael looked forward to Saturdays at the Malibu Hills ranch, when Ronnie took them riding, and Nancy often stayed home. "I planned all week what I wanted to say to him," Patti later wrote. "I thought if I found the right words, shared enough thoughts with him, he would reach across the distance."[92] "I didn't dare talk with Dad about my feelings," recalled Michael, "because he always seemed to be uncomfortable whenever he and I embarked on anything resembling a personal discussion."[93]

"Ronnie certainly wasn't given to sitting down

and psychoanalyzing himself with the children," Nancy Reagan admitted. "How many fathers did in those days?" But he made an effort, she pointed out: "There was an empty lot at the top of our street, and Ronnie would take the children and their friends up there on windy days to fly kites."[94] In 1961, when Maureen, who had dropped out of Marymount and was working as a typist in Washington, announced that she was marrying a policeman, Ronnie and Nancy attended the wedding. Jane, who remarried Fred Karger that year, did not. Jane's fifth and final marriage would last four years; Maureen's first—to a wife beater, as it turned out—less than one.[95]

Michael's grades were still perilously low, and he was suspended from Loyola several times for unruly behavior. He recalled that Nancy was furious when she saw his report card. "You're not living up to the Reagan name or image," she told him, "and unless you start shaping up, it would be best for you to change your name and leave the house." He snapped back, "Why don't you just tell me the name I was born with, so at least when I walk out the door I'll know what name to use."

According to Michael, Nancy took up his challenge and managed to get ahold of his adoption papers. She told him his real name was John L. Flaugher and that his birth parents had not been married.[96] "My relationship with Nancy was now strained to the point where we spoke to each other only when necessary," he writes.[97] His father blamed him for "pressuring" her into giving him the information, but tried to encourage Michael by offering to get him into Eureka College if he made it through high school. Michael had a counterproposal: "If you send me out of state to a coed high school for my last year, I promise to get good grades."[98]

Loyal Davis pulled some strings, and in September 1962, Michael was enrolled at the Judson School in Arizona, where his grades improved and he became the quarterback on the football team and the star pitcher on the baseball team. When his parents couldn't make a baseball game just before Easter the following year, Loyal and Edith filled in for them. "My first time up at bat with two men on base," Michael remembered, "I heard DeeDee yell, 'You better hit a home run, you little sonofabitch.' . . . I was so excited that I pounded out my first and last home run."[99]

On July 25, 1962, Nelle Reagan died of a cerebral hemorrhage at the age of seventy-nine in a nursing home in Santa Monica.[100] "Mother's passing was peaceful and without pain," Reagan wrote to Lorraine Wagner, a fan who had become a regular correspondent. "It was just a matter of going without waking. I'm sure it was what she wanted, too, because these past few years have found her unable to do any of the things that had always made her life meaningful."[101] Neil's wife, Bess, told me that she thought Nelle had Alzheimer's, though it wasn't called that then, and Reagan himself said as much to Edmund Morris.[102] In 1954, Nelle had told Wagner in a letter, "I have hardening of the arteries in my head—and it hurts just to think."[103] By 1957 she was complaining of memory lapses and heart problems. That summer she wrote friends in Dixon: "I am a shut in. I can't drive a car any more so it was sold this last week. I will be 74 years young this month of July, and am grateful to God, to have been spared this long life. Yet when each attact [sic] comes I whisper—'Please God, let it be now, take me home.'"[104]

"She had a lady who came and lived with her," Bess Reagan told me, adding, "Ronald paid for it."[105] In 1958, Nancy arranged for Nelle to be put into the nursing home, and most of her possessions were moved to Neil's house in Bel Air, which burned to the ground in 1961. The only things Neil and Bess managed to save were their silverware and Nelle's Bible.[106]

In 1962, Nancy was made a member of the Colleagues, signifying her full acceptance into Los Angeles's hardest-to-crack social clique. Betsy Bloomingdale, Marion Jorgensen, Betty Wilson, and Betty Adams had all been members for several years. The private charity had been founded in 1950 by nine society women headed by Lucy Toberman, whose husband's grandfather was mayor of Los Angeles in the 1870s—and who had introduced Marion to Earle Jorgensen—and Onnalee Doheny, whose husband's grandfather discovered oil downtown in 1892. "I was part of the original group," said Erlenne Sprague, who was then married to her first husband, Voltaire Perkins, a wealthy lawyer who played the judge on television's *Divorce Court*. "They just picked out women that were very socially involved."[107]

The Colleagues met once a month for lunch at one another's houses, which was one reason they limited membership to fifty. Every Saturday before Mother's Day, they held their annual "Glamour Sale," at which the ladies—clad in "Colleagues Blue" smocks—sold their old furs, designer clothes, and jewelry and gave the proceeds to the Big Sister League's homes for unwed mothers. The sale was originally held in Carlotta Kirkeby's ballroom—her husband owned the Sherry-Netherland Hotel in New York, the Drake in Chicago, the Fontainebleau in Miami Beach, and La Quinta resort near Palm Springs. By 1960 it had become so popular that it was moved to the Santa Monica Civic Auditorium, and everything from art and antiques to sheets and children's clothes were added to the inventory. At the time Nancy joined, the Colleagues was almost exclusively Gentile, and only a few Hollywood wives had made the cut, including Mal Milland and Clark Gable's fourth wife, Kay Spreckels, an heiress to the sugar fortune. The membership was expanded to sixty-five in the early 1970s, which is when Harriet Deutsch and Fran Stark, among others, were asked to join.[108]

"I sponsored Nancy," said Erlenne Sprague. "I sponsored a lot of these girls—Marion, Betsy, Betty Adams—because they were good workers and good friends and it just made the whole group so special." As Sprague explained, the Colleagues continued to grow over the years, adding two auxiliary organizations—Les Amis ("the mothers and aunts and grandmothers of some of us") in 1962, and the Chips ("our daughters and granddaughters") in 1966—and raising millions for both unwed mothers and abused children while maintaining its cachet as L.A.'s chicest charity.[109]

The year Nancy became a Colleague, Kurt Niklas, the popular maître d' at Romanoff's, opened the Bistro in Beverly Hills with the director Billy Wilder. Backed by Alfred Bloomingdale and David May, among others, the restaurant became the Group's canteen. Nancy and her friends now had their own charity, their own designer, Jimmy Galanos, their own hairdresser, Julius of Saks, their own flower arranger and party planner, David Jones, and their own interior decorator, Billy Haines, as well as a regular place to lunch. They also had their own resident political philosopher—and no one found him boring. "Ronnie was always so fantastic about talking after dinner," said Erlenne Sprague. "He would talk about the government and how it was just too big and this and that. And we would sit there absolutely spellbound, listening to him. Everybody thought he was great."[110]

Betty Adams agreed: "Ronnie was easy to understand, and he was one of the sweetest, most thoughtful men I ever met. I would have rather talked to Ronnie at a dinner party than anybody.

We'd get talking head to head, because we talked politics. He was interested in history and remembered everything. This country was his life. He felt it was the greatest in the world, and he brought it up to people everywhere. And we all thought he and Nancy were so wonderful together."[111]

"Our next anniversary will be our tenth," Nancy told Lydia Lane of the *Los Angeles Times*, who interviewed her while she was visiting her husband on the *G.E. Theater* set in June 1961. "So I feel [our marriage is] a success. A man should be the captain of the ship. I don't feel it's the woman's place to run things." She added, "A wife can't let her housework and her children blot out her husband. I know this isn't easy when she does all the work herself, but we can't get away from the fact that romance is kept alive by keeping up appearances."[112]

CHAPTER THIRTEEN

THE KITCHEN CABINET
1963–1966

I know it sounds corny, but these men were good men. They believed in the good. They believed in this country and all it stood for.

> Marion Jorgensen to author,
> November 4, 1997

Most of them were self-made men. They were all tough and crusty and very patriotic and strongly anti-Communist. They really felt that the system had allowed them to come from very humble beginnings to wonderful lives that I don't think they had ever even dreamed of when they were small children—and they were very, very grateful for that. I think those were the values they shared with Ronald Reagan. What really irritated all of these guys was to be called fat cats. That was how you got under their skin. Boy, my dad hated that.

> Robert Tuttle, son of Holmes Tuttle,
> to author, November 19, 1997

About the same time Nancy Reagan became a Colleague, Ronald Reagan became a Republican. As she moved up socially, he moved right politically. He had supported Eisenhower and voted Republican for the first time in 1952. But his instincts remained liberal, and he campaigned for Los Angeles's reformist mayor Fletcher Bowron against a Republican candidate handpicked by Asa Call and the Committee of 25, whom he then characterized as "a small clique of oil and real estate pirates."[1] Just seven years later he and Nancy were among a handful of stars who refused to attend a gala at 20th Century Fox for Russian premier Nikita Khrushchev.[2] The following year he wrote *Playboy* publisher Hugh Hefner to complain about favorable articles on Charlie Chaplin and Dalton Trumbo, who was writing his first screenplay under his own name since the blacklist, for *Spartacus*, starring Kirk Douglas. Unlike most people in Hollywood, Reagan still refused to admit that there had ever been a blacklist.

He backed Richard Nixon against John F. Kennedy in the 1960 election, even though he had long-standing doubts about the vice president's integrity. After a conversation with G.E. chairman Ralph Cordiner, whom he greatly admired, he even agreed to head Democrats for Nixon in California.[3] Reagan later wrote that he was ready to change parties at that point, but "[Nixon] said I'd be more effective if I campaigned as a Democrat." Joe Kennedy, he said, tried to persuade him to support his son, "but I turned him down."[4] Reagan had an "almost visceral loathing" of JFK's New Frontier agenda, historian Matthew Dallek observes in *The Right Moment*, and was soon urging Nixon to expose Kennedy as a socialist at heart. "Shouldn't someone tag Mr. Kennedy's *bold new imaginative* program with its proper age?" he wrote Nixon shortly after Kennedy's nomination. "Under the tousled boyish haircut it is still old Karl Marx." Nixon passed Reagan's letter on to his campaign staff, after scrawling across it, "Use him as speaker whenever possible. He *used* to be a liberal."[5]

Reagan was swimming against the tide, since Hollywood was solid Kennedy territory. The sexy young Democrat became a familiar presence at his brother-in-law Peter Lawford's parties in Malibu, and Frank Sinatra was busy rallying everyone from Gregory Peck to Marilyn Monroe to back him. Only the most diehard Republicans—Dick Powell, Edgar Bergen, George Murphy, John Wayne, Irene Dunne—supported Nixon. At a Nixon rally in Beverly Hills, Reagan met William F. Buckley Jr., who had founded the *National Review* in 1955—Reagan was a charter subscriber—and was already considered the country's leading conservative intellectual. Shortly after that Reagan initiated a correspondence with Buckley that would go on for decades and greatly influence his political thinking; Nancy, in turn, would become close to Buckley's outspoken socialite wife, Pat.

"I was having dinner at a restaurant across from the hall where I was to give this speech, and Reagan was there with Nancy," Bill Buckley recalled. "He got up and introduced himself. He had just read my book *Up from Liberalism,* and he rambled off a couple of lines that had amused him. We went into the auditorium together, and there was this great panic because the kid who was supposed to turn on the loudspeaker system couldn't be found. Reagan jumped up on the stage and tried to soothe the crowd while we waited for the superintendent to bring a key to the control room. They couldn't find him, so Reagan asked, 'Where is this machine?' They pointed way up to the balcony to a room abutting the street. The next thing we knew, he had poked his head out the window—there was a little ledge there—and he did one of those Cary Grant things. Nancy was practically ready to kill herself. I stuck my head out and thought, How is he going to do this? He got up to the window that corresponded to where the speaker system was, then sort of jutted his elbow in and broke the window, climbed in, turned on the loudspeaker system, and the show went on. That was a great introduction to Reagan."[6]

Over the next two years, Reagan traveled as far right as he would ever go. He gave several speeches for Fred Schwarz's Christian Anti-Communism Crusade in 1961 and was campaign chairman for Loyd Wright, the archconservative Los Angeles lawyer who challenged moderate Republican senator Thomas Kuchel in the 1962 primary. (Wright won only 15 percent of the vote, perhaps because he made statements such as "If we have to blow up Moscow, that's too bad.")[7]

Reagan was also the featured speaker at a 1962 fund-raiser for Republican congressman John Rousselot, who was a member of the John Birch Society.

This highly controversial organization—named after a Christian missionary and U.S. Army intelligence officer killed by the Chinese Communists— had been founded by Massachusetts candy manufacturer Robert Welch in 1958. It claimed 100,000 members, at least a quarter of them in Southern California, where the Birchers, as they were called, were systematically taking over local Republican clubs and volunteer organizations—much as the Communists had tried to take over liberal groups affiliated with the Democrats in the 1930s and 1940s. Welch actually accused former president Eisenhower of being a Communist agent, and while Reagan was not willing to go that far, he saw little to disagree with in the Birchers' attack on the graduated income tax, Social Security, and school busing. Two of his longtime allies in the battle against the Communists in Hollywood, Adolphe Menjou and John Wayne, were members.

Reagan devoted most of his efforts in 1962, however, to Nixon's unsuccessful bid for the California governorship. It was at a Nixon fund-raiser that Reagan officially switched parties. As he told it, a woman in the audience stood up in the middle of his speech and asked, "Mr. Reagan, are you *still* a Democrat?" He replied that he was. "Well, I'm a deputy registrar, and I'd like to change that," she announced, then marched to the stage with a registration form in hand. "I signed it and became a Republican," Reagan recalled, "then said to the audience, 'Now, where was I?'"[8]

From then on, he liked to say, "I didn't leave the Democrats, they left me." He never made the connection that his decision to abandon the party of his father came a month or so after his mother's death.

The conventional wisdom is that Reagan's decision to switch parties and shift to the far right was heavily influenced by Loyal Davis. Nancy Reagan objected strongly to the notion: "It's always written that my father was a rich, conservative John Bircher. That is untrue. He was *not* rich. He was *not* a John Bircher. . . . And he did *not* influence Ronnie's views. Ronnie made up his own mind about things. And once he did, it was very hard for anyone to change it."[9]

Richard Davis agreed with her. "This business of Dr. Loyal convincing Ronald Reagan that he should be a Republican, and a conservative Republican at that, is absolute nonsense," he told me. "Whenever I saw Edith and Loyal with Ronnie and Nancy, the dinner-table conversation was about family affairs, the children, that sort of thing. They didn't really talk politics."[10] Alice Pirie Wirtz, who was married to Colleen Moore's stepson, Homer Hargrave Jr., recalled rather differently a dinner with Reagan, the Davises, and her in-laws when he was passing through Chicago on a G.E. trip. "He was talking politics during the *whole* dinner," she said, "and they were all urging him to run for office."[11]

Homer junior told me that Loyal paid him very little notice until he ran for Congress in Chicago in 1958, as a conservative Republican. "He was way to the right, further to the right than I am," said Hargrave.[12] "He had fairly strong political opinions," said Nancy's friend Kenneth Giniger, who helped Loyal write his autobiography. "Yes, I would call them right-wing." Giniger doubted, however, that Loyal would have joined the John Birch Society, which attracted mostly middle-class suburbanites. "It wasn't his kind of thing. He wouldn't have liked the other people. He was a considerable snob."[13]

In fact, Ronnie and Loyal were already in agreement on the big issues when they met. Both had a burning antipathy for the Soviet Union and "confiscatory taxes," and no doubt fueled each other's fire when it came to denouncing Communist sympathizers and "encroaching government control," the dominant themes of Reagan's G.E. speeches by the late 1950s. On certain issues, including abortion and separation of church and state, the irreligious Loyal was more liberal than his son-in-law. Loyal's novel, Go in Peace, a defense of euthanasia in hopeless cases, caused quite a stir when it was published in 1954. After Kennedy took office, Ronnie was only too happy to oblige Loyal when he asked him to record an album, Ronald Reagan Speaks Out Against Socialized Medicine, which the American Medical Association distributed as part of its campaign against what would become the Medicare program. A year later Reagan, in a speech on the same subject titled "Losing Freedom by Installments," warned that "you and I are going to spend our sunset years telling our children and our children's children what it once was like in America when men were free."[14]

Often overlooked is Edith Davis's role in Reagan's rise. A year after Nancy and Ronnie married, Edith accosted the Reverend Billy Graham on the Biltmore golf course and dragged him into the house to meet her son-in-law. The politically conservative evangelical minister would say that the two-hour talk he and Reagan had that afternoon was the beginning of a lifelong friendship, and that Reagan was the president to whom he was closest.[15] After Mayor Kelly's death, Edith herself apparently switched parties. "I can assure you that she worked for Republican candidates starting already in 1960, and maybe before that," Loyal's partner Dr. Daniel Ruge told me.[16]

Edith's greatest influence continued to derive from the fact that she, not her husband, decided whom they saw for dinner. By the early 1960s, Loyal was semiretired, and the Davises had given up their lakefront maisonette for a pied-à-terre in a new high-rise off Michigan Avenue. Although they had finally made the Chicago Social Register— Cleveland Amory in *Who Killed Society?* listed Edith as one of the city's leading grande dames[17]— Phoenix was now their primary residence. Edith had encouraged her Chicago friend Abra

Rockefeller Prentice to build a house down the street, and Colleen Moore and Homer Hargrave took a casita at the Biltmore Hotel for several months each winter. Edith and Loyal's group also included Donald Harrington, a right-wing oilman from Amarillo, Texas, and his wife, Sybil, who was known for her fabulous jewelry and for giving $1 million a year to the Metropolitan Opera. The Davises continued to spend Christmas in Pacific Palisades, and Nancy, Ronnie, and the children took the overnight train to Phoenix for Easter every year.

Henry Luce and his wife, Clare, who had been Eisenhower's ambassador to Italy, were also spending more time in Phoenix by then, though he remained editor in chief at Time-Life until 1964. The Luces were the king and queen of Biltmore Estates, and Edith sought eagerly to have them look favorably upon Ronnie. Apparently she succeeded, because Henry Grunwald, then managing editor of *Time*, recalled in his memoir that the magazine's "first significant political mention" of Reagan, in April 1961, was the result of a "suggestion" from Henry Luce, who later "groused" that he had had to push the editors to run the story. "The piece summarized Reagan's message about the excesses of government and described him as 'boyish of face and gleaming of tooth,'" recalled Grunwald, adding that he didn't take the G.E. spokesman very seriously back then.[18]

An anecdote told by Richard Davis indicates that Loyal sometimes made Edith's job more difficult.

"The Luces had a dinner party one night, and Henry Luce got to talking about marijuana and other drugs and the pharmacology on it. Dr. Loyal ate him alive. He didn't spare any language at all. He said Luce didn't know a goddamn thing about marijuana or cocaine or their effects on the brain. At that point Mrs. Luce got up and left the dining room in tears. Edith and the other women had to go and sympathize with her to get her back to the table. Loyal would not tolerate fools lightly. Unless you really had the facts, you were in no position to disagree with him. . . . I also think he resented people with money. And, of course, they were the poor kids on the block, there's no question about that."[19]

Edith assiduously cultivated another powerful figure in Arizona: the charismatic Senator Barry Goldwater. She and Loyal got to know Goldwater because his brother, Robert, was married to Donald and Sybil Harrington's daughter. "Mother and Barry were good friends," Nancy Reagan told me. "They were very close, actually."[20] When Reagan gave a speech to the Phoenix Chamber of Commerce in March 1961, the Davises took Goldwater to hear him. Goldwater's Polish-Jewish grandfather had founded Arizona's leading department store chain, and his mother was descended from New England Puritans, but like Reagan he identified strongly with the mythology of the West and saw himself as something of a cowboy. A year earlier he had published the best-selling *The Conscience of a Conservative*, which he wrote with

L. Brent Bozell, Bill Buckley's Yale roommate and brother-in-law (and a former speechwriter for Senator Joseph McCarthy). It made Goldwater the darling of the right and set off talk about his running for president in 1964. "I was one of the very early ones who . . . began saying that I thought he should be a candidate," Reagan recalled. "I must say . . . the first time I ever said it to him, he had no such thing in mind at all."[21]

The Davises had first introduced the two men shortly after Goldwater was elected to the Senate in 1952, but it was only after Reagan's Phoenix speech in 1961 that they had their first serious talk. It may be that was when Reagan initially urged him to run for president. The silver-haired Goldwater, who was only four years older than Reagan, had not yet made up his mind, but after he declared his candidacy in December 1963, he asked Reagan to help with his campaign in California.

There is reason to believe that Reagan's right-wing views cost him his job with *G.E. Theater* in 1962. Reagan recounted that the show was canceled on twenty-four hours' notice that March, after he had refused to drop the political content of his speeches and limit himself to promoting G.E. products. "I thought about the dates already set up for three years ahead—the first one the annual dinner of the Indiana Manufacturers Association. I couldn't quite see myself spellbinding this group with a description of the new 1963 coffee pot," he wrote. He told the BBD&O executive who delivered the unwelcome message that "if the speeches were an issue I could see no solution short of severing our relationship."[22]

In addition, several G.E. executives were under federal indictment for price-fixing at the time, and Reagan had become openly antagonistic toward the Kennedy administration in his speeches. Two months before he was severed, he attacked the President by name for the first time in a speech at Huntington Memorial Hospital in Pasadena. Kennedy's domestic policies, Reagan declared, were little more than warmed-over welfare-statism, and he questioned whether the young president was up to dealing with "the roughnecks in the Kremlin." Given the Bay of Pigs debacle and the erection of the Berlin Wall the previous year, such views were applauded by the rich burghers of Pasadena, but apparently they were less well received by some of the higher-ups at the company's headquarters in Schenectady.[23]

Another factor was at work as well. One month before G.E. canceled the show, Reagan had testified before a federal grand jury investigating MCA for alleged monopolistic practices, including the 1952 blanket waiver SAG had given to Revue Productions when he was Guild president. A week after his testimony, which was riddled with "I don't recalls," Robert Kennedy's Justice Department asked the IRS for Ronald and Nancy Reagan's tax returns for the years 1952 to 1955, obviously looking for evidence of a bribe from MCA (none was found).[24] Reagan blamed this on politics, implying that the Kennedys were out to get him for supporting Nixon in 1960. Although the grand jury proceedings were closed, there was much speculation in the press that the MCA investigation could turn into a major scandal for the forgetful Reagan and his powerful friends Jules Stein, Lew Wasserman, and Taft Schreiber.

According to Nancy Reagan, *G.E. Theater* came to an end after NBC moved *Bonanza*, "a big-budget one-hour show in color," to Sunday nights at nine. "The competition was simply too much," she said, adding that the wholesome Western was "a program Ronnie loved to watch."[25] Lou Cannon backs her up, pointing out that because *Bonanza* was "routing" *G.E. Theater* in the ratings, Ralph Cordiner could do nothing to save Reagan's job.[26] Cordiner himself would step down the following year, after G.E. was convicted of price-fixing, and go to work for the Goldwater campaign.[27]

Losing his G.E. job was an unexpected blow to Reagan. Though he denied the story, the widow and sons of BBD&O's then chief executive Charles Brower told Edmund Morris that Reagan had gone to see Brower in New York a few days after the cancellation. In Mrs. Brower's recollection, Reagan "begged" her husband to try and change G.E.'s decision, crying as he pleaded, "What can I do, Charley? I can't act anymore, I can't do anything else. How can I support my family?"[28]

Lew Wasserman was hardly more comforting when Reagan went to see him about reviving his movie career. "You've been around this business long enough to know that I can't force someone on a producer who doesn't want to use him," the MCA president told him. Reagan saw this rebuff as politically motivated, too, since Wasserman was one of Kennedy's most active supporters in Hollywood. He told Morris that he had felt "betrayed," and Nancy added, "Ronnie was devastated."[29]

However, Wasserman's Kennedy connection may have saved Reagan from more serious problems. In June 1962 the Justice Department filed a civil suit against MCA for conspiracy in restraint of trade and named SAG as a co-conspirator. A remarkably quick and favorable settlement was reached in July, when MCA agreed to dissolve its talent agency, which by then was only a small part of an empire that included Universal Studios and Decca Records, as well as Revue Productions.[30] While this was good news in terms of Reagan's legal situation, it meant that as of July 23, 1962, he and 1,400 other MCA clients no longer had an agent.[31]

At fifty-one, Reagan was forced to think about what he wanted to do with the rest of his life. Even though he had effectively given up a $200,000-a-year job because he would not stop talking about politics, he still found it hard to see himself professionally as anything other than an actor. The possibility of a career in politics was always there, looming from as far back as 1940, when Dick Powell tried to get him to switch parties and run for

Congress. He had been asked to run for Congress again in 1952, by the Democrats, and that same year for the Senate, as a Republican, by Holmes Tuttle. Ten years later the wealthy Ford dealer tried to get him to run for the Senate again, this time by challenging the incumbent Thomas Kuchel in the Republican primary.[32] He turned Tuttle down but agreed to chair the campaign of Loyd Wright, who ran instead. Perhaps he sensed that the race was unwinnable; perhaps he listened to Nancy, who craved security, and Loyal Davis, who, as he put it, "cringed at the prospect of his beloved son-in-law stepping into what he called 'a sea of sharks.'"[33] As it turned out, a few weeks later he was unemployed and had plenty of time to hit the hustings not only for Wright but also, in the general election, for John Rousselot and Richard Nixon—all of whom lost. In Phoenix that Easter, there was talk around the family table that maybe Ronnie should consider a political career of his own after all.[34]

Ronnie and Nancy were in much stronger shape financially in 1962 than they had been the last time he hit a fallow period, shortly after they married. Although G.E. was no longer acting as his booking agent, he was more in demand as a public speaker than ever, earning several thousand dollars a speech from business groups and conservative organizations around the country. In October he was honored by the Young Americans for Freedom at a rally on Long Island attended by thirteen thousand junior Cold Warriors.[35] He also agreed to serve on the advisory board of the fast-growing organization, which had been founded at the Buckley family's Connecticut estate in September 1960 and would provide an army of volunteers for Goldwater's 1964 campaign.

At some point in 1962 or early 1963, Reagan started working on his autobiography, *Where's the Rest of Me?,* with Richard Hubler, a Hollywood writer who specialized in as-told-to books. The longest passages focus on incidents and stories that highlight his leadership qualities, from his speech during the student strike at Eureka to his struggles against Hollywood's Communists in the 1940s and 1950s. The last five pages read like a campaign tract. Quoting Lord Macaulay, Thomas Paine, and Lincoln, he denies that he is part of "the right wing lunatic fringe" or a "warmonger," and renounces liberalism once and for all. "Sadly I have come to realize that a great many so-called liberals aren't liberal—they will defend to the death your right to agree with them. The classic liberal used to be the man who believed the individual was, and should be forever, the master of his destiny. That is now the conservative position."[36]

The book's last line, however, goes to Nancy— "the rest of me."

In late 1963, Lew Wasserman came through with a role in the film *The Killers*. Co-produced by Revue Productions and Universal Pictures, it was one of the first made-for-TV movies—a form for which Wasserman can be credited—but was ultimately shown in theaters after NBC decided it was too violent for home viewing. Reagan played a sinister underworld figure with a semipermanent scowl and got fourth billing, after Lee Marvin, Angie Dickinson, and John Cassavetes. Dickinson, who played Reagan's kept woman, remembered that their big scene came when she told Reagan she was going home with the Cassavetes character. "Reagan slaps me and says, 'I said, get home.' He *hated* doing that. He's just dreadful in that movie, because he could not be a bad man. He could not be bad. He was the most pleasant man I've ever dealt with. Every time I would see him for the next twenty years, it would be 'I'm still glad I didn't really have to hit you.'"[37]

The Killers, Reagan's last film, turned out to be a critical and commercial flop. "It's one I try to forget," Reagan told the *Saturday Evening Post* in 1974. "I let Lew Wasserman . . . talk me into doing [it]." Nancy interjected, "No—it was a personal favor."[38] Over lunch with me thirty years later, Nancy Reagan elaborated: "Lew said if Ronnie did this movie, he would get him other movies after that. But when Ronnie tried to hold him to his end of the deal—well, there weren't any movies. He never really forgave Lew."[39] Several of their friends told me that the Reagans and the Wassermans were on distant terms all through the 1960s and 1970s.

The Killers started filming the day after John F. Kennedy was assassinated. "It was a very, very tough time," said Dickinson, who at thirty-two was one of the most attractive actresses in town and rumored to have been one of JFK's girlfriends. Perhaps in deference to her, Reagan refrained from talking politics on the set. "You weren't about to talk politics when this man had just been murdered—and most of us were Democrats," she said. "But Ronnie was always studying on the set. He was knee-deep in all this political stuff."[40]

Nancy later wrote that she was driving down San Vicente Boulevard when the news from Dallas "came over the car radio," but neither she nor her husband make any further note in their books of an event that was as traumatic as Pearl Harbor.[41] Patti, who much to her parents' annoyance had a crush on the young president, claimed that her mother registered no emotion when she picked her up from school that afternoon, and that her father's only reaction as they watched the television coverage was to remark, when Jacqueline Kennedy stepped off the plane from Dallas, "Couldn't she have changed her suit? There's blood all over it." Patti said she begged her parents not to go ahead with a cocktail party planned for two nights later, but Nancy told her, "Stop being so dramatic."[42] The Reagans had the party, and the Bloomingdales, Bob and Ursula Taylor, Holmes and Virginia Tuttle, and John Wayne attended it.[43]

On January 3, 1964, Barry Goldwater, wearing a work shirt and blue jeans at his home in Phoenix, announced that he would seek the Republican nomination to run for president against Lyndon Johnson. "I will not change my beliefs to win votes," he said. "I will offer a choice, not an echo."[44] His principal rival was liberal New York governor Nelson Rockefeller, and the contest between them tore the Republican Party apart during the primaries leading up to the convention in San Francisco in July. Rockefeller's supporters portrayed Goldwater as "a captive of the radical right," an irresponsible militarist who would lead the country into a nuclear war. Goldwater's camp labeled Rockefeller a "Me Too" Republican, an arrogant patrician who would outspend the Democrats at home and appease the Soviets abroad. Rockefeller's 1963 divorce and remarriage a month later, to divorcée Margaretta "Happy" Murphy, was also used against him by the Goldwaterites, in an era when politicians stayed married no matter what. Nowhere was the battle fought more bitterly than in California.

Reagan became an almost full-time volunteer for Goldwater. At a breakfast rally in Inglewood in May, he accused Goldwater's "liberal Republican enemies" of conducting the "most vicious and venomous campaign against a candidate in our party we have ever seen." Mimicking Goldwater's detractors, he proceeded to introduce the candidate as "a Neanderthal man, a bigot, a warmonger, looking out at us from the 19th century." The joke fell flat.[45] Overall, though, Reagan was one of the campaign's most effective and popular speakers, drawing huge crowds wherever he appeared. At the Memorial Day finale at Knott's Berry Farm in Anaheim, he stood on the podium—flanked by

John Wayne and Rock Hudson—and led 27,000 Goldwater enthusiasts in a roaring Pledge of Allegiance.[46] The race was so close that on primary night Walter Cronkite was projecting Goldwater the winner at the same time the wire services were declaring a Rockefeller victory. The results were made official only after the absentee ballots were counted—Goldwater won by 68,000 votes out of more than two million cast.

A month later Nancy and Ronnie, who had been made an alternate delegate by the Los Angeles County Republican organization, were at the party's national convention in San Francisco's Cow Palace, which was completely dominated by Goldwater supporters, who were nearly hysterical at the thought of nominating a true-blue conservative for the first time since Calvin Coolidge in 1924. They shouted "lover" and booed during Nelson Rockefeller's speech, shook their fists at the TV anchormen in their booths above the convention floor, and triumphantly voted down every proposal to soften the platform committee's hard-line planks on civil rights, Social Security, and foreign policy. A horrified Gore Vidal, who was there as a commentator, happened to be standing near the box from which Ronnie and Nancy watched former president Eisenhower give his speech on the second night.

"Suddenly, I was fascinated by them," the acidic Vidal later wrote. "First, there was her furious glare when someone created a diversion during Ike's aria. She turned, lip curled with Bacchantish rage, huge unblinking eyes afire with a passion to kill the enemy so palpably at hand—or so it looked to me. . . . I had heard that Reagan might be involved in the coming campaign. So I studied him with some care. He was slumped in a folding chair, one hand holding up his chins; he was totally concentrated on Eisenhower. . . . I had seen that sort of concentration a thousand times in half-darkened theatres during rehearsals or Saturday matinees: The understudy examines the star's performance and tries to figure how it is done. An actor prepares, I said to myself: Mr. Reagan is planning to go into politics. With his crude charm, I was reasonably certain that he could be elected mayor of Beverly Hills."[47]

The convention was a major social event, with such Rockefeller friends as *New York Herald Tribune* publisher John Hay Whitney and CBS chairman William F. Paley and their wives—the fashionable Cushing sisters, Betsy and Babe—flying in from the East Coast, and oil-rich Goldwater backers from Texas entertaining lavishly in Nob Hill's grand hotels. Colleen Moore Hargrave and Hope McCormick were there to write an article for the society page of the *Chicago Tribune*. "They went to all the parties with their little notebooks," said Homer Hargrave Jr., who was a Goldwater delegate. "The California delegation was two sections behind Illinois, and every time Reagan came down the aisle, he'd stop and say hello to me."[48]

Eisenhower's entourage included the Justin Darts and the Freeman Gosdens—both couples had weekend houses at the Eldorado Country Club near Palm Springs, where the Eisenhowers had been given a retirement villa. According to Dart, no one was more upset by Goldwater's harshly uncompromising acceptance speech—which ended with those fatal lines "Extremism in the defense of liberty is no vice! Moderation in the pursuit of justice is no virtue!"—than Eisenhower, who had hoped Pennsylvania governor William Scranton would be able to stop the Arizonan at the last minute. "Ike was sick, absolutely sick," said Dart.[49] Ike and Mamie spent the weekend following the convention at the Darts' summer house in Pebble Beach. "Ike never liked Goldwater," one of the guests told me. "He'd get that pained Eisenhower expression on his face when Goldwater's name came up. He thought Goldwater was one-dimensional. Not subtle. He said the conservative cabal had taken over the party. We asked Ike, 'What do we do?' 'You're going to hold your nose and vote for him.' "[50]

Eisenhower was far from alone in his distaste for Goldwater's candidacy: the entire Eastern wing of the Republican Party was up in arms. Walter Annenberg's *Philadelphia Inquirer*, which had endorsed every Republican candidate since Lincoln, supported Lyndon Johnson. Goldwater "was a smart-aleck, a dope, and he drank too much," Annenberg later said. "He wasn't fit to be president."[51] Babe Paley stomped off the dance floor at a post-convention party in Los Angeles at Anita May's when her dancing partner, Billy

Haines, crowed, "Isn't it great? We got Goldwater nominated."[52]

The Reagans went to the convention with Holmes and Virginia Tuttle and Henry and Grace Salvatori. Henry Salvatori, the multimillionaire head of the Western Geophysical oil company, was Goldwater's finance chairman in California, and Holmes Tuttle was also heavily involved in fundraising for the campaign. "Holmes and Salvatori were true believers," a moderate Republican friend of theirs told me. "We'd roll our eyes when they got going. Not that they were John Birchers." Salvatori had found Goldwater's speech "exhilarating," and said years later, "I don't understand to this day what's wrong with that statement."[53] Both he and Tuttle had been greatly impressed by Reagan's ability to draw crowds and articulate the conservative message during the primary.

Although the Reagans didn't know the Tuttles or the Salvatoris well at that point, they had many mutual friends. Both couples went back a long way with Betty Adams, through her Republican Party connections. The Salvatoris lived next door to Bill and Betty Wilson and were friends of the Bloomingdales'—Grace was the godmother of Alfred and Betsy's second son. Holmes Tuttle, who had been selling cars to Ronnie since the 1940s, was a close pal of Earle Jorgensen's. Tuttle's son, Robert, told me, "My father could always count on Earle to write a check."[54]

* * *

"To look at Holmes Tuttle you would never believe that he was one of the biggest movers and shakers in L.A.," said David Jones, who did the flowers for the Tuttles' dinners at their Tudor mansion in Hancock Park. "He was a man who was at ease with himself, and very firmly grounded," said Robert Tuttle. There was something about this tall, balding, pleasant-looking man that inspired confidence. As Betsy Bloomingdale put it, "Everybody listened to Holmes. He was an oracle. He knew what should be done and saw that it got done."[55]

The seventh of ten children, Tuttle was born in 1905 on a cattle ranch in the Indian Territory of Oklahoma; his mother was half Chickasaw. The family fell on hard times after World War I, and upon his father's death in 1922, Holmes left high school to work on the assembly line at a Ford plant in Oklahoma City. Four years later he set out for California, hitchhiking part of the way and arriving, legend has it, in a boxcar. By the time he married Virginia Harris, a schoolteacher, in 1934, he had worked his way up to sales manager of Cook Brothers Ford in downtown Los Angeles. Charles and Howard Cook, who also owned the Community Bank, backed him in a dealership in West Hollywood in 1946, and by the 1960s, Tuttle had Ford and Lincoln-Mercury dealerships in Beverly Hills, Irvine, Tucson, and Spokane, making him one of the most successful automobile dealers in the country.

Tuttle was very much part of the downtown establishment—a director of the Los Angeles

Chamber of Commerce, a member of the California Club and the Los Angeles Country Club, and a bosom friend of the mighty Asa Call, whom he considered his political mentor. Virginia Tuttle was a founder of the Los Angeles County Museum of Art and the Music Center, and socially the couple, who had lived in Pasadena before moving to Hancock Park, saw mostly a WASPy, conservative crowd. "Virginia was a very nice woman, and she did a lot for Holmes," said a longtime friend from the business world. "Much as I hate to use the word, she was a little pushy, not ambitious exactly, but always very concerned about being in the right group. I don't think the other ladies—Betsy, Marion, and Betty Wilson—were all that fond of Virginia."[56]

Politically, Holmes Tuttle was not as conservative as he seemed. His father had been a Bull Moose Republican who supported Teddy Roosevelt against William Howard Taft in 1912, and Holmes himself got in trouble with his Pasadena cronies for switching his support from Senator Robert Taft (President Taft's son) to Eisenhower when the general entered the race in 1952. Some even whispered that Tuttle was a *liberal* Republican. "I have never liked that, when they begin to put labels on you," Tuttle later explained. "I was not a so-called liberal Republican; I was just a Republican. . . . Sure, I was a Taft man. I think he was a great man, a great senator, and would have made a great president. But I felt that Eisenhower . . . certainly had a better chance to win. . . . So I changed."[57]

Tuttle's political involvement began in earnest with Eisenhower's reelection campaign in 1956; that campaign also marked the beginning of his friendship with Justin Dart, who was Eisenhower's chief fund-raiser in California. "I never will forget the day that 'Jus' walked into my office, closed the door, and said, 'Holmes, I want a $5,000 contribution [for President Eisenhower].' I said, 'Jus, you've lost your cotton-pickin' mind!' Well, 'Jus' is a pretty persuasive person. He not only got the $5,000, but he put me to work. I was working morning, noon, and night assisting him in the fund-raising."[58]

"They were a formidable fund-raising pair," said Robert Tuttle. "They'd sit in Justin's office up on Beverly and La Cienega, get a guy on the speaker-phone, and go to work on him. They'd play good cop, bad cop. Millions and millions of dollars were raised in that office over the years."[59]

Dart put Tuttle on the board of his drugstore conglomerate in 1958, and the two tycoons raised money for Nixon in 1960 and 1962. In the 1964 primary, however, Dart joined forces with tire king Leonard Firestone to co-chair Rockefeller's campaign—"[Nelson] told me not to work too hard, because he financed most of it himself," Dart recalled. He claimed he was too busy expanding his business to help Tuttle raise money for Goldwater in the general election.[60] Tuttle, meanwhile, continued to give his all to the Goldwater campaign, even though he had been disappointed when the senator rejected his advice to balance the ticket by choosing the moderate Scranton as his running mate, instead of conservative New York congressman William Miller. Tuttle also kept quiet about how drunk Goldwater got after his "crazy acceptance speech," according to one insider, who said, "Holmes had to put him on a plane back to Arizona."

Tuttle's pragmatism and deep sense of loyalty appealed to Reagan, who trusted him immediately. Marion Jorgensen told me, "Holmes was the one. Ronnie had confidence in Holmes, and Holmes had tremendous confidence in him."[61]

Like Tuttle, Henry Salvatori was proud to call himself a self-made man, but he also saw himself as something of a classicist, a student of Socrates, Plato, and Cicero. Born near Rome in 1901, he had come to the United States with his parents as a toddler. His father started a small wholesale grocery business in Philadelphia, and the family lived on a farm in South Jersey. Henry attended a one-room rural schoolhouse, public high school in Philadelphia, and the University of Pennsylvania, graduating with a BS in electrical engineering in 1923. He was hired by Bell Telephone Laboratories in New York and given a scholarship to Columbia, where he earned a master's degree in physics in 1926. For the next six years he worked in oilfields in Oklahoma and California, helping to develop the science of prospecting for oil by seismic methods. In 1933, with $9,000 in capital, he started the Western Geophysical Company in Los Angeles, and by 1955 he had built it into the largest offshore seismic contractor in the world, with operations in twenty-six countries. He merged the company with Litton Industries in 1960 but remained CEO until 1967.[62]

Salvatori met bubbly Grace Ford in Oklahoma in 1936, and she moved to Los Angeles later that year. He courted her by sending a rose to her hotel room every fifteen minutes from morning until midnight. "Mother was a ballet teacher in Tulsa," their daughter, Laurie, told me. "One day a screenwriter from MGM came to her school and asked if Mother would take her students to Los Angeles for an audition. She was the chaperone, but at the end of the day, she got the contract and they didn't. I have her 1936 Screen Actors Guild card. She was in the first horror movie Lionel Barrymore made, *The Devil Doll*. She played a mute. . . . Mother was not at all mute in real life."[63]

That was Grace's only movie. She married Henry in November 1937, and they soon had two children, Laurie Ann and her brother, Henry Ford. The Salvatoris built their first house in 1940, on Bellagio Road in Bel Air, and quickly hit it off with their neighbors, Bill and Betty Wilson, whose girls went to Marymount with Laurie. Grace threw herself into philanthropic work, most notably for the ten-year, $30 million drive to build the Los Angeles County Music Center, which was spearheaded by Buff Chandler, the wife of the *Los Angeles Times* publisher. After Grace raised almost $400,000 by raffling off a Cadillac Eldorado at the campaign's kickoff event in 1955, she was named *"Times*

Woman of the Year" and made vice chairman of the campaign's executive board. "Grace Salvatori was Buff Chandler's bag woman," said Connie Wald. "She raised more money for the Music Center than anyone."[64]

Meanwhile, Henry was embraced by the Committee of 25, becoming finance chairman of the L.A. County Republican Party in 1949 and state finance chairman two years later. Salvatori had been brought up a Republican—unlike Tuttle's father, however, the senior Salvatori not only admired President Taft but also named one of Henry's brothers William Howard in his honor. "It was only in the late 1940s when I became concerned with the Communist threat to the free world that I began to take an interest in politics," Salvatori said years later. "I was in San Francisco during the formation of the United Nations. I believed then that it was a mistake, and I thought that the Democratic Party was totally unaware of the future threat of Communist Russia."[65]

If Tuttle was the conciliator among Reagan's backers, Salvatori was the ideologue, the most committed to the conservative cause. A founding investor in the *National Review,* Salvatori also funded Fred Schwarz's Christian Anti-Communist Crusade and started his own Anti-Communism Voters League, "whose purpose was the evaluation of all candidates for all offices on the basis of how well they were aware of the Communist threat."[66] He was a major contributor to the American Security Council, which was founded by

General Douglas MacArthur and Henry and Clare Booth Luce in 1954 and aided the U.S. government's anti-Soviet efforts overseas. (It would be repeatedly branded a CIA front by its leftist critics.) In the early 1960s, the Salvatoris gave $1 million to the University of Southern California to establish the Research Institute of Communist Strategy and Propaganda. "My father was very proud of being an American," Laurie Salvatori said. "He believed that capitalism and the freedoms we enjoy as Americans have to be defended at all costs."[67]

Salvatori was a consistent supporter of opportunities for African-Americans, making six-figure donations to Howard University and the Lincoln Institute for Research and Education. After the 1965 Watts riot, he anonymously gave $250,000 to rebuild community institutions. "I'm a member of a minority myself," he liked to say, and his daughter pointed out that her parents had no hesitation about bringing the distinguished black architect Paul Williams to dinner at Chasen's. "They didn't get their usual table," she said, "and there were quite a few people staring at them."[68]

In 1964 the Salvatoris commissioned Williams, who had designed the MCA headquarters for Jules Stein and Saks Fifth Avenue in Beverly Hills, to build their new house. Williams was popular with conservatives—one of his earliest clients was ZaSu Pitts—who loved his "historical revival fantasies."[69] Williams was actually quite conservative himself and kept his distance from the civil rights movement. ("I am an architect . . . I am a Negro," he once wrote. "We march forward singly, not as a race. Deal with me, and with the other men and women of my race, as individual problems, not as a race problem, and the race problem will soon cease to exist!")[70]

For the Salvatoris he created a $700,000, thirty-three-room, twelve-thousand-square-foot neo-Georgian colonial that looked like Mount Vernon transported to a Bel Air hilltop. Betsy Bloomingdale declared it the most beautiful house in Los Angeles. Billy Haines did the interiors and designed most of the furniture, but at one point he walked off the job because he found Salvatori overbearing. "He and Henry had words," recalled Haines's associate Jean Hayden Mathison, who conspired with Grace to persuade Haines to complete the project. "Grace Salvatori was a delight— a crazy, wonderful lady, always enthused about everything," Mathison added.[71] "Oh, she was something," a friend said. "She had this *extremely* outgoing personality."

After the San Francisco convention, the Goldwater cause became something of a family affair for the Reagans. With Salvatori's backing, Reagan was made co-chair of California Citizens for Goldwater-Miller, the campaign's main volunteer organization. At Ronnie's suggestion, Neil Reagan, who was West Coast vice president of the McCann-Erickson advertising agency, was hired to produce Goldwater's TV and radio ads. In Phoenix, Edith threw herself into raising money for her neighbor

Barry. Nancy did her bit, too, plastering "Vote Goldwater" bumper stickers on their station wagon and her late-model Lincoln Continental.

As Anne Douglas remembered, Nancy was at least as gung ho for Goldwater as Ronnie was. "Young Ron and my son Eric were best buddies at John Thomas Dye," she told me. "They would spend one weekend with us and one weekend with the Reagans at the ranch. You know how kids pick up what they hear at home—my husband and I didn't care for Goldwater, and we must have discussed it. Anyway, I dropped Eric off at their house one Saturday morning, and about fifteen minutes later I got a call from him, crying and saying, 'Come and pick me up.' What happened was, he saw the Goldwater sign on the station wagon and said, 'Boo Goldwater!' Nancy was so furious she gave him a dressing down, and he started to cry. He didn't know what he had done. He was only six. Later on Nancy laughed about it, but at that moment she was serious. I went to pick him up, and that evening I talked to Nancy. She said, 'I don't know what your political opinions are, but you should keep the kids out of it.' So she was off me for a while. It was the one time Nancy and I had a falling out."[72]

Reagan had recommended Neil to Goldwater during the primary. Though the brothers were finally in the same party, they had hardly seen each other since Nelle died. "All of a sudden, one day, I got a call from Ronald," Neil recounted. "Ronald said, 'I told Barry Goldwater to call you. I think you can help him.' I said, 'What's the problem?' And he said, 'Well, he's getting all kinds of criticism of his TV commercials.' Well, the criticism they were getting—I found out—was not necessarily [on the] content; it was the production. . . . [But] I was the most surprised person in the world that he told Barry to call me, because I always operate on the theory that he doesn't even know I'm breathing, and he's probably suspicious that I don't know or care whether he's breathing or not."[73]

Neil spent sixty-five days that summer and fall flying around the country on a Boeing 727 with Goldwater and his wife, Peggy—this was the first presidential campaign in which candidates chartered their own jets.[74] But nothing McCann-Erickson came up with could match Lyndon Johnson's famous "Daisy" commercial, in which an image of a little girl picking the petals off a daisy is followed by one of a nuclear bomb exploding into a mushroom cloud. Goldwater's name was never mentioned, but the ad recalled all the fears Rockefeller had stirred up about him in a devastating thirty-second spot. From then on everything seemed to work against Goldwater, including his own slogan, "In Your Heart You Know He's Right." "In your heart you know he might," hecklers would chant at his appearances. "In your guts you know he's nuts."[75]

Late that summer, Tuttle asked Reagan to be the speaker at a $1,000-a-plate Goldwater fundraiser—"which was unheard of at that time," the car dealer noted—at the Cocoanut Grove nightclub in the Ambassador Hotel. "After he got through," Tuttle said, "I was besieged—my goodness—by people that said, 'He spoke of the issues, of the things that we are concerned about: government involvement, all these social programs, and all this 'womb to tomb' spending and so forth. We feel our federal government is taking a position that the Constitution never intended for it to do.' "[76]

Reagan titled his speech "A Time for Choosing," and it was a remarkably lucid distillation of everything he had been saying on the road for years, a mix of high-flying rhetoric and down-to-earth anecdotes that made ordinary people feel that he cared about their concerns and respected their intelligence. In contrast to Goldwater's disastrous acceptance speech, he opened on a conciliatory note:

> On the one hand, a small group of people see treason in any philosophical difference of opinion and apply the terms "pink" and "leftist" to those who are motivated only by humanitarian idealism in their support of the liberal welfare philosophy. On the other hand, an even greater number of people today, advocates of this liberal philosophy, lump all who oppose their viewpoint under the banner of right-wing lunacy.

But he quickly put the choice facing the electorate in stark terms:

Either we believe in our traditional system of individual liberty, or we abandon the American Revolution and confess that an intellectual elite in a far distant capital can plan our lives for us better than we can plan them ourselves.

By the end of the speech he had made this choice apocalyptic. "You and I have a rendezvous with destiny," he declared, echoing FDR. He then turned to Lincoln again. "We will preserve for our children this, the last best hope of man on earth, or we will sentence them to take the last step into a thousand years of darkness."[77]

As Nancy recalled the evening, "Ronnie's speech went over so well that [Holmes] came to him afterwards and said 'We've got to get that speech on television.'" Tuttle and Salvatori quickly came up with the money to buy a half hour of airtime on NBC so that Reagan could deliver his speech nationwide a week before the election. In Nancy's recollection and most other versions, Goldwater's advisers tried to stop the telecast, claiming it was "too emotional." Goldwater himself called Reagan at home, and Reagan suggested he view a taped film of the speech that had been made for fund-raising events in California. After he had seen it, the candidate asked his staff, "What the hell was wrong with that?"[78]

Laurie Salvatori, however, recalled a conversation with her mother that indicates that it was actually Grace who raised much of the money, and that a jealous Goldwater wanted the airtime for himself.

"My first memory of this whole Reagan business," she told me, "was walking into my mother's study, and her shushing me. When she got off the phone she said, 'You won't believe who called—Barry Goldwater. He was calling from his airplane. Some girlfriends and I have bought the airtime for Ronald Reagan to go on television to talk about Barry Goldwater.' Goldwater was asking my mother if he could have the time back, so he could talk for himself. And my mother said, 'Well, do you have the money?'—which she knew he probably didn't. And she said in the loveliest way possible, 'Well, Barry, if you don't . . .' As you know, this particular speech that Ronald Reagan gave for Barry Goldwater was the highlight of the whole campaign."[79]

The final version of the speech was taped before an invited audience outfitted with Goldwater signs in a studio in Phoenix; Patti remembered that half the audience, including her mother, was in tears by the time her father finished.[80] NBC broadcast the speech on October 27, 1964, at 8:30 in the evening, and Ronnie and Nancy watched it at Bill and Betty Wilson's house with the Salvatoris and the Tuttles. Over the next week $500,000 poured into the campaign's coffers, and another half million soon followed. According to Nancy, some $8 million was generated for the Republican Party as a result of the speech.[81] A new political star was born. *Washington Post* columnist David Broder declared that Reagan had made "the most successful national political debut since William

Jennings Bryan electrified the 1896 Democratic convention with his 'Cross of Gold' speech."[82]

No one seemed to notice that Barry Goldwater's name was mentioned only once, and then almost as an afterthought, following the rousing climax. Except, that is, Goldwater himself. "To his discredit, Goldwater always seemed to resent being superseded by Reagan," says Lyn Nofziger, who covered the 1964 election for the Copley newspapers and went on to become Reagan's press secretary two years later, in his eponymous memoir. "Probably Reagan was too effective from Goldwater's point of view because Reagan, not Goldwater, emerged from that campaign as the conservative hero."[83]

"Ronnie always believed that we're all put here for a purpose," Nancy Reagan told me. "We might not know now why or what the purpose is, but eventually we will. Barry opened the door. And then Ronnie took it along."[84]

Goldwater's defeat was the worst the Republicans had suffered since the Roosevelt years. Johnson carried forty-four states, winning even in such bastions of Midwestern Republicanism as Galesburg, Illinois, which so upset Loyal Davis that he announced he no longer wanted to be buried in his hometown.[85] Reagan took the loss more evenly, giving a brief pep talk to dejected campaign workers at an election night party at the Ambassador Hotel and encouraging them not to give up on the conservative cause.[86]

"We didn't want that to be the demise of the Republican Party," said Tuttle, "so we thought the best way to start rebuilding was here in California."[87] Tuttle got together with Salvatori and A. C. "Cy" Rubel, a key Goldwater supporter who had recently retired as chairman of the Union Oil Company, to discuss the future of the party, including whom they could run for governor against the Democratic incumbent, Edmund "Pat" Brown, in 1966. "Gentlemen," Tuttle told his cohorts, "I think we've got a candidate right here. How about Ron?"[88]

It didn't take much convincing. As Laurie Salvatori said, "My father felt that, unlike Goldwater, Ronald Reagan could get elected because he spoke better than anybody else in the world."[89] Furthermore, George Murphy's victory in the 1964 Senate race demonstrated that Californians were willing to elect an actor to high office; Reagan had campaigned for his old friend from SAG. "So I went to see him," Tuttle said. "In fact, Mrs. Tuttle went with me, and we spent the evening at Ron's home."[90] It is not clear whether this visit took place in late December 1964 or early January 1965. In either case, it was followed by more visits to San Onofre Drive by Tuttle, Salvatori, and Rubel.

"I knew those people were going to come up to the house after that disastrous election," Nancy Reagan told me. "I knew it. And they did. At first Ronnie said, 'Well, let me think about it.' And then finally he said to me, 'You know, the party is in such bad shape, if I felt that I could do something to help it, and I didn't do it, I'd feel terrible.' So he said to them, 'Let me go out and see what the response of the people is.' And there we were. On a road we never intended to be on. Ever."[91]

It was certainly a hard decision for the Reagans to make; on the other hand, there was also an air of inevitability about it, as if they had known all along where they were heading. Nancy's old friend Bruce McFarland vividly remembered her telling him on a visit to Chicago shortly after Patti was born, "Mark my words, Ronnie will be governor of California someday."[92] Others, including Ardie and Harriet Deutsch, remembered Nancy dropping similar comments over the years. Arlene Dahl recalled that Nancy had asked her to read her tea leaves at their hairdresser's in early 1965; she told Nancy that she would soon receive important news having to do with California's government.[93]

Ronnie and Nancy were naturally cautious, however, especially when it came to their financial security, and he had just signed a two-year contract to host a TV series called *Death Valley Days.* Although it wasn't nearly as prestigious as *G.E. Theater*, it paid a comparable salary and required nothing more than taping short introductions and doing the occasional star turn on horseback. The program was sponsored by U.S. Borax, a McCann-Erickson client handled by Neil Reagan, who had pushed his brother for the job. "There was a little method in my madness," Neil admitted.

"It kept him in the public eye for what I figured might be helpful if he ran for governor."[94]

Neil was included in some of the early meetings with Tuttle, Salvatori, and Rubel at the Reagan house, and he attested to the fact that his brother struggled with his decision. These "long sessions," Neil said, "used to start at eight o'clock in the evening and wind up at three and four the next morning. . . . [Ron] held out for a long time. . . . He was very noncommittal."[95]

"I dismissed them lightly and quickly to begin with, but they just kept coming back," Ronald Reagan recalled. "[They] kept insisting that I offered the only chance of victory and to bring the party back into something viable. It got to the place where I said, no, and no, and no. And Nancy and I couldn't sleep anymore. You know, we wondered, 'Are you making the right decision? Are you letting people down? What if they're right?' "[96]

The pressure was coming from all sides, according to Jack Wrather, the husband of Bonita Granville, who had made a movie with Reagan at Warners before moving to MGM, where she became friendly with Nancy. The Texas-born Wrather, a Marine commander during the war, whose family was in oil and whose first wife was the daughter of Governor Pappy Daniels, had moved to Los Angeles in 1946 and assembled an entertainment-and-real-estate-empire that included the rights to *Lassie* and *The Lone Ranger*, the Muzak Corporation, the Disneyland Hotel, and the Balboa Bay Club in Newport Beach, where

Barry and Peggy Goldwater kept a weekend apartment. Jack and Bunny lived a few houses down from the Bloomingdales in Holmby Hills, and they were very close to the Wilsons and the Jorgensens, as well as the Tuttles and Salvatoris.

"We all saw each other very often . . . at dinners and barbecues and cocktail parties and things," Wrather recalled. "We'd sit and discuss what the hell happened to Barry, why, and how terrific that commercial was of Ron's. . . . I remember one night at Bill Wilson's . . . all the men were gathered kind of English-style after dinner together and the ladies were in the other room . . . and talk got around to Ron and how much we needed somebody like Ron in the governorship; Pat Brown had to be gotten out, that he was a disaster, a do-nothing and worse than that. . . . We just sat and talked to Ron and said, 'Ron, God, you've got to run for governor. You've just got to. And we talked and talked. The gals finally came in and said, 'We've got to go home. It's late.'

"We all assured Ron at one time or another that if he would run we'd be available to him, any of us or all of us," Wrather continued, "for any kind of advice or help, or helping him put together any business plans or helping with personnel selection. And that we would obviously get behind him financially and that we would raise money for him; we'd do everything possible so that he wouldn't have to worry about the campaign funds to run on—which, of course, even in those days, was a big worry. . . . In between these affairs, Holmes would get all hot and bothered and call Ron, like Holmes does. You know, he's a great salesman!"[97]

By the end of the January, even *The New York Times* was asking Reagan if he was running. "I'm honored by all the interest," he told them. "Politics is nothing I'd ever thought of as a career. But it's something I'm going to give deep consideration and thought."[98]

In February, Reagan finally made up his mind. "He called me and told me that he would run if we still felt the same way," Tuttle said. "He and Nancy had discussed it and decided we should try it. He suggested that instead of announcing that he was going to run, we should just kind of put feelers out."[99] Tuttle, Salvatori, and Rubel formed an exploratory committee, which also included Tuttle's longtime business partner, Charles Cook, chairman of the Community Bank; Ed Mills, the bank's vice president and regional head of the Boy Scouts; and attorney William French Smith, who was brought in by Tuttle to oversee the campaign's legal affairs. French Smith, a *Mayflower* descendent from Boston and a partner in Gibson, Dunn & Crutcher, one of the largest law firms in Los Angeles, would soon become Reagan's personal lawyer. His wife, Jean, a third-generation Angeleno whose family owned the city's first lumber mill, had known the Tuttles for years, and she got along with Nancy right away.

Tuttle also sent Reagan to San Francisco to meet with Jaquelin Hume, the founder of Basic

Vegetable Products, the world's largest processor of dehydrated onions and garlic. Hume, who had been one of Goldwater's key supporters in Northern California, immediately agreed to come on board and gave a breakfast for Reagan to meet other prominent San Francisco conservatives. "I thought he was as sound as he could be," Hume said of his first meeting with Reagan. "He advocated the political and economic philosophy of which I approved and he seemed to have the ability to express it even better than Goldwater. . . . He is an extremely able individual, much more so than most people realize. . . . Most people had no comprehension that he had such an excellent mind."[100]

These men constituted the original nucleus of what would come to be known as the Kitchen Cabinet, though they would not actually be called that until after Reagan's election.[101] As William French Smith explained, "We had social contacts and political contacts, and the relationships just grew. I think what is now referred to as the Kitchen Cabinet was not known by any title. It was just a group of friends that became an executive committee. And I think that group of friends probably may be unique in the annals of American political history, because it started with him, and at least the nucleus has been with him ever since. I don't know of any other situation where it has been quite like that, people are both social friends and then became active politically in furthering his candidacy."[102]

*   *   *

From the beginning, Tuttle, Salvatori, and Rubel were determined not to repeat the mistakes of Goldwater's narrowly based campaign; they saw Reagan as someone who could unify the party. One of their first and wisest moves was to seek out the political consulting firm of Spencer-Roberts, which had run Rockefeller's campaign in the 1964 primary. Stuart Spencer, a former parks-and-recreation director, and Bill Roberts, a onetime television salesman, had been active in the L.A. County Young Republicans in the 1950s and started their own business in 1960. In six years, Lou Cannon notes, "they had won 34 of 40 congressional races with Republican candidates of various views." These successful candidates included Betty Adams's first husband, Alphonzo Bell, a moderate, and John Rousselot, whom they refused to handle for reelection when his John Birch Society membership was revealed. Even Goldwater grudgingly admitted to Tuttle that they were the best.[103]

Spencer-Roberts had also been approached by Reagan's likely opponent, George Christopher, the moderate former mayor of San Francisco. As Stu Spencer told me, he first met with Tuttle, Mills, and the Cook brothers at the Cave de Roy, a Hollywood key club. "Then we met with the Reagans several times at their home. It was a really big decision for the company. George Christopher was the odds-on favorite, not this guy coming out of Hollywood who had given a great speech for

Goldwater. We spent quite a bit of time talking to him. He then went over to see his in-laws in Phoenix, and he called us from there and said, 'When the hell are you guys going to make your minds up?' We said, 'We're not finished checking yet. We don't want to find out you're a Bircher or something.' So we had one more meeting. I'll never forget, we got to the house, and he's sitting there with these big bright red socks on. It was his sense of humor. We agreed to do it."[104]

In May the exploratory committee launched Friends of Ronald Reagan, with Rubel, who at seventy was the oldest of the original triumvirate, as chairman of its executive committee. Their first move was to hire Spencer-Roberts to set up the "test-the-waters" tour at a reported fee of $50,000.[105] A few weeks later Friends of Reagan sent out a mailing with requests for donations, which quickly brought in $135,000, enough to cover expenses through the end of the year, when Reagan agreed to make his decision final. Among the forty-one names on the letterhead were James Cagney, Walt Disney, Robert Taylor, and Randolph Scott, as well as Nancy's friend Anita May, who had been predicting for years that Ronnie would run, and who was the only woman included in meetings of the Kitchen Cabinet's inner circle. Although Jack Wrather, Bill Wilson, Earle Jorgensen, and Alfred Bloomingdale were not actively involved at this point, they were early contributors. "I remember saying, 'But Ronnie's an actor. An actor can't be governor,'" Betsy

Bloomingdale told me. "'Well,' Alfred said, 'you just wait and see.'"[106]

Marion Jorgensen recalled how Tuttle got her and Earle to contribute. "We went to a party at the Beverly Wilshire and I was sitting next to Holmes. He said, 'I want to drop by and see Earle tomorrow.' He started telling me about how Ronnie would make a good governor, and he felt Nancy could be a good help to him. He said, 'I want Earle to give me $25,000.' In those days that was a *lot* of money. But I said, 'Sure, Earle will give it to you.' When I got in the car, I said, 'Earle, I committed you for $25,000.' He said, 'You did *what*?' I said, 'Yes, because I knew you would want to. You always do anything Holmes asks you to do.' So he did. And that's how he got there with Holmes, Jack Hume, Henry Salvatori, and Cy Rubel."[107]

Late that spring Reagan hit the road, literally. "They had a hell of a time getting him to go on a plane in 1965," Robert Tuttle recalled.[108] All summer and fall Reagan drove around the state, building grassroots support by giving speeches to local chapters of the Rotary Club, the Chamber of Commerce, and the United Way. Nancy accompanied him only occasionally during this period and found campaigning daunting at first. As she recalled in *My Turn*, "We went to a reception for Ronnie at one of the big hotels in San Francisco, where so many people wanted to meet him, that they were lined up through the lobby, and around the block, waiting to get in. This was my introduction to politics, and when I woke up the next morning I couldn't move my neck. We called a doctor, who explained that when people are nervous, they tend to raise their shoulders—which I had apparently done for four hours. That, plus standing in an unnatural position with my arm extended, shaking hands, had sent me into a spasm. When I came home, a friend put me in touch with a Swedish woman, who put me in hot packs, massaged my neck, and used traction. Ever since, I've kept my shoulders down in a receiving line."[109]

"Politically, they were both green as hell in 1965," said Stu Spencer. "She didn't know what she was getting into, I don't think. But it turned out Nancy was born a politician. They were a team. People have got to recognize that. We never held a meeting in the house with Ron and discussed strategic matters—which we did a lot of—that she wasn't present. Listening. And, as time went on, asking questions. The tough questions. She was on a learning curve of the political process. She would double-check with others. She's a great phone person—talking to her friends out there, getting a lot of feedback, some of it valid, some it off-the-wall. I'd talk to her every day, or one of us from the campaign did—and I could always tell that night that she had talked to five people on the telephone. I'm talking about the 1960s, but this was true all the way through the process. Her political skills were better, in terms of what was best for Ron, than even his own. His skills were in the communications aspect and the beliefs and ideology. She was the personnel director of the Reagan operation, so to speak. She wanted to know who was going to be around Ron and who they were. She made a lot of decisions about people coming and people leaving. She was right 90 percent of the time. Her instincts were good. She knew what worked well with him. I've always said he'd never have made it without her."[110]

The Reagan road show was a huge success. Spencer-Roberts cast its client as the Citizen Politician, and he played the role to the hilt. Despite initial concern on the part of his handlers and the Kitchen Cabinet, Reagan insisted on following his talks with a question-and-answer period to show that he could think on his feet, not just memorize scripts. Constantly asked about the John Birch Society, he came up with an answer that had managed to elude Nixon and Goldwater: the former had denounced the Birchers and narrowly lost in 1962 as conservative Republicans sat on their hands; the latter had refused to denounce the society and had it hung around his neck like an albatross by the Democrats. Reagan said again and again and again, "They're supporting *my* philosophy, I'm not supporting *their* philosophy."[111]

To bolster Reagan's new, middle-of-the-road image, Tuttle took him out to Eldorado for a round of golf with Eisenhower. Although Ike remained neutral in the Reagan-Christopher contest, he is said to have told Tuttle, "I like your boy."[112] In the meantime, Salvatori was quietly encouraging his friend Los Angeles mayor Sam Yorty to challenge Governor Brown in the Democratic primary. For his part, Cy Rubel set up a lunch at the California Club at which Reagan was given the blessing of Asa Call and the Committee of 25—some say it was Call who really decided to run Reagan in the first place. Rubel also provided the Friends of Reagan with office space in the Union Oil Building and persuaded former USC football star and fellow oil executive Joe Shell not to enter the race. The triumvirate also prevailed on Republican state chairman Dr. Gaylord Parkinson to issue his so-called Eleventh Commandment that spring: "Thou shalt not speak ill of another Republican." This enabled Reagan, who as someone who had never held public office was more vulnerable to criticism than his opponent, to take the high road. Christopher, who was reprimanded at least twice by Parkinson for violating his stricture, seethed, and his supporters accused Reagan's rich backers of buying the state chairman off.[113]

By September, polls were showing Reagan as the clear front-runner, but Christopher as more likely to beat Brown. So much mail was pouring in—hundreds of letters a day, according to Kathy Randall Davis, the Spencer-Roberts secretary assigned to Reagan—that she had to hide some of it from the still undeclared candidate in order to prevent him from trying to answer every letter himself, as was his custom. "He and Mrs. Reagan had this thing about mail," she later wrote, "they almost fought over who would get to open it."[114]

It was a thrilling time for Ronnie and Nancy. She started wearing a "Reagan for Governor" button even on her evening clothes, and had the house-keeper, Anne Allman, the gardener, her hairdresser, and the butcher at the Brentwood Country Market wearing them, too. Seven-year-old Ron plastered his bedroom walls with Reagan bumper stickers. Only Patti was unenthusiastic about the turn her father's career had taken, which left her over-whelmed with the feeling that she had little control over her own life. At Christmas that year, Patti was so sulky that Loyal pulled her aside and said, "I want you to show how proud you are of your father. You back him up, do you understand me?"[115]

Patti felt that her father had become more remote than ever since his big speech for Goldwater. "Often, I'd come into a room and he'd look up from his note cards as though he wasn't sure who I was." Her relationship with her mother had not improved either as she entered her teen years. There were scenes at I. Magnin and Saks over clothes, and shouting matches at home. Patti said her mother listened in on her phone calls with boys and tore up her emotionally dark, typically teenage poetry. She saw her relationship with her mother as a constant battle. When her father came home from a campaign trip or a day of work on *Death Valley Days*, he always dismissed her accu-sations against her mother. "Patti . . . what is it with you? Your mother does everything she can for you and all you do is talk back to her and hurt her. . . . All she wants is to have a daughter. She looks at friends of hers, like Mrs. Bloomingdale, and how nice a time she has with Lisa, and she doesn't understand why she can't have that with you."[116]

"All our classmates knew that Patti didn't like her mother," said Liza Lerner, a daughter of the lyricist Alan Jay Lerner, who was a friend of Patti's at John Thomas Dye. "When we started sixth grade, Patti was the most developed girl in the class, and she was insecure and self-conscious about it. You have to realize that all thirteen-year-olds complain about their mothers, but Patti particularly had a thing about hers. I would go over there sometimes in the afternoon, and we'd go into Patti's room and stay there. She used to complain that her mother would leave the intercom on and listen in to what was going on in her room. My impression was that it was a very disconnected family. Every time I went over there, her father was just sitting around reading the newspaper—he didn't seem very out-going to me. And Nancy seemed like someone with blind ambition, who just had a mission, and anything that got in her way . . . When you're a kid, you get a visceral sense of things. She wasn't a warm person. She was a cold person. I knew the Wicks slightly better. Mary Jane Wick was an out-going, sweet woman, and Mr. Wick was a nice guy. Their house was a more normal, inviting place to be than the Reagans'."[117]

"I don't know what it was with Patti and me," Nancy Reagan confided years later. "Maybe the way I looked, the way I dressed—I don't know. When she was in seventh grade at John Thomas

Dye, the principal said, 'I think Patti should go to this doctor.' So we went to this psychiatrist, a crippled woman, I remember. 'I think you'd better get Patti away from you for a year, because she has a real fixation about her mother.' That's what she told Ronnie and me."[118]

Nancy had hoped that Patti would go to Marlborough or Westlake, the two most social private girls schools in Los Angeles, but they wouldn't take her because she failed eighth grade at John Thomas Dye. Patti wanted to go to a public school, because they were coed and integrated, but Nancy would not hear of it. After Patti deliberately botched the entrance exam at the exclusive Bishop School in La Jolla because it was all-girls and required uniforms, Betsy Bloomingdale suggested the Santa Catalina School near Santa Barbara, which was run by nuns but attended by girls from some of San Francisco's WASPiest old families. But the nuns rejected Patti, too. In September 1965 she entered the coed Orme School, located in the desert outside Flagstaff, Arizona, which was also a functioning cattle ranch. She promptly grew her hair long, had her ears pierced, tightened her jeans and shortened her skirts, and took to wearing thick black eyeliner and white lipstick. "When you've been dressed like Little Bo Peep for years," she later explained, "the slut look is very desirable."[119]

According to Patti, just before she left for boarding school, she had overheard Nancy telling Stu Spencer that Reagan's campaign literature should say that Ronnie had two children and that no mention should be made of Reagan's first marriage. Spencer, who felt that Rockefeller's divorce had cost him the nomination, agreed with Nancy. This was particularly hurtful to Maureen, who had been remarried, to a Marine lieutenant stationed at nearby Camp Pendelton, and who liked nothing more than talking politics with her father over dinner. An enthusiastic conservative herself, she had been a full-time volunteer for Goldwater and had been encouraging her father to run for office since he switched parties. Michael, on the other hand, had again been cast out by the family. After graduating from Judson with honors and being rewarded with a new Ford Galaxie 500 by his father, he made it through only one year at Arizona State, and was working the night shift loading freight for a trucking company at the Port of Los Angeles.[120]

"The consultants were very nervous about Dad's previous marriage, and the very clear message I was getting was that Michael and I were not to be involved in any way in the campaign," Maureen wrote. "In fact, Stu Spencer later suggested to my husband that I dig a hole and pull the dirt in over me until after the election." When she called her father to discuss the situation, he told her, "If you pay someone to manage a campaign . . . then you've got to give them the authority to do it as they see fit."[121] He agreed to let her introduce him at an event put on by the San Diego Federation of Republican Women, and he let it pass when Maureen, who could be as feisty as her mother, discarded the text prepared by Spencer-Roberts. It would have required her to say that her father had two children, named Patti and Ron, and *that*, she wrote, "would have been the ultimate humiliation."[122]

Ronnie and Nancy saw in 1966 at the Bloomingdales'. "It was the first year I did a New Year's Eve party, and I had champagne, caviar, and chili," said Betsy Bloomingdale, reeling off the guest list from her party book. "Irene Dunne, the Lohmans—she's Beverly Morsey now, the Dominick Dunnes, Bill Frye, and Jim Wharton. And I had everybody's children—that was the idea, to keep it small and family." Dominick Dunne, who was a producer then, and his wife, Lenny, were on the Beverly Hills A-list, and Lew Lohman was a rich oilman from Texas whose wife was in the Colleagues.[123]

Four days later Ronald Reagan formally announced his candidacy for governor in a televised broadcast from Pacific Palisades. Nancy stood at his side, looking up at him lovingly. The candidate was wearing a dark-green-and-navy tartan jacket, a white shirt, a dark tie, and black slacks; his wife wore a suit of fire-engine red, a color that guaranteed she would stand out. "Ladies and Gentlemen," Reagan began, "for the last six months I've been traveling up and down this state meeting as many of you as I could—answering questions and asking a few. There isn't any secret as to why I've been doing this: I have said I'll be a candidate for Governor once I've found the answers to a few questions myself— mainly about my acceptability to you. Who would like to be Governor isn't important. Who the people would like to be Governor is very important."[124]

The presentation seemed deliberately Rooseveltian in its homey majesty, from the direct appeal to the people right down to the crackling logs in the living room fireplace behind him. As Lou Cannon writes, "Reagan found his true calling in politics. Reagan was a competent actor with a limited range. As a politician, however, he was so enormously gifted that he seemed a president-in-waiting almost as soon as he began campaigning."[125]

Reagan "fielded a variety of questions with impeccable nonchalance," said *The New York Times* about the press conference that followed at the Statler-Hilton downtown. Then came a reception for 150 reporters, a private party for the Kitchen Cabinet, and another reception for the Friends of Ronald Reagan, whose numbers had swelled to six thousand. The campaign now began in earnest. To comply with the equal-airtime laws, Reagan took a leave from *Death Valley Days*; Robert Taylor and John Wayne agreed to fill in for him. He even gave in to flying for the first time in some twenty-five years—"Holmes told him, 'If you want to run, you gotta fly,'" Betty Adams recalled.[126] The campaign chartered a DC-3 for trips to Northern California, but Reagan used a bus or chauffeured car in the south.[127] Nancy accompanied him almost everywhere.

So did a team of Republican psychology professors hired by Spencer-Roberts with the Kitchen Cabinet's approval. Stanley Plog and Kenneth Holden had recently started a company called Behavior Science Corporation of Los Angeles, and they would come to be seen as the precursors of today's campaign consultants, who mold, advise, and direct a candidate every step of the way. "We were with him every waking moment during the entire campaign, one of the three of us," said Plog, referring to himself, Holden, and their assistant. "You'd fly up on the plane with him to Sacramento. You'd follow him into the restroom before he goes on stage, giving him a last-minute bit of advice. We were over at his home a lot, talking over issues with him, feeding [him] things, telling him, 'Look, here's three alternate programs that could grow out of your belief about this. Now which one do you like? You choose the one you like, and then we'll develop information and support it.'" Plog added, "The primary thing was to educate him on the politics and issues of California because, all along, that guy has been focused on national politics."[128]

After being holed up with Reagan for three days in a borrowed Malibu beach house, Plog and Holden made thirteen black books, each covering an important state issue, with information on five-by-eight cards that Reagan could remove and insert into a speech. "The speeches were all his, we didn't touch that," Plog said. "His short little one-liners all came from him. His ability to ad-lib in a spot was just fabulous; he could handle any situation."[129] To complement Spencer-Roberts's Citizen Politician concept, Plog and Holden dubbed Reagan's program the Creative Society. The idea was to counteract the perception of conservatives' always being against something—welfare, busing, Russia—and to reinforce Reagan's natural optimism and good humor. "Our problems are many but our capacity for solving them is immense," Reagan told his audiences. "The government is like a baby's alimentary canal," he would joke, "with a healthy appetite at one end and no responsibility at the other."[130]

Reagan lost his cool only once during the months leading up to the June primary, at a convention of the National Negro Republican Assembly in Santa Monica, when Christopher and a minor candidate implied that he was a racist for opposing the 1964 Civil Rights Act. "I resent the implication that there is any bigotry in my nature," Reagan barked. Then, flipping one of his note cards into the audience, he stalked off the stage, muttering "sons of bitches" under his breath, and drove home. Lyn Nofziger, his press secretary, followed him and, with Nancy, persuaded him to return for the cocktail party that followed the debate. Henry Salvatori was so upset when he read of the incident the next day that he told Nofziger he thought Reagan was "not smart enough or stable enough to be governor." He threatened to get former governor Goodwin Knight to run against Reagan, but Nofziger managed to talk him out of it, and he didn't say anything to Ronnie or Nancy.[131]

In contrast to Salvatori's prima donna behavior—he also had run-ins with Spencer-Roberts and Plog and Holden—Holmes Tuttle never wavered in his support for or belief in Reagan through all the ups and downs of the campaign. In addition to constantly calming down Salvatori, he was besieged with phone calls from angry Birchers who thought Reagan was abandoning the cause, as well as fretful moderates who warned that Reagan was an irredeemable right-winger. (Among the most adamant of the latter was Congressman Alphonzo Bell.) "It was a lonely and difficult time for my father," Robert Tuttle told me. "Because, of the three original Reagan supporters, he was the one who really worked day to day on the campaign. Mom and Dad were both very involved. They'd go down to the Reagan for Governor headquarters on Wilshire and Vermont, near the old I. Magnin's, and just work their hearts out. A lot of his close friends supported George Christopher, and would say to him, 'Why are you supporting this actor? Look at what Goldwater did to the party. Now you're going to do it again.' But he managed to continually reach out to the other side and say, 'If Christopher wins, we'll be on board the next day.' And he got *them* to say, 'If Reagan wins, *we'll* be on board.' And many of those people—the most prominent one was Justin Dart—came right on board.'"[132]

Reagan beat Christopher with a solid 65 percent of the vote, and several top Christopher backers were enlisted into the Kitchen Cabinet, including Dart and Leonard Firestone; Ted Cummings, the founder of the Food Giant supermarket chain and a leader in the Los Angeles Jewish community; and Arch Monson Jr., owner of a San Francisco–based theater supplies business and a prominent member of the exclusive and influential Bohemian Club. Taft Schreiber, who had also supported Christopher, was made vice chairman of the campaign's finance committee, and Jules Stein stepped up his behind-the-scenes activities. (Lew Wasserman raised money for Brown, another strike against him in Nancy's book.) After a public unity meeting of the two candidates' financial supporters at the Los Angeles Press Club, Henry Salvatori told reporters that Reagan's campaign had cost a little more than $500,000, compared to Christopher's $450,000, and that the combined forces were prepared to raise up to $700,000 for the general election.[133]

This merger of millionaires was not altogether cordial at first. Justin Dart, in particular, was seen as a Johnny-come-lately, who now wanted to run the show. As Frances Bergen said, "Justin was the original bull in the china shop. He had an enormously strong presence and could antagonize people at times." Bill Wilson remarked, "You can describe Justin in the one sentence that's been said so many times about him: Sometimes right, sometimes wrong, but never in doubt."[134] Another insider explained, "Justin thought Reagan didn't have a snowball's chance in hell of winning. That's exactly what he said. Then he and Leonard Firestone wanted to get on the bandwagon when Reagan won the primary—and there was lots of tension and anger about that. I remember Freeman Gosden had to get them all together at Eldorado to patch things up."

Still, Tuttle was happy to be working with his old fund-raising partner again. Nancy Reagan also found it reassuring to have the very rich and well-connected Dart on their side; she liked him precisely because he was so tough and effective. "The combination of Holmes and Justin, I tell you, that was a powerhouse," Nancy Reagan told me with laugh. "They did raise a lot of money. And in completely different ways. Holmes was a little smoother about it, but, boy, was he persistent."[135]

Nancy took an active interest in the fund-raising side of the campaign and kept track of who gave what. When Lee Annenberg donated $1,000 but Walter refrained, she wondered why, and he wrote a letter explaining that as a resident of Pennsylvania and a newspaper publisher he didn't think it was appropriate for him to be directly involved.[136] The Deutsches staged a melodramatic scene shortly after Reagan won the primary. "When Ronnie first ran for governor, I was a registered Democrat," Ardie recounted. "And I said to Harriet, 'I better tell Ronnie.' So the Reagans came over here for dinner, and I said, 'Ronnie, I have to tell you something. I can't vote for you. I'm not telling you because I'm such a great guy, but I don't want those vultures—Holmes and Justin—

coming at me.' I said, 'Of course I won't vote for Brown. I wouldn't vote against you. And if I were in your position, it would break up a friendship.' Ronnie got up, walked around the table, put his hands on my shoulders, and said, 'Nothing's going to break up our friendship. Vote for whoever you want.' Nancy and Harriet were crying—well, they were teary-eyed anyway."[137]

"Ronnie was wonderful," said Harriet Deutsch. "And so was Nancy." But perhaps her friend was not as pleased as Harriet seemed to think. For whatever reason, Harriet was not included in the small lunch Betsy Bloomingdale gave at home for Nancy's forty-fifth birthday—officially her forty-third.[138]

As the pace of the campaign intensified after Labor Day, Stu Spencer told Nancy that it would be helpful if she did some campaigning on her own. "I was shy in those days," she later wrote, "and terrified that I'd have to give a speech. I have often been asked why I felt that way, given all the years I had spent in theater and in film. But to me the difference is enormous. When I was acting, I wasn't being myself—I was playing a role that had been created for me. But giving a political speech is completely different. You can't hide behind a made up character, and I was far too private a person to enjoy playing myself." She finally agreed, with the proviso that she wouldn't make speeches, just take questions. As she put it, "This was a big step from simply standing up and taking a bow, but I was surprised that in fact I came to enjoy it."[139]

Spencer and Nancy had grown quite close by then, and he would remain one of her most steadfast allies. He was one of the first to understand a key factor in Ronnie's relationships: "Reagan didn't have any close friends to speak of. They were all acquaintances. Well, Robert Taylor was close. . . . Reagan went home to Mommy."[140] The wife of a prominent California Republican said, "Nancy was the one and only influence on Ronnie. The men in the Kitchen Cabinet went riding with him—they were always riding like a bunch of cowboys—but they were no closer to Ronald Reagan than those leaves on the ground over there. No matter how close you got to him, or how long you talked to him, you never got that close. No one did."

Stanley Plog took note of another lack in Reagan's makeup. While he had the capacity to engender great loyalty in the people who worked for him, he found it difficult to mediate when differences arose among them. "He would not do that," Plog said. "He is not an executive in that sense, of stepping in between his staff and saying, 'You do this and you do that.' . . . Others have traditionally done that for him. The personal relationships that are sticky like that are very disquieting for Reagan, very uncomfortable."[141]

Plog mentioned Tuttle and Salvatori as people who would handle personnel problems for the candidate. Stu Spencer realized that Nancy could also play that role.

*   *   *

Governor Brown was pleased by Reagan's victory—he considered him a lightweight who would be much easier to beat than Christopher. "Ronald Reagan for Governor of California? Absurd!" he scoffed when the actor's name first came up as a possible candidate, and his attitude hadn't really changed despite Reagan's impressive performance on the campaign trail. For a hard-bitten political veteran like Pat Brown, the so-called Citizen Politician would always be the "Professional Amateur," even when he took the Governor's Mansion right out from under his nose.[142]

It turned out that the bumbling old pro—his malapropisms were so frequent that they became known as "Brownisms"—was no match for the articulate, energetic, and astonishingly youthful-looking fifty-five-year-old movie star. During Brown's two terms, the state's population had zoomed from 15 million to 19 million,[143] and he had kept pace with new freeways, new water projects, new schools and colleges, and new jobs. By 1966, California had the highest personal income in the nation. But it also had high taxes, huge welfare rolls, and a rapidly rising crime rate. In addition, Brown was cursed with a calamitous sense of timing. He was vacationing in Greece when the Watts riots broke out in the summer of 1965, and when César Chávez and his striking grape pickers marched on Sacramento, Brown was spending Easter at Frank Sinatra's compound in Palm Springs. His inability to handle the ongoing student unrest at Berkeley—home of the Free Speech,

Filthy Speech, and Free Love movements—played into Reagan's moralistic law-and-order campaign. And when the Governor ran an ad reminding voters that an actor had shot Lincoln, even Hollywood liberals were disgusted. Up to then only a handful of entertainment personalities had actively campaigned for Reagan, including Pat Boone, Gene Autry and Dale Evans, John Wayne, and Piper Laurie. (Dick Powell had passed away in 1963, and Bill Holden, after leaving Ardis, had become such a heavy drinker that Ronnie and Nancy hardly ever saw him.) "All of a sudden Sinatra's in our camp, and a lot of others," Stu Spencer said. "Frank came aboard and stayed there."[144]

According to Henry Salvatori, Spencer-Roberts had a mole in the Brown camp who told them that the Governor's team was planning to run "a series of ads against Reagan besmirching his character involving some sexual misconduct." No such ads ever ran, but Tuttle and Salvatori felt they had to ascertain from Reagan whether there was any basis for concern. "Five or six members of our group met with him at his home and we commenced the conversation: 'Now, Ronnie, you understand that in politics you must tell us everything that has happened in your life, otherwise, you know . . .' Then we told him what Roberts's inside spy had reported, and it was at this point in the conversation when Nancy crossed the room to go out the front door. The instant we saw her, we became apprehensive and stopped talking. Reagan quickly sensed that we had come to bring up some sensitive matters, and he said, 'Fellows, I can tell from the way you stopped talking when Nancy appeared that you have something on your mind. Now, what exactly do you have in mind?' We replied by saying that we wanted to know if he ever had had any affairs with women, or something like that, that might be exploited by the opposition. He replied: 'Look, since I have known Nancy I can assure you that there is nothing to any rumor of any kind of misbehavior on my part. You can be assured that there is nothing to worry about.' "[145]

On election night, the Reagans and some of their friends gathered at Earle and Marion Jorgensen's place on Bel Air Road, which had a commanding view of Los Angeles. It would be the first of four election night buffets at the Jorgensens' house, a low-slung, spread-out ranch decorated by Billy Haines with his signature mix of Coromandel screens, Chippendale furniture, and long sofas upholstered in bold prints.

"You know how that came about?" Marion Jorgensen explained. "I was speaking to Nancy on the telephone about three o'clock in the afternoon on election day. And she said, 'I guess Holmes told you, we invited some of our friends to come down to the Biltmore Hotel at eight o'clock.' And she said, 'It's awful being here.' I said, 'Well, what are you doing?' 'Nothing.' I said, 'Well, what are you going to do until you go?' 'Nothing.' I said, 'Look, it's three o'clock. If I can get some of your friends, how about coming over to our house? I mean, very informal. Just come over about 5:30.' And they did. That was the first one, the first governor's election. I always had Ronnie's favorite thing to eat—veal stew. Loved it. And fresh coconut cake.' "[146]

The General got it all together in less than three hours, managing to round up the Salvatoris, the Wilsons, the Wrathers, Bob and Ursula Taylor, Irene Dunne, and Lorena Nidorf, Louis B. Mayer's widow, who was remarried, to Hollywood businessman Mike Nidorf.[147] The Reagans heard the news of Ronnie's victory over the radio on their way from the Jorgensens' to the Biltmore. In the end Reagan carried all but three counties. The final tally: Reagan, 3,742,913; Brown, 2,749,174.

The following night, Holmes and Virginia Tuttle gave a celebratory dinner at Perrino's for the Kitchen Cabinet, Betty Adams recalled. The biggest bash was given by Billy Haines and Jimmie Shields a few weeks later, at their house in Brentwood. Candlelit tables covered in turquoise linen cloths and spilling over with flowers were set around the pool, and the jubilant Haines toasted the Governor-elect and his wife, who, like most of her friends, was wearing a Galanos gown.[148]

CHAPTER FOURTEEN

SACRAMENTO
1967–1968

This imaginative state that popularized free-ways, supermarkets, swimming pools, drive-ins, backyard barbecues, the bare midriff, house trailers, Capri pants, hot rods, sports shirts, split-level houses and tract living has a former B-movie actor in the Governor's chair at Sacramento.

Charlotte Curtis, *The New York Times*, June 2, 1968

That is not Ronald Reagan's MO, ever, to go choose people, but instead, they gravitate to him. They would come to his attention only by getting there themselves. He would never go out and get them, or notice them and say, "Hey, come and follow me." That's not the way he operates. This is an idiosyncrasy. He never hires nor fires. He delegates and acquiesces.

Robert Walker, political adviser to Governor Reagan, 1968–1974[1]

I spent years defending *his* hair and *her* stare.

Nancy Reynolds, assistant press secretary
to Governor and Mrs. Reagan,
to author, April 2, 2003

"After Ronnie was elected, we flew up to Sacramento one morning—Nancy, Betty Wilson, and I," recalled Marion Jorgensen. "We flew up in the Fluors' airplane—Fluor Construction—in those days they could lend you an airplane and the government wouldn't get down your neck. We separated at the airport. Betty was going to help Nancy decorate Ronnie's office—she was always an amateur decorator and she had a decorating license. Well, she never did anything for anybody, but she did have a license. I was to find a restaurant where we could give a party for the Reagans before the swearing-in ceremony. See, he was going to be sworn in at one minute past midnight on New Year's Day evening. But when I went to these places, they were all going to be shut that day. I had read in a magazine about the Firehouse, so I went over there, and I thought it was charming. The owners were two brothers from San Francisco who happened to be good Republicans, and they said, 'All right, you can have it for a private party.' So that's where we gave the dinner. I remember they had those big flares as you walked through the walkway to go into the restaurant. There was a toast given that night, and I know

Earle gave it, and he said, 'To the Governor! Who knows, one day he may be our president.'"[2]

Among those applauding Earle Jorgensen's toast were the three men most responsible for launching Ronald Reagan's political career: Cy Rubel, Holmes Tuttle, and Henry Salvatori. The Bloomingdales and the Deutsches were there, too, as were the Jaquelin Humes from San Francisco. The Wilsons and the French Smiths had flown up from Los Angeles with Jack and Bunny Wrather on the company Convair.

The Firehouse guest list also included Loyal and Edith, Richard Davis and his second wife, Patricia, and Neil and Bess Reagan. Nancy's cousins Charlotte Ramage and Marguerite Grebe came from Atlanta and Chicago, respectively, with their families. Three of the four Reagan children were there: Maureen with her then husband, Lieutenant David Sills; fourteen-year-old Patti, who had complained, "How could you do this to me?," when her father phoned her at Orme on election night;[3] and eight-year-old Ron, whom everyone called the Skipper, accompanied by the Reagan housekeeper, Anne Allman. Michael was snowed in at Lake Tahoe, where his mother had taken him for the holidays.[4] Jane Wyman was not invited to any of the five-day inaugural festivities. "Why would she be?" said Marion Jorgensen, who recalled flying back to Sun Valley, the fashionable Idaho ski resort where the Jorgensens owned a condominium, the next day and skipping the rest of the week's events. "Can you imagine staying in Sacramento that long?"[5]

According to Nancy Reagan, the Sunday night swearing in was supposed to be a private affair for family and friends, to be followed by the official inauguration on Thursday, January 5. But more than thirty TV crews were waiting in the ornate rotunda of the capitol to watch Ronald Reagan assume the governorship of the most populous state in the union. As State Supreme Court Justice Marshall McComb held the four-hundred-year-old Bible of Father Junipero Serra, one of the state's first Spanish settlers, Reagan repeated the oath of office, and Nancy stood by, her big eyes brimming with pride and adoration. "Well, George, here we are on *The Late Show* again," the freshly installed Governor quipped to his old co-star Senator George Murphy, who had preceded him at the rostrum. When the laughter died down, Reagan delivered a brief and surprisingly religious speech in which he promised to try to "bring to public office the teachings and the precepts of the Prince of Peace."[6] This was clearly the son of Nelle speaking, not the heir of Barry Goldwater.

There has been much speculation as to why this ceremony was held at such an odd hour. The reason, Reagan always said, was to put a stop to Pat Brown's last-minute judge-appointing binge as soon as legally possible. The outgoing Governor had another theory. "My only guess is that it's because he believes in astrology," Brown told a reporter. "I understand he does." A San Francisco astrologer was quoted as saying, "No better time could be picked": Jupiter, the planet of kings, he explained, was high in the sky that night.[7] Even Stu Spencer had his doubts about the putative reason for the late hour. "That was the party line," he told me. "It was held at midnight because Nancy talked to [psychic] Jeane Dixon or somebody like that."[8]

After Spencer's remark was printed in *Vanity Fair* in 1998, Nancy Reagan called me to object. "It was exactly what Ronnie said. Pat Brown had sworn in eighty-four judges since the election, and Ronnie wanted to cut him off. I didn't even know Jeane Dixon at the time. I met her once in Washington. I never had any conversation with her." In his book on Reagan's governorship, Lou Cannon concludes, "The real reason for the timing of the midnight ceremony was not astrological but political," and he confirms that Brown appointed or promoted some eighty judges in the last two months of 1966, including his own brother, and that as late as January 1, 1967, he appointed his son, future governor Jerry Brown, to the State Narcotics Board.[9]

Ed Helin told me that both Pat Brown and his predecessor, Goodwin Knight, were clients of his boss, Carroll Righter. According to Helin, Righter also advised "almost all of the Kitchen Cabinet," though he was vague on specific names. Marion Jorgensen said she was not a devotee of Righter's but had consulted with other astrologers on occasion. "A lot of us did that," she said. "It was fun. But one of them said I would have a serious automobile accident in the next three months. I was so frightened I almost did have an accident. I said, 'Never again.'" What did she think of the rumor that Nancy had set the swearing-in time based on the advice of a stargazer? "Horsefeathers. She was never that big on that astrology stuff. It was not serious. At least I didn't think it was serious."[10] It seems only fair to note that while Nancy usually took the heat for relying on astrologers, Ronnie was also "incurably superstitious," in the words of Michael Deaver, who would soon become one of the Governor's closest aides. "If he emptied his pants pocket you would always find about five good-luck charms that people had sent him. I am sure he read his horoscope every day."[11]

It was almost one in the morning on January 2 when the limousine of California's new chief executive and first lady, followed by those of the Kitchen Cabinet and their wives, made its way to the Governor's Mansion, where Betty Wilson had organized a buffet supper. The ninety-year-old Victorian house bore a marked resemblance to the Addams family's residence and was in obvious need of extensive repairs, but the Infanta had done the best she could to camouflage the superficial defects of its main rooms. "Betty went in there and really fixed it up," Harriet Deutsch recalled. "She had everything done in candlelight. She didn't want the cobwebs to show. She put white camellias everyplace. Very dim lights." Marion Jorgensen added, "We all looked very peculiar. It was the day of the very short sleeveless dress—you know, Norell, Courrèges, the whole bit."[12]

Sacramento, a city of 200,000 whose major

industry after politics was fruit canning, had never seen anything quite like Nancy and her fashion-plate friends. The women of the Group may have been in their forties and fifties, but there was nothing matronly or dowdy about the way they looked. These were Sunbelt socialites, sleek, up-to-the-minute, almost Pop. The *Sacramento Union*'s Mae Belle Pendergast devoted many column inches to describing the designer outfits Nancy wore to the week's inaugural events. For the swearing in, she borrowed a black-and-white sequined Galanos cocktail dress so shiny that in photographs it looked as if it were coated in plastic. For Wednesday night's inaugural concert, which featured the San Francisco Symphony Orchestra, opera singer Marilyn Horne, and Jack Benny, she was in a "bright orange wool crepe formal gown with matching long coat." For Thursday's inaugural address on the steps of the capitol, it was a "bright-red" suit from Seventh Avenue's Ben Zuckerman. The dress that caused the most talk was the one-shoulder white Galanos gown sprinkled with diamanté daisies that Nancy wore to that evening's inaugural ball.[13] ("That was mine," she told me. "I bought it and still have it.")[14] The *Union*'s reporter was not alone in observing that the former actress, with her size-five figure, perfect tan, and stylish "artichoke" hairdo, looked a good ten years younger than her official forty-three years.[15] Others noted the resemblance to Jacqueline Kennedy, particularly in the wide-spaced eyes, the full eyebrows, the chestnut-brown bouffant, the consciously elegant clothes. And just as Jackie had had her New York hairdresser, Kenneth Battelle, fly down to Washington regularly, Nancy had Julius Bengtsson from Saks Fifth Avenue Beverly Hills spend the week in Sacramento.

In a 1979 interview for a University of California oral history project on his governorship, Reagan looked back on this first inauguration with humble pride. He recalled that after the swearing in, he took Holmes Tuttle to see the governor's office in the east wing of the capitol. Speaking on behalf of the Kitchen Cabinet, Tuttle told Reagan "to sit down in the governor's chair there, at the desk, and I did. Then he said, 'I don't know whether anyone has ever been able to say this before to a governor of California. But now you are sitting in that chair. And you don't owe any of us anything.' He said, 'All we wanted was good government. We believed that you could do that. You have no commitment, no promise to keep to anyone at all. You just do what you believe should be done.'"[16]

"And, by that time, I must say, I was eager to deal with the things that up to then I'd only been talking about," Reagan continued. "I also have to say that it wasn't too long after that Nancy and I looked at each other and said that this made anything else we'd ever done in our lives seem dull as dishwater. It was the most personally fulfilling experience I've ever had. Some nights you come home feeling ten feet tall."[17]

*　*　*

During the transition period between the election and the inauguration, the Friends of Ronald Reagan's executive committee had renamed itself the Major Appointments Task Force—with Cy Rubel staying on as chairman—and at Reagan's behest set about recruiting managers and administrators from the business world to fill the cabinet and other high positions. As Reagan explained, "I went to some of the people who had talked me into running after I was elected and I said, 'Look, I told you all I don't want to go up there alone. Now, *you* know where the bodies are. You know where the talent in California is. I don't want a screening committee to screen applicants for jobs. I want a *recruiting* committee.'"[18]

In addition to Rubel, the task force included Tuttle, Salvatori, Ed Mills, Jaquelin Hume, Leonard Firestone, Taft Schreiber, Arch Monson, and Leland Kaiser, a retired investment banker and self-described "card-carrying capitalist" from San Francisco.[19] Two weeks into their deliberations, Rubel fell seriously ill and was replaced as chairman by William French Smith, who at forty-nine was the youngest of the group. (Rubel died in June 1967.) Contrary to later accounts, Justin Dart was not a leading player at that point. Explaining that his still-growing business required his full attention, Dart said in a 1981 interview, "I was not involved with the 'nitty-gritty' of Ronald Reagan's state government anything like Holmes or Ed Mills." (Mills had recently gone to work for Holmes Tuttle Enterprises, as vice president, and was also made treasurer of the California Republican Party, part of the takeover of the party apparatus by the Kitchen Cabinet.) Dart couldn't resist adding, "I could get Ronald Reagan on the telephone any time of the day or night. He knew I would be [behind] him all the way."[20]

Gordon Luce, a banker who had headed Reagan's campaign in San Diego and who would soon be appointed secretary for business and transportation in Reagan's cabinet, recalled attending several task force meetings in Los Angeles. "We used to meet at the California Club, which was a popular place for those gentlemen, have lunch, have an all-day meeting, go through boxes full of people's names and personnel folders. Holmes Tuttle dominated those meetings. He was probably the closest of all the Kitchen Cabinet at that time to the Reagans. He gave it all day, all night—I mean, he worked, worked, worked."[21]

Jaquelin Hume outlined the criteria they set for appointees: "We were trying to find people who, if they took a political office, would do a good job rather than people with experience as political officeholders. And people who were philosophically dedicated to a private enterprise, conservative, profit-oriented society. . . . We felt that you do not get a clean house unless you clean house."[22]

Meanwhile, two of the bright young men from Reagan's campaign, Philip Battaglia and Thomas C. Reed, had set up a transition office at the IBM Building near the capitol in Sacramento and were also vetting applications. This parallel structure,

pitting Reagan's private court against his professional staff, would create some tensions but produce generally good results. Battaglia, a thirty-
two-year-old lawyer from Los Angeles, had been
hired as campaign chairman by Tuttle after Reagan
won the primary. His résumé was impressive:
accepted at USC law school at twenty; partner in
a top-notch firm at twenty-seven; head of the L.A.
Junior Chamber of Commerce. Battaglia made a
point of being deferential to Reagan and Nancy;
others found him high-handed and abrupt. By
election day it was clear that he would be chief of
staff for the new governor, who referred to him as
"my strong right arm."[23]

Reed, a millionaire land developer from Marin
County in his early thirties, had been the campaign's Northern California chairman. He, too, had
the credentials: first in his class at Cornell's engineering school and a master's degree from USC;
stints in the Air Force and at the Lawrence
Radiation Laboratory, where he helped design the
first hydrogen bomb. Reed had worked on
Goldwater's campaign, and began promoting
Reagan as a candidate for the presidency in 1968,
almost from the moment the governorship was
won. When he was offered the job of appointments
secretary in the new administration, he accepted
on the condition that he would serve only for the
first hundred days. Reed would remain a key political strategist for Reagan, however.[24]

The key post to fill was that of finance director,
the most powerful executive position after gover-

nor. Battaglia, Lyn Nofziger, who stayed on as press secretary, and Stu Spencer, who continued to advise Reagan, recommended Caspar Weinberger, an attorney and former assemblyman from San Francisco, but he was blackballed by Salvatori because he had supported Rockefeller in 1964 and Christopher in the primary before joining the Reagan campaign. Salvatori's personal choice for the job was Walt Disney, who declined. "We had set our sights entirely too high," the oil tycoon later said. "Our group was a little unsophisticated to think that a fellow like Walt Disney would quit his job to accept the position of finance director simply because he was a strong Reagan supporter."[25]

The $31,835 job went to Gordon Smith, who took a 75 percent cut in salary from his position at Booz Allen Hamilton, one of the four head-hunting firms that had been asked to help the task force.[26] The way Smith came to be hired says a lot about how the Kitchen Cabinet operated. William French Smith was impressed by the recommendations Gordon Smith (no relation) had made for other positions, and suggested that he himself might be suited for the finance job. French Smith took the headhunter for a drink at the home of Salvatori, who grilled him on a wide range of issues, including capital punishment. Satisfied that Smith was sufficiently conservative, Salvatori invited him for breakfast the next day with Tuttle and Schreiber. They then recommended Smith to Reagan, who had reservations about him and asked for two or three more choices. But Tuttle persisted, and

Gordon Smith was hired. "As it turned out Reagan's perception was right," Salvatori conceded. "Gordon Smith had all the necessary qualifications but he did not know how to handle people and he had no political know-how."[27]

The Kitchen Cabinet's choice, in Spencer's word, was a "disaster. They got practical when they realized, *Whoa, got a problem! This guy can't even add up what the deficit is.*"[28] Smith resigned a year later and was replaced by the pros' choice, Weinberger, who would earn Reagan's unshakable respect for his intellectual perspicacity and diligence. "Cap [is] an unusual man," Reagan said in 1979. "It is absolutely true when Cap Weinberger was only fourteen years old, he used to read the *Congressional Record* for pleasure. Cap has *a mind,* and a mind for finance; I've never seen anything like it."[29]

Nonetheless, Reagan continued to rely heavily on his rich backers for advice and support. Ronnie and Nancy returned to Pacific Palisades almost every weekend during their first two years in Sacramento, and while Nancy had fittings at Galanos or lunched at the Bistro with the gals from the Group, Reagan got together with the Kitchen Cabinet. "They would meet on Saturdays up at the Reagan home," Robert Tuttle said. "They'd just sit around and talk. They were a very congenial group of strong-willed guys. They would argue over things, there were disagreements, but basically they were all strong economic conservatives. Dad actually became assistant chief of protocol for the state. He didn't really want the job, and sure enough along comes his first duty and he has a stomach attack and couldn't fulfill it. We always teased him about it. So he promptly resigned." According to his son, Holmes Tuttle continued to spend at least half his time on politics all through Reagan's time in Sacramento. "It got to the point," Robert Tuttle said, "where our business was actually suffering because of it."[30]

Stu Spencer elaborated: "Holmes did the things that had to be done. During the first term, for example, when I said, 'Hey, we got to get the legislature back,' Holmes raised the money to let us go out and do the job. And we got it and we won it. . . . He spent a lot of time. I mean, I'd come to him at midnight and say, 'I need thirty grand for something.' He'd say, 'Go spend it!' That's the way he was."[31]

"We were in and out of Sacramento fairly often," said Hume,[32] who, along with Tuttle, became heavily involved in the Task Force on Government Efficiency and Economy, which was established shortly after Reagan took office. This project, which brought some two hundred corporate executives to government agencies for six months to find ways to cut spending on everything from telephone bills to use of office space, was the flagship of Reagan's promised Creative Society. It was also one of the more public ways in which the Kitchen Cabinet made its influence felt in Sacramento.

In April 1967, the *Los Angeles Times* ran an article by Carl Greenberg titled "Ronald Reagan's

'Kitchen Cabinet' "—the first documented use of this term in reference to the tycoons behind Reagan. Salvatori boasted that he talked to Reagan's chief of staff, Phil Battaglia, once a week, and Tuttle, French Smith, Schreiber, and Monson admitted to frequent phone calls and meetings with the Governor. But each assured the *Times* that, as Leland Kaiser put it, "There's one boss— and that's Reagan. Nobody is controlling *him*."[33] Still, the impression lingered that somehow they were.

"When I got in office then, I must say those first days were very dreary, very dark," Reagan recalled. "First of all, January and February in Sacramento are dreary and dull. Those damn tule fogs! And Nancy had to stay [in Los Angeles] till the semester ended, with our son. . . . I was over in that *old* mansion. Oh, that was the most dreary, *dismal* place in the world. It was just—to go home from the office to that—alone you know." What's more, Reagan complained, there was "controversy about everything," and he was "constantly being attacked."[34]

Even before the inauguration, Reagan's team discovered that Brown had used accounting tricks to cover up an estimated $400 million deficit.[35] In an effort to bring the budget under control, Reagan ordered a 10 percent across-the-board cut in spending for all government departments, includ- ing the state's much-heralded higher-education system. He also proposed charging tuition at state universities and colleges for the first time and, to make matters worse, in late January he helped engineer the firing of University of California president Clark Kerr by the Board of Regents, who were dissatisfied with his handling of the ongoing student unrest. Within days Reagan, who had railed against campus "beatniks and malcontents" during his campaign, was hung in effigy at Sacramento State, and protestors at U.C.-Davis staged a mock burial. California was "the laughingstock of the nation, as far as the academic community is concerned," declared the Democratic speaker of the State Assembly, Jesse "Big Daddy" Unruh.[36]

Uproar followed uproar. In February, when Battaglia asked state employees to work on Washington's and Lincoln's birthdays to save money, only 2 percent showed up. In March, Reagan asked for a $1 billion tax hike—then the largest tax increase ever proposed by a governor in the nation's history—including higher rates on personal income, corporate profits, retail sales, liquor, and cigarettes.[37] Conservatives in his own party howled even louder than the opposition. But Reagan fought back, turning to Asa Call for help in getting corporate chieftains to rein in their lobbyists.[38] Tuttle supplied the funds for a series of ninety-second filmed messages that were distributed to local TV stations, a new technique in political public relations that upset reporters, who felt they were being bypassed. Nofziger told them that was the point. "It's not a happy picture," Reagan informed his audience in the first message aired. "Our state has been looted and drained of its financial resources in a manner unique in our history," he said, laying the blame for the state's fiscal crisis at the feet of the previous administration with his usual dramatic flair. The public loved it, and his poll numbers remained high.[39] After extensive wrangling between Reagan and Unruh, the tax increase and a record $5 billion budget squeaked through the legislature.

During these same few months, Reagan was confronted with what he said were the two most difficult decisions he would make as Governor. In April he refused a plea for clemency from a black man who had murdered a white police officer while out on bail for a robbery charge; it was the first execution in the state in four years (and would be the last—the California Supreme Court overturned the state's capital punishment law in Reagan's second term).[40] Also in April, State Senator Anthony Beilenson—whose lawyer father, Laurence, had arranged the 1952 MCA waiver from SAG—introduced the Therapeutic Abortion Act, which permitted abortion in cases of rape or incest, and when the physical or mental health of the mother was endangered. Reagan anguished over his decision for months while being pulled from all sides. His top aides were split, as was the Kitchen Cabinet, and Catholic friends, including the Wilsons and Betsy Bloomingdale, made their views known to both Ronnie and Nancy. The archdiocese of Los Angeles had hired Spencer-

Roberts, and the firm arranged a meeting between Reagan and Francis Cardinal McIntyre, which only added to the controversy. Nancy suggested that Ronnie consult with Loyal, whom she called every day, according to her stepbrother, "to talk about the children or to get his advice." As a physician, Loyal approved of legalizing abortion, and Richard Davis believes that this was one instance where the doctor's purported influence was real.[41]

Reagan finally signed what was then the country's most liberal abortion law, on June 14, 1967 (and promptly wrote a letter to Betsy Bloomingdale asking her to forgive him). A year later he told a reporter that he had done "a lot of soul-searching" and had ultimately concluded that the legal concept of self-defense meant that a "woman had a right to defend herself from her unborn child."[42] (Legal abortions in California would jump from 518 in 1967 to 199,089 in 1980, and the Governor and his wife blamed psychiatrists for making a mockery of the law by recommending an abortion for any woman who claimed she might become depressed or suicidal if she gave birth to an unwanted child.)[43]

These early policy decisions surprised and disappointed Reagan's most right-wing supporters. "I really think that he is taking us for granted," said State Senator John Schmitz, a John Birch Society member and one of the few Republican legislators willing to criticize the Governor publicly. "As far as I'm concerned the words don't match up with the action." As Schmitz and other conservatives saw it, Reagan was making the government bigger, not smaller. Reagan responded in a late 1967 interview with CBS's Harry Reasoner: "I think we've got some narrow groups on both sides of the spectrum, who are well-meant and sincere," he said. "But I think that sometimes they would rather see someone go down in glorious defeat, jump off the cliff with flag flying, than recognize the practicality of trying to promote your philosophy and get it a step at a time. I try to point out to Republicans that it has taken the opposition thirty-five years to accomplish many of the things we're opposing. We can't believe that someplace out of the sunrise a man on a white horse is going to wave a wand and, if we get elected, change everything all at once."[44]

Nancy had an even harder time than Ronnie adjusting to life in Sacramento, where it seemed that her every move was scrutinized by the local press. She told *Hollywood Reporter* columnist George Christy, "When Ronnie was first elected, someone said that it wouldn't be much of a change for us, that politics was just like the picture business, that both were such public lives. But they were wrong. Politics is a completely different life. In the picture business you're protected somewhat—by the studio, by your producer, and so on. In politics you aren't protected in any way. You don't belong for a night to a theater audience; you belong to everyone all the time."[45]

Her first run-in with the press came when the

Reagans moved out of the Governor's Mansion three months after they had moved in. Nancy hated living in the old gingerbread pile, which had been built for a Gold Rush merchant in 1877 and occupied by governors and their families since the turn of the century. It was already rat-infested and creaking by the time Earl Warren lived there in the 1940s, and Goodwin Knight's wife would chide legislators who came for dinner about the need for a new official residence. Although the three-story, white frame structure had six Italian marble fireplaces in its reception rooms, beautifully carved paneling and moldings, and a lovely cupola rising above its mansard roof, it stood on a major thoroughfare in the middle of downtown and faced two gas stations and a motel. Because of the traffic, Earl Warren Jr. remembered, it was "like living over an earthquake fault."[46] Nancy worried about the Skipper being run over or the whole place going up in flames. When the fire alarm went off one afternoon that first winter, the fire marshal who came to the house told Nancy that the only way to get out of her son's room was to break a window with a dresser drawer. "That was it," said Nancy.[47]

At their own expense, the Reagans rented a six-bedroom Tudor-style house with a pool on 45th Street, a wealthy enclave on the eastern edge of the city. They called it the Executive Residence and had stationery and matchbooks made up with that moniker. When the owner put the house up for sale two years later, seventeen California businessmen, including Tuttle, Dart, Hume, Earle

Jorgensen, the Cook brothers, the Fluor brothers, and Irene Dunne's husband, Z. Wayne Griffin, purchased and remodeled it for $170,000. The Reagans continued to pay $1,250 a month in rent, until the state took over the payments in 1970.[48] Marion Jorgensen pointed out that when the group sold the house after Reagan left office, "We all made $5,000 profit—we never felt Ronnie and Nancy owed us anything."[49] Nonetheless, the press carped.

Reporters also carped when Nancy turned to her friends for help in furnishing the house and arranged for their gifts to be tax-deductible. Betsy gave her an English-style mahogany dining room table that seated twenty-four, and Marion provided the chairs. Virginia Milner, the wife of steel heir Reese Llewellyn Milner and a member of the Colleagues, donated Nancy's favorite piece—an antique French Regency fruitwood secretary—and other items reportedly totaling $17,000.[50] "The furniture belongs to the state, not to us," Nancy explained to George Christy, "but wouldn't you know that some politicians tried to make a brouhaha of it."[51]

Meanwhile, Reagan asked Leland Kaiser to raise $500,000 to build a new Governor's Mansion. The legislature had gone along with Pat Brown when he submitted plans for a glass-and-marble palazzo that would have cost $750,000; the only reason it wasn't built was that there were disagreements over its location. But Reagan's effort came under heavy attack for relying on private funding, and

Kaiser compounded the problem by sending a letter to lobbyists asking them for contributions. The project was temporarily shelved, and Kaiser was eased out of the Kitchen Cabinet.[52] However, Nancy kept on complaining—"When I go to other states and see how the governors live, I'm embarrassed"—and the press kept on carping.[53]

Nothing wounded Nancy more than a June 1968 *Saturday Evening Post* profile by Joan Didion, the dryly brilliant chronicler of California's history and society. Didion was the sister-in-law of Dominick Dunne, a good friend of the Bloomingdales', and Nancy thought the day they spent together at the 45th Street residence had gone well. Unbeknownst to Nancy, Didion had once stayed at the Governor's Mansion with Earl Warren's daughter and considered it her "favorite house in the world."[54] It is hardly surprising that she mocked the suburban Tudor Nancy was so proud of as "a stage set . . . for a woman who seems to be playing out some middle-class American woman's daydream, circa 1948."[55] Nancy was furious at Didion for implying that her constant smiling was nothing more than the obvious insincerity of a second-rate actress. From then on, whenever Didion's name came up, Nancy would snap, "Would she have liked it better if I had snarled?" Because of Didion's skill and reputation this piece would set the tone for much of the coverage of Nancy that followed—at least that is what Nancy and her friends believed.

"That article hugely affected how Nancy Reagan

responded to the press," said Betsy Bloom-ingdale's daughter-in-law Justine. "Betsy told me that Nancy was just stunned by the way she was ripped up one end and down the other. It was the first time she had been excoriated like that." As it happened, Justine's sister Serena Carroll was tak-ing a writing course taught by Joan Didion at UCLA that summer. "She talked about interviewing Nancy Reagan—repeatedly—and about how *cold* she was," Carroll told me. "Joan Didion *intensely* disliked Nancy Reagan."[56]

Apparently Didion wasn't alone. An article pub-lished a year earlier in the *California News Reporter* summed up the contradictory impressions people had of the controversial First Lady:

> She is a beautiful, charming, talented lady, a devoted mother and wife, a warm, friendly, gentle and unpretentious human being with a deep interest in flowers, art, animals and music, a frail and uncomplaining little girl out of place in the rough-and-tumble world of pol-itics.
>
> Or—she is an ambitious, shrewd, domineer-ing woman, a cold and brittle professional actress, a self-centered, demanding and determined extrovert, the cleverly-concealed but constant driving force behind a husband of far less social and political ambition.[57]

Underlying much of the criticism of Nancy during her first two years in Sacramento was the feeling that, as Bill Boyarsky writes in *The Rise of Ronald Reagan*, "Mrs. Reagan had considerable influence in running the state government." Boyarsky had been covering Reagan for the Associated Press since 1965, and later recounted being in the Governor's office one day early in the first term when Nancy happened to call. Apparently Gordon Smith, Reagan's ill-fated first finance director, had said something in a speech that contradicted a previous statement by the Governor. As Boyarsky listened, after several "Yes, dears," Reagan told his wife, "No, dear, I don't think he was being insubordinate."[58]

Lou Cannon, the capital correspondent for the *San Jose Mercury News* in those days, recalled a similar phone call from Nancy after the Black Panther leader Eldridge Cleaver had made derogatory and threatening remarks about Reagan. "But, honey," the Governor was overheard saying, "I can't have him arrested just because he said those things." Cannon was one of the first to make note of The Gaze, though he didn't use the term. "The adoration that Nancy displays for her husband is publicly expressed every time she watches a Reagan speech," he writes in *Ronnie and Jesse*, which was published in 1969. "During these moments, while other Reagan fans alternately applaud or laugh at the governor's one-liners, Nancy composes her features into a kind of transfixed adoration more appropriate to a witness of the Virgin Birth." In Cannon's estimation, Nancy was "the most formidable personality of the Reagan administration."[59]

When Reagan was asked by Harry Reasoner if he discussed major decisions with his wife, he was more frank than his aides may have wanted him to be. "We have no secrets," Reagan told the CBS newsman. "She usually knows what's on my mind and knows what's bothering me. She also, I think, knows by now . . . that a lot of my thinking is done out loud. So she usually hears a few different approaches to it, and suddenly one hits, and that's the script we go with." Reasoner also asked Nancy about the common perception that she was behind her husband's conversion to conservatism. "No, that's just not true at all," she answered, looking directly at him and smiling sweetly. "My husband is not that weak a man. And I'm not that strong a woman."[60]

Reagan tended to dismiss criticism of himself as just so many bad reviews; it was box office he cared about. But, as he explained in another 1967 TV interview, his wife had the "greatest sense of loyalty" of almost anyone he knew, especially when it came to her family. "She mans the barricades when the attacks start," he said with an admiring chuckle, "whether it's editorially, or a cartoon, or a fight here in the legislature, or someone making a statement on some controversy that we're engaged in. I have to bar the door every once in a while or she'll march forth and do battle."[61]

The Governor's wife wasn't above canceling their subscription to the relentlessly critical *Sacramento Bee*, or calling the publisher of the *Los Angeles Times* at home to complain about yet another Paul Conrad cartoon making fun of her husband. Reagan's assistant press secretary, Nancy Reynolds, who was assigned to travel with the First Lady, remembered that on their very first trip her charge lit into a fellow passenger. "I was sitting next to her," Reynolds said, "and right behind us was some guy who was tearing into Reagan's budget. She flipped that seat back, damn it, and turned around to him and said, 'You don't know what you're talking about—*that's my husband*—and you don't have the facts right!' Well, you can imagine, this guy was so *stunned* that he was like a fish. He never said another word. Then she flipped the seat back up and just sat there until we landed in L.A."[62]

Reynolds, who had covered politics for the CBS affiliate in San Francisco before being hired by Lyn Nofziger, learned early on that the Governor would not tolerate the slightest questioning of his wife's judgment. "The first week Reagan was Governor, I had set up an interview with a TV reporter from L.A., and I had him waiting in a room. I walked out into the hall and there was Nancy Reagan with Curtis Patrick, a young man who worked for the Governor. They were discussing something she wanted off the wall, and he was saying, 'Gee, I don't think we should do this.' She said, 'I want this taken down, and I want that put up.' I was afraid the reporter would hear this—it wasn't anything bad, but for some reason I thought, Oh, gee. So I went into the Governor's office, and I said, "Governor, Mrs. Reagan is out in the hall with Curtis Patrick, and they're having a lively discussion about the placement of something. I thought since we have a TV reporter in the next room, you might want to step out and tell Mrs. Reagan that there's somebody down the hall.' He looked at me in amazement and said, 'You must be mistaken. Nancy would never say or be in a position to cause any problem.' I realized from that moment that I was mistaken, and that he would always see her as he really thought about her—as the perfect wife and mother."[63]

The biggest crisis of Reagan's first year in office came in the summer of 1967, when he was forced to fire Phil Battaglia because of rumors that he was the leader of a "homosexual ring" on the Governor's staff. These charges were never proven, and, because Battaglia was married and had two adopted children, it was reported that he was leaving to return to his law practice. All this was actually the result of a coup against the egotistical and aggressive chief of staff led by Tom Reed, Lyn Nofziger, and Bill Clark, the Governor's appointments secretary, who would take Battaglia's job. "Battaglia behaved as if he ran the place," Lou Cannon later observed. "And some reporters sarcastically called him 'deputy governor' before Nofziger began using this phrase. My opinion at the time was that Battaglia patronized Reagan. He acted as if he were smarter than his boss."[64]

Battaglia had raised suspicions by the keen interest he took in Jack Kemp—the Buffalo Bills quarterback (and future congressman) who was working on the Governor's staff during his off-season that year—with whom he bought a cabin at Lake Tahoe. Kemp denied any sexual involvement with Battaglia. Battaglia was also close to the Governor's young scheduler, Richard Quinn, which added to the speculation about "homosexual activities," in Nofziger's words. "My concerns were purely political and they had to do with Reagan," Nofziger claimed. "Because he came out of the Hollywood scene, where homosexuality was almost the norm, I . . . feared that rumors would insinuate that he, too, was one. In those days that would have killed him politically."[65]

Reed, Nofziger, and Clark tried to bug Battaglia's office, had him and Kemp followed, and tracked them to a San Francisco hotel, only to discover that they stayed in separate rooms. Still, they were convinced that some kind of "hanky panky" was going on, and produced a report to give to Reagan that was mostly based on circumstantial evidence. Reed, who by then had returned to his real estate development business, informed Tuttle and French Smith that the Governor was facing a "Walter Jenkins situation," referring to the 1964 scandal surrounding the arrest of a close adviser to President Johnson in a YMCA men's room.[66]

Reagan was surprised when Tuttle, French Smith, and nine of his top aides came to see him in late August at the Hotel del Coronado in San Diego, where he was recuperating from a minor prostate operation. Reed said that Reagan "initially made excuses for Battaglia, suggesting he had been ill or under strain."[67] After an hour, however, according to Nofziger, "Reagan agreed that Battaglia and Quinn would have to go."[68] But he wouldn't confront Battaglia himself; he had Holmes Tuttle do it for him the next day. "You know who fired Phil Battaglia? Dad," Robert Tuttle told me. "I remember hearing raised voices downstairs at our house in Hancock Park. Phil was trying to get a judgeship out of it, and my father told him, 'Phil, when you walk out that door, you are no longer employed by Governor Reagan.'"[69]

Instead of disappearing, Battaglia remained in Sacramento and began using his Reagan connections on behalf of clients. Nofziger recalled, "Battaglia's behavior infuriated Nancy Reagan," who asked in exasperation, "Why doesn't someone do something about Phil?" Nofziger set about "destroying Battaglia's credibility" by confiding the details of his demise to several reporters he thought he could trust. In late September, *Newsweek* ran a blind item referring to a "top GOP presidential prospect" who had a "potentially sordid scandal on his hands," and a month later syndicated columnist Drew Pearson broke the story. Pearson inaccurately claimed that Reagan's security chief had a tape recording of a "sex orgy" at the Lake Tahoe cabin, and ominously asserted, "The most interesting speculation among political leaders in this key state of California is whether the magical charm of Governor Ronald Reagan can survive the discovery that a homosexual ring has been operating in his office."[70]

Reagan denied the story with increasing indignation at his weekly press conferences well into November, despite articles in *The New York Times* and the *Washington Star* stating that Nofziger had indeed talked to at least three journalists. Nancy was so mad at Nofziger for mishandling the situation that she refused to speak to him for five months. She had never really approved of the press secretary because of his rumpled appearance, and now she conspired with Stu Spencer, Tuttle, and Salvatori to get him fired. Nofziger finally offered to resign, telling the Governor, "I'm tired of Nancy cutting me up. . . . It just isn't worth it." Reagan replied that Nancy was doing no such thing, and persuaded Nofziger to stay through the 1968 elections. "Those who think that Ronald Reagan is run by Nancy should know that almost immediately I ceased hearing about demands that I be fired," he later wrote. "In fact, it wasn't long before she and I were back on speaking terms, where we have pretty much remained ever since."[71]

This was apparently an instance where Reagan put his foot down with his wife, but even though she had to wait several more months, in the end she got her way. And the campaign against

Nofziger may have continued without his knowing it. "We'd get phone calls from Henry Salvatori after he had seen Nofziger on the six o'clock news with his tie down and hair messed up," said Battaglia's successor, Bill Clark. "'Can't you straighten him up?' Henry would say. I heard that from several of the Kitchen Cabinet—almost in concert. 'Think about it for a moment,' I'd say, 'with Lyn standing there disheveled, doesn't it make Ron look better?'"[72]

Battaglia's downfall led to the rise of the team that would follow Reagan all the way to Washington: William P. Clark, Edwin Meese III, and Michael Deaver. As the Governor's new chief of staff, Clark, a thirty-five-year-old county lawyer and rancher who loved horseback riding, would become closer to Reagan than any other aide. In 1969, when he was appointed to a judgeship, he was succeeded by Ed Meese, a former prosecutor from Oakland who had been the Governor's legal affairs adviser. Mike Deaver served as deputy chief of staff to both Clark and Meese in Sacramento, where he became the personal favorite and political ally of Nancy Reagan. Then there was Helene von Damm, the Austrian-born dynamo who started out as Clark's secretary and then became Reagan's. Nancy Reynolds, who would grow as close to the First Lady as Deaver, completed the Reagan team.

"Ronald Reagan was the sweetest, kindest, most wonderful man to work for," Reynolds told me. "One of the great things about him was that he never equated disagreement with disloyalty. That was really important, because Mike and Lyn and I and many others could disagree with him even on policy matters. He would listen and then he'd argue back. He'd say, 'Well, now here's why I believe such-and-such.' Or, 'This is what I'm thinking.' And yet when you parted, you knew he'd never say, 'Sounds like disloyalty to me.'"[73]

The low-key, soft-spoken Clark brought an openness and calm to the Governor's office that had been missing under the controlling, peripatetic Battaglia. A fourth-generation Californian and churchgoing Catholic with a German wife and five kids, Clark had been raised as a "Jeffersonian Democrat" but changed parties in 1964 because he was impressed with the Goldwater message. He had met Reagan—on horseback, appropriately enough—when he managed his campaign in Ventura County in 1966. Both men were asked to join Rancheros Vistadores, the private riding club of which Justin Dart and Bill Wilson were long-standing members. Clark invented the "mini-memo" for Reagan, "a form of communication which the Governor liked very much—one page, four paragraphs, which started the discussion in cabinet meetings," he explained. "But I never had any aspirations for government or political work," he added. "I didn't have the fire in the belly."[74] Clark's laid-back attitude was reassuring to Reagan, but others felt that he was much more dogmatic and ambitious than he seemed.

It was Clark who assigned Deaver to what was

derisively referred to as the "Mommy watch" by staffers who found dealing with the First Lady difficult. As Clark told me, "My workload got so heavy—in the reorganization of state government, in working with the Democratic legislature—and Nancy's calls were so frequent, that I asked her first, and then the Governor, to understand that Mike could handle her requests, up to a point. But I told them that he would always keep me informed."[75] Helene von Damm noted that "Mrs. R," as everyone in the office called her, "was an extremely persistent person. If she called when Bill was in a meeting, I knew that she'd call back in half an hour. If Bill's meetings ran long enough to provoke a third call from Mrs. R, I'd call Mike Deaver and ask him to talk to her rather than have to tell her that Bill was still unavailable." According to von Damm, that was how the Nancy Reagan–Mike Deaver friendship began.

"Mrs. R didn't have the skill with people that her husband had," von Damm wrote in her memoir, *At Reagan's Side.* "In fact, where he always gave people the impression that he liked them, she, probably without knowing it, gave the opposite impression. Everyone tensed when she came into the office. I have to admit that when I heard her voice on the other end of the phone I'd always stiffen a little bit in anticipation of some criticism or other. Mrs. R was goal-oriented with people. If you were someone she thought important enough to befriend, she could pour on the charm. And she usually got the friendships she wanted. Similarly, if you worked for her or her husband, she wanted things done a certain way and would make constant demands until she was satisfied. In both cases, it seemed to me that she saw people, potential friends or employees, as means to an end, not as ends in themselves."[76]

Von Damm, a buxom brunette who was not yet thirty in 1967—and who had flown herself to San Francisco and begged for a job with Reagan's campaign after hearing him give a speech in Chicago—aroused suspicions in Nancy from the first. They gave each other a wide berth and would become openly hostile in the years to come, so there is a strong element of score-settling in von Damm's account. But even Nancy's close friends remarked about her tenaciousness. "When she gets onto something," Betsy Bloomingdale told me, "she is like a dog with a bone."[77]

"From the beginning, everybody was scared to death of Nancy," Deaver admitted. "Nancy's only interaction with the staff would be when there was a problem. She'd call up and say, 'Well, why did this happen?' Or, 'Why is Ronnie doing that?' My reaction was to tell her the truth. 'We did it because it's the right thing to do, and here's why.' 'Oh, okay.' And so pretty soon people would say, 'You can deal with *her*.' And I didn't have a problem with that. Because I liked her. So I developed a kind of personal relationship with Ronald *and* Nancy Reagan. I wasn't intimidated by either of them."[78]

According to Nancy Reynolds, "Mike had the

personality and the ability to anticipate her needs, and that's always a helpful thing. He had a great sense of PR, although that was not what he was hired for at the time. He had good instincts and she liked him. She trusted him. But she didn't just rush into it."[79] Stu Spencer, who was Deaver's political mentor, described the evolution of the alliance between the First Lady and her husband's deputy more cynically. "In the early days Mike worked at it," Spencer told me. "And then she found somebody who would carry the water when she wanted it carried."[80]

Deaver was a twenty-eight-year-old Republican Party field worker when Spencer put him in charge of the Reagan campaign in Santa Clara County. The first time Deaver saw the candidate, he thought, "My God, he has on rouge," but he soon realized that Reagan's rosy cheeks were as real as his convictions.[81] He had come to politics more by accident than by choice: he was playing piano in a San Jose cocktail lounge "for beer and sand-wiches," according to Republican politician Vernon Cristina, who "hired him for a damn little amount of money" to work for the local party organization in 1962.[82] In his senior year at San Jose State, Deaver had flirted with the idea of becoming an Episcopalian priest, but upon graduation in 1960 he opted for a job in sales with IBM, which he found so boring that he took off on an around-the-world trip with a college buddy. Restless by nature, easily impressed by glamour and power, gregari-

ous and charming, Deaver was one of those people who needed to be in the middle of things.

"My roots were lower middle class, not unlike
Reagan's," he wrote in his memoir, *Behind the
Scenes.* "We Deavers had what we needed and
not much else." His father was a Shell Oil distributor in Bakersfield, and Deaver had after-school and
summer jobs as a paper boy, soda jerk, fry cook,
ditch digger, meter reader, and offset printer. His
family was the last on the block to have a TV set;[83]
perhaps he watched it more intently as a result, for
somehow he developed a keen visual sense that
would serve him well in the image-obsessed world
of modern American politics. This attribute had
particular appeal to Nancy Reagan, who shared
his understanding of how much appearances mattered, even if she seemed better at shaping her
husband's public persona than her own. In fact,
Deaver later said, it was Nancy who first saw in
him "a quality I wasn't at all sure I possessed: the
instinct for how the media operates and how to
best present Ronald Reagan to it."

Soon we were huddling on scheduling, politics, the press, speeches, and other affairs
of state. I had fully expected to learn the
lion's share of politics at the side of Ronald
Reagan. . . . But Nancy proved to be a shrewd
political player in her own right. She forced me
to get in front of the governor, promoting
issues where [she] and I found common
cause. She also taught me ways to win him

over, ones other aides were unaware of. If you want to prevail on Reagan, she advised, never use blatant, crass politics as a tool to pull him in your direction. If I were to say that going to a certain event or supporting a certain bill would mean "political death" for him, he would dismiss my argument out of hand. But if I said that his support of this bill or his attendance at this event would hurt folks or damage a cause, Reagan would want to know more and would often end up taking my side if I could prove my case. . . . Nancy knew this was often the only way to move an inherently stubborn man, perhaps because she had a stubborn streak of her own.

Reagan surely had an inkling of what was going on—in conversations with Deaver he would refer to Nancy as "your phone pal." But, Deaver recalled, he "never once questioned my relationship with Nancy or asked how I was able to get along with her so well. I think he was comforted knowing his wife had a confidant within the inner circle."[84]

Deaver had one more thing going for him with Nancy. He could make her laugh, even when he was telling her something she didn't want to hear.

Shortly after going to work for Reagan in Sacramento, Deaver met his future wife, the California-born, Smith-educated Carolyn Judy, who had also worked on the campaign. "I was dating Helene von Damm," he recalled. "We drove to the opera one night in San Francisco and she suggested we stop by a party at the apartment of a friend of hers. The friend was Carolyn."[85] Six months later Mike and Carolyn were married; their first child, Amanda, was born in Sacramento, their second, Blair, just after the end of Reagan's second term. "Nancy liked Carolyn," Reynolds said, and she sometimes turned to the younger woman for advice on how to deal with Patti's rebelliousness. Reagan also became fond of both Deavers; looking back on her husband's long career with the future president, the down-to-earth Carolyn joked, "When I married Mike Deaver, I didn't know I was also marrying Ronald and Nancy Reagan."[86]

As close as they were, the Deavers were invited to the Executive Residence mostly for major functions, and then Mike would liven things up by playing the piano. Helene von Damm told me, "I would say the Reagans were rather—I don't know if 'aloof' is the right word—not unfriendly, but there was always a certain distance with the staff. Ronald Reagan was always a rather formal person, very respectful. He would hold the door open for the last file clerk. He was extremely easy to work for, totally undemanding, grateful for whatever you brought him—he would even sharpen his own pencils. But he didn't socialize in that sense."[87]

It was the same way with Nancy Reynolds, who von Damm insists was the closest of all during the gubernatorial years, and whom Nancy Reagan called "my close friend and right arm." "I never had dinner with just Ron and Nancy at the house in Sacramento," Reynolds told me. "They really wanted to be private people. They loved being alone. You know, Ronald Reagan was a gregarious guy, but he could spend many days and nights alone, or with Nancy, and be perfectly happy. When he came in that door after a terrible day with the legislature, there were always flowers and a wonderful, quiet meal, with no telephone going off. I think he was enormously grateful to Nancy for creating this wonderful sanctuary."[88]

"The pols never could figure it out," Deaver said. "They kept asking, 'Why doesn't this guy go out and drink with us?' Because the Reagans were kind of a fifties family, that's why. They wanted to be together in the evening." Nancy agreed: "I remember in Sacramento there was a place called Frank Fat's, and they would all go over there. Not Ronnie. Ronnie would come right home."[89]

Other staffers found the Governor remote, the First Lady dismissive, and their standoffishness problematic. "In his initial years in Sacramento [Reagan] exuded an attitude of intolerance for legislators," said Paul Haerle, who succeeded Tom Reed as appointments secretary. "This was reinforced by the fact his wife [was] hardly the ideal person to rub shoulders with legislators. None of them were wealthy. None of them, with very few exceptions, measured up socially to what she was used to in Pacific Palisades and the group they ran with socially there. So there was a sort of an ill-

disguised contempt running from Nancy to legislators and legislators' wives."

Clark attempted to rectify the problem by setting
up meetings between Reagan and individual legislators or small groups, rather than having him "just
go make speeches to them en masse and then
leave." Haerle continued, "It was very difficult still,
to get him to mix *socially*. The thing Ronald
Reagan did least well is go across to the
Comstock Club in Sacramento and have a drink
with *the boys*. It was like pulling teeth to get him to
do that. He would invite them out to his . . . rented
mansion . . . and there would be dinner parties
there for groups of legislators and their wives. But
the parties were quite rigid, and the legislators
were always let know one way or another that
about 9:30 or ten o'clock they were expected to go
home, please."[90]

There is a scene in the 1967 documentary
Nancy: Portrait of a Politician's Wife that shows
how naive she was about her role, and how different or disconnected she was from the typical
spouse of a government official. California's new
First Lady is giving a tour of the office she redeco-
rated for her husband to the new First Ladies of
Arizona and Oregon. Nancy is perfectly coiffed and
made up, with the barest hint of coral lipstick,
wearing a trendy chemise in a black-and-white Op
Art print. Her guests are wearing prim blouses over
straight skirts and have schoolteachers' hairdos.
"This is the study I did for Ronnie's birthday,"
Nancy tells them as they enter the wood-paneled

inner office, which has English-style mahogany furniture and warm red carpeting.

"What a nice present," says the First Lady of Oregon, Mrs. Tom McCall.

"And there are the jellybeans," says Nancy, pointing to a big apothecary jar on the Governor's desk. "You've heard about our jellybeans?"

"No, I don't know about your jellybeans," Mrs. McCall replies.

"Well, Ronnie loves jellybeans, and I discovered over many years that there are jellybeans—and *jellybeans*."

"You mean they aren't all the same?" asks Arizona's first lady, Mrs. Jack Williams.

"Uh-uh. Uh-uh. And the best kinds are little tiny ones—they have the best flavor."

"Is this your son's decision?" Oregon again.

"This is my husband! When I said Ronnie, I meant big Ronnie."

The wives of the Governors of Arizona and Oregon try hard not to look too amazed, then titter along with the Governor of California's wife, who goes on about the jellybeans: "So anyway, there's a special place that I get them. And this friend of ours gave us this container to have in the office. And when I first put it in here, all the other men would come in and say, 'Oh, really, jellybeans.' Now the first thing they do is come in and head for this, and I have to constantly keep it filled."[91]

"July 8, 1967: Dinner for Governor and Mrs. Reagan . . ." Betsy Bloomingdale was reading from her party book. "Caviar cream cheese, quenelles of salmon, medallions of veal. We had eighty-six people. It was an interesting sort of list." She reeled off the names: "Bill and Betty Adams, the Brissons—that's Rosalind Russell—the Bennys, the Bergens, the de Cordovas, Lady Colefax, Sammy Cahn—you know, the famous songwriter—the Dohenys, the Douglases, the Deutsches, one Dunne—that would be Dominick, or was it Irene? Bill Frye, Sophie Gimbel—oh, yes, she came from New York—Jimmy Galanos, Richard Gully, the Jorgensens, the Tom Joneses—he's Northrop Aviation, the LeRoys, the Lohmans, the Millands, one May—it must have been Anita because Tom died somewhere in there—the Minnellis, Lorena Nidorf, the Perkinses—that would be Erlenne and Voltaire—the Starks, the Steins, the Schreibers, the Smiths—Jean and Bill—the Thorntons—Tex Thornton was Litton Industries—Lady Caroline Townshend—whoever the hell that is—and, of course, the Wilsons." The indefatigable Betsy had also recorded those unable to attend, including the Tuttles, the Salvatoris, and the Darts, as well as the Jimmy Stewarts and Cesar Romero.[92]

Carolyn Deaver told me, "The Reagans had two lives, one in Sacramento and one in Los Angeles."[93] The couple who had once been thought of as hopelessly B-list were now the highest-ranking personages in the state, and the social stock of their friends and backers in Beverly Hills and Bel Air was soaring. Even stuffy San Francisco society had to take notice; Nancy seized every opportunity to flee Sacramento for luncheons and charity events in the City by the Bay, only an hour's drive away. At the September 1967 opening of the San Francisco Opera, she stole the show in a black-velvet Galanos coatdress set with crystals and rhinestones, and the Reagans would continue to attend the opera's white-tie opening night throughout his governorship.

But it was in Los Angeles that the couple truly reigned, and there that the social rituals that would turn the Reagan Group into something akin to a royal court took hold. The first of these was Nancy's annual birthday celebration, which began as a ladies' lunch at Betty Adams's house in July 1967. "I had a cozy little group—Amelia Gray, Betsy, Harriet, Marion, Erlenne, Mary Jane, and Betty Wilson," Betty Adams told me.[94] This lunch was later moved to the Bistro, and some years was supplemented by a coed dinner at Chasen's for a larger group, including Mervyn and Kitty LeRoy, Jules and Doris Stein, Billy Haines and Jimmie Shields, and, if they were in town, Walter and Lee Annenberg. The Tuttles, Salvatoris, and Darts were included in the dinners, but Virginia, Grace, and Punky were not part of the lunches. "She usually had the same group," Betsy Bloomingdale explained. "Because what we did then was to have her pick one thing out, and everybody bought it— maybe a very nice chain from Ruser, which used to be *the* jeweler. You know, instead of everybody bringing her lots of things that she didn't need."[95]

In 1968, Betty Wilson launched the Western-theme party that would be given every Fourth of July weekend as part of Nancy's birthday festivities. The first two or three were tailgate picnics on an undeveloped piece of property the Wilsons had bought in Temecula, a remote area of Riverside County southeast of Los Angeles. "It was pretty land," said Bill Wilson. "It had some nice oak trees. But there was nothing there, so we had to take tables and benches and barbecues down there. Ronnie used to insist on taking a couple of .22 rifles, because he couldn't stand the idea of these little ground squirrels chewing up the roots of the trees. So if one of them would pop his head out of a hole, Ronnie would take a shot at him and see if he could get him. His security guys would really go into orbit when Ronnie would hand me a rifle and we'd start walking out through the bushes. But I think Ronnie did that pretty much to tease them, as well as so the two of us could just go out and have some fun shooting gophers or ground squirrels together."[96]

"There was nothing there," Marion Jorgensen said of the first party at Temecula. "They had a little landing strip, and Tex Thornton flew us down on his plane—Irene Dunne, Earle, and me. It was a Cessna, it didn't hold more than about six people. I remember sitting on logs. We spread out everything on the ground. It really was a picnic."[97]

The Reagans, the French Smiths, and the Schreibers had all bought tracts adjoining the Wilsons' that year. The developers of the area called it Rancho California, and there was an understanding that roads and utilities would be extended into it. The Reagans paid $347,000 for their 778 acres, which they could well afford, having sold the Malibu Canyon ranch to 20th Century Fox for $1.9 million just before he became Governor. By the early 1970s, with Rancho California still undeveloped, the Wilsons bought an avocado farm north of Santa Barbara, and Betty started giving Nancy's Western parties there. A few years later, the Wilsons acquired a huge spread in northern Mexico, and the Reagans bought the 688-acre Rancho del Cielo, on a mountaintop above the Wilsons' old avocado farm, for $527,000, and sold their Rancho California tract for $856,000. From then on, Betty Wilson, joined by Marion Jorgensen, hosted the outdoor parties for Nancy at the Reagans' ranch. By then the hot dogs and hamburgers were catered by Chasen's, but everyone still came in checked shirts, jeans, boots, and cowboy hats.[98]

According to both Ronnie and Nancy, selling their beloved Malibu Canyon ranch was an emotional wrench; it was where they had courted, where Nancy got to know Maureen and Michael, where they took Patti and the Skipper on weekends. It also made Reagan an out-and-out millionaire for the first time in his life; he told Lou Cannon in 1968, "I could not have run for office unless I sold the ranch." Sacramento reporters, including Cannon, "smelled a sweetheart deal," as the highly lucrative sale had been worked out by Jules Stein and Taft Schreiber with Fox chief Darryl Zanuck, who was also a Reagan supporter.[99]

Reagan had paid $85,000 for the 290-acre property in 1951, or about $293 an acre. In December 1966 he sold 236 acres to Fox, which owned 2,500 adjacent acres that the studio used as a location for its Westerns. The $1.9 million purchase price worked out to $8,178 per acre, or a profit of more than 2,500 percent. French Smith was Reagan's lawyer for the sale and became one of three trustees of the blind trust established for the Reagans the day he became Governor—the other two were Bill Wilson and Jules Stein. Justin Dart would replace the aging Stein a few years later, but Oppenheimer Industries, a Kansas City–based investment firm run by a son of Doris Stein's from her first marriage, continued to manage the trust's assets. Meanwhile, Reagan had retained fifty-four acres at Malibu Canyon and used it as a down payment of $165,000 on the Rancho California land in 1968; a year later a New York–based corporation controlled by Jules Stein bought the fifty-four acres from the Rancho California developers for the same price.

Two more factors would make these transactions appear suspicious: in 1968, Reagan signed a tax bill advantageous to Fox and several other movie companies that had been vetoed by Pat Brown; and in 1974, just before he left office, the State Park and Recreation Board purchased the entire Fox property, including the former Reagan ranch, for $4.8 million, or $1,800 an acre.

Numerous investigations and a lawsuit by a local Democrat, however, produced conflicting opinions regarding fluctuating real estate values but no evidence of wrongdoing on the part of Stein or Reagan.[100]

One last note about Malibu Canyon: in the next-to-last segment of *Portrait of a Politician's Wife*, Nancy and Betsy are sitting in the back of a Lincoln Continental, being driven to the ranch for a farewell visit, Nancy in a white button-down shirt, jeans, and Keds, Betsy in an apricot silk blouse and pants with matching sandals. "Does the ranch have a name?" asks Betsy. "We named it Yearling Row," says Nancy, "because yearling was the business of the ranch, and row after *Kings Row*." "Oh, that's marvelous," says Betsy, presumably unaware of the Jane Wyman connection.[101]

In August 1968, Betsy Bloomingdale was at Nancy's side at the Republican National Convention in Miami Beach, where Reagan sought the party's presidential nomination, some felt prematurely. So were Marion Jorgensen and Betty Wilson—all the women chipped in and brought along Julius Bengtsson to keep their bouffants crisp and high in the humidity of South Florida in summer. Alfred Bloomingdale, Earle Jorgensen, and Bill Wilson were part of the California delegation, which was chaired by William French Smith and pledged to Reagan as a favorite son. Although most observers thought Richard Nixon, making an extraordinary comeback from the defeats of 1960 and 1962, was all but assured of the nomination, the Kitchen Cabinet was not about to give up. As Holmes Tuttle recounted, "We went from delegation to delegation. Len Firestone was right there. He would talk to one, I'd talk to the next one. Justin Dart, Henry Salvatori, Taft Schreiber, Raymond Lee, Lee Kaiser, [Jack] Hume, all of us were there. There wasn't any question who we wanted. We knew the kind of Governor he had been; we knew what he stood for; we knew that was who we needed back at the White House."[102]

More than the stay-at-home evenings and the run-away weekends, Reagan's ostensibly reluctant quest for the presidency barely a year after he had arrived in the state capital made many feel that the movie star governor and his social queen wife saw Sacramento as a mere stepping-stone to higher ground. During his campaign, he had promised to serve a full term as governor, and he continued to insist until the very eve of the balloting in Miami that he wasn't running for anything, just keeping his delegation unified. As far as the press was concerned, Reagan had been thrust into the front row of possible GOP nominees simply by virtue of his landslide victory in 1966: three days after that election, *The New York Times* ran a front-page story listing him as one of four leading contenders, along with Nixon, who had moved to New York and turned himself into the workhorse of the Republican Party; Governor George Romney of Michigan, a likable centrist; and Senator-elect Charles Percy of Illinois, a forty-eight-year-old corporate star with a handsome wife.[103] Nixon worried about Reagan from day one. Bill Buckley told me, "Nixon asked me how did I account for Reagan's success. This was just after he was elected Governor. And he spoke about him in terms of a presidential perspective. I said, 'He's a Hollywood actor.' And he said, 'Anybody who wins California by one million votes is a presidential candidate.'"[104] One suspects that the savvy Nixon also realized that Reagan's public appeal far outdistanced his. As Sue Cummings, the wife of Kitchen Cabinet member Ted Cummings, who knew both men quite well, said, "You had to know Nixon to like him. You didn't have to know Reagan to love him."[105]

As both Cannon and Garry Wills have pointed out, the anointing triumvirate of Rubel, Tuttle, and Salvatori had always wanted to elect a president; they had become interested in the charismatic actor only after their original favorite, Goldwater, stumbled. The idea of taking Reagan all the way to the White House was, at the very least, in the air early on. Jean French Smith told me that after hearing Reagan speak at the Ambassador Hotel the night of Goldwater's defeat, she turned to her husband and said, "That man ought to run for president."[106] Robert Tuttle remembered his father coming home from one of the first Major Appointments Task Force meetings and repeating what Jaquelin Hume had said: "Gentlemen, we don't have gubernatorial material here, we have presidential material."[107]

Henry Salvatori didn't discourage the notion in an interview he gave a couple of months into the first gubernatorial term. "People criticize Ronnie for having no political experience," he told Doris Klein of the Associated Press. "But he has a great image, a way to get through to people. . . . Look at John F. Kennedy. He didn't have much of a record as a senator. But he made a great appearance—and he had a beautiful wife. So does the governor. Nancy Reagan doesn't have to take a back seat to anyone. And the governor has plenty of time between now and the nomination to make a record as an administrator. But I don't believe people in other states really care much about what's happening in California anyway."[108]

As for Reagan's own ambitions, political consultant Stanley Plog, who traveled with him during the 1966 campaign, said, "He has always wanted to be president, not governor."[109] Also worth mentioning is Reagan's reply to a letter from his most politically minded child, Maureen, written shortly after he switched parties in 1962. She had seen a newspaper item about his being approached to run for governor, and urged him to do so. "Run . . . you can win back California" were her words. "Mermie, I really appreciate your support," her father wrote in return, "but if we're going to talk about what could be, well, I could be president—ha, ha!—but of course, that's not going to happen, is it?"[110]

This attitude, at once boastful, ambivalent, and self-deprecating, would characterize the entire

1968 Reagan for President campaign. Like his run for the governorship, it began with a meeting at the house on San Onofre Drive of the Reagans and their rich backers, who would eventually spend nearly half a million dollars on the effort.[111] As Theodore H. White revealed in *The Making of the President 1968*:

> Within ten days of his election, Reagan had gathered his inner circle together, on Thursday, November 17, 1966, at his home in Pacific Palisades for a first discussion of the Presidency. There, too, was named a captain for the adventure—young Tom Reed. . . . Reed, in the next two weeks, was to engage as counsel for the campaign the master architect of the Goldwater nomination of 1964, F. Clifton White of New York. Together, the two were to draw up a meticulous master plan for seizure of the nomination, timed in five phases and date-deadlined from December, 1966 to nomination in August, 1968.[112]

Lyn Nofziger, who was present at that meeting and was one of those pushing hardest for Reagan to run, named the other participants as Battaglia, Tuttle, Salvatori, Schreiber, and Mills, all of whom were also raring to go. Only Nancy and her ally Stu Spencer, it appears, were counseling caution. According to Mike Deaver, Nancy "was skeptical from the start. I can still hear her telling Reagan and me that it was 'way too early for this kind of thinking.' "[113] Deaver, however, didn't come into the picture until after Battaglia's exit, in August 1967, and the scandal that ensued convinced nearly everyone in the Governor's office, especially the new chief of staff, Bill Clark, that it would be wise to pull back. "My position throughout was that first we had to prove ourselves in Sacramento," Clark told me. "And I thought we had a lot of work to do."[114]

That summer, Reagan saw Nixon at the Bohemian Grove, the annual encampment of the Bohemian Club of San Francisco's members and guests, an all-male event that went back to the 1870s and that in the postwar years had become the most important conclave of mainly Republican politicians and corporate chieftains in the country. The club's secret membership was said to include such Reagan backers as Asa Call, Justin Dart, Earle Jorgensen, Leonard Firestone, and Northrop chairman Thomas V. Jones. Barely a handful of staunchly conservative Hollywood people belonged—Bing Crosby, Edgar Bergen, Art Linkletter. Bill Buckley was a guest of Senator George Murphy that year, and as Buckley's biographer John Judis recounts: "At that gathering, Reagan and Nixon, who were both members, met frequently and agreed finally that Reagan would stay out of the primaries unless Nixon faltered."[115] Buckley, who had been actively courted by Nixon over the past year, had also begun a regular correspondence with Nancy Reagan at this time, and he may have influenced her cautious attitude about having her husband run.[116]

Ed Meese and Casper Weinberger also opposed a run, but Nofziger, Reed, and Clifton White, backed by the Kitchen Cabinet, pushed ahead. As Rus Walton, a junior aide close to Clark, explained, "I think [Reagan] was reluctant at first. I can't pretend that I really know personally his inner thoughts. I think that he was had. I think what came into play were not necessarily his ambitions but other people's ambitions. Maybe some of it was anti-Nixon. I don't know. What I'm trying to say is, I don't think he pushed and shoved his way to get there in '68. I think he was dragged rather than he led."[117]

As far as Nofziger could tell, Reagan "believed that if God wanted him to be President He would see that it got done."[118] Usually accompanied by Nofziger and Reed, he began flying around the country giving speeches at GOP fund-raisers while maintaining that he was a "noncandidate." When delegates to the South Carolina state convention in September started chanting, "Reagan '68! Reagan '68!" he gave them his best aw-shucks look, then blushed bright red before breaking into a great big grin that indicated how happy their chanting made him. Earlier in the year, he had agreed to debate Robert Kennedy, who had been elected to the Senate from New York after his brother's death, on the CBS program *Town Meeting of the World*, and after standing up to intense questioning by European students about the Vietnam War, he emerged as the surprise victor. That fall, following in the footsteps of such heavyweights as Harry Truman and Adlai Stevenson, he spent four days as a Chubb Fellow at Yale and again made a positive impression on those who were prepared to dismiss him as a dimwitted cowboy. After a brief visit to her alma mater, Smith College, Nancy joined him in New Haven—she wore a leopard coat over a bright green trapeze dress to one lecture—and the Reagans visited Bill and Pat Buckley at their weekend house in nearby Stamford.

By the end of 1967, Reagan had raked in some $1.5 million for the party, and a Gallup Poll of Republican county chairmen had him in second place after Nixon.[119] "There is a very real possibility," intoned Harry Reasoner on *CBS Reports*, "that Ronald Reagan, an actor who ran for his first public office just over a year ago, will be the next Republican candidate for president. This frightens some people and delights others. The people who are delighted and those who are frightened are responding to the same feeling: that the man might go all the way."[120]

To say 1968 was a tumultuous year in American politics is both an understatement and a cliché. One shocking and calamitous event followed another, throwing the plans of candidates in both parties, including the sitting President himself, into constant disarray. For Reagan, the year began with a celebration: a $1,000-a-ticket ball in Sacramento co-chaired by Tuttle and Salvatori to congratulate their protégé on completing his first year as governor. At that point, President Lyndon Johnson and Vice President Hubert Humphrey seemed all but certain to be renominated, and George Romney, backed by Nelson Rockefeller, who had vowed not to run again, was still Nixon's strongest rival for the Republican nomination. Then came the Tet Offensive on January 30, in which North Vietnamese and Vietcong forces attacked Saigon and thirty South Vietnamese provincial capitals. They were driven back after three weeks, but the sight of Communist fighters storming the American embassy on the evening news was enough to propel Senator Eugene McCarthy of Minnesota, the hero of the antiwar movement, to a near victory over Johnson in the March 12 New Hampshire primary. The next morning Robert Kennedy, realizing that the President was vulnerable, jumped into the race, and at the end of the month a worn-out LBJ gave up the fight. Vietnam also did in Governor Romney, who claimed he had been "brainwashed" by American generals and diplomats on a tour of the battlefields, a remark that sent his poll numbers into a free fall that ended with his withdrawal in late February. Nixon now looked unassailable, unless Rockefeller made a move, or Reagan got serious. Maryland's cagey Governor Spiro Agnew was trying to start a "Draft Rocky" movement and writing letters to Reagan urging him to sign on for the vice presidency.

The country was stunned once again on April 4,

by the assassination of civil rights leader Martin Luther King Jr. in Memphis and the rioting that broke out almost immediately in Washington, Boston, Chicago, Philadelphia, Detroit, and more than a hundred other cities. With thirty-nine dead, twenty thousand arrested, and fifty thousand Army troops and National Guardsmen on the streets, the political climate heated up all the more. Alabama's racist former governor George Wallace managed to get his third party registered in all fifty states; Hubert Humphrey stepped forward as the mainstream alternative to the liberal RFK and the peacenik McCarthy; Rockefeller decided to run after all; and Reagan got a little more serious by letting his name stay on the ballot in the May 28 Oregon primary. Nixon trounced him, 73 percent to 23 percent.[121] A week later Reagan's favorite-son slate was unopposed in the California primary, and Kennedy beat McCarthy decisively. Then, as the heir to Camelot exited his victory party through the Ambassador Hotel's kitchen, he was shot by Sirhan B. Sirhan, a young Palestinian disgusted by Kennedy's support of Israel in the Six Day War, and America turned upside down again.

This second Kennedy assassination seemed to have more of an effect on the Reagans than the first. It happened in their own city, in the very hotel where Reagan's political career had been launched, and like the stricken Bobby, Ronnie was running for president. "It was a terrible tragedy that all Californians took to heart," Nancy later wrote.[122] Kathy Davis, Reagan's secretary at the time, recorded her boss's state of mind the following morning, when Kennedy's condition was listed as extremely grave. The Governor looked as if he "had been up all night in front of the television. As I later found out he had. First, he asked me to reach Ethel Kennedy on the phone. I tried all day long and was never successful in getting through to her. I'm sure to this day that she doesn't know that the Governor wanted to offer the services of his father-in-law, Dr. Loyal Davis, the world renowned neurosurgeon."

Reagan's secretary also typed a soothing letter he had handwritten to Patti that day, with a curious final paragraph that seems to refer to the seer Jeane Dixon: "Isn't it strange, a few months ago our friend in Washington told me that she foresaw a tragedy for him before the election. She didn't know whether it would be in the nature of illness or of accident, but that there would be a tragedy befall him."[123]

RFK's death made Nancy even more uncertain about the wisdom of pursuing the nomination. President Johnson ordered around-the-clock Secret Service protection for all the candidates, but Nancy still worried and kept track of every death threat, even though her husband tried to keep her from finding out about them.[124] The King assassination had also shaken Nancy, as she and Ronnie had happened to be in Washington when the news broke, and witnessed the city go up in flames from their penthouse suite at the Madison Hotel. Reagan went ahead with his scheduled speech at the Women's National Press Club, but they had to be escorted to the airport by National Guardsmen.[125]

The results of the California primary should have discouraged Reagan for another reason: only 48 percent of the Republicans who turned out bothered to vote for his unopposed favorite-son slate.[126] The previous week, a *San Francisco Chronicle* poll had shown that a paltry 30 percent of Californians thought he was doing a good job. Meanwhile, a petition to have him recalled had garnered two thirds of the 780,000 signatures needed to place the proposition on the ballot in November. Though it would ultimately fall short, this uprising in his own backyard was an embarrassment to Reagan at a time when he was attempting to make a good impression on the national stage. Aside from accusing him of being generally incompetent and endangering the state's health programs and educational system, the petition charged, "Ronald Reagan is attempting to further his personal ambitions at the expense of the people of California."[127]

But adversity had a way of energizing Reagan and bringing out his competitive side. As political operative Robert Walker observed, "When we got into the summer and things began to heat up, Reagan became considerably more enthusiastic about the possibility of being nominated. We were able to get him out of Sacramento more frequently for speeches. By the time he came to the convention in Miami Beach, a great deal of his reluctance had been overcome and he felt that lightning might strike and he would have to be ready."[128]

When Goldwater wrote Reagan a letter in mid-June all but telling him to release his delegates and take the credit for clinching Nixon's inevitable victory, Reagan dismissed his advice.[129] When Rockefeller sent a secret emissary to Pacific Palisades in early July, Reagan assured him that he was "in this race for keeps."[130] With the convention only a month away, the hope was that if the two governors from opposite ends of the party could keep Nixon from winning on the first ballot, the convention would break open and one of them might emerge the nominee.

Two weeks later, on July 19, Reagan took off in a chartered jet with Tuttle, the increasingly important French Smith, White, Reed, Nofziger, and "all the reporters whom Nofizger could induce to come along" for a delegate-hunting swing through the South. Grassroots support was strong for Reagan in Dixie, but the powers that be, such as South Carolina senator Strom Thurmond and Texas senator John Tower, had been rounding up delegates for Nixon for months.[131] As Tuttle remembered the tour, from Charlottesville to Amarillo, Reagan's team heard the same refrain: "'But is he going to run?' And I said, 'Well, look, fellows, you're running if you are a "favorite son."'" But they kept pressing: 'Why doesn't he come out and say, "I'm going to be a candidate"?'"[132] Lou Cannon, who was on the trip, wrote, "Delegates in every state left me with the impression that Reagan was their emotional first choice but that the California governor's official non-candidacy had persisted for so long that Nixon had become their intellectual commitment."[133]

The Reagans arrived in Miami on Saturday, August 3, on a private plane chartered by Alfred Bloomingdale. The California delegation was housed at the Deauville Hotel. "For some reason, it had this terrible smell," said Betsy Bloomingdale, who recalled that she had to lend Nancy an iron because the hotel staff "didn't know how to press a dress properly."[134] On Sunday morning Reagan appeared on *Face the Nation* and reiterated that he was just a favorite-son candidate. He then spent the day being driven from hotel to hotel on Collins Avenue, seeking support from half a dozen state delegations. In between there was the Bloomingdales' lunch on their chartered yacht, and later Jack and Bunny Wrather's dinner at the Jockey Club "for all the Kitchen Cabinet and Ron and Nancy." Like many in the Reagan Group, Jack Wrather was worried about his friend's chances. "I don't know the best way to say it," the oil-and-entertainment tycoon later confessed, "I just thought that [it] was a little early, that the situation wasn't right for him . . . and I didn't want to see him beaten."[135]

The latest reports had Nixon anywhere from ten to fifty votes short of the 667 needed for the nomination.[136] He had also pulled ahead of Rockefeller for the first time, in a Gallup Poll released that weekend. The New York governor retained his lead in the Harris Poll and bravely stuck to his line that only he could win in November against Humphrey or McCarthy. Rockefeller's entourage included his three brothers—David, chairman of the Chase Manhattan Bank, Laurence, one of the country's foremost conservationists, and Winthrop, governor of Arkansas—as well as Professor Henry Kissinger of Harvard and the philanthropic widow Brooke Astor. (Society reporter Charlotte Curtis of *The New York Times* reported that Mrs. Astor had to cancel her private dinner dance "after complaints about its being scheduled at a beach club that excludes Jews and Negroes.")[137] The New York delegation was headquartered at the Americana Hotel, but Rocky and Happy spent much of their time at the Indian Creek Island home of Gardner Cowles, where the publisher's very social second wife, Jan, got the New York and California groups together for cocktails and, presumably, a bit of stop-Nixon plotting. The Rockefellers and the Reagans knew each other slightly from governors conferences, and Happy much preferred Ronnie to his wife. "They were so *different,*" she confided to me years later. "He was this big, warm, funny Irishman. And she was this, well, Birchite, as far as I was concerned. Now I think I was probably wrong."[138]

For his part, a confident Richard Nixon was fishing for bass in far-off Montauk, Long Island, with his buddy Robert Abplanalp, the aerosol king, and wasn't planning to arrive in Florida until Tuesday afternoon. He had his daughters, Tricia and Julie, represent him at Sunday night's obligatory gala at the Fontainebleau, along with Julie's fiancé, David Eisenhower, Ike's grandson. The Rockefellers and the Reagans breezed in and out of this $500-a-ticket Republican Party fund-raiser for two thousand, with its life-size pink pachyderm in the hotel lobby and its "special surprise guest," Thomas Dewey. Also making the Miami Beach GOP scene: Teddy Roosevelt's eighty-four-year-old daughter, Alice Longworth; A&P heir Huntington Hartford; Kleenex heir James Kimberly; New York power lawyer—and former Joe McCarthy aide—Roy Cohn; and Walter and Lee Annenberg, who were remaining studiously neutral between their good friends Nixon and Reagan.[139]

The twenty-ninth Republican National Convention officially opened on Monday morning, August 5, with an "inspirational reading" by John Wayne, titled "Why I Am Proud to Be an American." But Reagan stole the day's show by unexpectedly announcing that he was a real candidate after all. While he was making his announcement at an impromptu press conference in the Deauville's Napoleon II Room, Nancy, who was upstairs having her hair done by Julius, heard the news on the radio. She was about to have a press conference of her own, but she was so thrown by the sudden development that she had her mother, who had arrived from Chicago with Loyal the day before, greet the reporters for her. "I only know about my children from what I read in the papers," claimed Edith, who was then asked if she was a Republican. "'Oh, heavens,' she exclaimed, as if to say, perish any other thought," reported *The Washington Post*. She then declared that she was too nervous to answer any more questions.[140] When Nancy finally appeared, in a blue-and-white cotton dress by Chester Weinberg, she told the reporters, "I think it is important to a man to do something about the things he feels strongly about. Whatever satisfies and fulfills him makes for a better marriage."[141]

According to Bill Clark, "Nancy and I were in total agreement in Miami that he should not go for the presidency. And he was in agreement, too. If she hadn't been under a hairdryer when that came up, and if she had joined me, it probably could have been stopped."[142] Clearly Reagan and the Kitchen Cabinet got carried away by the intrigue, plots, and flattery of Convention Hall. As French Smith recalled, "Everywhere he went, he evoked such enthusiasm that it sort of became contagious."[143] There were rumors that morning, based on what turned out to be a fraudulent telegram, that Rockefeller's backers within the California delegation were about to bolt, breaking the unity that Reagan—and Tuttle and Salvatori—so cherished.[144] So they listened to the fired-up Nofziger and the supposedly brilliant White; to bitter William Knowland, the former senator who hated Nixon for having deprived him of the vice presidential nomination back in 1952; to Governor James Rhodes of Ohio, himself a favorite son but really a Rockefeller stalking horse—all of whom were saying that

Reagan would not be taken seriously unless he made his candidacy explicit. His announcement made headlines, though it was overshadowed a few hours later by that of Governor Agnew, who withdrew his favorite-son candidacy and threw Maryland's delegates to Nixon.

Nofziger was ecstatic about Reagan's decision to announce. Reagan aide Rus Walton remembered being greeted by the Governor's press secretary as he arrived at the Deauville. "The first thing he said to me [was], 'I want you to go down to your room and start writing an acceptance speech.' . . . I said, 'You got to be kidding.' He said, 'No, sir.' He said, 'You get down there and start drafting the acceptance speech.' Well, I tell you, I didn't put one word on a piece of paper. I sat there and thought, 'What if something happens?' Because this guy does have the luck of the Irish. You've seen it time and time again. I thought, 'Oh, boy, if he gets the nomination, I'm dead.' But he didn't."[145]

"Nancy Reagan was a model of serenity and composure as her husband was nominated Wednesday night," *Women's Wear Daily* reported. "Thousands of colored balloons tumbled from the ceiling, hundreds of neon-orange-shawled demonstrators paraded around the floor stamping on them, Reagan banners jumped in the air while the slide-trombone band blared 'California Here I Come.' The deafening noise didn't faze Nancy. Facing TV cameras at the edge of her box, in her orange-lavender-and-white high-belted Galanos with the gold buckle, she waved and shook hands with all the passersby she knew. Does she ever tire of smiling, she was asked. 'No, not now,' she smiled. She said Ronnie wouldn't be here, but that was all right. 'I'm very proud and pleased.'" (*WWD* added, "She's been perfectly groomed at every moment. She also gets first prize for looking divine under intense floodlights which do devastating damage to both Pat Nixon and Loraine Percy.")[146]

Reagan was still working the delegates on the floor and in caucus rooms around the hall when his name was placed in nomination by Ivy Baker Priest, a former U.S. treasurer and the first woman to nominate a major presidential candidate. No fewer than eleven more candidates were put forward, including favorite sons from Alaska and Hawaii. Convention chairman Congressman Gerald Ford had called the proceedings to order at 5:30, and the roll call of the states would not begin until after one in the morning. Compared to the hysterical ideological warfare of the 1964 convention, this was torture by tedium: "Hour upon hour of thundering cliché, of enervating restatement of the obvious, of prancing up and down the hall in exhaustively planned 'demonstrations'—the whole soggy business relieved only by an occasional burst of asininity," as Russell Baker so brilliantly put it.[147]

In the end, the South held for Nixon, who had spent Tuesday afternoon reassuring Southern delegates that he was against busing, Communism, and an activist Supreme Court, and who was said to have given Strom Thurmond a veto over the pick for vice president. In what *The New York Times* called "the greatest comeback since Lazarus,"[148] Nixon received 692 votes to Rockefeller's 277 and Reagan's 182. But it wasn't until Wisconsin, the next-to-the-last state, that Nixon went over the top, and for Reagan's men that was proof of how close they had come.

"We were just outgunned," said Robert Walker, who had spent five months working the South for Reagan. "They had more power than we had. If you really want to know what stopped it . . . Barry Goldwater, Strom Thurmond are the ones that stopped it. Because they were establishment Republicans at the time, in reaction to their being ostracized, if you will, by their abysmal defeat in '64. They wanted nothing more than to be respectable again and Richard Nixon gave them respectability within the Republican party." As Walker saw it, "It would have just taken one state to deny him that nomination on the first ballot, and that could have been South Carolina, it could have been Florida, it could have been Mississippi. We had all these states under the gun, and we even had Mississippi off of the floor—with [Reagan] pleading with them, when the people running the convention started calling the first ballot. So they had, of course, to go back in order to answer the call. The Governor didn't even get to finish his pitch."[149]

It was two in the morning when Reagan marched to the platform to propose that the convention make the nomination unanimous. Ford, citing the rules, tried to stop Reagan from taking this honor, just as he had hurried the roll call to keep Reagan from prying Mississippi out of Nixon's grasp. These were the kinds of machinations, the not-so-subtle slights, that Nancy Reagan noticed and remembered.

The Reagans were less unhappy with Goldwater, for whose reelection campaign in Arizona, Edith Davis had again been a significant fund-raiser.[150] After all, his advice had proven to be correct. Nor were they angry with Thurmond, who, along with Goldwater, had been very vocally urging Nixon to take Reagan as his running mate. By some accounts Reagan was on the short list until the last cut, when Spiro Agnew, the man Dick Nixon was most comfortable with, emerged as the surprise choice. That was okay with the Reagans, too. As Nancy told *The Washington Post*, "My husband feels he can implement his philosophy and ideas more as governor of California than as vice president, and I agree with that."[151]

Only the postmortems remained:

"I wrote in a column from Miami that Reagan's candidacy was almost certainly something that he undertook to do something nice for his friends. It was so obvious he was not going to win," said Bill Buckley. "Reagan called to tell me that was exactly correct—it was only because he felt an obligation to them."[152]

"I think Cliff [White] gave us a little bad advice," said Holmes Tuttle. "He felt we couldn't convince some of these people unless he was a definite candidate, you understand, instead of just being a 'favorite son.' I think we were just overoptimistic. . . . Well, we were a little premature, I'll put it that way. . . . But it was a good start."[153]

"What I remember most," said Betsy Bloomingdale, "was there were so many Secret Service we could hardly move. And the night Ronnie didn't make it, we came back to the hotel, and there was not a soul around."[154]

Ronnie and Nancy stayed in Florida for the weekend, cruising through the Keys on Alfred Bloomingdale's yacht. "Only the two of us and the crew," Reagan wrote. "That first night, we slept fourteen hours, and we felt the greatest sense of relief either of us had ever known."[155]

"Reagan limped back to Sacramento, more than a little embarrassed, to lick his political wounds," Mike Deaver recalled. "For Nancy, the convention fiasco served as confirmation of her own political antennae. After Miami, she would never again hold back her opinion on major political decisions, whatever the Gipper might be thinking; but it was always about protecting her husband, not about driving him on."[156]

"He told me afterward," Lyn Nofziger confided, "and I know he told other people, too, that he was not disappointed. He did not feel that he was really ready for the presidency."[157]

CHAPTER FIFTEEN
SACRAMENTO II
1969–1974

It was in the California period that I began to understand that there was a Reagan mystique, that it carried a force of its own, and that no matter how you tried you couldn't pin it down. I saw Reagan run for reelection as governor by running against the government. He campaigned as if he had not been part of it for four years. I can't explain it either. I only know it worked.

Michael Deaver, *Behind the Scenes*[1]

Reagan is a closet moderate and regularly practiced compromise with other consenting adult politicians in Sacramento.

Richard Whalen, *The New York Times*, February 22, 1976

Princess Salima, English-born wife of Aga Khan IV, was named the best-dressed woman in the world yesterday, nosing out the leading American entry, Mrs. Ronald Reagan.

Frederick Winship, UPI, January 7, 1972

Ronald Reagan had good reason to be pleased with himself on December 5, 1968, as he headed to Palm Springs to host the Republican Governors' Conference. The state budget was now running a surplus, and Reagan had been able to announce the first of four rebates he would give to taxpayers during his governorship. In November the Republicans had won control of the state legislature, and Nixon had beat Hubert Humphrey, the Democratic nominee, by a hair in the popular vote but decisively in the Electoral College. No governor had campaigned harder for Nixon than Reagan, who traveled to twenty-two states in the ten weeks between the convention and the election and was credited with helping Nixon keep most of the South out of George Wallace's hands.[2]

Nancy was in a cheerful mood, too, since the Reagans would be staying at Sunnylands, the Annenbergs' sumptuous estate in Rancho Mirage, along with the President-elect and his daughter Tricia. The 32,000-square-foot neo-Mayan palace had been completed two years earlier at a cost of $5 million. Set on a square mile of erstwhile desert and enclosed by pink stucco walls, with a gatehouse at the corner of Frank Sinatra and Bob Hope Drives, the house had been designed by Quincy Jones, the dean of USC's architecture school, and decorated by Billy Haines and Ted Graber in vibrant corals, yellows, and greens. Its 6,400-square-foot living room was shaped like a tent, with walls of volcanic rock and enormous picture windows looking out onto Walter's private nine-hole golf course. There was a meditation garden for Lee, still a devoted Christian Scientist, as well as a cactus garden and two hothouses, one just for orchids. The house contained a good part of the Annenbergs' art collection, including master-pieces by Monet, Renoir, Degas, Cézanne, van Gogh, Gauguin, Picasso, and Matisse.[3] The first time the Reagans had visited Sunnylands in 1967, Nancy wrote in the guest book, "Sheer heaven! How can you ever bear to tear yourself away?"[4]

"The Eisenhowers came to us for lunch while Nancy and Ronnie were our guests," Lee Annenberg said of that visit. After leaving the White House in 1961, Ike and Mamie spent their winters in a bungalow on the eleventh fairway of the Eldorado Country Club, the most exclusive of the private gated communities around Palm Springs, and the Annenbergs became their friends. "You know, when you played golf with General Eisenhower, no one ever spoke," she continued. "There was this silence. He was very serious about his golf. And he always wanted to be called 'General.' He was a chef. He loved to cook steaks, and he would put on an apron and a high, tall chef hat and do delicious barbecued steaks. They had their friends at the club—the Darts and the Gosdens and the Tuttles. The Firestones were at Thunderbird. It was like a big, happy group. They had us over from time to time, and they came here from time to time. He came here for golfing and fishing. We had the lake stocked with fish, and as he got older and it was harder for him to play golf, he would come over here and fish."[5]

The three-day Republican Governors' Conference was "quite a production," according to Helene von Damm, who was there as Bill Clark's secretary. "The Walt Disney studio masterminded the weekend. They issued each Governor a car with a personalized license plate. The entertainment, including a manufactured 'afternoon on the range' complete with cowboy hats and chaps for the men and bonnets and umbrellas for the women, and a western barbecue made getting any work done pretty challenging."[6]

Most of the governors were staying at the Riviera Hotel, but the real action was at Sunnylands. On Saturday, Walter invited Nelson Rockefeller and Gerald Ford, then the GOP minority leader in the House, to join him, Nixon, and Reagan in a round of golf. (Eisenhower had been hospitalized earlier that year and could not attend the conference.) Pointedly excluded was Maryland governor and vice president–elect Spiro Agnew, who Walter thought was "the bottom of the barrel" and who had embarrassed himself at the opening ceremony the night before by saying how pleased he was to be in "Palm Beach."[7]

"That weekend was when Nixon asked Walter to be his ambassador to Great Britain, right then and there on the spot," Lee Annenberg told me. "Walter said, 'Leave my paper? Well, maybe for two years.' Nixon said, 'Oh, you'll love it. I know you'll stay longer.'"[8] According to other accounts, a stunned

Annenberg—fearful that the confirmation process would dredge up his father's imprisonment and overturn everything he had done to restore the family name—gave Nixon a flat no at first. But Reagan, Rockefeller, and Ford all urged him to accept, and by the end of the day he had. As Nancy put it, "It was such a great opportunity for Walter, and for Lee, too."[9] The Annenbergs would be in London for almost six years, from 1969 to late 1974, and become bosom friends of the royal family.

On December 13, 1968, the *Los Angeles Times* named Nancy "Woman of the Year," an honor accompanied by an article titled "A Model First Lady." "Nancy Reagan treaded the intricate paths of politics, state and national, with never a misstep," the paper declared, and went on to commend her for doing "a job few women would envy for long if they understood the day in, day out grind that ceremonial duties can become. She was poised, friendly, informed, interested and beautifully turned out day after day, not just when she felt like it." There were laudatory quotes from her mother, Marion Jorgensen, Betty Wilson, and the recently widowed Anita May, who said, "Nancy has never changed. She has always been a wonderful wife and mother with time for her family, time for her friends, time for everybody. When my husband was ill she never came to town without coming up to see him."[10]

The kudo was but a temporary truce in the ongoing battle between the Reagans and the paper's publisher, Otis Chandler. The liberal Otis had succeeded his father as publisher in 1960 at age thirty, though the conservative Norman remained chairman of the Times Mirror Company. Under Norman the paper had turned big profits; under Otis it started winning Pulitzers. The younger Chandler's elevation had been pushed by his mother, the formidable "Buff" Chandler, over the objections of the rest of the family, who favored Norman's younger brother, Philip, a patron of the John Birch Society. The *Times* had endorsed Reagan for governor, but as David Halberstam has written in *The Powers That Be*, both Otis and Buff disapproved of him and his policies.[11] Unfortunately, Buff also found Nancy insufferable, and Buff was the power behind her son's throne.

According to Marion Jorgensen, "Otis never really took over. He was the most useless human being I ever saw in my life. It was Buff. It was all Buff. The paper gave a hard time to the Reagans. She was very snobbish about it. She had no reason not to like them. But the Chandlers were used to having their hand in, and she didn't pick Ronnie."[12]

Dorothy Buffum, as she was christened in 1901, was the daughter of the owner of Buffum's department stores in déclassé Long Beach, and she was always looked down on by her right-wing Pasadena in-laws, which may explain why she constantly nudged her husband toward the center. When Norman refused to switch his support from

Taft to Eisenhower in 1952, she told him, "No Ike, no sex," or words to that effect, and it worked.[13] The paper had been in the Chandler family—and the Republican Party's vest pocket—since 1882, when it was bought by Norman's maternal grandfather, Colonel Harrison Grey Otis. Norman took over in 1944, upon the death of his father, Harry, who was said to be the richest man in Los Angeles. Shortly after that, Buff went to work as her husband's "administrative assistant." She helped him start the afternoon *Los Angeles Mirror* in 1947, launched the Times Woman of the Year award in 1950, and won it herself the following year, for heading the Save the Hollywood Bowl Committee. Her most important accomplishment was the building of the $30 million Los Angeles County Music Center. When the downtown elite didn't come up with enough money, she turned to the Westside and ended up naming two of the center's three buildings, the Mark Taper Forum and the Ahmanson Theater, after rival Jewish savings-and-loan tycoons.[14] The third, and largest, was named the Dorothy Chandler Pavilion.

"She was tough, old Buff," said producer Jim Wharton. "She had a list of what she thought everybody should give, and you were on that list for $25,000, $50,000, $1 million, or whatever. And, boy, if you didn't come through."[15] Betsy Bloomingdale concurred: "I was terrified of her. I remember she came to dinner one night and I had on these new earrings from Harry Winston that Alfred had given me. They had these marvelous pear-shaped diamonds, and she said to Alfred, 'Just one of those little diamonds, if you gave it to the Music Center . . .' Alfred did give money, and our name is on the wall."[16] Among the Reagan Group, it was gospel that Grace Salvatori had been the *real* rainmaker of the ten-year building drive. "Gracie Salvatori raised more money right out of her telephone than Buff Chandler ever thought of raising," Marion Jorgensen told me. "We were with the Salvatoris the night the Music Center opened, in 1964. Buff Chandler got up and made a speech, talked about Welton Beckett, the architect, and never ever said one word about Gracie Salvatori. It was the worst thing I ever saw in my life. The *cruelest* worst."[17]

When the Mark Taper Forum opened in April 1967, Governor and Mrs. Reagan were photographed with Buff Chandler; Nancy was wearing her white Galanos gown from the inaugural ball. Buff Chandler liked clothes, too, and she had her dresses made by Balenciaga in Paris and Norman Norell in New York. She was also a devotee of Carroll Righter's, so much so that she once threatened to fire an editor who wanted to drop his astrology column.[18] In the picture, the two women seem worlds apart. Only a week before, Reagan's then chief aide Philip Battaglia had gone public about the Governor's unhappiness with his press coverage. Battaglia complained that it was considered perfectly proper for Mrs. Chandler to raise money from the private sector for her Music Center, "yet when a bipartisan group of private donors started a fund drive for a new Governor's residence, a seemingly parallel situation, it's tagged editorially as illegal. It makes you wonder."[19] Mrs. Chandler was not amused. The Reagans and the Bloomingdales slipped out during intermission because, it was said, they disapproved of the opening night play, John Whiting's *The Devils*, about a libertine priest and a wanton nun, which had been condemned by the archdiocese of Los Angeles and the County Board of Supervisors.[20]

In 1968, when Buff Chandler launched the Blue Ribbon 400—a women's group that would provide continuing funds for the center by requiring each of its four hundred members to donate $1,000 a year—the Governor's wife was conspicuous in her lack of support. The first meeting was held at Doris Stein's Misty Mountain, with Grace Salvatori and Anne Douglas as co-chairs, and everyone from Anita May to Virginia Tuttle as founding members. "Nancy *loathed* Buff Chandler," Betsy Bloomingdale told me. "She didn't want us to join the Blue Ribbon 400. Punky Dart and I were the last holdouts, as I recall. Marion, Betty Wilson, Erlenne, Harriet—they all joined. I never joined. I didn't really need to be involved in that, and Nancy didn't want us to be."[21]

"The paper was terrible to Ronnie all during the governor's years," Nancy Reagan recalled wearily. "And Buff was a very strong woman. But at least we knew where we stood with her. Her son was trickier. I remember the son asked us to dinner and afterward we had to go into his trophy room. It was filled with all these animal heads and guns. And he told us about shooting each one. It was as if he was trying to prove his masculinity."[22]

The fact that Betsy was almost alone in taking Nancy's side against the fearsome matriarch of the *Los Angeles Times* was an indication that by the second year of the governorship she had become first among equals at the budding Reagan court. Her husband's behind-the-scenes role had also grown during that time; it was said that Nancy called Alfred frequently to ask for his advice on anything from staff problems to how to help Ronnie deal with recalcitrant legislators. On December 31, 1968, Ronnie and Nancy were at the Bloomingdales' New Year's Eve party for the fourth year running, along with Patti and Ron and the three Bloomingdale children. That year's guest list included Cecil Beaton, Jules and Doris Stein, Freddie and Janet de Cordova, Ray and Mal Milland, Bill Frye and Jim Wharton, and Father Bill Kenney, the Paulist priest who had brought Alfred into the church. Also partaking of the champagne, caviar, and chili was the gadabout New York real estate heir who was fast becoming Nancy Reagan's best male friend: Jerry Zipkin.

Neither Nancy nor Betsy could ever remember when they met "the divine Jerome," as Pat Buckley called him, but from the late 1960s until his death in 1995 the three seemed inseparable. Betsy Bloomingdale told me that the commonly held assumption that he and Alfred had grown up together in Manhattan was not true, though they probably crossed paths at Elberon, a New Jersey shore resort frequented by well-to-do Jewish families in the 1920s. "Alfred and Jerry used to call it Albumen-by-the-Sea," she said, and her party books show that the first time Zipkin went to dinner on Delfern Drive was in 1960. Nancy Reagan told me she thought she met Zipkin at one of Anita May's parties in the 1950s. "But I'm really not sure," she said. "It just seems like he was always part of my life."[23]

In later years, Zipkin sometimes claimed that *he* had introduced Nancy and Betsy to each other. "All of a sudden, he was there," said a friend of both women, who remembered meeting him at a dinner at the Jorgensens' around the time Reagan became Governor. "Justin Dart took an instant dislike to him at that dinner. A lot of us wondered what Nancy and Betsy saw in Zipkin—all that spewing venom."

"I'll never forget, one day there was a lunch at Betsy and Alfred's," said Marion Jorgensen. "It was right after Ronnie was elected, and I don't think he was there. Jerry was walking beside me as we were leaving the dining room, and Nancy was just ahead of us with Alfred. And Jerry said, 'Look at her. She looks awful. Everything is wrong—the hair, the dress, the shoes.' And she heard him and turned around. He said, 'I *said* you look awful.' She gave him a look. But a few minutes later I see them in a corner talking. And that's when it began—their great friendship—I think."[24]

For Nancy, their bond was based on much more than clothes: "Jerry had an eye," she said in a long, wistful conversation we had a few days after he died, in 1995. "And whenever Jerry said something, he was right. He was very instinctive about people. He was a great teacher. You could learn a lot from Jerry—about art, about books, about history—if you left yourself open to it. He enjoyed teaching you. Friendship was the basis of it all. Ronnie was very fond of Jerry, too. Jerry was a big defender. God help anybody who said anything against Ronnie to Jerry. And he never forgot. *I'd* forget, but he wouldn't."[25]

Controversial, cultivated, outspoken, and hilarious, Jerry Zipkin was a know-it-all who knew everybody from Diana Vreeland and Doris Stein to Liza Minnelli and Mick Jagger. Maniacally well organized, he traveled with greeting cards, wrapping paper, and Scotch tape, "in case I'm invited to a birthday party," and finished his Christmas shopping by September, but didn't feel left out of the holiday spirit because, as he told *The New York Times*, "I'm usually advising others what to buy."[26] His fourteen-room apartment on upper Park Avenue was a jungle of objets: eighteenth-century Meissen leopards, miniature Henry Moore sculptures, a gold-leaf portrait of his shoe done by Andy Warhol in the 1950s. He played up his reputation for nastiness by collecting all kinds of snakes— vipers, asps, cobras, pythons—in crystal, bronze, silver, and porcelain, or on needlepoint pillows. But he told *House and Garden*, "If I saw a real snake, I think I'd pass out."[27]

Every June, Zipkin was at Claridge's in London for the season; every July, at the Plaza Athénée in Paris for the haute couture, followed by two or three weeks in the South of France at the Cap Ferrat villa of W. Somerset Maugham, the rich, cynical, and closeted homosexual British author who entertained international society and deposed royalty in the grand manner that Zipkin came to assume as his own. After Maugham's death in 1965, Zipkin took to floating around the Mediterranean on cosmetics king Charles Revson's yacht, the *Ultima II*. In August he headed to L.A. "He would come out with all his vermeil boxes," said set designer Jacques Mapes, "and spread them out in his room at the Beverly Hills Hotel." Mapes also told me about the night in 1965 when Zipkin came to pick him up at Kennedy Airport and insisted they have dinner in Queens. "Jerry wasn't invited to Truman Capote's Black and White Ball," Mapes explained. "He was really very, very distraught about that. And he wanted to be able to truthfully say he was out of town."[28]

Jerome Robert Zipkin, the son of Annette Goldstein and David Zipkin, a real estate operator, was born on December 18, 1914, in New York City. The family was well off but not particularly social, something young Jerry seemed determined to change as soon as possible. He first attracted the notice of *The New York Times* at age fifteen, when he recited a hymn at the dedication of the new Temple Emanu-El on Fifth Avenue. In 1932 he entered Princeton University, which accepted very few Jewish students in those days. Although he kept it secret from almost all of his friends, he was quietly expelled in his junior year for stealing a copy of Terrasi's *Life of van Gogh* from the university store. According to one friend, he had a nervous breakdown. He completed his education at Rollins College, in Winter Park, Florida, where, he liked to joke, he "majored in canoeing."[29] Mickey Ziffren, the wife of the prominent Los Angeles lawyer Paul Ziffren, was his classmate there: "We both fell in love with the same Italian exchange student—a count to boot—and I got him. Jerry wasn't visibly anything. He always kept a veil around his private life."[30]

Zipkin liked to tell friends that he spent the war "gathering information for the OSS at the Stork Club." The Veterans of the Office of Strategic Services have no record of him working for the precursor to the CIA, but it is fascinating to speculate that he may have been the agency's man on Nancy Reagan. In any case, he was always very mysterious about what he did between lunch and dinner. "I've never worked a day in my life," he would proudly announce to anyone who inquired. But he was listed as president of his father's company as early as 1941, and his good friend the designer Bill Blass told me that in the 1950s "Jerry went to his office every day. He ran the business until he realized it was interfering with his social life, so he sold it. And from then on he specialized in friendship. It became his profession."[31]

After his father's death in 1944, Zipkin started taking his mother on shopping trips to Europe. "He bought her *a lot* of clothes," said family friend Steven Kaufman, of the Pittsburgh department store dynasty. "Jerry was madly insane for her, and she for him. They were both ardent Republicans, to the point of nausea."[32] Zipkin and his mother shared the Park Avenue apartment until she died in 1974, which might explain why he was so good with grande dames—that and his passion for card games. In fact, it was a letter of introduction from his canasta chum Sophie Gimbel that brought him to his original Los Angeles patroness, Anita May. Soon he counted Claudette Colbert, Joan Bennett, and ZaSu Pitts among his closest friends. He also became "inty-inty" with Billy Haines and Jimmie Shields, as well as Mapes's companion, Ross Hunter, the producer of the 1950s Doris Day movies. In 1963, when Zipkin found out that ZaSu Pitts was terminally ill, he persuaded Hunter to offer her a part. Given this roster of friends, it seems as if a friendship with Nancy Reagan was all but inevitable.

By the late 1960s he was close to not only California's First Lady but also half the women in the Colleagues. "We always got along very well," said Marion Jorgensen. "He used to call me and say, 'I'm coming out. Can you arrange a card game?' He loved to play 10-cent canasta. So it was Carlotta Kirkeby, Kay Gable, Jerry, and me. That was our usual game. We'd start at eleven in the morning, have sandwiches right at the card table, and keep playing until 5:30. There was a lot more to Jerry than some people gave him credit for. Betty Wilson was *hysterical* over him. She never understood him at all. He scared her to death. I think she was afraid of him criticizing and going out and talking about her. She covered that up by saying she couldn't stand him."[33]

Zipkin befriended the Governor's wife's staff as well as her social set. Nancy Reynolds, the daughter of an Idaho senator, was his favorite, which meant she was not exempt from his unsolicited fashion critiques. "One time when we were in New York, I wore a sweater that I just loved, and he said, 'That is the most awful thing that I have ever seen in my life! Are you going to a Mexican fiesta?' It had bright colors, which is why I liked it, but I never wore it again."[34]

According to Reynolds, Nancy Reagan knew that Zipkin was not universally liked among her friends. "She definitely was very defensive of him. She just loved him, and she looked forward to his calls. I think she really relied on his judgment and followed his advice. She learned a lot about New York and a lot about Europe, which she didn't really have much knowledge of, from Jerry. And Jerry entertained Ronald Reagan, who was delighted his wife had that friendship she could count on. The Reagans felt he was a hundred-percenter, and in politics there are very few hundred-percenters."[35]

In January 1968, Nancy Reagan was named to the International Best Dressed List, coming in ninth out of twelve, ahead of Princess Alexandra of Kent and Faye Dunaway but behind Gloria Vanderbilt Cooper, Charlotte Ford Niarchos, Lee Radziwill, Lauren Bacall, and Lynda Bird Johnson. The list, started in Paris in 1922 and taken over by New York fashion publicist Eleanor Lambert after the war, was based on the votes of two thousand "fashion experts, designers, socialites and other observers of the international scene."[36] A place on it became so coveted in café society and jet-set circles that Lambert found herself being offered bribes of as much as $50,000 to jigger the results.[37]

Nancy was named again in 1971, and by the following year she was in second place; the Begum Aga Khan led that year's list, which included Parisian hostess São Schlumberger, designer Carolina Herrera, Cher, and Twiggy.[38] In 1974, having been on the list the requisite three times, she was elevated to the Hall of Fame, "the Valhalla of clotheshorses," as the society columnist Suzy wrote, "may they dress in peace."[39] Nancy had finally caught up with Anita May, who made the Hall of Fame in 1964, and Betsy Bloomingdale, who ascended in 1970. It took Jerry Zipkin until 1985 to get on the men's list.[40] (I can still hear the shrieks from some of the fashion editors who determined the final cut over lunch at Lambert's apartment every year whenever his name came up: "Those horrible bright linings he has put into his suits!" "Those big vulgar cuff links!" "So what if he's the First Lady's best friend!")

In January 1969, the Reagans attended the inauguration of Richard Nixon, who, according to Barry Goldwater, made a point of snubbing them.[41] They had barely arrived back in Sacramento when the Governor was confronted with a strike at Berkeley called by the Third World Liberation Front, a newly formed alliance of student radicals and outside agitators who demanded that the university set up an autonomous college for black, Asian, and Mexican studies. On February 5, after two weeks of escalating violence, including numerous attempts to firebomb university buildings and assaults on students trying to attend classes, Reagan declared "a state of extreme emergency" and sent in the California Highway Patrol. "Those who want to get an education," he said, "should be protected . . . at the point of a bayonet if necessary."[42]

Reagan's hard-line approach to campus unrest, which bedeviled him throughout his first term, won him the approval of the middle-class, law-abiding parents whose ungrateful children were taking over administration buildings at Columbia and Duke, staging sit-ins at Harvard and teach-ins at the University of Michigan, shutting down San Francisco State for months on end. "We have been picked at, sworn at, rioted against, and downgraded until we have a built-in guilt complex," he told *The New York Times* in August 1968:

> This has been compounded by the accusations of our sons and daughters who pride themselves on "telling it like it is." . . . [A]s for our generation I will make no apology. No people in all history paid a higher price for freedom. And no people have done so much to advance the dignity of man. We are called materialistic. Maybe so. . . . But our materialism has made our children the biggest, tallest, most handsome, and intelligent generation of Americans yet. They will live longer with fewer illnesses, learn more, see more of the world, and have more successes in realizing their personal dreams and ambitions than any other people in any other period of our history— because of our materialism.[43]

For Reagan, it was the Hollywood strike of 1945–46 all over again: Berkeley was a hotbed of "communism and blatant sexual misbehavior"; the protesters were "criminal anarchists" and "off-campus revolutionaries."[44] His sarcasm knew no bounds. A hippie, he liked to crack in speeches, is "a fellow who dresses like Tarzan, has hair like Jane, and smells like Cheetah." Another oft-repeated line: "Their signs said, 'Make love, not war.' But it didn't look like they could do either."[45] For some, such gauche remarks were indicative of Reagan's fundamental anti-intellectualism. Buff

21 Ronnie and Nancy at their Malibu Canyon ranch, 1954. *(Murray Garrett/Getty Images)*

22 The Reagans at the 1958 baptism of their son, Ronald Prescott, with their daughter, Patti, and the boy's godparents, Robert and Ursula Taylor. *(Reagan Family Photo Collection)*

23 Nancy in 1956 at their Pacific Palisades home, which General Electric called the House of the Future. *(A.P. Wide World Photos)*

24 Nancy with her longtime favorite designer, James Galanos, in Los Angeles, 1967. *(Bob Willoughby/ MPTV)*

25 The Reagans arriving at the funeral of their close friend Dick Powell in Beverly Hills, 1963. *(A.P. Wide World Photos)*

26 The Reagans celebrating his victory in the 1966 Republican primary for governor of California, with actor Cesar Romero. *(A.P. Wide World Photos)*

27 Nancy gazing at her husband after his swearing-in as governor in Sacramento, January 2, 1967. *(Reagan Family Photo Collection)*

28 Governor and Mrs. Reagan backstage at the opening of the San Francisco Opera with tenor Franco Bonisolli, 1969. *(A.P. Wide World Photos)*

29 The Reagans with their children, Ron and Patti, moving into the old Governor's Mansion, January 1967. *(A.P. Wide World Photos)*

30 Alfred and Betsy Bloomingdale greeting guests at a 1967 dinner they gave for Governor and Mrs. Reagan. *(Bob Willoughby/MPTV)*

31 Ronnie and Nancy with former president Dwight Eisenhower and Lee Annenberg at Sunnylands, the Annenbergs' Palm Springs estate, 1967. *(Reagan Family Photo Collection)*

32 Nancy with her New York confidant Jerry Zipkin in the 1970s. *(Reagan Family Photo Collection)*

33 Ladies of the Group in 1980: from left, Marion Jorgensen, Betty Wilson, Erlenne Sprague, Bunny Wrather, Harriet Deutsch, and Betty Adams. *(Reagan Family Photo Collection)*

34 Oilman Henry Salvatori, one of the original members of the Kitchen Cabinet, with his wife, Grace, in Los Angeles, 1979. *(George Rose/Los Angeles Times)*

35 Drugstore tycoon Justin Dart, another prominent Reagan backer, with an assortment of his company's products, 1966. *(Steve Fontanini/Los Angeles Times)*

36 Car dealer Holmes Tuttle, the leader of the Kitchen Cabinet, at home in Hancock Park, 1973. *(Fitzgerald Whitney/Los Angeles Times)*

37 Reagan's 1976 and 1980 campaign manager, John Sears III, center, with his lieutenants, Charles Black and James Lake. *(The New York Times)*

38 Reagan with his longtime press secretary, Lyn Nofziger, 1967. *(©Bettmann/Corbis)*

39 Stuart Spencer, who ran Reagan's gubernatorial campaigns but worked for Gerald Ford in 1976. *(The New York Times)*

40 Michael Deaver, the aide closest to the Reagans personally, in Sacramento and afterward. *(John Barr)*

41 Ronald Reagan campaigning for president in 1980, flanked by former president Ford and Reagan's running mate, George H.W. Bush. *(A.P. Wide World Photos)*

42 Nancy and Ronnie at Rancho del Cielo in the canoe he gave her as an anniversary gift, 1976. *(A.P. Wide World Photos)*

PHOTOS 21–42

23

24

25

26

27

28

29

30

31

32

33

34

35

36

37

38

39

40

41

42

Chandler, for example, stepped down from the University of California's Board of Regents in 1968. Reagan was happy to see her go. He appointed William French Smith in her place and made him chairman.[46]

Reagan's crackdown on the Berkeley agitators was overwhelmingly endorsed by the regents at their March 1969 meeting. Even Jesse Unruh voiced approval of the Governor's handling of the situation, perhaps because the Democrats' own polls "showed 80 percent in favor of disciplinary action against students and teachers engaged in disrupting campus life."[47] On March 14, the Third World Liberation Front announced that it was suspending the strike and entering negotiations with university officials. A "gratified" Reagan said he was glad they were taking their dispute indoors, where it should have been all along.

On March 17, Reagan bragged about the turnaround in a letter to fellow Republican governor Jack Williams of Arizona, who evidently had also had a run-in with campus rebels. "I'm convinced we win when we defy the little monsters, as you did," Reagan wrote. "Two days ago at Berkeley an outdoor rally was broken up by a thunder shower, and now the students have called off hostilities while they take their quarterly exams. We are still on the side of the angels, but a little clout here and there is in order. After all, the Lord took a club to the money changers in the temple."[48]

* * *

The Governor and First Lady began *their* spring break in Los Angeles, at a black-tie dinner dance for six hundred given by Jules and Doris Stein to celebrate the opening of the Sheraton-Universal hotel at MCA's Universal City. The Steins had flown in two planeloads of friends from New York and Paris—Emilio Pucci, Estée Lauder, Oscar and Françoise de la Renta, Kenneth Jay Lane, Adam and Sophie Gimbel, Prince Johannes von Thurn und Taxis, Clare Booth Luce, Artur Rubinstein— and greeted them at the airport with "a kilted band of Scottish bagpipers." The three-day extravaganza—medical philanthropist Mary Lasker called it "the most wonderful weekend in the history of mankind"—included the premiere of Universal Pictures's *Sweet Charity* the following night, but the Reagans, more cognizant now of how their highfalutin socializing played in Sacramento, had decided to skip that.[49]

It was just as well, because that morning brought sad news: Dwight Eisenhower had died at Walter Reed Hospital in Bethesda after a long struggle with heart disease. The Reagans went on to Phoenix as planned, but then flew to Washington for the March 31 funeral. Edgar Gillenwaters, who worked as the Governor's liaison in Washington, accompanied them to the National Cathedral and later remembered that General Charles de Gaulle, the President of France, was seated in the pew in front of them. "I was fascinated at one point to notice that his aide was writing on a small piece of paper,"

Gillenwaters said. " 'Ronald Reagan' was all I could read; it was in French. De Gaulle put the paper in his pocket and, in a most uncharacteristic move, did a complete turn around in the pew of the church and looked eyeball to eyeball with Ronald Reagan for an extended period of time. He was fascinated and probably had heard—must have heard—so much about him in order to do that uncharacteristic thing in a serious funeral setting. Then after the services were over, as we were leaving the pew, de Gaulle made a move to come to Ronald Reagan and shake his hand. It was a very extended handshake and, if you believe in 'vibes,' the exchange was loaded with vibes, back and forth. No conversation, nor [the] usual courtesies, no 'nice-to-meet-you' type exchange. He also took Nancy Reagan's hand and made the same gesture to her."[50]

Perhaps de Gaulle, whose government had nearly been toppled by rioting Paris students in 1968, and who himself would pass on in 1970, was trying to express his support for Reagan's tough stance against California's alienated youth.

On April 18, the *Berkeley Barb*, a local underground newspaper, ran a column calling for the establishment of "a cultural, political, freak-out and rap center for the Western world" on a vacant plot of university-owned land four blocks from the campus. Two days later, about one hundred street people, hippies, and New Left activists, dragging sod, plants, and playground equipment, occupied the site, which they named People's Park.[51] On April 30 the university announced that it was going ahead with plans to convert the land into athletic fields, but the squatters refused to leave. At dawn on May 15, 250 policemen moved into the makeshift park and forcibly evicted them; by noon an eight-foot-high steel-mesh fence surrounded the area, and three thousand protesters, mostly students, had gathered in Sproul Plaza outside the university's main gate. "Let's go down and take over the park!" shouted student president-elect Dan Siegal.[52]

In the ensuing "Battle of Berkeley," heavily out-numbered police and Alameda County sheriff's deputies used tear gas and shotguns loaded with birdshot to control the rock-throwing crowd. When they ran out of birdshot, they switched to buck-shot; one demonstrator was hit in the stomach and later died, another was blinded, and a highway patrolman was stabbed. In response to pleas from local law enforcement authorities, Reagan sent in two thousand National Guardsmen and imposed a curfew on the city, in effect placing Berkeley under martial law. The protesters, he said, were "chal-lenging the right of private ownership in this coun-try."[53] But the marches, violence, and arrests con-tinued for four more days, until May 20, when a low-flying National Guard helicopter tear-gassed the campus, outraging students and professors but quelling the unrest. It wasn't until June 2 that Reagan withdrew the National Guard, commending its troops for "the remarkable restraint they displayed in the face of extreme provocation."[54]

The Governor was weeping a few days later as he delivered the eulogy at the funeral of his close friend Robert Taylor, dead of lung cancer at fifty-seven. Nancy was distraught, too. "I think Bob's death hit me as hard as anything in my life," she later wrote. "The last time I saw him, I left the hospital to go back to Sacramento, telling Ursula I'd see her in a few days. I got out in the hall, and something made me turn back. I returned to his room and kissed him on the cheek. When I landed in Sacramento, they told me he had died . . . I flew back on the next plane to be with Ursula. She asked if Ronnie would deliver the eulogy and, of course, he said yes. But the morning of the funeral he confessed to me that he was afraid he wouldn't be able to get through it without breaking up."[55]

Ursula Taylor would later tell Laurence Leamer that Nancy "took over for me. . . . I was in shock. She made all the phone calls, all the arrangements, picked out my wardrobe—everything. Nancy could never separate herself from Ronnie for more than a day if she could help it, and she stayed with me several days and took care of me." Within the week, Ursula turned to Nancy again, when her twenty-three-year-old son by her first marriage, Michael Theiss, was found dead in his bed of a drug overdose. Ursula recalled that of all the condolence notes she received, sixteen-year-old Patti's was "so sensitive . . . the most beautiful."[56]

Patti, who had just started her summer vacation from Orme, remembered her father being despondent over Robert Taylor's death. He would come home from work at five every day," she recalled, "but he didn't seem part of those months." Perhaps because the double tragedy in the Taylor family made them appreciate each other more, Patti and her mother enjoyed "one of our rare cease-fires" that summer, taking sun by the pool and discussing books they'd give each other to read.[57] In August the Reagans left Sacramento for the beach house they had started renting every summer in Trancas, just north of Malibu. Nancy recalled Bill Buckley spending a night with them there when he was in Los Angeles to give a speech. "He really endeared himself to the kids," she told me. "First of all, he went swimming at midnight with flashlights. The kids thought that was just wonderful. 'Why don't you two do that?' Then the next morning he had peanut butter on toast for breakfast. That sealed it."[58]

Trancas brought out the best in the Reagans. "That was where we'd do most of our visiting as a family," Maureen wrote. "I'd try to get out there one or two days each week, depending on my work schedule. On the days that all of us were there at the same time, we'd be out body-surfing and Dad would look around and marvel, 'My goodness, all four of my pupils, all here at the same time!' "[59]

Maureen was single again, having divorced

Lieutenant Sills in 1967, and had a public relations job with Pacific Southwest Airlines. Michael was trying to make a name for himself by racing speedboats—he had won the Outboard World Championship in 1967—even while trading on his father's name by endorsing products, including the Power Mac-Six chainsaw and Hart, Schaffner and Marx suits. He had been called up for the draft in 1968, but was excused owing to a variety of medical problems, including a chronic ulcer. After he had a serious accident in a race in Texas, his father urged him to "make your hobby your real job" by selling boats instead of racing them, advice Michael chose not to take.[60]

Patti, meanwhile, was earning high grades at boarding school and fantasizing "about being in Haight-Ashbury, plaiting flowers in my hair, or at Berkeley, protesting the war."[61] In her sophomore year she had tried to run away to Alaska with the school dishwasher, but that had been forgiven; her parents didn't know she was now having an affair with her married English teacher. After she had been caught smoking in March 1968, her father wrote her a four-page letter, reminding her that cigarettes were addictive and unhealthy—Nancy had given them up under pressure from Loyal the year before—and indicating that he realized her problems went beyond sneaking smokes. "You broke not only school rules but family rules and to do this you had to resort to tricks and deception. Why is this of such great concern to the school or to me and your mother? The answer is very simple. We are concerned that you can establish a pattern of living wherein you accept dishonesty as a way of life."[62]

Young Ron was still the model son and favorite. "Why don't we just nuke 'em?" he would say when his father complained about antiwar "flag-burn-ers."[63] "Nancy was crazy about that boy, just crazy about him," said Marion Jorgensen. "And for him to say his father didn't spend enough time with him, I'm here to tell you that's not true. In fact, I think they spent too much time with him—he was spoiled rotten. They'd drag him everywhere—to the Wilsons' ranch when there were no other kids around. Earle used to say to me, 'I don't know what they're doing, bringing that kid along.' They had him underfoot every five seconds."[64] According-ing to Nancy, she tried to make her son's life as normal as possible and even had the security man who drove him to school wear a sweater instead of a jacket and a cap. But he had a hard time adjust-ing to the move from Pacific Palisades, switching schools twice before settling in at Sacramento Country Day. He was beaten up by three class-mates one day, and later told Patti that the boys had called him "warmonger" as they pummeled him.[65]

"I remember going out to watch Ron play foot-ball on his sixth-grade team," Nancy said, "and hearing the boys on the other team saying, 'There's Reagan. Let's hit him hard.' They practi-cally had to hold me back to keep me from going after those kids."[66] Nancy Reynolds told me that the Governor soon realized that his presence at the games aggravated the situation, but he tried to make it up to his son in other ways. When the assistant principal took Ron's class on a tour of the capitol, for example, Reagan not only showed them around his office but also invited them to lunch at the Executive Residence.[67]

Still, there was something odd about Ronald Reagan's approach to fatherhood. He would never let his son win a swimming race, explaining that his pretending to lose would undermine the boy's confidence "in a genuine victory achieved at a later date." After Ron finally bested him at age twelve, they never raced again.[68] When Arizona governor Jack Williams, whose daughter also attended Orme, wrote to Reagan to say that he had seen Patti singing in the school choir, and commented on her "eloquently beautiful dark eyes," as well as the loveliness of the Western sky on that particular evening, Reagan replied: "It was very kind of you to write about Patti as you did, and both Nancy and I are grateful. We would have enjoyed your letter even without reference to our daughter—your description of the beauty of the setting was so vivid."[69]

"Mike came home one day and he was very excited—'Oh, we're going to the Orient! We're going to Manila!,'" Carolyn Deaver recalled. "I heard the 'we' and was beginning to jump up and down. He said, 'No, no, no, not you. I'm going with the Reagans.' The next day I was in quite a funk about the whole thing when he came home. And he said, 'I don't know what you've done, but Nancy Reagan suggested that you come along. She said it would be fun, because they're taking Patti and Ron.'"[70]

In early September 1969, President Nixon asked Governor Reagan to represent him at the opening of the Cultural Center of the Philippines, the pet project of that country's first lady, Imelda Marcos. As much as Nixon resented Reagan's popularity, he also feared that he might mount a challenge from the right in 1972, and the largely ceremonial trip to Manila was one way of keeping Ronnie and Nancy happy. Nixon was well aware that Nancy, whom he considered "smart and tough," was her husband's "chief advisor." As he once told an aide, "Nancy Reagan runs Ronald Reagan. . . . You just can't afford to alienate [her]."[71]

The Reagans were provided with an Air Force jet and Secret Service protection, and put up at the four-hundred-year-old Malacañang Palace of President Ferdinand Marcos. "When we got off the plane, this little man kept running after me with a tape measure," Carolyn Deaver told me. "And I kept saying, 'Get away.' The next day on my bed was laid out the most beautiful Philippine dress that he had done his best to make to my size—it had those great big butterfly sleeves, and it was like getting into a birdcage. There was a little note that it was from Mrs. Marcos, and it was quite clear that she wanted me to wear it to that evening's dinner. Mike said, 'You look gorgeous.' I couldn't stand, but I did look pretty good. And I walked into the Reagans' suite, and Nancy has got on the worst-looking outfit I've ever seen. It doesn't have huge sleeves, it's not beaded, it's like a proletariat farmer's dress. This had not been by accident. Nancy said, 'Where did you get *that* dress?' I said, 'It was on my bed.' She said, '*This* was on my bed. Can you believe it?' Of course, Imelda came out in something more resplendent than ever."[72]

On their second day, while Reagan met with President Marcos, Nancy and the children were given a tour of Manila. When they passed a river-bank slum, Patti asked her mother if she felt guilty. "Of course not," Nancy answered.[73] Their cease-fire was obviously over by then. For Nancy Reynolds, who was also on the trip, "Patti was a sullen, ungrateful little girl with a lot of anger and bitterness. I never saw her have a warm glance, a warm word, a warm anything toward Nancy."[74]

"The favorable remarks about the exceptionally able manner in which you, Nancy and your children represented the United States at the opening of the Philippine Cultural Center continue to reach me," Nixon wrote to Reagan on October 8. "You were superb Ambassadors of goodwill and I just wanted you to know how much I appreciated your efforts. . . . Pat joins me in sending warm personal regards to you and Nancy."[75]

The following month the Reagans were off to London and Paris with the Bloomingdales. It was Nancy's first trip to Europe since she had toured the Continent with Edith and Loyal when she was twelve, and Ronnie's since 1949, when he filmed *The Hasty Heart* in London. "The wives flew over on one plane, and the husbands on another," Betsy Bloomingdale told me. "In those days Ronnie and Nancy didn't fly together because of the children."[76] Although this was a private trip, in London the Reagans stayed with the Annenbergs at the ambassador's residence, Winfield House. The Bloomingdales, who were not as close to Walter and Lee, took a suite at Claridge's.

As Walter Annenberg had predicted, his confirmation had been a real struggle. His predecessor at the Court of St. James's had been the quintessential Eastern establishment career diplomat David K. Bruce, whose elegant and erudite wife, Evangeline, made no secret of her dismay at their being followed by a couple she considered nouveau-riche social climbers from California. "I've never even heard of these strange people," Evangeline told friends as she set about poisoning the well for Walter and Lee in both London and Washington.[77] The Bruces' choice for the most desirable post in the U.S. diplomatic service had been CBS chairman William Paley, who along with his wife, Babe, had openly sought the appointment.[78]

More seriously, Annenberg's nomination was opposed by Democratic senator William Fulbright, chairman of the Foreign Relations Committee, and strongly criticized by *The New York Times*, which editorialized that Annenberg had bought the nomination with campaign contributions. (In fact, he had not given money to Nixon's 1968 campaign, but several of his sisters had.) When *The Washington Post* joined in with a Drew Pearson column reminding readers that Moses Annenberg had been jailed for tax evasion in the 1940s, Walter called the *Post*'s owner, Katharine Graham, and accused her of betraying their friendship. Graham found herself in an awkward position: she was scheduled to host a dinner in honor of the Annenbergs at her house in Georgetown a few days later, following Walter's Senate confirmation hearings. Wanting to make the evening as enjoyable as possible—and supposedly unaware of the tensions between the Annenbergs and the Bruces—she invited David and Evangeline Bruce. At the dinner, Evangeline refused to make conversation with Lee, and Walter later declared that he would never speak to Katharine Graham again.[79] According to Marguerite Littman, a longtime American resident in London and a leading hostess, the fault lay as much as with the Annenbergs as with the Bruces. "They went around trashing the Bruces. Lee said they didn't use fingerbowls, and silly things like that—that Winfield House was falling apart."[80]

Even before Annenberg presented his credentials to Queen Elizabeth that April, his wife had flown over Billy Haines and Ted Graber to begin work on a six-month, $1 million renovation of the ambassador's residence. The thirty-five-room Georgian-style mansion in Regent's Park had been built in 1937 by Woolworth heiress Barbara Hutton, who donated it to the American government after the war. "The first dinner we gave at Winfield House was for Governor and Mrs. Reagan," Lee Annenberg told me. "Walter had arranged for Ronnie to be a speaker at the Institute of Directors, held in the Royal Albert Hall. There must have been six thousand people there, and then we gave a dinner for thirty or forty."[81]

Although no one realized it at the time, among the corporate executives at the Royal Albert Hall that night in November 1969 was Denis Thatcher, who went home and told his wife, Margaret, then minister of education in the government of Conservative prime minister Edward Heath, how impressed he had been by the California governor's ideas and delivery. Reagan had received a standing ovation, apparently a tribute that only former prime minister Harold Macmillan had ever received. "I started to cry," Nancy later said. "I noticed a woman next to me also crying, and I was touched that she'd been as moved as I was."[82]

"That was the English part of the trip," Betsy Bloomingdale said. "I was in charge of the French part." The high point of their Paris stay was a dinner in the Reagans' honor at Versailles, hosted by its then curator, Gerald van der Kemp, and his American wife, Florence. "I had called Florence," Betsy Bloomingdale said, "because Nancy had always been so fascinated by the stories of the dinners we'd gone to in Versailles. And being a big Republican anyway, Florence was thrilled to give a dinner for the Governor of California. . . . The Duke and Duchess of Windsor were there, and a lot of terribly sophisticated French people—you know, Alexis de Redé, Ghislaine de Polignac, all that crowd that we'd known for years. Real sophisti-cates. So nobody really cared who Ronald Reagan was. He was a nice, handsome-looking actor from Hollywood, I think they thought, with a very pretty wife and what have you. But Ronnie was fabulous that night. He got up—did a little bit in French—and then really started to speak. And after dinner they all knew who Ronald Reagan was. They were *mad* for Ronald Reagan."[83]

For Nancy, nothing compared with meeting the woman for whom a king had given up his throne. The aging Windsors, who were renowned for their exquisite taste in everything from decor to dogs, held sway over international society from a *petit palais* in the Bois de Boulogne. "The Duchess was the star of the evening, the absolute star," Nancy told *Women's Wear Daily*'s Jody Jacobs. "Her yel-low Givenchy dress over pants was so beautiful even Ronnie mentioned it. . . . It's not just that she looks so good. It's her charm and the way she has of making you feel you're the most important per-son in the world when she's talking to you." Nancy said of the Duke, "Oh, he was wonderful. . . . He told Ronnie, 'I'm completely behind what you stand for.'"[84] Jacobs had hoped to conduct her interview with Nancy at Winfield House, but Lee nixed that. According to Jacobs, Lee said that "she had spent too much time and effort on the house to have anyone but herself be the first one interviewed there."[85]

A year later, at the 1970 Republican Governors' Conference in Sun Valley, Nancy made a new friend, Katharine Graham. The shy, vaguely dowdy publishing heiress, who had taken over *The Washington Post* after her husband's suicide seven years earlier, and the fashion-conscious former actress were an unlikely match, but they seemed to have an immediate affinity for each other. They had been encouraged to seek each other out by an even more unlikely go-between. "I must say, we kept this rather a dark secret," Graham told me in 1998, sitting beneath a Diego Rivera painting in the drawing room of her R Street mansion. "Because what we actually did was meet through Truman Capote. And both of us felt slightly embarrassed—you know, because people kept asking all through the Reagan years, 'How did you happen to meet? How did you happen to be friends?' And at that point, for some reason, we didn't think it was suitable. I don't exactly know why. But we never much said that in fact we did meet through Capote. After *In Cold Blood* he was very interested in the death penalty, and he had gone out to California in pursuit of death row interviews. In the course of doing that he met Governor and Mrs. Reagan. He said to me, 'I know you won't believe me, honey, but you'd really like them,' and encouraged me to look them up. It happened quite accidentally, because I was invited to speak at the Republican governors' meeting in Sun Valley, on a panel about the press. I flew out there all alone and feeling very unsure of myself—I'd only gone to work in '63. At one of the first receptions—it was a terribly cold winter night and everyone went out to the dinner in sleds—I met the Reagans. And because of Truman, you know, Nancy and I got to know each other."[86]

"Truman Capote came to the house for lunch a few times in Sacramento," Nancy Reagan told me. "And he said, 'You know, you really should know Kay Graham. If you knew her, you'd like her.' Ronnie used to do a funny imitation of him. So we went to Sun Valley, and I walked into this lodge where we were having dinner. And there was Kay standing in front of the fireplace. So I walked up to her and said, 'Well, I think it's time we really met.' "[87]

California's First Lady had become much more sure of herself by the end of her husband's first term. Since 1968 she had been hosting annual poolside parties at the Executive Residence for legislators and their wives with entertainment provided by Hollywood friends such as Jack Benny, Danny Thomas, and Red Skelton. She had found a cause she loved in the Foster Grandparents Program, which arranged for lonely senior citizens to spend time with institutionalized children. As she told the *Sacramento Union*, "I think it is wonderful because it benefits both sides—the older people whose families are grown, and the children who receive an extra amount of love and attention."[88] The federally funded program had been started by Kennedy in-law Sargent Shriver in 1965, and was still quite small when Nancy became aware of it on a visit to Pacific State Hospital. She soon took charge, and eventually expanded the program to all state hospitals. She also made regular visits to soldiers wounded in Vietnam at military hospitals around the state. "Hospital visiting is a natural thing for me to do," she said. "I used to watch my father operate."[89] After these visits, she would call the servicemen's parents, wives, or girlfriends and pass on messages. These activities were well suited to Nancy's nurse's side—they also were her way of showing her support for Ronnie's very vocal pro-war stance. On October 15, 1970, as hundreds of thousands of demonstrators marched on Washington to demand that Nixon pull out of Vietnam, the Governor's press office invited TV crews to accompany the First Lady on a visit to an Army hospital in San Francisco. "It's a symbolic visit," Nancy admitted. "I want the boys here to know there are a lot of people in California who are grateful to them."[90]

Reagan's decision to seek reelection surprised no one, as he said in a fifteen-minute televised speech on March 10, 1970. Less than two weeks earlier he had been forced to call upon the National Guard again, when students at U.C.-Santa Barbara, shouting "Death to corporations" and "Burn, baby, burn," set fire to a Bank of America branch. The attacks on businesses continued on and off for three months, and at one point a frustrated Reagan snapped at a reporter, "If it takes a bloodbath, let's get it over with. No more appeasement."[91] Nancy told columnist George Christy, "From a woman's standpoint, it frightens me when I see students shouting obscenities; I think of Hitler's Nazi youth movement."[92] "Every time you and Ronnie open your mouths you echo my thoughts," a supportive Lillian Gish wrote Nancy from New York.[93]

Reagan was opposed by the Democrats' State Assembly leader, Jesse Unruh, who opened his campaign on Labor Day weekend by taking two busloads of reporters to the gates of Henry Salvatori's estate in Bel Air. As the TV cameras rolled, Unruh asserted that a property-tax-relief bill proposed by Reagan would save his wealthy friend $4,113 a year, whereupon Salvatori, in tennis whites, appeared and yelled through the gates, "Oh, you ass! Is this the way you have to get your publicity?" Grace was right behind him, shouting, "We worked for the money to pay for it!"[94]

Unruh was playing on the lingering perception that the Kitchen Cabinet was running the state— he also staged a showy scene outside the 45th Street house to remind voters that it had been bought by a group headed by Holmes Tuttle and Jaquelin Hume—but his antics backfired. "In a single stroke Unruh had revived the image of 'Big Daddy,' the domineering political bully who had no respect for the rights of others," Lou Cannon observes. "Californians value both their holidays and their privacy, and they identified with the nice-looking elderly couple whose castle had been invaded on a holiday by the dread Unruh. Rarely has a self-inflicted wound so thoroughly under-mined what might have been a promising cam-paign."[95]

"We just stood on Ron's record, and ran on it and ran on it and ran on it, and we won again," said Tuttle. "Of course, we didn't win by a million votes, but we won by over a half million."[96] Despite a recent hospitalization for his chronic stomach problems, Tuttle co-chaired the campaign with Tom Reed. Tuttle's fund-raising partner, Justin Dart, replaced Salvatori as finance chairman, but in most respects 1970 was a carbon copy of 1966, with Hume heading the Northern California effort and Ed Mills serving as Tuttle's deputy in the south. Spencer-Roberts managed the campaign, and Neil Reagan's agency, McCann-Erickson, handled the advertising. However, there was one big new name on the campaign's organizational chart, Frank Sinatra, who was a co-chair of Californians for Reagan, which was made up of Democrats and independents.[97]

It is commonly thought that Sinatra, who was once so far left that both MGM and MCA dropped him in the blacklist days, had switched sides after his buddy President Kennedy opted to stay with Bing Crosby instead of him on a 1962 visit to Palm Springs. According to Sinatra's valet, George Jacobs, Attorney General Robert Kennedy had told Sinatra, "We can't have the president sleeping in the same house where Sam Giancana slept."[98]

"The Kennedy slight hurt him deeply," his daughter Tina Sinatra told me. "But he did *not* sledgehammer his helipad when he found out the President wasn't coming, and the new guesthouse had been built for my sister, brother, and me, not Kennedy." In Tina's view, her father had little truck with "the far-right Minutemen—John Wayne, Randolph Scott, Ward Bond," who were Reagan's most faithful Hollywood supporters. He saw his role, she said, as "nudging Ronnie toward the middle. . . . I also think he thought the Democratic Party was going to take a major nosedive. Once he went off to the Reagan camp, he stayed there, but he remained a registered Democrat until the day he died. He loved politics. He loved to put his money where his mouth was, to entertain and put his voice into the electoral process, to help make something happen."[99]

Sinatra had made a few appearances for Reagan in 1966, after taking offense at Pat Brown's an-actor-killed-Lincoln ad. This time around, he was angry at Jesse Unruh, who had been a major Bobby Kennedy booster, for not doing enough to carry California for his friend Hubert Humphrey in 1968. In the intervening years Sinatra had seen more of the Reagans socially through the Annenbergs and the Deutsches; the latter had been spending New Year's at the singer's desert compound since the early 1960s. He went all-out for Reagan in 1970, staging glitzy benefits throughout the state, usually with Dean Martin at his side, and raising more than $500,000 of the campaign's $3.5 million total.[100]

On election night in November, the Reagans went to the Jorgensens' before proceeding to the Biltmore, as they had four years earlier. "Ronnie decided it was good luck," explained Marion Jorgensen. "So when he ran a second time, Nancy called me up. I said, 'Oh, are we having the cocktail party?' She said, 'Yes, but there will be a few more people.' It was astonishing how many more popped up that night." Almost the entire Kitchen Cabinet was on hand this time, as well as outgoing Nevada governor Paul Laxalt, who had become a close ally of Reagan's; the Deavers and Nancy Reynolds; and Gloria and Jimmy Stewart. Marion made a point of having not only the same food—veal stew and coconut cake—but also the same employees from the same caterer.[101]

Demonstrators carrying Vietcong flags hurled four-letter words and oranges at Ronald Reagan as he was sworn in for a second term on the steps of the capitol, on January 4, 1971. But that didn't stop the Governor, who was only a month away from his sixtieth birthday, from completing his address. "They're like mosquitoes and flies. They're part of the world, and you have to put up with them, I guess," he said of the protesters who now plagued most of his public appearances.[102] For them, he was now "Ronald Ray-gun," a term that Joan Baez had coined at Woodstock in 1969.

Nancy had decided that the inaugural ball

should be white-tie, and had asked Sinatra to produce the inaugural gala at the Sacramento Municipal Auditorium. She also asked Frank, who was between marriages to flower-child actress Mia Farrow and former Las Vegas showgirl Barbara Marx, to escort Patti to the ball. Years later, after Kitty Kelley alleged that Nancy had a long-term affair with the crooner that began around this time, Patti told an interviewer, "When I read about my mother and Sinatra in Kitty's book, I thought, Well, God, I spent this whole evening with him and he never came on to me. Of course, I was jailbait at the time, but he was very gentlemanly. We talked about music; he was going to teach me to sing. And then I thought, Maybe he did come on to me and I just didn't recognize it. . . . Maybe there was something to those singing lessons after all."[103]

By then Patti was a freshman at Northwestern University, her grandfather's alma mater. That wasn't why she chose it; she had thought her English teacher from Orme was going to get a job there, but that didn't work out, and he ended up at the University of Pennsylvania. Her father had spoken at her high school commencement the previous June, and she had agreed to make her debut at Las Madrinas, the top cotillion for Los Angeles society girls, in December to appease her mother, but in Evanston she drew the line at pledging for a sorority. Instead, she befriended the very person her father had warned her to avoid, student body president Eva Jefferson, who he had been told was a radical black activist. When Patti finally managed to fly to Philadelphia to see her paramour, he picked her up at the airport with his wife and kids. He then promised her a rendezvous in Chicago, but didn't show up on the appointed weekend.[104]

A few weeks later, perhaps sensing something was wrong, Nancy invited her daughter to join her in New York, where she was speaking at a United Community Campaign of America luncheon. This had been Edith's primary charity in Chicago, and now Nancy was national chairman of its women's committee. Although Patti had not planned on even mentioning her failed affair, she was so upset that she found herself telling her mother the whole sad story. Much to her surprise, Nancy was understanding and comforting. Patti's analysis of her mother's reaction is insightful:

> There have been comments from the media that she is more liberal politically than my father, but I don't think her ideology or her morality are rooted in either liberalism or conservatism. One of my mother's complexities is her ability to transform, adapt to situations for personal reasons. I was bringing her a personal crisis, showing her I needed her, and she adapted to that, became gentle, nurturing, and non-judgmental.[105]

Yet when *The New York Times*'s Judy Klemesrud turned up at Nancy's Waldorf Towers suite, she reverted to her public role as the no-nonsense wife of a conservative politician. She was "shocked," she said, to read that a welfare family had recently been housed at the Waldorf. "I think the people of New York should be shocked, too. There must be somewhere else to put these people." She was "appalled and ashamed" by the sex-oriented films Hollywood was turning out. "I think they've shown no sense of responsibility, no taste. . . . I've often said that it's going to be cured at the box office if people stop going. But some people, even my friends, say they go 'out of curiosity.' I don't see why they are so curious. A dirty picture is a dirty picture, and that's that." Even *Love Story* with Ryan O'Neal and Ali MacGraw went too far for her. "I thought it leaned too heavily on the four-letter words. I would have liked a little more tenderness." As for Women's Lib, "I'm in agreement with equal pay for equal jobs. . . . After that, I'm afraid they kind of lose me." Hot pants? "I think a woman should look like a woman, with a little more femininity and elegance than hot pants offer. I don't like fads."[106]

As fate would have it, Patti no sooner returned to Northwestern than she was embroiled in what came to known as "the hot pants incident." This brouhaha started when she and a friend were approached in their dormitory lobby by a black man selling shorts out of a cardboard box; the friend called security, the man was arrested, and the press ran away with the story. REAGAN'S DAUGHTER IN HOT PANTS HASSLE was the headline on the *Chicago Tribune*'s front-page story the next day. Soon everyone from Loyal Davis to Eva

Jefferson to the peddler's brother, a local alderman, became involved. When Frank Sinatra read about the upcoming trial, he called Nancy, who told him she was on her way to Chicago. "He was in New York for some big fight," recalled Nancy, "and he said, 'Well, I'll stop there on my way back to the Coast.' We had dinner with Patti at the Drake." As Patti remembered it, Sinatra gave her a lecture on law and order and sticking up for her rights, but others have suggested the dinner was merely a cover for an assignation between the singer and Nancy, who was staying at the hotel rather than at her parents' one-bedroom pied-à-terre. "Oh, please," said Nancy when I asked her about these allegations. "Frank? There was nothing."[107] It seems unlikely that someone as controlled as Nancy Reagan would have risked her husband's political career for a fling with a man who was known to brag about his conquests.

In any event, the trial was postponed, perhaps because strings were pulled by Sinatra or the Davises, all of whom were friendly with Mayor Richard Daley, and Patti left Northwestern at the end of that semester. She spent the summer of 1971 at Oxford and then transferred to USC as a drama major. After two years she dropped out. "I can't say we're surprised," her father told her. "Maybe I'll go back and finish college someday," Patti replied. "No, you won't," said Nancy.[108]

The great achievement of Reagan's second term, indeed of his entire governorship, was the

California Welfare Reform Act of 1971. It took him six months of struggle with the cocky new Democratic speaker of the assembly, Bob Moretti, to get the bill through the legislature, and when he first asked his aides, including Meese and Deaver, what they thought his chances of success were, their answers ranged from "We shouldn't try" to "None."[109] Since coming into office, Reagan had been determined to get what he called "the welfare monster" under control—one out of nine Americans was on some form of relief by the early 1970s, and in California the Aid to Families with Dependent Children caseload was increasing by forty thousand a month.[110] On March 3, 1971, Reagan unveiled the "lengthiest, most detailed and specific legislative proposal ever originated by a California governor," which called for cutting welfare expenditures by as much as $800 million annually by tightening eligibility requirements and closing loopholes while increasing funds for "the truly needy."[111] Reagan's most controversial proposal would force able-bodied fathers—and mothers with older children—to work at public service for their AFDC checks.[112]

The bill became law on August 13, after a final version had been hammered out in three weeks of face-to-face negotiations between Reagan and Moretti, which involved a fair degree of cursing as well as nitty-gritty haggling over nearly every subclause. "Both he and I developed a grudging respect for each other," said the thirty-four-year-old speaker, who came from a poor, half-Italian, half-Armenian family in Detroit. "I don't think that socially we'd ever have mixed, but when the governor gave a commitment he kept it, and when I gave a commitment, I kept it. So that working on the development of legislation with him was relatively easy because we always knew where the other guy stood."[113]

"Reagan always prided himself on his ability to compromise," said Mike Deaver, who had been given the fancy new title director of administration at the start of the second term. "And he understood that there always was going to *be* compromise. He would tell you stories about what he learned in his work with the unions and the studios and the Screen Actors Guild. That's where he really learned how to compromise—*when* to make the move and so forth."[114]

The path to reform had taken Reagan to the Winter White House at San Clemente that April for a "welfare summit" with President Nixon, who had proposed his own Family Assistance Plan in 1969 and was not happy about the California Governor stealing his thunder. Nixon's plan essentially amounted to a guaranteed minimum income for welfare recipients and was seen by conservatives as yet another example of his inability to control spending and his lack of principles. Reagan had even testified against Nixon's plan in U.S. Senate hearings the previous summer.[115] Their three-hour meeting in San Clemente was mediated by Caspar Weinberger, who had left Sacramento to become Nixon's budget director. Reagan essentially got what he wanted, the presidential blessing for his work-for-checks reform. In exchange he agreed to stop opposing Nixon's plan, which would be shelved in 1972.[116] Reagan's reform legislation, on the other hand, would become the model for other states, and eventually for the federal government during the Clinton administration.

For Nixon, struggling with a recession, inflation, and soaring deficits, as well as a war in Southeast Asia he could neither win nor end, Reagan increasingly represented a looming threat to his renomination in 1972. Despite Reagan's assurance at a White House meeting in January 1971 that he "would not in any way allow himself to become a candidate," as Nixon's chief of staff H. R. Haldeman noted in his diary, the President's paranoia was set off by the slightest sign of a Reagan surge. When the Young Americans for Freedom came out for Reagan that May, for example, Nixon ordered Attorney General John Mitchell to "straighten them back out."[117] But Reagan was both sincere and realistic about not running this time around. In July, responding to a letter from Vermont governor Deane Davis urging him to make another try for the White House, Reagan joked, "Just between us, though, I think we'd better settle for the North Pole—it's easier to reach than that other place you mentioned."[118]

"They got along fine," Nancy Reagan said of her husband and Nixon, adding, "We were never *close*."[119] Nixon seemed to alternate between slighting the Reagans and courting them. Nancy

Reagan told me that they were never invited to a state dinner by Nixon, though they were by Lyndon Johnson, who seated her at his table. They were asked to San Clemente in the summer of 1970 for an intimate dinner with the Nixons and Henry Kissinger, who was then national security adviser. Reagan wrote Kissinger a cryptic note the following day: "It was good seeing you last night—my mind is busy but my lips are sealed. Enclosed is the Patton speech made to his 3rd Army before it left England to cross the Channel."[120]

On July 15, 1971, Nixon startled the nation—and Ronald Reagan—when he announced that he would be paying an official visit to Communist China the following year. Bill Buckley, who was in Sacramento to tape a session of his talk show, *Firing Line*, with Reagan, was at the Governor's house when "there was a call from his office saying that it was very important to hear a special broadcast that Richard Nixon was making at six o'clock. It was the announcement that he was going to China, which was a very anti-right-wing thing to do in those days. So we sat and watched it. And then the phone rang, and someone came in and said, 'Dr. Kissinger for Governor Reagan.' Henry was losing no time."[121] As Buckley recalled, Kissinger guaranteed Reagan "that the strategic intentions of the President were in total harmony with the concerns of the conservative community."[122]

In October, Nixon sent Reagan on a two-week tour of Asia to reassure our allies that his historic opening to China would not change their relationships with the United States. In Japan the Reagans were the first foreign visitors who were not heads of state to have an audience with Emperor Hirohito, and in Thailand they were received by King Bhumibol—Ronnie bowed and Nancy curtsied. In Singapore, Reagan met with Prime Minister Lee Kuan Yew, and in South Korea with President Park, who told him how *he* dealt with student unrest. "Just before our arrival there was rioting on the campus of the University of Seoul," Nancy recalled. "It was interesting to see how such things are handled in these countries. First, let me say there was irrefutable evidence that the rioting was engineered by Communist infiltrators. The president simply closed the university, and the young men were drafted into the army. President Park told Ronnie that after they had a little taste of military life, he'd reopen the university, and he was sure the returning students would have a greater appreciation of their educational opportunity."[123]

There was also a quick, unannounced detour to Saigon, where Reagan was helicoptered to lunch with President Thieu while Nancy and young Ron took a second helicopter to the American ambassador's residence. Nancy also made a point of visiting an American military hospital in the South Vietnamese capital. Between official duties, the superstitious Reagans bought a "spirit house" at Bangkok's floating market for their garden in Sacramento, and Nancy found time for a visit to Hanae Mori's couture house in Tokyo. "Skipper was the best traveler of all," Nancy Reynolds told the *Sacramento Union* upon their return. "He certainly developed the most sophisticated palate and was quite an expert with chopsticks by the time we left."[124]

Reagan's most important stop was Taiwan, where he and Nancy dined with Generalissimo Chiang Kai-shek and the formidable Madame Chiang. The eighty-five-year-old Nationalist Chinese leader, who had been driven from the mainland by Mao Zedong's Red Army in 1949, was understandably concerned by Nixon's surprise announcement, and pleased to receive his personal message of reassurance from Reagan. But two days after Reagan returned to Sacramento, the U.N. General Assembly, with tacit U.S. approval, voted to expel Taiwan in favor of Communist China. "Reagan tracked me down in Madrid," Bill Buckley told me. "He was as mad as I ever heard him. He said, 'What am I going to do? Here I just reassured all of our friends that nothing that matters is going to change, and I come back and now this terrible thing happens.'"[125]

According to Haldeman's *Diaries*, a "very upset" Reagan tried to reach Nixon after midnight on the day of the vote, and when the President returned his call the next morning, Reagan pushed him to go on TV and denounce the U.N. When Nixon said that wasn't possible, an infuriated Reagan called Secretary of State William Rogers and Attorney General John Mitchell. "The P makes the point that we need to keep the right wing on track,"

Haldeman wrote. "We have to see if K[issinger] can keep Reagan in line and try to do so with Buckley also, and we've just got to keep Reagan from jumping off the reservation."[126]

Nixon sent Reagan off on an Air Force plane again in July 1972—this time to Europe—perhaps to prevent his making any last-minute waves before the August convention in Miami. Reagan met with the prime ministers of Britain, France, Italy, and Denmark, and was given a full day's briefing by NATO secretary general Joseph Luns in Brussels. In Madrid he and Nancy dined with both Generalissimo Franco and the future king and queen, Juan Carlos and Sofia. There was also a glamorous lunch on the Queen of Denmark's yacht, and an audience with Pope Paul VI. Their final stop was in the Governor's ancestral land, Ireland, where they threw coins in a wishing well at Cashel Rock.[127]

It was all fun and unity at the 1972 Republican National Convention in Miami Beach, which opened with a filmed tribute to the late President Eisenhower in which Mamie urged the delegates to give Nixon "the full eight years." The following night Nancy sat beside Happy Rockefeller and right behind Pat Nixon as Nixon's was the only name placed in nomination. The President himself was at a Republican youth rally headlined by Sammy Davis Jr., reminding the assembled throng that he had not only ended the draft but also lowered the voting age to eighteen. The Reagans were staying with the Leonard Firestones on Key Biscayne, as were the Bloomingdales and the Annenbergs. So was Frank Sinatra. Vice President Agnew, who was now a regular at Sinatra's Palm Springs compound, had also stayed on at least one occasion with the Reagans in Sacramento. The only jarring note came when angry young demonstrators, "in a symbolic protest of the poor against the rich," started ripping designer dresses off the backs of women arriving at a Republican Party reception at the Fontaineblean Hotel.[128] "Our car was almost turned over by these hoods," Betsy Bloomingdale told me. "Alfred saved our lives—he told the driver to step on it. The driver floored the accelerator, the car shot ahead, and the people fell off, or stopped chasing us."[129]

The California delegation, chaired by Governor Reagan, included most of the Kitchen Cabinet, as well as the Gosdens' nineteen-year-old daughter, Linda, whom Reagan had chosen over Walter Annenberg's daughter, Wallis, to represent the newly enfranchised teenage voters. Henry Salvatori, who had given $90,000 to Nixon's last campaign, and would throw in another $100,000 in 1972, was hoping to be made ambassador to his native Italy. (It didn't happen, perhaps because his FBI background check turned up the $5 dues he had paid to something called the Dante Alighieri Society, a reputedly pro-Mussolini group, in 1940.) Several other Reagan friends were among Nixon's largest contributors, including Firestone ($113,000), Jules Stein ($118,000), and Thomas V. Jones, whose Northrop Corporation gave a $150,000 donation that was later deemed illegal.[130] In total, the Nixon campaign's California finance committee, run by Tuttle, Dart, and Schreiber, raised more that $9 million, and was rewarded with a pre-inaugural dinner with the President at Blair House.[131] Reagan campaigned throughout the South and West for Nixon, who carried forty-nine states, leaving only Massachusetts to his Democratic opponent, George McGovern.

Tuttle later explained the logic behind the Kitchen Cabinet's all-out effort for Nixon: "There was no question in our minds at that time . . . that we were going to run Ron for office in 1976 after Nixon left office. Make no mistake about it, we were all primed. Our whole activity down at the convention in 1972 was to acquire friends and get commitments. We were working hard. Ron worked hard for Nixon. He spoke and raised money; we all did. Mr. Dart and I put on one of the biggest fundraisers in history out here for President Nixon in 1972. But make no mistake about it, we were all ready to go. Don't you think we weren't building for 1976. . . . In fact, there was a great deal of pressure for the Governor to run for a third term, but we couldn't convince him. He said, 'No, I said I don't believe in a third term. I tried to get a bill through the legislature for a two-term limit. I'd make a hypocrite of myself, and I'm not going to do it.' We thought maybe it might hurt his chances [in 1976] by being out of office. He could have won the governorship without any problems."[132]

* * *

Nancy arrived at Nixon's January 1973 inauguration with a complete Galanos wardrobe, which met with the full approval of Jerry Zipkin, who had come down from New York for the festivities. The Reagans hosted one of the four inaugural balls, Nancy in white satin embroidered with black beaded tulips. There was a wonderful photograph in the *Los Angeles Times* of her embracing Martha Mitchell, soon to be the uncontrollable loose lips of the Watergate affair, and another of Imelda Marcos with her arm in a sling from a recent assassination attempt. There was also one of the Reverend Billy Graham greeting Republican National Chairman George H. W. Bush and his wife, Barbara, at Ross Perot's dinner at the Madison Hotel, which the Reagans attended with the Annenbergs, Lee dripping rubies and diamonds over her yellow lace gown.[133]

Later they all took their limousines to the Fairfax Hotel's Jockey Club, where a boozed-up Frank Sinatra, who had performed at the inaugural gala, called *Washington Post* reporter Maxine Cheshire a "two-dollar broad" and much worse, and stuffed a couple of bills in her champagne glass.[134] Sinatra had been out to get Cheshire ever since she humiliated him in front of Reagan a month earlier, when the two men arrived for a dinner Agnew was giving for Republican governors, by loudly asking, "Mr. Sinatra, aren't you afraid that your alleged Mafia associations are going to prove to be the same kind of embarrassment to Mr. Agnew that they were to the Kennedys?"[135]

But not even the ugly scene at the Jockey Club, which was widely reported, could mar the Reagans' sense that the next inauguration in Washington would be their own. As the kingmakers of the Kitchen Cabinet reasoned, when Nixon stepped down in four years the lackluster Agnew would be brushed aside, and their man would have an open path to the nomination. Nancy had already made it clear that, while her husband was not going to run for a third term as governor in 1974, he wasn't planning to retire. "He is very concerned as to the direction the Republican Party takes, not only in California, but in the country," she wrote in a weekly Q&A column she had started contributing to the *Sacramento Union*, "and he certainly wants to have a voice in that determination."[136]

Ronnie and Nancy, primed to move on to bigger things, seemed to do everything right in the last two years of his governorship. They highlighted their patriotism by giving dinners for prisoners of war returning from Vietnam after the Paris Peace Accord was signed in January 1973, and their steadfastness by hosting a controversial reception for South Vietnamese president Thieu a few months later. They made another trip to the Far East for Nixon in late 1973, even as the deepening Watergate scandal was causing other Republicans to keep their distance. They cultivated the grandees of the national press, growing ever closer to the Annenbergs, Gardner and Jan Cowles, and Kay Graham. By the end of 1974, Reagan could proudly point to the more than $5 billion given back to taxpayers in rebates, credits, and property tax cuts, and the 300,000 names taken off the state's welfare rolls as a result of his reforms.[137] He had gone from the candidate who was scorned for saying "A tree is a tree is a tree—how many more do you need to look at?" to a governor who oversaw the creation of the Redwoods National Park, added 145,000 square miles to the state park system, sponsored the nation's toughest water pollution control laws, and established the Air Resources Board to deal with smog-causing automobile emissions. He shared credit for what *The New York Times* would call "a first-rate environmentalist" record with his resources director, Norman Livermore, a lumberman who belonged to the Sierra Club and, like Bill Clark, rode horseback with him.[138]

For her part, Nancy's persistent lobbying for a new Governor's Mansion had finally paid off, even though, as she liked to point out, she and Ronnie would never spend a night in the $1.4 million, thirty-one-room, yellow-stucco edifice rising on eleven acres of riverfront land given to the state by the Kitchen Cabinet.[139] She had also seen to it that the old gingerbread mansion would be preserved as a State Historic Site, and diplomatically gave a few official functions there, with Mike Deaver pounding away at the piano in the parlor.[140]

"Ronnie accomplished a great deal during his eight years as governor of California, and in my own way, I suppose I did too," Nancy later wrote. "But for me, the return of the POWs marked the high point of Ronnie's administration."[141] The Reagans hosted four dinners for the returning servicemen, two at the Executive Residence and two in Pacific Palisades. "When they were landing in California, we saw them on TV," Nancy Reagan told me. "And I said to Ronnie, 'I just can't wait to get my arms around them and tell them how I feel.' They would get up and toast Ronnie for what he'd done. And Ronnie would say, 'That's not what we're doing—we're toasting you.' I remember one man gave me the tin spoon he had eaten with in prison. Patti came to one of the dinners—I thought it might be good for her to hear their stories—but she was very bored by the whole thing."[142]

One of the returnees, Nancy recalled, was future Arizona senator John McCain, who would become a close friend of theirs. "We met John in Sacramento. He had been seven years in solitary confinement, and the ones there the longest came back first. He could have been released earlier, but the North Vietnamese wanted him to meet with Jane Fonda when she went to Hanoi. And he wouldn't do it."[143]

Nancy also prevailed upon Justin and Punky Dart to lend their Holmby Hills house for two large receptions for the POWs on March 28 and April 10, 1973. In between these two parties, the Governor and First Lady gave their dinner for Thieu at the

Beverly Wilshire Hotel, where guests were greeted by picketing protesters led by Jane Fonda and her second husband, Tom Hayden, a founder of the radical Students for a Democratic Society.[144] Nancy seated the South Vietnamese President between her and Irene Dunne, and Reagan's table included Doris Stein, John Wayne, and Cy Ramo, the chairman of TRW, a major defense contractor based in Los Angeles.[145] "Tell Jane Fonda what a dope she is," Zsa Zsa Gabor told reporters as she arrived.[146]

Nancy donated her fees from her newspaper column to the National League of Families of American Prisoners of War and Missing in Action. The "Dear Abby" format allowed her to voice her opinion on such subjects as the legalization of marijuana (against), the death penalty (for), and teenage marriage (wait). The column also spawned a parody in the National Lampoon, titled "Nancy Reagan's Dating Do's and Don'ts." A typical installment:

Dating is like dynamite. Used wisely, it can move mountains and change the course of mighty rivers. Used foolishly, it can blow your legs off. Scientists have calculated, for example, that if a man could harness even a fraction of the kinetic energy wasted in a single session of Post Office or Spin the Bottle, he could light up the entire city of Wilmington, Delaware, and have enough left over to discover and mass produce a cheap, effective cure for cancer of the larynx.[147]

There were a few glitches, such as a 1974 *Los Angeles Times* exposé involving Anita May. Seven months after Reagan was given the National Jewish Hospital Tom May Award at a gala in Beverly Hills, the *Times* accused him of reversing a decision made by the state parks department not to renew the lease on a private beach club in Santa Monica as a favor to Anita May. The Sand and Sea Club, of which May was a member, occupied three acres of state-owned land that was slated to be turned into a parking lot to provide public access to the beach. May had written a letter to Reagan in 1971, which led to a meeting between her and parks commissioner William Penn Mott, shortly after which the lease was renewed for another ten years. After the *Times* story appeared, a Democratic state senator declared that "a few rich individuals have no right to monopolize state park lands." But Reagan and Mott denied the allegations, and the eighty-one-year-old May, pleading illness, refused to comment.[148]

The worst glitch of all was one over which the Reagans had no control—the ongoing scandal in Washington, which would completely upend their hopes for a smooth ride to the 1976 nomination. "I think the situation is being taken care of," Nancy placidly told a reporter in April 1973, ten days after Watergate had claimed its first high-level casualties, H. R. Haldeman and John Erlichman, who had been forced to resign their White House posts. "The American people are always fair people; they're not going to condemn a whole party for the actions of a few."[149]

The first real jolt to the Reagans' plans was the October 10, 1973, resignation of Vice President Agnew, who had pleaded no contest to unrelated corruption charges that went all the way back to his days as a Maryland county executive. His replacement by House minority leader and party stalwart Gerald Ford meant Nixon now had a much more palatable heir apparent—a prospect that did not warm the hearts of the Reagans, who remembered how Ford had tried to keep Ronnie from the podium at the 1968 convention. The Kitchen Cabinet actually tried to get Nixon to appoint Reagan instead of Ford. "Oh, yes," said Tuttle. "I took quite an active part in that, and I think President Nixon made a very bad mistake when he didn't appoint him. I did my best, and so did Mr. Dart, to convince Nixon that he should. You bet I did." Would Reagan have accepted the vice presidency then? "Nobody ever turns it down," Tuttle said, not quite answering the question.[150]

By the spring of 1974, when Haldeman, Erlichman, and John Mitchell had been indicted and Nixon had been ordered to turn over his White House tapes by the Supreme Court, Ronnie and Nancy were losing their cool. "Nixon should have destroyed the tapes," said Ronnie, according to Patti. "It's a witch-hunt. It's just because he's a Republican." "[It's] terrible what they are doing to this man," said Nancy, adding, "It's wonderful that his daughters are sticking by him."[151]

But life—and strengthening ties to those who could be helpful—had to go on. In August 1973, Nancy gave the first of several dinners at Pacific Palisades for Jan and Gardner Cowles, whose Cowles Communications owned TV stations in Des Moines, Memphis, and Orlando as well as *Look* and *Family Circle* magazines. There were three tables of eight with David Jones centerpieces on the deck, and not a single unfamiliar name on the guest list. Except for Jerry Zipkin, who escorted the recently widowed Irene Dunne, it was the same set of couples who saw one another all the time: the Darts and the Gosdens, who were both very close to the Cowleses, the Bloomingdales and the Annenbergs and the Deutsches, the Jorgensens and the Wilsons, the Tuttles, and Tex and Flora Thornton of Litton Industries.

In January 1974, Kay Graham gave a dinner for Nancy in Washington. The Reagans and the owner of the *Post* had seen quite a bit of each other since they met at Sun Valley four years earlier. In February 1971, the Governor had been the guest speaker at an editorial lunch at the paper, and that evening Graham gave a dinner at home for the Reagans. As Katharine Graham told me, "We kept up. When I went to California, I'd call them and receive them in some way. Nancy and I always liked each other, I believe. And I was interested in getting to know the Governor as a person who was on the conservative side of the Republican Party. And Nancy and I got to be friends. I think our friendship was sealed in a really odd way. They came back to Washington after the dinner for both of them, and I said to Nancy, 'Would you like to come to dinner when you're here?' She said they couldn't, because he was going to some male din-ner—the Alfalfa Club dinner, I think. I said, 'That's too bad, but why don't *you* come?' And she said, 'Oh, you don't want me without Ronnie.' I said—because the light had started to dawn at that point about women—'Nancy, that's not where it's at any-more. Of course, I want you.' She said, 'You do?' I mean, she had apparently never gone out without him. So she was very pleased to be asked on her own."[152]

Graham put together a serious group for Nancy's solo dinner, including the man who was trying to save Nixon from Watergate, White House special counsel Leonard Garment; Helmut Sonnenfeld from the State Department; columnists James Reston, William Safire, and James Kilpatrick; and Clay Felker, the publisher and editor of *New York* magazine. In her thank-you note, Nancy wrote, "You can't tell what might happen now that I've made the plunge."[153]

Two months later Ronnie and Nancy were back in Palm Springs with the Annenbergs and their houseguest, Prince Charles. The Prince of Wales, then twenty-six, was in the Royal Navy, on shore leave from his ship, HMS *Jupiter.* Lee Annenberg recalled that "Nancy phoned and said, 'Prince

Charles is going to be in San Diego. What do you think we should do?' I suggested they come down to Sunnylands, and I would invite him. He came with his equerry for the weekend. And that's when they got to know him very well."[154]

While the Reagans and "the With-It Prince," as he was sometimes called, were the only house-guests that weekend, a small group including Bob and Dolores Hope and Frank Sinatra, unrepentant but apparently absolved, came for dinner on Saturday night. The caviar Lee served was a personal gift, she told her guests, from the Shah of Iran.[155]

That summer, as the House Judiciary Committee began drawing up articles of impeachment, everyone knew that it was only a matter of time before the nation really wouldn't have Nixon to kick around anymore. He resigned on August 9, 1974, and was succeeded by Gerald Ford, who under the terms of the Twenty-fifth Amendment was charged with nominating a new vice president for Congress to approve. According to Ed Mills, the Kitchen Cabinet made another play to get the vice presidency for Reagan. "I'm sure that Justin Dart and Holmes Tuttle made contact, but there was never any invitation, to my knowledge, for Reagan to come back and be interviewed relative to the situation," Mills said, adding, "Rockefeller was actually selected. Maybe it's a good thing it didn't happen. Sometimes fate seems to dictate how these things ultimately work out."[156]

On December 15, 1974, the *Sacramento Union* ran a farewell interview with Nancy Reagan. In eight years the First Lady had not given a single interview to the much more important *Sacramento Bee*—as many a former friend and ex-employee knew, when Mrs. Reagan was crossed, she stayed crossed. Mae Belle Pendergast, the society reporter who had gushed over Nancy's inaugural wardrobe in 1967, was asking the questions. "What is ahead for the Reagans?" she wondered. "We'll take that day by day," said Nancy.[157]

In one of his end-of-term interviews, Ronnie told the *Saturday Evening Post,* "I've heard Nancy's father say he could not possibly accomplish what he did—even with his skill as a surgeon—without her mother. I could never do what I'm doing without Nancy. When you want to go home as much as I do, you work at it."[158]

Shortly after Ronnie and Nancy left Sacramento, Jesse Unruh summed up the Reagan governorship: "I think he has been better than most Democrats would concede and not nearly as good as most Republicans and conservatives might like to think. As a politician I think he has been nearly masterful." He added, "I do not like Ronald Reagan. I find him cold, withdrawn, shallow, sanctimonious and with very little personal warmth in spite of his appeal to people from the platform and the television tube."[159]

CHAPTER SIXTEEN

REAGAN VS. FORD

1975–1976

Once upon a time [Reagan] said [something] to me on an airplane about the future and about the presidency, and about any possibilities in '76. He was telling me that I was perhaps overly concerned; that I should not be concerned so much about the future, about the planning, and about making sure you meet all the right people or enough of them, and that sort of thing. He said, "Bob, if the Lord wants me to be president of the United States, I'll *be* president of the United States, and you don't need to worry."

Bob Walker, political aide to Governor Reagan[1]

Of Ronnie's five campaigns for public office, the one I remember most vividly is the only one he lost. That was in 1976, when he challenged President Gerald Ford for the Republican nomination. That campaign was so exciting, so dramatic, and so *emotional*—especially at the convention—that in my mind it almost overshadows Ronnie's four victories.

Nancy Reagan, *My Turn*[2]

One result of Nixon's downfall was that the Annenbergs came home from London and made their presence felt much more in the Reagan Group. On December 31, 1974, they had the first of their New Year's Eve parties at Sunnylands, and it would become Reagan court ritual. "Lee called and said, 'Could I take over your whole New Year's Eve party?'" recalled Betsy Bloomingdale. "They wanted to have the Governor and Mrs. Reagan, you see. She said she would have everyone we had, but she didn't have Connie Wald, which kind of put me in the thickety-wicket with Connie, whom I adore. She did have Jules and Doris Stein. I remember Doris changing into her long dress in the car on the way out, because she didn't want to spend the night in Palm Springs."[3]

This passing of the torch did not go smoothly; in fact, it created something of a power struggle between Betsy Bloomingdale and Lee Annenberg, with Nancy caught in the middle, juggling her steel-beneath-the-bubbles best friend and the titanium-tough wife of the man who could be most useful to Ronnie's political future. "I told Lee, 'I always spend New Year's with my children,'" Betsy Bloomingdale went on, "and she said, 'That's okay, I'm inviting them.' She invited the children the first year, but for *after* dinner. The second year she didn't invite them. And the third year she didn't invite Alfred and me. Alfred said, 'I don't care about going all the way out to Palm Springs anyway. We're not going to beg for an invitation.' Apparently it was all because that summer, when Walter and Lee came out here, as they did every year in August, and stayed in the bungalow at the Beverly Hills Hotel, I didn't entertain them. I don't know why I didn't. I must have been busy with other things. But I didn't have a lunch or dinner for them, and all the others would line up to give dinners for the Annenbergs every single night. So Lee got miffed, and Nancy and I understood: one must pay attention."[4] Stirring the pot was Jerry Zipkin, who also spent Augusts at the Beverly Hills Hotel and had not made Lee's New Year's Eve list.

Nancy and Ronnie went to the Annenbergs' again in 1975, the year that Lee codified the houseguest roster. From then on, the same five couples—the Reagans, the Jorgensens, the Wilsons, the French Smiths, and the Deutsches—would stay in the same five guest suites, each done up by Billy Haines in a single cheery California color, with everything matching from the curtains to the wastebaskets. In 1976, however, Nancy favored Betsy, and they went there on New Year's Eve. The matter was finally resolved the following year. "Ardie Deutsch made it up," Betsy Bloomingdale told me. "He said, 'This is ridiculous, that we're all there and Alfred and Betsy aren't.' "[5]

* * *

President Ford called Governor Reagan over the 1974 holidays and, already nervous, tried to tempt him with a choice of jobs: he could go to Washington as secretary of transportation or take the post Walter Annenberg had just left at the Court of St. James's. Reagan declined, saying, "Hell, I can't afford to be an ambassador."[6] He agreed, however, to serve on a commission to investigate alleged CIA abuses connected to Watergate; the eight-man panel was chaired by Vice President Nelson Rockefeller and included former secretary of the treasury C. Douglas Dillon, former NATO supreme commander General Lyman Lemnitzer, and Lane Kirkland, the secretary-treasurer of the AFL-CIO.[7]

The sixty-four-year-old Reagan was leaving office on a wave of high approval ratings and flattering editorials and about to embark on a lucrative career as a private citizen. By January 6, 1975, he was on his way back to Pacific Palisades, after seeing his successor, Edmund "Jerry" Brown Jr., the son of his predecessor, sworn in. The thirty-six-year-old, unmarried Jerry had already annoyed Nancy by announcing that he would not live in the new Governor's Mansion upon its completion, referring to it as "a Taj Mahal" and suggesting that it be used as "a halfway house for lobbyists."[8] Both Ronnie and Nancy were relieved to be leaving the drab state capital and eager to get on with the next stage of their life. As Lyn Nofziger, who had reconciled with the Reagans when he ran Nixon's 1972 campaign in California, later wrote, "I think he was tired of the job, tired of dealing with the petty personalities in the legislature, tired of commuting to Los Angeles on most weekends so his wife could socialize with their rich friends, tired of the small-town atmosphere of Sacramento."[9]

Three months earlier, Michael Deaver and Peter Hannaford, a public relations specialist who joined the Governor's staff in his last year, had presented Reagan with a "comprehensive plan" for his immediate future, including a syndicated newspaper column, a daily radio program, and frequent speaking engagements. Both aides relocated to Los Angeles, where they opened Deaver & Hannaford, in a high-rise on Wilshire Boulevard in Westwood, fifteen minutes from San Onofre Drive. The corner office was reserved for Reagan and decorated by Nancy with mostly the same furniture and in the same warm reds as his office in the state capitol. The jellybean jar was on his desk, Helene von Damm was office manager, and Nancy Reynolds was in charge of advance work.[10] Only Ed Meese, who took a job as vice president and general counsel of the Rohr Corporation, an aircraft manufacturer based in San Diego, was missing, but he was in constant touch.[11] Although Ronald Reagan was the raison d'être of Deaver & Hannaford, the PR firm would pick up a few other clients, including the Dart Corporation, the government of Taiwan, and Rockwell International, one of the major Southern California defense firms.[12]

Reagan's income reportedly jumped to more than $800,000 that year.[13] His five-minute radio

program, titled *Viewpoint,* was aired every week-
day on nearly three hundred stations, his column ran
in more than two hundred newspapers, and he
commanded up to $10,000 for each of the eight to
ten speeches he gave every month.[14] In all three
formats his message was basically the same as it
had been since the 1950s: only conservatism
could save America from economic disaster and
the world from Communist domination. As
always, he wrote the bulk of his own material,
scratching out his radio addresses on yellow pads
as he flew around the country on his speaking
tours. It was a clever way to keep Reagan in the
public eye—by his own calculation he was reaching 20 million Americans each week[15]—and a fairly
exhausting routine even for someone half his age.
But Nancy made sure his itineraries allowed for an
afternoon nap, and Ronnie kept up his exercise
regime on the road. He was constantly telling
Deaver and Hannaford, "Remember to build some
ranch time into that schedule."[16]

"From the first day we saw it, Rancho del Cielo
cast a spell over us," Reagan would write of his
fourth and last ranch. "No place before or since
has ever given Nancy and me the joy and serenity
it does."[17] The Reagans had closed on their 688-
acre hideaway in the Santa Ynez Mountains north
of Santa Barbara just a few weeks before the end
of the governorship. It had been found for them by
Bill Wilson, whose avocado ranch was a few miles
away. Nancy was nervous at first about the tortur-

ously twisting seven-mile-long road that led to the remote property, but as Wilson recalled, "Ronnie fell in love with the place immediately—before we got anywhere near the house. As we got closer to it, he said, 'It's absolutely gorgeous here. I love it.'"[18] Nancy, too, was swept away by the sheer beauty of the place, with its old oaks and madrones, riding trails crisscrossing the chaparral, and views of the Pacific in one direction and the horse farms and vineyards of the Santa Ynez Valley in the other.

A tiny—"and I mean tiny," as Nancy put it— adobe house built in 1871 by the property's first owner, José Jesús Pico, a homesteader from Mexico, sat in the middle of a rolling pasture, and cattle grazed under a smog-free blue sky. A subsequent proprietor had named the place Tip Top Ranch, and while the Reagans changed the name, they maintained it as a working livestock operation, with twenty-two head of cattle and four horses, to take advantage of California tax breaks for agricultural preserves. *The New York Times* estimated that the $900 in property tax they paid in 1979 would otherwise have been closer to $42,000.[19]

Over the next two years, Ronnie spent most of his free time fixing up his "Ranch in the Sky," usually making the two-hour drive from Pacific Palisades with Barney Barnett, the retired California highway patrolman who had been his driver in Sacramento, and Dennis LeBlanc, the young former state trooper who had been his security man and now traveled with him on his speaking trips. "Sometimes the three of us would go up and back every day for three days in a row," LeBlanc recalled. "Anne, the Reagans' housekeeper, would pack a lunch for us or we'd stop at a Kentucky Fried Chicken place on the way up." They completely gutted the house, converting its screened-in wrap-around porch into an L-shaped living room and dining area, replaced the asbestos roof with Spanish-style tiles, repaired old fences and built new ones. Nancy helped Ronnie paint the house and lay a new floor in the kitchen. They also dug a pond behind the house and named it Lake Lucky.[20]

The end result was an exceedingly modest, 1,500-square-foot cottage heated only by two fireplaces. There were two bedrooms, one off the kitchen for Anne Allman. The master bedroom had sunny yellow walls and a matching chenille bedspread. The living room sofas were covered in brown cotton, the armchairs in the den were done in orange plaid, and paintings of horses, cowboys, and Western landscapes hung in every room. As I toured the place in 1999, I kept thinking, Nancy Reagan stayed *here*? It was a far cry from Sunnylands, or even her parents' villa in manicured Biltmore Estates. But it had a simplicity and coziness that said a lot about the couple that spent so much time there together.

On a rise just above the house were a tack barn and a spruced-up trailer, where the kids stayed. "There was always a project at the ranch, and if you went up there to stay, you helped," said the Wicks' son C.Z., who had become close to young Ron. "On one of the first weekends I went there, they were building a patio in front of the house. Ron and I quarried the rocks for that—putting them in the back of their ancient Ford station wagon and bringing them down to the house."

C. Z. Wick explained that when guests arrived at the turnoff from Pacific Coast Highway, "you'd call from the gas station down at the bottom of Refugio Road and say you were coming up. The Governor would always be waiting to unlock the gate for you. Inevitably, something would catch his interest while he was waiting. I remember once he'd been creosoting those telephone poles that he used to make the fences around the house—you know, this greasy stuff that would make them waterproof and keep the termites away. And he had found some berries that when you rubbed them together acted like soap. I walked up, and there he was rubbing these things between his hands, cleaning the creosote off."[21]

"Since the day we bought the ranch," Ronnie said, "if Nancy or I wanted to think something out, there's been no better place to do it than Rancho del Cielo. . . . During those first months after we left Sacramento, I spent a lot of time . . . riding around the ranch thinking about the future."[22]

On Halloween 1975, Ronnie and Nancy called a family meeting at San Onofre Drive to tell the children that he had decided to run for president.

Maureen, the self-described "political junkie" of the family, arrived first.[23] She had campaigned hard for Nixon in 1972—George Shultz, then secretary of the treasury, even wrote Reagan a note calling her "terrific." But, at thirty-four, Maureen was not having much success in launching an acting career, and had taken up with a fifty-five-year-old song-and-dance man named Gene Nelson. Her new beau had actually acted with her father in one of his last films for Warner Bros., but that did not endear him to Ronnie or Nancy.

Then came Michael with his fiancée Colleen Sterns. After a brief first marriage—to an eighteen-year-old belle from Mobile, Alabama—that pro-duced a son in 1973, Michael had finally found a source of stability in Colleen, "a girl who was equal in strength to Mom or Nancy."[24] He had a good job selling boats in Costa Mesa, and with Colleen's help he was working off his considerable debts, while trying to follow the advice his father had given him about marriage: "You'll never get in trou-ble if you say 'I love you' at least once a day."[25]

Patti was not at the meeting. Her parents claimed she didn't want to come; she said she hadn't been asked.[26] A year earlier, while working as a singing hostess at the Great American Food and Beverage Company in Santa Monica, she had met Bernie Leadon, the pot-smoking steel guitarist for the Eagles, one of the most popular rock bands of the early 1970s. They were now living together in Topanga Canyon, the hippie haven near Malibu, which her angry father told her was a sin.[27] Marion

Jorgensen told me that Nancy tried to get along with Patti during this period and even had her friends buy "these little beaded things she was making out there in the woods."[28] In 1974, when Patti and Bernie co-wrote a song for the Eagles called "I Wish You Peace," her album credit read Patti Davis. Patti saw dropping her father's name as a "turning point." As she wrote, "There was an underlying reason for choosing my mother's maiden name. . . . It was a child's way of asking for a parent's approval."[29]

The youngest Reagan, who was still living at home but refused to be called the Skipper, had also turned rebellious as he approached eighteen. In the summer of 1973, Ronnie and Nancy had taken him on a four-day horseback trip through Yosemite National Park, with no tents, just sleeping bags, and Ron was so proud of his mother that he had her tin cup engraved, "To the World's Greatest Camper—Sport—and Mom."[30] The following year, however, he was expelled from Webb, one of the top boarding schools in California. "They threw me out halfway through my junior year," Ron said. "I was too much of a troublemaker. Too prankish. My mother was mortified. . . . She thought my life was over. But my father had a good sense of humor about that sort of thing. He took it with a little more grace." Now that he was back in Pacific Palisades and enrolled at the prestigious Harvard School, the neighbors often heard him screaming at his mother, "Leave me alone! . . . All I want is to be left alone."[31]

A likely source of these arguments was the affair he was having with an older, married woman. "She was terrible," Nancy Reagan told me. "She looked like a child, but she certainly wasn't a child. She had a daughter whom Ron should have been going out with."[32]

In considering the problems and rebellions of the Reagan children, one has to realize that things could have been much worse, given the turbulence of the times and their parents' celebrity. No fewer than five of the Reagans' friends' children had overdosed or committed suicide. Like Bob and Ursula Taylor's boy, Charles Boyer's twenty-one-year-old son, Michael, was found dead in his bed. Art Linkletter's twenty-year-old daughter, Diane, and Ray and Fran Stark's twenty-five-year-old son, Peter, both jumped out of windows, reportedly while high on LSD. Gregory Peck's son, Jonathan, was thirty when he shot himself in 1975. By her own admission, Patti was taking psychedelics, including peyote, and had a "six month bout with cocaine" later in the 1970s, but she was so estranged from the family that her mother could only imagine what was going on.[33] In Ron's case, Nancy had found a bag of marijuana in his room during the summer before he was expelled from Webb, and was so upset that for the first time she tried to hit him.[34] Her suspicion that he was using drugs would continue to be another source of contention between them, and lead her to the sort of overbearing motherly behavior—monitoring his phone calls, grilling him about his friends—that drives teenagers to despair.

That evening in October 1975, as Ron slouched on the living room sofa, impatient to get into his costume for a Halloween party, his father explained why he had called the family together. "Dad had a speech all prepared," Maureen recalled, "and it was clear to me as we all sat down that he had thought about this meeting for a good long while before we all got there."[35]

"Whenever I check into a hotel, the bellhop asks, 'Why don't you run for President?'" Ronnie told his children. "The next morning, when I leave, the chambermaids come up to me and say the same thing. When I walk through the airports, people are always stopping me and saying, 'Please, we *need* you to run.' It won't be easy but the grassroots support is there. I've been speaking out on the issues for quite a while now, and it's time to put myself on the line. In three weeks I'm going to announce that I'm entering the race. Otherwise, I'd feel like the guy who always sat on the bench and never got into the game."[36]

"You might think that Ronnie's decision to run for president was a big turning point for our family or for us as a couple," Nancy later wrote. "While it was in certain ways, in others it wasn't. We didn't agonize over whether or not Ronnie should run. Quickly enough, it just became obvious that running for president was what Ronnie was going to do and that I was going to support him. If Ronnie was worried after he made his decision, he never let on. If I sometimes knew he was worried, it wasn't because he told me; it was just because I knew him so well. I never heard him express real fear or self-doubt; I don't think he really felt either. As I've said before, he liked a good competition."[37]

And that's what he would get.

"The potential risks of his candidacy were not lost on any of us," wrote Mike Deaver. "Ford was a sitting, if unelected, president, and Reagan considered himself a loyalist, a consummate party man. No Republican president had been denied his party's renomination in one hundred years. None had been challenged within the party since Teddy Roosevelt did so in 1912, against William Howard Taft, and lost."[38] More recently, however, two Democratic presidents, Truman in 1952 and Johnson in 1968, had given up the fight in the face of strong opposition in the primaries.

As with Reagan's first race for governor in 1966 and what Nofziger called his "quarter-hearted" presidential effort in 1968, the planning for 1976 began early but the announcement came late. This time, however, the candidate's delaying tactics were based on calculation rather than doubt— Reagan wanted to keep making money for as long as possible before he formally declared, when federal law would require him to give up his lucrative radio commentaries. As usual, the first strategy meeting, in May 1974, took place in Pacific Palisades, with Nancy present. The cast included Deaver, Hannaford, Meese, and Nofziger, as well as Holmes Tuttle and Justin Dart, who was eclipsing Henry Salvatori as the co-leader of the Kitchen Cabinet. There were also some new faces, including David Packard, the billionaire founder of the Hewlett-Packard computer company; Clarke Reed, the chairman of the Republican Party in Mississippi; and, most importantly, John P. Sears III, a well-connected Washington lawyer and the wunderkind tactician of Nixon's 1968 campaign.[39]

The shadow of Watergate, which was still three months from resolution, hung over the gathering. According to Jules Witcover in *Marathon: The Pursuit of the Presidency, 1972–1976*, "Meese summarized the morning's discussion and the general agreement that Reagan should run, but that the effort would have to be contingent on Nixon's remaining as President through 1976." When Reagan asked if anyone disagreed, only Sears contradicted the consensus. "I think it can be done, I think it should be done; the party needs it, the country needs it; but I disagree that Nixon has to stay as President," Sears asserted. "In fact, Nixon will be gone in six months." Furthermore, Sears told Reagan, "Jerry Ford can't cut the mustard, he's not perceived as a leader; he can't lead the Congress or the country. He will be vulnerable and we can beat him. He will not be seen as a true incumbent; you have as much support around the country as he has."[40]

The thirty-four-year-old Sears had studied chemistry at Notre Dame, in hopes of pursuing a career in psychiatry, but he wound up at

Georgetown Law School. "He's cool and unflappable and has a great capacity to size other people up," a friend once described him. "In that way he's never really abandoned his wish to be a psychiatrist."[41] Sears had been recruited for the 1976 effort by the Governor's top political aide, Bob Walker, who had worked for Nixon in 1968 before defecting to Reagan and heading his delegate hunt in the South, where he found himself outsmarted at almost every turn by Sears. Nixon had taken the cunning young lawyer to the White House with him, but he was quickly forced out by John Mitchell. The attorney general "neither liked nor trusted him," said Nofziger, who had also worked in the Nixon White House, "feelings I grew to understand and appreciate." As Nofziger tells it, Walker "persuaded Deaver to invite [Sears] to some early organizational meetings. Deaver became enamored of Sears, whose line of political chatter impressed almost all of us, including the Reagans."[42]

"John Sears was urbane and articulate," Nancy recalled in *My Turn.* "And he knew as much about politics as anyone I had ever met. I loved having lunch with him because he was bright, knowledgeable, and fascinating to listen to. John was not a dyed-in-the-wool conservative, and some of Ronnie's supporters didn't trust him. His mission was to bring home a winner, and he would do everything possible to make that happen." She added, "He also had excellent contacts with the Washington press corps, which would be very important if Ronnie entered the race."[43] In fact, a decade after Nancy penned those words, Nixon's lawyer Leonard Garment published *In Search of Deep Throat*, in which he came to the well-considered conclusion that John Sears had been Bob Woodward and Carl Bernstein's infamous secret source.

In the event, Nixon resigned three months earlier than Sears had predicted, but that still made Sears something of a prophet for Ronnie, Nancy, and Mike Deaver. "Our long national nightmare is over," declared Gerald Ford on August 10, 1974, after being sworn in as the first man to assume the presidency without having been elected to that office or to the vice presidency. This precedent would subtly undermine Ford's legitimacy and provide justification for Reagan's challenge, but for the moment the entire nation was relieved to have a "regular guy" from Grand Rapids, Michigan, replacing the dour, paranoid, and downright weird Richard Milhous Nixon. Betty Ford, a former modern dancer who still liked to kick up her heels on the dance floor, was also a breath of fresh air in contrast to the sad, uptight, isolated Pat Nixon. And the four Ford children, all in their early twenties and late teens, were athletic and outgoing, not prim and prissy like the Nixon girls. That fall, after the new First Lady underwent a radical mastectomy, she spoke openly about the previously taboo subject of breast cancer and earned the respect of the country for her honesty and bravery.

By then her husband's popularity had been severely damaged by his unconditional pardon of Nixon, and there was audible grumbling on the right about his selection of Rockefeller for vice president, his offer of amnesty to Vietnam War evaders, and his proposed deficit to stimulate the lagging economy. In the November 1974 midterm elections, the Democrats picked up forty-nine House seats, five Senate seats, and four governorships. Reagan, winding down in Sacramento and wanting to be seen as giving Ford a chance, remained temporarily above the fray, though he publicly supported the pardon, saying Nixon had "suffered as much as any man should."[44]

In December, Tuttle, Dart, and Jack Wrather hosted a lunch at the Downtown Los Angeles Club for Senator Lloyd Bentsen, a conservative Texas Democrat who was thinking of running for president. The lunch was widely seen as a warning signal to Ford, and The New York Times quoted unnamed guests as saying that the Kitchen Cabinet big shots would never have given the lunch without Reagan's prior knowledge.[45] Meanwhile, John Sears was letting it drop that he had been offered a job in the Ford White House, and pressuring Deaver to get Reagan to announce as soon as possible in the new year.[46]

That would have to wait, since Reagan was just embarking on the radio, newspaper, and speaking schedule put together by Deaver and Hannaford. In February 1975, "immaculate in a carefully pressed blue suit and highly polished loafers," he was the star speaker at a conference sponsored by the Young Americans for Freedom and the American Conservative Union to explore the possibility of forming a third party. Introduced by Bill Buckley's brother, Senator James Buckley of New York, as "the Rembrandt of American conservatism," Reagan brought the crowd to its feet. "Is it a third party we need?" he bellowed. "Or is it a new and revitalized second party, raising a banner of no pale pastels, but bold colors which make it unmistakably clear where we stand on all the issues troubling the people?"[47]

In early March, at a Republican leadership conference in Washington, Reagan rejected appeals by Ford and Rockefeller to broaden the party base by asserting, "A political party cannot be all things to all people. . . . It is not a social club or fraternity engaged in intramural contests to accumulate trophies on the mantel over the fireplace."[48] A *Newsweek* cover story later that month, titled "Ready on the Right," called him "the most kinetic single presence in American political life."[49] Ford's chief of staff, Donald Rumsfeld, contacted Reagan and offered him the post of secretary of commerce, which Reagan politely turned down. On March 30, an increasingly edgy President Ford invited the Reagans for dinner at the Palm Springs house he and Betty were renting from one of his golfing partners. If his purpose was to dissuade Reagan from running, he obviously didn't succeed. Betty Ford later said of Nancy, "She's a cold fish. . . . Nancy could not have been colder. Then the flashbulbs went off, and she smiled and kissed me—suddenly an old friend. I couldn't get over that. Off camera—ice. On camera—warmth."[50]

Two days later the Reagans flew to London, where Ronnie gave a speech to the Pilgrim Society, an organization founded by Cecil Rhodes to promote unity among English-speaking nations, and met with the first woman to head the Conservative Party, Margaret Thatcher. Justin Dart, who kept an apartment near Hyde Park, and Walter Annenberg had helped arrange the meeting. "I'd planned on spending only a few minutes with Margaret Thatcher but we ended up talking for almost two hours," Reagan recalled. "I liked her immediately—she was warm, feminine, gracious, and intelligent—and it was evident from our first words that we were soul mates when it came to reducing government and expanding economic freedom."[51]

Thatcher felt the same way. "It was clear that Ron Reagan was in politics out of passionate belief," she told me in 1998. "This is the century when we have had the biggest battle of ideas in history. Between totalitarianism and freedom. Coercion versus liberty. Ron Reagan was a passionate warrior in this battle. I was also a warrior."[52] The Iron Lady, as she came to be known, had taken over the Tory leadership only two months before meeting Reagan, and had immediately declared "an all-out war on Socialism." With an approval rating of 64 percent, she was the most popular politician in Britain at the time, well on her way to 10 Downing Street.[53]

Shortly after Reagan returned to Los Angeles, he met with his inner circle, "confessed his increasing disillusion with Ford's leadership and said he was willing to run."[54] Had Thatcher provided him with the example—and extra dose of affirmation—that he needed to commit to taking on the White House and its ideologically impure occupant? In a Memorial Day speech in Atlantic City, Reagan sounded the theme that would propel his campaign against Ford: "The free world—indeed, the entire non-Communist world—is crying out for strong American leadership, and we are not providing it. Neither are we providing a strong, lasting, consistent foreign policy." The next morning on *Face the Nation* he promised he would make his plans known by the end of the year.[55]

A few days later, Reagan's principal boosters in the Senate, Jesse Helms of North Carolina, James McClure of Idaho, and James Buckley, issued a statement that could only make Ford more uncomfortable: "As neither the President nor the Vice President was elected to office, it would be in the best interest of the Republican Party and of the country for the 1976 presidential and vice-presidential nominations to be sought and won in an open convention. . . . The merits of the current administration must be judged in 1976 by delegates pledged only to support the principles of their party. The President can ask for no more—and he deserves no less."[56]

Meanwhile, at a secret meeting in San Francisco with Deaver, Hannaford, and Nofziger, Sears was given the go-ahead to put together a Reagan for President committee. Nofziger soon moved to Washington, where he and Sears started working out of a makeshift headquarters at Sears's law firm. They had already approached Senator Paul Laxalt about heading the committee. Laxalt, a tall, rugged conservative, had been governor of Nevada during Reagan's first term, and the two men got along well. As a freshmen senator from a small state, however, he wanted to be sure Reagan was serious before he brought the ire of the White House down upon himself. In a July 4 phone call, Laxalt asked Reagan, "You've got a fire burning in your gut to do this, don't you?" "I have to tell you I have," Reagan answered. "Well, tell me, on a scale of one to ten," Laxalt persisted, "where would you place yourself in terms of a candidacy?" "Oh, right about eight," said the ever cautious Reagan. "That's good enough for me," his fellow Westerner told him. "I guess I'm your man."[57]

On July 15, Laxalt announced the formation of the Citizens for Reagan Committee, with himself as chairman and Sears as executive vice chairman. Asked about a recent Gallup Poll showing Reagan as the first choice of 20 percent of Republicans as opposed to 41 percent for President Ford, Laxalt maintained that was a strong position for a noncandidate against an incumbent.[58] Ford had officially declared he was running in a July 8 speech from the Oval Office;

two days later forty-four prominent California Republicans, including several longtime Reagan associates, came out for the President. The defectors included state party chairman Paul Haerle, who had been Reagan's appointments secretary in Sacramento and did not get along with Nancy, and computer tycoon David Packard, who had been at the first strategy meeting in Pacific Palisades in May 1974, but who now signed on as Ford's national finance chairman. The most surprising name on the list was Henry Salvatori.

"I felt this way very strongly," Salvatori later explained, "that an incumbent President should not be opposed by a member of his own party. At no time has such a man won. If he wins the nomination, he loses the election. I thought of it strictly as a practical situation. I felt for Reagan. Through no fault of his own, lightning struck, and he had to face an incumbent President when he shouldn't have. If Nixon hadn't gotten involved in Watergate, Reagan would have marched right in. I understood how a lot of people felt. It was hard for them and it was hard for Reagan to say, 'Let's wait for next time.' I was hoping he wouldn't run for his own ultimate good. I asked him before I committed to Ford if he was going to run and he hadn't decided. I don't think he would have run if he hadn't felt a responsibility to various people around the country who liked him so much and urged him to run. It proved me wrong, but I really thought that if one or two guys like me would go for Ford that maybe he wouldn't run. I really believed that."[59]

Salvatori tried to talk Tuttle into seeing things his way, but as far as Tuttle was concerned whatever Ronnie wanted Ronnie got. This split in the Kitchen Cabinet was some time in coming, and it would never quite be repaired. At the root of it was an antagonism between Salvatori and Justin Dart that went all the way back to 1964, when they were on opposite sides of the Goldwater-Rockefeller divide. Both men tended toward the pugnacious and arrogant, and both were fond of publicizing their wealth and power. Salvatori, whose influence in Reagan's first term had nearly equaled Tuttle's, resented the sudden rise of Dart in the second term. The change in the federal campaign finance law after Watergate, limiting individual donations to $1,000 to any one candidate and $25,000 to any party in each campaign cycle, further strengthened Dart's position as an ace fund-raiser against the big-check writer Salvatori.

Nancy also played a significant role in this shifting dynamic. Although she and Punky Dart hadn't hit it off at first—and Punky would never become a lady-in-waiting like Betsy, Marion, and Betty Wilson—Nancy had come to appreciate her discretion and independence. The fact that Punky had refused to join the Blue Ribbon 400, while Grace Salvatori remained Buff Chandler's right arm despite being publicly humiliated by her, no doubt contributed to Nancy's growing affection for Dart's wife. The elegant champagne receptions the Darts gave for the POWs had also made points with the Governor's wife. Moreover, Nancy had developed her own relationship with Justin Dart; she frequently called him about fund-raising and personnel matters, just as she had been doing with Alfred Bloomingdale for years.

Though such subtle social shifts may seem inconsequential, the decline of the archconservative Salvatori and the rise of the more corporate-minded Dart, especially when seen in the light of Nancy's increasing closeness to the Gosdens, the Cowleses, Kay Graham, and other establishment types, represented a small step in the long process of moving her husband toward the center. In any event, Nancy would never fully forgive Henry Salvatori for his 1976 defection. The Salvatoris were off Marion Jorgensen's guest list as early as May 1975, and when the Jorgensens had a big cocktail party for the Reagans on the night of the California primary in June 1976, everyone from Betty Adams to Jerry Zipkin was there nibbling on the guacamole in toast cups with bacon bits— everyone except Henry and Grace.[60]

Leonard Firestone and Taft Schreiber also backed Ford, though the latter would die before the Kansas City convention. In addition, the Reagan campaign found itself without two key strategists: Tom Reed and Stu Spencer. Reed, a driving force behind the 1968 presidential run and co-chair of the 1970 gubernatorial campaign, had been made an assistant secretary of defense by Nixon and would soon be promoted to secretary of the Air Force by Ford. Spencer would become the chief strategist in the Ford campaign, though, as he told me, he didn't jump to the other side—he was pushed.

"My problem was never with the Reagans," he confided, explaining that during the Governor's second term his top staffers moved to consolidate their power. "I had total access to the Reagans. They [the staffers] had a problem with that. The Reagans didn't even know it was happening, and I'm not the kind of guy to go around and whine. I fight my battles." Although he counted Ed Meese among those who undermined him, Spencer was most disappointed by his old protégé, Mike Deaver. "He was a very big part of it. We had some real problems. This started in the last two years of the governorship, and it got worse. I just walked away. And then in 1976 there was no way that those people were going to let me in, even if I wanted in—it was obvious to me. I had known Ford for years, and his campaign started having some problems, and all of a sudden they came to me. Actually, I agreed to do something for two months, and I ended up there for eighteen months. The point is it was not a falling out with the Reagans. But when I got into the Ford thing, I took some good shots at the Reagans, and they were pretty mad. But the reason I was there was, hey, Ford was the only show in town for me."[61]

The Ford-Reagan contest was an exceptionally personal one, not only because the candidates had very little respect for each other's abilities but also because their wives seemed to be innately antipathetic. The two women could not have been more different. For Nancy Reagan, for instance, a trip to New York meant lunch at Le Cirque with Jan Cowles and Jerry Zipkin, a fitting at Adolfo or Bill Blass, and dinner at the Buckleys' Park Avenue maisonette. Betty Ford's best friend in New York, on the other hand, was her former teacher Martha Graham, the matriarch of modern dance, who introduced her to Halston, the hippest designer in town, and Andy Warhol, the wildest artist. Whereas Nancy was a virtual teetotaler, Betty liked to drink, and she would later admit to a problem with alcohol and pills. Even while she was First Lady, she talked about the nervous breakdown she had had in the 1960s and how much psychiatry had helped her—something the secretive, image-driven Nancy would never dream of doing.

In August 1975, Betty Ford gave an interview on *60 Minutes.* When Morley Safer asked her how she would react if her eighteen-year-old daughter told her she was having an affair, the First Lady answered, "Well, I wouldn't be surprised. I think she's a perfectly normal human being, like all girls. If she wanted to continue it, I would certainly counsel and advise her on the subject." While not exactly condoning premarital sex, she did say that it "might lower the divorce rate," and she also blithely suggested that if she were a young person today she might try marijuana. She called the Supreme Court's 1973 *Roe v. Wade* decision "great," saying that it had brought abortion "out of the backwoods and put it in the hospitals where it belongs."[62]

The reaction from Republican right-wingers was instantaneous. William Loeb, the ultraconservative publisher of New Hampshire's leading newspaper, the *Manchester Union Leader*, condemned the immorality and the "utter stupidity" of Betty Ford's remarks. "Involving any prominent individual, this would be a disgusting spectacle," he wrote. "Coming from the First Lady in the White House, it disgraces the nation itself."[63] So many angry phone calls, telegrams, and letters deluged 1600 Pennsylvania Avenue that the President was only half joking when he said that he was afraid his wife's remarks would cost him 20 million votes. The very next week, however, a Harris Poll showed that she was a lot more popular than he was, and in analyzing the results, Louis Harris said, "Mrs. Ford's outspoken statements have won support from those younger and more independent elements in the electorate who are indispensable to her husband in a contest for the White House next fall." Feminist leader Betty Friedan anointed the First Lady "the best kind of liberated woman."[64]

None of this went over well with Nancy. In mid-September she took it upon herself to attack the increasingly admired First Lady. She didn't mention Betty Ford by name in the speech she gave to the Women's Republican Club of Grosse Pointe, the richest town in the Fords' home state of Michigan, but everybody knew exactly whom she was referring to when she said, "I am disturbed about the growing immorality. . . . Our sons and daughters are told not only that it's all right to break our rules of morality, but that there should be no rules at all. . . . I believe it is time the great majority of us said, 'Enough already. Stop.'"[65]

The great issue of the day for American women was the Equal Rights Amendment, which had been passed by Congress but had not been ratified by the required three quarters of the states. Among the wives of potential presidential candidates from both parties, a field that included Georgia governor Jimmy Carter, Arizona congressman Morris Udall, and Sargent Shriver, only two opposed the ERA—Cornelia Wallace, the wife of the Alabama governor, and Nancy Reagan. As First Lady, Betty Ford became the amendment's most prominent supporter, spending countless hours calling state legislators and urging them to vote for it. Her progressive views endeared her most of all to women in the media, just as Nancy's obsession with tradition and appearance worked against her. As Helen Jackson, the wife of another prospective candidate, Senator Henry "Scoop" Jackson of Washington, said, "More is expected of wives this year than at any other time in a Presidential campaign. We all discuss cerebral things. . . . I think it's all because of Watergate and the women's movement. Watergate made people more concerned about the kind of people elected to public office, and because of the women's movement, wives are now expected to be able to talk issues. It takes a lot more energy now than when all we did was drink tea and shake hands with the ladies."[66] At the end of 1975, *Newsweek* put Betty Ford on its cover as "Woman of the Year" and *Time* named her its "Man of the Year," making her only the eleventh woman to receive that distinction.

Ironically, in private Nancy Reagan, because of her glamorous upbringing and her years in Hollywood, was much more sophisticated than Betty Ford. As the editor of *Interview* in those days, I had occasion to see Mrs. Ford at Halston's dinners, where she was really a fish out of water—extremely pleasant but at a loss with guests such as Diana Vreeland and Truman Capote, who had both hit it off perfectly with Nancy. One of the new friends Nancy made during this period was Barry Diller, who was a senior ABC executive when he met her at a dinner given by Oscar and Françoise de la Renta in Los Angeles. "I was seated next to her, and instantly we got it," Diller recalled. "It didn't really make any sense—we weren't of the same age, I was hardly a Republican—but within twenty minutes we were telling each other about our lives." After the Reagans left Sacramento and Diller took over Paramount in 1974, he continued to see her, and when his relationship with Diane von Furstenberg was in trouble, he told me, "one of the people I really talked about it with was Nancy. And I did not talk to too many of the older folks about my personal life. But with her I talked about everything, and I totally trusted her."[67]

But then again, Nancy was always at ease with men. Merv Griffin, who had known the Reagans since he was under contract to Warner Bros. in the 1950s, regularly put her, with or without Ronnie, on his nightly talk show throughout the governorship and afterward. Mike Wallace, who went even further back with Nancy, aired an interview with her and Ronnie and Maureen for *60 Minutes* on December 14, 1975, three weeks after Reagan formally announced his candidacy. CBS ran a full-page ad in *The New York Times*: "Tonight, Ronald Reagan tells how he'd play the role of President."

Up to the last minute, Gerald Ford did everything possible to stop Reagan from entering the race. In early October he put the super-professional Stu Spencer in charge of his campaign's day-to-day operations, in effect turning the campaign manager, the feckless Howard "Bo" Callaway of Georgia, into a figurehead. A month later the President shook up his foreign policy team and top staff. Secretary of Defense James Schlesinger, a hard-liner who opposed the Nixon-Kissinger policy of détente with the Soviet Union and Communist China, was replaced by the more moderate Donald Rumsfeld, who had been White House chief of staff. Rumsfeld's deputy, Richard Cheney, took his boss's job, and, as a supposed sop to conservatives, Henry Kissinger, who had been serving as both secretary of state and national security adviser since Watergate, gave up the latter post to his right-hand man, Lieutenant General Brent Scowcroft. In the midst of this upheaval, Vice President Rockefeller, tired of the constant chorus of criticism aimed at him by Southern Republicans, including Bo Callaway, told Ford that he was taking himself out of consideration for the 1976 ticket.

Reagan promptly went on the record with his reaction. He said he was "shocked" at the dismissal of Schlesinger, calling him "the most articulate voice" on national defense in the administration, and expressed dismay at the "shabby treatment" of Rockefeller. "I'm certainly not appeased," he told the press with a laugh. Speaking at Florida Atlantic University in Boca Raton on November 3, he answered a student's question about his intentions by saying, "On a scale of 1 to 10, I'm about a 9."[68]

Meanwhile Tom Reed, who had become Air Force secretary in the November shuffle, advised Dick Cheney to call the only person who could persuade Reagan to pull out—Holmes Tuttle. According to Tuttle, however, another move Ford had made around this time to burnish his image with the right actually worked against him with Reagan. In late October, when New York mayor Abe Beame begged the federal government to guarantee the bonds of his nearly bankrupt city, Ford refused, which resulted in the notorious *Daily News* headline FORD TO CITY: DROP DEAD. "The governor had been talking about all the cities being in bad shape," Tuttle recalled. "That convinced us. We took a poll throughout this country, and the poll showed us there was strong support for what

Governor Reagan was talking about. He was the man, so we decided to run. . . . [But] we said, 'Well, maybe we'll wait for another poll.' So we waited three weeks or thirty days, and we took another one. When that happened, we met up at the governor's house. It was a go, and we went."[69]

On November 20, Reagan, having informed Ford the day before, held a news conference at the National Press Club in Washington to announce officially that he was a candidate for president. Presenting himself once more as a Citizen Politician and vowing to respect the Eleventh Commandment, "Thou shalt not speak ill of another Republican," he nevertheless declared, "Our nation's capital has become the seat of a buddy system that functions for its own benefits—increasingly insensitive to the needs of the American worker who supports it with his taxes. Today it is difficult to find leaders who are independent of the forces that have brought us our problems: the Congress, the bureaucracy, the lobbyists, big business and big labor."[70]

The reference to big business was the idea of John Sears, who quite brilliantly realized that Reagan could appeal to traditionally Democratic blue-collar workers in the Rust Belt as well as to his base of affluent Sun Belt suburbanites. It did not endear Sears to Tuttle, Dart, and the rest of the Kitchen Cabinet, though they had to marvel at the efficiency with which he launched the new Reagan campaign. Immediately following the press conference, the Reagans, accompanied by a large contingent from the national media, boarded a chartered 727 for a two-day blitz of the four key early-primary states: New Hampshire, Florida, Illinois, and North Carolina. The Secret Service attached to the Reagans assigned the couple the code names that would follow them the rest of their lives: his was Rawhide, hers Rainbow.[71]

At every stop, Sears had organized well-planned, well-controlled, and well-timed-for-TV events. For a brief frightening moment, however, at the first stop in Miami, a rally outside a Ramada Inn near the airport, things went awry when a young man waving a toy pistol was wrestled to the ground by the Secret Service as the Reagans stepped off the platform. A terrified Nancy blamed Ronnie for not precisely following the Secret Service's instructions. "From now on," she told him, "if the Secret Service tells you to turn to the left, turn left! Do what they tell you to do!"[72]

Nancy's hysteria was somewhat justified. In September two assassination attempts with real guns had been made on President Ford's life. The first, in Sacramento, was by Lynette "Squeaky" Fromme, a member of the Charles Manson Family; the second, in San Francisco, was by Sara Jane Moore, a prisoners' rights fanatic.

Three weeks after Reagan announced, the latest Gallup Poll had him at 40 percent, Ford at 32 percent—numbers that boded well for Sears's blitzkrieg strategy of knocking the President out of the race with quick wins in New Hampshire in

February and Florida in March. By the end of the year, the Reagan campaign had raised $2 million, against $1.7 million raised for Ford.[73] After spending Christmas Eve at the home of Charles and Mary Jane Wick—the start of another Reagan ritual—and New Year's Eve at the Annenbergs', the Reagans headed for New Hampshire.

On his first day in the Granite State, wearing two sweaters and a ski jacket in 7-degree weather, Reagan told three hundred residents of Moultonborough that détente with the Soviet Union had become a "one-way street." He continued, "I think it's time for us to straighten up and eyeball them, and say, 'Hey, fellas, let's get this back on the track where it's something for something, not all one way.'" If he were president, he added, he would tell the Russians for starters to get out of Angola, where they were backing the pro-Communist side in a civil war—"or you're going to have to deal with us." The next day *New York Times* columnist James Reston wrote, "The more bonnie Ronnie talks, the better President Ford looks. . . . For delicacy of language and precision of policy, [Reagan] makes Mr. Ford's statements on détente and Angola seem almost eloquent and statesmanlike."[74]

On a second trip to New Hampshire, Reagan went after the welfare system. "There's a woman in Chicago," he said. "She has 80 names, 30 addresses, 12 Social Security cards, and is collecting veterans' benefits on four nonexisting deceased husbands. And she's collecting Social

Security on her cards. She's got Medicaid, getting food stamps and she is collecting welfare under each of her names. Her tax-free cash income alone is over $150,000." His listeners, however, kept bringing up his proposal to save the federal government $90 billion annually by transferring most of its welfare and social service programs to the states. No, he had to keep telling them, that did not mean that New Hampshire would have to enact an income tax or a sales tax to cover the costs. A Gallup Poll released on January 10 now had Ford and Reagan running neck and neck, with 45 percent each. On January 12, Reagan disavowed his proposal, calling it a "mistake"; one day later he disavowed his disavowal.[75] Under Stu Spencer's guidance, Ford made hay of his opponent's gaffes, calling his economic plan "pure political demagoguery" and asserting that Reagan was too "extreme" a conservative to win against the Democrats in November.[76]

On February 24, Ford beat Reagan by 1,300 votes out of 108,000 cast, and took seventeen of the state's twenty-one convention delegates. Reagan, who had celebrated his sixty-fifth birthday in New Hampshire, called it a "virtual tie."[77] But Paul Laxalt, who had spent the previous night with Ronnie and Nancy waiting to uncork the champagne, saw it for what it was. "We couldn't believe it," he wrote. "Ron Reagan had never lost a race."[78]

He lost three more states in early March, Massachusetts and Vermont on the 2nd, and a week later, more significantly, Florida, where his state campaign chairman had originally predicted a two-to-one victory—and where Ford beat him by ten points. But in his speeches around Florida he had found his issue, the Panama Canal, his bogey-man, Henry Kissinger, and his voice. In Winter Haven, on February 29, he accused the secretary of state of having a secret plan to give sovereignty over the canal to Panama, then ruled by a leftist military dictator, General Omar Torrijos. "If these reports are true," he asserted, "it means that the American people have been deceived by a State Department preoccupied by secrecy. They are due a full explanation. Presumably Mr. Ford has not been fully informed by the State Department, for if he were, I cannot imagine he would knowingly endorse such action. . . . When it comes to the Canal, we bought it, we paid for it, it's ours, and we should tell Torrijos and company that we are going to keep it!"[79]

He went even further in Orlando four days later, especially regarding Kissinger, whom he con-demned as the architect of America's retreat in the face of "Soviet imperialism" in Southeast Asia, the Middle East, and Africa. "Last year and this, the Soviet Union, using Castro's mercenaries, inter-vened decisively in the Angola civil war and routed the pro-Western forces. Yet, Messrs. Ford and Kissinger continue to tell us that we must not let this interfere with détente. We have given the Soviets our trade and our technology. At Kis-singer's insistence, Mr. Ford snubbed Aleksandr

Solzhenitsyn, one of the great moral heroes of our time. . . . Mr. Ford and Dr. Kissinger ask us to trust their leadership. I confess I find that more and more difficult to do. Henry Kissinger's stewardship of United States foreign policy has coincided precisely with the loss of United States military supremacy."[80] Reagan's attacks on Kissinger were so strident that Bill Buckley, whose *National Review* was enthusiastically "plugging for Reagan," called him on Kissinger's behalf and argued that the Panama Canal issue was more complicated than he was making it out to be.[81]

The day after Reagan's Florida defeat, *The New York Times* reported that Ford's campaign advisers were sending signals to Reagan "to end his insurgency—and perhaps join the Republican ticket as a running mate." Dick Cheney was quoted as saying that the White House would not hold a grudge against the Californian for things said in "the heat of the campaign." With Nancy at his side, Reagan dug in his heels and told the press, "The incumbent in these first couple of primaries has thrown the whole load at us, he has shot all the big artillery there is, used everything in the incumbency he can, and we are still possessing almost half the Republican vote."[82]

The following Tuesday, Ford took Reagan's native state of Illinois, 61 percent to 39 percent. Ford declared "a great victory and another real clincher in our effort to win the nomination and go on to victory in 1976." Stu Spencer said that Reagan should withdraw, "the sooner the better."[83]

Eleven out of twelve living former Republican National Committee chairmen had already endorsed Ford, the only exception being George H. W. Bush, who had been made director of the CIA by Ford and was therefore obliged to remain neutral.[84] The National Republican Conference of Mayors and seven of the thirteen Republican governors called on Reagan to quit the race. All of this only served to fuel Reagan's stubbornness. Arriving at a rally in Greensboro, North Carolina, with Jimmy Stewart, who called Reagan "a friend of mine," Reagan told reporters to tell Ford to quit.[85]

Laxalt recalled that the campaign was so broke by then that they had barely been able to pay for the 727 to fly them to North Carolina, and according to Nofziger even Nancy Reagan had come to the conclusion that it was time to throw in the towel. Nofziger was stunned when a frazzled Mike Deaver told him, "You've got to talk her out of it." He knew he was not Nancy's favorite, but he agreed to give it a try. "Ronnie has to get out," Nancy blurted when Nofziger walked into their hotel suite. "He's going to embarrass himself if he doesn't." At that moment Reagan walked out of the bedroom and, realizing what was going on, said, "Lynwood," using his pet name for Nofziger, "I'm going to stay in this thing until the end. I still think we can win."[86]

Nancy helped save the day in North Carolina, however, by strongly supporting Thomas Ellis, the local campaign chairman, when he pleaded with

Harry Treleaven, the campaign media consultant, to air a half-hour videotape of one of Reagan's hard-hitting Florida speeches. For Ellis, the tape of Reagan sitting at a desk in a studio and talking directly into the camera was reminiscent of his 1964 Goldwater speech. Until then Treleaven had insisted on thirty-second spots filmed at Reagan rallies, and he feared that Reagan's professionalism in a studio setup would remind voters of his career as an actor. In the four days before the primary, the campaign ran the Florida tape on fifteen of North Carolina's seventeen TV stations, and it is generally credited with turning the tide in the state, which Reagan won with 52 percent of the vote.[87]

There were twenty-one more primaries to go. In April and May, Reagan won Texas, Alabama, Georgia, Indiana, and Arizona while Ford took Wisconsin, West Virginia, and Michigan. In Nebraska, the Ford campaign ran radio ads in which Barry Goldwater attacked Reagan's stand on the Panama Canal, saying it was based on "gross factual errors" and could "needlessly lead this country into open military conflict." Flabbergasted, Nancy told reporters, "I feel as if I have been stabbed. . . . Of course, everyone knows what my husband did in 1964 for him." According to Nofziger, the spots continued to run "until Nancy personally called [Goldwater] and complained. Reagan won Nebraska anyway by a lopsided margin, but things were never the same again between Goldwater and the Reagans."[88]

Edith Davis also made a call to her Phoenix neighbor. "She called him up in his Senate office," Richard Davis told me, "and she called him a cocksucker. That was all over Washington and Phoenix—see, Barry Goldwater wanted to be secretary of defense under Ford."[89]

The primaries ended on June 8, with Reagan winning California by two to one and Ford sweeping New Jersey and garnering most of the delegates in Ohio. On the last weekend, Ford ran the most negative TV ads of the campaign, focusing on Reagan's recent comments on the situation in Rhodesia, where black guerrillas were fighting against the white government of Ian Smith: "Last Wednesday, Ronald Reagan said he would send American troops to Rhodesia. On Thursday he clarified that. He said they could be observers, or advisers. What does he think happened in Vietnam? . . . When you vote Tuesday, remember: Governor Ronald Reagan couldn't start a war. President Ronald Reagan could."[90] Once again Nancy was outraged, but this time the focus of her fury was Stu Spencer, whom she blamed for the ads. "It was quite a while before I could forgive Stu for that one."[91]

By July 18, after the eleven states that didn't hold primaries had chosen their delegates in conventions, *The New York Times* had Ford with 1,102 delegates, only 28 short of the number required for nomination. But Reagan was not far behind with 1,063. About 100 delegates were still uncommitted, and they were fought over fiercely in the month leading up to the convention. According to Laxalt, "We soon realized that competing for these delegates against the White House wasn't a fair fight. Ron would call them—even visit with them personally—and did reasonably well. But then Jerry Ford would invite them to a meeting in the Oval Office. It was like a guy with a Volkswagen vying for the attention of a girl against a competitor who has a Rolls-Royce."[92]

"I was furious," Nancy later wrote. "President Ford took full advantage of his office. He brought dozens of uncommitted delegates to the White House for lunches, cocktails, meetings, and dinners. He invited an entire state delegation to have lunch with him. In July, he invited Clarke Reed, the chairman of the Mississippi delegation, to a State Dinner for Queen Elizabeth. . . . Over the July 4 weekend, he invited seven uncommitted delegates to watch the tall ships sail into New York Harbor from the flight deck of an aircraft carrier."[93] The 1976 Bicentennial celebrations marked a turning point in the national mood: patriotism was suddenly back in style.

On July 11, the Reagans were in Palm Springs for the wedding of Frank Sinatra and Barbara Marx, a tall, gorgeous blonde who three years earlier had divorced her first husband, Zeppo Marx. The ceremony took place at Sunnylands, with Freeman Gosden as Frank's best man and Bea Korshak, the wife of the shadowy Beverly Hills lawyer Sidney Korshak, as the maid of honor. The 130 guests included Spiro Agnew, Sammy Davis Jr., the Armand Deutsches, and the Gregory Pecks. *The New York Times* noted, "Reporters were made to stand outside the gates in temperatures approaching 115 degrees." The reception was held at the Sinatra compound, a mile down Frank Sinatra Drive from the Annenbergs'.[94]

After the wedding, Reagan flew east with Sears on a two-day "raiding expedition" to try to turn around delegates pledged to Ford in New Jersey and Pennsylvania. The head of the Pennsylvania delegation, Drew Lewis, was "rumored to be unhappy" with Ford, according to Nofziger.[95] Sears, who realized that things were looking grim, had come up with the bold idea of having Reagan announce his choice for vice president prior to the convention—which had never been done before—in hopes of winning over enough delegates from the Northeast to put him over the top. Now he decided that the best choice to accomplish that was Pennsylvania senator Richard Schweiker, who was a childhood friend of Lewis's and a member of the same small religious sect, the Schwenkfelders. The only problem was that Schweiker was seen as a liberal who might turn off Reagan's core supporters.

Before going to Reagan, Sears convinced Laxalt, Nofziger, and Deaver one by one of the wisdom of this maneuver. On July 20, Laxalt got his fellow senator and Sears together in his Capitol Hill office, and Schweiker, after deliberating with his wife for two days, agreed to fly to Los Angeles for a secret meeting with Reagan. Sears flew out a day in advance and sold Reagan on the idea of a liberal running mate while simultaneously making the argument that Schweiker was not really a liberal. "He's against gun control, he's a big man in the Captive Nations movement, and he's against abortion," Sears told Reagan.[96] On July 24, Nancy had a lunch at home for the Schweikers, Sears, and Laxalt. According to Sears, "I remember that it was paramount that Justin Dart and Holmes Tuttle be there to meet them as well. 'We have to do this, John,' Nancy said to me. 'It won't change anything, of course. You understand that, but we've got to have them here so they can think they have okayed the decision.' "[97] After three hours of talking, Reagan told the younger man, "I've made a decision, Senator, and I'd like you to be my running mate."[98]

On the morning of July 26, Reagan made his announcement on television in Los Angeles, and Schweiker called Drew Lewis, who not only refused to switch sides but also called President Ford and reaffirmed his support. The right wing was outraged; Howard Phillips, director of the Conservative Caucus, said Reagan had "betrayed the trust of those who look to him for leadership."[99] "Never mind that Kennedy had picked Johnson in 1960 to unify the Democrats," an exasperated Nancy said. "Never mind that two conservatives on the same ticket had no chance of winning. As always, some of Ronnie's supporters insisted on putting ideological purity ahead of victory."[100] Bill

Buckley, who was supporting Reagan, came to his defense. "It is worth recalling just how traditional, in essence, such a choice actually is," he reminded his readers in a column defending the Schweiker ploy.[101]

But in the few days left before the convention, it became clear that Reagan would not pick up more than a handful of delegates in the Northeast, and, to make matters worse, the Mississippi delegation, which had been leaning toward Reagan, was now completely up in the air. Reagan and Schweiker flew to Jackson, to meet directly with the delegates, taking along John Wayne, who told a reporter that he had always thought "Schweiker was a commie, but if he's good enough for Ronnie, that's enough for me."[102]

At the 1964 convention in San Francisco, Ronald Reagan had been a bit player. In Miami Beach in 1968, he had taken a more important part but was not quite sure how to play it. In 1972, in Miami Beach again, he had performed perfectly, but his was still a supporting role. Now, as the Grand Old Party gathered in Kansas City, Ronnie was definitely a star, playing his part to the hilt. And so was Nancy. In fact, she and Betty Ford nearly upstaged their husbands. As Jerald terHorst, Ford's former press secretary, wrote in his syndicated column:

The impact of the "presidential women," their importance in making or breaking a ticket—perhaps even in shaping it—is now of such significance that we should no longer discount or disguise it. The Republican scene in Kansas City last week was a testimonial to the fact. Betty Ford and Nancy Reagan were more than symbols in the intense rivalry between their husbands. They were competitors in their own right, vying for space in the papers and a place in the spotlight, their entrances to the convention hall carefully stage-managed to extract maximum attention from delegates and television viewers. On the sidewalks, street vendors hawked buttons reading "Vote for Betty's Husband" and "Betty Can Dance But Nancy Can Lead." Except for the two principals, no other Republican politician in the hall rated the special salute and the acknowledgement of personal influence and popularity accorded the First Lady. One cannot imagine Bess Truman, Mamie Eisenhower, Jackie Kennedy, or even Pat Nixon standing at the lectern with upturned face, right fist punching the air, while defiantly shouting, "We're going to win!"[103]

The Reagans arrived in Kansas City on Sunday, August 15, the day before the convention opened. Flying with them were Maureen, Michael and Colleen, who was now his wife, and Ron, all of whom had done their part in the primary campaigns, and would surround Nancy in her skybox at the Kemper Arena for the next four nights. Though *The New York Times* delegate count now showed Ford only ten votes short, Reagan maintained that he could still win. In a last-ditch effort to pull off an upset, Sears had proposed a rule change that would require candidates to name a running mate before the presidential roll call. Reagan's choice, Richard Schweiker, was waiting at the airport with the news that thirteen uncommitted Pennsylvania delegates were finally ready to come aboard, though he refused to provide their names to the press. The in-fighting among the Pennsylvanians had become so bitter that Schweiker's children slipped a note under Drew Lewis's door, saying, "Caesar had his Brutus, Jesus had his Judas, and Schweiker has his Lewis."[104]

Once again the Kitchen Cabinet comprised a large part of the California delegation: Tuttle, Dart, William French Smith, Jack Wrather, Earle Jorgensen, Bill Wilson, and Alfred Bloomingdale had seats on the convention floor. Their wives had brought Julius again, who spent much of his time coiffing Nancy in the Reagans' suite at the Alameda Plaza Hotel. The Bloomingdales and Jerry Zipkin had arrived two days earlier for a round of parties, including one given by Kansas City banker Charles Price II and his wife, Carol, a Swanson frozen food heiress, who were good friends of the Annenbergs and the newest additions to the Group.

"It's really quite civilized here," Zipkin told *The New York Times*'s Charlotte Curtis. "I wasn't sure what I was getting into. I've been up at the Olympics with the Jaggers and out in Beverly Hills with Ronnie and Nancy just oozing charm out of every pore. I brought some cheese and that nice pita bread just in case."[105] On Tuesday he had a tête-à-tête lunch with Nancy in her suite and caught her up on the parties she had missed over the weekend.[106] A few eyebrows were raised when he and Betsy Bloomingdale were photographed sitting in the Reagan box, just behind Nancy and the children.

On the opening night, Vice President Rockefeller's keynote speech was completely overshadowed by the boisterous demonstrations set off by the back-to-back arrivals of Nancy, in a crimson Galanos, and Betty Ford, in an aquamarine Halston. The band got so mixed up that it switched abruptly from "California, Here I Come" to "The Michigan Fight Song" and back again, squeezing a few bars of "The Sidewalks of New York" in between as Rockefeller took the podium.[107] During the course of the day, Ford had won enough public commitments to give him a majority of the delegates, but the Reagan forces were still counting on fights over their proposed rule change and an anti-Kissinger platform plank they had introduced at the last minute to undo the inevitable.

The following night, Ford wisely accepted this so-called Morality in Foreign Policy plank, complete with its praise for Solzhenitsyn, overruling the protests of Rockefeller and Kissinger himself. The climactic moment came when the rule change was narrowly defeated after Mississippi's Clarke Reed, under heavy pressure from White House chief of staff Dick Cheney, threw in his lot with Ford. "So close and yet so far," an unnamed Reagan supporter told the *Times*.[108] "That was when we knew for certain that the race was over," said Nancy, who had suffered a defeat of her own that evening when Betty Ford upstaged her entrance by dancing in the aisles with pop singer Tony Orlando.[109]

"The next evening, before the nominations were made, our family had a quiet dinner together in our suite," Nancy later wrote. "Then we all gathered in the living room, where Ronnie explained what we already knew—that our long, emotional struggle was about to end in defeat." Facing his teary-eyed family, Reagan said, "I'm sorry that you all have to see this." Characteristically, he then tried to lighten the mood. "You know what I regret the most? I had really looked forward to sitting down at the table with Brezhnev to negotiate on arms control. He would tell me all the things that our side would have to give up. And then, when he was finished, I was planning to stand up, walk around the table, and whisper one little word in his ear: *Nyet*." Nancy proposed a toast: "Honey, in all the years we've been married, you have never done anything to disappoint me. And I've never been prouder of you than I am now."[110]

At 12:30 it was all over when West Virginia put Ford over the top on the first ballot. But it was close: Ford 1,187; Reagan 1,070. Several delegations then moved to switch their votes and make it unanimous for Ford. The California delegation would not go along with this customary gesture, and knowing how bad that would look for Reagan, Nofziger called Tuttle and asked him to make them switch. For once, even Tuttle couldn't deliver, so Nofziger went down onto the convention floor and pleaded with the delegates himself. "We came here to vote for Reagan and we're going to keep voting for him," Bill Wilson snapped. The matter was resolved when convention chairman Governor James Rhodes decided the appearance of party unity was more important than the fine points of procedure, pounded his gavel, and declared "The vote is unanimous."[111] "In the heat of the moment I thought this was outrageous," Nancy said. "But in retrospect, it was probably a wise move."[112]

"All at once I began to cry, not just a few tears but real sobs," Nofziger recalled. "I couldn't figure it out. In the back of my head I was calm and rational but still, there I was, crying like a girl."[113] Back at the hotel, Helene von Damm was crying "so hard I had to take big gulps of air between sobs."[114] By that time Wilson, Earle Jorgensen, and Alfred Bloomingdale had come to the Reagan suite. "I'll never forget the sight of those three great big grown-up men crying when Ronnie lost," Nancy told me.[115]

Sometime after one in the morning, a victorious Gerald Ford was driven to the Alameda Plaza to meet with his vanquished foe. Sears had agreed to this meeting in advance on the condition that Ford not ask Reagan to be his running mate, so that Reagan would not be put in the awkward position of having to turn the President down.[116] Many in Kansas City believed a Ford-Reagan ticket was the Republicans' best chance of winning against Jimmy Carter and Walter Mondale, who had been nominated by a strong and unified Democratic Party the previous month. According to Nofziger, however, one of Ford's top aides told him the President "absolutely refused to discuss the possibility of picking Reagan."[117] For his part, Reagan said, "I just wasn't interested in being vice-president."[118] According to her friends, Nancy was even less interested. During their twenty-seven-minute meeting, Ford did not extend an offer, and Reagan extolled the virtues of Senator Robert Dole of Kansas. Yet at the "unity press conference" that followed, Reagan waffled when asked what he would do if he were drafted at the convention the following night. A smiling Ford then wrapped things up by saying he was sure there would be a place for Reagan in his administration.[119]

Back at his own hotel, the Crown Plaza, on what was now Thursday morning, Ford and his advisers held two meetings to pick the vice presidential candidate from a list of sixteen names that included one woman, Ambassador Anne Armstrong of Texas (whose strongest advocate among the Ford insiders was Stu Spencer). The first meeting went from 3:15 to 5:00 A.M., the second started at 9:30.

"At seven o'clock there was a knock on the door of my hotel room," recalled Mike Deaver. "I go to the door bleary-eyed in my pajamas, and there are Jus Dart, Holmes Tuttle, and William French Smith, all in their blue blazers, rep ties, gray slacks, and loafers. 'We want to see Ron,' Jus said. They wanted him to be vice president in the worst way. My room was right next to the Reagans' suite, so I let them into the living room, got some coffee for them, went into the Reagans' bedroom—they were sound asleep—woke them up, and said, 'I'm sorry, but Jus and Holmes and Bill Smith are out there and want to talk to you about the vice presidency.' Reagan said, 'Tell them I don't want the vice presidency.' I said, 'They're not going to take that from me. You have to tell them.' The guy was ticked, but he got up and got dressed, and just as he came into the living room the telephone rings. I pick it up and say, 'Governor, it's President Ford.' Reagan takes the phone. 'Right, right, right. Great. I'll do everything I can to help. Wonderful.' He puts the phone down and says, 'Guys, I know what you came here for, but he's picked Bob Dole.' Jus Dart put his arms around Reagan and *wept.*"[120]

Justin Dart later maintained that he *had* convinced Reagan to take the nomination if it were offered. As he remembered it, he had cornered Ronnie in his suite after it became obvious that Ford would win—and at a moment when Nancy was at the convention hall. "I was there begging, arguing," Dart said. "I said, 'Look, your first duty is to your country—not to your wife, not to your family, not to anything, just your country. And Ford needs you to get elected.' He would give me every reason in the world why he shouldn't take it. . . . In any event I finally convinced him on a one-on-one basis that he owed it to his country. He said, 'I don't want to sit there presiding over that Senate with a gag on my mouth.' . . . In his own way he was absolutely right and he was totally sincere, but the final line was, 'Yeah, I'll do it if he offers it.'"

In Dart's account, he then sent a message to Ford, but there was no response. "Well, Ford didn't offer it for two reasons," Dart said. "First, he thought he didn't need Ronald Reagan to win. And second, he was upset with Ronald Reagan for opposing him for the nomination, which is understandable. I like Jerry Ford. I don't think he's in the same class with Ronald Reagan either as a leader or a thinker or a statesman, but he had a right to those opinions."[121] Tuttle backed up Dart in saying that Reagan "would have accepted. No question about it. He was not asked."[122] But Ed Mills, who was also at the convention, was not so sure. "After it was all over, whether Reagan would have considered it, I don't know to this day."[123]

Later on Thursday morning, with Nancy standing at his side, Reagan spoke to about two hundred of his campaign workers in the Alameda Plaza's ballroom. "The cause goes on," he told them. "Nancy and I aren't going [to go] back, sit on a rocking chair and say that's all there is for us. We're going to stay in there and you stay in there with me." Nancy, obviously upset, turned her back to the crowd so that no one would see her openly sob.[124] "There wasn't a dry eye in the room, including my own," said Mike Deaver.[125]

Cary Grant, white-haired but debonair, introduced a sparkling Betty Ford on the last night of the convention, and then the First Lady presented her husband. The President, who was famous for his dull delivery and clumsy manner, managed to give a rousing and polished acceptance speech, probably because he had rehearsed it for two weeks.[126] In a magnanimous gesture, Ford then invited his would-be usurper to join him on the stage. "I don't have the foggiest idea what I'm going to say," Reagan told Deaver as he took Nancy's hand and led her from their box.[127] In his brief extemporaneous remarks, the once-and-future candidate sounded a cry to battle that brought him the longest, loudest ovation of the entire convention. "In some campaigns," columnist Tom Wicker wrote, "the loser is the biggest winner."[128]

"After he lost the nomination in Kansas City in 1976," Marion Jorgensen told me, "we were all at the Wilsons' ranch, the one they had up in Santa Barbara. And we'd go for dinner, you know, at the neighbors'. And now Ronnie wasn't being seated so well. He had lost and they put him next to me, an old friend, instead of next to the hostess, where he'd always been seated as Governor. You see what I mean? And I said to him one night, 'It must be hard, losing like that.' And he looked at me and said, 'Marion, you don't understand. I *am* going to be President of the United States. I *am not* giving up.'"[129]

CHAPTER SEVENTEEN

REAGAN VS. CARTER
1977–1980

[Reagan in 1976] was convinced that if he had won he would have beaten Jimmy Carter. The thought of getting his own shot at Carter certainly pushed him toward his eventual decision to run again. I'm sure that Nancy, too, wanted him to run again. They had come so close. And there was no doubt in her mind or her husband's that he was the best man, better than Ford, better than Carter.

Lyn Nofziger, *Nofziger*[1]

"Fate" as a character in legend represents the fulfillment of man's expectation of himself.

Barbara Tuchman, *The March of Folly: From Troy to Vietnam*[2]

Bush was the last-minute choice for vice president, because what's-his-name—Ford—asked to be co-president. That made Ronnie so mad that he picked up the phone and called George Bush.

Betsy Bloomingdale to author,
September 26, 1999

A week after the convention in Kansas City, President Ford called Ronald Reagan and invited him and Nancy "to come to Washington and spend a night in the White House." Reagan declined, and while he assured Ford that he would do whatever he could to help the ticket, he added, "I've also got to get back to making a living." Mike Deaver, who had already started putting Reagan's speaking schedule together for the fall, explained that this should not be interpreted as a rebuff, and issued a pro forma statement of support: "The Governor sincerely believes that the country cannot afford four years of Jimmy Carter and the stakes are too high to wallow in recriminations."[3]

Over the next nine weeks Reagan campaigned in more than twenty states, but exclusively for Republican candidates who had supported his challenge to Ford. Just as pointedly, his speeches emphasized the party's platform, with its anti-détente and anti-abortion planks, which had been included to mollify his conservative supporters. Likewise, when he finally agreed to do television ads for the Ford-Dole effort, they focused almost entirely on the virtues of the platform.[4] There were no joint appearances with Ford, and when the President appeared in California in late October, with John Wayne at his side, Reagan remained at Rancho del Cielo, sending his regrets by telegram, which an annoyed Ford staff released to the press.[5] After Lyn Nofziger, who was working for Dole, pleaded with him, Reagan acquiesced to a photo op with the vice presidential candidate, on the condition that it take place in Pacific Palisades.[6] When Ford's campaign chairman, James Baker III, called Holmes Tuttle and begged him to persuade Reagan to make a quick swing through Florida, Mississippi, and Texas in the final days before the election, Reagan said no.[7] According to Nofziger, Reagan wouldn't even accept an invitation to a Salute to Ford fund-raiser in Los Angeles unless Paul Haerle, the California Republican Party chairman who had deserted him early on, was disinvited.[8] Nancy later admitted, "It took years for the scars of 1976 to heal between the Fords and the Reagans. . . . You can't work that hard and that long without being frustrated, and Ronnie and I were both deeply disappointed that he didn't win the nomination in 1976."[9]

"To my surprise, Reagan, who is seldom bitter, went to California a bitter man, convinced that Ford had stolen the nomination from him," Nofziger would write. "While I'm certain he would have beaten Jimmy Carter, I'm still not sure that things didn't work out for the best in the long run. The nation needed a Jimmy Carter in order truly to appreciate a Ronald Reagan."[10]

"I'm at peace with the world," Reagan told reporters standing outside his polling place in Pacific Palisades on November 2. In response to their questions, he said he "wouldn't rule out and wouldn't rule in" another try for the presidency in 1980.[11] Two days later, after Ford had lost to Jimmy Carter, a small-town peanut farmer who had served a single term as governor of Georgia, *The*

New York Times reported that Reagan was refusing requests for interviews because, as an aide relayed, "he doesn't want to get bogged down in saying I told you so."[12] The country's lack of enthusiasm for both candidates was evident—it was the lowest turnout since the Truman-Dewey race of 1948—and many wondered if a more committed Reagan would have been able to save Ford, who lost by only 2 percent of the popular vote and failed to carry any Southern state other than Virginia.

Three weeks after the election, the old Reagan team—Ed Meese, Deaver, Hannaford, and Nofziger—convened at the Pacific Palisades house to decide what to do with the $1.2 million left over from their 1976 campaign fund (which had been flooded with donations after the North Carolina victory). Conspicuously absent was John Sears, who had returned to his Washington law practice, having alienated the Kitchen Cabinet as well as most of the Sacramento staffers, who felt he had been condescending to them and to the candidate. Sears's one ally, Mike Deaver, had unthinkingly okayed Nofziger's offer to close down the convention operation. "My reason was simple: money," said Nofziger. "I didn't want Sears or one of his cronies controlling it. I didn't like Sears, didn't respect him, didn't trust him; I'm confident the feeling was mutual. And I didn't want him to have any say in how it was to be used."[13]

At the meeting, Nofziger and Meese proposed using the money to form a political action committee, Citizens for the Republic, which was officially launched in early January 1977, with Nofziger in charge. Under federal campaign finance law, Reagan could have kept the money after paying taxes on it; the fact that he didn't was seen as a sure sign that he had already made up his mind to run again. Nofziger, however, claimed that was not really the case:

I had given the situation a lot of thought, based on the belief that Reagan would not run again. Too old. Nor was I alone in this belief. Among others, it was shared by Deaver, who was closest to the Reagans. . . . On several occasions during the next two years, he was to confide to Meese, Hannaford, and me over breakfast that he thought Reagan was too old to run again. On my part, I thought that at age sixty-four [sic] he had had his shot at the Presidency and had missed. By the time he could run again he would be sixty-eight, an age which in general is a little long in the tooth to be seeking the presidency. But though I thought Reagan would not run again I was convinced he could continue to be an effective force in the Republican Party and a strong advocate for his philosophy of government. He was, after all, the unquestioned leader of the conservative wing of the party, now the dominant wing. At our meeting we concluded that the best way to keep Reagan effective was to form a political action committee (PAC) with Reagan as chairman. The leftover money would serve as seed money—a million bucks buys a lot of seed—and using Reagan's name we could raise a lot more. The PAC would finance Reagan's political activities—his speeches, appearances, travel—and allow him to support candidates who shared his political views. . . . My dream was to use it to build a political power base that would effectively carry on the Reagan philosophy long after he had retired to Rancho [del] Cielo in the mountains above Santa Barbara.[14]

According to Deaver, whose PR firm collected a monthly consulting fee from Citizens for the Republic, Reagan was simply doing what a candidate does: keeping his options open.[15] For Nancy, a run in 1980 "seemed preordained, really, after the 1976 campaign. Ronnie was ready, and everything seemed to fall into place."[16] Reagan himself would write, "I think we both knew it wouldn't—couldn't—end in Kansas City. After committing ten years of our lives to what we believed in, I just couldn't walk away and say, 'I don't care any more.'"[17]

All the Reagans' closest friends seemed to feel he would run again. Marion Jorgensen recalled, "We flew to Oklahoma City with Nancy and Ronnie and the Wilsons and the Tuttles—Holmes was being inducted into the Oklahoma Hall of Fame. Ronnie was giving a speech in honor of Holmes in this great big auditorium, and we had a table right in front of the podium. I went to the ladies' room, and there, standing in the door to the auditorium, was Mike Deaver, holding a raincoat. It was a miserable night, pouring rain and thunder and lightning. I said, 'Mike, what are you doing here?' He said, 'I'm waiting for Ronnie. We're flying to Albuquerque as soon as he finishes his speech.' I said, 'You can't go out on a night like this on some charter plane.' He said, 'We have to. He's giving a breakfast speech, he's got a coffee meeting, he's speaking to the Rotary at lunch, he has a late-afternoon speech, and he has a dinner speech.' *Five*. In Albuquerque in one day. So, you see, after he was beaten in Kansas City, he started all over again."[18]

"Ronnie's schedule was unbelievable," Marion Jorgensen continued. "Earle and I used to travel quite a bit, going from one of his plants to another. And we never got on a plane back in those days that Ronnie wasn't there with Mike Deaver, going somewhere to speak. Nancy was always all alone—oh, it was terrible. But Ronnie never gave up, and she was such a good wife. I remember there was a big fire in Pacific Palisades and she was frightened, so we went out there and got her. She came here and stayed the night."[19]

Reagan had resumed his radio commentaries and newspaper column in September 1976, and by Deaver's reckoning he "could do 20 speeches a month for the next year, and that would add up to $100,000 a month in speaking fees. But he won't do that many of course." Nofziger found it annoying that Deaver & Hannaford would bill the standard $5,000 fee to the campaigns of candidates Reagan was supposed to be helping. According to *The New York Times*, Reagan expected his income to be about $750,000 in 1977.[20]

Traveling with Reagan was an ongoing education in stagecraft for Deaver. "The meticulous care I learned to take in staging an event down to checking the mark—where the performer stands—and camera positions, I picked up from Reagan. He would come out of a ballroom after making a speech and say, 'Mike, don't ever let them turn down the house lights again. It causes me to lose my eye contact.' Another of his rules was not to set up the first row of tables or seats more than eight feet away from him. He wanted to be able to look at the faces. Once, I tried to convince him he didn't have to sit through every dinner, he could just go in and make his speech. He said, 'No, you'd be surprised how much I learn about my audience, watching them during the meal and the early part of the program.'" Above all, Deaver said, Reagan "did not want to do things that were out of character. You might say to him, 'Why don't you take off your jacket and sling it over your shoulder?' He would say, 'No, I don't do that with my jacket.'"[21]

For Reagan a show was a show, as it had been for his mother, whether it was a Disciples of Christ reading or a Republican stump speech, whether it was performed in a county jail or at the Cocoanut

Grove. Giving dinner speeches, however, he would turn into his father, the great big Irish raconteur with an endless store of jokes and tales. But unlike Jack, Ronnie didn't need alcohol to turn on the charm, and Nancy always saw to it that he kept his drinking to a single vodka and orange juice or a glass of wine with meals.

On February 14, 1977, he gave Nancy a letter addressed to "St. Valentine":

> I'm writing to you about a beautiful young lady who has been in this household for 25 years now—come March 4th. I have a request to make of you but before doing so feel you should know more about her. For one thing she has 2 hearts—her own and mine. I'm not complaining. I gave her mine willingly and like it right where it is. Her name is Nancy but for some time now I've called her Mommie and I don't believe I could change. My request of you is—could you on this day whisper in her ear that someone loves her very much and more and more each day? Also tell her, this "someone" would run down like a dollar clock without her so she must always stay where she is.[22]

For their silver anniversary three weeks later, Ronnie gave Nancy a canoe he named *Tru Luv.* She later wrote that she had always teased him about the offhand way he had proposed, and this was his way of finally fulfilling her fantasy of the perfect proposal. "I had envisioned that Ronnie would take me out in a canoe as the sun was setting and would strum a ukulele as I lay back, trailing my fingers in the water, the way they used to do in the old movies I saw as a little girl. Twenty-five years later . . . [he] took me out on the little lake at our ranch. 'I didn't bring a ukulele,' he said. 'So would it be all right if I just hummed?' I know it sounds unbelievably corny, but I loved it."[23] That summer Ronnie found a boulder on one of the trails, carved his and Nancy's initials into it, and drew a heart around them.

By then most of the alterations on the ranch house were complete, but Ronnie kept busy with Dennis LeBlanc and Barney Barnett building fences, clearing brush from riding trails, and chopping wood for the fireplaces. As LeBlanc told Peter Hannaford for his book *Ronald Reagan and His Ranch,* "He never asked Barney or me to do anything he wouldn't do. It was wonderful to watch the two of them together. They were only a year apart in age, and their birthdays were on the same day, February 6. Barney would talk to him as if they were brothers. They'd be working on something and Barney would say, 'Damn it, Governor, you can't do it that way.' He'd reply, 'But Barney, I'm doing it.' He attributed his physical well-being, his longevity to being able to go to the ranch, both for the physical nature of the work and for riding his horses. . . . He rode on an English saddle and everyone else up there rode Western. When you look at pictures of the group, he is always sitting straight as an arrow, while the others are slouching."[24]

While her parents were celebrating the durability of their love, Patti, at twenty-four, decided to have her fallopian tubes tied, fearing, as she later wrote, that if she had a child, "I would become like my mother." Like many of her generation, she felt it was wrong to bring a child into a world that was overpopulated, polluted, and threatened with nuclear extinction.[25] Her decision coincided with the end of her relationship with Bernie Leadon; an affair with the Beach Boys' Dennis Wilson led to a pregnancy scare a month after she had been sterilized. In desperation Patti turned to her parents and told Nancy what she had done. "Only a crisis could have sent me to their front door," Patti wrote, adding, "For the next three years, we had the longest truce in our battle-scarred history."[26]

The previous fall, Ron had announced that he was dropping out of Yale University after only two months to pursue a career in ballet. The issue had been brewing since his senior year at the Harvard School, where he started studying dance after it was introduced into the curriculum. Nancy, who tended to blame Patti's transgressions on her but Ron's on anyone else, told me that her son's interest in ballet stemmed from his relationship with the older woman, which was a continuing source of contention between him and his mother. Ron had moved in with the Wicks during his last year of high school, partly because his parents were away campaigning so much, partly because he wanted to avoid confrontations with his mother, who had told off his married girlfriend one day when she ran into her at the Bistro.

His father had handed him his diploma at the Harvard School graduation in June 1976, and his mother was elated when he was accepted at Yale, after Bill Buckely wrote a strong letter of recommendation. Ron broke the news that he was casting aside an Ivy League education over dinner in New York the night before he and his parents were to spend Thanksgiving at the Buckleys' in Connecticut. Nancy and Ronnie were extremely upset and shared their concern with Pat and Bill. "Such a decision is not easily received in any household," Bill Buckley wrote in his 1983 memoir, *Overdrive.* "In their household, it was received with True Shock."[27]

Among the traits Ron had inherited from his father were a passion for debate, a flair for sarcasm, and a fierce stubborn streak. When his parents realized they could not change his mind, he once told me, "My father offered to call Gene Kelly and ask him about studios in Los Angeles. He thought it would be a better idea if I came back there rather than go right to New York." Reagan's old colleague from the SAG board recommended the Stanley Holden Dance Center in West Los Angeles, where Ron worked hard to catch up with boys who had started studying ballet in their early teens. He also met and fell in love with Doria Palmieri, who worked at the school, came from a middle-class Italian-American family, and was seven years his senior. Nancy was not warm to the idea of another older woman, but at least Doria wasn't married.[28]

In 1977 and 1978, Nancy stepped up her entertaining at San Onofre Drive. The Reagans gave a dinner for the Buckleys on their next visit, and another for the Edmund Borys, who owned Fauchon's, the gourmet food emporium, in Paris. "Her dinner parties are lovely, formal but casual with great warmth," said Jerry Zipkin, sizing up Nancy as a hostess. "And Ronnie always makes an amusing toast that is pertinent." Betsy Bloomingdale added, "If there are 16 guests, Nancy . . . has two or three round tables in the atrium off the living room. The dinners are usually seated and served, with place cards and imaginative centerpieces like pottery centerpieces from Thailand."[29]

Nancy even started her own party book, like Betsy's and Marion's, "but I wasn't as good at keeping it up," she told me. One dinner she recorded was for Jan and Gardner Cowles, on August 16, 1977. "We had," she recited, "crudités, salmon mousse with sauce *verte*, chicken parmesan, corn sauté, vegetable platter, raspberries and blueberries with Kirsch and whipped cream, brownies, and Mouton Rothschild '52—Ronnie knew about wine." Their guests were the Tuttles, the Darts, the Jorgensens, the Bloomingdales, Zipkin, and Buff Chandler—the last a conciliatory gesture, Nancy Reagan said. It helped that the widow Chandler's date, F. Patrick Burns, was a Reagan contributor.[30]

Since leaving Sacramento, Nancy had maintained her association with the Foster Grandparents Program. She also attended Colleagues meetings to plan the annual Glamour Clothes Sale, which drew as many as six thousand bargain hunters to the Santa Monica Civic Auditorium the day before Mother's Day. Marion was the head cashier, and Betsy ran the "fur department," with help from the florist David Jones, who remembered, "One year this beautiful black lady came in and said she would buy this long mink Fendi coat with a mandarin collar and no sleeves if Betsy would autograph it. Betsy said, 'Why does she want my autograph?' I said, 'Listen, we're not going to make this sale.' So I gave Bets a brown paper bag, and she autographed it, and we made the sale. The most amazing thing was when Marion Jorgensen donated a full-length lynx coat, which was probably worth $300,000."[31] Connie Wald told me, "Nancy and her friends—Betsy, Marion, Harriet, Erlenne, Mary Jane—always sat together at the Colleagues meetings. They moved as a herd, and were quite content being part of the Group."[32]

In December 1977, Betsy took Ronnie and Nancy to the New York Metropolitan Museum's Costume Institute Ball, which every year celebrated the opening of a new exhibition curated by Diana Vreeland, the former *Vogue* editor known as "the Empress of Fashion." The ball was chaired by Jacqueline Onassis, and one had to be invited to buy a ticket by a committee of society ladies headed by Pat Buckley. That year's exhibition was titled "Vanity Fair," after a passage in John Bunyan's *Pilgrim's Progress* about a town called Vanity, where "lusts, pleasures and delights of all types" were sold—a description Vreeland thought fit 1970s New York to a tee.[33] Nancy, who had never attended the party before, was one of the stars of the evening, in a black strapless Yves Saint Laurent, with Ronnie behind her in the photographs, looking a little perplexed in his tuxedo. A big part of their allure stemmed from the assumption, held with much hope on the Upper East Side, that they would be the next occupants of 1600 Pennsylvania Avenue. I remember Estée Lauder, the cosmetics tycoon, rushing over to say hello during the long cocktail hour in the grand foyer, and Jerry Zipkin and Betsy Bloomingdale, in her usual Dior, standing on either side of the Reagans with a proprietary look.

Several months earlier, UPI had reported:

Betty Newling Bloomingdale, a wealthy person prominent in fashionable society, was fined $5,000, given a one-year suspended prison sentence and placed on a year's probation . . . for not declaring the full value of two Christian Dior dresses she brought to the United States from France. Testimony showed the true value of the dresses was $3,880, but Mrs. Bloomingdale presented an invoice to a customs agent showing the purchase price as $518.65. The reduction was made to avoid the import duty. Mrs. Bloomingdale, who lives in Beverly Hills and whose husband is a member of the New York department store family, pleaded guilty last August 23 to a charge of concealing an invoice from a customs inspector. Federal District Court Judge Lawrence T. Lydick, who imposed the sentence, told the defendant that she "deserved the contempt of society which has served you so well." Mrs. Bloomingdale told the court she was "truly sorry."[34]

The close connection between the Reagans' social and political lives during this period is perhaps best illustrated by Justin Dart's promotion of Arthur Laffer, the brilliant young economist whose revolutionary "supply-side theory" would provide a major theme for Reagan's 1980 campaign and greatly influence his economic policies as President. Laffer was one of a group of economists who had attended a December 1975 meeting with Reagan organized by Martin Anderson, a former Nixon aide who had been Reagan's senior policy adviser on domestic issues for the 1976 campaign. It was at that meeting, Anderson recalled, that Reagan probably first heard the supply-side gospel as preached by the thirty-five-year-old Laffer: "If you cut tax rates, revenues may go up. If you raise tax rates too much, income goes down."[35] As Anderson pointed out, the work done by Laffer and Robert Mundell, his mentor at the University of Chicago, on the relationship between tax rates and incentives to invest and produce "was way, way outside the mainstream of the current economic thinking."[36] Mundell would eventually win a Nobel Prize, and Laffer would become a near household name for the Laffer Curve, a simple, graphic illustration of their theory.

For Reagan, who had been railing against the graduated income tax since his days as a high-bracket Hollywood star, Laffer's ideas had natural appeal. It wasn't until the following year, however, when Laffer left Chicago for the Charles B. Thornton chair of business economics at USC—and Dart, a USC trustee, "adopted" him—that he began to see Reagan frequently. "I got very involved with Reagan through Justin Dart," the economist told me. "I was very impressed with Reagan. He knew his stuff, he talked about it, he'd come to meetings with congressional testimony paper-clipped where he had a question he wanted to ask."[37]

A month after Laffer arrived in Los Angeles, in September 1976, Reagan wrote a column titled "Tax Cuts and Increased Revenue":

Warren Harding did it. John Kennedy did it. But Jimmy Carter and President Ford aren't talking about it. That "it" that Harding and Kennedy had in common was to cut the income tax. In both cases, federal revenues went up instead of down . . . the presidential candidates would do us all a service if they would discuss the pros and cons of the concept. Since the idea worked under both Democratic and Republican administrations before, who's to say it couldn't work again?[38]

A person close to the Group told me Laffer was a regular guest at Punky and Justin Dart's dinner parties, where "he was always going on about cutting taxes." According to Laffer, he was in and out of the Dart house almost every day, and he and his wife vacationed at the Darts' place in Pebble Beach. "USC had the Dart Center for the Study of Private Enterprise, which I was head of," Laffer explained. "And I got to know Jus. I adored that man. He was one of the neatest guys I ever met in my life, a guy who did things and was not afraid to overstep himself. His basic political principles were simply pro-growth, pro-business, supply-side intuitively. He was not Holmes Tuttle, who said balance the budget, don't cut taxes. For a crusty old curmudgeon, Justin Dart got it."[39]

Laffer's heterodox views and brash personality made him a contentious figure within the Reagans' inner circle. One who was not so sure about him was Nancy herself. He, in turn, found her impressive but intimidating. "She was very strong, and everyone knew how much influence she exerted," Laffer told me. "There was no ambiguity *ever* with regard to her power—personally, socially, and on policy levels. If she really had a strong view on something, she could put it out there. If she thought someone was disloyal to her Ronnie, that was a nuclear holocaust! She was probably the most loyal wife that ever walked the planet—and you just love her for that. But any dealings with her were difficult at best."[40]

To illustrate how tough Nancy could be, Laffer told me about a dinner at the Darts' in the spring of 1978 with her and William E. Simon, the Wall Street wheeler-dealer who had been secretary of the treasury under Nixon and Ford. "It was just the five of us—Ronnie couldn't make it," Laffer said. "Jeff Bell, who had been a top policy guy on Reagan's staff in the 1976 campaign, was running for senator in New Jersey in the primary against Clifford Case, the liberal Republican incumbent. I said, 'Hey, what's the boss doing? Is he support-ing Jeff?' 'No, he's not,' she said. I said, 'What? He's not supporting Jeff?' And I could tell she col-ored a little bit. When you saw that you knew, 'Stand down, officer, right now.' So I shut up. Bill Simon, who was from New Jersey, said, 'Yeah, what *is* this?' He just goes right into it. And she gets up and walks around the table, and she's got her face this close to his. 'Don't you *ever* say any-thing nasty about my husband.' Right in Simon's face."[41]

By 1977 the supply-side doctrine had been taken up in a big way by the *Wall Street Journal* as a miracle cure for stagflation—the combination of low growth and high inflation that plagued the economy for most of the decade. In early 1978, Representative Jack Kemp and Senator William Roth of Delaware introduced legislation to cut taxes by 30 percent over three years. Reagan, who had kept on friendly terms with his onetime staffer and football star turned politician, was one of the first Republican leaders to endorse the Kemp-Roth Bill, which was dismissed out of hand by congressional Democrats and President Carter. Reagan also lent his support that spring to Proposition 13, the California property-tax-limitation initiative, which was overwhelmingly approved by voters in June. Reagan, who as governor had watched a similar proposal of his go down to defeat—and who was not above seeing himself as a prophet ahead of his time—felt vindicated.

"By early 1978 we all thought he'd decided to run again," said Lyn Nofziger. "Not that he told us, because he didn't. He had a thing about throwing his hat into the political ring too soon and his idea of too soon was a lot later than mine."[42] Following his usual pattern, Reagan finally allowed a so-called exploratory committee to be formed in the spring of 1979. The formal announcement of his last-chance quest for the presidency, and the forsaking of his very profitable private career, would not come for another nine months.

Until then Reagan continued to give speeches across the country to groups spanning the social spectrum from the National Roofing Contractors Association to the California Thoroughbred Breeders Association. In January 1978 alone he gave twelve speeches in seven states, and one night in Chicago that April he squeezed in both the Eisenhower Silver Jubilee Gala at the Palmer House and a Bonds for Israel dinner at the Hyatt Regency.[43] Reagan grossed $817,000 during 1978 and the first six months of 1979, more than three quarters of it from speaking fees, including the $72,000 he charged Republican organizations and candidates. His highest fee, $10,572, was for a speech at USC.[44]

To burnish his image as a statesman, Reagan, accompanied by Nancy, traveled to Asia in the spring and Europe in the fall of 1978. In Japan he met with Prime Minister Fukada, had dinner with the leaders of the Diet, and addressed the Keideran, the country's most important business association. In a pair of gestures designed to please his right-wing base and show support for longtime American allies, he also stopped in Taipei, to pay a call on Chiang Kai-shek's son, who had succeeded him as president, and Tehran, where Shah Reza Pahlavi's regime was struggling to subdue a revolution in the making. Britain, France, and Germany were on Reagan's European itinerary, which included a second tête-à-tête with Conservative Party leader Margaret Thatcher, meetings with Chancellor Helmut Schmidt and future chancellor Helmut Kohl, and a visit to East Berlin via Checkpoint Charlie. In July 1979, the Reagans made an overnight trip to Mexico City to meet President López Portillo.

Through his Citizens for the Republic, Reagan assured himself a prominent role in the 1978 midterm elections. But, unlike 1976, when he had restricted his support to conservative Republicans, this time, Nofziger said, "[we] became more interested in making friends and picking up brownie points for Reagan than in helping elect a select few. . . . We wanted broad party support for Reagan come 1980. So we contributed about $800,000 to campaigns that year and bought a lot of friends for him. What we sought was enough political support to create an impression of inevitability about a Reagan candidacy."[45] Among the more moderate Republicans Reagan hit the stump for was Senator Charles Percy of Illinois, who publicly credited him with his razor-thin win.

Nancy also worked to further the cause. "I remember the night they had the Nixons up from San Clemente to ask him for his help," a close friend told me. According to Nancy's records, she gave a dinner in August 1978 for the Nixons *and* the Annenbergs, with the Gosdens and the Deutsches as the only other guests. She served pea soup, fried chicken, and coconut mousse. Ronnie brought out a Haut Brion '47 for the former president and his ambassador to London.[46] Keeping the Annenbergs happy was more important than ever, since Gerald Ford had recently become a resident of Palm Springs—where he and Betty would grow closer to Walter and Lee—and was considered the only Republican who could spoil Reagan's plans by seeking a rematch with

Jimmy Carter. Despite Reagan's loyalty during Watergate, Nixon's allegiance would also come into question if the man who pardoned him ran. Asked about his plans by a reporter a few weeks earlier, Ford had declined to answer, but he pointed out that since leaving the White House he had traveled more than 400,000 miles on behalf of the Republican Party and some "deserving charities."[47]

As 1979 began, Reagan was far ahead of a crowded field of potential contenders for the GOP crown. In a Gallup Poll released on January 10, he was the favorite of 40 percent of Republicans, followed by Ford with 24 percent, Senate Minority Leader Howard Baker of Tennessee with 9 percent, and former Texas governor John Connally with 6 percent.[48] Lagging behind were two Illinois congressmen, John Anderson, a liberal, and Philip Crane, a conservative. As winter turned into spring, two more big names were added to the list: Senator Robert Dole and former CIA director George Bush, but Reagan remained the clear front-runner. One major worry, however, was that Jack Kemp, the forty-four-year-old champion of the supply-side movement, would listen to the clamoring of *Wall Street Journal* editorial writer Jude Wanniski, neoconservative intellectual Irving Kristol, and Jeff Bell, whom Reagan had declined to support in New Jersey only a few months earlier, and throw his Buffalo Bills helmet into the ring.

On March 7, in Washington, Paul Laxalt announced the formation of Reagan's exploratory committee, with himself as chairman and John Sears as executive vice chairman and chief strategist.[49] "Sears was firmly in control," a let-down Nofziger wrote. "He named Jim Lake press secretary and put his other crony, Charlie Black, in charge of the field operation. Both were well qualified. Deaver, as usual, was the majordomo, taking care of the Reagans, worrying about logistics, and serving as the deputy campaign manager and general manipulator of people and things. Ed Meese was the overall issues man while Marty Anderson was again in charge of domestic issues and Richard Allen headed up foreign affairs. . . . As for me, Sears, in another stroke of genius, decided that I should be the fund-raiser, the one position where he was confident I would fail."[50]

Nofziger had done everything he could to prevent Sears's return, including traveling to Houston in the spring of 1978 to persuade James Baker to join the Reagan team. Baker said he had already made a commitment to support his good friend George Bush if he decided to run.[51] Meanwhile Mike Deaver, with Nancy's approval, had sent out feelers to Sears about taking an advisory role in the campaign. When Sears hinted that he might go to work for Senator Howard Baker unless he was put in charge, Deaver, who had been angling to run the campaign himself, caved in. Nancy invited Sears to Rancho del Cielo, where the wily Washington lawyer convinced Reagan that he couldn't win with any other campaign manager.[52] Nofziger told me that Reagan's decision was all the more disheartening because "he had made a commitment that he would not bring Sears back in."[53]

Deaver later explained, "It was at my insistence that John Sears was brought back to head the 1980 primary campaign, over the objections of Paul Laxalt and other Reagan intimates. I still believed that we needed the Eastern access that Sears could provide. I had a healthy respect for his tactical skills, and his calm, almost laid-back manner. A cherubic-looking guy, Sears was no ideologue. He was . . . a brain for hire who wanted to play on a winning team. And those were terms I understood."[54]

In announcing Reagan's campaign committee, Sears played up the presence of four of Ford's cabinet members, including Bill Simon and Caspar Weinberger, who had been secretary of health, education, and welfare. Buried among the 365 names on the twenty-three-page list of committee members that Jim Lake handed out to the press were the Kitchen Cabinet veterans who had always run these things—Tuttle, Dart, Mills, Hume, French Smith. Henry Salvatori was missing altogether. This was in keeping with Sears's strategy of toning down Reagan's wealthy, conservative image and highlighting his appeal to the average American. It was also typical of Sears's control-freak personality.

Sidelining the Kitchen Cabinet, however, created an immediate problem: money. Without Tuttle and Dart pounding on boardroom doors, much of the corporate cash that would have been Reagan's went to Connally, a conservative and former Democrat who had bravely switched parties at the height of Watergate. By late April the campaign was having a hard time meeting its payroll. Sears blamed Nofziger for not raising enough money; Nofizger blamed Sears for spending too much. Enter Charles and Mary Jane Wick, who were personally close to the Reagans but not part of the Kitchen Cabinet clique. Charlie Wick was actually a registered Independent, though he agreed with Reagan's basic philosophy and considered him "a man of destiny." Mary Jane, a Republican, thought of herself as "a little to the right of Louis XIV," but, like her husband, she had never been involved in politics. In 1978, Charlie had sold his nursing home chain for millions and, aside from looking after his investments, now had very little to do with his time.

One night in late April, the Wicks had dinner with Nancy at an Italian restaurant in Westwood and told her they would like to help raise money for Ronnie. "I said that we were thinking of having a lunch and inviting heads of different major corporations whom we knew and they knew," Charles Wick told me. "But then we thought, The only problem with a lunch is if certain guys can't show up, then we've kind of blown it with them. She looked at us somewhat plaintively and said, 'Gee, I wish you really could think of something.' So we decided to give a cocktail party and bill it as the formation of the Ground Floor Committee—to try and give some characterization as to there's always a reward if you're on the right side."[55]

The Wicks sent out telegrams on behalf of the Ground Floor Committee, which consisted of them and ten other couples, saying: THE FIRST MEETING WILL BE AT OUR HOUSE, JUNE 28, 1979. THE NEXT MEETING WILL BE AT THE WHITE HOUSE. P.S. RONNIE AND NANCY WILL BE AT OUR RECEPTION. "Ronnie and Nancy had been going to different cocktail receptions in an effort to raise money," Wick continued. "And if they raised $17,000 or $18,000 in one evening, they felt that was a pretty good success. Well, we charged a thousand bucks—that was the maximum you *could* charge. And the dramatic thing is, we wound up with $80,000. Freeman Gosden's daughter, Linda, stood at the door collecting the checks. Mary Jane designed large, attractive nametags for everyone. And I'm sort of short and resent having to stand at the edge of a crowd and not being able to see over people's heads. So we had Ronnie speak from a riser right out here by the pool. We had these two giant speakers, and Ronnie addressed those people in those booming terms, and it was fabulous."[56]

A month later, *The New York Times Magazine* ran the kind of article that Sears was so adept at eliciting from the national media. Titled "Reagan: The 1980 Model," the piece was as flattering to Sears as it was to the candidate. "Ronald Reagan is setting out on his third campaign for the Republican Presidential nomination, and his first truly well-prepared campaign," Adam Clymer wrote. "This time he may win. A late June Gallup Poll gave him an edge over President Carter for the first time—49 percent for Mr. Reagan as opposed to 45 percent for President Carter. Indeed, repackaging Ronald Reagan is the key growth industry in American politics today. In Washington and Los Angeles, experienced politicians are plotting the finances, the branch offices and franchise distributorships, the sales pitches and the promotional tours of the new candidate Reagan."[57]

Sears let Laxalt try out the slogan for the new, middle-of-the-road Reagan: "You're not talking about a right-wing nut with horns growing out of his ears. You're talking about a responsible conservative." He had Reagan himself confront the "age problem" head-on, believing that the electorate would get bored with the subject if it were openly aired. As the *Times* noted, if Reagan were elected, he would be the oldest incoming president in U.S. history, and while his opponents promised that they would not make an issue of his age, they found ways to get in their digs—Howard Baker said after a meeting with Reagan that they had had a good "father-son talk."[58] On the campaign trail, Reagan joked about his longevity—"I can remember when a hot story broke and the reporters would run in yelling, 'Stop the chisels.'" But he was serious with the *Times*: "The world has changed. The advances that have been made in every form of health care are such that I don't think you go by numbers anymore with regard to age. It's an individual and his capacity, and I feel fine."[59] As the columnist Robert Novak observed, "The tone of the campaign was set by Sears: dull, noncontroversial sameness—sitting on the immense Reagan lead in the public opinion polls."[60]

On August 24, Sears moved to strengthen his position even more by forcing Nofziger to quit. The "dirty work," as Nofziger called it, was done by Deaver, who informed his old colleague that he would be taking over the fund-raising operation. Turning down the consolation prize of running the campaign in California and Texas, Nofziger resigned on the spot. Reagan, who was spending most of that month vacationing at the ranch, called and told him, "I don't want you to quit. . . . We've been together too long." But, according to Nofziger, at a meeting held two days later at the Pacific Palisades house, Sears, Black, Lake, and Deaver voted to let him go, with only Meese and Reagan himself defending him. "I was an example of what could happen if you stood up to [Sears]," Nofziger said.[61]

Nancy didn't cast a vote on Nofziger's fate, but one can trace her invisible hand working in other ways. Two weeks before Nofziger's ouster, Sears and Deaver had been asked by the Reagans to meet with Charlie Wick to discuss fund-raising ideas. "We had rented a place out in Malibu that summer," Wick explained. "We're walking on the beach, Nancy and Mary Jane in front and Ronnie and I in back. We're talking about the campaign and when and where he was going to announce. I said, 'I think you ought to announce in New York. That is the citadel of the world's media. I'm sure we could do a Ground Floor Committee dinner there and get at least 250 people. That would take care of the whole week's expenses.' Ronnie said, 'Let me talk to Mike and John Sears.' We had lunch at the Beverly Wilshire Hotel, and they thought it was a fabulous idea. They said, 'The only way it can be done is if you go to New York for a couple of months to put it together.' I said, 'Forget it.' Deaver and Sears then called Mary Jane, and that did it."[62]

In September the Wicks took a suite at the Mayfair Regent on Park Avenue, the hotel that housed Le Cirque. "At eight o'clock in the morning it became the office," said Mary Jane Wick. "It was just work, work, work all day long. We started by calling a number of the big CEOs in the city, and much to my surprise there weren't too many of them who were interested in Reagan. Their feeling was that, even though he had been governor for eight years, he was still an actor, and they couldn't quite see him as president. A lot of them preferred John Connally or George Bush." Through Helene von Damm, who had been running the campaign's fund-raising efforts in the Northeast, the Wicks found two prominent New York Republicans to co-chair the announcement dinner: William Casey, a Wall Street lawyer who had headed the Securities and Exchange Commission under Nixon, and Maxwell Rabb, who was also a lawyer and had served in Eisenhower's cabinet.

"We had to get a ballroom in a hotel for the dinner, but there always was the money problem,"

Mary Jane Wick told me. "Fortunately, Charlie had a friend from college who was president of Hilton Hotels, and he let us have the New York Hilton ballroom without a down payment. When we were planning the dinner, I called a florist we all knew in L.A., and he had all these tablecloths from a benefit he had done in Palm Springs. Anyhow, Marion Jorgensen and Betty Wilson put them in their luggage and brought them to New York."[63]

"Little by little it looked like we could exceed 250," said Charlie Wick. "On the night of the dinner there were 1,800 people in the ballroom, and in the balcony there were 250 of the world's press." Mary Jane Wick added, "Our daughter Cindy was going with this young man whose father was a political cartoonist for a well-known newspaper in Paris, so he came over to cover this. Of course, with his son going with our daughter, we knew he wouldn't do anything that wouldn't be acceptable. And our other daughter, Pam, is married to the son of Bob Michel—he was the minority leader in the House of Representatives. So Bob, who has a great voice, sang 'The Star-Spangled Banner.' "[64]

The Bloomingdales, the Deutsches, the Darts, and the Tuttles flew in for the announcement dinner, which was held on November 13, and Jerry Zipkin was there with the Cowleses and the Buckleys. All four Reagan children attended, and Jimmy Stewart narrated the official campaign film, which introduced the new, supposedly improved Ronald Reagan. "I believe this country hungers for spiritual revival; hungers to once again see honor placed above political expediency; to see government once again the protector of our liberties, not the distributor of gifts and privilege," Reagan intoned. In keeping with Sears's cautious, above-the-fray approach, the speech recycled Reagan's criticism of big government and support of a strong national defense, but without the hard-edged rhetoric that had thrilled conservative audiences but frightened almost everyone else. Its most daring proposal was a call for a new economic and military partnership with Canada and Mexico, and no mention was made, for example, of the seizure of the American embassy in Tehran nine days earlier. A headline in the following morning's *New York Times* said it all: THE 1980 MODEL REAGAN: STRIDENT CAMPAIGN TONE IS GONE.[65]

That morning Reagan flew to Washington for a news conference, at which he announced that he would not participate in debates or other public appearances with his rivals for the nomination. He was introduced by Representative Jack Kemp as the "oldest and the wisest candidate," an unfortunate choice of words that annoyed Reagan's handlers and led journalists to refer to him among themselves as "the O & W."[66] Sears had cut a deal with Kemp in October: in exchange for the congressman's agreement to endorse Reagan instead of running himself, he would be made campaign chairman in place of Laxalt. When Laxalt got wind of the plot, however, he went directly to the Reagans, who overruled Sears. At the news conference in Washington, Reagan presented Kemp as the campaign's "chief spokesman."

Arthur Laffer disclosed to me that Kemp's real goal from the beginning was to be Reagan's running mate. Laffer had therefore advised the young congressman not to give up his bargaining power by dropping out too early. "I had a little dinner party for Jack Kemp at my home in Rolling Hills Estates with the Reagans and the Tuttles and the Darts. I have a little guesthouse in the back. I told him, 'Jack, what you've got to do is walk down to the guesthouse with Ron. I'll set it all up, and you and Ron just sit down and have a little private chat for a while. And you tell him this: "Sir, you know I adore you. I think the world of you. I've worked for you, you've been my hero, my role model, all my life. What I'm going to do, sir, is I'm going to run, and every delegate I get, come convention time, I'm going to instruct all those delegates to vote for you." Jack, that's what you've got to tell him.' And they were down there for half an hour. My scheme was working. When they came back up, they were chatting away, all smiles. Then I finally got to Jack. 'Jack, did you do it? Did you tell him that?' He said, 'Oh, no, Art, I couldn't. I told him I'd never run against him. I'd give him all the support I could.' I said, 'Jack, you just lost the vice presidency. He's not going to pick a wuss for a vice president. He's going to pick someone who shows vote-getting ability. Why would he take someone who doesn't run?' And, of course, that's Jack's history. He's made an ever greater reputation by not running for ever higher offices."[67]

On Thanksgiving, nine days after the announcement, Nancy called Mike Deaver and asked him to come up to San Onofre Drive. As he came into the foyer, he could see Ronnie in the living room with Sears, Black, and Lake, but Nancy surprised him by asking if he would mind waiting in their bedroom. After twenty minutes, Deaver later recalled, "I decided this was ridiculous. I walked into the living room and said, to no one in particular, 'What's going on?' No one looked directly at me, almost always a bad sign. Then Reagan said, 'Mike, the fellows here have been telling me about the way you're running the fund-raising efforts, and we're losing money. As a matter of fact, they tell me I have to pay thirty thousand dollars a month to lease my space in your office building.' I was more stunned than angry."

Deaver, who knew that Reagan's monthly charges, including everything from secretaries to limousines, ran from only about $5,000 to $10,000, told him, "If these gentlemen have convinced you that I am ripping you off, after all these years, then I'm out. I'm leaving." Reagan followed him out of the room, saying, "No, this is not what I want." Deaver snapped, "I'm sorry, sir, but it's what I want."[68]

Deaver's departure shocked Reagan's entourage. As one insider told The New York Times, "There's a new Ronald Reagan who wants the Presidency so bad that he's willing to dump old friends."[69] Nancy Reynolds told me, "John Sears got Mike fired. Boy, that was a tough one. I was furious and sick and hurt that he had that much influence. Mike was really hurt, and Nancy Reagan wasn't happy either."[70]

The following Monday, Martin Anderson, who was close to both Deaver and Nancy, announced that he was leaving the campaign to return to his position as senior fellow at Stanford University's Hoover Institution.[71] Anderson put all the blame on Sears. As he told me, "Sears was a brilliant strategist, but he developed what I'd call an incipient megalomania. He did not like any criticism. At policy meetings he would propose something as a political stroke. And I'd say that's great but it wouldn't work, and I'd tell him why, and he did not like that. So he took a couple of hundred thousand bucks of campaign money and set up a competing policy shop in Washington, without telling me. I found out about that and had a long talk with him. Anyways, I went on strike. I quit. I walked away. He spent about six hours trying to talk me out of it, but there was no way to deal with him."[72] Perhaps Sears was aware of the nickname people were using with increasing frequency about him: Rasputin.[73]

In his memoir, *Revolution*, Anderson attributes all this court intrigue partly to Reagan's "highly unusual" and "unique" managerial style:

* * *

He made no demands, and gave almost no instructions. Essentially, he just responded to whatever was brought to his attention and said yes or no, or I'll think about it. At times he would just change the subject, maybe tell a funny story, and you would not find out what he thought about it, one way or the other. His style of managing was totally different from the model of the classic executive who exercised leadership by planning and scheming, and barking out orders to his subordinates.

It was something that all those who had worked closely and intimately with Ronald Reagan knew. Ed Meese knew. Mike Deaver knew. And so did Dick Allen and Lyn Nofziger and Peter Hannaford and John Sears. . . . But we rarely talked about it among ourselves and never to outsiders.

We kept it a secret.

We just accepted Reagan as he was and adjusted ourselves to his manner. If that was the way he wanted to do things, fine. At the time it seemed like a small thing, an eccentricity that was dwarfed by his multiple, stunning qualities.

So everyone overlooked and compensated for the fact that he made decisions like an ancient king or a Turkish pasha, passively letting his subjects serve him, selecting only those morsels of public policy that were especially tasty. Rarely did he ask searching questions and demand to know why someone had or had not done something. He just sat back in a supremely calm, relaxed manner and waited until important things were brought to him. And then he would act, quickly, decisively, and usually, very wisely. . . .

This kind of behavior in a political candidate is unheard of. From the viewpoint of a jealous, competitive staff it is potentially chaotic.[74]

How did Nancy perceive her role in this competitive cast of characters? "I was always conscious of people who were trying to end-run Ronnie, who were trying to use him for their own agendas," she told me. "And all my little antennae would go up. It never occurred to him, because he didn't work that way. He wouldn't think anybody would work that way. But they do. So I'd point things out to him."[75]

Now the only Californian left at the top of Reagan's campaign was Ed Meese, and he was extremely upset over the departures of Nofziger, Deaver, and Anderson. In early December, Morgan Mason, the handsome young son of the actor James Mason and a favorite of Betsy Bloomingdale's and Nancy Reagan's, applied for a job at campaign headquarters in Los Angeles. Among the restricted personal papers at the Reagan Library is a record of his interview with Mike Wallace, a staffer close to Sears. The handwritten notes make clear the extent to which Sears sought control of access to the Reagans:

Mike Wallace said:

New team in ctrl here

Sears, Wallace, Black, Lake

"Meese if he comes out of his pout"

Conc. re allegiance to MKD [Deaver] & your relationship to NR [Nancy Reagan]

JPS [Sears] wary of peo in contact w. Reagans

That was MKD's problem. Instead of fighting it out down here, he would just call the Reagans.

Anything said to Reagans must be cleared w. Wallace or Sears[76]

Morgan Mason did not get the job. A month later, however, he was hired as a consultant by the newly formed Reagan Executive Advisory Committee, which was comprised mainly of Kitchen Cabinet members who had decided that the time had come for them to get more involved. "The original group was Holmes Tuttle, Jack Wrather, Bill French Smith, Bill Wilson, Ted Cummings, Charles Wick, and me," said Arthur Laffer, who was named the EAC's secretary and kept minutes of its meetings, some of which can be found in the Reagans' restricted papers. "The first meeting was in Justin Dart's office, with all the eagles flying—Jus had big wooden eagles everywhere. All those guys just loved eagles." According to Laffer, Dart was the driving force of the group, and he chose Bill Simon as the chairman. They decided to keep the membership to about two dozen and to bring in prominent business leaders from other parts of the country, including David Packard of Hewlett-Packard, Bill Boeing of Boeing Aircraft, Don Kendall of Pepsico, and Joe Coors, the Colorado beer king who had been a major contributor to Reagan's 1976 effort. "We had the word come down that Alfred Bloomingdale was also to be in the group," recalled Laffer. "Betsy had asked Nancy, and Nancy asked Ronnie, and Ronnie said, 'Yes, sir.' "[77]

The EAC's mission, spelled out in notes from a meeting on February 5, 1980, was "to advise and assist RR on all aspects of the campaign, with particular attention to policy and issue positions and to recommending qualified individuals who might serve as advisors and consultants to RR and the campaign. The EAC will be organizationally responsible directly to RR." Among the illustrious figures the EAC would enlist as advisers were the economists Milton Friedman and George Shultz, former ambassador to South Vietnam Robert Ellsworth, and retired admiral Elmo Zumwalt.[78]

Michael Deaver wrote that, except for infrequent phone conversations with Nancy, he was out of touch with the Reagans for five months after he quit. But the February 5 notes say, "Michael K. Deaver has been appointed as his personal liaison to the E.A.C. by RR." While Dart went on about the "need to combat Soviets in Middle East by any means necessary," the notes indicate that Deaver was suggesting "2 things this group can do— broad strategy priorities; get management into campaign."[79] Ed Meese was also involved with the EAC from the beginning, and as early as January

14 he was making sure that copies of his memos to Bill Simon went to Deaver.[80]

Around the same time, Nancy, who talked regularly with Justin Dart, asked him to look into the campaign's hemorrhaging finances. Dart turned to William Casey, who had co-chaired the announcement dinner in New York and had recently joined the EAC.[81] Casey undertook an audit of Sears's costly operation, which included eighteen regional offices with more than two hundred employees, and was said to be paying $50,000-a-year consulting fees to scholars for position papers. According to his biographer Joseph E. Persico, after Casey finished his "management audit," he met with the Kitchen Cabinet at Tuttle's house and told them, "Ronald Reagan hasn't got a campaign organization. He's got a civil war. There's Ed Meese and the California guys in one camp. There's John Sears and his technocrats on the other side. Between the two, the campaign's paralyzed. I also looked at the books. You're going broke."[82]

Meanwhile, a few days after Reagan suffered a wholly unexpected early defeat to George Bush in Iowa, Casey sat down and wrote a six-page letter to the candidate urging him to rethink his entire campaign strategy. The letter ended with a call for "a sharp assertive stance."[83]

The Iowa caucuses on January 21 were the first contest of the primary season, and Reagan had been expected to win handily in a state where he was still remembered fondly as the Des Moines sports announcer who had made it big in Hollywood. Following Sears's above-it-all strategy, Reagan spent only six days in the state and refused to join six other candidates in a televised debate, which Iowans saw as a snub. Despite a precipitous drop in local polls within days of the debate, and a second-place finish six points behind Bush, Reagan refused to blame his campaign manager, telling reporters, "If I had to do it over I'd do it the same way again."[84] But even Sears conceded, "The public's perception of the campaign has changed. People now think there's a race where they didn't think there was one before. In some ways, that's sort of a relief for us. We won't have a motivational problem anymore."[85]

For all his spin, Sears was in trouble and he knew it. According to reporter Lally Weymouth, the daughter of Kay Graham, who wrote a profile of Nancy Reagan for *The New York Times Magazine*, Sears went to Nancy and told her that he had overheard Meese "telling some staff members that Sears would be fired the day after the New Hampshire primary, along with Lake and Black." Sears said that put him in an intolerable position, and he suggested bringing in Bill Clark—whom Reagan had elevated to the California Supreme Court—presumably to ease out Meese, Sears's archenemy. Nancy agreed to call Clark, but, according to the Judge, as he was known, she didn't make the offer Sears had suggested.[86]

"On Lincoln's Birthday," Clark told me, "Nancy

and Ron asked me to come to the ranch. I spent most of the day and the evening with them—it was just the three of us. They wanted me to replace Sears. I didn't say no, because you don't say no to Ronald Reagan—or to Nancy—but, as the Irish would say, I sorted it out. I explained that my position on the Supreme Court was critical at the time, and if I left we would probably lose three or four cases that were under submission. Ron looked me in the eye and said, 'Bill, I understand. But if I make it, you're going to hear from me again.'" Furthermore, Clark disclosed, after the Reagans ran down a list of prospective replacements for Sears with him, "I suggested that Bill Casey be tagged."[87]

Matters came to a head at a Holiday Inn in Worcester, Massachusetts, three days later. That afternoon the Reagans held a meeting in their room with Casey, Meese, Richard Wirthlin, the campaign pollster, and Richard Allen, the foreign policy adviser, who had complained that he was being cut out of the loop by Sears. Casey's report on the campaign's finances and management so impressed everyone present that it was agreed that he should join the team immediately, though no announcement would be made until after New Hampshire. That evening Reagan summoned Sears, Black, and Lake to discuss restructuring the campaign. One of the three later told Lally Weymouth it was "a very contentious meeting. Anger, a great deal of anger, was displayed by [Reagan], and after two hours we were at the point where Sears said something to the effect of 'I cannot work here as long as Ed Meese continues to be in the spot he is in.' The clear intent was: 'Him or me.' At that point, Reagan blew up. He jumped out of his chair and shouted."[88]

As Nancy remembered the scene, things got even more dramatic: "Ronnie rarely loses his temper, but he certainly was angry that night. 'You got Deaver,' he told John, 'but, by God, you're not going to get Ed Meese! You guys have forced me to the wall.' I was sure he was going to hit John, so I took his arm and said, 'It's late, and I think we should all get some sleep.' "[89]

"We tried to work it out," she explained at the time, "and I tried to be helpful, but by the time we got to New Hampshire, it was obvious to all of us that we were kind of applying Band-Aids. It was a situation that just wasn't going to work. Ronnie decided that, before he knew what the results were, he would make a change, so that if he lost it wouldn't seem that this had come about because he had lost—which I thought was very nice of Ronnie."[90]

Reagan later discussed Sears with presidential historian Theodore White, saying, "I don't fault his ability at political analysis, but he wanted to do *everything.* And when I wanted to bring someone in to really handle an office situation where the morale was at zero . . . he delivered an ultimatum . . . that he would leave if that was done. So I just knew that it could not go on that way. . . . There was . . . a feeling that I was just kind of a spokesman for John Sears."[91]

On the afternoon of February 26, while New Hampshire voters were still going to the polls, Reagan again summoned Sears, Black, and Lake to his hotel suite. As Nancy and Casey sat nearby, he handed Sears a statement that began, "Ronald Reagan today announced that William J. Casey has been named campaign director . . . replacing John Sears, who has resigned to return to his law practice."[92] Sears's two colleagues were also dismissed. Reagan announced later that day that Ed Meese had been promoted to chief of staff and Richard Wirthlin to chief of strategy and planning. The new triumvirate would soon be joined by Nofziger, who took over as press secretary; Anderson, who came back to oversee policy; and Deaver, who resumed traveling with the Reagans on the campaign plane, a Boeing 727 named *LeaderShip '80.*

Reagan overwhelmed Bush in New Hampshire, 50 percent to 23 percent. Trailing behind were Howard Baker with 13 percent, John Anderson with 10 percent, and John Connally, Robert Dole, and Philip Crane with less than 3 percent each. These last three would soon drop out and endorse Reagan, who in this state had not only agreed to underwrite a debate with Bush but also generously invited the other candidates, who had been excluded by the newspaper sponsoring the event, to join them on the platform. When the moderator threatened to shut off Reagan's microphone, he seized the moment and famously declared, "I *paid* for this microphone," while Bush just stood there, not knowing what to do. It was in New Hampshire, too, that Bush coined the all-too-memorable phrase "voodoo economics" to put down Reagan's supply-side-based promises of tax cuts, a balanced budget, and increased military spending.

Over the next three months the new campaign team "let Reagan be Reagan" once again—attacking Carter for his feeble response to the Soviet invasion of Afghanistan, criticizing him for not doing enough to free the fifty-two American hostages seized at the American embassy in Tehran, railing against the Panama Canal Treaty, even after it had been ratified by the Senate. Turning to the economy, a rejuvenated Reagan said, "I suggest that when one administration can give us the highest inflation since 1946, the highest interest rates since the Civil War, and the worst drop in value of the dollar against gold in history, it's time that administration was turned out of office and a new administration elected to repair the damage done."[93]

Meanwhile, no detail was too small for Nancy to notice. When French Smith told her about an article in the Republican National Committee's March newsletter about Ford addressing a group of party fund-raisers, she asked him to send it to her. She then passed it along to Meese with a cover note saying, "Before your meeting with Bill Brock—Bill

Smith sent this—no mention of RR in this at all— you wouldn't even know he was running."[94] Brock, the RNC chairman, had been installed by Ford, and some of Reagan's advisers, particularly Paul Laxalt, who was close to Nancy, thought he should be replaced.

That month Reagan took Vermont, South Carolina, Florida, Alabama, Georgia, Illinois, and most of New York, leaving Bush only Massachusetts, the state he was born in, and Connecticut, the state where he went to school. Howard Baker dropped out of the race, Gerald Ford got cold feet about a last-minute entry, and Henry Kissinger, who had been pushing Ford the hardest, announced that he would have no problem supporting Reagan against Carter. In April, Reagan won Wisconsin and Kansas, but Bush scored an upset in Pennsylvania and prevailed in Maine, the state where he summered. On May 3, however, Bush lost his home state of Texas, and Reagan then went on to sweep North Carolina, Indiana, Tennessee, Maryland, and Nebraska. Bush had one more important win, in Michigan, on May 20, but Reagan's victory in Oregon that same day left him only six delegates short of the 998 required for nomination, and California, the biggest prize and a sure thing for its golden boy, was still to come. On May 26, George Bush announced that he was giving up and would ask his 202 delegates to vote for Reagan at the convention. When a reporter asked Reagan how he felt, he replied, "I don't think it's quite sunk in yet. Maybe someplace along the line later today I'll go home by myself and let out a loud yell."[95]

The only remaining question was who Reagan's running mate would be. The two leading contenders were his strongest primary opponents, George Bush and Howard Baker, who as moderates would balance the ticket ideologically. However, Reagan told confidants that he would not feel personally comfortable with Bush, and Nancy was still smarting from his voodoo economics line. The Reagans liked Howard Baker—in 1976 he and his wife, Joy, had invited them to stay at their home in Tennessee even though he was Ford's state campaign chairman—but the Republican right wing was still fuming at Baker for voting for the Panama Canal Treaty. Then there was Paul Laxalt, whom Nancy favored, but who as a fellow conservative from a small Western state would do little to broaden Reagan's appeal. On July 1, five more individuals were asked by Bill Casey to submit financial and health information for screening—Jack Kemp, Bill Simon, Donald Rumsfeld, Senator Richard Lugar of Indiana, and Representative Guy Vander Jagt of Michigan. A few days later, after it was decided that a woman should be considered, former ambassador Anne Armstrong was added to the list. But, amazingly, the name that drew the highest numbers in the polls was former president Gerald Ford.

Two days after Reagan clinched the nomination, at the end of May, Ford had publicly endorsed him, though he categorically ruled out becoming his running mate.[96] On June 5, Ford invited Reagan to his house near Palm Springs. At the end of their ninety-minute meeting, Ford reiterated that he had taken himself out of consideration because he and Reagan were both residents of California, and the Constitution prohibits electors from voting for both a presidential and a vice presidential candidate from their own state. Still, the idea of a Reagan-Ford "dream ticket" hung in the air right up to the convention, kept aloft by senior Republican senators and mutual friends of both men within the Kitchen Cabinet.[97]

June was a month for reconciliation. Henry Salvatori was welcomed back into the Kitchen Cabinet at a dinner Holmes and Virginia Tuttle gave at their Hancock Park home the night of the California primary.[98] On June 13, Reagan held a joint news conference with Bill Brock and announced that the moderate RNC chairman would be staying on. That evening, 1,100 of the party faithful paid $500 a plate for a "unity dinner" organized by the Wicks to help pay off the campaign debts of Bush, Baker, Connally, Dole, and Crane, all of whom made speeches extolling the victor. Ford repeated his pledge of support via speakerphone. Efrem Zimbalist Jr. was the emcee, and Jimmy Stewart, Irene Dunne, Robert Stack, and Joseph Cotten lent a dash of Old Hollywood glamour.[99]

On June 20 the EAC gathered at the Palmer House in Chicago. "The meeting began with Bill

Casey's update on the campaign," Arthur Laffer's minutes read. "In an upbeat discussion, President Ford's total support of the Reagan candidacy after a meeting in Palm Springs was described, as well as a successful Unity Dinner." The Kitchen Cabinet and their new corporate allies were so sure of a Reagan victory in the fall, it seems, that a large portion of the meeting was taken up by Ed Meese's discussion of plans for "the Transition to a Reagan Presidency." One member, New York businessman George Champion, even proposed having Reagan publicly designate George Shultz and Bill Simon as his choices for secretary of state and secretary of the treasury, respectively. "This would have substantial beneficial effects on Eastern attitudes toward Reagan, as well as being exceptionally good appointments," Champion argued. But John Connally, who had been added to the EAC roster, worried that anyone named so prematurely might become a campaign issue, and he was backed up by Casey and others.[100]

In early July the Reagans spent five days at the Wilsons' new ranch in northern Mexico, resting up for the convention. (The Wilsons owned the ranch in partnership with Diego Redo, a hotel tycoon from one of the oldest Mexican families, and his wife, Norma.) Only Earle and Marion Jorgensen and Bob and Betty Adams were invited along. "Ronnie brought three acceptance speeches written for him by three different people," Bill Wilson told me. "I remember him sitting out on the front porch of our house reading those three speeches, and he finally put them all back in his briefcase and took out the yellow pad and started writing his own. How much he kept of each one of the three, I have no idea, but he wrote his own from scratch."

Wilson also told me, "Earle and Ronnie and I were on horses, riding around the ranch, when Ronnie asked each of us who we thought he should pick for vice president. The interesting thing about that was that Betty had anticipated that this might happen, and she said, 'Don't suggest George Bush'—though he was the one I would have suggested, and I actually did, but I had to wait. I said, 'Ronnie, wait until this evening at cocktails and I'll tell you who I think.' But I had to go back to the house and tell Betty, 'Yes, it did happen, and I honestly think George Bush would be the person. Even though he may have made some adverse comments during the campaign, between the two of them they have the chance of getting the most electoral votes—and that's the name of the game right now.'"[101]

According to Wilson, Earle Jorgensen recommended Jack Kemp—Marion, along with Betty and Nancy, was still mad at Bush for his disparaging remarks about Ronnie. "I don't know whether our suggestions had any effect on him or not," Wilson concluded. "I think by the time they got to the convention, there was so much politics and so much backroom maneuvering that I'm sure he didn't remember what we had said."[102]

The day after they returned from Mexico, Marion and Betty hosted Nancy's birthday party at

Chasen's. It was the biggest one yet, with everyone from the Annenbergs to the Sinatras crammed into the private room upstairs. Sinatra had done a benefit concert for the campaign in Boston in late 1979, when its coffers were nearly empty. In early 1980, however, the press had reported that he was under investigation for alleged Mafia associations in Nevada, where he had applied for a gambling license using Reagan as a reference, so on Ed Meese's advice the singer's role in the campaign was played down.[103] The only photographer at Chasen's was the Bloomingdales' son Robert, who had been hired by Marion so that she would have a record of the night. In his pictures, Nancy, who had just turned fifty-nine, is wearing a sexy, low-cut dress and glowing with happiness. Not known for long speeches, she did what for her was a rare thing; after cutting the cake and making a wish, she gave an extended toast thanking all of the Reagans' friends for always being there for them. Bandleader Joe Moshay, who played at most of the Group's parties, was so touched that he wrote Nancy a note. "In all honesty, I feel that you could never give a more sincere and from the heart speech to your close friends as you did that night. YOU WERE PRECIOUS!!!"[104]

On the afternoon of July 14, 1980, Ronnie and Nancy made a triumphal entrance into Detroit for what some commentators were calling a coronation. They were both wearing white—he a tropical linen jacket, she a trim Adolfo suit—as they stepped out of their limousine at the Detroit Plaza Hotel in the Renaissance Center, a soaring downtown redevelopment project completed in 1977. When they entered the lobby, a modernistic five-story atrium, several hundred delegates and supporters on the balconies started chanting, "Reagan! Reagan! Reagan!" while showering them with ticker tape and confetti.

After being escorted to their sixty-ninth-floor suite, the Reagans proceeded directly to the suite of Gerald and Betty Ford, one floor up. The convention city was abuzz with rumors of a Reagan-Ford ticket, even though the former president had declared upon arriving two days earlier, "Under no circumstances would I be the candidate for the Vice Presidency."[105] But Wirthlin's polls still showed that Ford was the only prospect who boosted Reagan's numbers, and Reagan agreed to try to persuade Ford to change his mind. It was Ford's sixty-seventh birthday, and as he later recalled, "Ron presented me with an Indian peace pipe. He was making amends for running against me in 1976. Following the presentation, Ron said that he and Nancy wanted me to be his running mate in 1980! I was overwhelmed and flattered. In deference to his request, I said I would think about it and talk to Betty."[106]

According to Bill Wilson, Reagan's offer was not entirely sincere. "There was some thought that maybe you could get him to consider it—not accept it—and get his support in the campaign," Wilson told me.[107] Meese called Reagan's offer "pro forma" and said Reagan "was surprised when Ford in essence said he would think about it."[108] There was another surprise that evening—causing delight among the press, who were desperate for something to dramatize what promised to be an unsuspenseful convention—when Ford quipped in his opening-night remarks, "I am not ready to quit yet. . . . Count me in."[109] Thus began one of the most bizarre episodes in modern political history, which nearly resulted in Reagan's decapitating himself before he was crowned.

Ford went to Reagan's suite the following day for an hour-long meeting about the vice presidency. Although a still reluctant Ford reportedly recommended Bush, Reagan sources let it leak that he was definitely the first choice of an increasingly enthusiastic Reagan. Reagan also met with Henry Kissinger, who told reporters as he left the suite that he was *not* seeking a position in a Reagan administration. He would nevertheless take a leading role in the events of the next forty-eight hours, in what his enemies saw as a bold-faced attempt to assure just the opposite. The man who invented détente was anything but beloved by right-wing Republicans, and many in the Kitchen Cabinet viewed him with suspicion. A notation from the minutes of an April 4 EAC meeting says it all: "discussion was centered on the potential role of ex-Secretary of State, Henry Kissinger. Consensus did not result."[110] Kissinger's most vociferous enemy within Reagan's inner circle was foreign policy adviser Richard Allen, who had been an unhappy subordinate of his in the Nixon White House.[111]

Conservatives had attempted to bar Kissinger from addressing the convention, but in the speech he gave that evening he tore into Carter's foreign policy and came out sounding like Reagan at his most apocalyptic. "The Carter Administration has managed the extraordinary feat," he intoned in his heavy German accent, "of having at one and the same time the worst relations with our allies, the worst relations with our adversaries and the most serious upheavals in the developing world since the end of the Second World War. We can assert that these multiplying crises are the natural result of a naïve philosophy, which, since 1977, has recoiled from our power and fled from our responsibilities. Sooner or later our weakness will produce a catastrophe."[112]

At midnight Kissinger proceeded to Ford's suite and made what several sources have called an "impassioned plea" for the former president to consider Reagan's offer in light of the dire international situation. After forty-five minutes, Alan Greenspan, who had served as chairman of the Council of Economic Advisers under Ford, joined the discussion. According to Theodore White, over the next two hours Kissinger and Greenspan developed the concept that "the President would be the Chief Policymaker, but the Vice-President would be the Chief Operator." In this proposed scheme of things, Ford would oversee the Office of Management and Budget as well as the National

Security Council. "All agreed," White writes, "that the next morning Ford's councillors would meet with Reagan's and see if a new definition of the roles of President and Vice-President could be worked out."[113]

On Wednesday morning, Kissinger, Greenspan, and Dick Cheney, Ford's former chief of staff, presented their ideas for a power-sharing arrangement to Casey, Meese, and Wirthlin. As Lyn Nofziger recalled, Meese "wrote down Ford's demands and showed them to me. Among other things Ford, or at least those negotiating for him, was demanding that the White House staff report to the president through him—Ford would decide who on the staff would and would not see the president. He also wanted to pick the secretary of state and secretary of defense, although he generously offered Reagan a veto. But in turn, he wanted veto rights on Reagan's other cabinet picks."[114]

"From my perspective as negotiator," Meese later wrote, "this was a complete nonstarter. . . . I had no doubt that, from Kissinger's standpoint, this meant control over important facets of foreign policy and arms control, in which Kissinger himself, it's safe to say, would have played a prominent role. . . . I didn't think that Ronald Reagan had campaigned for president in 1976 and again in 1980 to wind up with others calling the shots on foreign policy—or to barter away any other aspects of the executive authority conferred on the president by the Constitution."[115]

Nonetheless, the Reagan and Ford teams continued to negotiate throughout the day, and the principals met again at five that afternoon. Reagan remained noncommittal, however, when the former president said that if he were to return to Washington, he would need to have some of his key people come back with him, starting with Kissinger and Greenspan.[116] Meanwhile, everyone wanted to get their two cents in. As Deaver remembered the scene, it seemed as if the entire Republican Party leadership was in Reagan's suite at one time or another, including Bill Brock, Bob Dole, Bob Michel, Congressman John Rhodes of Ohio, and Governor Jim Thompson of Illinois—all giving the candidate advice.[117]

"From the start, I vigorously opposed the Ford gesture. . . . My man was George Bush," wrote Deaver, who had developed a friendly relationship with Bush's campaign manager, James Baker. "I saw him as a class person and I thought he would bring the right assets to the ticket. A moderate, with ties to the East (Yale) and the oil fields of Texas. The son of a former senator, Prescott Bush of Connecticut. Handsome, youthful, sharp."[118] Nancy Reynolds, who had taken time off from Bendix to help Nancy with her press at the convention, told me, "Elizabeth Dole, whom I knew personally, called and wanted to see me right away. She was promoting Bob for vice president. And I was sort of stunned, because we had never thought about it."[119] Jack Kemp, meanwhile, was going ahead with plans to have his name placed in nomination, so there was some apprehension that things could get out of hand on the convention floor.

During most of this back and forth on Tuesday and Wednesday, Nancy Reagan was busy with her own schedule—lunch with *Newsweek*'s editorial board, an interview for *Vogue*, meet-and-greets with various state delegations, a photo-op with unemployed automobile workers and their wives. Accompanied by all four children—even Patti made it—she represented her husband at the Joe Louis Arena Tuesday night while he remained at the hotel, as convention protocol dictated. A rotating cast of Republican leaders' wives occupied the seat beside her, including Nancy Kissinger, Peggy Goldwater, Nellie Connally, Teresa Heinz (wife of Senator John Heinz, later wife of John Kerry), and an old acquaintance from MGM, Elizabeth Taylor, whose sixth husband was Senator John Warner of Virginia.[120] Nancy had to miss another event that evening. As reported by Eugenia Sheppard the previous day in her "Around the Town" column in the *New York Post,* "Jerome Zipkin will give a dinner for 17 ladies at the London Chop House. He will be the only male present. The ladies he's invited are Mrs. Alfred Bloomingdale . . . Mrs. William Buckley Jr. . . . Mrs. Guilford Dudley, from Nashville . . . Mrs. Justin Dart, Mrs. Earl [sic] Jorgensen, Mrs. William Wilson . . ."[121]

Nancy was also enlisted in the effort to make the dream ticket a reality, even though she was still plugging for Laxalt. "I thought the whole idea was ridiculous," she said of a Reagan-Ford combination. "I didn't see how a former president—*any* president—could come back to the White House in the number-two spot. It would be awkward for both men, and impractical, and I couldn't understand why that wasn't obvious to everybody. 'It can't be done,' I told Ronnie. . . . But he didn't see it that way." Nancy halfheartedly agreed to call Betty Ford and feel her out. "I was relieved to find that Betty felt pretty much as I did," she later wrote. " 'No,' she said. 'As much as we'd like to help, I don't think it's a good idea.' "[122]

Nancy was in the suite with Ronnie at 7:00 P.M. on Wednesday when, to their astonishment, they turned on the *CBS Evening News* and saw Gerald Ford giving a live interview to Walter Cronkite. "If I go to Washington, and I'm not saying that I'm accepting, I have to go there with the belief that I would play a meaningful role, across the board, in the basic, crucial, tough decisions that have to be made in the four-year period." Cronkite asked Ford, "It's to be something like a co-presidency?" Ford answered, "That's something that Governor Reagan really ought to consider. . . . The point you raise is a legitimate one."[123]

"As far as Ronnie was concerned," Nancy said, "that did it."[124]

Society columnist Aileen "Suzy" Mehle, who had come to the convention with Zipkin, recalled a conversation she had had with Nancy that evening about Ford and Kissinger's power play. " 'How dare they,' she said. And I said, 'You'd have to watch *them.* There wouldn't be any co-presidency. They would be president, and maybe they'd let Ronnie be vice president—let us guide you. *Right.*' Nancy was miffed. She was *very* miffed."[125] Nancy later admitted, "I think I would have done almost anything to prevent Ronnie from picking a former president as his running mate."[126]

Reagan immediately ordered Deaver to get Kissinger on the phone, saying, "This has gone too far." On Reagan's behalf, Deaver told Kissinger that it was time for Ford to put up or shut up. At the same time, Reagan dispatched Casey to Ford's suite with the message that if the former president accepted his offer, it "had to be based on faith and understanding; it could not be a written compact."[127] Shortly after eleven o'clock, Ford appeared at Reagan's suite and gracefully withdrew. "Then [Reagan] picked up the phone and said, to the amazement of everyone in the room, 'I'm calling George Bush. I want to get this settled. Anyone have any objections?' "[128]

"Out of a clear blue sky, Governor Reagan called me up and asked if I would be willing to run with him on the ticket," an elated Bush told reporters the next day. "I was surprised, of course, and I was very, very pleased. I feel honored. . . . I told him I would work, work, work."[129] It is clear from Barbara Bush's memoir that she wanted her husband to be on the ticket. George Bush had addressed the convention earlier that evening, assuming, as the rumor mill had it, that Ford had already been chosen. "We went right back to the Pontchartrain Hotel and our whole floor was filled with many close friends and family," Mrs. Bush wrote. "It was like a funeral. George found Jeb [Bush] in our bedroom really upset. 'It's not fair, it's not fair,' he said. George and I put on old clothes, and I urged him to let us pack up and get out of there. George gave both Jeb and me a talking-to: 'We came to this convention to leave politics with style and we are going to do it.' Almost immediately, the phone call came to our room from Ronald Reagan and the rest is history."[130]

Nancy had been in the convention hall for three hours by then. After watching the Ford-Cronkite interview, she had taken Patti, Ron and his girl-friend Doria, and Michael and Colleen to the Joe Louis Arena. Maureen, who was a delegate from California, had been there all day. Several of Nancy's friends were also with her that night, including Betty Wilson, Norma Redo, and Betty Adams, who remembered how surprised Nancy was when "she was called out of the box and told that they chose Bush."[131]

"On 'decision night,' I went to the convention hall totally in the dark," Paul Laxalt recalled. "Before long, I had an urgent call from Ron, which I took in a trailer outside the arena. 'Paul,' Ron said, 'I've decided to go [with] George Bush. I know that many of the delegates will be unhappy, so George and I are coming to the arena together. Will you please join us?' In a few minutes, George and Barbara Bush and Ron and Nancy Reagan arrived. Nancy rushed to me and took my hand. 'I'm so sorry, Paul. I wish it had been you.' "[132]

Nancy grudgingly came to see things Mike Deaver's way. As he wrote, "You could not have invented a more balanced ticket than Ronald Reagan and George Bush. One, a Midwesterner, up from poverty, a performer, outdoorsman, and regular guy, strong in the West. The other, a child of wealth, of prep schools, a war hero—a commissioned navy pilot at eighteen—captain of the Yale baseball team, now a transplanted Texas oilman. Bush had credentials where Reagan needed them most. He had served in Congress, as ambassador to the United Nations, as chairman of the Republican National Committee, as director of the CIA, as envoy to China. He was a professional who came across as earnest, well-bred, squeaky-clean."[133]

But, Nancy Reynolds told me, "I don't think Nancy Reagan and Barbara Bush ever developed a great, warm, cozy relationship."[134] Although both women went to Smith, and Barbara was only four years younger than Nancy, their backgrounds, styles, and personalities contrasted sharply. Even in Detroit, the buzz was that the two women didn't get along. "Why that's silly," Barbara Bush told *Los Angeles Times* reporter Bella Stumbo, who had bluntly asked about the rumors. "We've only met twice. And from what I've seen of Nancy so far, I like her and she likes me. Furthermore, I think she's ravishingly beautiful. When we were with them, I could hardly take my eyes off her . . . and she's been just darling to us. If anything, I think she's just shy."

"People say there is a big difference between you and Mrs. Reagan. Can you describe the difference?"

"Why, yes," Barbara Bush answered. "Nancy is a size four, and I'm a size forty-four."[135]

In a well-orchestrated show of camaraderie, the Reagans flew to Houston with the Bushes at the end of the convention. After lunch at the Bush home in the old-money Memorial section, the two couples made the first public appearance of the Republican ticket at the upscale Galleria shopping mall. Five days later, Reagan, Bush, and Anne Armstrong, who was named co-chairman of the campaign with Paul Laxalt, met with the Executive Advisory Committee at the Los Angeles Hyatt. Laffer's deadpan minutes are quite revealing:

> Tuttle and Smith both were exceptionally pleased with the convention and praised the way Ford handled himself and the outcome of the entire process. Dart thought the entire process was great with the best of all possible worlds with George Bush. . . . Max Rabb noted that Henry Kissinger did not demand any conditions and is fully on board with the Reagan efforts. . . . Coors said that any controversy over Gerald Ford was as a result of Cronkite's mistakes and not anything to do with Ford or anyone else. . . . George Bush

then expressed his pleasure at being at the meeting. . . . His major point was that he and Mrs. Bush had developed an extraordinary personal relationship with the Reagans. . . . The meeting broke up at approximately the predetermined time with a mad dash to waiting vehicles as the Dart-Kendall cabal headed en masse toward The Grove (most of the others were right with them).[136]

After making a brief appearance at the Bohemian Grove, the candidate headed straight for his mountaintop ranch. He kept a low profile during August, while the Democrats met in New York City and renominated President Jimmy Carter and Vice President Walter Mondale. One of the social highlights of the convention week was a birthday lunch for Miss Lillian, the President's eighty-two-year-old mother. The guest list included Mayor Ed Koch; Ambassador Angier Biddle Duke and his wife, Robin; real estate queen Alice Mason, who was Carter's number-one fund-raiser in New York; Walter Cronkite's wife, Betsy; and former California governor Pat Brown. The host, Richard Weisman, a rich young art collector, had called the Warhol Factory and asked us to bring a few celebrities: Andy took Patti LuPone, the star of *Evita*; I invited Jerry Zipkin. When reporter Enid Nemy asked him what such a good friend of Nancy Reagan's was doing there, Zipkin snapped, "I had to eat lunch somewhere."[137] He was then introduced to the guest of honor by Oatsie Charles, an old friend of his who was one of Georgetown's leading hostesses. "This is Jerome Zipkin, he's a Republican," Charles told Miss Lillian. "That's okay," she said good-naturedly, "I have lots of Republican friends." "So do I," replied Zipkin.

At the end of the month, the Reagans moved to Wexford, the former weekend house of Jack and Jackie Kennedy in the Virginia hunt country, which would be their East Coast base for the duration of the campaign. National campaign headquarters had already been set up in Arlington, Virginia, just across the Potomac from Washington. Reagan had come out of the Detroit convention with a 55–24–15 lead over Jimmy Carter and John Anderson, who was running as an independent. But after a week of being portrayed as a simple-minded, heartless, nostalgic fantasist by the Democrats in New York—and making a couple of gaffes on his own, such as calling for renewed diplomatic relations with Taiwan, and then having to admit he had misspoken—Reagan found his lead over Carter had shrunk to only six points.

On August 30, the Reagan team gathered at Wexford. In addition to Casey, Meese, Wirthlin, Nofziger, Anderson, Allen, and Deaver, there was a new face: James Baker, who was put in charge of debates. With Deaver's encouragement, the suave, impeccably groomed, fourth-generation Houston lawyer had managed to win over Nancy, despite his closeness to the Bushes. As Nancy Reynolds told me, "Jim Baker really had a great sense of humor, and he could kid her in a nice way. If you could kid her, that was a big plus."[138] Baker was also seen as a pragmatist who would bolster the basic campaign strategy of keeping the focus on Carter's "failure of leadership" while at the same time helping Reagan moderate his positions in order to broaden his appeal, particularly to ethnic and blue-collar voters in the big industrial states of the Northeast and Midwest. A tricky balance would have to be maintained, however, for if Reagan came across as abandoning his conservative principles, he would forfeit his hopes of making significant inroads into Carter's native South. "Peace through strength" was the new Reagan slogan. In essence, this was a Sears campaign without Sears.

The three candidates went into action on Labor Day: Anderson at a parade in Calumet City, Illinois, his home state; Carter at a picnic in Tuscumbia, Alabama, in the Baptist heart of the South; and Reagan at an "ethnic festival" in Jersey City, New Jersey. With the Statue of Liberty looming in the background and the flags of Eastern European countries flanking him, Reagan took off his jacket and tie in the sweltering heat and launched into his familiar criticism of Carter's handling of the economy, which was languishing from 13 percent inflation, 8 percent unemployment, and 12 percent interest rates.[139] At the end of the speech, Reagan was joined on the stage by the father of Lech Walesa, the Polish union leader who had defied his

country's Communist regime by taking his shipyard workers out on strike.

A day that started out so well, however, ended in
near disaster at Reagan's last stop, the Michigan
State Fair, where he told a predominantly black
audience how happy he was to be there "while
[Carter] is opening his campaign down there in the
city that gave birth to and is the parent body of the
Ku Klux Klan." The crowd gasped, and Reagan
knew he had made a major mistake. Not only were
his facts wrong—Tuscumbia was neither the Klan's
birthplace nor its headquarters—but his remark
came across as an incredibly cheap shot. The next
day Carter assailed him for insulting the South,
and although Reagan had already rushed to apologize to the governor of Alabama, six other
Southern Democratic governors, including Bill
Clinton of Arkansas, publicly denounced him.[140]

Lyn Nofziger, who had supplied Reagan with the
erroneous information, persisted in telling
reporters that they were making a mountain out of
a molehill, which only made the situation worse.
Since this fracas came right on top of the Taiwan
brouhaha, Nancy realized that there was no one in
the top staff who could handle her husband with
the subtlety and candor required. The sixty-seven-
year-old Casey, who was called "Spacey" behind
his back, had never run a national campaign, and
while Baker had done a good job for Ford in 1976
and for Bush in the primaries, he wasn't familiar
with Reagan's idiosyncrasies. Nancy was aware
that Deaver had patched things up with his old

mentor, Stu Spencer, and while she and Ronnie hadn't spoken to Spencer in four years, she asked Deaver to see if he would come back. Spencer agreed and came aboard as national political director three days after the Labor Day fiasco.[141] "I started flying with Reagan again," he told me. "I let him vent his spleen on me about going with Ford in '76. He had a good time, and from then on it was like the way it was before."[142]

That weekend, in another sign of the campaign's tilt to the center, Reagan invited Henry Kissinger to lunch at Wexford, and that evening Kissinger and his wife were among one hundred guests at a private dinner Nancy gave for Mary Jane and Charlie Wick. The guest list also included David Rockefeller, Estée and Joseph Lauder, Drew Lewis, Charles and Carole Price from Kansas City, Jane and Guilford Dudley from Nashville, and Senator John Warner, who had a place nearby. Elizabeth Taylor, who was suffering from a bad back, could not attend.[143] While Nancy was wary of Kissinger's intentions, she realized his presence at her husband's side was reassuring to the Eastern foreign policy establishment. On a personal level, the Reagans had grown more comfortable with the Kissingers after having spent time with them at the Buckleys' in New York and Connecticut. Later in the campaign, Henry and Nancy Kissinger would give a dinner for Nancy Reagan at their River House apartment in New York.[144]

Meanwhile, James Baker was trying to arrange a

debate with Carter and Anderson, to be sponsored by the League of Women Voters. But Carter refused to participate if Anderson was included, considering the renegade liberal Republican more likely to draw votes from the left than from the right. After several compromises were rejected by the White House, the League agreed to go along with a Reagan-Anderson debate on September 21, though they refused Baker's request that Carter be represented by an empty chair. The gangly, bespectacled Anderson was no match for a well-briefed and dynamic Reagan, who made a point of referring to "the man who isn't here" as often as possible. Prior to the debate, Carter had pulled slightly ahead of Reagan in the polls; afterward, Reagan regained the lead, with Anderson remaining at around 10 percent.[145]

The two major candidates' numbers would seesaw back and forth all through October, as Carter abandoned his Rose Garden strategy of remaining cool and presidential and came out swinging. Campaigning in Chicago and Milwaukee on October 6, Carter called Reagan's foreign policy "jingoistic" and "macho" and said it "would lead our country to war." In Philadelphia the next day, Reagan responded, "Well, I think he's a badly misinformed and prejudiced man. Certainly he's reaching a point of hysteria that's hard to understand."[146] Three days later, in Florida, the President stepped up his attacks, saying, "I don't know what he would do in the White House, but his opposition to the SALT II treaty, his opposition to Medicare, his opposition to many of the programs that are important like the minimum wage or unemployment compensation, his call for the injection of American military forces into place after place after place around the world indicate to me that he would not be a good president or good man to trust with the affairs of this nation in the future."[147]

Carter, like Pat Brown and Jesse Unruh before him, had not figured out that going negative on Reagan had a boomerang effect—the meaner his opponent got, the nicer Ronnie seemed. Based on Wirthlin's research that the "most salient issue" for voters was high prices, Reagan hammered away at the administration's inability to control inflation. At first he largely ignored the President's attempt to portray him as a recycled Barry Goldwater. After Carter's campaign introduced TV ads implying that Reagan viewed arms control negotiation as "a poker game" and nuclear war as "just another shoot-out at the O.K. Corral,"[148] however, Nancy decided to take the highly unusual step of taping a one-minute commercial of her own.

"I don't often speak out in campaigns," she began, "but I think this campaign now has gotten to the point and the level where I have to say something. I am deeply, deeply offended by the attempts of Mr. Carter to paint my husband as a man he is not at all. I'm offended when he tries to portray him as a warmonger, as a man who would throw the elderly out on the street and cut off their Social Security when, in fact, he never said anything of the kind at any time. That's a cruel thing to do. It's cruel to the people. It's cruel to my husband. I deeply, deeply resent it as a wife and a mother and a woman."[149]

From the start of the campaign, the national press, particularly female reporters, fixated on what came to be called The Gaze. "When I would look at Ronnie when he spoke, that wasn't an act," Nancy Reagan told me with an exasperated sigh in 1997. "That was the way I felt—no matter how many times I had heard a speech. The audience reaction always varies a bit—and I *like* to hear him speak. I adore him! And when I said, 'My life began with Ronnie,' well, it's true. I mean, I had a wonderful life before then, but it really *began*."[150]

There were also innumerable references to Nancy Reagan's influence and behind-the-scenes machinations, especially after her part in the Sears purge was made known. As always, Nancy sought to downplay her role, repeatedly telling interviewers that she would never sit in on cabinet meetings the way Rosalynn Carter did. Ironically, whenever Mrs. Carter tried to defend herself from those who criticized her for being too powerful, she tended to come out sounding like Nancy. "Jimmy makes the decisions. All I do is tell him what I think. He takes it or leaves it. He might be influenced to a certain degree, but people just don't know Jimmy Carter if they think I can persuade him to do something he doesn't want to do." The White House communications chief Patrick Caddell once even said of Rosalynn, "She's got great antennae."[151]

Unlike Rosalynn Carter, however, who usually campaigned on her own, Nancy didn't like leaving Ronnie's side. But as the race tightened, Stu Spencer convinced her that two could do more than one, and Peter McCoy—a Sotheby's executive whose mother-in-law, Onnalee Doheny, was a friend of Nancy's from the Colleagues—was hired to travel with her. "Nancy and I would go off on our own trips for three or four days at a time," McCoy told me. "The campaign plane would come into a city, and we'd jump on a small jet and go do a little outside business, and then join up with the tour later. Nancy is quite remarkable. We'd be up at eight in the morning and go all day long until ten or eleven at night, and then go back to the hotel—and Ronnie would be off on the main tour somewhere else. I think they both really found it difficult to be separated. I've never seen anything quite like that. They would talk every night."[152]

Reagan himself tried to explain their relationship to Lally Weymouth, who, for her *Times* article on Nancy, asked him what he thought his life would have been like if he hadn't met her. "I don't know," he answered, "except I know I wouldn't have been happy. I was well aware that I was very lonely, although I guess I was a success in Hollywood and had all the perquisites that go with that. But I felt the need to love someone. . . . Has she influenced my life? Yes, because I've never been happier in my life than I have been with her. She is very much what you see. There is a gentleness to her, a fierce feeling of family loyalty. I miss her very much when we're not together. We're very happy. I imagine if I sold shoes, as my father did, she would have wanted to help me sell shoes. . . . She's a very intelligent person. I don't know of anything we don't talk about. When anything happens that's interesting or exciting, the first thought that enters my mind is how I'm going to tell her."[153]

The press also tried to make an issue of the Reagan children's not quite measuring up to the standards of the Republican Party platform, with its high moral tone and disapproval of anything but the most traditional values. In an interview with Mike Wallace on *60 Minutes*, Patti, who had just come from Jane Fonda's exercise class, defended her family:

Q: Somebody else in New York wrote a fascinating piece about the Reagan children and said, Can you imagine four children, one an E.R.A. organizer and an actress, divorced twice; second, divorced once, sells gasohol and races boats; third, a rock musician and composer and actress; fourth, a ballet dancer, 22 years old. Does this sound like the children of Ronald and Nancy Reagan?

A: Well, you know, each of us are very individual and we have our own careers and our own interests that we've been working towards—I mean, what would make us normal? If we were bookkeepers or waitresses or gas station—I mean, what do they want? Not that I would give them what they wanted anyway, but I'd be curious to know. You know, I don't think that anything that any of us is doing is so alarming, you know.

Q: It's just unexpected, apparently, to some people.

A: I think it's kind of refreshing. . . .

Q: You gonna vote?

A: Yes.

Q: Jimmy Carter, John Anderson, Ronald Reagan?

A: I'm gonna vote for my father. It wouldn't be very nice not to vote for him, would it?

Q: That's the only reason?

A: No. I'm gonna vote for him because I think he'd be a good President. I do.[154]

On October 28, Ronald Reagan and Jimmy Carter had their only debate. "[It was] scheduled for 8 P.M. in Philadelphia," Deaver recalled. "I had planned a quiet, early dinner, topped off with a 1964 Cabernet. I let Reagan have one glass of wine before the debate . . . a little color for his cheeks. The Reagans, Stu Spencer, and I were the only ones in the room. Then he went into the bedroom for half an hour to rest. When I walked in, to let him know it was time to leave, he was standing at the mirror, practicing his lines, rehearsing his opening statement."[155]

Some people thought it was all over when the President told the audience that he had asked his twelve-year-old daughter, Amy, what she thought the most important issue was. "She said she thought nuclear weaponry and the control of nuclear arms," said Carter, as the audience groaned. "I knew the race was won," wrote Deaver later.[156]

As Jack Wrather put it, "It was a cut-and-dried situation at the end, because Carter made such an ass of himself. Again, I'm sure he's a very decent, and, I think, even intelligent guy, but he just made an ass of himself. He didn't do anything; he went from one side to the other. And he gave people of this country such a sense of insecurity that, during that last famous debate that he and Ron had, it was just so obvious that he really didn't know what he was talking about. You know, when Ron said, 'Jimmy, there you go again,' or something like that, everybody in the United States said, 'That's it.' They said, 'We agree with you, Ron.' Everybody talked back to the television set."[157]

On Thursday, October 30, the Reagan campaign's worst nightmare seemed to be coming true: the Iranian majlis, or parliament, had started debating whether to release the American hostages held in Tehran for nearly a year. Carter's failure to secure their freedom continued to be the great disgrace of his administration, especially after an attempted rescue mission in April had ended with four Army helicopters crashing in the Iranian desert. Now, as Reagan's advisers had feared, it looked as if he might be able to cut a deal just before the election. On Halloween there were reports that a DC-8 was waiting in Europe to fly the hostages home. On Saturday night, White House chief of staff Hamilton Jordan caught up with the President in Chicago and told him that the Iranians were offering terms. Canceling the next day's campaign events, Carter flew back to Washington at four in the morning, only to realize that the Iranians were playing games: they wanted to release their captives one by one over a period of time. Meanwhile, all three networks were running hour-long specials on the first anniversary of the embassy seizure, which would fall on election day.[158]

That weekend, an article headlined CLOSE REAGAN BUSINESS FRIENDS; THEY SEEM TO PERSONIFY HIS VALUES appeared on the first page of *The New York Times* business section, with profiles of Holmes Tuttle, Justin Dart, Ted Cummings, Earle Jorgensen, Jack Wrather, and William French Smith, who was described as "a possible Attorney General." Tuttle, the *Times* reported, "expects to help screen appointees for Mr. Reagan, as he did in California." Dart, still feisty at seventy-three, despite a hip replacement and heart troubles, announced that he would head a presidential advisory board on productivity, "the nation's No. 1 problem."[159] The Executive Advisory Committee was so sure their boy was going to win that they started calling themselves the Transition Advisory Committee.

On election night, Tuesday, November 4, 1980, they were all at Earle and Marion Jorgensen's house in Bel Air: Holmes and Virginia Tuttle, Henry and Grace Salvatori, Justin and Punky Dart, Bill and Betty Wilson, Jack and Bunny Wrather, William and Jean French Smith, Armand and Harriet Deutsch, Charles and Mary Jane Wick, Bob and Betty Adams, Voltaire and Erlenne Perkins, Tex and Flora Thornton from Litton, Tom and Ruth Jones from Northrop. Alfred and Betsy Bloomingdale took Jerry Zipkin, who wore a "Reagan for President" button on his lapel and, for a change, told all the women how fabulous they looked. Walter and Lee Annenberg had voted early that morning in Philadelphia, then boarded their jet and picked up Charles and Carol Price in Kansas City on the way out. The Jaquelin Humes arrived from San Francisco, and Old Hollywood was represented by the Jimmy Stewarts, the Robert Stacks, and the Ray Starks. Of the campaign staff, only Ed and Ursula Meese, Mike and Carolyn Deaver, and Peter and Casey McCoy were included. Nancy's hairdresser, Julius Bengtsson, was there, too. So were the Reagan children—Patti, Ron with Doria, Michael with Colleen, Maureen with her new fiancé, Dennis Revell, a lawyer she had met through the Young Republicans—and Neil and Bess Reagan.[160] Ronnie's brother, now seventy-two and retired to posh Rancho Santa Fe, told everyone not to worry, Dutch was going to win in a landslide.[161]

Marion Jorgensen told me she served the same food she served at her election night parties in 1966 and 1970—veal stew and coconut cake. "But that night was so different than when he was governor," she said. "The Secret Service came five or six days ahead and put telephones all over my house. They even put in the 'red telephone.' They were looking for a private place to put it, so they put it in Earle's dressing room. I have a picture of Ronnie sitting in a chair in Earle's dressing room with that phone—it was a call from the King of Saudi Arabia, congratulating him on just being elected president."[162]

The party began at the usual time—4:30 in the afternoon. By then the polls had started closing in the East, and forty-five minutes later NBC's John Chancellor was the first to call the election. "NBC News now makes its projection for the presidency," he announced, as a hush fell over the Jorgensens' party and the Reagans' closest friends and family stood transfixed in front of the five television sets Marion had placed around the living room, library, and den. "Reagan is our projected winner. Ronald Wilson Reagan of California, a sports announcer, a film actor, a governor of California, is our projected winner at 8:15 Eastern Standard Time on this election night."[163] Reagan would carry forty-four states and trounce Carter 51 percent to 41 percent in the popular vote, with 7 percent going to John Anderson.

Ronnie was in the shower, and Nancy was in the bathtub, with the TV in the bedroom turned up extra loud, when she heard Chancellor declaring her husband the winner. "I leaped out of the tub," she recalled, "threw a towel around me, and started banging on the shower door. Ronnie got out, grabbed a towel, and we ran over to the television set. And there we stood, dripping wet, wearing nothing but our towels, as we heard that Ronnie had just been elected! Then the phone started to ring. It was President Carter, calling to concede, and to congratulate Ronnie on his victory. I was thrilled, and stunned. We hadn't even gone to the Jorgensens' yet!"[164]

"They were late," Marion Jorgensen recalled, "and they were *never* late. I got a call from Nancy's secretary, Elaine Crispin, who said they were just a little bit detained. And pretty soon the helicopters and the motorcade came—I never saw anything like it. A Secret Service man came in and tapped me on the shoulder, so we knew, Earle and I, to go out and greet them. And he said to us, 'Now, you know how to do this?' I said, 'Sure, I know how to do it. We've done this many times before.' And he said, 'Oh, no, you haven't. You haven't greeted the president of the United States before.' . . . The minute Ronnie became president, I called him 'Mr. President.' And he said to me, 'Wait a minute. What's this?' I said, 'Well, you *are*. And that will be forevermore now.' And he said, 'Not with you, my friend. Not with Earle. Not with my good friends.' I said, 'Well, I will say this: Around anybody, it'll be

Mr. President. When we're just a few of us long-time friends, O.K., it'll be Ronnie.' "[165]

"Oh, what an evening that was," said Betsy Bloomingdale, recalling the triumphant procession of the Reagans and their friends from the Jorgensen house in Bel Air to the official victory party at the Century Plaza Hotel in Century City.[166] "Jerry was with us, and Alfred was a fast driver and he followed the Reagan motorcade, and all along Beverly Glen there were crowds of people screaming and yelling and waving flags. Alfred had a Mercedes with a sunroof, and Jerry was hanging out of the sunroof, screaming and yelling, and we were waving at the people—oh, that was such fun! When we got to the Century Plaza Hotel, we all *ran* in. Alfred just left the car there. He said, 'The hell with the car.' And we went upstairs to the suite where Nancy and Ronnie were."

Acknowledgments

I owe so much to so many, starting with Nancy Reagan, without whose cooperation this book would not have been possible. Mrs. Reagan has been extraordinarily generous with both her time and memories; she made herself available to my seemingly endless phone calls, granted me special access to the personal papers of the Reagan and Davis families held at the Ronald Reagan Presidential Library, and on two occasions invited me to her house in Bel Air, which was generally off limits to visitors during the former president's long illness. I especially valued our lunches at the Hotel Bel Air, sometimes with the tape recorder running, sometimes not. I am also exceedingly grateful for her introduction to her stepbrother, Dr. Richard Davis, at the 2000 Republican convention in Philadelphia, and to Dr. Davis for the five lengthy telephone interviews he gave in which he shared his recollections and insights regarding their family life with frankness and sensitivity.

In addition, because I had Nancy Reagan's blessing, her closest friends, many of whom have a built-in allergy to journalists and biographers, welcomed me into their homes in Los Angeles and Palm Springs and granted me interviews. These include Betty Adams, Lee Annenberg, Frances Bergen,

Armand and Harriet Deutsch, Anne Douglas, Marje Everett, William Frye and the late James Wharton, Merv Griffin, David Jones, Jean French Smith, Erlenne Sprague, Robert Tuttle, Connie Wald, Charles and Mary Jane Wick, William Wilson, and Mignon Winans. I am especially grateful to Betsy Bloomingdale and Marion Jorgensen for opening their social records to me, and for never tiring of my requests for yet another guest list or menu. I am also indebted to Jane Gosden, Wendy Stark Morrissey, and Denise Hale for their wisdom and advice about the world of the Reagans and their friends.

I am deeply beholden to Joanne Drake at the Office of President and Mrs. Reagan for reviewing and granting permission to quote from documents in the personal papers of President and Mrs. Reagan; to archivist Cate Sewell for her cheerful and unstinting help at the Ronald Reagan Library; and to Frederick Ryan, chairman of the Ronald Reagan Presidential Foundation, for including me among the foundation's friends at such events as the Reagan administration alumni reunion in Simi Valley in 1999 and the christening of the USS *Ronald Reagan* in Newport News, Virginia, in 2002. Also deserving of special mention is Robert Higdon, for employing his special brand of diplomacy on my behalf in countless ways, including arranging an interview with former prime minister Margaret Thatcher in London.

Others who gave me very useful and much appreciated interviews for this first of two volumes and the *Vanity Fair* articles that preceded it were

Martin and Annalise Anderson, Brooke Astor, Howard Baker, James A. Baker III, the late Bill Blass, Robert and Justine Bloomingdale, Frank Bogert, Tom Bolan, William F. Buckley Jr., Serena Carroll, William Clark, Eleanor O'Connor Clarke, Judy Hargrave Coleman, Jan Cowles, Douglas Cramer, Sue Cummings, Arlene Dahl, Michael Dart, Carolyn Deaver, Michael Deaver, the late Fred de Cordova, Janet de Cordova, Angie Dickenson, Barry Diller, Eric Douglas, Mica Ertegun, William Fine, Ron Fletcher, James Galanos, Angie Galbraith, John Gavin, Kenneth Giniger, the late Katharine Graham, the late C.Z. Guest, the late Richard Gully, Homer Hargrave Jr., Ed Helin, Reinaldo Herrera, Marcia Hobbs, Nancy Holmes, Leonora Hornblow, Linda LeRoy Janklow, Morton Janklow, the late Steven Kaufman, Nan Kempner, Arthur Laffer, Kenneth Jay Lane, Paul Laxalt, Liza Lerner, Gordon Luce, Aerin Magnin, Martin Manulis, the late Jacques Mapes, the late Jean Wescott Marshall, Jean Hayden Mathison, Peter McCoy, Bruce McFarland, Edwin Meese III, Nolan Miller, George Montgomery, Chase Morsey, Patricia Neal, Lyn Nofziger, China Ibsen Oughton, Charlotte Galbraith Ramage, Bess Reagan, Lyn Revson, Nancy Reynolds, Daniel Ruge, Ann Rutherford, Lily Safra, Laurie Salvatori, São Schlumberger, Peter Shifando, George Shultz, Tina Sinatra, Stuart Spencer, the late Robert Stack, Rosemarie Stack, Kevin Starr, Baroness Margaret Thatcher, Michael Thornton, Tucker Trainor, Florence van der Kemp, Helene von Damm, Lanetta Walhgren, Mike

Wallace, Anne Washburn, John Wellborne, Nicholas Wetzel, Abra Rockefeller Wilkin, Pete Wilson, Alice Pirie Wirtz, Mickey Ziffren, and Peg Zwecker.

During the six years since I decided to write this book, I have been dependent on an ever-changing but consistently able team of editorial assistants, researchers, and transcribers, including Georgia Flight, Chris Lawrence, Frank Banfi, Ted Panken, and Jonelle Lennon in New York and Long Island; Lisa Leff, Mack Polhemus, Todd O'Keeffe, Iris Berry, and Carol Bua in Los Angeles; and Steve Hammons in Washington, D.C. Bill Troop has stuck with this project almost from the beginning; I most appreciate his creative suggestions and persistence in tracking down those elusive things called facts. In the final crunch Matt Pressman, helped by Molly Fox and Matthew Williams, did an exceptionally thorough job on my endnotes, bibliography, and permissions.

Photo researcher Ann Schneider brought her usual diligence and taste to ferreting out previously unseen, striking, and revealing images of the vast cast of characters who were part of the Reagans' lives. She was aided considerably in this task by Steve Branch, the audio-visual archivist at the Reagan Library.

Special thanks to Slim Aarons for his glamorous jacket photograph of the Reagans, taken in Acapulco on a weekend hosted by D.K. Ludwig, and to my pal Jonathan Becker for his most flattering author's photo. Thanks also to graphic designer Martin Saar for his overall visual advice.

I would also like to thank Brian and Mila Mulroney, Kiron Skinner, Maureen Smith, Kristina Stewart, and John Loring for their suggestions and introductions to sources, Bennett Ashley of Janklow, Newborn & Ashley for drawing up my contracts, Devereux Chatillon of Sonnerschein Nath & Rosenthal for her legal reading of my manuscript, Norman Switzer for showing me the General Electric house, Marc Short, former Executive Director of Young America's Foundation, for his tour of Rancho del Cielo, Judith Wolfe at the Amagansett Public Library, Ron Marlow of the First Christian Church of Dixon, Valerie Yaros at the Screen Actors Guild, Nancy Young at Smith College, Judy Canter at the *San Francisco Chronicle* Library, radio historian J. David Goldin, Marion Jorgensen's social secretary Diane Felterer, Chris Harris and Gary Bradherring of MapEasy, Inc., and Frank Bowling, formerly of the Hotel Bel Air, my home away from home on my research trips.

At *Vanity Fair* I am most indebted to Graydon Carter for his original assignment and his continuing support after it turned into a seemingly never-ending book project, Chris Garrett for her patience and fairness in working out my numerous leaves of absence, Aimee Bell, David Harris, Lindsay Bucha, and Abby Field.

At Warner Books, my gratitude goes to Jamie Raab for being the first to see that there was a book in those articles, and for her many extensions; Rick Horgan for his most useful editorial comments and guidelines; Anne Twomey, Ivan Held, Robert Castillo, Harvey-Jane Kowal, and Jimmy Franco.

For constant moral support and encouragement over the long haul, I thank my agents Anne Sibbald and Mort Janklow; my friends Brigid Berlin, Colin Shanley, Claudia Cohen, Virginia Coleman, Isabel Rattazzi, Eric Freeman, Ross Bleckner, Paul Wilmot, Adam Lippes, Doris Ammann, and George Frei; and my sisters Suzanne Mead and Barbara Williams.

After Nancy Reagan, there is no one more responsible for making this book a reality than my longtime *Vanity Fair* editor and friend, Wayne Lawson, whose intelligence, taste, and sense of fairness are reflected on every page.

Bob Colacello
Amagansett, New York
August 2004

Notes

Chapter One: Early Ronnie, 1911–1932

1. Neil Reagan oral history, p. 9.
2. Edwards, *Early Reagan*, p. 33; Cannon, *Reagan*, p. 23; E. Morris, *Dutch*, pp. 14, 688.
3. Ronald Reagan with Hubler, *Where's the Rest of Me?*, p. 3.
4. Neil Reagan oral history, p. 38.
5. Ibid., p. 43.
6. Cannon, *Reagan*, p. 22.
7. Edwards, *Early Reagan*, p. 57.
8. Ronald and Nancy Reagan's personal papers, held at the Ronald Reagan Presidential Library, box 84, "Letters/Nelle Reagan, Reagan family letters (early)," "My Sonnet," by Nelle Reagan; Wills, *Reagan's America*, p. 23.
9. Ronald Reagan with Hubler, *Where's the Rest of Me?*, p. 9.
10. Edwards, *Early Reagan*, p. 62.
11. John Wilson obituary, *Whiteside Sentinel*, circa March 10, 1883, Ronald and Nancy Reagan's personal papers, held at the Ronald Reagan Presidential Library, box 84, "Letters/Nelle Reagan, Reagan family letters (early)"; Edwards, *Early Reagan*, pp. 23–25, pp. 29–30.
12. Wills, *Reagan's America*, p. 10; Edwards, *Early Reagan*, pp. 26–28.
13. Edwards, *Early Reagan*, p. 28.
14. E. Morris, *Dutch*, p. 688. Anne Edwards states that Nelle Wilson was born on July 24, 1883 (Edwards, *Early Reagan*, p. 31).
15. John Wilson obituary, *Whiteside Sentinel*, circa March 10, 1883, Ronald and Nancy Reagan's personal papers, held

at the Ronald Reagan Presidential Library, box 84, "Letters/Nelle Reagan, Reagan family letters (early)."

16. Edwards, *Early Reagan*, pp. 31–32.
17. Ibid., p. 32; E. Morris, *Dutch*, pp. 16–17; Wills, *Reagan's America*, p. 16; Neil Reagan oral history, p. 10.
18. E. Morris, *Dutch*, p. 13.
19. Ibid.
20. Neil Reagan oral history, p. 12.
21. Wills, *Reagan's America*, pp. 16–17; p. 23. See also Edwards, *Early Reagan*, pp. 34–36.
22. Wills, *Reagan's America*, pp. 19–24; Barbara A. Chernow and George A. Vallasi, eds., *The Columbia Encyclopedia: Fifth Edition* (New York: Columbia University Press, 1993), p. 770.
23. Wills, *Reagan's America*, p. 24; *Encyclopaedia Britannica*, 1960 edition, "Disciples of Christ," "Carry Nation."
24. E. Morris, *Dutch*, pp. 18, 22.
25. Edwards, *Early Reagan*, p. 37; E. Morris, *Dutch*, pp. 25–26. Some sources say that Jack Reagan worked at Marshall Field's rather than at the Fair Store (Cannon, *Reagan*, p. 24).
26. E. Morris, *Dutch*, pp. 27–29; Edwards, *Early Reagan*, pp. 37–38, 40.
27. Edwards, *Early Reagan*, p. 39.
28. E. Morris, *Dutch*, p. 30.
29. Ronald Reagan with Hubler, *Where's the Rest of Me?*, p. 13.
30. Ibid.; E. Morris, *Dutch*, p. 30; Edwards, *Early Reagan*, pp. 42, 44; Ronald Reagan, *An American Life*, p. 58.
31. Edwards, *Early Reagan*, p. 40.
32. Wills, *Reagan's America*, p. 29.
33. Ronald Reagan with Hubler, *Where's the Rest of Me?*, pp. 14–15.
34. Ibid., p. 17.
35. E. Morris, *Dutch*, pp. 31, 53; Edwards, *Early Reagan*, pp. 47–48.
36. Edwards, *Early Reagan*, p. 49.

37. Ibid., pp. 45, 51.
38. Wills, *Reagan's America*, p. 14.
39. R. Morris, *Encyclopedia of American History*, p. 509; E. Morris, *Dutch*, p. 692.
40. Neil Reagan oral history, pp. 8–9.
41. Marlow, "First Christian Church (Disciples of Christ) and the Reagan Family," p. 36.
42. Neil Reagan oral history, p. 2.
43. Healy in *Saturday Evening Post*, April 1974, p. 76.
44. Neil Reagan oral history, p. 2.
45. Marlow, "First Christian Church (Disciples of Christ) and the Reagan Family," p. 59.
46. Wills, *Reagan's America*, p. 27.
47. Cannon, *Reagan*, p. 26.
48. Wills, *Reagan's America*, p. 27.
49. E. Morris, *Dutch*, pp. 42, 694.
50. *Los Angeles Times*, November 28, 1980, "Neil May Give Advice but Promises Not to Sell Beer."
51. Marlow, "First Christian Church (Disciples of Christ) and the Reagan Family," p. 50.
52. Ronald Reagan with Hubler, *Where's the Rest of Me?*, p. 15.
53. Marlow, "First Christian Church (Disciples of Christ) and the Reagan Family," p. 196.
54. Wills, *Reagan's America*, p. 25.
55. Cannon, *Reagan*, p. 26.
56. Letter from Ronald Reagan to Pat York, May 2, 1989. Obtained courtesy of Pat York.
57. Vaughn, *Ronald Reagan in Hollywood*, p. 57, citing a 1943 *Modern Screen* interview.
58. Ibid., p. 11.
59. Cannon, *Ronnie and Jesse*, p. 6.
60. Marlow, "First Christian Church (Disciples of Christ) and the Reagan Family," pp. 71–72.
61. E. Morris, *Dutch*, pp. 59, 696.
62. Ronald Reagan, *An American Life*, p. 41.
63. Edwards, *Early Reagan*, pp. 68–69.
64. Ibid., p. 73.

65. Wills, *Reagan's America*, p. 58.
66. Walgreen, *Never a Dull Day*, p. 298.
67. *San Diego Tribune*, November 20, 1984, "Reagan Pitched His Way on First Job."
68. Wills, *Reagan's America*, p. 30.
69. Cannon, *Reagan*, p. 25.
70. Ronald Reagan, *An American Life*, p. 45.
71. Ronald Reagan with Hubler, *Where's the Rest of Me?*, p. 23.
72. Wills, *Reagan's America*, pp. 44–49.
73. Ronald Reagan with Hubler, *Where's the Rest of Me?*, p. 28.
74. Wills, *Reagan's America*, p. 48.
75. Cannon, *Ronnie and Jesse*, p. 8.
76. Marlow, "First Christian Church (Disciples of Christ) and the Reagan Family," p. 261.
77. E. Morris, *Dutch*, p. 699.
78. Ibid., p. 702.
79. Ibid., p. 87.
80. Ibid., pp. 91, 703.
81. Ronald Reagan, *An American Life*, p. 75.

Chapter Two: Early Nancy, 1921–1932

1. Kelley, *Nancy Reagan*, p. 38.
2. Cannon, *Reagan*, p. 142.
3. Nancy Reagan with Libby, *Nancy*, p. 25.
4. Ibid., pp. 20–21.
5. Root, *Root Genealogical Records, 1600–1870*, pp. 314–15.
6. Ibid., p. 357.
7. Edwards, *Early Reagan*, pp. 382–83; Kelley, *Nancy Reagan*, p. 28.
8. Edwards, *Early Reagan*, p. 379.
9. Nancy Reagan with Libby, *Nancy*, p. 21. Kitty Kelley in her unauthorized biography asserts that there were only seven Luckett children, and that they were born in Washington, D.C., because the Lucketts did not have the

means to travel 130 miles for each pregnancy (Kelley, *Nancy Reagan*, pp. 23–24).

10. Edwards, *Early Reagan*, p. 379; Lambert, *Nazimova*, p. 188; Kelley, *Nancy Reagan*, p. 23.
11. Nancy Reagan with Libby, *Nancy*, p. 21.
12. Ronald and Nancy Reagan's personal papers, held at the Ronald Reagan Presidential Library, box 20A, clipping dated September 22, 1900, from Edith Luckett's scrapbook.
13. Ronald and Nancy Reagan's personal papers, held at the Ronald Reagan Presidential Library, box 20A, undated clipping from a Dallas newspaper, circa 1926, from Edith Luckett's scrapbook.
14. *Los Angeles Times*, October 27, 1987.
15. *New York Times*, December 18, 1910.
16. Lambert, *Nazimova*, pp. 4, 22, 81–86, 72–73, 108–14.
17. McClellan, *The Girls*, pp. 3–5.
18. Ibid., pp. 14, 21–22.
19. Ronald and Nancy Reagan's personal papers, held at the Ronald Reagan Presidential Library, box 20A, unidentified newspaper clipping dated December 22, 1924, from Edith Luckett's scrapbook.
20. Kelley, *Nancy Reagan*, p. 28.
21. *Los Angeles Times*, January 20, 1981, "Nancy Reagan's Early Years: A Matter of Relativity."
22. Ibid.
23. Kelley, *Nancy Reagan*, p. 29; Edwards, *Early Reagan*, p. 383.
24. McClellan, *The Girls*, p. 21.
25. Wills, *Reagan's America*, p. 182.
26. Lambert, *Nazimova*, pp. 162–63.
27. Ibid., pp. 189–90.
28. Edwards, *Early Reagan*, p. 383; Kelley, *Nancy Reagan*, p. 29.
29. Kelley, *Nancy Reagan*, p. 31.
30. Nancy Reagan with Novak, *My Turn*, p. 69.
31. Ronald and Nancy Reagan's personal papers, held at the Ronald Reagan Presidential Library, box 20A,

unidentified 1924 clipping from Edith Luckett's scrapbook.

32. Edwards, *Early Reagan*, p. 384 (Edwards's source notes state that this quotation is from an Edith Luckett interview with Jean Kinney on "Around About").

33. Nancy Reagan with Novak, *My Turn*, p. 71.

34. Nancy Reagan with Libby, *Nancy*, p. 24.

35. Charlotte Galbraith Ramage, to author, April 19, 2001.

36. Nancy Reagan, to author, March 9, 2004.

37. Kelley, *Nancy Reagan*, p. 33.

38. Charlotte Galbraith Ramage, to author, April 19, 2001.

39. Ibid.

40. Nancy Reagan with Novak, *My Turn*, p. 77.

41. Kelley, *Nancy Reagan*, p. 32.

42. *People*, July 16, 1983, "A Find at a Flea Market Sheds Light on Nancy Reagan's Life with Her Real Father," p. 24; *Los Angeles Times*, January 20, 1981, "Nancy Reagan's Early Years: A Matter of Relativity."

43. Edwards, *Early Reagan*, p. 385.

44. L. Davis, *A Surgeon's Odyssey*, p. 225.

45. Richard Davis, to author, September 29, 2000.

46. L. Davis, *A Surgeon's Odyssey*, p. 84.

47. Richard Davis, to author, September 29, 2000, April 10, 2001.

48. L. Davis, *A Surgeon's Odyssey*, p. 22.

49. Richard Davis, to author, April 10, 2001.

50. L. Davis, *A Surgeon's Odyssey*, p. 10.

51. *Chicago Tribune*, November 14, 1965.

52. L. Davis, *A Surgeon's Odyssey*, p. 34.

53. Ibid., p. 64.

54. Ibid., p. 55.

55. Ibid., p. 103.

56. Ibid., p. 155.

57. Nicholas Wetzel, to author, April 11, 2001.

58. L. Davis, *A Surgeon's Odyssey*, pp. 186–87.

59. Nicholas Wetzel, to author, April 11, 2001; *Who's Who in America, 1980–1981* (Chicago: Marquis Who's Who, 1981), p. 816.

60. L. Davis, *A Surgeon's Odyssey*, p. 221.
61. Nicholas Wetzel, to author, April 11, 2001.
62. L. Davis, *A Surgeon's Odyssey*, pp. 226–27.
63. Richard Davis, to author, April 10, 2001.
64. Nancy Reagan with Libby, *Nancy*, p. 26.
65. *Los Angeles Times*, January 20, 1981, "Nancy Reagan's Early Years: A Matter of Relativity"; *People*, July 18, 1983, "A Find at a Flea Market Sheds Light on Nancy Reagan's Life with Her Real Father," p. 25.
66. Mantle, ed., *The Best Plays of 1927–28*, p. 402; clipping of theater review from an unidentified Chicago newspaper, April 1928.
67. Kelley, *Nancy Reagan*, p. 34.
68. Mantle, ed., *The Best Plays of 1928–29*, pp. 377–78; *New York Evening Post*, September 22, 1928; Richard Davis, to author, April 10, 2001.
69. L. Davis, *A Surgeon's Odyssey*, p. 228.
70. Richard Davis, to author, April 10, 2001.
71. Nancy Reagan, to author, June 4, 2000.
72. Charlotte Galbraith Ramage, to author, April 19, 2001.
73. Mantle, ed., *The Best Plays of 1928–1929*, pp. 377–78; Lardner, *The Lardners*, p. 179.
74. Grobel, *The Hustons*, p. 122.
75. Author's diary, April 3, 2001.
76. Richard Davis, to author, April 10, 2001.
77. Nancy Reagan with Novak, *My Turn*, p. 73.
78. Kelley, *Nancy Reagan*, p. 36.
79. L. Davis, *A Surgeon's Odyssey*, p. 228.
80. Nancy Reagan, to author, March 26, 1998.
81. Richard Davis, to author, April 10, 2001.
82. Spatz Leighton, *The Search for the Real Nancy Reagan*, p. 16.
83. Nancy Reagan with Novak, *My Turn*, pp. 76–77.
84. Ibid., p. 76.
85. Lambert, *Nazimova*, p. 320.
86. Nancy Reagan with Novak, *My Turn*, p. 74.
87. Ronald and Nancy Reagan's personal papers, held at the

Ronald Reagan Presidential Library, box 84, "Dr. Loyal Davis, In Memoriam."

88. Ronald and Nancy Reagan's personal papers, held at the Ronald Reagan Presidential Library, box 84, "Letters/Dr. Loyal Davis."

89. *People,* July 18, 1983, "A Find at a Flea Market Sheds Light on Nancy Reagan's Life with Her Real Father," pp. 23–24; *Los Angeles Times*, January 20, 1981, "Nancy Reagan's Early Years: A Matter of Relativity." Both stories were illustrated with photographs from a Robbins family album that was put together by Patsie Robbins and later surfaced in a New Jersey flea market.

90. Kelley, *Nancy Reagan*, p. 35.

91. Nancy Reagan with Libby, *Nancy*, p. 25.

92. *People,* July 18, 1983, "A Find at a Flea Market Sheds Light on Nancy Reagan's Life with Her Real Father," pp. 23–24; *Los Angeles Times*, January 20, 1981, "Nancy Reagan's Early Years: A Matter of Relativity."

93. Richard Davis, to author, September 29, 2000.

94. Nancy Reagan, to author, April 30, 2001.

95. Jean Wescott Marshall, to author, April 19, 2001.

96. L. Davis, *A Surgeon's Odyssey*, p. 242.

97. Ibid., pp. 238–40.

98. Dunning, *Tune in Yesterday*, pp. 61–62; Lackmann, *The Encyclopedia of American Radio*, p. 38.

99. Kelley, *Nancy Reagan*, p. 37.

100. L. Davis, *A Surgeon's Odyssey*, p. 231.

101. Richard Davis, to author, April 10, 2001.

102. Ronald and Nancy Reagan's personal papers, held at the Ronald Reagan Presidential Library, box 84, "Mrs. Loyal Davis (Edith), In Memoriam."

Chapter Three: Iowa, 1933–1937

1. "B. J. Palmer's Epigrams," from the Web site of Palmer Chiropractic University, www.palmer.edu/pfch/Epigrams. htm.

2. Ronald and Nancy Reagan's personal papers, held at the

Ronald Reagan Presidential Library, box 84, "Letters/Nelle Reagan, Reagan family letters (early)," "My New Year Poem, 1935–36," by Nelle Reagan.

3. Ronald Reagan with Hubler, *Where's the Rest of Me?*, p. 17.
4. Edwards, *Early Reagan*, p. 43.
5. Nachman, *Raised on Radio*, p. 16.
6. E. Morris, *Dutch*, pp. 37, 693.
7. Ronald Reagan with Hubler, *Where's the Rest of Me?*, pp. 42–43.
8. Ibid., pp. 43–44; Ronald Reagan, *An American Life*, pp. 59–60.
9. Ronald Reagan, *An American Life*, pp. 59–60.
10. Ronald Reagan with Hubler, *Where's the Rest of Me?*, p. 45.
11. Ibid., p. 46.
12. Ibid.
13. Ronald Reagan, *An American Life*, p. 63. Garry Wills says that it was an "old Chevrolet" (Wills, *Reagan's America*, p. 59).
14. Cannon, *Reagan*, p. 44; Edwards, *Early Reagan*, pp. 121–23.
15. Edwards, *Early Reagan*, p. 124.
16. Ibid., pp. 125–26. Lou Cannon differs slightly, saying that Reagan's room cost $18 per month (Cannon, *Reagan*, p. 44).
17. Ronald Reagan with Hubler, *Where's the Rest of Me?*, p. 55.
18. Ronald Reagan, *An American Life*, p. 66.
19. Ibid., pp. 66–67.
20. Wills, *Reagan's America*, p. 61.
21. Edwards, *Early Reagan*, pp. 138–39.
22. Ibid., pp. 133, 143.
23. Ronald Reagan with Hubler, *Where's the Rest of Me?*, pp. 56–58; Wills, *Reagan's America*, p. 99.
24. Wills, *Reagan's America*, p. 97.
25. Ibid., pp. 97, 99.
26. Vaughn, *Ronald Reagan in Hollywood*, p. 24.

27. Ibid.
28. Ibid., pp. 23–25.
29. Ronald Reagan, *An American Life*, p. 71; E. Morris, *Dutch*, pp. 116, 708.
30. Ronald Reagan with Hubler, *Where's the Rest of Me?*, p. 48.
31. Edwards, *Early Reagan*, p. 131.
32. Ronald Reagan, *An American Life*, p. 75; Edwards, *Early Reagan*, pp. 134–35.
33. Ronald Reagan with Hubler, *Where's the Rest of Me?*, p. 45.
34. E. Morris, *Dutch*, pp. 122, 709.
35. Neil Reagan oral history, pp. 13–16.
36. Edwards, *Early Reagan*, pp. 143–44.
37. Ronald Reagan with Hubler, *Where's the Rest of Me?*, p. 59.
38. Ibid.
39. Ibid., p. 60.
40. Wills, *Reagan's America*, p. 110.
41. Cannon, *Reagan*, p. 46.
42. Wills, *Reagan's America*, pp. 112–13.
43. Ronald Reagan, *An American Life*, p. 74.
44. Edwards, *Early Reagan*, p. 145; Ronald Reagan with Hubler, *Where's the Rest of Me?*, pp. 67–68.
45. Wills, *Reagan's America*, p. 113; Edwards, *Early Reagan*, p. 134. Note that her surname has been withheld at the request of her family.
46. E. Morris, *Dutch*, p. 119; Wills, *Reagan's America*, p. 114.
47. Edwards, *Early Reagan*, p. 149.
48. Ibid.
49. Wills, *Reagan's America*, p. 108.
50. Edwards, *Early Reagan*, pp. 150–51.
51. E. Morris, *Dutch*, p. 124.
52. Ronald Reagan with Hubler, *Where's the Rest of Me?*, p. 70.
53. Ibid., p. 72; Ronald Reagan, *An American Life*, pp. 78–79.
54. Ronald Reagan with Hubler, *Where's the Rest of Me?*, p. 72; Wills, *Reagan's America*, p. 114.

55. Ronald Reagan, *An American Life*, pp. 79–80; E. Morris, *Dutch*, p. 131.
56. Ronald Reagan with Hubler, *Where's the Rest of Me?*, p. 74.
57. Ibid.
58. Edwards, *Early Reagan*, p. 166; *Dixon Telegraph*, April 16, 1937, "Thrilled: Ronald Reagan Reveals His Reaction Over Success."
59. Wills, *Reagan's America*, p. 114.
60. Ronald Reagan with Hubler, *Where's the Rest of Me?*, p. 76.
61. Ronald and Nancy Reagan's personal papers, held at the Ronald Reagan Presidential Library, box 84, "Letters/Nelle Reagan, Reagan family letters (early)."

Chapter Four: East Lake Shore Drive, 1933–1939

1. Kelley, *Nancy Reagan*, p. 39.
2. Nancy Reagan with Novak, *My Turn*, p. 78.
3. Barbara A. Chernow and George A. Vallasi, eds., *The Columbia Encyclopedia: Fifth Edition* (New York: Columbia University Press, 1993), p. 450.
4. Biles, *Big City Boss in Depression and War*, p. 21.
5. Ibid., p. 24.
6. Nicholas Wetzel, to author, April 11, 2001.
7. Ronald and Nancy Reagan's personal papers, held at the Ronald Reagan Presidential Library, box 84, "N. Reagan—Letters," undated letter to Loyal Davis from Nancy at Camp Ketchuwa.
8. Jean Wescott Marshall, to author, April 19, 2001.
9. China Ibsen Oughton, to author, February 21, 2001.
10. Ibid.
11. Bruce McFarland, to author, February 14, 2002.
12. China Ibsen Oughton, to author, February 21, 2001.
13. Angie Johnson Galbraith, to author, February 27, 2001.
14. Jean Wescott Marshall, to author, April 19, 2001.

15. "Nancy Reagan," *A&E Biography*, A&E Television Network, March 31, 1997.
16. Jean Wescott Marshall, to author, April 19, 2001.
17. Bruce McFarland, to author, February 14, 2002.
18. *Chicago Tribune*, June 13, 1980.
19. Jean Wescott Marshall, to author, April 19, 2001.
20. *Vita Scholae*, The Girls Latin School of Chicago, June 1948, p. 48.
21. Wills, *Reagan's America*, p. 182.
22. Grobel, *The Hustons*, p. 168.
23. Lambert, *Nazimova*, p. 346.
24. Ibid., pp. 347–48.
25. Nancy Reagan, to author, March 25, 2002.
26. Lambert, *Nazimova*, pp. 356–57.
27. Grobel, *The Hustons*, p. 176.
28. Nancy Reagan with Libby, *Nancy*, p. 62.
29. Grobel, *The Hustons*, pp. 122–23.
30. Richard Davis, to author, April 10, 2001.
31. Huston, *An Open Book*, p. 182.
32. Grobel, *The Hustons*, p. 175.
33. Richard Davis, to author, April 10, 2001.
34. Weld, *September Song*, pp. 130–31; Grobel, *The Hustons*, p. 188.
35. Nancy Reagan, to author, March 19, 2003.
36. Moore, *Silent Star*, p. 250.
37. Ibid., pp. 22–24.
38. *Los Angeles Times*, January 26, 1988, "Colleen Moore, Film Star of Flapper Age, Dies at 87."
39. Moore, *Silent Star*, pp. 231–45.
40. Ibid., p. 245.
41. Ibid., pp. 252–55.
42. Homer Hargrave Jr., to author, February 22, 2002.
43. Abra Rockefeller Wilkin, to author, January 17, 2002.
44. Homer Hargrave Jr., to author, February 22, 2002.
45. Judy Hargrave Coleman, to author, January 28, 2002.
46. Ibid.
47. Homer Hargrave Jr., to author, February 22, 2002.
48. Judy Hargrave Coleman, to author, January 28, 2002.

49. Unidentified clipping from *Chicago American*, article by Lois Baur, from clippings file at Ronald Reagan Presidential Library.
50. Abra Rockefeller Wilkin, to author, January 17, 2002.
51. Nancy Reagan with Novak, *My Turn*, p. 306.
52. Nancy Reagan, to author, February 4, 2002, March 25, 2002.
53. Nancy Reagan, to author, March 25, 2002.
54. Judy Hargrave Coleman, to author, January 28, 2002.
55. "Nancy Reagan," *A&E Biography*, A&E Television Network, March 31, 1997.
56. Kelley, *Nancy Reagan*, p. 41.
57. Richard Davis, to author, April 10, 2001.
58. Ibid.
59. Kelley, *Nancy Reagan*, pp. 37–38.
60. Biles, *Big City Boss in Depression and War*, p. 28.
61. Ibid., p. 39.
62. L. Davis, *A Surgeon's Odyssey*, p. 294.
63. Ibid., p. 249.
64. Dunning, *On the Air*, pp. 636–37.
65. *Vita Scholae*, The Girls Latin School of Chicago, 1937, p. 27.
66. Richard Davis, to author, April 10, 2001.
67. Nancy Reagan with Novak, *My Turn*, pp. 74–75.
68. Nancy Reagan with Libby, *Nancy*, p. 27.
69. Cannon, *Reagan*, p. 142.
70. Nancy Reagan with Novak, *My Turn*, p. 75.
71. Kelley, *Nancy Reagan*, p. 42.
72. Abra Rockefeller Wilkin, to author, January 17, 2002.
73. Marjorie Everett, to author, September 25, 1999.
74. Nancy Reagan with Libby, *Nancy*, pp. 30–31.
75. Ibid., p. 25.
76. *Los Angeles Times*, January 20, 1981, "Nancy Reagan's Early Years: A Matter of Relativity."
77. Ibid.
78. Nancy Reagan, to author, August 25, 2001.
79. Nancy Reagan with Novak, *My Turn*, p. 78.
80. Nancy Reagan to author, August 25, 2001.

81. L. Davis, *A Surgeon's Odyssey*, p. 231.
82. Kelley, *Nancy Reagan*, p. 43.
83. Nancy Reagan with Novak, *My Turn*, p. 74.
84. Grobel, *The Hustons*, p. 198.
85. Nancy Reagan with Novak, *My Turn*, pp. 80–81.
86. Nancy Reagan with Libby, *Nancy*, pp. 62–63.
87. Ibid., p. 63.
88. Nancy Reagan with Novak, *My Turn*, p. 82.
89. *Vita Scholae*, The Girls Latin School of Chicago, 1939, p. 12.
90. Homer Hargrave Jr., to author, February 22, 2002.
91. Ibid.
92. *Vita Scholae*, The Girls Latin School of Chicago, 1939, p. 12.
93. Kelley, *Nancy Reagan*, p. 55; Nancy Reagan with Libby, *Nancy*, pp. 52–53; Edwards, *Early Reagan*, p. 389.
94. Kelley, *Nancy Reagan*, pp. 56–57.

Chapter Five: Warner Bros., 1937–1941

1. Pitt and Pitt, *Los Angeles A to Z*, pp. 339–40.
2. Ibid., p. 403.
3. Population figures for various cities from *Encyclopaedia Britannica*, 1960 edition.
4. M. Davis, *City of Quartz*, p. 118.
5. *New York Times*, July 7, 2002, "The Endless City vs. Its Closing Frontier."
6. Pitt and Pitt, *Los Angeles A to Z*, p. 578.
7. Mike Davis, *City of Quartz*, p. 25.
8. *New York Review of Books*, May 28, 1998, "Angels of L.A.," pp. 17–18.
9. *Encyclopaedia Britannica*, 1960 edition, "Los Angeles."
10. Mike Davis, *City of Quartz*, p. 160.
11. Higham, *Merchant of Dreams*, pp. 434, 201.
12. Ibid., p. 215.
13. Warner with Jennings, *My First Hundred Years in Hollywood*, p. 223.
14. Edwards, *Early Reagan*, pp. 163, 578.

15. *Des Moines Dispatch*, June 13, 1937, "The Making of a Movie Star," by Ronald "Dutch" Reagan.
16. Ronald Reagan, *An American Life*, p. 83.
17. Ogden, *Legacy*, pp. 135–38; Cooney, *The Annenbergs*, pp. 71–73, 382.
18. Ronald Reagan with Hubler, *Where's the Rest of Me?*, p. 84; Edwards, *Early Reagan*, p. 176.
19. Neil Reagan oral history, p. 18.
20. Wills, *Reagan's America*, p. 143.
21. Edwards, *Early Reagan*, p. 178; Ronald Reagan with Hubler, *Where's the Rest of Me?*, p. 88.
22. Edwards, *Early Reagan*, p. 173.
23. Ronald Reagan with Hubler, *Where's the Rest of Me?*, p. 89.
24. Edwards, *Early Reagan*, p. 184.
25. Ronald Reagan with Hubler, *Where's the Rest of Me?*, p. 89.
26. Edwards, *Early Reagan*, p. 183.
27. Ronald and Nancy Reagan's personal papers, held at the Ronald Reagan Presidential Library, box 84, Reagan family letters, "Letters/Nelle Reagan."
28. E. Morris, *Dutch*, p. 720; Edwards, *Early Reagan*, pp. 182–84.
29. E. Morris, *Dutch*, p. 164.
30. *Los Angeles Times*, October 3, 1948.
31. Edwards, *Early Reagan*, pp. 188–90; E. Morris, *Dutch*, pp. 153, 717–18.
32. Edwards, *Early Reagan*, pp. 188–89.
33. Quirk, *Jane Wyman*, p. 13.
34. Ibid., p. 14.
35. Morella and Epstein, *Jane Wyman*, pp. 6–8; Quirk, *Jane Wyman*, pp. 13–14.
36. Quirk, *Jane Wyman*, p. 13; Edwards, *Early Reagan*, p. 189.
37. Quirk, *Jane Wyman*, p. 14.
38. Morella and Epstein, *Jane Wyman*, p. 7.
39. Quirk, *Jane Wyman*, p. 14
40. Ibid., p. 16; Edwards, *Early Reagan*, p. 190.

41. Morella and Epstein, *Jane Wyman*, p. 9; Quirk, *Jane Wyman*, p. 18.
42. 1964 *Guidepost Magazine* interview, quoted in Quirk, *Jane Wyman*, p. 17.
43. Quirk, *Jane Wyman*, p. 16.
44. Edwards, *Early Reagan*, pp. 190–91.
45. Quirk, *Jane Wyman*, pp. 16–17.
46. Ibid., p. 25.
47. Morella and Epstein, *Jane Wyman*, p. 14; Quirk, *Jane Wyman*, p. 32.
48. E. Morris, *Dutch*, pp. 140, 715.
49. Quirk, *Jane Wyman*, pp. 30–31.
50. Edwards, *Early Reagan*, p. 192.
51. E. Morris, *Dutch*, p. 157.
52. Leonora Hornblow, to author, February 10, 2000.
53. E. Morris, *Dutch*, p. 161.
54. Ronald Reagan with Hubler, *Where's the Rest of Me?*, p. 88.
55. Richard Gully, to author, October 1, 1999.
56. E. Morris, *Dutch*, p. 718; Edwards, *Early Reagan*, p. 192.
57. E. Morris, *Dutch*, p. 720.
58. Edwards, *Early Reagan*, p. 193; Quirk, *Jane Wyman*, p. 43.
59. Wills, *Reagan's America*, p. 145.
60. Quirk, *Jane Wyman*, p. 42.
61. McClelland, *Hollywood on Ronald Reagan*, p. 46 (citing a 1944 *Movieland* article co-authored by Jane Wyman).
62. Edwards, *Early Reagan*, p. 193.
63. Ronald Reagan with Hubler, *Where's the Rest of Me?*, p. 87.
64. McClelland, *Hollywood on Ronald Reagan*, p. 6.
65. E. Morris, *Dutch*, p. 162.
66. Edwards, *Early Reagan*, pp. 197–98.
67. E. Morris, *Dutch*, p. 163.
68. Edwards, *Early Reagan*, pp. 199–200. See also E. Morris, *Dutch*, pp. 161–64; Eells, *Hedda and Louella*, pp. 190–91.
69. Leonora Hornblow, to author, February 10, 2000.

70. Maureen Reagan, *First Father, First Daughter*, p. 36.
71. Edwards, *Early Reagan*, pp. 200–201; E. Morris, *Dutch*, pp. 165–66; Fine Collins in *Vanity Fair*, April 1997, p. 368.
72. Leonora Hornblow, to author, February 10, 2000.
73. Eells, *Hedda and Louella*, p. 23.
74. Jane Wyman, to author, February 21, 1999.
75. Quirk, *Jane Wyman*, p. 45.
76. Edwards, *Early Reagan*, p. 213; E. Morris, *Dutch*, p. 725.
77. E. Morris, *Dutch*, p. 185.
78. *Movie-Radio Guide*, September 20, 1941, "The Ten Richest Women in Movies," quoted in Schultz, *Irene Dunne*, p. 253, entry B-319.
79. Ronald Reagan with Hubler, *Where's the Rest of Me?*, p. 86.
80. E. Morris, *Dutch*, p. 185.
81. Nancy Reagan, to author, July 10, 2000.
82. Schary Zimmer (now Jill Robinson), *With a Cast of Thousands*, p. 110.
83. *Current Biography 1941*, "Benny, Jack."
84. McClelland, *Hollywood on Ronald Reagan*, p. 26.
85. Leonora Hornblow, to author, February 10, 2000.
86. Edwards, *Early Reagan*, p. 230.
87. Maureen Reagan, *First Father, First Daughter*, pp. 27–28.
88. William Frye, to author, October 27, 1999.
89. Wright Cobb and Willems, *The Brown Derby Restaurant*, pp. 7, 72–73.
90. Robert Stack, to author, March 16, 2000.
91. Ibid.
92. Vaughn, *Ronald Reagan in Hollywood*, pp. 105–6. Other sources say that the film's budget was $750,000.
93. Ronald Reagan with Hubler, *Where's the Rest of Me?*, pp. 97–98.
94. Ibid., p. 81.
95. Maureen Reagan, *First Father, First Daughter*, pp. 60–61.
96. Ibid., p. 61; E. Morris, *Dutch*, p. 177.
97. Maureen Reagan, *First Father, First Daughter*, p. 61.
98. Vaughn, *Ronald Reagan in Hollywood*, p. 39.
99. Edwards, *Early Reagan*, pp. 245–50.

100. Vaughn, *Ronald Reagan in Hollywood,* p. 39.
101. Spada, *Ronald Reagan*, p. 39.
102. E. Morris, *Dutch*, p. 184.
103. Ann Rutherford, to author, January 22, 2001.
104. PBS Online, *American Experience: Lindbergh*, special features, "Fallen Hero: Charles Lindbergh in the 1940s," http://www.pbs.org/wgbh/amex/lindbergh/sfeature/fallen.html.
105. Affron, *Lillian Gish*, pp. 285–86.
106. Schlesinger Jr., *A Life in the 20th Century*, p. 242.
107. Gabler, *An Empire of Their Own*, pp. 351–53.
108. Billingsley, *Hollywood Party*, pp. 70–71; Koch, *Double Lives*, pp. 78, 225.
109. Billingsley, *Hollywood Party*, p. 75; Koch, *Double Lives*, p. 225.
110. Gabler, *An Empire of Their Own*, p. 354.
111. Buhle and Wagner, *Radical Hollywood*, p. 56.
112. Lardner Jr., *I'd Hate Myself in the Morning*, p. 98.
113. E. Morris, *Dutch*, pp. 157–59, 719.
114. Leonora Hornblow, to author, February 10, 2000.
115. Vaughn, *Ronald Reagan in Hollywood*, p. 93.
116. Affron, *Lillian Gish*, p. 291.
117. Gabler, *An Empire of Their Own*, p. 345; *New York Times*, September 12, 1941, "Lindbergh Sees a 'Plot' for War."
118. Edwards, *Early Reagan*, p. 258.
119. Vaughn, *Ronald Reagan in Hollywood*, pp. 99–100.
120. Ibid., p. 34.
121. Ibid., p. 35.
122. Ibid., p. 67.
123. Ibid., p. 79.
124. Ibid., p. 72.
125. Ibid., p. 70.
126. Ibid., p. 67.
127. Ronald Reagan with Hubler, *Where's the Rest of Me?*, p. 102.
128. Vaughn, *Ronald Reagan in Hollywood*, p. 68.
129. Ibid., p. 102.

Chapter Six: Nancy at Smith, 1939–1944

1. Nancy Reagan with Novak, *My Turn*, p. 82.
2. Richard Davis, to author, September 29, 2000, April 25, 2002.
3. Richard Davis, to author, April 25, 2002.
4. Horowitz, *Alma Mater*, p. 70.
5. Kelley, *Nancy Reagan*, p. 49.
6. Nancy Reagan with Libby, *Nancy*, p. 52.
7. China Ibsen Oughton, to author, February 12, 2001.
8. Nancy Reagan with Novak, *My Turn*, pp. 82–83.
9. Nancy Reagan with Libby, *Nancy*, p. 52.
10. "Nancy Reagan: An American Story," Fox News Channel, July 6, 2002.
11. Letter from Loyal Davis to Nancy Davis, postmarked December 6, 1939, provided courtesy of Nancy Reagan.
12. L. Davis, *A Surgeon's Odyssey*, p. 252.
13. Richard Davis, to author, April 10, 2001.
14. Richard Davis, to author, April 25, 2002.
15. "Nancy Reagan," *A&E Biography*, A&E Television Network, March 31, 1997.
16. Richard Davis, to author, April 25, 2002.
17. Lambert, *Nazimova*, p. 370.
18. "Nancy Reagan," *A&E Biography*, A&E Television Network, March 31, 1997.
19. Grobel, *The Hustons*, p. 176.
20. Affron, *Lillian Gish*, p. 200.
21. Ibid., pp. 20–21, 39.
22. Ibid., p. 270.
23. Ibid., pp. 272, 389.
24. Ibid., p. 158.
25. Ibid., p. 175.
26. Ibid., p. 287.
27. Ibid., p. 289.
28. Moore, *Silent Star*, p. 66.
29. Affron, *Lillian Gish*, pp. 286, 391.
30. Ibid., p. 290.
31. Berg, *Lindbergh*, pp. 421–22.

32. Ibid., p. 419.
33. McDaniel in *Los Angeles Herald Examiner*, October 28, 1980, "Dr. Loyal Davis—the Stepdaddy of Kingmakers."
34. Richard Davis, to author, April 25, 2002.
35. Homer Hargrave Jr., to author, February 22, 2002.
36. Higham, *Merchant of Dreams*, pp. 270–71; Lardner Jr., *I'd Hate Myself in the Morning*, p. 89.
37. Homer Hargrave Jr., to author, February 22, 2002.
38. Richard Davis, to author, April 25, 2002.
39. Richard Davis, to author, April 10, 2001.
40. Brown and Brown, *Reagan*, p. 165.
41. Nancy Reagan, to author, October 27, 1997.
42. Richard Davis, to author, April 25, 2002.
43. Barbara A. Chernow and George A. Vallasi, eds., *The Columbia Encyclopedia: Fifth Edition* (New York: Columbia University Press, 1993), p. 1092.
44. Kelley, *Nancy Reagan*, p. 39.
45. Richard Davis, to author, April 10, 2001.
46. Mike Wallace, to author, May 30, 2002.
47. Nicholas Wetzel, to author, April 11, 2001.
48. Richard Davis, to author, September 29, 2000.
49. Nicholas Wetzel, to author, April 11, 2001.
50. L. Davis, *A Surgeon's Odyssey*, pp. 10–11.
51. Nancy Reagan with Novak, *My Turn*, p. 75.
52. Cannon, *Ronnie and Jesse*, p. 158.
53. Kelley, *Nancy Reagan*, p. 39.
54. Nicholas Wetzel, to author, April 11, 2001.
55. Daniel Ruge, to author, April 11, 2001.
56. Richard Davis, to author, April 10, 2001.
57. Biles, *Big City Boss in Depression and War*, p. 107.
58. Ibid., p. 145.
59. Nancy Reagan, to author, April 30, 2001.
60. Richard Davis, to author, April 25, 2002; April 10, 2001.
61. L. Davis, *A Surgeon's Odyssey*, p. 294.
62. Leamer, *Make-Believe*, p. 46.
63. *New York Times*, December 11, 1941, "Mrs. Davis Named to Smith Deanship"; *New York Times*, July 24,

1969, "Hallie Flanagan Davis Is Dead; Headed Federal Theater in 30's."

64. Leamer, *Make-Believe*, pp. 52–53.
65. Ronald and Nancy Reagan's personal papers, held at the Ronald Reagan Presidential Library, box 20, Nancy Reagan scrapbook #1, 1946–1950.
66. Nancy Reagan with Libby, *Nancy*, p. 64.
67. Martin Manulis, to author, May 4, 2002.
68. Ibid.
69. Nancy Reagan with Libby, *Nancy*, p. 64.
70. Ibid., p. 65.
71. *People,* July 18, 1983, "A Find at a Flea Market Sheds Light on Nancy Reagan's Life with Her Real Father"; *Los Angeles Times*, January 20, 1981, "Nancy Reagan's Early Years: A Matter of Relativity."
72. Jean Wescott Marshall, to author, April 19, 2001.
73. Kelley, *Nancy Reagan*, pp. 51–52.
74. Richard Davis, to author, April 25, 2002.
75. Ibid.
76. Nancy Reagan with Novak, *My Turn*, p. 82.
77. Nancy Reagan with Libby, *Nancy*, p. 53.
78. Bruce McFarland, to author, February 14, 2002.
79. Gauss Jackson and Haydn, *The Papers of Christian Gauss*, pp. 118–20.
80. Edwards, *Early Reagan*, p. 390, quoting *Daily Princetonian*, December 16, 1941.
81. Kelley, *Nancy Reagan*, pp. 57–59.
82. Edwards, *Early Reagan*, p. 390.
83. Kelley, *Nancy Reagan*, p. 57.
84. Nancy Reagan with Novak, *My Turn*, p. 83.
85. Bruce McFarland, to author, February 14, 2002.
86. Richard Davis, to author, April 25, 2002.
87. Leamer, *Make-Believe*, p. 53; Kelley, *Nancy Reagan*, p. 59.
88. Leamer, *Make-Believe*, pp. 46–49.
89. Richard Davis, to author, April 25, 2002.
90. Edwards, *Early Reagan*, p. 389.
91. Ronald and Nancy Reagan's personal papers, held at the

Ronald Reagan Presidential Library, box 20, Nancy Reagan scrapbook #1, 1946–1950.

92. Nancy Reagan with Novak, *My Turn*, p. 84.
93. Richard Davis, to author, April 17, 2003.
94. L. Davis, *A Surgeon's Odyssey*, p. 256.
95. Richard Davis, to author, April 25, 2002.
96. Richard Davis, to author, September 29, 2000, April 10, 2001, April 25, 2002.
97. L. Davis, *A Surgeon's Odyssey*, pp. 256–57.
98. Bulletin of the American College of Surgeons, Vol. 67, No. 10 (October 1982), p. 3 (from main clippings file at Ronald Reagan Presidential Library).
99. L. Davis, *A Surgeon's Odyssey*, pp. 263–69.
100. Richard Davis, to author, September 29, 2000.
101. Dunning, *On the Air*, pp. 81, 636, 420.
102. Richard Davis, to author, April 25, 2002.
103. Kelley, *Nancy Reagan*, pp. 61–62.
104. Biles, *Big City Boss in Depression and War*, p. 119.
105. Edwards, *Early Reagan*, pp. 390–91.
106. Ibid.
107. Kelley, *Nancy Reagan*, p. 60.
108. Ibid., p. 62; Leamer, *Make-Believe*, p. 54.
109. Leamer, *Make-Believe*, pp. 54–55.
110. Kelley, *Nancy Reagan*, pp. 63, 536.
111. Nancy Reagan with Novak, *My Turn*, p. 77.
112. Richard Davis, to author, April 25, 2002.
113. Grobel, *The Hustons*, p. 176.
114. Richard Davis, to author, April 25, 2002; Jean Wescott Marshall, to author, April 19, 2001; Kelley, *Nancy Reagan*, p. 64.
115. Nancy Reagan with Libby, *Nancy*, p. 32.
116. Ibid., p. 66.
117. L. Davis, *A Surgeon's Odyssey*, pp. 278–80.
118. Ibid., pp. 281–82.
119. Ibid., pp. 283–86.
120. Shepherd in *The American* (Chicago), November 11, 1962.
121. L. Davis, *A Surgeon's Odyssey*, pp. 292–93.

122. Richard Davis, to author, April 10, 2001.
123. Ibid.
124. Daniel Ruge, to author, April 11, 2001.
125. Davidson, *Spencer Tracy*, p. 2.
126. Nancy Reagan, to author, June 4, 2000.
127. Richard Davis, to author, April 25, 2002.
128. Nancy Reagan with Libby, *Nancy*, p. 53; Kelley, *Nancy Reagan*, pp. 64–65; Richard Davis, to author, April 25, 2002.
129. Nancy Reagan, to author, May 3, 2002.
130. Lambert, *Nazimova*, pp. 288, 7.
131. Ibid., pp. 382–83.
132. Leamer, *Make-Believe*, p. 55; Kelley, *Nancy Reagan*, p. 65.
133. Nancy Reagan with Libby, *Nancy*, p. 54.
134. Richard Davis, to author, April 25, 2002.
135. Robert Higdon, to author, May 2002.
136. Nancy Reagan with Libby, *Nancy*, pp. 66–67.
137. Edwards, *Early Reagan*, p. 391.
138. *Chicago Tribune*, June 8, 1963, "Zasu Pitts, 63, Film Comedienne, Is Dead."
139. Nancy Reagan with Libby, *Nancy,* p. 67.
140. Nancy Reagan, to author, June 4, 2000.

Chapter Seven: Ronnie and Jane, 1941–1946

1. Vaughn, *Ronald Reagan in Hollywood*, p. 168.
2. Leamer, *Make-Believe*, p. 119.
3. Vaughn, *Ronald Reagan in Hollywood*, p. 37.
4. Ronald Reagan with Hubler, *Where's the Rest of Me?*, pp. 99–100.
5. E. Morris, *Dutch*, p. 180.
6. Jacques Mapes, to author, September 29, 1999.
7. E. Morris, *Dutch*, pp. 184–85, 189.
8. Leonora Hornblow, to author, February 10, 2000.
9. Edwards, *Early Reagan*, p. 261; Vaughn, *Ronald Reagan in Hollywood*, p. 108.
10. E. Morris, *Dutch*, p. 727.

11. Leamer, *Make-Believe*, pp. 119–20; Vaughn, *Ronald Reagan in Hollywood*, pp. 108–9.
12. Wright Cobb and Willems, *The Brown Derby Restaurant*, p. 115.
13. Ronald Reagan with Hubler, *Where's the Rest of Me?*, p. 107; Ronald Reagan, *An American Life*, p. 97.
14. Ronald Reagan with Hubler, *Where's the Rest of Me?*, pp. 111–12.
15. E. Morris, *Dutch*, p. 192.
16. Vaughn, *Ronald Reagan in Hollywood*, pp. 109–10; E. Morris, *Dutch*, p. 192.
17. McClelland, *Hollywood on Ronald Reagan*, p. 34.
18. Bowman, *Los Angeles*, pp. 330–35. Pitt and Pitt, in *Los Angeles A to Z*, say that the battle was three nights later (p. 579).
19. Bowman, *Los Angeles*, pp. 330–31; Pitt and Pitt, *Los Angeles A to Z*, p. 558.
20. Wills, *John Wayne's America*, pp. 107, 105.
21. Friedrich, *City of Nets*, p. 105.
22. Benjamin and Simon in *New York Review of Books*, December 20, 2001.
23. Friedrich, *City of Nets*, p. 106.
24. Brownstein, *The Power and the Glitter*, p. 80.
25. Friedrich, *City of Nets*, pp. 108, 158.
26. Ibid., pp. 106–7; Donnelly, *Fade to Black*, p. 368; E. Morris, *Dutch*, p. 729.
27. Ronald Reagan with Hubler, *Where's the Rest of Me?*, p. 117.
28. Vaughn, *Ronald Reagan in Hollywood*, pp. 112–13.
29. Ibid., p. 116.
30. Ronald Reagan with Hubler, *Where's the Rest of Me?*, p. 113.
31. E. Morris, *Dutch*, p. 202; Morella and Epstein, *Jane Wyman*, p. 58; Edwards, *Early Reagan*, pp. 267–68.
32. Ronald Reagan, *An American Life*, p. 102; E. Morris, *Dutch*, pp. 207, 731.
33. Thomas, *Golden Boy*, p. 49.
34. Edwards, *Early Reagan*, pp. 274–75.

35. E. Morris, *Dutch*, pp. 209, 732.
36. McClelland, *Hollywood on Ronald Reagan*, p. 109; Vaughn, *Ronald Reagan in Hollywood*, pp. 117–18.
37. Edwards, *Early Reagan*, p. 281; Quirk, *Jane Wyman*, pp. 74–75.
38. Ronald Reagan with Hubler, *Where's the Rest of Me?*, p. 119.
39. Ibid.
40. Ibid., pp. 123–24.
41. Ronald Reagan, *An American Life*, pp. 101–2; Ronald Reagan with Hubler, *Where's the Rest of Me?*, pp. 124–25.
42. Wills, *Reagan's America*, p. 245.
43. Ronald Reagan with Hubler, *Where's the Rest of Me?*, p. 179.
44. Billingsley, *Hollywood Party*, pp. 95, 89–90.
45. E. Morris, *Dutch*, pp. 205–6.
46. Brownstein, *The Power and the Glitter*, pp. 81–82.
47. Ibid., p. 81.
48. Ibid., pp. 87–90; Friedrich, *City of Nets*, pp. 167–68; Billingsley, *Hollywood Party*, p. 111.
49. Friedrich, *City of Nets*, p. 168.
50. Excerpt from *Hollywood Renegades: The Society of Independent Motion Picture Producers*, by J. A. Aberdeen, available on the Web site of Cobblestone Entertainment Publishers at http://www.cobbles.com/simpp_archive/huac_alliance.htm.
51. *New York Times*, April 23, 1944, "Tempest in Hollywood."
52. Brownstein, *The Power and the Glitter*, pp. 100–101.
53. Vaughn, *Ronald Reagan in Hollywood*, p. 124.
54. Neil Reagan oral history, p. 22.
55. E. Morris, *Dutch*, pp. 215, 733.
56. Ibid., p. 216.
57. Ibid., p. 737.
58. Ronald Reagan with Hubler, *Where's the Rest of Me?*, p. 138.
59. E. Morris, *Dutch*, p. 198.

60. Ronald Reagan with Hubler, *Where's the Rest of Me?*, p. 202.
61. Michael Reagan with Hyams, *On the Outside Looking In*, pp. 7, 14–15, 275.
62. McClelland, *Hollywood on Ronald Reagan*, p. 52.
63. Maureen Reagan, *First Father, First Daughter*, pp. 49–50.
64. Ibid., p. 51.
65. E. Morris, *Dutch*, pp. 218, 734.
66. Morella and Epstein, *Jane Wyman*, pp. 87–88; Edwards, *Early Reagan*, p. 285.
67. Neil Reagan oral history, p. 37.
68. Maureen Reagan, *First Father, First Daughter*, pp. 39–41; p. 44.
69. E. Morris, *Dutch*, p. 220.
70. Quirk, *Jane Wyman*, pp. 86–87.
71. McClelland, *Hollywood on Ronald Reagan*, pp. 52–54.
72. Ronald Reagan with Hubler, *Where's the Rest of Me?*, p. 187.
73. Ibid., p. 188.
74. Ibid., pp. 141, 191.
75. Kotkin and Grabowicz in *Esquire*, August 1980, p. 27.
76. Edwards, *Early Reagan*, pp. 294, 583.
77. Ibid.
78. Vaughn, *Ronald Reagan in Hollywood*, pp. 162–63; E. Morris, *Dutch*, p. 222.
79. Ronald Reagan with Hubler, *Where's the Rest of Me?*, p. 141.
80. Vaughn, *Ronald Reagan in Hollywood*, p. 163; E. Morris, *Dutch*, pp. 222, 735.
81. *Time*, September 9, 1946, "Political Notes: Glamour Pusses"; Vaughn, *Ronald Reagan in Hollywood*, p. 123.
82. *Time*, September 9, 1946, "Political Notes: Glamour Pusses."
83. Ronald Reagan with Hubler, *Where's the Rest of Me?*, p. 141.
84. E. Morris, *Dutch*, p. 228.
85. Vaughn, *Ronald Reagan in Hollywood*, pp. 121–22.
86. E. Morris, *Dutch*, p. 229.

87. Ibid.
88. Ronald Reagan with Hubler, *Where's the Rest of Me?*, p. 142.
89. Ronald Reagan, *An American Life*, p. 106; Ronald Reagan with Hubler, *Where's the Rest of Me?*, p. 142.
90. E. Morris, *Dutch*, p. 230.
91. Ronald Reagan with Hubler, *Where's the Rest of Me?*, p. 165.
92. E. Morris, *Dutch*, p. 231; Vaughn, *Ronald Reagan in Hollywood*, p. 164.
93. Edwards, *Early Reagan*, p. 306.
94. Vaughn, *Ronald Reagan in Hollywood*, p. 128.
95. Ronald Reagan with Hubler, *Where's the Rest of Me?*, pp. 166–67.
96. Ibid., pp. 167–68.
97. Vaughn, *Ronald Reagan in Hollywood*, p. 132.
98. Schlesinger Jr. in *Life*, July 29, 1946.
99. Vaughn, *Ronald Reagan in Hollywood*, p. 131; Wiener in *New Republic*, March 31, 1986.
100. *Time*, September 9, 1946, "Political Notes: Glamour Pusses."
101. Brownstein, *The Power and the Glitter*, p. 109.
102. Schlesinger Jr., *A Life in the 20th Century*, p. 409; Brownstein, *The Power and the Glitter*, p. 109.
103. Neil Reagan oral history, pp. 30–31.
104. Ibid., p. 31.
105. Vaughn, *Ronald Reagan in Hollywood*, p. 132; E. Morris, *Dutch*, pp. 234, 740; Wills, *Reagan's America*, p. 249.
106. Edwards, *Early Reagan*, pp. 304–5.
107. Wills, *Reagan's America*, pp. 246–47. See also Vaughn, *Ronald Reagan in Hollywood*, pp. 130, 278 (notes 49 and 50).
108. Vaughn, *Ronald Reagan in Hollywood*, p. 164.
109. Ronald Reagan with Hubler, *Where's the Rest of Me?*, pp. 169–70.
110. Vaughn, *Ronald Reagan in Hollywood*, p. 130.
111. Ronald Reagan, *An American Life*, p. 111.
112. Wills, *Reagan's America*, p. 249; *New York Times*, May 6,

1993, "Disney Link to the F.B.I. and Hoover Is Disclosed"; *Las Vegas Life*, October 1999, "Billy Wilkerson: The First Big Link to Hollywood"; *Las Vegas Sun*, February 15, 2000, "Book Examines 'The Man Who Invented Las Vegas.'" See also Vaughn, *Ronald Reagan in Hollywood*, p. 130.

113. Ronald Reagan with Hubler, *Where's the Rest of Me?*, p. 139.

114. Edwards, *Early Reagan*, p. 300; *Current Biography 1949*, "Reagan, Ronald."

115. Vaughn, *Ronald Reagan in Hollywood*, p. 129.

116. Ibid.

117. Ibid., p. 277 (note 43).

118. Ronald Reagan with Hubler, *Where's the Rest of Me?*, p. 179.

119. Ibid., pp. 145–46.

120. Vaughn, *Ronald Reagan in Hollywood*, p. 138.

121. Billingsley, *Hollywood Party*, pp. 106–12; *Current Biography 1953*, "Reagan, Ronald."

122. Billingsley, *Hollywood Party*, p. 121.

123. *Los Angeles Times*, August 5, 2001.

124. Vaughn, *Ronald Reagan in Hollywood*, p. 159.

125. Wills, *Reagan's America*, pp. 233–35; Vaughn, *Ronald Reagan in Hollywood*, pp. 138–39.

126. Vaughn, *Ronald Reagan in Hollywood*, pp. 139, 282 (note 32).

127. E. Morris, *Dutch*, p. 239.

128. Edwards, *Early Reagan*, p. 311; Vaughn, *Ronald Reagan in Hollywood*, p. 139.

129. Edwards, *Early Reagan*, p. 311.

130. Ronald Reagan with Hubler, *Where's the Rest of Me?*, pp. 171, 172–73; Vaughn, *Ronald Reagan in Hollywood*, p. 140.

131. Ronald Reagan with Hubler, *Where's the Rest of Me?*, pp. 174–75.

132. Friedrich, *City of Nets*, p. 279; Vaughn, *Ronald Reagan in Hollywood*, p. 139.

133. Billingsley, *Hollywood Party*, pp. 151, 332.

134. Friedrich, *City of Nets*, p. 277.
135. Vaughn, *Ronald Reagan in Hollywood*, p. 139.
136. Robert Stack, to author, March 16, 2000.
137. Ibid.
138. E. Morris, *Dutch*, p. 243.
139. Billingsley, *Hollywood Party*, p. 158.
140. Ronald Reagan with Hubler, *Where's the Rest of Me?*, p. 155; *New York Times*, November 13, 1946, "Bomb Blasts Home of Film Technician"; *New York Times*, November 14, 1946, "Violence Spreads in Movie Dispute."
141. Vaughn, *Ronald Reagan in Hollywood*, p. 140; Edwards, *Early Reagan*, p. 319.
142. E. Morris, *Dutch*, pp. 240, 741.
143. *New York Times*, November 16, 1946, "679 Pickets Seized in Film Strike After 1,500 Protest Injunctions."
144. Vaughn, *Ronald Reagan in Hollywood*, p. 142.
145. Ronald Reagan with Hubler, *Where's the Rest of Me?*, p. 183.
146. Vaughn, *Ronald Reagan in Hollywood*, p. 143.
147. Ibid., p. 133.
148. Lindfors, *Viveka-Viveca*, p. 154.
149. McClelland, *Hollywood on Ronald Reagan*, p. 152.
150. *Current Biography 1949*, "Wyman, Jane."
151. Leonora Hornblow, to author, February 10, 2000.

Chapter Eight: Nancy in New York, 1944–1949

1. Mantle, *The Best Plays of 1944–1945*, pp. 9–10.
2. Ibid., pp. 8–9.
3. Leamer, *Make-Believe*, p. 57.
4. Nancy Reagan, to author, April 7, 1998.
5. Kelley, *Nancy Reagan*, p. 68; Kenneth Giniger, to author, April 11, 2003.
6. Nancy Reagan, to author, March 10, 2003, March 19, 2003.
7. Affron, *Lillian Gish*, p. 220.
8. Nancy Reagan with Novak, *My Turn*, pp. 84–85.

9. Kanin, *Tracy and Hepburn*, pp. 95–98; Davidson, *Spencer Tracy*, pp. 94–98.
10. Kanin, *Tracy and Hepburn*, p. 98.
11. Davidson, *Spencer Tracy*, pp. 100–102.
12. Richard Davis, to author, April 17, 2003.
13. Leamer, *Make-Believe*, p. 60; Anne Washburn, to author, May 7, 2003.
14. Nancy Reagan with Libby, *Nancy*, pp. 70–71.
15. Nancy Reagan with Novak, *My Turn*, pp. 85–86.
16. Edwards, *Early Reagan*, p. 392.
17. Nancy Reagan, to author, March 10, 2003.
18. "Nancy Reagan," *A&E Biography*, A&E Television Network, March 31, 1997.
19. Nancy Reagan, to author, November 27, 1997.
20. Richard Davis, to author, April 17, 2003.
21. Nancy Reagan, to author, October 27, 1997.
22. Anne Washburn, to author, May 7, 2003.
23. "Nancy Reagan," *A&E Biography*, A&E Television Network, March 31, 1997.
24. Leamer, *Make-Believe*, p. 61.
25. Kelley, *Nancy Reagan*, p. 67.
26. Nancy Reagan with Libby, *Nancy*, pp. 68–69.
27. Leamer, *Make-Believe*, p. 61.
28. Nancy Reagan with Libby, *Nancy*, p. 69.
29. Ronald and Nancy Reagan's personal papers, held at the Ronald Reagan Presidential Library, box 20, Nancy Reagan scrapbook #1, 1946–1950, undated clipping from *New York Mirror*, "Only Human," by Sidney Fields.
30. Kenneth Giniger, to author, April 11, 2003, April 15, 2003.
31. Ronald and Nancy Reagan's personal papers, held at the Ronald Reagan Presidential Library, box 20, Nancy Reagan scrapbook #1, 1946–1950, clipping from an unidentified Boston newspaper, dated September 1, 1946.
32. Ibid., unidentified newspaper clipping, dated November 1946.
33. Ibid., unidentified newspaper clipping, dated December 3, 1946.

34. "Application for Class A Junior Membership," Nancy Davis, dated at New York offices of the Screen Actors Guild, May 20, 1947, held at the current offices of the Screen Actors Guild, 5757 Wilshire Boulevard, Los Angeles, CA.
35. Grobel, *The Hustons*, p. 237.
36. Weld, *September Song*, p. 190.
37. Nancy Reagan, to author, March 10, 2003.
38. Kelley, *Nancy Reagan*, pp. 68–69.
39. Ronald and Nancy Reagan's personal papers, held at the Ronald Reagan Presidential Library, box 20, Nancy Reagan scrapbook #1, 1946–1950.
40. Ibid.
41. Ibid., clipping from *Washington Post*, July 19, 1947.
42. Ibid., unidentified newspaper clipping, dated July 31, 1947.
43. Ronald and Nancy Reagan's personal papers, held at the Ronald Reagan Presidential Library, box 20, Nancy Reagan scrapbook #1, 1946–1950.
44. Ibid., clipping from *Chicago Daily News*, October 21, 1947.
45. Richard Davis, to author, April 10, 2001.
46. Bruce McFarland, to author, February 14, 2002.
47. Nancy Reagan, to author, March 10, 2003.
48. Ronald and Nancy Reagan's personal papers, held at the Ronald Reagan Presidential Library, box 20, Nancy Reagan scrapbook #1, 1946–1950.
49. Kenneth Giniger, to author, April 11, 2003.
50. Kelley, *Nancy Reagan*, p. 69; Ronald and Nancy Reagan's personal papers, held at the Ronald Reagan Presidential Library, box 20, Nancy Reagan scrapbook #1, 1946–1950, unidentified newspaper clipping dated March 1948.
51. Nancy Reagan with Libby, *Nancy*, p. 69; Nancy Reagan with Novak, *My Turn*, p. 86.
52. Nancy Reagan with Novak, *My Turn*, p. 87; Ronald and Nancy Reagan's personal papers, held at the Ronald Reagan Presidential Library, box 20, Nancy Reagan

scrapbook #1, 1946–1950, clippings dated October 1948.
53. Vidal in *New York Review of Books*, September 29, 1983.
54. Leamer, *Make-Believe*, p. 58; Nancy Reagan with Libby, *Nancy*, p. 69.
55. Nancy Reagan with Libby, *Nancy*, pp. 69–70.
56. Nancy Reagan with Novak, *My Turn*, pp. 86–87.
57. Leamer, *Make-Believe*, p. 58; Ronald and Nancy Reagan's personal papers, held at the Ronald Reagan Presidential Library, box 20, Nancy Reagan scrapbook #1, 1946–1950, clippings dated October 1948.
58. Nancy Reagan with Novak, *My Turn*, pp. 87–88.
59. *New York Times*, March 28, 2002, "Milton Berle, TV's First Star As 'Uncle Miltie,' Dies at 93"; Nancy Reagan with Novak, *My Turn*, p. 88.
60. Ronald and Nancy Reagan's personal papers, held at the Ronald Reagan Presidential Library, box 20, Nancy Reagan scrapbook #1, 1946–1950; *Mademoiselle*, November 1948.
61. Nancy Reagan with Libby, *Nancy*, p. 89.

Chapter Nine: Divorce, 1947–1948

1. Edwards, *Early Reagan*, p. 322; Vaughn, *Ronald Reagan in Hollywood*, p. 224.
2. McClelland, *Hollywood on Ronald Reagan*, p. 70.
3. *New York Times*, March 12, 1947, "7 Quit Film Guild Posts."
4. Edwards, *Early Reagan*, p. 321.
5. Wills, *Reagan's America*, p. 249; E. Morris, *Dutch*, p. 288.
6. Edwards, *Early Reagan*, p. 322.
7. Schweizer, *Reagan's War*, p. 14.
8. Wills, *Reagan's America*, pp. 249, 427–28; Billingsley, *Hollywood Party*, p. 127.
9. Ronald Reagan with Hubler, *Where's the Rest of Me?*, pp. 156–57.
10. E. Morris, *Dutch*, p. 246.

11. Buhle and Wagner, *Radical Hollywood*, pp. 376–77; Gellman, *The Contender*, pp. 111–12.
12. Brownstein, *The Power and the Glitter*, p. 110; Hollywood Democratic Committee Records, 1942–1950, held at the University of Wisconsin library archives main stacks, MAD 3M/32/C2–3.
13. Schlesinger Jr., *A Life in the 20th Century*, p. 410.
14. Ibid., p. 412; Vaughn, *Ronald Reagan in Hollywood*, p. 166.
15. Schlesinger Jr., *A Life in the 20th Century*, pp. 411, 413.
16. Ibid., p. 413.
17. Vaughn, *Ronald Reagan in Hollywood*, p. 167.
18. Brownstein, *The Power and the Glitter*, p. 110.
19. Vaughn, *Ronald Reagan in Hollywood*, pp. 164–65.
20. Ibid., p. 161.
21. Ibid., p. 144.
22. Gellman, *The Contender*, p. 108.
23. Friedrich, *City of Nets*, pp. 299–300.
24. Gabler, *An Empire of Their Own*, p. 362; Friedrich, *City of Nets*, p. 303.
25. Eells, *Hedda and Louella*, p. 267.
26. Edwards, *Early Reagan*, pp. 340–41; Vaughn, *Ronald Reagan in Hollywood*, p. 144; Tavistock College (UK) Media Department, "Perceived Communist Influence in Hollywood Film: The HUAC Years," www.tavistockcollege.devon.sch.uk.
27. Laurents, *Original Story By*, p. 84.
28. Thomas, *Golden Boy*, p. 11; E. Morris, *Dutch*, p. 252.
29. Allyson with Spatz Leighton, *June Allyson*, p. 95.
30. Ibid., p. 94.
31. Ibid., pp. 94–96.
32. *The "Kitchen Cabinet"* oral history, Justin Dart, OH 1676, p. 37; *New York Times*, January 27, 1984, "Bluntest and Most Outspoken of Circle" (obituary).
33. *Los Angeles Times*, February 6, 1982, "For Justin Dart, No Time to Rest."
34. Ibid.
35. Ibid.

36. *Current Biography 1946*, "Dart, Justin."
37. *Los Angeles Times*, February 6, 1982, "For Justin Dart, No Time to Rest."
38. Ibid.
39. *Current Biography 1946*, "Dart, Justin."
40. Sellmer in *Business Week*, July 13, 1946.
41. *Los Angeles Times*, February 6, 1982, "For Justin Dart, No Time to Rest."
42. *The "Kitchen Cabinet"* oral history, Holmes Tuttle, OH 1675, p. 113.
43. Marsha Hunt interviewed by Glen Lovell in January 1998, from Spartacus Educational, "Marsha Hunt": www.spartacus.schoolnet.co.uk/USAhuntM.htm.
44. Author's diary, July 28, 2000.
45. Quirk, *Jane Wyman*, p. 63.
46. Leonora Hornblow, to author, February 10, 2000.
47. Edwards, *Early Reagan*, pp. 324–25; Ronald Reagan with Hubler, *Where's the Rest of Me?*, p. 194.
48. Maureen Reagan, *First Father, First Daughter*, p. 52.
49. E. Morris, *Dutch*, pp. 250–52; Ronald Reagan with Hubler, *Where's the Rest of Me?*, p. 195. Reagan says this is when his interest in wine began, as his doctor recommended a glass of wine with dinner to build up his strength.
50. *New York Times*, July 16, 1947, "Refugee Relief Unit Set Up in Hollywood."
51. Michael Reagan with Hyams, *On the Outside Looking In*, p. 20; Quirk, *Jane Wyman*, pp. 101, 110.
52. McClelland, *Hollywood on Ronald Reagan*, pp. 68–70.
53. Quirk, *Jane Wyman*, p. 99; Morella and Epstein, *Jane Wyman*, p. 111.
54. Morella and Epstein, *Jane Wyman*, p. 117; Quirk, *Jane Wyman*, p. 111.
55. Edwards, *Early Reagan*, p. 330.
56. Quirk, *Jane Wyman*, p. 112.
57. Donnelly, *Fade to Black*, p. 44.
58. Quirk, *Jane Wyman*, p. 101.
59. Ronald Reagan with Hubler, *Where's the Rest of Me?*, p. 198.

60. Vaughn, *Ronald Reagan in Hollywood*, p. 161.
61. *Current Biography 1949*, "Reagan, Ronald."
62. Vaughn, *Ronald Reagan in Hollywood*, p. 161; Edwards, *Early Reagan*, pp. 335–37; E. Morris, *Dutch*, p. 752.
63. Bentley, ed., *Thirty Years of Treason*, p. 110.
64. Vaughn, *Ronald Reagan in Hollywood*, p. 145.
65. E. Morris, *Dutch*, p. 743.
66. Gellman, *The Contender*, p. 117.
67. Buhle and Wagner, *Radical Hollywood*, p. 382.
68. P. Dunne, *Take Two*, p. 293.
69. Friedrich, *City of Nets*, p. 306.
70. Huston, *An Open Book*, p. 129.
71. Grobel, *The Hustons*, p. 300.
72. Huston, *An Open Book*, pp. 131–32.
73. P. Dunne, *Take Two*, p. 201; Brownstein, *The Power and the Glitter*, p. 113; *New York Times*, October 26, 1947, "Hollywood Split by Hearings."
74. P. Dunne, *Take Two*, p. 206.
75. Lester Cole, *Hollywood Red*, as quoted in McClelland, *Hollywood on Ronald Reagan*, pp. 190–92.
76. Vaughn, *Ronald Reagan in Hollywood*, p. 167.
77. *New York Times*, October 26, 1947, "Un-American Committee Puts on Its 'Big Show'"; *New York Times*, October 20, 1947, "Radio, Television and Floodlights Will Open Red Film Inquiry Today."
78. Edwards, *Early Reagan*, p. 340.
79. Friedrich, *City of Nets*, pp. 314–15.
80. Ibid., pp. 311–16.
81. *New York Times*, October 23, 1947, "79 in Hollywood Found Subversive, Inquiry Head Says."
82. Bentley, ed., *Thirty Years of Treason*, pp. 112, 118.
83. Vaughn, *Ronald Reagan in Hollywood*, p. 147.
84. *New York Times*, October 21, 1947, "Film Men Admit Activity by Reds; Hold It Is Foiled."
85. *New York Times*, October 25, 1947, "Critics of Film Inquiry Assailed; Disney Denounces 'Communists'"; *New York Times*, October 26, 1947, "Congress Is Urged to Alter Inquiries."

86. Bentley, ed., *Thirty Years of Treason*, p. 140.

87. Ibid., pp. 124, 125.

88. Ibid., p. 131.

89. Edwards, *Early Reagan*, p. 341; Cannon, *Reagan*, p. 82.

90. Cannon, *Reagan*, p. 83; E. Morris, *Dutch*, pp. 255–56.

91. Bentley, ed., *Thirty Years of Treason*, pp. 143–47; Edwards, *Early Reagan*, p. 349.

92. Nixon, *In the Arena*, p. 190; Vaughn, *Ronald Reagan in Hollywood*, p. 166.

93. *New York Times*, October 24, 1947, "Hollywood Communists 'Militant,' but Small in Number, Stars Testify"; Cannon, *Reagan*, p. 84; Vaughn, *Ronald Reagan in Hollywood*, p. 148.

94. *New York Times*, October 28, 1947, "Films of 11 U.S. Stars Are Banned by Rumania."

95. Grobel, *The Hustons*, p. 304.

96. Bentley, ed., *Thirty Years of Treason*, p. 154.

97. Ibid., pp. 158–61.

98. Huston, *An Open Book*, p. 133.

99. Friedrich, *City of Nets*, p. 321.

100. *New York Times*, October 31, 1947, "The News of Radio: Hollywood Group Buys More Time on Air to Oppose Washington Hearing"; *New York Times*, November 2, 1947, "The Nation: Hollywood Fights Back."

101. Friedrich, *City of Nets*, p. 326; Vaughn, *Ronald Reagan in Hollywood*, p. 148; Huston, *An Open Book*, p. 134.

102. P. Dunne, *Take Two*, p. 202; Huston, *An Open Book*, p. 134; Friedrich, *City of Nets*, p. 237.

103. Ronald Reagan with Hubler, *Where's the Rest of Me?*, p. 200.

104. Friedrich, *City of Nets*, p. 333; Cannon, *Reagan*, p. 84.

105. Cannon, *Reagan*, p. 85.

106. Gabler, *An Empire of Their Own*, p. 373; *New York Times*, November 26, 1947, "Movies to Oust Ten Cited for Contempt of Congress"; Billingsley, *Hollywood Party*, p. 200.

107. *New York Times*, November 26, 1947, "Movies to Oust Ten Cited for Contempt of Congress."

108. Ibid.
109. *New York Times*, November 30, 1947, "'Safe and Sane' Films New Hollywood Rule."
110. Kahn, *Hollywood on Trial*, p. 186.
111. Vaughn, *Ronald Reagan in Hollywood*, p. 154; Cannon, *Reagan*, p. 85.
112. "Statement Proposed by Ronald Reagan Discussed at the Board Meeting of December 8, 1947, for Further Discussion at Special Meeting December 12, 1947." Document 3414, from Screen Actors Guild files, held at SAG offices, 5757 Wilshire Boulevard, Los Angeles, CA.
113. E. Morris, *Dutch*, p. 261.
114. Wills, *Reagan's America*, p. 253.
115. Huston, *An Open Book*, p. 135.
116. Vaughn, *Ronald Reagan in Hollywood*, pp. 185–87; E. Morris, *Dutch*, pp. 278, 748–49.
117. Ronald Reagan with Hubler, *Where's the Rest of Me?*, p. 201.
118. Nancy Reagan, to author, October 1, 1999.
119. Leonora Hornblow, to author, February 10, 2000.
120. Ronald Reagan with Hubler, *Where's the Rest of Me?*, p. 201.
121. Leamer, *Make-Believe*, p. 115.
122. Edwards, *Early Reagan*, p. 353.
123. Morella and Epstein, *Jane Wyman*, p. 121.
124. E. Morris, *Dutch*, pp. 258, 744.
125. Morella and Epstein, *Jane Wyman*, p. 122.
126. Ibid., p. 123; McClelland, *Hollywood on Ronald Reagan*, p. 74.
127. Quirk, *Jane Wyman*, p. 113; Morella and Epstein, *Jane Wyman*, p. 123.
128. E. Morris, *Dutch*, pp. 259, 744.
129. Morella and Epstein, *Jane Wyman*, pp. 123–24.
130. Ibid., p. 124; Vaughn, *Ronald Reagan in Hollywood*, p. 230; McClelland, *Hollywood on Ronald Reagan*, p. 74.
131. McClelland, *Hollywood on Ronald Reagan*, p. 164.
132. Ibid., pp. 78–80.

133. Morella and Epstein, *Jane Wyman*, p. 125; Quirk, *Jane Wyman*, p. 113; Cannon, *Reagan*, p. 64.
134. Scheer in *Playboy*, August 1980. See also Edwards, *Early Reagan*, p. 355.
135. Cannon, *Reagan*, p. 64.
136. Maureen Reagan, *First Father, First Daughter*, p. 68.
137. McClelland, *Hollywood on Ronald Reagan*, p. 80.
138. Allyson with Spatz Leighton, *June Allyson*, p. 96.
139. Cannon, *Reagan*, p. 64.

Chapter Ten: Ronnie and Nancy in Hollywood, 1949–1952

1. Nancy Reagan with Libby, *Nancy*, p. 91.
2. Ibid.; Kelley, *Nancy Reagan*, p. 70.
3. Nancy Reagan, to author, May 29, 2003.
4. Leonora Hornblow, to author, February 10, 2000.
5. Higham, *Merchant of Dreams*, p. 132.
6. Ibid., pp. 308, 174; Donnelly, *Fade to Black*, pp. 231–32; Associated Press, July 5, 1983, "Former Studio Executive Dead at 84"; *Los Angeles Times*, July 6, 1983, "Film Executive Benjamin Thau Is Dead at 93."
7. Nancy Reagan, to author, May 29, 2003.
8. Richard Davis, to author, May 30, 2003.
9. Ronald and Nancy Reagan's personal papers, held at the Ronald Reagan Presidential Library, box 20, Nancy Reagan scrapbook #1, 1946–1950, photo entitled "Phoenicians, Visitors Turn Out for Play." The caption states it was taken during the intermission of *Born Yesterday* "at the new Sombrero Playhouse." The photograph is undated in the scrapbook, but it appears on a page with several other items from early 1949. Ann Lee Harris, the founder of the Sombrero Playhouse, confirmed that the Sombrero opened in January 1949, with the first off-Broadway production of Garson Kanin's *Born Yesterday* (to author, May 29, 2003). *The Best Plays of 1948–1949* also states that *Born Yesterday* played at the

Sombrero Playhouse in the winter of 1948–49 (Mantle, ed., p. 51).

10. Edwards, *Early Reagan*, pp. 393–94; Kelley, *Nancy Reagan*, pp. 70–71; Leamer, *Make-Believe*, pp. 63–65.
11. Leamer, *Make-Believe*, p. 63; Mantle, ed., *The Best Plays of 1945–1946*, p. 406.
12. Nancy Reagan, to author, May 17, 2003, May 29, 2003.
13. Edwards, *Early Reagan*, p. 393.
14. Ronald and Nancy Reagan's personal papers, held at the Ronald Reagan Presidential Library, box 20, Nancy Reagan scrapbook #1, 1946–1950, unidentified clipping.
15. Kenneth Giniger, to author, April 11, 2003.
16. Leamer, *Make-Believe*, p. 65.
17. Kelley, *Nancy Reagan*, p. 71.
18. Ibid.
19. Nancy Reagan, to Sydney Guilaroff, April 15, 1992. Unpublished material from Sydney Guilaroff's memoir, *Crowning Glory*, published 1996. Obtained courtesy of Cathy Griffin.
20. Nancy Reagan with Libby, *Nancy*, pp. 91–92.
21. Levy, *George Cukor, Master of Elegance*, p. 325.
22. Kelley, *Nancy Reagan*, p. 72; Nancy Reagan with Libby, *Nancy*, p. 92; Nancy Reagan with Novak, *My Turn*, p. 88.
23. Nancy Reagan with Libby, *Nancy*, p. 92.
24. McDaniel in *Los Angeles Herald Examiner*, October 27, 1980, "Part 2: Hurray for Hollywood"; Kelley, *Nancy Reagan*, pp. 72–73; Edwards, *Early Reagan*, p. 376.
25. Laurents, *Original Story By*, p. 81.
26. Ann Rutherford, to author, January 22, 2001.
27. Higham, *Merchant of Dreams*, pp. 70, 2.
28. Nancy Reagan, *I Love You, Ronnie*, p. 18.
29. Ronald and Nancy Reagan's personal papers, held at the Ronald Reagan Presidential Library, box 20, Nancy Reagan scrapbook #1, 1946–1950, *Cleveland Plain Dealer*, February 12, 1950, "M-G-M, Mum on Television, Signs Video Star Anyhow."
30. Bill Fine, to author, January 10, 2001.
31. Nancy Reagan, to author, March 22, 2000.

32. James Galanos, to author, October 12, 1999.
33. Nancy Reagan, to author, March 22, 2000.
34. Ronald and Nancy Reagan's personal papers, held at the Ronald Reagan Presidential Library, box 20, Nancy Reagan scrapbook #1, 1946–1950, unidentified clipping from a Chicago newspaper, dated August 10, 1949.
35. Nancy Reagan with Libby, *Nancy*, p. 95.
36. Bruce McFarland, to author, February 14, 2002.
37. Ronald and Nancy Reagan's personal papers, held at the Ronald Reagan Presidential Library, box 20, Nancy Reagan scrapbook #1, 1946–1950, *Cleveland Plain Dealer*, February 12, 1950, "M-G-M, Mum on Television, Signs Video Star Anyhow."
38. Leonora Hornblow, to author, February 10, 2000.
39. Armand Deutsch, to author, September 30, 1999.
40. Deutsch, *Me and Bogie*, pp. 11, 126–27, 197.
41. Williams with Diehl, *The Million Dollar Mermaid*, p. 186.
42. Connie Wald, to author, July 24, 2003.
43. Author's diary, November 23, 2001.
44. Richard Davis, to author, May 30, 2003.
45. Ibid.
46. Ronald and Nancy Reagan's personal papers, held at the Ronald Reagan Presidential Library, box 20, Nancy Reagan scrapbook #1, 1946–1950, *Modern Screen*, June 1949, "Which Girl Has the Gable?"
47. Kelley, *Nancy Reagan*, p. 74.
48. Leonora Hornblow, to author, February 10, 2000.
49. Leamer, *Make-Believe*, p. 65.
50. Richard Davis, to author, May 30, 2003.
51. E. Morris, *Dutch*, p. 280.
52. LeRoy with Kleiner, *Take One*, p. 192.
53. Laurents, *Original Story By*, p. 91.
54. Gottlieb and Wolt, *Thinking Big*, p. 301; Digital History, "Chronology of Film History," available online at: www.digitalhistory.uh.edu/historyonline/film_chron.cfm?#anticommunism.
55. "The Enemy Pool," from Myron Fagan, *Red Stars in Hollywood: Their Helpers . . . Fellow Travelers . . . and*

Co-conspirators (St. Louis: Patriotic Tract Society, 1948), available online from the Michigan State University Digital Library at http://digital.lib.msu.edu/onlinecolls/subcollection.cfm?CID=1&SCID=9.

56. Higham, *Merchant of Dreams*, p. 387; Friedrich, *City of Nets*, p. 377; Gabler, *An Empire of Their Own*, pp. 371–72.

57. *Hollywood Reporter*, October 28, 1949, "Signers of Appeal to High Court for Lawson, Trumbo."

58. Ronald and Nancy Reagan's personal papers, held at the Ronald Reagan Presidential Library, box 20, Nancy Reagan scrapbook #1, 1946–1950.

59. Nancy Reagan with Libby, *Nancy*, p. 110.

60. McDaniel in *Los Angeles Herald Examiner*, October 27, 1980, "Part 2: Hurray for Hollywood."

61. Nancy Reagan with Libby, *Nancy*, pp. 110–11; Nancy Reagan with Novak, *My Turn*, p. 94.

62. Ronald Reagan with Hubler, *Where's the Rest of Me?*, p. 235.

63. Leamer, *Make-Believe*, p. 147.

64. Ibid., p. 148.

65. Kelley, *Nancy Reagan*, pp. 85–88.

66. Morella and Epstein, *Jane Wyman*, p. 131.

67. Doris Lilly in *Quest* magazine, October 1988, "All for the Love of Ronnie," quoted in E. Morris, *Dutch*, pp. 279, 749.

68. McClelland, *Hollywood on Ronald Reagan*, p. 86.

69. Leamer, *Make-Believe*, p. 148; Richard Gully, to author, October 1, 1999.

70. Edwards, *Early Reagan*, p. 370; Morella and Epstein, *Jane Wyman*, p. 128.

71. Morella and Epstein, *Jane Wyman*, p. 147; Edwards, *Early Reagan*, p. 356.

72. Connie Wald, to author, July 24, 2003.

73. Edwards, *Early Reagan*, pp. 362–63; Vaughn, *Ronald Reagan in Hollywood*, p. 231; Leamer, *Make-Believe*, p. 149.

74. *New York Times*, April 21, 1949, "Reagan Refusing Role at Columbia."

75. *New York Times*, April 30, 1949, "Reagan Signs Pact to

Make U-I Films"; Edwards, *Early Reagan*, p. 395; Ronald Reagan with Hubler, *Where's the Rest of Me?*, p. 213.

76. Nancy Reagan, *I Love You, Ronnie*, p. 13; E. Morris, *Dutch*, pp. 278, 748; Michael Reagan with Hyams, *On the Outside Looking In*, p. 20.

77. Edwards, *The Reagans*, pp. 17–18; Edwards, *Early Reagan*, p. 394.

78. Ronald Reagan with Hubler, *Where's the Rest of Me?*, pp. 222–27. Reagan made at least two trips to New York before late October.

79. Minutes from SAG board meeting, August 14, 1950, held at SAG offices, 5757 Wilshire Boulevard, Los Angeles, CA. See also E. Morris, *Dutch*, p. 280.

80. Edwards, *Early Reagan*, p. 394.

81. Nancy Reagan with Novak, *My Turn*, pp. 94–95.

82. Ronald Reagan with Hubler, *Where's the Rest of Me?*, p. 235.

83. Nancy Reagan with Novak, *My Turn*, p. 95.

84. E. Morris, *Dutch*, p. 628.

85. Nancy Reagan, *I Love You, Ronnie*, pp. 10–11.

86. Ronald and Nancy Reagan's personal papers, held at the Ronald Reagan Presidential Library, box 20, Nancy Reagan scrapbook #1, 1946–1950, newspaper clipping dated November 29, 1949; undated newspaper clipping; newspaper clipping dated December 6, 1949; newspaper clipping dated December 12, 1949.

87. Nancy Reagan, *My Turn*, p. 97.

88. McClelland, *Hollywood on Ronald Reagan*, p. 130, quoting *Doris Day: Her Own Story*, by Doris Day and A. E. Hotchner.

89. E. Morris, *Dutch*, p. 835.

90. Ibid., p. 235.

91. McClelland, *Hollywood on Ronald Reagan*, p. 98.

92. Ronald and Nancy Reagan's personal papers, held at the Ronald Reagan Presidential Library, box 20, Nancy Reagan scrapbook #1, 1946–1950, "Nancy Davis Back Home for Yule," December 24, 1949; Bruce McFarland, to author, February 14, 2002.

93. Robert Stack, to author, March 16, 2000.
94. Ronald and Nancy Reagan's personal papers, held at the Ronald Reagan Presidential Library, box 20, Nancy Reagan scrapbook #2, 1950–1952, newspaper clipping dated October 13, 1950.
95. *New York Times*, August 30, 1951, "Actor Walker Dies After Drug Dosage."
96. Kelley, *Nancy Reagan*, p. 77.
97. Ronald and Nancy Reagan's personal papers, held at the Ronald Reagan Presidential Library, box 20, Nancy Reagan scrapbook #1, 1946–1950, unidentified newspaper clipping dated April 24, 1950.
98. Schary with Palmer, *Case History*, pp. 42–43.
99. Ibid., pp. 44–45.
100. Note held in a display case at the Ronald Reagan Presidential Library.
101. *New York Times*, February 17, 1950, "Metro Is Testing Low-Budget Plan"; *New York Times*, April 2, 1950, "Hollywood Postscript to the Academy Awards."
102. Kelley, *Nancy Reagan*, p. 82.
103. Nancy Reagan with Libby, *Nancy*, pp. 96–97.
104. Ronald and Nancy Reagan's personal papers, held at the Ronald Reagan Presidential Library, box 20, Nancy Reagan scrapbook #1, 1946–1950, *New York Herald Tribune*, April 5, 1950.
105. Ronald and Nancy Reagan's personal papers, held at the Ronald Reagan Presidential Library, box 20, Nancy Reagan scrapbook #1, 1946–1950, unidentified newspaper clipping; Paul Morrissey, to author, April 15, 2003.
106. Richard Davis, to author, April 17, 2003.
107. Huston, *An Open Book*, p. 185.
108. Ronald and Nancy Reagan's personal papers, held at the Ronald Reagan Presidential Library, box 20, Nancy Reagan scrapbook #1, 1946–1950, newspaper clipping dated June 15, 1950.
109. Ibid., newspaper clipping dated June 3, 1950.
110. Ibid., undated clipping.
111. *New York Times*, June 30, 1950, "The Screen in Review:

'The Next Voice You Hear . . . ,' Dore Schary Production, Opens at Music Hall"; Ronald and Nancy Reagan's personal papers, held at the Ronald Reagan Presidential Library, box 20, Nancy Reagan scrapbook #2, 1950–1952, *Time*, July 10, 1950, review of *The Next Voice You Hear*.

112. Ronald and Nancy Reagan's personal papers, held at the Ronald Reagan Presidential Library, box 20, Nancy Reagan scrapbook #2, 1950–1952, clipping dated August 1950.

113. Ibid., unidentified clipping, circa September 1950.

114. Nancy Reagan, to author, May 17, 2003, May 29, 2003.

115. Leamer, *Make-Believe*, pp. 65–66.

116. Richard Davis, to author, May 30, 2003.

117. Richard Davis, to author, April 17, 2003.

118. Ronald and Nancy Reagan's personal papers, held at the Ronald Reagan Presidential Library, box 20, Nancy Reagan scrapbook #2, 1950–1952, unidentified clippings.

119. Ibid., clipping dated September 1950.

120. Ibid., "In Hollywood with Louella O. Parsons: Nancy Davis," September 24, 1950.

121. Nancy Reagan, *I Love You, Ronnie*, p. 8.

122. Ronald and Nancy Reagan's personal papers, held at the Ronald Reagan Presidential Library, box 20, Nancy Reagan scrapbook #2, 1950–1952, clipping dated December 28, 1950; clipping dated January 1950; undated clipping.

123. Ibid., "Edith Gwynn's Hollywood," October 17, 1950.

124. *New York Times*, July 14, 1962, "Jerry Wald Is Dead; Movie Producer, 49."

125. Nancy Reagan, *I Love You, Ronnie*, p. 19.

126. Nancy Reagan, to author, June 4, 2000.

127. Minutes from SAG board meeting, October 9, 1950, held at SAG offices, 5757 Wilshire Boulevard, Los Angeles, CA.

128. Nancy Reagan, to author, March 22, 2000.

129. Ibid.

130. Ronald Reagan with Hubler, *Where's the Rest of Me?*, p. 196.
131. Ann Rutherford, to author, July 22, 2001.
132. Leamer, *Make-Believe*, p. 162.
133. Nancy Reagan with Libby, *Nancy*, p. 110.
134. Vaughn, *Ronald Reagan in Hollywood*, p. 201.
135. Schweizer, *Reagan's War*, p. 25.
136. Vaughn, *Ronald Reagan in Hollywood*, p. 203; Schweizer, *Reagan's War*, p. 25; SAG press release dated September 17, 1950, held at SAG offices, 5757 Wilshire Boulevard, Los Angeles, CA.
137. Schweizer, *Reagan's War*, pp. 19–20.
138. Brownstein, *The Power and the Glitter*, pp. 120–21.
139. Nancy Reagan, to author, November 12, 2002.
140. Ronald Reagan with Hubler, *Where's the Rest of Me?*, p. 234.
141. Nancy Reagan, to author, March 22, 1999.
142. Gahagan Douglas, *A Full Life*, p. 323.
143. Edwards, *Early Reagan*, p. 417.
144. McClelland, *Hollywood on Ronald Reagan*, p. 229.
145. Schweizer, *Reagan's War*, p. 25.
146. Vaughn, *Ronald Reagan in Hollywood*, pp. 210–11.
147. *New York Times*, April 15, 1951, "Hollywood Is Calm: Hayden's Frank Admission of Red Ties Not Likely to Hurt Career."
148. SAG press release, dated April 11, 1951, held at SAG offices, 5757 Wilshire Boulevard, Los Angeles, CA.
149. *New York Times*, July 4, 1952, "Film Writers Shy From Guild Action"; Vaughn, *Ronald Reagan in Hollywood*, pp. 213–18.
150. *Hollywood Citizen News*, July 30, 1951, "Inside Labor," by Ronald Reagan, held at SAG offices, 5757 Wilshire Boulevard, Los Angeles, CA.
151. Ronald and Nancy Reagan's personal papers, held at the Ronald Reagan Presidential Library, box 20, Nancy Reagan scrapbook #2, 1950–1952, clipping circa June 1951.
152. Ibid., clipping dated February 12, 1951; clipping dated

February 1951; clipping dated May 21, 1951; undated clipping.

153. Donnelly, *Fade to Black*, pp. 603–4.
154. Nancy Reagan with Novak, *My Turn*, p. 97.
155. Maureen Reagan, *First Father, First Daughter*, pp. 87, 90.
156. Ibid., p. 91.
157. Michael Reagan with Hyams, *On the Outside Looking In*, pp. 34–35.
158. Maureen Reagan, *First Father, First Daughter*, p. 93.
159. Michael Reagan with Hyams, *On the Outside Looking In*, pp. 35–36.
160. Nancy Reagan, to author, July 22, 2001.
161. Leamer, *Make-Believe*, p. 165.
162. Morella and Epstein, *Jane Wyman*, pp. 161–64; Donnelly, *Fade to Black*, pp. 63–65.
163. Nancy Reagan, *I Love You, Ronnie*, p. 13.
164. Nancy Reagan with Novak, *My Turn*, p. 98.
165. Leamer, *Make-Believe*, p. 162.
166. *Life*, April 5, 1954, "Stargazer for Stars"; Kelley, *Nancy Reagan*, p. 215.
167. Arlene Dahl, to author, May 16, 2001.
168. Ed Helin, to author, August 11, 2003.
169. *Time*, February 22, 1960, "Hollywood: Hi There, Sagittarius," p. 76.
170. *Life*, April 5, 1954, "Stargazer for Stars"; *Current Biography 1972*, "Righter, Carroll"; Ed Helin, to author, August 11, 2003.
171. *Life*, April 5, 1954, "Stargazer for Stars."
172. Ronald and Nancy Reagan's personal papers, held at the Ronald Reagan Presidential Library, box 20, Nancy Reagan scrapbook #2, 1950–1952, clipping dated January 20, 1950.
173. Weld, *September Song*, pp. 136–37.
174. Edwards, *Early Reagan*, p. 420.
175. Kelley, *Nancy Reagan*, p. 94.
176. Nancy Reagan with Novak, *My Turn*, p. 100.
177. Kelley, *Nancy Reagan*, p. 90.
178. Edwards, *Early Reagan*, pp. 432–33.

179. Nancy Reagan, *I Love You, Ronnie*, p. 24.
180. Ronald Reagan with Hubler, *Where's the Rest of Me?*, p. 237.
181. Kelley, *Nancy Reagan*, p. 93.
182. Ronald and Nancy Reagan's personal papers, held at the Ronald Reagan Presidential Library, box 20, Nancy Reagan scrapbook #2, 1950–1952, "Davis-Reagan Nuptials Set," by Louella Parsons, February 21, 1952.
183. Ibid., undated clipping entitled "File for Marriage License."
184. Nancy Reagan with Libby, *Nancy*, p. 25. Kitty Kelley's account of Nannee Robbins's death differs slightly. Kelley claims that Robbins suffered a heart attack while waiting for Nancy and Reagan to arrive, and that Nancy's father, Kenneth, her son, flew her home to Los Angeles (see Kelley, *Nancy Reagan*, p. 114).
185. Ed Helin, to author, August 11, 2003.
186. Goldschneider and Elffers, *The Secret Language of Relationships*, p. 518.

Chapter Eleven: Pacific Palisades, 1952–1958

1. Nancy Reagan, to author, March 22, 2000.
2. Ronald Reagan with Hubler, *Where's the Rest of Me?*, pp. 239–40.
3. Nancy Reagan, to author, March 22, 2000.
4. Nancy Reagan with Libby, *Nancy*, p. 123.
5. Bill Fine, to author, January 10, 2001.
6. Maureen Reagan, *First Father, First Daughter*, p. 94.
7. Ronald Reagan with Hubler, *Where's the Rest of Me?*, p. 240.
8. Richard Davis, to author, September 29, 2000, April 25, 2002.
9. Heather Schader of the Arizona Biltmore, to author, September 9, 2003.
10. L. Davis, *A Surgeon's Odyssey*, pp. 298, 333; *Chicago Daily News*, October 14, 1960, "Top Surgeon Post Going to N.U. Professor."

11. Ronald and Nancy Reagan's personal papers, held at the Ronald Reagan Presidential Library, box 20, Nancy Reagan scrapbook #2, 1950–1952, clipping dated October 1951.
12. Ronald and Nancy Reagan's personal papers, held at the Ronald Reagan Presidential Library, box 84, "R. Reagan—Letters," telegram dated March 18, 1952.
13. Ronald Reagan, *An American Life*, p. 123.
14. Morella and Epstein, *Jane Wyman*, pp. 168–70.
15. Richard Gully, to author, October 1, 1999.
16. Nancy Reagan, to author, September 18, 1999.
17. Nancy Reagan, to author, March 22, 2000.
18. Friedrich, *City of Nets*, p. 413.
19. Edwards, *Early Reagan*, pp. 539–42.
20. Vaughn, *Ronald Reagan in Hollywood*, pp. 3–4.
21. Nancy Reagan, to author, July 24, 1998.
22. P. Davis, *The Way I See It*, p. 20.
23. Nancy Reagan with Novak, *My Turn*, p. 103.
24. Nancy Reagan, to author, September 18, 1999.
25. Ronald Reagan with Hubler, *Where's the Rest of Me?*, p. 243.
26. Nancy Reagan, to author, October 22, 1999.
27. Morella and Epstein, *Jane Wyman*, p. 174.
28. Michael Reagan with Hyams, *On the Outside Looking In*, p. 38.
29. Ibid., pp. 38–39.
30. Nancy Reagan, to author, March 22, 2000.
31. Nancy Reagan with Novak, *My Turn*, p. 125.
32. McDougal, *The Last Mogul*, pp. 184–87; Wills, *Reagan's America*, p. 264.
33. Wills, *Reagan's America*, pp. 264–65; Bruck, *When Hollywood Had a King*, pp. 120–21.
34. Brownstein, *The Power and the Glitter*, p. 183.
35. Nancy Reagan, to author, October 18, 2003.
36. Ibid.
37. Nancy Reagan with Novak, *My Turn*, p. 125.
38. Leamer, *Make-Believe*, p. 171; Nancy Reagan with Novak, *My Turn*, p. 125.

39. Nancy Reagan with Novak, *My Turn*, p. 125.
40. Edwards, *Early Reagan*, p. 445; *Us Weekly*, March 16, 1982, "Looking Back with Us."
41. Nancy Reagan, *I Love You, Ronnie*, p. 36.
42. Ibid., pp. 37–38.
43. Ronald Reagan with Hubler, *Where's the Rest of Me?*, p. 248.
44. Ibid., pp. 248–49.
45. Moldea, *Dark Victory*, pp. 107–8.
46. Kelley, *Nancy Reagan*, pp. 100–101.
47. Edwards, *Early Reagan*, p. 446.
48. Nancy Reagan, *I Love You, Ronnie*, p. 41.
49. Nancy Reagan with Novak, *My Turn*, pp. 126–27.
50. Ronald Reagan with Hubler, *Where's the Rest of Me?*, p. 251.
51. Edwards, *Early Reagan*, pp. 452–53.
52. Nancy Reagan with Novak, *My Turn*, p. 127; Moldea, *Dark Victory*, p. 199; E. Morris, *Dutch*, pp. 304–5.
53. Nancy Reagan with Novak, *My Turn*, p. 127; Wills, *Reagan's America*, pp. 267–68; *New York Times*, October 10, 1954, display advertisement, "Tonight: Ronald Reagan, the Long Way Round."
54. William Frye, to author, October 27, 1999.
55. Edwards, *Early Reagan*, pp. 454, 455.
56. Nancy Reagan, *I Love You, Ronnie*, p. 53.
57. Moldea, *Dark Victory*, p. 199; Nancy Reagan, *I Love You, Ronnie*, p. 55.
58. *TV Guide*, November 22, 1958, "Hey, Ronnie—Did the Guy Get the Girl? Ronald Reagan May Be On Film—But He's Got to Answer Questions in the Flesh."
59. Cannon, *Reagan*, p. 94.
60. Nancy Reagan, *I Love You, Ronnie*, pp. 54–55.
61. Nancy Reagan, to author, March 22, 2000, March 19, 2003.
62. Kelley, *Nancy Reagan*, p.106; Moldea, *Dark Victory*, p. 109; Edwards, *Early Reagan*, p. 459.
63. Nancy Reagan with Novak, *My Turn*, p. 128.
64. Norman Switzer, to author, November 9, 1999.

65. Nancy Reagan, to author, March 22, 2000.
66. Ronald Reagan with Hubler, *Where's the Rest of Me?*, p. 273.
67. Richard Gully, to author, October 1, 1999.
68. Nancy Reagan, to author, October 27, 1997.
69. Thomas, *Golden Boy*, pp. 101–2.
70. Arlene Dahl, to author, May 16, 2001.
71. Patti Davis, *The Way I See It*, p. 25.
72. Nancy Reagan, to author, September 18, 1999.
73. Allyson with Spatz Leighton, *June Allyson*, p. 98.
74. Bergen, *Knock Wood*, pp. 12, 47.
75. Frances Bergen, to author, March 30, 2000.
76. Ronald Reagan with Hubler, *Where's the Rest of Me?*, p. 241.
77. Dunning, *On the Air*, p. 35.
78. Allyson with Spatz Leighton, *June Allyson*, p. 139.
79. Edwards, *Early Reagan*, p. 444.
80. Wills, *Reagan's America*, p. 283.
81. Ronald Reagan with Hubler, *Where's the Rest of Me?*, p. 263.
82. Ibid., pp. 266–67.
83. Cannon, *Reagan*, p. 96.
84. William Frye, to author, October 27, 1999.
85. Author's diary, August 12, 1999.
86. William Frye, to author, October 27, 1999.
87. Ibid.; author's diary, August 12, 1999.
88. Author's diary, October 24, 1999.
89. Nancy Reagan, to author, October 18, 2003.
90. Leonora Hornblow, to author, February 10, 2000.
91. Richard Gully, to author, October 1, 1999.
92. Author's diary, October 24, 1999.
93. McDougal, *The Last Mogul*, p. 77.
94. Ann Rutherford, to author, January 22, 2001.
95. *Current Biography 1967*, "Stein, Jules"; Richard Gully, to author, October 1, 1999; *New York Times*, April 30, 1981, "Jules Stein, Philanthropist, Doctor, Film Mogul, Dies"; Bruck, *When Hollywood Had a King*, pp. 86–87.
96. William Frye, to author, October 27, 1999.

97. William Frye, to author, October 27, 1999, November 27, 2002.
98. Ronald Reagan, "On Becoming Governor," an oral history conducted 1979, Regional Oral History Office, University of California, Berkeley, 1986, p. 5. Courtesy, The Bancroft Library.
99. Ronald Reagan with Hubler, *Where's the Rest of Me?*, p. 274.
100. Arlene Dahl, to author, May 16, 2001.
101. Ronald Reagan with Hubler, *Where's the Rest of Me?*, pp. 274–75.
102. P. Davis, *The Way I See It*, p. 24.
103. Wills, *Reagan's America*, p. 268; Moldea, *Dark Victory*, p. 199.

Chapter Twelve: The Group, 1958–1962

1. Harriet Deutsch, to author, November 7, 1997.
2. Ibid.
3. Armand Deutsch, to author, September 30, 1999.
4. Harriet Deutsch, to author, November 7, 1997.
5. Lee Annenberg, to author, November 18, 1997.
6. Ogden, *Legacy*, p. 491.
7. Lee Annenberg, to author, November 18, 1997.
8. Ogden, *Legacy*, p. 305.
9. Gabler, *An Empire of Their Own*, pp. 152, 284; Ogden, *Legacy*, p. 305.
10. Ogden, *Legacy*, pp. 309–10.
11. Ibid., p. 302.
12. Ibid., pp. 313, 314, 317–18.
13. Ibid., p. 315.
14. Ibid., p. 372.
15. Ibid., p. 375.
16. Leonora Hornblow, to author, February 10, 2000.
17. Ogden, *Legacy*, p. 315.
18. Richard Gully, to author, October 1, 1999.
19. Ann Rutherford, to author, January 22, 2001.
20. Nancy Reagan, to author, October 27, 1997.

21. Author's diary, November 7, 1999.
22. David Jones, to author, March 12, 2000.
23. Ibid.
24. Leonora Hornblow, to author, February 10, 2000.
25. Anne Douglas, to author, November 29, 1999.
26. Ann Rutherford, to author, January 22, 2001.
27. Author's diary, October 4, 1999.
28. Ann Rutherford, to author, January 22, 2001.
29. Schary Zimmer, *With a Cast of Thousands*, p. 140.
30. Amory, *Who Killed Society?*, pp. 36, 49.
31. *New York Times*, February 18, 1957, "California Society Stems from Gold Rush."
32. Betty Adams, to author, October 12, 1999.
33. Marion Jorgensen, to author, October 6, 1999.
34. Ibid.
35. Connie Wald, to author, July 24, 2003.
36. Marion Jorgensen, to author, October 6, 1999.
37. York, *Going Strong*, pp. 152, 155.
38. Ibid., p. 152.
39. Marion Jorgensen, to author, October 6, 1999.
40. *Los Angeles Times*, August 13, 1999, "Earle Jorgensen, Wealthy Reagan Confidant, Dies."
41. *Los Angeles Times*, October 26, 1961, "Earle M. Jorgensen Earnings Reported Up."
42. Marion Jorgensen, to author, October 6, 1999.
43. Frances Bergen, to author, March 30, 2000.
44. Author's diary, March 29, 2003.
45. Bill Wilson, to author, November 7, 1997.
46. Marcia Hobbs, to author, November 8, 1997.
47. Betsy Bloomingdale, to author, January 3, 2004, January 2, 2004.
48. Betsy Bloomingdale, to author, November 1, 1997.
49. Betsy Bloomingdale, to author, January 2, 2004.
50. David Jones, to author, March 12, 2000.
51. Bloomingdale with Whitney, *Entertaining with Betsy Bloomingdale*, p. 10.
52. *New York Times*, December 29, 1941, "Gloria Vanderbilt Is Wed While 1,000 Wait in Rain."

53. Betsy Bloomingdale, to author, January 2, 2004.

54. Fred de Cordova, to author, April 5, 2000.

55. Federal Bureau of Investigation file on Alfred S. Bloomingdale, obtained under the Freedom of Information Act, December 22, 2000; *New York Times*, February 8, 1944, "New Treasurer Chosen by Tammany Committee."

56. *New York Times*, April 4, 1941, "Play and Ice Show Opening Tonight"; *New York Times*, April 11, 1941, "News of the Stage: Alfred Bloomingdale to Be Independent Producer"; *New York Times*, August 31, 1941, "News and Gossip of the Rialto."

57. Fred de Cordova, to author, April 5, 2000.

58. *New York Times*, September 26, 1943, "Reno Decree to Dancer."

59. *New York Times*, February 8, 1944, "New Treasurer Chosen by Tammany Committee."

60. *New York Times*, May 4, 1944, "'Allah Be Praised' to Close Saturday."

61. Marion Jorgensen, to author, October 6, 1999.

62. Betsy Bloomingdale, to author, November 1, 1997, January 2, 2004.

63. About.com, 20th Century History, "Just Charge It! The Invention of the First Credit Card," by Jennifer Rosenberg, http://history1900s.about.com/library/weekly/aa081601a.htm; Milton and Bardach, *Vicki*, p. 43.

64. Richard Gully, to author, October 1, 1999.

65. Betsy Bloomingdale, to author, November 1, 1997; Nancy Reagan, to author, October 27, 1997.

66. Betsy Bloomingdale, to author, January 3, 2004.

67. Patti Davis, to author, May 30, 2003.

68. Nancy Reagan, to author, June 4, 2000, June 28, 2001.

69. P. Davis, *The Way I See It*, p. 23.

70. Lanetta Wahlgren, to author, November 20, 1999.

71. Betty Adams, to author, October 12, 1999.

72. Mary Jane Wick, to author, October 14, 1999.

73. Charles Wick, to author, November 3, 1997.

74. Mary Jane Wick, to author, November 3, 1997.

75. Betty Adams, to author, October 12, 1999.
76. C. Z. Wick, to author, October 19, 1999.
77. Lanetta Wahlgren, to author, November 20, 1999.
78. Betty Adams, to author, October 12, 1999.
79. Betsy Bloomingdale, to author, November 1, 1997.
80. Collins in *Vanity Fair*, July 1991, p. 131.
81. P. Davis, *The Way I See It*, pp. 28–29.
82. Ibid., p. 27.
83. Ibid., pp. 39–40.
84. Ibid., p. 66.
85. Nancy Reagan, to author, October 22, 1999.
86. *George*, February 1999, "To Sir with Love," p. 72.
87. Michael Reagan with Hyams, *On the Outside Looking In*, pp. 41–48.
88. Ibid., p. 71.
89. Ibid., pp. 74, 76.
90. Ibid., pp. 79–80.
91. P. Davis, *The Way I See It*, p. 49.
92. Ibid., p. 53.
93. Michael Reagan with Hyams, *On the Outside Looking In*, pp. 76–77.
94. Nancy Reagan, to author, June 4, 2000.
95. Maureen Reagan, *First Father, First Daughter*, pp. 114–31.
96. Michael Reagan with Hyams, *On the Outside Looking In*, p. 89.
97. Ibid., p. 91.
98. Ibid., p. 92.
99. Ibid., pp. 92–93.
100. E. Morris, *Dutch*, p. 301.
101. Angelo, *First Mothers*, p. 331.
102. E. Morris, *Dutch*, p. 754.
103. Angelo, *First Mothers*, p. 329.
104. Edwards, *The Reagans*, Appendix III, p. 370.
105. Bess Reagan, to author, November 2, 2000.
106. Neil Reagan oral history, p. 4.
107. Erlenne Sprague, to author, October 21, 1999.
108. *New York Times*, May 13, 1973, "Couture Clothes Sold

2d Hand to Aid Charity"; "A History of the Colleagues, Inc.," an unpublished pamphlet from the Colleagues archives; Jill Carter (longtime Colleagues member), to author.

109. Erlenne Sprague, to author, October 21, 1999.
110. Ibid.
111. Betty Adams, to author, October 12, 1999.
112. *Los Angeles Times*, June 15, 1961, "It Begins at Home, Says Star."

Chapter Thirteen: The Kitchen Cabinet, 1963–1966

1. E. Morris, *Dutch*, p. 293.
2. Kelley, *Nancy Reagan*, p. 121.
3. Perlstein, *Before the Storm*, p. 123.
4. Ronald Reagan, *An American Life*, pp. 133–34.
5. Dallek, *The Right Moment*, p. 38; E. Morris, *Dutch*, p. 316.
6. William F. Buckley Jr., to author, November 19, 1997.
7. Hill, *Dancing Bear*, p. 182; Dallek, *The Right Moment*, p. 39.
8. Nancy Reagan with Novak, *My Turn*, p. 129; Ronald Reagan, *An American Life*, pp. 135–36.
9. Colacello in *Vanity Fair*, July 1998, p. 82; Nancy Reagan, to author, October 27, 1997.
10. Richard Davis, to author, April 10, 2001.
11. Alice Wirtz, to author, January 14, 2002.
12. Homer Hargrave Jr., to author, February 22, 2002.
13. Kenneth Giniger, April 11, 2003.
14. Dallek, *The Right Moment*, p. 39.
15. Author's recording of Billy Graham speech, April 5, 2000, at the Beverly Hilton, Beverly Hills, CA.
16. Daniel Ruge, to author, April 11, 2001.
17. Amory, *Who Killed Society?*, p. 392.
18. Grunwald, *One Man's America*, p. 528.
19. Richard Davis, to author, April 10, 2001.
20. Nancy Reagan, to author, October 27, 1997.

21. Ronald Reagan, "On Becoming Governor," an oral history conducted 1979, Regional Oral History Office, University of California, Berkeley, 1986, p. 1. Courtesy, The Bancroft Library.
22. Ronald Reagan with Hubler, *Where's the Rest of Me?*, p. 273.
23. E. Morris, *Dutch*, pp. 320, 759.
24. McDougal, *The Last Mogul*, pp. 293–94.
25. Nancy Reagan with Novak, *My Turn*, p. 129.
26. Cannon, *Governor Reagan*, pp. 113–14.
27. E. Morris, *Dutch*, p. 760; Cannon, *Reagan*, p. 97.
28. E. Morris, *Dutch*, p. 321.
29. Ibid., pp. 323, 760.
30. Edwards, *Early Reagan*, p. 478.
31. McDougal, *The Last Mogul*, p. 300.
32. *The "Kitchen Cabinet"* oral history, Ed Mills, OH 1677, pp. 66–67.
33. Nancy Reagan with Novak, *My Turn*, p. 75.
34. Edwards, *Early Reagan*, p. 478.
35. Perlstein, *Before the Storm*, p. 499.
36. Ronald Reagan with Hubler, *Where's the Rest of Me?*, pp. 297–98.
37. Angie Dickinson, to author, October 1, 1999.
38. Healy in *Saturday Evening Post*, April 1974.
39. Nancy Reagan, to author, March 1, 2004.
40. Angie Dickinson, to author, October 1, 1999.
41. Nancy Reagan with Novak, *My Turn*, p. 5.
42. P. Davis, *The Way I See It*, p. 61.
43. Ibid., p. 62; Kelley, *Nancy Reagan*, p. 129.
44. Goldwater with Casserly, *Goldwater*, pp. 155–56; Perlstein, *Before the Storm*, p. 260.
45. *New York Times*, May 30, 1964, "Attacks Provoke Goldwater Camp."
46. Dallek, *The Right Moment*, p. 64.
47. Vidal in *The New York Review of Books*, September 29, 1983.
48. Homer Hargrave Jr., to author, February 22, 2002.

49. *The "Kitchen Cabinet"* oral history, Justin Dart, OH 1676, p. 41.
50. Author's diary, September 22, 1999.
51. Ogden, *Legacy*, p. 378.
52. Jean Hayden Mathison, to author, October 5, 1999.
53. *The "Kitchen Cabinet"* oral history, Henry Salvatori, OH 1674, p. 11.
54. Robert Tuttle, to author, November 18, 1997.
55. David Jones, to author, March 12, 2000; Robert Tuttle, to author, November 18, 1997; Betsy Bloomingdale, to author, November 4, 1997.
56. Author's diary, March 25, 2003.
57. *The "Kitchen Cabinet"* oral history, Holmes Tuttle, OH 1675, p. 112.
58. Ibid., p. 111.
59. Colacello in *Vanity Fair*, July 1998.
60. *The "Kitchen Cabinet"* oral history, Justin Dart, OH 1676, p. 40.
61. Marion Jorgensen, to author, November 4, 1997.
62. *The "Kitchen Cabinet"* oral history, Henry Salvatori, OH 1674, pp. 2–3; *Los Angeles Times*, July 8, 1997, "Henry Salvatori, Major Donor to GOP, Dies"; Federal Bureau of Investigation file on Henry Salvatori, obtained under the Freedom of Information Act, December 6, 2001.
63. Laurie Salvatori, to author, October 29, 1997.
64. Connie Wald, to author, July 24, 2003.
65. *The "Kitchen Cabinet"* oral history, Henry Salvatori, OH 1674, p. 3.
66. Ibid.
67. Laurie Salvatori, to author, October 29, 1997.
68. Proubasta in *Geophysics*, August 1983; Federal Bureau of Investigation file on Henry Salvatori, obtained under the Freedom of Information Act, December 6, 2001; Laurie Salvatori, to author, October 29, 1997.
69. Viladas in *New York Times Magazine*, August 18, 2002, p. 189; *Life*, October 3, 1938, "Negroes: The U.S. Also Has a Minority Problem," p. 54.
70. Williams in *American Magazine*, July 1937, p. 59.

71. Jean Hayden Mathison, to author, October 5, 1999.
72. Anne Douglas, to author, November 29, 1999.
73. Neil Reagan oral history, pp. 46–49.
74. Ibid., p. 30; Nofziger, *Nofziger*, p. 13.
75. Kelley, *Nancy Reagan*, p. 133.
76. *The "Kitchen Cabinet"* oral history, Holmes Tuttle, OH 1675, p. 114.
77. Ronald and Nancy Reagan's personal papers, held at the Ronald Reagan Presidential Library, box 795, "A Time for Choosing: An Address by Ronald Reagan."
78. Nancy Reagan with Novak, *My Turn*, p. 130; Dallek, *The Right Moment*, p. 67; Cannon, *Governor Reagan*, pp. 132–33.
79. Laurie Salvatori, to author, October 29, 1997.
80. P. Davis, *The Way I See It*, p. 72.
81. Nancy Reagan with Novak, *My Turn*, p. 131.
82. Perlstein, *Before the Storm*, p. 504.
83. Nofziger, *Nofziger*, p. 12.
84. Nancy Reagan, to author, October 27, 1997.
85. Nicholas Wetzel, to author, April 11, 2001.
86. Dallek, *The Right Moment*, p. 71. See also French Smith, *Law and Justice in the Reagan Administration*.
87. *The "Kitchen Cabinet"* oral history, Holmes Tuttle, OH 1675, p. 114.
88. *New York Times*, May 31, 1980, "Reagan's Inner Circle of Self-Made Men."
89. Colacello in *Vanity Fair*, July 1998.
90. *The "Kitchen Cabinet"* oral history, Holmes Tuttle, OH 1675, pp. 114–15.
91. Colacello in *Vanity Fair*, July 1998.
92. Bruce McFarland, to author, February 14, 2002.
93. Arlene Dahl, to author, May 16, 2001.
94. Neil Reagan oral history, p. 22.
95. Ibid., p. 23.
96. Ronald Reagan, "On Becoming Governor," an oral history conducted 1979, Regional Oral History Office, University of California, Berkeley, 1986, pp. 3–4. Courtesy, The Bancroft Library.

97. Jack Wrather, "On Friendship, Politics, and Government," an oral history conducted 1982, Regional Oral History Office, University of California, Berkeley, 1984, pp. 3–5. Courtesy, The Bancroft Library.

98. *New York Times*, January 23, 1965, "Reagan Weighing a New Role in Gubernatorial Race on Coast."

99. *The "Kitchen Cabinet"* oral history, Holmes Tuttle, OH 1675, p. 115.

100. Jaquelin Hume, "Basic Economics and the Body Politic: Views of a Northern California Reagan Loyalist," an oral history conducted 1982, Regional Oral History Office, University of California, Berkeley, 1984, pp. 17, 22. Courtesy, The Bancroft Library.

101. *The "Kitchen Cabinet"* oral history, Ed Mills, OH 1677, p. 80; *The "Kitchen Cabinet"* oral history, Holmes Tuttle, OH 1675, p. 134.

102. William French Smith, "Evolution of the Kitchen Cabinet, 1965–1973," an oral history conducted 1988, Regional Oral History Office, University of California, Berkeley, 1989, pp. 7–8. Courtesy, The Bancroft Library.

103. Cannon, *Governor Reagan*, pp. 134–35; *New York Times*, October 16, 1966, "Pat Brown vs. Ronnie Reagan; Political Fun and Games in California."

104. Stuart Spencer, to author, November 5, 1997.

105. Leamer, *Make-Believe*, p. 196.

106. Betsy Bloomingdale, to author, November 1, 1997.

107. Marion Jorgensen, to author, October 6, 1999.

108. Robert Tuttle, to author, November 18, 1997.

109. Nancy Reagan with Novak, *My Turn*, pp. 131–32.

110. Colacello in *Vanity Fair*, July 1998, p. 135.

111. Ibid.

112. Robert Tuttle, to author, November 18, 1997.

113. *New York Times*, October 16, 1966, "Pat Brown vs. Ronnie Reagan; Political Fun and Games in California"; Dallek, *The Right Moment*, pp. 179, 184.

114. Randall Smith, *But What's He Really Like?*, p. 19.

115. P. Davis, *The Way I See It*, pp. 72, 80–81.

116. Ibid., pp. 72, 66, 52, 69.

117. Liza Lerner, to author, December 12, 1999.
118. Nancy Reagan, to author, September 18, 1999.
119. P. Davis, *The Way I See It*, pp. 73–79.
120. Maureen Reagan, *First Father, First Daughter*, pp. 140–43; Michael Reagan with Hyams, *On the Outside Looking In*, pp. 97–105.
121. Maureen Reagan, *First Father, First Daughter*, pp. 146–47.
122. Ibid., p. 149.
123. Betsy Bloomingdale, to author, October 25, 1999.
124. *New York Times*, January 5, 1966, "Reagan Enters Gubernatorial Race in California"; Edwards, *Early Reagan*, p. 491; Randall Smith, *But What's He Really Like?*, p. 4.
125. Cannon, *Governor Reagan*, p. 140.
126. *New York Times*, January 5, 1966, "Reagan Enters Gubernatorial Race in California"; Betty Adams, to author, October 12, 1999.
127. Cannon, *Governor Reagan*, p. 144.
128. Stanley Plog oral history, pp. 5–6, 10.
129. Ibid., p. 7.
130. *New York Times*, January 5, 1966, "Reagan Enters Gubernatorial Race in California"; *New York Times*, November 14, 1965, "The Ronald Reagan Story; Or, Tom Sawyer Enters Politics."
131. Cannon, *Reagan*, p. 111; Nofziger, *Nofziger*, pp. 38–42.
132. Colacello in *Vanity Fair*, July 1998, p. 135.
133. *New York Times*, June 14, 1966, "Reagan Receives Pledge of Unity."
134. Frances Bergen, to author, March 30, 2000; Colacello in *Vanity Fair*, July 1998, p. 135.
135. Nancy Reagan, to author, June 1998.
136. Ogden, *Legacy*, p. 493.
137. Armand Deutsch, to author, November 7, 1997.
138. Harriet Deutsch, to author, November 7, 1997.
139. Nancy Reagan with Novak, *My Turn*, pp. 132–33.
140. Stuart Spencer, to author, November 5, 1997.
141. Stanley Plog oral history, p. 20.

142. Brown and Brown, *Reagan*, pp. 11, 35.
143. California Department of Finance, Demographic Research Unit, Reports and Research Papers, "E-7 Historical California Population Estimates," http://www.dof.ca.gov/HTML/DEMOGRAP/e-7.xls.
144. McClelland, *Hollywood on Ronald Reagan*, p. 210; Stuart Spencer, to author, November 5, 1997.
145. *The "Kitchen Cabinet"* oral history, Henry Salvatori, OH 1674, pp. 15–16.
146. Colacello in *Vanity Fair*, July 1998, p. 136.
147. Marion Jorgensen and Nancy Reagan, to author, March 1, 2004.
148. Mann, *Wisecracker*, p. 345; Jean Hayden Mathison, to author, October 5, 1999.

Chapter Fourteen: Sacramento, 1967–1968

1. Robert Walker, "Political Advising and Advocacy for Ronald Reagan, 1965–1980," an oral history conducted 1982, 1983, Regional Oral History Office, University of California, Berkeley, 1985, p. 52. Courtesy, The Bancroft Library.
2. Marion Jorgensen, to author, October 6, 1999, March 1, 2004.
3. P. Davis, *The Way I See It*, p. 83.
4. Maureen Reagan, *First Father, First Daughter*, p. 155.
5. Marion Jorgensen, to author, March 1, 2004.
6. Nancy Reagan with Novak, *My Turn*, pp. 134–35; Hill, *Dancing Bear*, p. 222; Cannon, *Governor Reagan*, pp. 171–72.
7. Boyarsky, *The Rise of Ronald Reagan*, p. 14.
8. Colacello in *Vanity Fair*, July 1998, p. 136.
9. Cannon, *Governor Reagan*, pp. 172–73.
10. Marion Jorgensen, to author, March 1, 2004.
11. Deaver with Herskowitz, *Behind the Scenes*, p. 35.
12. Colacello in *Vanity Fair*, July 1998, p. 136.
13. *Sacramento Union*, January 5, 1967, "Charming Figure: Inaugural Spotlight Turns on Nancy Reagan Tonight."

14. Nancy Reagan, to author, March 13, 2004.
15. *Sacramento Union*, January 5, 1967, "Charming Figure: Inaugural Spotlight Turns on Nancy Reagan Tonight."
16. Ronald Reagan, "On Becoming Governor," an oral history conducted 1979, Regional Oral History Office, University of California, Berkeley, 1986, p. 6. Courtesy, The Bancroft Library.
17. Ibid., p. 28.
18. Ibid., pp. 29–30.
19. Greenberg in *Los Angeles Times West*, April 23, 1967.
20. *The "Kitchen Cabinet"* oral history, Justin Dart, OH 1676, pp. 45–47.
21. Gordon Luce, to author, April 4, 2000.
22. Jaquelin Hume, "Basic Economics and the Body Politic: Views of a Northern California Reagan Loyalist," an oral history conducted 1982, Regional Oral History Office, University of California, Berkeley, 1984, pp. 26–27. Courtesy, The Bancroft Library.
23. Cannon, *Governor Reagan*, p. 176; *The "Kitchen Cabinet"* oral history, Holmes Tuttle, OH 1675, p. 124.
24. Cannon, *Governor Reagan*, pp. 176–78; *The "Kitchen Cabinet"* oral history, Ed Mills, OH 1677, p. 74.
25. *The "Kitchen Cabinet"* oral history, Henry Salvatori, OH 1674, p. 21.
26. Cannon, *Governor Reagan*, p. 182.
27. *The "Kitchen Cabinet"* oral history, Henry Salvatori, OH 1674, p. 22.
28. Colacello in *Vanity Fair*, July 1998, p. 136.
29. Ronald Reagan, "On Becoming Governor," an oral history conducted 1979, Regional Oral History Office, University of California, Berkeley, 1986, p. 37. Courtesy, The Bancroft Library.
30. Robert Tuttle, to author, November 18, 1997.
31. Colacello in *Vanity Fair*, July 1998, p. 137.
32. Jaquelin Hume, "Basic Economics and the Body Politic: Views of a Northern California Reagan Loyalist," an oral history conducted 1982, Regional Oral History Office,

University of California, Berkeley, 1984, p. 37. Courtesy, The Bancroft Library.

33. Greenberg in *Los Angeles Times West*, April 23, 1967.

34. Ronald Reagan, "On Becoming Governor," an oral history conducted 1979, Regional Oral History Office, University of California, Berkeley, 1986, pp. 33, 43. Courtesy, The Bancroft Library.

35. Cannon, *Governor Reagan*, p. 180.

36. "Reagan: The Governor," KCRA-TV, circa 1975, Steve Swatt, producer-reporter, Pamela J. Morgan, director, provided courtesy of the Ronald Reagan Presidential Library.

37. Boyarsky, *The Rise of Ronald Reagan*, p. 174; Cannon, *Governor Reagan*, p. 194.

38. Ronald Reagan, "On Becoming Governor," an oral history conducted 1979, Regional Oral History Office, University of California, Berkeley, 1986, p. 44. Courtesy, The Bancroft Library.

39. "CBS Reports: What About Ronald Reagan?" CBS News, December 12, 1967, Harry Reasoner and Bill Stout, reporters, Gene DePoris, producer, Sam Zelman, executive producer; Nofziger, *Nofziger*, p. 62.

40. Boyarsky, *The Rise of Ronald Reagan*, p. 196; Cannon, *Governor Reagan*, p. 218.

41. Cannon, *Governor Reagan*, p. 211; Richard Davis, to author, April 25, 2002, September 29, 2000.

42. "Reagan: The Governor," KCRA-TV, circa 1975, Steve Swatt, producer-reporter, Pamela J. Morgan, director, provided courtesy of the Ronald Reagan Presidential Library.

43. Cannon, *Reagan*, pp. 131–32.

44. "CBS Reports: What About Ronald Reagan?" CBS News, December 12, 1967, Harry Reasoner and Bill Stout, reporters, Gene DePoris, producer, Sam Zelman, executive producer.

45. Christy in *Los Angeles Times West*, June 27, 1971.

46. McHugh in *Los Angeles Times West*, April 23, 1967.

47. *New York Times*, February 11, 1967, "False Alarm at

Reagan Home"; Nancy Reagan with Libby, *Nancy*, p. 178.

48. *New York Times*, March 25, 1969, "Reagan's Friends Buy House so He Can Stay in It"; *New York Times*, February 2, 1970, "Influence of Reagan's Landlords Questioned in California Governorship Race"; *New York Times*, September 12, 1970, "Unruh Fights Hard to Overcome Campaign Lead Held by Reagan."
49. Marion Jorgensen, to author, March 1, 2004.
50. Leamer, *Make-Believe*, p. 211.
51. Christy in *Los Angeles Times West*, June 27, 1971.
52. Cannon, *Ronnie and Jesse*, pp. 139, 196; McHugh in *Los Angeles Times West*, April 23, 1967; Hill, *Dancing Bear*, p. 230.
53. Christy in *Los Angeles Times West*, June 27, 1971.
54. Wills, *Reagan's America*, p. 300.
55. Didion in *Saturday Evening Post*, June 1968.
56. Justine Bloomingdale and Serena Carroll, to author, November 6, 1999.
57. *California News Reporter*, October 6, 1967, "California's 'Elusive' First Lady."
58. Boyarsky, *The Rise of Ronald Reagan*, p. 6.
59. Cannon, *Ronnie and Jesse*, pp. 158–61.
60. "CBS Reports: What About Ronald Reagan?" CBS News, December 12, 1967, Harry Reasoner and Bill Stout, reporters, Gene DePoris, producer, Sam Zelman, executive producer.
61. "Nancy: Portrait of a Politician's Wife," television news profile circa 1975, courtesy of the Ronald Reagan Presidential Library.
62. Nancy Reynolds, to author, April 2, 2003.
63. Ibid.
64. Cannon, *Governor Reagan*, p. 240.
65. Nofziger, *Nofziger*, pp. 75–77.
66. Cannon, *Governor Reagan*, pp. 243–44.
67. Ibid., p. 245.
68. Nofziger, *Nofziger*, p. 78.

69. Robert Tuttle, to author, March 19, 2003; Nofziger, *Nofziger*, p. 78.
70. Cannon, *Governor Reagan*, pp. 247–49.
71. Nofziger, *Nofziger*, pp. 82–83.
72. William Clark, to author, March 14, 2000.
73. Nancy Reynolds, to author, April 2, 2003.
74. William Clark, to author, March 14, 2000.
75. Ibid.
76. Von Damm, *At Reagan's Side*, p. 70.
77. Betsy Bloomingdale, to author, November 4, 1997.
78. Colacello in *Vanity Fair*, July 1998, p. 136.
79. Nancy Reynolds, to author, April 2, 2003.
80. Stuart Spencer, to author, November 5, 1997.
81. Deaver with Herskowitz, *Behind the Scenes*, p. 36.
82. Vernon Cristina, "A Northern Californian Views Conservative Politics and Policies, 1963–1970," an oral history conducted 1983, Regional Oral History Office, University of California, Berkeley, 1986, p. 35. Courtesy, The Bancroft Library; Rus Walton, "Turning Political Ideas into Government Program," an oral history conducted 1983, Regional Oral History Office, University of California, Berkeley, 1985, pp. 1–2. Courtesy, The Bancroft Library.
83. Deaver with Herskowitz, *Behind the Scenes*, pp. 47–50.
84. Deaver, *Nancy*, pp. 46–48.
85. Deaver with Herskowitz, *Behind the Scenes*, p. 46.
86. Nancy Reynolds, to author, April 2, 2003; Carolyn Deaver, to author, April 17, 2000.
87. Helene von Damm, to author, May 23, 2000.
88. Nancy Reynolds, to author, April 2, 2003; Nancy Reagan with Libby, *Nancy*, p. 303.
89. Colacello in *Vanity Fair*, July 1998, pp. 136–37.
90. Paul R. Haerle, "Ronald Reagan and Republican Party Politics in California, 1965–1968," an oral history conducted 1982, Regional Oral History Office, University of California, Berkeley, 1983, pp. 13–14. Courtesy, The Bancroft Library.
91. "Nancy: Portrait of a Politician's Wife," television news

profile circa 1975, courtesy of the Ronald Reagan Presidential Library.

92. Betsy Bloomingdale, to author, January 3, 2004.
93. Carolyn Deaver, to author, April 17, 2000.
94. Betty Adams, to author, October 12, 1999.
95. Betsy Bloomingdale, to author, January 3, 2004.
96. Colacello in *Vanity Fair*, July 1998, p. 138.
97. Marion Jorgensen, to author, October 6, 1999.
98. Colacello in *Vanity Fair*, July 1998, p. 138.
99. Cannon, *Governor Reagan*, p. 304.
100. Moldea, *Dark Victory*, pp. 240–41, 255–56; *New York Times*, February 26, 1976, "Reagan Puts His Net Worth at $1,455,571"; *New York Times*, August 13, 1976, "Reagan Resists Financial Disclosure."
101. "Nancy: Portrait of a Politician's Wife," television news profile circa 1975, courtesy of the Ronald Reagan Presidential Library.
102. Kelley, *Nancy Reagan*, pp. 172–73; The *"Kitchen Cabinet"* oral history, Holmes Tuttle, OH 1675, p. 142.
103. *New York Times*, November 10, 1966, ". . . and New Republicans Win."
104. William F. Buckley Jr., to author, November 19, 1997.
105. Sue Cummings, to author, March 22, 2000.
106. Jean French Smith, to author, November 8, 1997.
107. Robert Tuttle, to author, November 18, 1997.
108. Boyarsky, *The Rise of Ronald Reagan*, pp. 158–59.
109. Stanley Plog oral history, p. 6.
110. Maureen Reagan, *First Father, First Daughter*, pp. 138–39.
111. Cannon, *Governor Reagan*, p. 265.
112. White, *The Making of the President 1968*, p. 35.
113. Deaver, *Nancy*, p. 44.
114. William Clark, to author, March 14, 2000.
115. Judis, *William F. Buckley, Jr.*, p. 327.
116. Ibid., pp. 207, 283, 291; Domhoff, *The Bohemian Grove and Other Retreats*, pp. 14, 116–245.
117. Rus Walton, "Turning Political Ideas into Government Program," an oral history conducted 1983, Regional Oral

History Office, University of California, Berkeley, 1985, p. 31. Courtesy, The Bancroft Library.

118. Nofziger, *Nofziger*, p. 69.
119. Boyarsky, *The Rise of Ronald Reagan*, pp. 249, 254–55.
120. "CBS Reports: What About Ronald Reagan?" CBS News, December 12, 1967, Harry Rearsoner and Bill Stout, reporters, Gene DePoris, producer, Sam Zelman, executive producer.
121. Cannon, *Governor Reagan*, p. 262.
122. Nancy Reagan with Libby, *Nancy*, p. 165.
123. Randall Davis, *But What's He Really Like?*, pp. 79–80.
124. Nofziger, *Nofziger*, p. 72; Nancy Reagan with Novak, *My Turn*, p. 142.
125. Nofziger, *Nofziger*, pp. 70–71.
126. Cannon, *Ronnie and Jesse*, p. 269.
127. *New York Times*, June 2, 1968, "Petitioners Seek Reagan's Ouster."
128. Robert Walker, "Political Advising and Advocacy for Ronald Reagan, 1965–1980," an oral history conducted 1982, 1983, Regional Oral History Office, University of California, Berkeley, 1985, p. 41. Courtesy, The Bancroft Library.
129. Cannon, *Governor Reagan*, p. 265.
130. White, *The Making of the President 1968*, p. 236.
131. Cannon, *Governor Reagan*, p. 265.
132. *The "Kitchen Cabinet"* oral history, Holmes Tuttle, OH 1675, p. 141.
133. Cannon, *Reagan*, p. 162.
134. Betsy Bloomingdale, to author, March 15, 1984.
135. Jack Wrather, "On Friendship, Politics, and Government," an oral history conducted 1982, Regional Oral History Office, University of California, Berkeley, 1984, p. 8. Courtesy, The Bancroft Library.
136. White, *The Making of the President 1968*, p. 239.
137. *New York Times*, August 5, 1968, "The Republican Way: A Gala for the Adults and a Bash for the Young Set."
138. Happy Rockefeller, to author, December 19, 2000.
139. *New York Times*, August 5, 1968, "The Republican Way:

A Gala for the Adults and a Bash for the Young Set";
Women's Wear Daily, August 8, 1968, "Elephant's Eye."

140. *Washington Post*, August 6, 1968, "A Spotlight on Nancy."

141. *Washington Evening Star*, August 6, 1968, "Leading Lady Big Role."

142. William Clark, to author, March 14, 2000.

143. William French Smith, "Evolution of the Kitchen Cabinet, 1965–1973," an oral history conducted 1988, Regional Oral History Office, University of California, Berkeley, 1989, p. 40. Courtesy, The Bancroft Library.

144. *New York Times*, August 6, 1968, "Reagan Officially in Race; Acts to Bar Nixon Sweep."

145. Rus Walton, "Turning Political Ideas into Government Program," an oral history conducted 1983, Regional Oral History Office, University of California, Berkeley, 1985, p. 32. Courtesy, The Bancroft Library.

146. *Women's Wear Daily*, August 8, 1968, "Elephant's Eye"; *Women's Wear Daily*, August 7, 1968, "Those Republican Stars."

147. *New York Times*, August 8, 1968, "That Time When Minutes Last Hours."

148. *New York Times*, August 8, 1968, "News Summary and Index; The Major Events of the Day; Republican Convention."

149. Robert Walker, "Political Advising and Advocacy for Ronald Reagan, 1965–1980," an oral history conducted 1982, 1983, Regional Oral History Office, University of California, Berkeley, 1985, pp. 10, 42. Courtesy, The Bancroft Library.

150. *Chicago Daily News*, July 11, 1968, "Society in Chicago: Davises Sure of Seat."

151. *Washington Post*, August 6, 1968, "A Spotlight on Nancy."

152. William F. Buckley Jr., to author, November 19, 1997.

153. *The "Kitchen Cabinet"* oral history, Holmes Tuttle, OH 1675, pp. 140–41.

154. Betsy Bloomingdale, to author, March 15, 2004.

155. Ronald Reagan, *An American Life*, p. 178.
156. Deaver, *Nancy*, p. 44.
157. Lyn Nofziger, to author, April 19, 2000.

Chapter Fifteen: Sacramento II, 1969–1974

1. Deaver with Herskowitz, *Behind the Scenes*, p. 44.
2. Cannon, *Ronnie and Jesse*, p. 276.
3. Colacello in *Vanity Fair*, July 1998, p. 138; Cooney, *The Annenbergs*, pp. 314–17; Ogden, *Legacy*, pp. 398–99.
4. Ogden, *Legacy*, p. 401.
5. Lee Annenberg, to author, November 18, 1997; Colacello in *Vanity Fair*, June 1999.
6. Von Damm, *At Reagan's Side*, p. 63.
7. Ogden, *Legacy*, pp. 402–3.
8. Colacello in *Vanity Fair*, July 1998, p. 138.
9. Cooney, *The Annenbergs*, p. 17; Nancy Reagan, to author, January 4, 2004.
10. *Los Angeles Times*, December 13, 1968, "Times Woman of the Year: Nancy Reagan: A Model First Lady."
11. Halberstam, *The Powers That Be*, p. 560.
12. Marion Jorgensen, to author, October 6, 1999.
13. Halberstam, *The Powers That Be*, p. 275.
14. Rabbi Edward Feinstein sermon, September 2000, "City of Angels," from Rabbi Edward Feinstein archives, www.vbs.org/rabbi/rabfeins/city_bot.htm.
15. James Wharton, to author, October 27, 1999.
16. Betsy Bloomingdale, to author, January 4, 2004.
17. Marion Jorgensen, to author, October 6, 1999.
18. Ed Helin, to author, August 11, 2003.
19. *New York Times*, April 2, 1967, "Reagan Unhappy at Press Notices."
20. Kelley, *Nancy Reagan*, p. 177.
21. Betsy Bloomingdale, to author, January 2, 2004.
22. Nancy Reagan, to author, January 4, 2004, October 4, 1999.
23. Betsy Bloomingdale, to author, November 4, 1997; Nancy Reagan, to author, October 27, 1997, May 27, 2001.

24. Marion Jorgensen, to author, October 6, 1999; author's diary, May 12, 2002.
25. Colacello in *Vanity Fair*, September 1995, p. 102.
26. *New York Times*, November 21, 1979, "New Yorkers, etc."
27. Buckley in *House and Garden*, October 1987.
28. Jacques Mapes, to author, September 29, 1999.
29. Mickey Ziffren, to author, March 29, 2001.
30. Colacello in *Vanity Fair*, September 1995, p. 102.
31. Ibid., pp. 102–11.
32. Ibid., p. 102.
33. Marion Jorgensen, to author, November 4, 1997, October 6, 1999.
34. Nancy Reynolds, to author, April 2, 2003.
35. Nancy Reynolds, to author, June 21, 1995.
36. *New York Times*, January 11, 1968, "It Was Warm Inside Lord & Taylor."
37. Fine Collins in *Vanity Fair*, April 2004, p. 328.
38. *Chicago Tribune*, January 7, 1972, "Salima's Best Dressed."
39. *Chicago Tribune*, January 11, 1972, "Suzy Says: Worldly Dressers."
40. "The International Best-Dressed List Hall of Fame," *Vanity Fair*, April 2004.
41. Goldwater with Casserly, *Goldwater*, p. 256.
42. Cannon, *Governor Reagan*, p. 291; *New York Times*, February 6, 1969, "Reagan Declares an Emergency in Berkeley Campus Disorders."
43. Schweizer, *Reagan's War*, p. 50.
44. Cannon, *Reagan*, p. 148; Cannon, *Governor Reagan*, p. 291.
45. Cannon, *Governor Reagan*, p. 285.
46. French Smith, *Law and Justice*, pp. 239–40.
47. *New York Times*, February 23, 1969, "After Two Years in Office, Reagan Confounds Critics with Growing Strength."
48. Ronald and Nancy Reagan's personal papers, held at the Ronald Reagan Presidential Library, box 915, "Ronald Reagan's Letters as Governor, 1966–1974."

49. *New York Times*, March 30, 1969, "The Jules Stein Party: A 3-Day Extravaganza for 600 Fashionable Guests."

50. Edgar Gillenwaters, "Washington Office Troubleshooter and Advocate for Commerce in California, 1967–1973," an oral history conducted 1983, Regional Oral History Office, University of California, Berkeley, 1985, pp. 35–36. Courtesy, The Bancroft Library.

51. Griffith in *New York Times Magazine*, June 29, 1969.

52. *New York Times*, May 16, 1969, "Shotguns and Tear Gas Disperse Rioters Near the Berkeley Campus."

53. Ibid.; *New York Times*, June 14, 1969, "Reagan Links 'People's Park' Battle to Politics."

54. *New York Times*, May 25, 1969, "Education: The War Between Reagan and Berkeley"; *New York Times*, June 8, 1969, "Berkeley Police Raid Park Annex"; *New York Times*, June 3, 1969, "Reagan Removing Berkeley Troops."

55. Noonan, *When Character Was King*, p. 73; Nancy Reagan with Libby, *Nancy*, p. 138.

56. Leamer, *Make-Believe*, p. 223.

57. P. Davis, *The Way I See It*, p. 92.

58. Author's diary, July 10, 2000.

59. Maureen Reagan, *First Father, First Daughter*, p. 207.

60. Michael Reagan with Hyams, *On the Outside Looking In*, pp. 115–19.

61. P. Davis, *The Way I See It*, p. 94.

62. Skinner, Anderson, and Anderson, eds., *Reagan: A Life in Letters*, p. 53.

63. P. Davis, *The Way I See It*, p. 106.

64. Marion Jorgensen, to author, October 6, 1999; author's diary, November 3, 1999.

65. P. Davis, *The Way I See It*, p. 94.

66. Nancy Reagan with Novak, *My Turn*, p. 170.

67. Leamer, *Make-Believe*, p. 220.

68. Ron Reagan Jr. in *Esquire*, June 2003, pp. 108, 111.

69. Ronald and Nancy Reagan's personal papers, held at the Ronald Reagan Presidential Library, box 914, "Ronald Reagan's Letters as Governor, 1966–1974," letter from

Jack Williams to Ronald Reagan, May 15, 1967, letter from Ronald Reagan to Jack Williams, May 22, 1967.
70. Carolyn Deaver, to author, April 17, 2000.
71. Crowley, *Nixon in Winter*, p. 369; Anson, *Exile*, p. 144.
72. Carolyn Deaver, to author, April 17, 2000.
73. P. Davis, *The Way I See It*, p. 103.
74. Nancy Reynolds, to author, April 2, 2003.
75. Ronald and Nancy Reagan's personal papers, held at the Ronald Reagan Presidential Library, box 915, "Ronald Reagan's Letters as Governor, 1966–1974," letter from Richard Nixon to Ronald Reagan, October 8, 1969.
76. Colacello in *Vanity Fair*, July 1998, p. 139.
77. Cooney, *The Annenbergs*, p. 321.
78. Ogden, *Legacy*, p. 405.
79. Colacello in *Vanity Fair*, July 1998, p. 138.
80. Marguerite Littman, to author, June 2001.
81. Colacello in *Vanity Fair*, July 1998, pp. 138–39.
82. Christy in *Los Angeles Times West*, June 27, 1971.
83. Colacello in *Vanity Fair*, July 1998, p. 139.
84. Kelley, *Nancy Reagan*, p. 183.
85. Ibid., p. 181.
86. Colacello in *Vanity Fair*, July 1998, p. 139.
87. Ibid.
88. *Sacramento Union*, January 30, 1972, "She's a Wife First."
89. Ibid.
90. Kelley, *Nancy Reagan*, p. 195.
91. Cannon, *Governor Reagan*, pp. 294–95.
92. Christy in *Los Angeles Times West*, June 27, 1971.
93. Affron, *Lillian Gish*, p. 322.
94. Colacello in *Vanity Fair*, July 1998, p. 137; Cannon, *Reagan*, p. 172.
95. Cannon, *Reagan*, p. 172.
96. *The "Kitchen Cabinet"* oral history, Holmes Tuttle, OH 1675, p. 129.
97. Edgar Gillenwaters, "Washington Office Troubleshooter and Advocate for Commerce in California, 1967–1973," an oral history conducted 1983, Regional Oral History

Office, University of California, Berkeley, 1985, p. 25a. Courtesy, The Bancroft Library.

98. Jacobs with Stadiem, *Mr. S*, p. 163.
99. Tina Sinatra, to author, March 28, 2001.
100. Cannon, *Governor Reagan*, p. 448; Kelley, *Nancy Reagan*, p. 185.
101. Marion Jorgensen, to author, November 4, 1997.
102. Schweizer, *Reagan's War*, pp. 65–66.
103. Collins in *Vanity Fair*, July 1991, p. 130.
104. P. Davis, *The Way I See It*, pp. 107–10.
105. Ibid., p. 110.
106. *New York Times*, February 3, 1971, "Nancy Reagan May Be Shy—But She Still Takes a Stand."
107. P. Davis, *The Way I See It*, pp. 112–16; Kelley, *Nancy Reagan*, pp. 188, 204; Edwards, *The Reagans*, p. 118; Nancy Reagan, to author, March 26, 1998.
108. P. Davis, *The Way I See It*, p. 130.
109. E. Morris, *Dutch*, p. 369.
110. Ibid., p. 373; Cannon, *Governor Reagan*, p. 350.
111. Cannon, *Governor Reagan*, p. 351; E. Morris, *Dutch*, pp. 372–73.
112. Cannon, *Reagan*, pp. 182–83.
113. E. Morris, *Dutch*, p. 376; Cannon, *Governor Reagan*, p. 357.
114. Michael Deaver, to author, November 21, 1997.
115. Cannon, *Governor Reagan*, pp. 352–53.
116. E. Morris, *Dutch*, p. 373.
117. Haldeman, *The Haldeman Diaries*, pp. 238, 291.
118. Ronald and Nancy Reagan's personal papers, held at the Ronald Reagan Presidential Library, box 915, "Ronald Reagan's Letters as Governor, 1966–1974," letter from Deane Davis to Nancy Reynolds, July 8, 1971, with Ronald Reagan's handwritten response.
119. Nancy Reagan, to author, October 22, 1997.
120. Ronald and Nancy Reagan's personal papers, held at the Ronald Reagan Presidential Library, box 915, "Ronald Reagan's Letters as Governor, 1966–1974," handwritten letter dated June 28, [1970].

121. William F. Buckley Jr., to author, November 19, 1997.
122. Judis, *William F. Buckley, Jr.*, p. 328.
123. Ronald and Nancy Reagan's personal papers, held at the Ronald Reagan Presidential Library, box 84, memo to Don Oliver from Pete Hannaford dated February 20, 1980, forwarded to Ronald Reagan; Nancy Reagan with Libby, *Nancy*, p. 206.
124. *Sacramento Union*, November 1, 1971, "On the Reagan Tour."
125. William F. Buckley Jr., to author, November 19, 1997.
126. Haldeman, *The Haldeman Diaries*, p. 368.
127. Ronald and Nancy Reagan's personal papers, held at the Ronald Reagan Presidential Library, box 84, memo to Don Oliver from Pete Hannaford dated February 20, 1980, forwarded to Ronald Reagan; Nancy Reagan with Libby, *Nancy*, p. 210.
128. Cheshire with Greenya, *Maxine Cheshire, Reporter*, p. 122.
129. Betsy Bloomingdale, to author, March 15, 2004.
130. Federal Bureau of Investigation file on Henry Salvatori, obtained under the Freedom of Information Act, December 6, 2001; Sale, *Power Shift*, pp. 231, 77; *New York Times*, October 12, 1974, "Northrop Admits to a Secret Fund."
131. *Los Angeles Times*, March 8, 1973, "Gubernatorial Race: Top GOP Money Raisers to Meet."
132. *The "Kitchen Cabinet"* oral history, Holmes Tuttle, OH 1675, pp. 145–46.
133. *Los Angeles Times*, January 22, 1973, "Inaugural Whirl Produces Party Crush"; *Los Angeles Times*, January 18, 1973, "On Fashion: 'Me-Too' Coat for Nancy."
134. Cheshire with Greenya, *Maxine Cheshire, Reporter*, p. 124.
135. Ibid., p. 121.
136. *Los Angeles Times*, April 2, 1972, "The State."
137. Meese, *With Reagan*, p. 33; E. Morris, *Dutch*, p. 372.
138. Cannon, *Governor Reagan*, Chapter 21; Whalen in *New York Times Magazine*, February 22, 1976.
139. Kelley, *Nancy Reagan*, p. 158.

140. Robert Higdon, to author, March 10, 2004.

141. Nancy Reagan with Novak, *My Turn*, p. 141.

142. Nancy Reagan, to author, April 19, 1998.

143. Ibid.

144. Kelley, *Nancy Reagan*, p. 194.

145. Ronald and Nancy Reagan's personal papers, held at the Ronald Reagan Presidential Library, box 920, guest list and seating chart for Beverly Wilshire reception, undated.

146. Kelley, *Nancy Reagan*, p. 194.

147. *New York Times Magazine*, December 10, 1972, display ad entitled "So You're Growing Up?," accompanying article by Mopsy Strange Kennedy, "Juvenile, Puerile, Sophomoric, Jejune, Nutty—and Funny."

148. *Los Angeles Times*, October 2, 1974, "Beach Club Gets Favor Following Letter to Reagan"; *Los Angeles Times*, October 10, 1974, "Sen. Roberti Demands Removal of Beach Club."

149. *New York Times*, May 11, 1973, "While Governors Were Doing Business, Wives Did the Town."

150. *The "Kitchen Cabinet"* oral history, Holmes Tuttle, OH 1675, p. 146.

151. P. Davis, *The Way I See It*, p. 138.

152. Colacello in *Vanity Fair*, July 1998, p. 139.

153. Ibid.

154. Ibid.

155. *New York Times*, March 19, 1974, "Prince Charles's Palm Springs Visit: Film Stars, Caviar and Golf."

156. *The "Kitchen Cabinet"* oral history, Ed Mills, OH 1677, p. 93.

157. *Sacramento Union*, December 15, 1974, "Nancy Reagan Looks Back on 8 Years."

158. Healy in *Saturday Evening Post*, April 1974.

159. Whalen in *New York Times Magazine*, February 22, 1976.

Chapter Sixteen: Reagan vs. Ford, 1975–1976

1. Robert Walker, "Political Advising and Advocacy for Ronald Reagan, 1965–1980," an oral history conducted

1982, 1983, Regional Oral History Office, University of California, Berkeley, 1985, p. 26. Courtesy, The Bancroft Library.

2. Nancy Reagan with Novak, *My Turn*, p. 178.
3. Author's diary, September 17, 1999; Betsy Bloomingdale, to author, October 25, 1999.
4. Author's diary, September 17, 1999; Betsy Bloomingdale, to author, March 15, 2004.
5. Author's diary, September 17, 1999.
6. Hannaford, *Ronald Reagan and His Ranch*, p. 34; Cannon, *Reagan*, p. 195.
7. *New York Times*, January 6, 1975, "8 on the President's Panel Span Wide Range of Belief."
8. *New York Times*, January 7, 1975, "Brown, Stressing Change from Reagan Era, Sworn In As California Governor."
9. Nofziger, *Nofziger*, p. 154.
10. Skinner, Anderson, and Anderson, eds., *Reagan, in His Own Hand*, p. xiv; Hannaford, *Ronald Reagan and His Ranch*, pp. 34–36.
11. Cannon, *Reagan*, p. 196.
12. Kotkin, Grabowicz, and Stein in *Esquire*, August 1980, p. 34.
13. Cannon, *Governor Reagan*, p. 399. See also *New York Times*, February 26, 1976, "Reagan Puts His Net Worth at $1,455,571." Reagan's declared income for 1975 was $282,253.
14. Skinner, Anderson, and Anderson, eds., *Reagan, in His Own Hand*, p. xv; Cannon, *Governor Reagan*, p. 399.
15. Skinner, Anderson, and Anderson, eds., *Reagan, in His Own Hand*, p. xv.
16. Hannaford, *Ronald Reagan and His Ranch*, p. 38.
17. Ronald Reagan, *An American Life*, p. 194.
18. Hannaford, *Ronald Reagan and His Ranch*, p. 30.
19. *Sacramento Union*, December 15, 1974, "Nancy Reagan Looks Back on 8 Years"; *New York Times*, October 6, 1980, "Reagan More than a Millionaire but Extent of Wealth Is Hidden."

20. Hannaford, *Ronald Reagan and His Ranch*, pp. 38–40.
21. C. Z. Wick, to author, October 19, 1999.
22. Ronald Reagan, *An American Life*, p. 195.
23. Maureen Reagan, *First Father, First Daughter*, p. 99.
24. Michael Reagan with Hyams, *On the Outside Looking In*, p. 138.
25. Ibid., p. 124.
26. P. Davis, *The Way I See It*, p. 152.
27. Ibid., p. 146.
28. Marion Jorgensen, to author, October 6, 1999.
29. P. Davis, *The Way I See It*, pp. 147–48.
30. Nancy Reagan with Novak, *My Turn*, p. 171.
31. Kelley, *Nancy Reagan*, p. 210.
32. Nancy Reagan, to author, January 4, 2004, June 4, 2000.
33. P. Davis, *The Way I See It*, p. 150; Collins in *Vanity Fair*, June 1991.
34. P. Davis, *The Way I See It*, pp. 139–40, 150.
35. Maureen Reagan, *First Father, First Daughter*, p. 227.
36. Nancy Reagan with Novak, *My Turn*, p. 181.
37. Nancy Reagan, *I Love You, Ronnie*, pp. 125–26.
38. Deaver with Herskowitz, *Behind the Scenes*, p. 64.
39. Witcover, *Marathon*, pp. 65–66.
40. Ibid., p. 66.
41. *New York Times*, August 2, 1976, "Bold Reagan Tactician: John Patrick Sears 3d."
42. Nofziger, *Nofziger*, p. 165.
43. Nancy Reagan with Novak, *My Turn*, p. 180.
44. *New York Times*, September 15, 1974, "Mercy Was Satisfied, but the Constitution Requires Justice."
45. *New York Times*, December 18, 1974, "Reagan's G.O.P. Financial Backers, in Move Interpreted as Signal to Ford, Give Luncheon for Bentsen."
46. Witcover, *Marathon*, p. 68.
47. *New York Times*, February 17, 1975, "Study of 3d Party for '76 Approved by Conservatives."
48. *New York Times*, March 9, 1975, "Reagan Rejects Ford Plea to G.O.P. to Broaden Base."
49. Kelley, *Nancy Reagan*, p. 218.

50. Ibid.
51. Ronald Reagan, *An American Life*, p. 204.
52. Author's diary, August 1998.
53. Ronald and Nancy Reagan's personal papers, held at the Ronald Reagan Presidential Library, box 84, Associated Press wire, February 20, 1975, attached to correspondence between Walter Annenberg and Margaret Thatcher arranging the meeting of Thatcher and Ronald Reagan in London.
54. Witcover, *Marathon*, p. 70.
55. *New York Times*, June 2, 1975, "2 G.O.P. Leaders Score Ford Policy."
56. Witcover, *Marathon*, p. 51.
57. Laxalt, *Nevada's Paul Laxalt*, pp. 288–89.
58. *New York Times*, July 16, 1975, "Six Form a 1976 Group for Reagan."
59. The *"Kitchen Cabinet"* oral history, Henry Salvatori, OH 1674, pp. 35–36.
60. From the personal papers of Marion Jorgensen, guest list and menu for cocktail party honoring Governor Reagan, June 8, 1976.
61. Stuart Spencer, to author, November 5, 1997.
62. Boller Jr., *Presidential Wives*, p. 425; *New York Times*, April 12, 1976, "Wives in '76 Campaign Find the Going Difficult."
63. Boller Jr., *Presidential Wives*, pp. 425–26.
64. *Ibid*, pp. 426, 417.
65. Kelley, *Nancy Reagan*, p. 219.
66. *New York Times*, April 12, 1976, "Wives in '76 Campaign Find the Going Difficult."
67. Barry Diller, to author, October 16, 1999.
68. *New York Times*, November 4, 1975, "Reagan Shocked at Schlesinger Ouster."
69. The *"Kitchen Cabinet"* oral history, Holmes Tuttle, OH 1675, pp. 147–48.
70. *New York Times*, November 21, 1975, "Reagan Enters Campaign, Seeks a Curb on Spending."
71. Hannaford, *Ronald Reagan and His Ranch*, p. 58.

72. Nancy Reagan with Novak, *My Turn*, p. 183.

73. *New York Times*, December 12, 1975, "Reagan Tops Ford as Gallup Finds a Sharp Reversal"; *New York Times*, June 16, 1976, "Reagan Fund Raising Exceeds Ford's as the Convention Nears."

74. *New York Times*, January 6, 1976, "Reagan Opens Campaign for New Hampshire Vote"; *New York Times*, January 7, 1976, "Ford's Best Ally: Reagan."

75. *New York Times*, February 15, 1976, "'Welfare Queen' Becomes Issue in Reagan Campaign"; *New York Times*, January 7, 1976, "Reagan Defends His Plan to Cut Budget"; *New York Times*, January 11, 1976, "G.O.P. Seems Evenly Split Over Ford-Reagan Contest"; *New York Times*, January 14, 1976, "Reagan Disavows $90 Billion Figure."

76. *New York Times*, February 20, 1976, "Ford Intensifies Attack on Reagan"; *New York Times*, February 14, 1976, "President Terms Reagan Too Conservative to Win."

77. *New York Times*, February 26, 1976, "Reagan Claiming Victory; Some Aides Disappointed."

78. Laxalt, *Nevada's Paul Laxalt*, p. 291.

79. *New York Times*, February 27, 1976, "Reagan's Predicted Margin of Victory in Florida Revised Downward by Manager"; *New York Times*, March 10, 1976, "Ford Defeats Reagan in Florida; Carter Is Winner Over Wallace in Democratic Vote, Jackson 3d"; *New York Times*, February 29, 1976, "Reagan Sharpens His Criticism of Ford, Citing Canal Talks and Two in Cabinet."

80. *New York Times*, March 5, 1976, "Reagan, in Direct Attack, Assails Ford on Defense."

81. Judis, *William F. Buckley, Jr.*, pp. 387–88.

82. *New York Times*, March 10, 1976, "Ford's Aides Send Signal to Reagan"; *New York Times*, March 10, 1976, "Reagan Voices 'Delight' on Florida Vote."

83. *New York Times*, March 17, 1976, "Ford Decisively Defeats Reagan in Illinois Voting; Carter Is a Solid Winner."

84. *New York Times*, February 28, 1976, "11 Former Chiefs of G.O.P. Endorse Ford over Reagan."

85. *New York Times*, March 19, 1976, "Reagan Suggests Ford Quit the Race."

86. Laxalt, *Nevada's Paul Laxalt*, pp. 291–92; Nofziger, *Nofziger*, p. 179.

87. *New York Times*, March 29, 1976, "Reagan's Upset Victory in North Carolina Attributed to Impact of Last-Minute TV Speech."

88. Witcover, *Marathon*, p. 421; Kelley, *Nancy Reagan*, p. 237; Nofziger, *Nofziger*, p. 191.

89. Richard Davis, to author, April 25, 2002.

90. Witcover, *Marathon*, p. 431.

91. Nancy Reagan with Novak, *My Turn*, p. 191.

92. *New York Times*, July 18, 1976, "Democratic Slate Assailed by Ford; G.O.P. Unity Urged"; Laxalt, *Nevada's Paul Laxalt*, p. 295.

93. Nancy Reagan with Novak, *My Turn*, pp. 191–92.

94. *New York Times*, July 12, 1976, "Sinatra Wed in Palm Springs; Reagan, Agnew Among Guests."

95. Nofziger, *Nofziger*, p. 196.

96. Witcover, *Marathon*, p. 460.

97. Kelley, *Nancy Reagan*, p. 239.

98. Witcover, *Marathon*, p. 461.

99. Ibid., p. 463.

100. Nancy Reagan with Novak, *My Turn*, p.192.

101. Judis, *William F. Buckley, Jr.*, p. 389.

102. *Wall Street Journal*, July 27, 2000, "When a Convention Mattered."

103. *Chicago Tribune*, August 25, 1976, "Behind Every President . . ."

104. *Wall Street Journal*, July 27, 2000, "When a Convention Mattered."

105. *New York Times*, August 16, 1976, "Kansas City Dazzles the Chic."

106. *New York Times*, August 18, 1976, "New York Delegates Shut Out Both Sides' Celebrities."

107. *New York Times*, August 17, 1976, "Convention Erupts with Arrival of Candidates' Wives."

108. *New York Times*, August 18, 1976, "Ford Gains Edge

over Reagan; Baker or Ruckelshaus Listed as Likely Choice for No. 2 Spot."

109. Nancy Reagan with Novak, *My Turn*, p. 193; *New York Times*, August 18, 1976, "Betty Ford Bests Nancy Reagan on Applause Scale."
110. Nancy Reagan with Novak, *My Turn*, p. 193.
111. Nofziger, *Nofziger*, pp. 203–4.
112. Nancy Reagan with Novak, *My Turn*, p. 195
113. Nofziger, *Nofziger*, p. 204.
114. Von Damm, *At Reagan's Side*, p. 83.
115. Colacello in *Vanity Fair*, July 1998, p. 140.
116. Witcover, *Marathon*, p. 503.
117. Nofziger, *Nofziger*, pp. 202–3.
118. Ronald Reagan, *An American Life*, p. 202.
119. *New York Times*, August 19, 1976, "Ford Takes Nomination on First Ballot; Reveals Vice-Presidential Choice Today."
120. Colacello in *Vanity Fair*, July 1998, p. 140.
121. The *"Kitchen Cabinet"* oral history, Justin Dart, OH 1676, pp. 44–45.
122. The *"Kitchen Cabinet"* oral history, Holmes Tuttle, OH 1675, p. 146.
123. The *"Kitchen Cabinet"* oral history, Ed Mills, OH 1677, p. 93.
124. *New York Times*, August 20, 1976, "Reagan, on Dais, Spurs Party On."
125. Deaver with Herskowitz, *Behind the Scenes*, p. 72.
126. Witcover, *Marathon*, p. 509.
127. Deaver with Herskowitz, *Behind the Scenes*, p. 72.
128. *New York Times*, August 22, 1976, "A Few Good Words About Reagan."
129. Author's diary, September 24, 1999.

Chapter Seventeen: Reagan vs. Carter, 1977–1980

1. Nofziger, *Nofziger*, p. 221.
2. Tuchman, *The March of Folly*, p. 49.

3. *New York Times*, September 9, 1976, "Aides Say Reagan Will Campaign for Ford if He Gets Assignments."
4. *New York Times*, October 11, 1976, "Reagan Ads for G.O.P. Set for Television."
5. *New York Times*, October 30, 1976, "Reagan Shuns Role in Ford's Campaign."
6. *New York Times*, September 27, 1976, "Dole Succeeds in Meeting Reagan to Display G.O.P. Unity on Coast."
7. *New York Times*, October 28, 1976, "Reagan Bars Aiding Ford in 3 Key States."
8. Nofziger, *Nofziger*, p. 208.
9. Nancy Reagan with Novak, *My Turn*, pp. 201–2.
10. Nofziger, *Nofziger*, pp. 206–7.
11. *New York Times*, November 3, 1976, "Reagan Will Not Bar Another Try in 1980."
12. *New York Times*, November 5, 1976, "Reagan Hints at Active Role in Shaping G.O.P. Future."
13. Nofziger, *Nofziger*, p. 214.
14. Ibid., p. 215.
15. Deaver with Herskowitz, *Behind the Scenes*, p. 75.
16. Nancy Reagan, *I Love You, Ronnie*, p. 128.
17. Ronald Reagan, *An American Life*, p. 203.
18. Colacello in *Vanity Fair*, July 1998, p. 140.
19. Marion Jorgensen, to author, November 4, 1997, March 1, 2004.
20. *New York Times*, September 9, 1976, "Aides Say Reagan Will Campaign for Ford if He Gets Assignments."
21. Deaver with Herskowitz, *Behind the Scenes*, pp. 74–75.
22. Nancy Reagan, *I Love You, Ronnie*, p. 129.
23. Nancy Reagan with Novak, *My Turn*, p. 102.
24. Hannaford, *Ronald Reagan and His Ranch*, p. 45.
25. P. Davis, *The Way I See It*, p. 154.
26. Ibid., p. 161.
27. Buckley Jr., *Overdrive*, p. 95.
28. Warhol and Colacello in *Interview*, November 1980, p. 30.
29. *New York Times*, November 9, 1980, "Word from Friends: A New White House Style Is on the Way."
30. Nancy Reagan, to author, February 13, 2004.

31. David Jones, to author, March 12, 2000.
32. Connie Wald, to author, November 7, 1997.
33. *New York Times*, December 13, 1977, "Metropolitan Celebrates Fashion's Past, Present."
34. *New York Times*, September 29, 1976, "A Social Figure Is Fined $5,000 for Not Declaring $3,800 Dresses."
35. Anderson, *Revolution*, p. 166.
36. Ibid., p. 146.
37. Arthur Laffer, to author, April 4, 2000.
38. Anderson, *Revolution*, p. 151.
39. Arthur Laffer, to author, April 4, 2000.
40. Ibid.
41. Ibid.
42. Nofziger, *Nofziger*, p. 221.
43. Ronald and Nancy Reagan's personal papers, held at the Ronald Reagan Presidential Library, box 85 and box 450.
44. *New York Times*, August 16, 1979, "Reagan Got $72,840 in 18 Months for His Talks to G.O.P. Groups."
45. Nofziger, *Nofziger*, p. 222.
46. Nancy Reagan, to author, March 13, 2004.
47. *New York Times*, May 14, 1978, "Gallup Poll Says Carter Would Triumph over Ford or Reagan for Presidency."
48. *New York Times*, January 11, 1979, "Poll Shows Ford Trailing Reagan in a 1980 Race."
49. *New York Times*, March 8, 1979, "Backers of Reagan Open His Campaign."
50. Nofziger, *Nofziger*, p. 234.
51. Ibid., pp. 223–24.
52. Kelley, *Nancy Reagan*, pp. 249–50.
53. Lyn Nofziger, to author, April 19, 2000.
54. Deaver with Herskowitz, *Behind the Scenes*, p. 85.
55. Charles Wick and Mary Jane Wick, to author, November 3, 1997.
56. Ibid.
57. Clymer in *New York Times Magazine*, July 29, 1979.
58. Ibid.; *New York Times*, January 23, 1979, "Reagan Backers Decide to Meet Issue of Age Early and Head On."

59. Deaver with Herskowitz, *Behind the Scenes*, p. 75; Clymer in *New York Times Magazine*, July 29, 1979.
60. Evans and Novak, *The Reagan Revolution*, p. 74.
61. Nofziger, *Nofziger*, pp. 235–36.
62. Charles Wick, to author, October 14, 1999.
63. Mary Jane Wick, to author, October 14, 1999.
64. Charles Wick and Mary Jane Wick, to author, October 14, 1999.
65. *New York Times*, November 14, 1979, "Reagan Entering Presidency Race, Calls for North American 'Accord'"; *New York Times*, November 14, 1979, "The 1980 Model Reagan: Strident Campaign Tone Is Gone."
66. Cannon, *Governor Reagan*, pp. 453–54.
67. Arthur Laffer, to author, April 4, 2000.
68. Deaver with Herskowitz, *Behind the Scenes*, p. 87.
69. *New York Times*, December 4, 1979, "Shifts on Reagan Staff Strengthen Role of Campaign Chief."
70. Nancy Reynolds, to author, April 2, 2003.
71. *New York Times*, December 4, 1979, "Shifts on Reagan Staff Strengthen Role of Campaign Chief."
72. Martin Anderson, to author, March 27, 2000.
73. *New York Times*, January 27, 1980, "As Reagan Goes, So Goes John P. Sears 3d."
74. Anderson, *Revolution*, pp. 289–90.
75. Nancy Reagan, to author, October 27, 1997.
76. Ronald and Nancy Reagan's personal papers, held at the Ronald Reagan Presidential Library, box 507, handwritten notes on Executive Advisory Committee, note dated December 5, 1979, on the subject "Morgan Mason."
77. Arthur Laffer, to author, April 4, 2000.
78. Ronald and Nancy Reagan's personal papers, held at the Ronald Reagan Presidential Library, box 507, notes dated February 5, 1980, under heading "Purpose and Function."; ibid., page entitled "Consultants & Advisers."
79. Ronald and Nancy Reagan's personal papers, held at the Ronald Reagan Presidential Library, box 507, dated February 5, 1980, notes under heading "Composition

and Leadership"; ibid., page entitled "Exec. Adv. Comm., 2pm."

80. Ronald and Nancy Reagan's personal papers, held at the Ronald Reagan Presidential Library, box 503, memorandum from Ed Meese to William E. Simon on "Reagan for President" stationery, dated 14 January 1980, subject: Executive Advisory Committee.

81. Colacello in *Vanity Fair*, July 1998; Anderson, *Revolution*, p. 328.

82. White, *America in Search of Itself*, p. 249; Anderson, *Revolution*, p. 328; Persico, *Casey*, p. 175.

83. Ronald and Nancy Reagan's personal papers, held at the Ronald Reagan Presidential Library, box 507, letter from William J. Casey to Ronald Reagan, dated February 1, 1980.

84. *New York Times*, January 23, 1980, "Reagan to Reconsider His Decision Not to Debate with G.O.P. Rivals."

85. *New York Times*, January 27, 1980, "As Reagan Goes, So Goes John P. Sears 3d."

86. Weymouth in *New York Times Magazine*, October 26, 1980.

87. William Clark, to author, March 14, 2000.

88. Weymouth in *New York Times Magazine*, October 26, 1980.

89. Nancy Reagan with Novak, *My Turn*, p. 206.

90. Weymouth in *New York Times Magazine*, October 26, 1980.

91. White, *America in Search of Itself*, p. 251.

92. Ibid.

93. *New York Times*, February 29, 1980, "The Basic Speech: Ronald Reagan."

94. Ronald and Nancy Reagan's personal papers, held at the Ronald Reagan Presidential Library, box 919, cover page attached to Republican National Committee April 1980 Finance Committee Report, sent from William French Smith to Nancy Reagan, forwarded by Nancy Reagan to Ed Meese with handwritten note.

95. *New York Times*, May 27, 1980, "Bush Says He'll Quit Active Campaigning, Ending 2-Year Quest."
96. *New York Times*, May 28, 1980, "Campaign Report; Ford Endorses Reagan, Saying He Has Nomination."
97. White, *America in Search of Itself*, p. 321; *New York Times*, July 14, 1980, "At Center Stage, Ronald Reagan Takes His Biggest Role."
98. *New York Times*, May 31, 1980, "Reagan's Inner Circle of Self-Made Men."
99. *New York Times*, June 15, 1980, "Six Losing Candidates Vow Fealty to Reagan at G.O.P. Unity Fete."
100. Ronald and Nancy Reagan's personal papers, held at the Ronald Reagan Presidential Library, box 543, "Notes from the June 20th [1980] Reagan Executive Advisory Committee meeting held at the Palmer House in Chicago. (By Arthur B. Laffer)."
101. Bill Wilson, to author, October 30, 1999.
102. Ibid.
103. *New York Times*, June 18, 1980, "Campaign Report; Reagan Aides Are Reported Concerned by Sinatra Move."
104. Letter, Joe Moshay to Nancy Reagan, October 16, 1981, ID# 046371, GI002, WHORM: Subject File, Ronald Reagan Library.
105. *New York Times*, July 14, 1980, "A State of Some Confusion: Reagan's Search for Vice-Presidential Candidate Is Vital, Critical and Highly Important—Or Is It?"
106. Anthony and McCollister in *George*, February 1999.
107. Bill Wilson, to author, November 7, 1997.
108. Meese, *With Reagan*, p. 43.
109. *New York Times*, July 15, 1980, "Reagan Is Promising a Crusade to Make Nation 'Great Again.'"
110. Ronald and Nancy Reagan's personal papers, held at the Ronald Reagan Presidential Library, box 543, "Reagan Advisory Committee: Minutes of April 4, 1980."
111. *New York Times*, October 31, 1980, "Departing Adviser to Reagan: Richard Vincent Allen."

112. *New York Times*, July 16, 1980, "Reagan Woos Ford as Top Republicans Denounce President."
113. White, *America in Search of Itself*, pp. 321–22.
114. Nofziger, *Nofziger*, p. 242.
115. Meese, *With Reagan*, p. 44.
116. White, *America in Search of Itself*, p. 323.
117. Deaver with Herskowitz, *Behind the Scenes*, pp. 93–94.
118. Ibid.
119. Nancy Reynolds, to author, April 2, 2003.
120. Ronald and Nancy Reagan's personal papers, held at the Ronald Reagan Presidential Library, box 194, "Nancy Reagan: Detailed Schedule" for July 14 and July 15, 1980.
121. *New York Post*, July 14, 1980, "Around the Town with Eugenia Sheppard."
122. Nancy Reagan with Novak, *My Turn*, p. 211.
123. *New York Times*, July 17, 1980, "Reagan Says Bush Backs Platform; Ford Was Offered Major Authority"; White, *America in Search of Itself*, pp. 323–24.
124. Nancy Reagan with Novak, *My Turn*, p. 212.
125. Aileen Mehle, to author, March 28, 2004.
126. Nancy Reagan with Novak, *My Turn*, p. 212.
127. Deaver with Herskowitz, *Behind the Scenes*, p. 96; White, *America in Search of Itself*, p. 325.
128. Deaver with Herskowitz, *Behind the Scenes*, p. 96.
129. *New York Times*, July 17, 1976, "Reagan Wins Nomination and Chooses Bush as Running Mate After Talks with Ford Fail."
130. Barbara Bush, *Barbara Bush*, p. 154.
131. Betty Adams, to author, October 12, 1999.
132. Laxalt, *Nevada's Paul Laxalt*, p. 314.
133. Deaver with Herskowitz, *Behind the Scenes*, p. 97.
134. Nancy Reynolds, to author, April 2, 2003.
135. *Los Angeles Times*, July 16, 1980, "Mrs. Bush Happy to Settle for Second."
136. Ronald and Nancy Reagan's personal papers, held at the Ronald Reagan Presidential Library, box 543, "Reagan

Executive Advisory Committee Meeting; Friday, July 25, 1980, Boston Room, L.A. Hyatt."

137. *New York Times*, August 14, 1980, "A Confident Miss Lillian Marks Her 82nd Birthday."

138. Nancy Reynolds, to author, April 2, 2003.

139. Cannon, *Governor Reagan*, p. 490; White, *America in Search of Itself*, p. 391.

140. *New York Times*, September 3, 1980, "Carter Assails Reagan Remark About the Klan as an Insult to the South."

141. Cannon, *Governor Reagan*, pp. 483–84.

142. Stuart Spencer, to author, November 5, 1997.

143. Ronald and Nancy Reagan's personal papers, held at the Ronald Reagan Presidential Library, box 490, "Guest List for Private Wick Dinner; Friday, September 5, 1980."

144. *New York Times*, October 31, 1980, "Reagan Advisers Ponder Kissinger Foreign Policy Role; Mrs. Reagan as Guest of Honor."

145. *New York Times*, October 28, 1980, "Carter and Reagan to Meet Tonight in Debate That Could Decide Race."

146. *New York Times*, October 7, 1980, "Carter Presses Issue of 'War and Peace'"; *New York Times*, October 8, 1980, "Reagan Declares Carter Is at 'a Point of Hysteria.'"

147. *New York Times*, October 11, 1980, "Carter Asserts Reagan Presidency Would Be 'Bad Thing' for Country."

148. *New York Times*, October 19, 1980, "Carter and Reagan Go on Attack in Ads."

149. *New York Times*, October 26, 1980, "Mrs. Reagan, in Campaign Ad, Assails Statements by Carter on Her Husband."

150. Nancy Reagan, to author, October 27, 1997.

151. *New York Times*, April 5, 1980, "Strong Wives Keeping Pace with Front-Runners."

152. Peter McCoy, to author, October 31, 1997.

153. Weymouth in *New York Times Magazine*, October 26, 1980.

154. Ronald and Nancy Reagan's personal papers, held at the

Ronald Reagan Presidential Library, box 543, Mike Wallace interview with Patti Reagan, pp. 8–9.

155. Deaver with Herskowitz, *Behind the Scenes*, p. 98.
156. Cannon, *Governor Reagan*, p. 504; Deaver with Herskowitz, *Behind the Scenes*, p. 98.
157. Jack Wrather, "On Friendship, Politics, and Government," an oral history conducted 1982, Regional Oral History Office, University of California, Berkeley, 1984, p. 9. Courtesy, The Bancroft Library.
158. White, *America in Search of Itself*, pp. 407–8.
159. *New York Times*, October 31, 1980, "Close Reagan Business Friends; They Seem to Personify His Values."
160. From the personal papers of Marion Jorgensen, guest list for Tuesday, November 4, 1980, election night.
161. Neil Reagan oral history, p. 55.
162. Colacello in *Vanity Fair*, July 1998, p. 141.
163. White, *America in Search of Itself*, p. 411.
164. Nancy Reagan with Novak, *My Turn*, p. 221.
165. Colacello in *Vanity Fair*, July 1998, p. 141.
166. Ibid.

Bibliography

Books

Affron, Charles. *Lillian Gish: Her Legend, Her Life*. New York: Scribner, 2001.

Allyson, June, with Frances Spatz Leighton. *June Allyson*. New York: G. P. Putnam's Sons, 1982.

Amory, Cleveland. *Who Killed Society?* New York: Harper & Brothers, 1960.

Anderson, Martin. *Revolution*. San Diego and New York: Harcourt Brace Jovanovich, 1988.

Angelo, Bonnie. *First Mothers: The Women Who Shaped the Presidents*. New York: William Morrow, 2000.

Anson, Robert Sam. *Exile: The Unquiet Oblivion of Richard M. Nixon.* New York: Simon & Schuster, 1984.

Benson, Gigi, ed., and Harry Benson, photographs. *The President and Mrs. Reagan: An American Love Story*. New York: Harry N. Abrams, 2002.

Bentley, Eric, ed. *Thirty Years of Treason: Excerpts from Hearings before the House Committee on Un-American Activities, 1938–1968*. New York: Viking, 1971.

Berg, A. Scott. *Lindbergh*. New York: G. P. Putnam's Sons, 1998.

Bergen, Candice. *Knock Wood*. London: Hamish Hamilton, 1984.

Biles, Roger. *Big City Boss in Depression and War: Mayor Edward J. Kelly of Chicago*. Dekalb, IL: Northern Illinois University Press, 1984.

Billingsley, Kenneth Lloyd. *Hollywood Party: How Communism Seduced the American Film Industry in the 1930s and 1940s*. Roseville, CA: Forum/Prima, 2000.

Bloomingdale, Betsy, with Catherine Whitney. *Entertaining with Betsy Bloomingdale*. Wilsonville, OR: Beautiful America, 1994.

Boller, Jr., Paul F. *Presidential Wives*. New York: Oxford University Press, 1998.

Bowman, Lynn. *Los Angeles: Epic of a City*. Berkeley, CA: Howell-North, 1947.

Boyarsky, Bill. *The Rise of Ronald Reagan*. New York: Random House, 1968.

Brown, Edmund G. (Pat), and Bill Brown. *Reagan: The Political Chameleon*. New York: Praeger, 1976.

Brownstein, Ronald. *The Power and the Glitter: The Hollywood-Washington Connection*. New York: Pantheon, 1990.

Bruck, Connie. *When Hollywood Had a King: The Reign of Lew Wasserman, Who Leveraged Talent into Power and Influence*. New York: Random House, 2003.

Buckley, Jr., William F. *Overdrive: A Personal Documentary*. Garden City, NY: Doubleday, 1983.

Buhle, Paul, and Dave Wagner. *Radical Hollywood: The Untold Story Behind America's Favorite Movies*. New York: New Press, 2002.

Bush, Barbara. *Barbara Bush: A Memoir*. New York: Charles Scribner's Sons, 1994.

Cannon, Lou. *Governor Reagan: His Rise to Power*. New York: PublicAffairs, 2003.

———. *Reagan*. New York: G. P. Putnam's Sons, 1982.

———. *Ronnie and Jesse: A Political Odyssey*. Garden City, NY: Doubleday, 1969.

Cheshire, Maxine, with John Greenya. *Maxine Cheshire, Reporter*. Boston: Houghton Mifflin, 1978.

Cooney, John. *The Annenbergs*. New York: Simon & Schuster, 1982.

Courtney, Marguerite. *Laurette*. New York: Rinehart, 1955.

Crowley, Monica. *Nixon in Winter*. New York: Random House, 1998.

Curtis, Charlotte. *The Rich and Other Atrocities*. New York: Harper & Row, 1976.

Dallek, Matthew. *The Right Moment: Ronald Reagan's First Victory and the Decisive Turning Point in American Politics*. New York: Free Press, 2000.

Davidson, Bill. *Spencer Tracy: Tragic Idol*. New York: E. P. Dutton, 1987.

Davis, Loyal. *A Surgeon's Odyssey*. Garden City, NY: Doubleday, 1973.

Davis, Margaret Leslie. *Dark Side of Fortune: Triumph and Scandal in the Life of Oil Tycoon Edward L. Doheny*. Berkeley and Los Angeles: University of California Press, 1998.

Davis, Mike. *City of Quartz: Excavating the Future in Los Angeles*. New York: Vintage, 1992.

Davis, Patti. *The Way I See It: An Autobiography*. New York: G. P. Putnam's Sons, 1992.

Deutsch, Armand. *Me and Bogie: And Other Friends and Acquaintances from a Life in Hollywood and Beyond*. New York: G. P. Putnam's Sons, 1991.

Deaver, Michael K. *Nancy: A Portrait of My Years with Nancy Reagan*. New York: William Morrow, 2004.

Deaver, Michael K., with Mickey Herskowitz. *Behind the Scenes: In Which the Author Talks About Ronald and Nancy Reagan . . . and Himself*. New York: William Morrow, 1987.

Dewey, Donald. *James Stewart*. Atlanta: Turner, 1996.

Domhoff, G. William. *The Bohemian Grove and Other Retreats: A Study in Ruling-Class Cohesiveness*. New York: Harper & Row, 1974.

Donnelly, Paul. *Fade to Black: A Book of Movie Obituaries*. London and New York: Omnibus, 2000.

Dunne, Dominick. *The Way We Lived Then: Recollections of a Well-Known Name Dropper*. New York: Crown, 1999.

Dunne, Philip. *Take Two: A Life in Movies and Politics*. New York: Limelight, 1980, 1992.

Dunning, John. *On the Air: The Encyclopedia of Old-Time Radio*. New York and Oxford: Oxford University Press, 1998.

———. *Tune in Yesterday: The Ultimate Encyclopedia of Old-Time Radio, 1925–1976*. Englewood Cliffs, NJ: Prentice Hall, 1976.

Edwards, Anne. *Early Reagan*. New York: William Morrow, 1987.

———. *The Reagans: Portrait of a Marriage*. New York: St. Martin's, 2003.

Eells, George. *Hedda and Louella*. New York: G. P. Putnam's Sons, 1972.

Eliot, Marc. *Walt Disney: Hollywood's Dark Prince*. New York: Birch Lane, 1993.

Evans, Rowland, and Robert Novak. *The Reagan Revolution*. New York: E. P. Dutton, 1981.

French Smith, William. *Law and Justice in the Reagan Administration: The Memoirs of an Attorney General*. Stanford, CA: Hoover Institution Press, 1991.

Friedrich, Otto. *City of Nets: A Portrait of Hollywood in the 1940's*. Berkeley and Los Angeles: University of California Press, 1986.

Gabler, Neal. *An Empire of Their Own: How the Jews Invented Hollywood*. New York: Anchor/Doubleday, 1988.

Gabor, Zsa Zsa, with Wendy Leigh. *One Lifetime Is Not Enough*. New York: Delacorte, 1991.

Gahagan Douglas, Helen. *A Full Life*. Garden City, NY: Doubleday, 1982.

Garment, Leonard. *In Search of Deep Throat: The Greatest Political Mystery of Our Time*. New York: Basic, 2000.

Gauss Jackson, Katherine, and Hiram Haydn. *The Papers of Christian Gauss*. New York: Random House, 1957.

Gebhard, David, and Harriette Von Breton. *Los Angeles in the Thirties, 1931–1941*. Los Angeles: Hennessey & Ingalls, 1989.

Gebhard, David, and Robert Winter. *Los Angeles: An Architectural Guide*. Salt Lake City: Gibbs-Smith, 1994.

Gellman, Irwin F. *The Contender: Richard Nixon, the Congress Years, 1946–1952*. New York: Free Press, 1999.

Goldschneider, Gary, and Joost Elffers. *The Secret Language of Relationships*. New York: Penguin, 1997.

Goldwater, Barry M., with Jack Casserly. *Goldwater*. New York: Doubleday, 1988.

Goodwin, Betty. *Chasen's: Where Hollywood Dined, Recipes and Memories*. Santa Monica, CA: Angel City, 1996.

Gottlieb, Robert, and Irene Wolt. *Thinking Big: The Story of the Los Angeles Times, Its Publishers and Their Influence on Southern California.* New York: G. P. Putnam's Sons, 1977.

Gould, Lewis L. *Grand Old Party: A History of the Republicans.* New York: Random House, 2003.

Grafton, David. *The Sisters: Babe Mortimer Paley, Betsey Roosevelt Whitney, Minnie Astor Fosburgh; The Lives and Times of the Fabulous Cushing Sisters.* New York: Villard, 1992.

Grobel, Lawrence. *The Hustons.* New York: Charles Scribner's Sons, 1989.

Grunwald, Henry. *One Man's America: A Journalist's Search for the Heart of His Country.* New York: Anchor/Doubleday, 1997.

Halberstam, David. *The Powers That Be.* New York: Alfred A. Knopf, 1979.

Haldeman, H. R. *The Haldeman Diaries: Inside the Nixon White House.* New York: G. P. Putnam's Sons, 1994.

Hannaford, Peter. *Ronald Reagan and His Ranch: The Western White House, 1981–1989.* Bennington, VT: Images from the Past, 2002.

Harris, Leon. *Merchant Princes: An Intimate History of Jewish Families Who Built Great Department Stores.* New York: Harper & Row, 1979.

Hepburn, Katharine. *Me: Stories of My Life.* New York: Alfred A. Knopf, 1991.

Higham, Charles. *Merchant of Dreams: Louis B. Mayer, M.G.M., and the Secret Hollywood.* New York: Donald I. Fine, 1993.

Hill, Gladwin. *Dancing Bear: An Inside Look at California Politics.* Cleveland and New York: World, 1968.

Horowitz, Helen Lefkowitz. *Alma Mater: Design and Experience in the Women's Colleges from Their 19th Century Beginnings to the 1930s.* New York: Alfred A. Knopf, 1984.

Huston, John. *An Open Book.* New York: Alfred A. Knopf, 1980.

Jacobs, George, with William Stadiem. *Mr. S: My Life with Frank Sinatra.* New York: HarperCollins, 2003.

Johnson, Paul. *A History of the American People.* New York: HarperCollins, 1997.

Judis, John B. *William F. Buckley, Jr.: Patron Saint of the Conservatives*. New York: Simon & Schuster, 1988.

Kahn, Gordon. *Hollywood on Trial: The Story of the Ten Who Were Indicted*. New York: Boni & Gaer, 1948.

Kanin, Garson. *Tracy and Hepburn: An Intimate Memoir*. New York: Viking, 1971.

Kelley, Kitty. *Nancy Reagan: The Unauthorized Biography*. New York: Simon & Schuster, 1991.

Koch, Stephen. *Double Lives: Spies and Writers in the Secret Soviet War of Ideas Against the West*. New York: Macmillan/Free Press, 1994.

Lackmann, Ron, ed. *The Encyclopedia of American Radio: An A-Z Guide to Radio from Jack Benny to Howard Stern*. New York: Checkmark, 1996, 2000.

Lambert, Gavin. *Nazimova: A Biography*. New York: Alfred A. Knopf, 1997.

Lardner, Ring, Jr. *I'd Hate Myself in the Morning: A Memoir*. New York: Thunder's Mouth/Nation, 2000.

———. *The Lardners*. New York: Harper & Row, 1976.

Laurents, Arthur. *Original Story By: A Memoir of Broadway and Hollywood*. New York: Alfred A. Knopf, 2000.

Laxalt, Paul. *Nevada's Paul Laxalt: A Memoir*. Reno: Jack Bacon, 2000.

Leamer, Laurence. *Make-Believe: The Story of Nancy & Ronald Reagan*. New York: Harper & Row, 1983.

LeRoy, Mervyn, as told to Dick Kleiner. *Mervyn LeRoy: Take One*. New York: Hawthorn, 1974.

Levy, Emanuel. *George Cukor, Master of Elegance: Hollywood's Legendary Director and His Stars*. New York: William Morrow, 1994.

Lindfors, Viveca. *Viveka-Viveca*. Don Mills, Ontario: Beaverbooks, 1981.

Mann, William J. *Wisecracker: The Life and Times of William Haines, Hollywood's First Openly Gay Star*. New York: Viking, 1998.

Mantle, Burns, ed. *The Best Plays of 1927–1928 and the Year Book of the Drama in America*. New York: Dodd, Mead, 1965.

———. *The Best Plays of 1928–1929 and the Year Book of the Drama in America*. New York: Dodd, Mead, 1965.

———. *The Best Plays of 1944–1945 and the Year Book of the Drama in America*. New York: Dodd, Mead, 1965.

———. *The Best Plays of 1945–1946 and the Year Book of the Drama in America*. New York: Dodd, Mead, 1965.

———. *The Best Plays of 1948–1949 and the Year Book of the Drama in America*. New York: Dodd, Mead, 1965.

Mantle, Burns, and Garrison P. Sherwood, eds. *The Best Plays of 1909–1919 and the Year Book of the Drama in America*. New York: Dodd, Mead, 1933.

Marlow, Ron. "First Christian Church (Disciples of Christ) and the Reagan Family: Dixon Illinois, 1920–1928." Unpublished, 2001.

Marton, Kati. *Hidden Power: Presidential Marriages That Shaped Our Recent History*. New York: Pantheon, 2001.

McClellan, Diana. *The Girls: Sappho Goes to Hollywood*. New York: St. Martin's, 2000.

McClelland, Doug. *Hollywood on Ronald Reagan: Friends and Enemies Discuss Our President, the Actor*. Winchester, MA: Faber & Faber, 1983.

McDougal, Dennis. *The Last Mogul: Lew Wasserman, MCA, and the Hidden History of Hollywood*. New York: Crown, 1998.

Meese, Edwin III. *With Reagan: The Inside Story*. Washington, DC: Regnery Gateway, 1992.

Milton, Joyce, and Ann Louise Bardach. *Vicki*. New York: St. Martin's, 1986.

Moldea, Dan E. *Dark Victory: Ronald Reagan, MCA, and the Mob*. New York: Viking Penguin, 1986.

Moore, Colleen. *Silent Star*. Garden City, NY: Doubleday, 1968.

Morella, Joe, and Edward Z. Epstein. *Jane Wyman: A Biography*. New York: Delacorte, 1985.

Morgan, Robin, and George Perry, eds. *The Book of Film Biographies: A Pictorial Guide of 1000 Makers of the Cinema*. New York: Fromm International, 1997.

Morris, Edmund. *Dutch: A Memoir of Ronald Reagan*. New York: Random House, 1999.

Morris, Richard B., ed. *Encyclopedia of American History*. New York: Harper & Row, 1961.

Nachman, Gerald. *Raised on Radio*. New York: Pantheon, 1998.

Nixon, Richard. *In the Arena: A Memoir of Victory, Defeat, and Renewal*. New York: Simon & Schuster, 1990.

Nofziger, Lyn. *Nofziger*. Washington, DC: Regnery Gateway, 1992.

Noonan, Peggy. *When Character Was King: A Story of Ronald Reagan*. New York: Viking, 2001.

Ogden, Christopher. *Legacy: A Biography of Moses and Walter Annenberg*. Boston and New York: Little, Brown, 1999.

Parmet, Herbert S. *George Bush: The Life of a Lone Star Yankee*. New York: Scribner, 1997.

Parsons, Louella O. *The Gay Illiterate*. Garden City, NY: Doubleday, 1944.

Perlstein, Rick. *Before the Storm: Barry Goldwater and the Unmaking of the American Consensus*. New York: Hill and Wang/Farrar, Straus and Giroux, 2001.

Persico, Joseph E. *Casey: From the OSS to the CIA*. New York: Viking, 1990.

Pitt, Leonard, and Dale Pitt. *Los Angeles A to Z: An Encyclopedia of the City and County*. Berkeley and Los Angeles: University of California Press, 1997.

Quirk, Lawrence J. *Jane Wyman: The Actress and the Woman*. New York: Dembner, 1986.

Randall Davis, Kathy. *But What's He Really Like?* Menlo Park, CA: Pacific Coast Publishers, 1970.

Reagan, Maureen. *First Father, First Daughter: A Memoir*. Boston: Little, Brown, 1989.

Reagan, Michael, with Joe Hyams. *On the Outside Looking In*. New York: Zebra, 1988.

Reagan, Nancy. *I Love You, Ronnie: The Letters of Ronald Reagan to Nancy Reagan*. New York: Random House, 2000.

Reagan, Nancy, with Bill Libby. *Nancy*. New York: William Morrow, 1980.

Reagan, Nancy, with William Novak. *My Turn: The Memoirs of Nancy Reagan*. New York: Random House, 1989.

Reagan, Ronald. *An American Life*. New York: Simon & Schuster, 1990.

Reagan, Ronald, with Richard G. Hubler. *Where's the Rest of Me?* New York: Elsevier Dutton, 1965. First Karz-Segil Publishers Edition, 1981.

Riese, Randall, and Neal Hitchens. *The Unabridged Marilyn: Her Life from A to Z*. New York and Chicago: Congdon & Weed, 1987.

Root, James Pierce. *Root Genealogical Records, 1600–1870: Comprising the General History of the Root and Roots Families in America*. New York: R. C. Root, Anthony & Co., 1870. Available at the Ronald Reagan Presidential Library, Simi Valley, CA.

Sale, Kirkpatrick. *Power Shift: The Rise of the Southern Rim and Its Challenge to the Eastern Establishment*. New York: Random House, 1975.

Schary, Dore, as told to Charles Palmer. *Case History of a Movie*. New York: Random House, 1950.

Schary Zimmer, Jill. *With a Cast of Thousands: A Hollywood Childhood*. New York: Stein & Day, 1963.

Schlesinger, Arthur, Jr. *A Life in the 20th Century: Innocent Beginnings, 1917–1950*. Boston and New York: Houghton Mifflin, 2000.

Schultz, Margie. *Irene Dunne: A Bio-Bibliography*. Westport, CT, and New York: Greenwood, 1991.

Schweizer, Peter. *Reagan's War: The Epic Story of His Forty-Year Struggle and Final Triumph Over Communism*. New York: Doubleday, 2002.

Sharp, Kathleen. *Mr. and Mrs. Hollywood: Edie and Lew Wasserman and Their Entertainment Empire*. New York: Carroll & Graf, 2003.

Skinner, Kiron K., Annelise Anderson, and Martin Anderson, eds. *Reagan: A Life in Letters*. New York: Free Press, 2003.

———. *Reagan, In His Own Hand*. New York: Free Press, 2001.

Smith, Jane S. *Elsie de Wolfe: A Life in the High Style*. New York: Atheneum, 1982.

Spada, James. *Ronald Reagan: His Life in Pictures*. New York: St. Martin's, 2000.

Spatz Leighton, Frances. *The Search for the Real Nancy Reagan*. New York: Macmillan, 1987.

Stuart, Sandra Lee. *The Pink Palace: Behind Closed Doors at the Beverly Hills Hotel*. Secaucus, NJ: Lyle Stuart, 1978.

Thomas, Bob. *Golden Boy: The Untold Story of William Holden*. New York: St. Martin's, 1983.

———. *King Cohn: The Life and Times of Harry Cohn*. New York: McGraw-Hill, 1990.

Tuchman, Barbara W. *The March of Folly: From Troy to Vietnam*. New York: Alfred A. Knopf, 1984.

Vaughn, Stephen. *Ronald Reagan in Hollywood: Movies and Politics*. Cambridge: Cambridge University Press, 1994.

Von Damm, Helene. *At Reagan's Side*. New York: Doubleday, 1989.

Wagner, Walter. *Beverly Hills: Inside the Golden Ghetto*. New York: Grosset & Dunlap, 1976.

Walgreen, Myrtle R., as told to Margueritte Harmon Bro. *Never a Dull Day*. Chicago: Henry Regnery, 1963.

Walker, John, ed. *Halliwell's Filmgoer's Companion*. New York: HarperPerennial, 1997.

Warner, Jack L., with Dean Jennings. *My First Hundred Years in Hollywood*. New York: Random House, 1965.

Weld, John. *September Song: An Intimate Biography of Walter Huston*. Lanham, MD: Scarecrow, 1998.

Weller, Sheila. *Dancing at Ciro's: A Family's Love, Loss, and Scandal on the Sunset Strip*. New York: St. Martin's, 2003.

White, Theodore H. *America in Search of Itself: The Making of the President, 1956–1980*. New York: Warner, 1982.

———. *The Making of the President 1968*. New York: Atheneum, 1969.

Williams, Esther, with Digby Diehl. *The Million Dollar Mermaid*. New York: Simon & Schuster, 1999.

Wills, Garry. *John Wayne's America: The Politics of Celebrity*. New York: Simon & Schuster, 1997.

———. *Reagan's America: Innocents at Home*. Garden City, NY: Doubleday, 1987.

Witcover, Jules. *Marathon: The Pursuit of the Presidency, 1972–1976*. New York: Viking, 1977.

Wright Cobb, Sally, and Mark Willems. *The Brown Derby Restaurant: A Hollywood Legend*. New York: Rizzoli, 1996.

York, Pat. *Going Strong*. New York: Arcade/Little, Brown, 1991.

Articles

Anthony, Carl S., and Anna McCollister. *George*, February 1999. "Ronald Reagan: The Role of a Lifetime."

Benjamin, Daniel, and Steven Simon. *New York Review of Books*, December 20, 2001. "A Failure of Intelligence?"

Buckley, Christopher. *House and Garden*, October 1987. "Man About Town at Home."

Christy, George. *Los Angeles Times West*, June 27, 1971. "Conversations with Nancy."

Clogher, Rick. *Mother Jones*, August 1981. "Weaving Spiders, Come Not Here."

Clymer, Adam. *New York Times Magazine*, July 29, 1979. "Reagan: The 1980 Model."

Colacello, Bob. *Interview*, November 1980. "Patti Davis: Limo to J.F.K. with Bob Colacello."

———. *Vanity Fair*, September 1995. "A Walker on the Wild Side."

———. *Vanity Fair*, July 1998. "Ronnie and Nancy."

———. *Vanity Fair*, August 1998. "Ronnie and Nancy: The White House Years and Beyond."

———. *Vanity Fair*, June 1999. "Palm Springs Weekends."

Collins, Nancy. *Vanity Fair*, July 1991. "Patti Dearest."

Didion, Joan. *Saturday Evening Post*, June 1968. "Pretty Nancy."

Dunne, Dominick. *Vanity Fair*, November 1989. "Jane's Turn."

Dunne, John Gregory. *New York Review of Books*, May 28, 1998. "Angels of LA."

Fine Collins, Amy. *Vanity Fair*, April 1997. "Idol Gossips."

———. *Vanity Fair*, April 2004. "The Lady, the List, the Legacy."

Greenberg, Carl. *Los Angeles Times West*, April 23, 1967. "Ronald Reagan's 'Kitchen Cabinet.'"

Griffith, Winthrop. *New York Times Magazine*, June 29, 1969. "People's Park—270′ × 450′ of Confrontation."

Healy, Paul F. *Saturday Evening Post*, April 1974. "Sunday Afternoon with the Ronald Reagans."

Kotkin, Joel, and Paul Grabowicz. *Esquire*, August 1980. "Dutch Reagan, All-American."

Kotkin, Joel, Paul Grabowicz, and Jeff Stein. *Esquire*, August 1980. "Life Begins at Seventy."

McDaniel, Wanda. *Los Angeles Herald Examiner*, October 26–30, 1980. "Nancy Reagan: The Woman Who Would Be Queen." "Part 1: Her Majesty, The Enigma," October 26, 1980. "Part 2: Hurray for Hollywood—The Honeymoon Begins," October 27, 1980. "Part 3: Dr. Loyal Davis—The Stepdaddy of Kingmakers," October 28, 1980. "Part 4: Behind the Steel Armor—What Makes Nancy Run," October 29, 1980. "Part 5: The Reagan Reign—Queen Nancy and Her Loyal Court," October 30, 1980.

McHugh, Vincent. *Los Angeles Times West*, April 23, 1967. "Last Stand for a Gracious Lady."

Meroney, John. *Architectural Digest*, April 2000. "Hollywood at Home: Ronald Reagan in Pacific Palisades."

Proubasta, Dolores. *Geophysics*. August 1983. "Henry Salvatori."

Reagan, Ron, Jr. *Esquire,* June 2003. "My Father's Memories."

Scheer, Robert. *Playboy*, August 1980. "The Reagan Question."

Schlesinger, Arthur, Jr. *Life*, July 29, 1946. "The U.S. Communist Party."

Sellmer, Robert. *Business Week*, July 13, 1946. "Super Druggist Dart."

Shepherd, C. Owsley. *The American* (Chicago), November 11, 1962. "A Sunday Profile: A Fighting Surgeon Makes Success a Habit."

Vidal, Gore. *New York Review of Books*, September 29, 1983. "Ronnie and Nancy: A Life in Pictures."

Viladas, Pilar. *New York Times Magazine*, August 18, 2002. "Star Turns."

Warhol, Andy, and Bob Colacello. *Interview*, November 1980. "Ron Reagan: Cream of Carrot Soup, Sauteed Frogs' Legs and Beer with Andy Warhol."

Weymouth, Lally. *New York Times Magazine*, October 26, 1980. "The Biggest Role of Nancy's Life."

Whalen, Richard J. *New York Times Magazine*, February 22, 1976. "Peach-Pit Conservative or Closet Moderate?"

Wiener, Jon. *New Republic*, March 31, 1986. "When Old Blue Eyes Was 'Red.'"

Williams, Paul. *American Magazine*, July 1937. "I Am a Negro."

Wills, Garry. *Esquire*, August 1980. "Ron and Destiny."

Oral Histories

Cristina, Vernon J, "A Northern Californian Views Conservative Politics and Policies, 1963–1970." An oral history conducted in 1983 by Sarah Sharp, in *Republican Campaigns and Party Issues, 1964–1976*. Regional Oral History Office, The Bancroft Library, University of California, Berkeley, 1986.

French Smith, William, *Evolution of the Kitchen Cabinet, 1965–1973*. An oral history conducted in 1988 by Gabrielle Morris. Regional Oral History Office, The Bancroft Library, University of California, Berkeley, 1989.

Gillenwaters, Edgar, "Washington Office Troubleshooter and Advocate for Commerce in California, 1967–1973." An oral history conducted in 1983 by Sarah Sharp, in *Internal and External Operations of the California Governor's Office, 1966–1974*. Regional Oral History Office, The Bancroft Library, University of California, Berkeley, 1985.

Haerle, Paul, "Ronald Reagan and Republican Party Politics in California, 1965–1968." An oral history conducted in 1982 by Sarah Sharp, in *Appointments, Cabinet Management, and Policy Research for Governor Ronald Reagan, 1967–1974*. Regional Oral History Office, The Bancroft Library, University of California, Berkeley, 1983.

Hume, Jaquelin, "Basic Economics and the Body Politic: Views of a Northern California Reagan Loyalist." An oral history conducted in 1982 by Gabrielle Morris, in *Republican*

Philosophy and Party Activism. Regional Oral History Office, The Bancroft Library, University of California, Berkeley, 1984.

The "Kitchen Cabinet": Four California Citizen Advisers of Ronald Reagan. Interviews conducted by Steven D. Edgington and Lawrence B. de Graaf in 1983. California Government History Documentation Project: The Reagan Era. Courtesy of the Center for Oral and Public History, California State University, Fullerton.

Plog, Stanley, "More Than Just an Actor: The Early Campaigns of Ronald Reagan." An interview conducted by Stephen Stern in June 1981 for the Oral History Program. Available through the UCLA Department of Special Collections in the Charles E. Young Research Library.

Reagan, Neil, "Private Dimensions and Public Images: The Early Political Campaigns of Ronald Reagan." An interview conducted by Stephen Stern in 1981. Oral History Program. Available through the UCLA Department of Special Collections in the Charles E. Young Research Library.

Reagan, Ronald, "On Becoming Governor." An oral history conducted by Gabrielle Morris and Sarah Sharp in 1981 and 1983. In *Governor Reagan and His Cabinet: An Introduction*. Regional Oral History Office, The Bancroft Library, University of California, Berkeley, 1986.

Walker, Robert, "Political Advising and Advocacy for Ronald Reagan, 1965–1980." An oral history conducted in 1982–83 by Gabrielle Morris and Sarah Sharp. Regional Oral History Office, The Bancroft Library, University of California, Berkeley, 1985.

Walton, Rus, "Turning Political Ideas into Government Program." An oral history conducted in 1983 by Gabrielle Morris. Regional Oral History Office, The Bancroft Library, University of California, Berkeley, 1985.

Wrather, Jack, "On Friendship, Politics, and Government." An oral history conducted in 1982 by Gabrielle Morris. In *Republican Philosophy and Party Activism*. Regional Oral History Office, The Bancroft Library, University of California, Berkeley, 1984.

Index